Michael Kühlenthal (Hrsg./Ed.)

Ostasiatische und europäische Lacktechniken

East Asian and European Lacquer Techniques

Internationale Tagung
des Bayerischen Landesamtes für Denkmalpflege
und des Deutschen Nationalkomitees von ICOMOS
in Zusammenarbeit mit dem
Tokyo National Research Institute of Cultural Properties
München, 11. – 13. März 1999

International Conference
of the Bavarian State Department of Historical Monuments
and the German National Committee of ICOMOS
together with the
Tokyo National Research Institute of Cultural Properties
Munich, 11 – 13 March 1999

ARBEITSHEFTE DES BAYERISCHEN LANDESAMTES FÜR DENKMALPFLEGE, BAND 112

Arbeitshefte des Bayerischen Landesamtes für Denkmalpflege

Umschlagabbildungen / *Cover*

Vorderseite: Stellschirm „Fortissimo“ von Jean Dunand und Seraphin Soudbinine, 1925/26, Ausschnitt; The Metropolitan Museum of Art, NewYork (50.102.4)

Front cover: 'Fortissimo' screen by Jean Dunand and Seraphin Soudbinine, 1925/26, detail; The Metropolitan Museum of Art, New York (50.102.4)

Rückseite: Stellschirm, China, Ausschnitt der Vorderseite; Museum für Lackkunst, Münster (Inv. Nr. AS-CH-a-8)

Back cover: Screen, China, detail of the front side; Museum für Lackkunst, Münster (Inv. No. AS-CH-a-8)

Umschlaginnenseiten

Tisch von Jean Dunand, ca. 1925, Details der Tischplatte in japanischer Eierschalentechnik; The Metropolitan Museum of Art, New York (1986.400)

Cover inside

Table by Jean Dunand, ca. 1925, details of table top decorated with eggshell lacquer inlay; The Metropolitan Museum of Art, New York (1986.400)

S. 5: Wien, Schloss Schönbrunn, Vieux Laque-Zimmer, Ausschnitt einer chinesischen Lacktafel (Schloss Schönbrunn Kultur- u. Betriebsges.m.b.H./Alexander Koller, Hg. 115.015)

P. 5: Vienna, Schönbrunn Palace, Vieux Lacquer-Room, detail of a Chinese lacquer panel (Schloss Schönbrunn Kultur- u. Betriebsges.m.b.H./Alexander Koller, Hg. 115.015)

Redaktion und Layout: Susanne Böning-Weis, Michael Kühlenthal, Christine Schuller, Susan Tipton

Gesamtherstellung: Lipp GmbH, Graphische Betriebe, Meglingerstraße 60, 81477 München

Vertrieb: Karl M. Lipp Verlag, Meglingerstraße 60, 81477 München

ISBN: 3-87490-710-4

Inhalt / *Contents*

Vorwort

Die internationale Tagung „Ostasiatische und europäische Lacktechniken" (München, 11.–13. März 1999) wurde vom Bayerischen Landesamt für Denkmalpflege und dem Deutschen Nationalkomitee von ICOMOS zusammen mit dem Tokyo National Research Institute of Cultural Properties veranstaltet. Der Kongress war als Abschluss des sechs Jahre laufenden deutsch-japanischen Projekts zur Erforschung und Restaurierung von Lacken und lackierten Oberflächen gedacht. Träger des Projekts waren das Bundesministerium für Bildung und Forschung auf deutscher und das Kultusministerium (Mombusho) auf japanischer Seite, mit der Leitung und Durchführung waren die Abteilung Restaurierung des Bayerischen Landesamtes für Denkmalpflege unter Hauptkonservator Dr. Michael Kühlenthal und das Department for Conservation Science des Tokyo National Research Institute of Cultural Properties unter seinem Direktor Sadatoshi Miura betraut.

Das Projekt hat für die deutsche Forschung und Denkmalpflege ein neues, bisher kaum beachtetes Fachgebiet erschlossen, das insofern von nicht zu unterschätzender Bedeutung ist, als große Teile der Ausstattung, d. h. das Mobiliar von Kirchen, Klöstern und Schlössern, ursprünglich mit Lacken beschichtet gewesen sind. Außerdem gehören alle nach Europa importierten ostasiatischen Lackarbeiten aus drei Jahrhunderten zu diesem Kulturerbe. So konnten seit 1993 unter Führung des Bayerischen Landesamtes für Denkmalpflege und Mitwirkung des Doerner-Instituts der Bayerischen Staatsgemäldesammlungen in München die Lackiertechniken und die hierfür relevanten Materialien des 17. und 18. Jahrhunderts erforscht werden.

Schwerpunktthema in der ersten Projektphase (1993–95) war die Erforschung europäischer Lackbeschichtungen und der Möglichkeiten ihrer Konservierung und Restaurierung, d. h. die Untersuchung von Lacken auf farbig gefassten Ausstattungsstücken und furnierten Oberflächen, sowie davon ausgehend die Entwicklung von Lacktrennungsverfahren und die gezielte Rekonstruktion bereits entfernter historischer Lacke. Die Forschungsergebnisse dieser ersten Phase wurden in einer Publikation von Katharina Walch und Johann Koller „Lacke des Barock und Rokoko" („Baroque and Rococo Lacquers") 1997 in der Reihe der Arbeitshefte des Bayerischen Landesamtes für Denkmalpflege veröffentlicht.

In der zweiten Projektphase (1996–99) konnte man sich dann auf die Analyse und Restaurierung europäischer Imitationslacke konzentrieren, d. h. auf lackierte Oberflächen, die in Imitation japanischer und im weitesten Sinn ostasiatischer Lackarbeiten im 17. und 18. Jahrhundert hergestellt worden sind. Untersucht wurden Objekte berühmter Lackwerkstätten, wie z. B. von Christian Reinow und Martin Schnell am Hof Augusts des Starken in Dresden, Gérard Daglys am Hof Friedrichs I. von Preußen oder Lackausstattungen der Schlösser in Rastatt, die unter dem Markgrafen von Baden-Durlach entstanden. Auch wichtige Werkstätten französischer Ebenisten wie Criard, Dubois und Vanrisamburgh wurden mit einbezogen, da man die deutsche Lackkunst nicht losgelöst von der französischen betrachten kann. Die Ergebnisse dieser Forschungen sind in einem weiteren, von Michael Kühlenthal herausgegebenen Band der Arbeitshefte des Bayerischen Landesamtes für Denkmalpflege, „Japanische und europäische Lackarbeiten" („Japanese and European Lacquerware") im Jahr 2000 veröffentlicht worden.

Für die japanischen Wissenschaftler und Restauratoren war mit dem Projekt die Erkenntnis verbunden, dass die bisher wenig beachteten Exportarbeiten ein wichtiger Teil des japanischen Kulturerbes sind. Im Zusammenhang damit hat die Projektarbeit auch zu einer neuen Einschätzung europäischer Lackarbeiten in Japan geführt. Außerdem konnte ein Verfahren (Pyrolyse-GC/MS) entwickelt werden, durch welches die Bestimmung ostasiatischer Lacke und ihrer Herkunft nun eindeutig möglich ist.

Das interdisziplinär angelegte Projekt hat auf historisch-kunsthistorischer Ebene zur Erforschung der Wechselbeziehungen und der Art des Handels zwischen Japan und Europa seit dem 16. Jahrhundert beigetragen, auf naturwissenschaftlicher Ebene die Entwicklungen neuer Analysemöglichkeiten erbracht und auf restauratorischer Ebene zu einer Umsetzung der naturwissenschaftlichen Ergebnisse in Form praktikabler Restaurierungsmethoden geführt. Es wurden zwei deutsch-japanische Seminare am Tokyo National Museum und zwei weitere am Bayerischen Landesamt für Denkmalpflege abgehalten, um Zwischenbilanzen zu ziehen und die erzielten Ergebnisse auszutauschen. Mit der internationalen Tagung von 1999, deren Beiträge hier vorgelegt werden, aber sollten Experten aus möglichst vielen lackverarbeitenden Ländern und von Institutionen, die sich mit historischen Lackarbeiten beschäftigen, zusammengeführt werden. Dem interdisziplinären Charakter des Projekts entsprechend wurden Kunsthistoriker, Naturwissenschaftler und Restauratoren aus Ost und West eingeladen, über ihre Arbeit zu referieren und die Ergebnisse zu diskutieren und auszutauschen. Und wie die zahlreichen Reaktionen im Anschluss an die Tagung zeigten, hat diese Initiative ein höchst positives Echo gefunden.

Die Tagung und die hier vorgelegte Veröffentlichung wurde aus Mitteln des Beauftragten der Bundesregierung für Angelegenheiten der Kultur und der Medien gefördert. Zu danken ist außerdem dem japanischen Kultusministerium (Mombusho) und dem Bundesministerium für Bildung und Forschung, welche das Projekt zur Erforschung und Restaurierung von Lacken finanziert haben. Die Tagung wurde außerdem vom Bayerischen Staatsministerium für Wissenschaft, Forschung und Kunst unterstützt.

Die Bayerische Verwaltung der Staatlichen Schlösser, Gärten und Seen hat den Max-Joseph-Saal in der Münchner Residenz für die Tagung zur Verfügung gestellt, da der Säulensaal des Landesamts für die mehr als 350 Teilnehmer aus aller Welt zu klein war. Dr. Michael Kühlenthal, dem Spiritus Rector und Organisator dieser Veranstaltung, hat Christine Schuller in der gesamten Vorbereitung und Organisation der Tagung tatkräftig zur Seite gestanden. Zahlreiche Mitglieder der Abteilung Restaurierung des Bayerischen Landesamtes für Denkmalpflege, vor allem Susanne Frowein, Anja Fuchs, Rupert Karbacher, Mathias Kocher, Erwin J. Mayer, Helga Prettner, Laura Resenberg, Hans Stölzl, Marlies Vaeßen, Peter Weinzierl, Milena Zebera und Reinhard Zehentner, haben durch ihre Mithilfe zum Gelingen der Tagung beigetragen. Für die redaktionelle Arbeit sei schließlich Christine Schuller und Dr. Susan Tipton sowie dem Pressereferat des Bayerischen Landesamtes für Denkmalpflege, Dr. Karlheinz Hemmeter und Susanne Böning-Weis gedankt.

Ganz besonderer Dank gilt schließlich Herrn Ministerialrat Dr. Bernhard Döll, auf dessen Initiative die Zusammenarbeit mit Japan auf dem Gebiet der Denkmalpflege und des Denkmalschutzes zustande gekommen ist. Die Ergebnisse haben seinen Einsatz und seine stete Unterstützung gerechtfertigt.

Prof. Dr. Michael Petzet
Präsident von ICOMOS

Dr. Egon Johannes Greipl
Generalkonservator des
Bayerischen Landesamtes
für Denkmalpflege

Foreword

The international congress on 'East Asian and European Lacquer Techniques' held from March 11th until March 13th 1999 has been organised by the Bavarian State Department of Historical Monuments and the German Committee of ICOMOS in co-operation with the Tokyo National Research Institute of Cultural Properties. The symposium was the conclusion of a six years German-Japanese project of research and conservation of lacquers and varnished surfaces. The project was supported by the Federal Ministry for Education and Research on the German side and the Ministry for Cultural Affairs (Mombusho) on the Japanese side. The realisation of the project was entrusted to the Restoration Department at the Bavarian State Department of Historical Monuments under chief conservator Dr. Michael Kühlenthal and the Department for Conservation Science at the Tokyo National Research Institute of Cultural Properties under its director Sadatoshi Miura.

In Germany the project has opened a completely new and until recently almost neglected field of research in monument conservation insofar as large parts of the entire interior decoration, i. e. the furnishing of churches, convents, castles and palaces, have originally been coated with lacquers. Besides it must be noted that all pieces of East Asian lacquerware, that have been imported to Europe during the past three centuries and their imitations created in Europe, form part of this cultural heritage. So it was a big chance for the Bavarian State Department of Historical Monuments in collaboration with the Doerner-Institute at the Bavarian State Gallery to study historical lacquer techniques and the respective materials used in the 17th and 18th century more carefully in the framework of the German-Japanese project on lacquer techniques since 1993.

In the first stage of the project (1993–95) the main emphasis was laid on the investigation of European lacquer coatings and the possibilities of their conservation and restoration, i. e. the investigation of varnishes on polychromed veneered surfaces and on pieces of interior decoration, furthermore on the development of methods for the separation of lacquers and the reconstruction of removed historical lacquers and varnishes as well. The results of this first phase of research have been published by Katharina Walch and Johann Koller in a bilingual volume entitled 'Baroque and Rococo Lacquers' ('Lacke des Barock und Rokoko') in 1997 in the series of the 'Arbeitshefte des Bayerischen Landesamtes für Denkmalpflege'. In the second stage of the project (from 1996–99), based on the results of the first phase of research, the work concentrated on the analysis and restoration of European imitation lacquers, i. e. on lacquered surfaces, that have been produced in imitation of Japanese and in a broader sense East Asian lacquerwork of the 17th and 18th centuries. Objects from famous lacquer workshops, like the ones of Christian Reinow and Martin Schnell at the court of August the Strong in Dresden, Gérard Dagly at the court of Frederick I. of Prussia or the lacquer rooms in the residential palace at Rastatt, made under the Margraves of Baden-Durlach, have been investigated. French workshops of ébénistes like Criard, Dubois and Vanrisamburgh have been included in this investigation as well since it is not possible to study the German art of lacquering without a close look on the French. The results of these investigations have been made accessible to the public in 2000 in a further volume of the 'Arbeitshefte des Bayerischen Landesamtes für Denkmalpflege' on 'Japanese and European Lacquerware' ('Japanische und europäische Lackarbeiten') edited by Michael Kühlenthal.

For the Japanese scientists and conservators the project has brought about the discovery, that Japanese export lacquers – almost unstudied until now – are an important part of the cultural heritage of Japan, and deserve special attention and careful study. In this respect the project has led to a completely new understanding of European lacquerware in Japan. Furthermore, a method (Pyrolysis-GC/MS) has been developed, which makes it now possible to provide an unequivocal definition of East Asian lacquers and their provenience.

The interdisciplinary project has from the historical and art historical point of view led to the investigation of the interrelations and the commercial exchange between Japan and Europe since the 16th century, to the development of new analytical methods on the side of the natural sciences and – from the conservatorial point of view – to a transfer of these scientific results into practicable restoration and conservation methods. Two seminars and workshops have been held at the Tokyo National Museum followed by another two held at the Bavarian State Department of Historical Monuments in order to discuss interim reports and to exchange investigation results. With the international conference in Munich in 1999, the contributions of which are published in this issue, experts from a wide range of lacquer producing and manufacturing countries as well as from institutions dealing with historical lacquerware have been brought together. According to the interdisciplinary character of the project art historians, natural scientists, conservators and restorers from East and West have been invited to refer about their work and to discuss and exchange their investigation results. As the various reactions in connection with the congress have proven, this initiative has found a most positive echo.

The conference and the publication have been supported with funds by the Federal Government Commissioner for Cultural Affairs and the Media. We have to thank on the Japanese side the Ministry for Cultural Affairs (Mombusho) and on the German side the Federal Ministry for Education and Research, which financed the research project on historical lacquer techniques. The symposium has furthermore been supported by the Bavarian State Ministry of Science, Research and Fine Arts.

The Bavarian Administration of Castles, Gardens and Lakes has kindly put the Max-Joseph Hall in the Residential Palace in Munich at our disposal, since the Hall of Columns in the Old Mint of the Bavarian State Department of Historical Monuments soon proved too small for the 350 participants. Dr. Michael Kühlenthal, the spiritus rector and organiser of the event, has been supported and most effectively assisted in the preparation and organisation of the conference by Christine Schuller. Various members of the Department of Restoration at the Bavarian State Department of Historical Monuments, and above all Susanne Frowein, Anja Fuchs, Rupert Karbacher, Mathias Kocher, Erwin J. Mayer, Helga Prettner, Laura Resenberg, Hans Stölzl, Marlies Vaeßen, Peter Weinzierl, Milena Zebera und Reinhard Zehentner, have by their constant help contributed in a decisive measure to the success of the conference. For the editorial work of the publication we would like to thank Christine Schuller and Dr. Susan Tipton as well as the press office of the Bavarian State Department of Historical Monuments, Dr. Karlheinz Hemmeter and Susanne Böning-Weis.

Very special thanks go to Federal Ministry Deputy, Dr. Bernhard Döll, on whose initiative the co-operation with Japan in the field of monument preservation and conservation has come into being. The results have justified his dedication and his constant support of the project.

Prof. Dr. Michael Petzet
President of
ICOMOS International

Dr. Egon Johannes Greipl
Conservator General of the
Bavarian State Department
of Historical Monuments

刊行に寄せて

1992年に始まった日独学術交流もラッカーに関する研究を重ねて、1999年始めには「日本と西洋のラッカー」に関する報告書を日独共同編集で出版し、再びここに昨年3月にミュンヘンで開催されたシンポジウムの報告書を刊行できたことは、大きな喜びである。

漆に関する共同研究を開始した当時、漆の研究者や修復技術者の数はヨーロッパではきわめて少なかった。また輸出漆器について見れば、日本でも事情はそれほど変わらず、その研究者や修復技術者はごく少数で、共同研究を進めるためには日独双方においてまず、多くの研究者や修復技術者の協力を得ることからはじめなければならなかった。そのため昨年3月にシンポジウムを開催する事を決めたとき、どの程度の参加者数になるか予想がつかなかったが、開催してみると日本からの参加者も含めて予想外の大人数で、いかに多くの人がわれわれの共同研究に対して興味を持ってくれるようになったかを知り、大変感激した。本研究を遂行するに当たり快くお力添えいただいた共同研究者の方々、特に加藤寛、松原美智子、北村昭斎、宮腰哲雄の各先生方に厚くお礼申し上げたい。またドイツ側研究のまとめ役となっていただいたキューレンタール先生の献身的な働きなくしては、本研究の成果を上げることはできなかったと考えられる。ここで、心からお礼申し上げたい。

近年、海外の美術館に収蔵されている輸出漆器の修復事業が日本で開始され、そこにわれわれの共同研究成果が早速生かされている。このシンポジウムの成果が今後さらに広がって、また新しい道が開かれることを願う。

三浦定俊（東京国立文化財研究所）

Foreword

It is a great pleasure for me to publish the proceedings of the Munich symposium on 'East Asian and European lacquer techniques' as the results of the joint research project between Japan and Germany on the Conservation of Cultural Heritage after the previous volume on 'Japanese and European Lacquerware'. When we began our collaborative studies on urushi (Japanese lacquer) in 1993, there were not so many researchers and restorers familiar with urushi in Europe.

The situation in Japan was not so different at that time, since only a few people worked on the topic of urushiware made for export. So we had to look around for members (scientists, restorers and conservators) for our joint studies in Japan and Germany. After six years, when we planned the symposium in Munich, I would not have expected so many participants to gather from Japan, Germany and other countries and was very pleased indeed to see so many people become interested in our project on lacquer art.

In 1997 the Japanese government (the Agency for Cultural Affairs, Bunkacho) started a project on the restoration of export urushiware in foreign countries. Our results contributed – in techniques and ideas – a lot to this project. I am convinced, that our collaboration will be a further substantial contribution to the field of lacquerware conservation.

Last, but not least, I would like to express my sincere appreciation to key members of the team, who continuously helped and supported me in the project: Mr. Kato, Mrs. Matsubara, Mr. Kitamura and Prof. Miyakoshi, and particularly my German colleague, Dr. Kühlenthal.

Sadatoshi Miura
Director of the Conservation Department,
The Tokyo National Research Institute of Cultural Properties

Japanische Exportlacke

Japanese Export Lacquer

Cabinet with pilasters, 19th century incorporating fragments, *c.* 1640; h. 178 cm, w. 119 cm, d. 58 cm; private collection; photograph courtesy Christie's

Oliver Impey

Japanese Export Lacquer: the Fine Period

Two famous boxes, the van Diemen box[1] (fig. 1) and the Buys box[2], both of which bear the names of the persons to whom they were given, have rather skewed our perception of the export trade in lacquer from Japan in the 1630s and 1640s. This is not to say that they are not important, for they are, nor that they are not of very fine quality, for they are; but they are not export works of art. Nor, *pace* so many authors, are they necessarily of more fine quality than some, admittedly few, pieces that are export art.

Part of the trouble is the subject-matter; Earle[3] has convincingly shown that they depict a variety of versions of scenes from the *Genji monogatari*, the Tale of Genji, the celebrated romance by the tenth century Court Lady Murasaki Shikibu. This, I suggest, is in this context virtually irrelevant.

According to Professor Christiaan Jörg's report in this publication it was at the instigation of the Dutch that the styles of export lacquer changed from the *namban* style through what we call the 'transitional' to the 'pictorial' style. This was a radical change, but a change already inherant in the later works of the *namban* style. Indeed it may be earlier than that, for we can only guess how the *namban* style evolved. If we suggest that it was originally made in the 1570s, we shall probably not be far wrong.

Sanz and Jordan[4] have demonstrated that *namban* cabinets and other works were used as gifts between the various members of the Habsburg Royalty and nobility of Spain, Austria and Tirol, possibly as early as the 1570s. A coffer they describe in the Convento de las Descalzas Reales, Madrid, was certainly there in 1616, almost certainly there in 1603, and probably there in 1582; if this is so then it is earlier than the Ambras cabinet.

Certainly the top of the Ambras cabinet[5], inventoried in 1596 but quite likely made a decade or two earlier, has the beginnings of a pictorial representation that goes beyond flower-and-bird patterns by the use of the fence in the lower left. What does this signify? Is it a subtle allusion to some literary *mitate*?

At any rate, it is a hint of things to come, as well as reflecting something with which the artist was familiar. I do not believe we can judge how well versed in literature a lacquer artist, or the supervisor of a lacquer artist might be, but *namban* cabinets and chests, avowedly for the export market, are not uncommonly found with scenes such as the Three Drinkers, which are part of the Japanese repertoire and would have no resonance to a westerner other than the decorative and the exotic. Why should Genji be any different? Admittedly, Genji was perhaps the most famous literary work in Japan in the Momoyama and early Edo periods; and admittedly, later, the customers for *Ukiyo-e hanga* were presumably well enough versed in Genji to understand the not so subtle *mitate* so common in the print-makers' repertoire. But that need not set it apart, nor need it disqualify it from being a standard set of motifs usable for any decorative medium for any customer however barbarian. Indeed, there is the remarkable case of the 'pictorial' style dish, of perhaps 1690, in the Pitti Palace which bears a decoration of Monju Bosatsu.[6]

Namban lacquer, then, although made for a western market, may bear scenes that reflect stories or situations familiar to the Japanese lacquerer, as well as the more anodyne *sansui* landscapes and flowers-and-birds.

When the style begins to change, in the 1630s and in the 1640s, just before and just after the expulsion of the Portuguese from Japan and the beginning of the Dutch and Chinese monopoly of the direct trade with Japan, it must change from some impulse. This impulse would be expected to have two components, a commercial demand, and a stylistic origin. The demand was obviously from the Dutch and the stylistic origin is purely Japanese, picked up by the Dutch. It did not stay pure for long; it was too expensive and it was too slow. If the Dutch merchandise missed the monsoon, then the cash-flow was impeded for a year. And in a year fashions and demand may have changed. So this must be the origin of the break-away from the *namban*. Usually such change was a gradual process as the merchants and the lacquerers accomodated to it, but sometimes, clearly, it was not. In the 1630s and '40s new words creep into the orders and the *facturen* (the shipping lists) of the East India Company (Vereenigde Oost-Indische Compagnie or VOC). The words *extraordinarij schoon* or *geheel schoon*[7] first appear in the *facturen* in 1643, the word *verheven*[8] work or *takamakie* as late as 1648.[9] This is so late, that I suspect that 1643 descriptions of quality referred to raised work, but I cannot prove it. And these surely follow the quasi-legal private trade rather that provoke it; doubtless the 'fine' style was established in private trade before it became a commercial commodity in commercial numbers.

Interestingly the word *rochevellen*[10] (shagreen, ray-skin, *samé*) first appears in 1635. Shagreen seems never to have been used for the finest pieces, but is very much a hall-mark of the early 'transitional' phase. The pieces with their interiors of red or green lacquer are first ordered in 1639.[11] It should be recalled that delivery, and *facturen* were the actual bills of lading, occurred some two to three years after the orders were made, so in calculating the date of the orders for such things, adjustment should be made accordingly.

The van Diemen box and the Buys box differ from all other of the pieces that I shall call the 'fine' style, in being of standard Japanese shapes. There must be a sharp distinction drawn between the two groups, wherever possible; possibly the 'FC' box[12] only is ambiguous in its shape. The export shapes of equivalent quality are well known and have been catalogued by Joe Earle[13] and by Julia Hutt[14]. Earle did not name the group, but included with the van Diemen and Buys boxes, the Mazarin chest (fig. 2) and the Lawrence chest (only known from a photograph), the Chiddingstone and Vienna caskets and the V&A and the Tokyo 'jewel coffers'; to the complete list should perhaps be added the 'FC' box and the V&A miniature wedding casket. But these are only the ones we know from extant complete examples, or in the case of the Lawrence coffer, from photographs; Earle also included the fragments of a third 'Mazarin' style chest incorporated into a piece of 19th century furniture; this is not of

Fig. 1. The van Diemen box, *c.* 1639; h. 16 cm, w. 48 cm, d. 26.7 cm; Victoria and Albert Museum, W. 49–1916

the same quality and should be discounted. However, inlays into French furniture of the eighteenth century can be used to demonstrate that there were originally more examples of this style and quality, as we shall see below.

The van Diemen and the Buys boxes have been convincingly dated to between 1635 and 1640. Each has on the reverse of the lid, the name of the owner, or recipient. Significantly these names are the names of the wives of the Governor-General in Batavia, Anton van Diemen, and of the Director-General (the second-in-command) Philips Lucasz. Thus the names, inlaid in unusually thick gold (*kimpaku*), are of Maria van Diemen and of Pieternellae Buys. Buys was the maiden name of the wife of Philips Lucasz, whom she married in 1634. There are two anomalies here; why use her maiden name, and why spell the name Pieternellae, where the final 'e' is not normal Dutch usage? There can be no doubt that the names are original, whereas the two other names in the Buys box, Anton: Vernatty and Will: Drinkwater have been added later in gold paint.

The van Diemen box and the Buys box are of the same shape, size and general conformation; each has or had a drop-in tray within. Both are of typical Japanese shape. The decoration is mostly in fine gold and silver *hiramakie* and *takamakie*. The panels of decoration are raised slightly from the corners and edges; this must have made Vulliamy's job marginally easier when dissecting the Buys box for William Beckford.[15] In each, the decoration is confined within complex borders, and the cartouche, where present, is within a narrow border of sheet metal, silver or gold. The panels of the sides are cut at about seven eighths of the way up, as the decoration continues onto the lid. These side panels contain fine *takamakie* landscapes, on both boxes.

Otherwise, the two boxes have little in common. The lid of the van Diemen box has a scene that covers all the area within the borders; the lid of the Buys box has a somewhat similar scene but within a complex shaped cartouche, with spandrels of *hanabishi*. The interior tray of the Buys box has another scene, but without human figures, within a cartouche similar to that on the lid, but with more complex spandrels; the interior of the van Diemen box has a cartouche containing a landscape in an unusual technique resembling ink-painting, which is in fact painted, not in *makie*. The sides of the tray of the van Diemen box are in *nashiji*; the sides of the tray in the Buys box were presumably in the cash pattern, with pearlshell, that is used as decoration inside both Vulliamy cabinets. It is possible that these are extraneous, for the drawers below the fall fronts do not belong to the Buys box, though they are in remarkably similar style and quality. Presumably these were provided by William Beckford who would have been able to distinguish such quality. One of them has been mounted upside down, as the cabinet-maker was not familiar with bamboo. Because the top and the tray of the Buys box are so similar, it was the obvious candidate for cutting up to make two cabinets; the van Diemen box would not have been suitable, and has thus survived intact.

The Chiddingstone (fig. 3)[16] and Vienna caskets[17] are the only known examples of the shape, a European shape derived from precious metal or mounted hardstone caskets of the late renaissance. Of two stages in height, roughly pyramidal in form, they open in the two registers to reveal shallow wells, the lower one above a single line of three drawers. There are pilasters at the corners, and flanking the central drawer on the front, of lacquered wood (Chiddingstone) or of decorated ivory (Vienna). It should be noticed that the pilasters on the Chiddingstone casket bear a marked resemblance to those we describe below and attribute to the bed-chamber balustrade of Amalia von Solms. The ivory pilasters on the Vienna casket resemble those on the jewel boxes to be described below. Both caskets have complex multiple mouldings and borders, with minute inlay of pearlshell. The Vienna casket has panels of black wood veneer, probably ebony, finely carved in relief to give the appearance of black *takamakie*; the Chiddingstone casket has panels of gold and silver lacquer *takamakie* scenes of landscape, flowers, birds or animals, though the lower panels (the flanking drawer-fronts) have quartered panelling with geometrical patterns. Each casket has a recessed centre drawer of arched shape and in each case a loose fitting to cover this drawer; the Chiddingstone fitting hangs awkwardly on the central pilasters, the Vienna fitting inserts into the recess. It is a wonder that both have survived. The Vienna casket has had ivory fittings placed above the central pilasters and *netsuke* (!) above the corners.

The interior of the two lids (one above the other) of each are finely decorated with landscapes in *takamakie* on a black ground. The interior of the lower part of each casket is in red lacquer and has or would have had a drop-in tray (the Chiddingstone tray is missing); the Vienna tray has red lacquered small open compartments around a well in black lacquer in which is a diamond-shaped cartouche containing a landscape in the *sumie* technique used on the tray on the van Diemen box and on the V&A jewel box (to be described below). The interior of the drawers are also in red lacquer while the exterior sides of the drawers are decorated with gold flower-work.

The two 'jewel boxes' are of a standard European shape; here they are of exceptional quality, but there are many other examples of the shape, which vary in quality from the very good to the mediocre. Perhaps this shape could be associated with mentions in the *facturen* in 1636 '*juweelcantoorkens*'[18] or '*juweelcoffertiens*'[19] in 1656.

The shape is rectangular, sometimes with pilasters at the corners, the lid having concave sides and a sliding horizontal door at the apex. One end of the box lifts up, revealing a secret drawer under the well in the interior. In Schloss Aschaffenburg is a painting by Simon Renard de Saint-André (1613–1677) which depicts an example of this shape.[20] Occasionally this basic shape is found with doors and drawers, instead of the open chest.

The V&A example (fig. 4) shares with the Vienna casket the presence of panels of a thin veneer of carved black wood, prob-

Fig. 2. Top of the Mazarin chest, *c*. 1640; Victoria and Albert Museum, 412–1882

Fig. 3. The Chiddingstone casket, *c.* 1640; h. 35.6 cm, w. 37.5 cm, d. 31 cm; Trustees of the Denys Eyre Bower Estate, on loan to the Ashmolean Museum, Oxford

ably ebony[21], covered in colourless lacquer, imitating fine raised lacquer, on the exterior. The interior of the lid has four panels of very fine *takamakie* landscapes (fig. 5). The concealed drawer in the base has countersunk *takamakie* panels on the front and, a most unusual feature, on the sides of the drawers. Where the top slides out, a shallow well is revealed which is decorated in a flat lacquered landscape, very much in Kano style, which is painted, not in *makie*, in the same technique as that found on the tray of the van Diemen box. I have not seen the Tokyo National Museum example and so cannot describe it; the exterior is much more in the style of the 'transitional' jewel boxes, though the quality seems to be equal to that of the V&A piece.

The Mazarin chest[22] is quite different. It is inconceivable that this and the pieces we have been discussing come from the same hand and highly unlikely that they come from the same workshop. The proportions of the chest are somewhat odd; it is too narrow for the depth and for the height; the decoration is of superb quality, comparable to that on the other pieces we have discussed, but in a style and technique different enough to set it apart. The lid, as well as the inside of the lid, have strongly depicted cartouches, with borders of birds and dragons in relief, within which detailed *sansui* landscapes are dotted with animals inlaid in solid metal; this we have not seen in the above examples. The wide borders are of a type that is to become more common, of *mon* and stylized flowerheads linked by scrollwork, with metal sheet as well as pearlshell and colours of gold and silver lacquer; this may be a development from the type of border on the van Diemen box. A red lacquer is found in the pictorial parts, but not in the borders. The back has a charming surprise; a painting in strong Kano (*Sanraku*?) style of a tiger and bamboo, asymmetrical and off centre; no concession to a foreign client.

The small box called the 'FC' box, from the thick silver monogram inlaid into the reverse of the lid (though it could be CF) fits closely but not integrally into this group. The *takamakie bonsai* on the lid, and the landscape inside the box are reminiscent of those on the pieces described above. The lid, however, is bordered with flower-filled half 'cloud-collars' quite atypical, and the exterior has borders which only resemble those on the V&A wedding casket. The attribution of the initials to François Caron, while perfectly possible, for he was Opperhoofd in Japan at this time is pure conjecture. The inclusion of the small 'wedding casket' shaped box now in the Victoria and Albert Museum in this group will be discussed by Julia Hutt in this publication.

Which are the finest pieces? It would seem to me that if we set apart the subject-matter, as predisposing towards Japanese taste and therefore 'Japanese market quality', then the van Diemen box and the Buys box are not of finer quality than the Chiddingstone and Vienna caskets and the V&A and Tokyo 'jewel boxes', but very much the same; they must surely, as Earle deduces, have come from the same workshop. The others, (the Mazarin chest and presumably the Lawrence chest, the 'FC' box and possibly the V&A wedding chest), I submit, do not. The 'third Mazarin chest' certainly does not.

It must be clear, however, that there is another category of 'fine' quality pieces that seem to be of slightly, but discernably lesser quality. These are also more evident from French furniture than from extant pieces, though enough whole pieces exist to give a firm basis for the category; these include the Arched cabinet[23] (colour plate III.1), the Trianon close-stool[24], and two very similar cabinets, one in the Peabody-Essex Museum[25], and the Chiddingstone cabinet (not to be confused with the Chiddingstone casket). It seems likely that the Trianon close-stool (and its companion, now dismembered, see below) was a product of the private trade, for nothing likely to be of this shape has been found in the VOC records; the other pieces are of standard shape, albeit of unusual decoration, which would not be detected by examination of the records. Thus these second category pieces could either be private trade or Company goods. These all have raised work, as have most pieces of good quality from this time on.

One piece, or series of pieces which we think we can detect both in partial existence and in detailed documentation are four pilasters, and possibly some of their top-rail, now included in a piece of French furniture of early nineteenth century date (colour plate II).[26] These are tall, turned, narrow pilasters of two different diameters, but of the same height (as far as we can detect), some 66.8 cm. The present conformation of the piece of furniture makes it impossible to tell whether or not the pilasters were originally free-standing. The quality of the lacquer on these is exceptional, with pictorial cartouches in shaped borders enclosed by *nashiji* and geometric borders. There is no raised work. Many of the subjects depicted in the small cartouches are most unusual or unique. There is no pearlshell on the pilasters themselves, though there is on what appears to be part of the top-rail.

We believe these to be the remnants of the balustrade in the bedchamber of Amalia von Solms, wife of the Stadholder, at Huis ten Bosch. This is described as being composed of seven parts each with eight pilasters, with the centre part opening as two gates. The room was 28 *voet* (feet) wide.[27]

Amalia von Solms ordered a model to be made of a wooden balustrade which she requested Philips Lucasz (Governor-General in Batavia and husband of Pieternella Buys) to have made and lacquered in Japan.[28] How the model reached Japan is not known, but it was returned to Batavia in 1640 in the *Castricum*. The balustrade itself was sent in two parts by François Caron (Opperhoofd in Japan) from Japan; the main part on 29 October 1639 on the *Breda*, the second part on 20 November 1640 on the *Witten Elephant*. Apparently the first part waited in Batavia for more than a year for the second part, but was eventually shipped on 30 November from Batavia to Holland on the *Salamander*, before the second part could have arrived in Batavia. That the whole balustrade was of first quality is confirmed by the price; the first, and larger part was valued at the huge price of 822 taels, the second part at 90.3 taels. The second part must have followed the first to Holland quickly, for on 19 August 1641 the Chamber of Amsterdam considered how to deal with the balustrade (as it was technically illegal private trade) and decided to present it to the Princess, at a value of 2342.14 florins. It turned out that it was a bit too large and five pilasters were omitted and stored.

In 1698 Thomas Bowrey[29] described the room as having 'a true Japan lackerd bed [of which, alas, we know nothing] and Inclosed with rails and Banisters of the same work'. On 16 August 1797, under the French regime, it was put up for auction (lot 162) as *een kostbaar Chinees verlakt hek met paerl d'amour ingelegt, lang 28, hoog 2.5 voet, met zijn voetbank* (a costly Chinese lacquered fence inlaid with pearlshell, 28 feet long, 2.5 feet high, with its plinth)[30], but was unsold. As the present piece of furniture was made up in the early nineteenth century, it is likely that the pilasters, if indeed they do originate as we suggest, came from after the sale, rather than being four of the five put into storage in the 1640s.

Fig. 4. The Victoria and Albert Museum jewel box, *c.* 1640; h. 20.1 cm, w. 28.4 cm, d. 19.6 cm; Victoria and Albert Museum, 628–1868

Fig. 5. The Victoria and Albert Museum jewel box, *c.* 1640; decoration within the upper compartment; Victoria and Albert Museum, 628–1868

Other pieces are documented in Europe, but not in the VOC records. A good example is the Trianon close-stool and its former 'pair', now dismembered and its parts incorporated into at least two, and possibly more, pieces of high quality French furniture by Adam Weisweiler under the direction of the *marchand-mercier* Dominique Daguerre.[31] The close-stool in the Petit Trianon appears not to be documented, but in the Garde Meuble in 1729 there is a description of what must have been its pair. When Weisweiler delivered the grand *secrétaire* for the Cabinet Intérieur du Roi to Versailles on 11 January 1784, it came with the side panels but without the front panels, which were to be supplied by the Garde Meuble. These were the front and sides of the close-stool. The top of the close-stool was made into the hinged top panel of a writing table supplied by Weisweiler to Marie-Antoinette at St Cloud in the same year. Furthermore there is a commode with *pietra dura* panels attributed to Weisweiler that incorporates borders that seem to come off the same close-stool. The point is that Daguerre knew exactly what lacquer he had to supply for the components not taken from the close-stool, for both the former pieces of furniture, and had them available to use. The side panels of the *secrétaire* and the flanking panels of the writing table are in the same style. As the borders of both close-stools and on these extra panels resemble closely those on the Mazarin chest, there must have been other pieces of similar type to be dismembered. Further examples of this type are found in the side-panels of other pieces of furniture by Weisweiler, notably the pair of *secrétaires* in the Metropolitan Museum[32], further evidence of the connoisseurship of Daguerre, but we do not know from what shapes they derive.

The problem is made more complex by the antiques trade of the eighteenth century; dealers were looking for 'old japan' which might equally have been straightforward export pieces, but also included pieces not originally made for export but which had nevertheless found their way to Europe. So much did this happen, that there must have been a flourishing private (and therefore undocumented) trade in Japanese-market lacquer among the Dutch merchants in Nagasaki. The *marchand-mercier* Edmé François Gersaint, who had several times been in Holland, wrote in 1745 'Les morceaux de choix sont de même extrêmement rares à trouver, particulièrement quand ils sont anciens. Ils sont quelquefois portez à des prix qui étonnent même en Hollande'[33]. Such pieces could be disassembled 'at a very great risque' as Vulliamy put it, just as could the export pieces. The fall front of the *secrétaire en cabinet* by Weisweiler now in the Huntington Art Gallery[34] cannot have come from a box, as the flanking panels on the centre row are upright and fit at either side of the central panel suggesting they were cut from it in order to balance the other panels, which are all horizontal in format and not consecutive in design.

Even more enigmatic is yet another cabinet by Weisweiler.[35] The doors are made from a large panel cut vertically; or are they the doors of a cabinet of European shape? As the picture on the doors is of the Yatsuhashi bridge, scarcely a European-taste subject, then this must have been an exceptional cabinet, of a type not known today. It may have been known only a hundred-odd years ago, for in the late 19th century, the cabinet-maker Henri Dasson made a cabinet much in the style of Weisweiler[36], and of the previously-mentioned cabinet in particular, using as doors two somewhat similar panels very much in Japanese taste and of Japanese pictorial subject-matter, deer and maples, chrysanthemum, bush-clover and bird-cages. These doors seem too large for a piece for Japanese use, even for a large *bunko* or document box.

Connoisseurship was not confined to the *marchants-merciers*; their clients must also have been well aware of the differences in quality available. Mme de Pompadour, for instance, who is always praised for her good taste, kept the van Diemen box in an ormolu-mounted glass case.[37] The Queen Marie-Antoinette had a collection of Japanese lacquer, most of it of non-export type, much of it 'enhanced' in ormolu; and it was for her that Weisweiler had made the writing table for St Cloud from the top of the close-stool.[38] William Beckford, that fanatic collector, was certainly able to distinguish the best from the second-best.

Lacquer of this 'fine period' was extremely expensive; as the Dutch grew more accustomed to the new styles of lacquer, the 'transition' from the *namban* into the 'pictorial', so demand must have grown wider, more was demanded of the lacquerers for less money (the documents are full of this) so that the quality suffered. The quality was still sufficient to satisfy demand, and today one has to look hard to discriminate. It was presumably the lacquerers refusal to lower the quality yet further that caused the Dutch finally to cease official orders for large pieces of lacquer furniture after 1693.

Notes

1 Victoria and Albert Museum, London. See Earle 1983.
2 Elton Hall, Peterborough. See Earle 1983.
3 Earle 1983.
4 Sanz/Jordan Gschwend 2000. We are grateful to them for allowing us access to their unpublished work.
5 For a photograph that shows some of the top, see Boyer 1959, pl. 57.
6 Unpublished; see Impey/Jörg/Viallé, forthcoming.
7 Rijksarchiv, The Hague, Factorij Japan, NFJ 767.
8 NFJ 772.
9 It could be that in this context, the word *geheel* implies raised work, *verheven*, but this is conjecture. The words do not appear ever to occur in the same *factuur*.
10 NFJ 763.
11 VOC 863.
12 Meech 1995, no. 3.
13 Earle 1983.
14 Hutt March 1998, pp. 3–9.
15 Roberts Oct. 1986, pp. 38–141.
16 Chiddingstone Castle, Kent; Trustees of the Denys Eyre Bower, on loan to the Ashmolean Museum, Oxford.
17 Museum für angewandte Kunst, Vienna.
18 NFJ 263.
19 NFJ 780.
20 Illustrated in Thornton 1978, pl. 239.
21 Ebony was frequently imported into Japan; see, for instance the letter from Richard Cocks, Chief Merchant of the English Factory in Hirado, to the East India Company, of 25 February 1616, reporting on the wreck of 'a Portingale [Portuguese] junk on the coast of Japon laden with ebony wood the greatest part'. Foster 1896–1902, 6 vols., vol. IV, p. 53.
22 Victoria and Albert Museum, London. See Earle 1983.
23 Private collection, Oxford. See *Lacquer* 1984, col. pl. on p. 127.
24 Petit Trianon, Versailles. See Impey/Whitehead Sept. 1990, pp. 159–165, pl. 1.
25 Sold by Christie's, London, 12 November 1996, lot 257.
26 Private collection. Sold by Christie's, London, 14 June 1993, lot 427.
27 For this room, see Scheurleer 1969, no. 1, pp. 29–66. The sales catalogue (1797) is Lugt, *Repertoire des ventes*, no. 5641.
28 This is documented in the Rijksarchiv, The Hague; NFJ 764, 839, 840, and VOC 101, 1133. See also Impey/Jörg/Viallé, forthcoming.
29 Temple 1927.
30 Sales catalogue (1797) Lugt, *Repertoire des ventes*, no. 5641.
31 See Impey/Whitehead Sept. 1990.
32 See Impey/Kisluk-Grosheide Jan. 1994, pp. 48–61. See especially fig. 4. Note (pl. 2) that the front panels have been replaced.
33 Sales catalogue of the Chevalier de Roque, 1745. Quoted in Whitehead 1992, p. 188 and note on p. 248.
34 Illustrated in Pradère 1989, pl. 482.
35 Pradère 1989, p. 42.
36 Sold Christie's, London, 16 June 1992, lot 333.
37 See Cordey 1939.
38 Impey/Whitehead Sept. 1990.

Acknowledgment

The work in this paper is part of the research undertaken for the forthcoming book *Japanese export lacquer*, by Oliver Impey, Christiaan Jörg and Cynthia Viallé. I am grateful to both my colleagues for allowing me to use this work.

References

Boyer, Martha: *Japanese export lacquers of the seventeenth century in the National Museum of Denmark*, Copenhagen, 1959

Cordey, J.: *Inventaire des biens de Mme de Pompadour rédigé après son décès*, Paris, 1939

Crowood Press (ed.): *Lacquer*, Marlborough, Wilts., 1984

Earle, J. J.: 'Genji meets Yang Guifei. A group of Japanese export lacquers', *Transactions of the Oriental Ceramic Society*, vol. 47, 1983, pp. 45–76

Foster, William: *Letters received by the East India Company from its servants in the East,* London, 1896–1902, 6 vols., vol. IV

Hutt, Julia: 'A Japanese lacquer chest in the V&A: A seventeenth-century wedding casket for the Dutch market', *Apollo*, vol. CXXXXVII, no. 433, March 1998, pp. 3–9

Impey, Oliver/Jörg, Christiaan/Viallé, Cynthia: *Japanese export lacquer*, forthcoming

Impey, Oliver/Kisluk-Grosheide, Danielle: 'The Japanese connection. French eighteenth-century furniture and export lacquer', *Apollo*, vol. CXXXIX, no. 383, Jan. 1994, pp. 48–61

Impey, Oliver/Whitehead, John: 'From Japanese box to French Royal Furniture', *Apollo*, vol. CXXXII, no. 343, Sept. 1990, pp. 159–165

Meech, Julia: *Lacquerware from the Weston Collection*, New York, 1995

Pradère, Alexandre: *French Furniture Makers. The Art of the Ébéniste from Louis XIV to the Revolution*, London, 1989

Roberts, Hugh: 'Beckford, Vulliamy and Old Japan', *Apollo*, vol. CXXIV, no. 296, Oct. 1986, pp. 338–341.

Sanz, Ana Garcia/Jordan Gschwend, Annemarie: 'Via Orientalis. Asian and Far Eastern objects in the Descalzas Reales', *Realos Sitios,* no. 138, 2000, pp. 25–39

Scheurleer, Th. H. Lunsingh: 'De woonvertrekken in Amalia's Huis in het Bosch', *Oud Holland*, 84, no. 1, 1969, pp. 29–66

Temple, R. C. (ed.): *The papers of Thomas Bowrey 1669–1713*, Hakluyt Society, second series, vol. 58, 1927

Thornton, Peter: *Seventeenth-century interior decoration in England, France and Holland*, New Haven/London, 1978

Whitehead, John: *The French Interior in the eighteenth century*, London, 1992

Photo Credits

Figs. 1, 2, 4, 5: Victoria and Albert Museum, London
Fig. 3: Ashmolean Museum of Art and Archaeology, Oxford
Colour plate II: photograph courtesy Christie's, London
Colour plate III.1: private collection

1

▽ 2

1 The Arched cabinet, *c.* 1640; h. 46.6 cm, w. 49 cm, d. 34.2 cm; private collection

2 Paulus Moreelse, *Allegory of Vanity* (detail), oil on canvas, 1627; Fitzwilliam Museum, Cambridge

3–5 Chest, gold and silver *hiramakie* and *takamakie*, gold foil and mother-of-pearl on a black lacquer ground, Japanese for the Western market, *c.*1640; Victoria and Albert Museum, FE.63–1997 (side: 8 x 7.2 cm, front and top: 8 x 15.3 x 7.2 cm)

3 ▽

4 ▽

5 ▽

Julia Hutt

East and West in Japanese Export Lacquerware: Some Problem Pieces in the Victoria and Albert Museum

The Victoria and Albert Museum (hereafter referred to as V&A) houses a small, but extremely important, group of seventeenth century Japanese export lacquerware, a number of which have been referred to by Oliver Impey in this publication. In addition, in 1997 the V&A was fortunate to acquire at auction an extremely small, high quality export lacquer chest (colour plate III.4) which posed many intriguing questions that were not immediately answerable. What makes it particularly interesting, moreover, is that it is of a type and size never seen before in a Japanese context, while its function initially remained uncertain.

In an attempt to answer some of these questions, it is necessary first to examine the chest in the overall context of Japanese lacquerware. A comparison with some of the key pieces of export lacquerware shows that it, too, belongs to the group of objects produced between approximately 1630 and 1640, referred to as the 'high quality' group. These were of a far higher standard of workmanship than earlier export pieces, which were produced up until the 1620s and termed *namban* ('southern barbarian'). In particular, the chest bears many points of similarity to the van Diemen[1] and Buys[2] boxes, as well as the Mazarin[3] and Lawrence[4] chests. The main characteristics shared by lacquerwork of this high quality group are the use of geometric borders, ogival cartouches and subject matter that alludes to the *Genji monogatari* ('The Tale of Genji'), in complex and expensive lacquer techniques, such as *takamakie* ('high sprinkled picture'), often combined with gold and silver inlay.

Up until around the 1640s, Japanese export lacquerware was characterised by designs that covered virtually the entire surface area of an object, a feature rarely encountered on examples for the domestic market. In addition, areas of decoration were surrounded by geometric borders or shaped cartouches. A thin strip of gold foil encloses the main designs on all four sides of the small chest, followed by thicker zigzag borders. By contrast, the rim of the lid is edged with a key-fret pattern in thin slivers of mother-of-pearl shell on a black lacquer ground (colour plate III.5). Although both zigzag and key-fret borders are commonly found on earlier examples of *namban* lacquerware, a key-fret border executed in an identical manner is also found as the outer border on all four sides and lid of the Mazarin chest (fig. 4).

Among the high quality group of export lacquerware, the most important areas of decoration were frequently surrounded by highly ornate cartouches, which were themselves one of the distinguishing characteristics of the group. The focal point of the small chest, for example, is a design of buildings in a landscape set within an ogival cartouche on the slightly domed lid (colour plate III.5). It was, in addition, common practice for such cartouches to be set against a repetitive ground pattern, in this case a *shokkō-kin* diaper pattern in gold on black lacquer. In such cases, the ornate cartouche served to distinguish and separate the strongly contrasting geometric ground from the main area of decoration, a distinction that was further emphasised by outlining the cartouche in gold foil. Although there are numerous examples of this stylistic feature, that which occurs on what would have been the flat top of the Buys box is especially worthy of comparison (fig. 1).

Another feature of the small chest also has close parallels with other examples of the high quality group of export lacquerware. The two semi-circular end panels of the lid are each decorated with a flower head among scrolling leaves in gold *hiramakie* ('low sprinkled picture') on black lacquer (colour plate III.3). An almost identical scrolling design also forms the borders immediately surrounding the name panel of the van Diemen (fig. 2) and Buys boxes. A similar, but more ornate scroll that incorporates other flower heads and motifs embellished with mother-of-pearl shell and gold foil, also forms the main borders on the exterior of the van Diemen box and Mazarin chest (fig. 4).

Another characteristic of high quality export lacquerware is that a high proportion is decorated with figural scenes that allude to the *Genji monogatari* ('The Tale of Genji'), the great classic of Japanese literature, written by Murasaki Shikibu around 1000 AD. This massive work follows the life of Prince Genji, recounting his numerous romantic associations with women of different backgrounds. Since Europeans did not reach Japan until 1543, comparatively little was known about Japan in the West in the early seventeenth century. The use of scenes from the *Genji monogatari* to decorate lacquerwork intended for this market was, therefore, somewhat curious. Lacquerware for the home market rarely portrayed figures as contemporary custom dictated that explicit narrative be avoided. In its place, the depiction of a few key elements from a particular event or chapter was sufficient to trigger the necessary association for any educated Japanese. Presumably Japanese craftsmen were equally ignorant of their Western customer and assumed they had a basic knowledge of the story but needed greater visual prompts. For this reason, normal convention was flouted in the decoration of export lacquerware and a few key figures from the novel were depicted in an appropriate setting. An understanding of the story was, in fact, of no importance whatsoever. What appealed to these foreign clients were figures in completely different dress and settings that came to embody the exoticism associated with Japan and the East.

Since it has already been suggested that the small chest shares many features in common with the high quality group of export lacquerwork, it would seem highly probable that it, too, is decorated with scenes from the *Genji monogatari*. However, the small size of the chest inevitably involves the simplification of a design to its barest components so that an association with a particular chapter or event is neither straightforward nor always possible. Only two of the five chest panels portray figures; although those on one side (colour plate III.3) are dressed in court attire, their allusion to a particular chapter is not precisely clear.[5] The figures on the chest front (colour plate III.4) possibly allude, in an abbreviated form, to *Nowaki* ('The Typhoon'), chapter 28, when women were sent to put out insect cages and search for stray flowers untouched by the storm. References to this chapter are also found on several other items of lacquerware

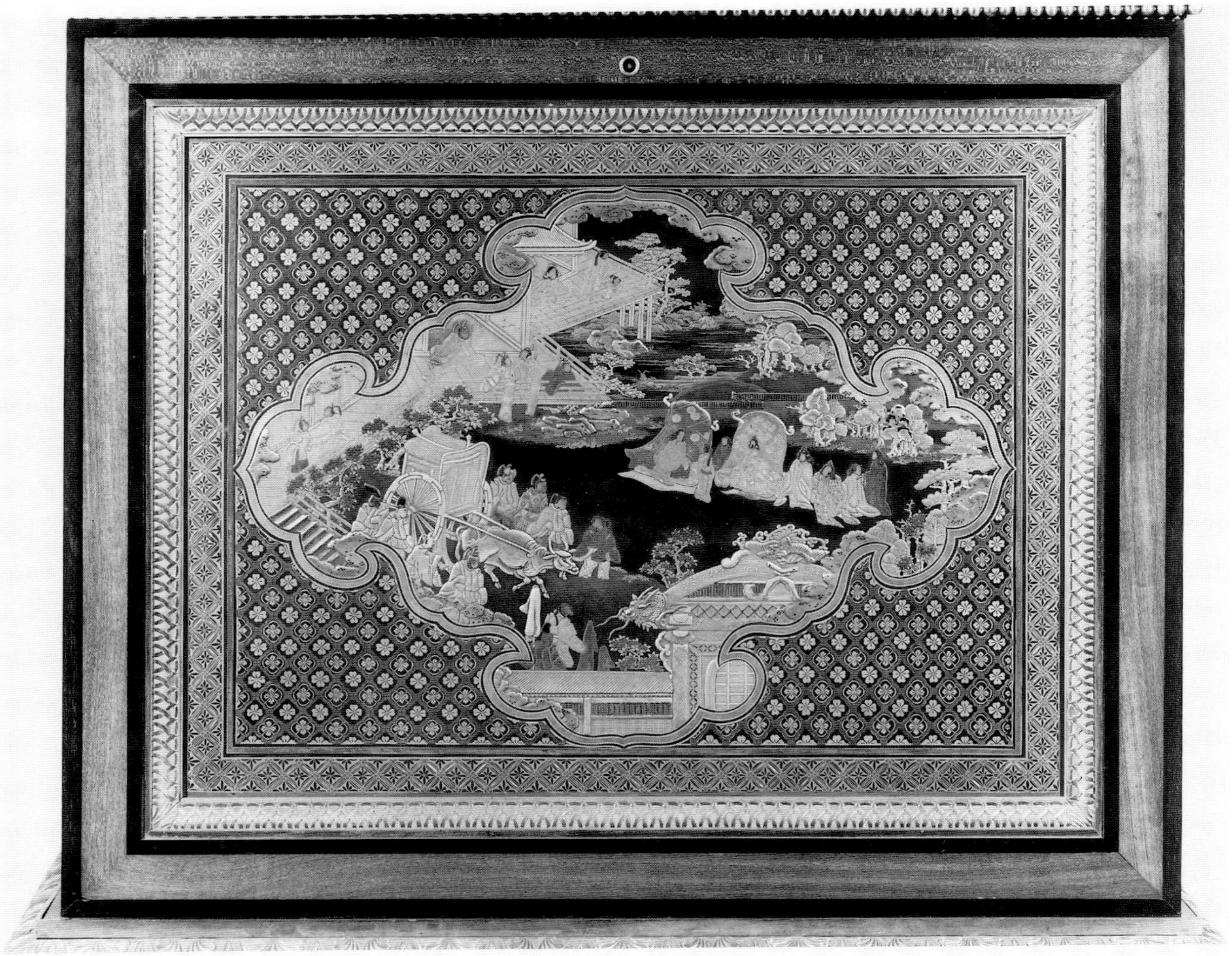

Fig. 1. Buys box (detail of what was the exterior of the lid), scene from chapter 1 *Genji monogatari*, on a *hanabishi* ('stylised flowers') ground, gold and silver *hiramakie* and *takamakie*, with gold foil on a black lacquer ground, Japanese for the Western market, 1636–1639; 34.4 x 45.7 cm; Elton Hall, Peterborough, Proby Collection

from this group, namely the front panels of the Mazarin (fig. 4) and Lawrence (fig. 6) chests, as well as what remains of the front panel (fig. 5) of a third chest, which will be discussed in greater detail later.

Apart from Genji-related scenes, other subjects portrayed on high quality export lacquerware were distinctive palatial buildings, often with a complex of interconnecting verandahs, bridges and gateways (colour plate III.5). One cannot help drawing a comparison between such a design within the ogival cartouche on the lid of the small chest and the top and inside of the lid of the Mazarin chest, which depicts palace buildings in their surrounding landscape within extremely elaborate cartouches formed by phoenixes and dragons.

But what was particularly intriguing about this small lacquer chest was its function, which was not immediately apparent. Export lacquerware is almost entirely composed of shapes or forms that had some practical function in a Western context, particularly the chest or coffer. In addition there were a small number of rare items, such as pipe cases or ruff boxes, which were the result of special commissions rather than regular trade goods.

Fig. 2. Van Diemen box (interior of lid), inscribed Maria van Diemen, gold *hiramakie* with gold foil on a black lacquer ground, Japanese for the Western market, *c.*1636–1639; 48.0 x 26.7 cm; Victoria and Albert Museum, W.49–1916

The chest which forms the main subject of this paper so far, is quite remarkable on account of its exceedingly small size (8 x 15.3 x 7.2 cm) and the fact that it is neither a flat-topped nor a domed chest, but a cross between the two. It is essentially a chest with an overhanging lid that also rises to a gentle curve. Such a form would appear to be quite unique in lacquer or any other medium in Japan during the early seventeenth century.

The auction catalogue[6] in which the chest was offered for sale noted that it had almost exactly the same height to width proportions as another high quality piece of export lacquerware, namely the Lawrence chest. It also suggested that, on the basis of this information, it could have been a scaled-down model of the Lawrence and very similar Mazarin chests, a sample to whet the appetite of Dutch officials and traders. This hypothesis, however, does not stand up to investigation. On the basis of shape alone, the small chest is fundamentally different, for it does not have a flat-topped lid. In addition, if the chest were intended as a sample or model to demonstrate the workshop's skills to the full, one would expect it to be of the highest quality. Even allowing for its size, the detail could have been much richer, particularly in the use of inlays; one such example is represented by the drawer sides of the contemporary export casket in the V&A.[7] Yet another possible function for the chest is that it could have been intended as a gift from Japanese to Dutch officials to smooth along complex negotiations in the purchase of the expensive larger chests.

It would seem far more likely, however, that a clue to its function lies in its distinctive shape and size. An examination of contemporary Dutch objects reveals unmistakable similarities with the chest to wedding caskets that were popular during the seventeenth century (fig. 3).[8] It was customary for such caskets to be filled with gold coins and offered by a man to his intended as a marriage token. Although the Dutch prototypes are generally deeper in form than the small lacquer chest, with a more pronounced dome to the lid, this is nevertheless combined with the unmistakable overhanging rim which is balanced by the base. The slight differences in form, together with the addition of a handle and feet, are acceptable when considering that Japanese craftsmen were working in a form unknown to them.

Wedding caskets were usually made of engraved silver as costly items in their own right. The fact that one such wedding casket was made of lacquer suggests that this, too, was considered a treasured medium. As there appear to be no other examples of lacquerwork in this form, it is highly likely that the small chest was specially commissioned either in Japan, Holland or by an official in the Dutch East Indies. On account of their quality, size and obvious cost of manufacture, the Mazarin and Lawrence chests must have been the result of a specific order. To these commissions must also be added at least three additional examples that were inscribed with Western names, namely the van Diemen and Buys boxes, as well as that of a box inscribed with the monogram 'F. C'.[9] These initials may well refer to François Caron, a highly successful individual who was initially made deputy Opperhoofd of the Dutch trading post at Hirado in 1633 and Opperhoofd in 1639. More particularly, the inside of the lid of the van Diemen box was inscribed with the name of Maria van Diemen, wife of Anton van Diemen, Governor-General of the Dutch East Indies from 1636–45 (fig. 2). Similarly the Buys box was also inscribed Pieternellae Buys, wife of Philips Lucasz, who was appointed Director-General, second-in-command to van Diemen, around 1635. Indeed it is on the basis of this biographical information that these boxes, and the whole group, may be loosely dated. It is highly probable that the small chest may have been made as the casket for the wedding of a high-ranking official, either that of Anton van Diemen in 1630 or, more probably, that of Philips Lucasz in 1634, during a two year return to the Netherlands. It is even possible that Lucasz returned to Holland with the explicit purpose of marriage and that he commissioned the casket prior to 1634 in anticipation of the event. Alternatively, a third party, such as François Caron, may even have commissioned it as a gift to his superior, Lucasz, to present to his wife.

Since a wedding casket was made of a costly material and was something of a status symbol, it was invariably utilised after a couple's betrothal, but probably for a slightly different function. Since most caskets were fitted with a lock, they were frequently used to store valuable items, especially rings, but also jewellery and gold coins.[10] This is well illustrated in a Dutch still life painting, *Allegory of Vanity*, by Paulus Moreelse, dated 1627 (colour plate III.2).[11] This portrays the lid of a small lacquer box open to reveal several ornate rings on a base covered in a red fabric, possibly velvet. As far as it is possible to be certain from the scale of the painting, shadow on the red lining of the lid's interior suggests that it was also domed, in keeping with a wedding casket. It is also worth noting that the V&A's small chest has a ledge running round the lower interior. The fact that the box in Moreelse's painting is fitted with a raised block to hold the rings possibly suggests a function for this ledge. Or was it simply designed to hold a removable tray, now missing?

The box portrayed in Moreelse's painting appears black covered with gold decoration, suggesting lacquerwork. The style of decoration, however, does not appear altogether typical of contemporary Japanese export lacquerwork. Since attempts to imitate Japanese lacquerware, termed japanning, could be observed during the first two decades of the seventeenth century in France, Italy, England, Denmark and Holland, it is possible that Moreelse's box was one such example. A surviving object of particular relevance in this context, datable to the first half of the seventeenth century, is a Dutch coffer, decorated with birds, flowers and scrollwork.[12] Although the overall form is that of a wedding casket, the dimensions of the coffer are slightly larger (22.5 x 25 x 17.5 cm).

Fig. 3. Wedding casket, engraved silver, Dutch; second half seventeenth century (mark crowned O); 8.4 x 8 x 5.1 cm; Victoria and Albert Museum, M.113–1923

The question of whether Moreelse's box was an example of japanning, Japanese lacquerware or was even produced in one of the areas serving the trading posts of the Dutch East India Company, has implications regarding the V&A's small lacquer chest. If Japanese, it probably represents the earliest portrayal of Japanese export lacquerware in a European painting and indicates the high esteem such work was accorded. It would also suggest, however, that the small chest was not the only one of its type to have been made, though it is the only one to have survived. If, on the other hand, the box in Moreelse's painting represents an example of japanning, this is nonetheless of considerable historical importance. It provides further evidence for the function of the V&A's chest, as a wedding casket and a box for rings. The scale of the box in the painting, however, is such that any conclusive judgement as to its place of manufacture is simply not possible.

I would now like to turn my attention to another different, but not unrelated, piece in the collection of the V&A, a composite object which has posed some interesting questions as to its original form. Japanese lacquerwork first reached Europe around 1560 and, being quite unlike anything seen before was enormously popular. The trees capable of producing lacquer were not native to Europe, while the knowledge of obtaining and working with the sap was simply not available. It not only became impossible to keep up with the demand for items decorated with this lustrous black and gold material, but prices also rose dramatically as a result. In time, the Dutch also began to find Japanese lacquerware too expensive and no more orders appeared in the books of the Dutch East India Company after 1693. Since examples of Japanese lacquerware could not be replaced at will, they became even more treasured, and worn or damaged objects could have relatively intact panels removed and reused. At a later date, furniture manufacturers and collectors felt no compunction at ordering the cutting of seventeenth century lacquerware from their original form. This was often for no reason other than to incorporate them into a piece of furniture of the latest fashion. The object under discussion, a French Boulle-work cabinet of early nineteenth-century date, is one such example, making use of three Japanese export lacquer panels around which the cabinet was designed. For conservation reasons, the cabinet has recently been dismantled, allowing an excellent opportunity for close examination of all constituent parts. It is immediately evident that the panels were cut from larger pieces; the compositions bear no apparent relation to where they were cut, while the details of the designs go right to the edges of the panels. The borders were then covered with black pigment, over which Boulle marquetry was placed.

Of the three lacquer panels that comprise the Boulle-work cabinet, one is larger than the others, while the remaining two are of equal size. In addition, one cannot help noticing the striking similarities between the largest panel (fig. 5) and the front of the Mazarin (fig. 4) and Lawrence (fig. 6) chests. Formerly in the collection of Sir Trevor Lawrence, the Lawrence chest was subsequently sold in 1916 and again in 1941 from Llantarnam Abbey near Cwmbran, Gwent, Wales, after which it completely disappeared. However, information concerning the chest may be obtained from the book of Sir Trevor Lawrence's collection privately published in 1895, which had, as its frontispiece, a black and white illustration of the chest. A comparison between the photograph and the Mazarin chest suggests that they were made in the same workshop. Both are large, flat-topped chests, sumptuously decorated with scenes from the *Genji monogatari*, with similar borders and large, ornate lock-plates. Calculations based on the photograph of the Lawrence chest, moreover, suggest that it was probably larger than the Mazarin chest.

Fig. 4. Mazarin chest, gold, silver and black *hiramakie* and *takamakie,* gold, silver and mother-of-pearl on a black lacquer ground, Japanese for the Western market, *c.*1640; 56.5 x 100.3 x 63.5 cm; Victoria and Albert Museum, 412–1882

Fig. 5. Panel, gold, silver and black *hiramakie* and *takamakie*, gold and mother-of-pearl on a black lacquer ground, Japanese for the Western market, *c.* 1640; 53 x 44 cm; Victoria and Albert Museum, 1084–1882

Fig. 6. Lawrence chest, scene from chapter 1 *Genji monogatari,* gold, silver and black *hiramakie* and *takamakie,* gold, silver and mother-of-pearl on a black lacquer ground, Japanese for the Western market, *c.* 1640

A stylistic comparison between the front of the Mazarin and Lawrence chests and the main panel of the Boulle-work cabinet, moreover, suggests that it, too, may also have derived from a third large chest similar to the other two. Among other important characteristics, all three are united by decoration from the *Genji monogatari*. The front of the Mazarin chest is unusual in that it depicts not a single episode but a number of different scenes from various chapters of the novel, including the aforementioned chapter 28 (*Nowaki* or 'The Typhoon') in the bottom left-hand corner. The front of the Lawrence chest, however, depicts women and girls among flowers and plants in a garden setting. This alludes to a single event, referred to in chapter 28, where females were sent to put out insect cages and search for stray flowers untouched by the storm. The main panel of the Boulle-work cabinet reveals striking similarities in composition to the front of the Lawrence chest, particularly to the bottom left-hand corner. Taking into account the respective sizes of the Lawrence and Mazarin chests, it is possible to suggest that the panel of the Boulle-work cabinet represents the left-hand side of a front of a third large chest. This would seem to be confirmed by the size of the panel itself; another panel of equal size, together with room for a large lock-plate, would roughly equal another chest of similar size.

It is also interesting to note that, whereas the materials and techniques of execution of the Lawrence and Mazarin chests are exceptional, those of the cut panel are less striking. If one were to imagine the constraints of time and money that the manufacture of two such chests would place on a workshop, it is easy to see how corners might be cut during the making of a third. It is even possible to see imperfections and signs of haste in the execution of its decoration. An examination of the open gateway in the bottom right corner of the cut panel, for example, reveals that the small roof is supported by poles and door panels to the front, but that it is unsupported to the rear, making it appear imbalanced.

It is also worth noting that the back of the main panel has been pared down to its pine base and bears an interesting inscription, roughly written in black ink. It reads 'Carter the bloke wants you

Fig. 7. Pair of panels, gold and silver *hiramakie* and *takamakie* on a black lacquer ground, Japanese for the Western market, *c.*1640; 43 x 24.7 cm each; Victoria and Albert Museum, 1084–1882

go at once keep ?rate'. The cabinet was very probably one and the same that was purchased from the Stowe sale of 1848 by Charles Cope for £37 12 shillings. It was restored some time later, possibly by the Carter whose name is mentioned. According to the Oxford English Dictionary, the expression 'bloke', meaning man or fellow, came into usage around 1851. The London Post Office Directory of 1872, moreover, lists a Thomas Arnold Carter, upholsterer, at 277, Euston Road, near Euston Square, the address given in the Stowe catalogue for Charles Cope.[13]

Fig. 8. Mazarin chest (side), gold, silver and black *hiramakie* and *takamakie,* gold, silver and mother-of-pearl on a black lacquer ground, Japanese for the Western market, *c.*1640; 56.5 x 63.5 cm; Victoria and Albert Museum, 412–1882

And what about the other two lacquer panels (fig. 7) of the Boulle-work cabinet? If one places them side by side, it is evident that the design continues from one panel to the other, such as the birds flying from one to the other, together with the shoreline in the very bottom of both compositions. It is evident, therefore, that the two panels were originally one larger panel, which was cut in two about a vertical axis. Bearing in mind the size and weight of the Mazarin chest, extremely robust handles with secure fixings were necessary to lift it. As a result, each side panel has a large handle with two fixing points (fig. 8). Each of the smaller panels of the Boulle-work cabinet has an oval repair that corresponds to the fixing point of one side of such a handle. The two panels together probably represent one side panel of a larger chest, though additionally trimmed down each side. Furthermore, before the original side panel was cut into two, the handle would need to be removed. This would leave two damaged, oval areas in panels that were otherwise in good condition. This problem was evidently overcome by filling the areas with material of comparable size and colour, and painting over details of the design at the joins so that they corresponded. As these areas of repair were undoubtedly inserted in Europe, one would expect them to be examples of japanning. However, an examination of the reverse of one of the panels throws up some unexpected information. The original panel was pared down on the back to its original pine body, leaving the lacquer decoration on the front untouched. The back of the oval inset is covered with *nashiji* ('pear-skin ground'), one of the most quintessential of Japanese lacquer techniques (fig. 9). This is unequivocal proof of Japanese, rather than European, manufacture for the repairs. Since the front of the inset is covered with black lacquer, two small pieces were evidently taken from an object, possibly already damaged, that was lacquered black on the outside and *nashiji* on the inside, a typical Japanese combination. These were then inserted into the damaged areas to produce a most satisfactory solution to the problem.

It is tempting to suggest that the two smaller panels of the Boulle-work cabinet originally formed one side panel of a chest, possibly the same chest from which the larger main panel also derived. It must be noted, however, that there is a difference in quality between the side and front panels. Is this, however, an acceptable discrepancy for panels belonging to one object? It is in-

Fig. 9. Panel (reverse; cf. fig. 7), pine wood, *nashiji* lacquer insert, Japanese for the Western market, *c.*1640; 43 x 24.7 cm; Victoria and Albert Museum, 1084–1882

terested to note that the same inconsistency may also be observed on the Mazarin chest. In the case of low chests, the focal point of decoration was invariably the top and front, with less attention being paid to the sides. The fact that the back panel of the Mazarin chest is striking in design but far inferior in terms of materials and techniques, was undoubtedly due to the fact that the back was often placed against a wall and was not immediately visible. Probably for the same reasons mentioned earlier, the two smaller panels are also not of the same quality as those of the Mazarin chest. It is also possible, of course that the panels are from a chest or chests altogether unconnected with the Lawrence and Mazarin chests. I think, however, that the similarities, particularly those of subject matter and composition, are more than mere coincidence. If one may propose that all three panels originally belonged to a third chest, similar to the Mazarin and Lawrence chests but of slightly inferior quality, it is interesting to speculate what might have happened to the other pieces of the chest, namely the top, back, other front half and the other side. Were they already worn or damaged before the chest was cut up, or were they so mutilated in the process as to be beyond recognition today and untraceable?

My paper has been concerned with 'problem pieces' of Japanese export lacquerware in the collection of the V&A. Although the state of our knowledge on the subject has greatly increased in recent years, there still remain many tantalising questions to which we shall probably never have satisfactory or conclusive answers. On the basis of a newly-discovered object that has only recently been added to the V&A's collection, and one that has been in the Museum's collection for over one hundred years, it has been instructive to re-examine a group of objects that share important key characteristics, namely the high quality group of export lacquerware.

Notes

1 Museum inventory number W.49–1916, V&A.
2 Elton Hall, Peterborough. Although the box was originally thought to have been of identical form to the van Diemen box, it was subsequently dismantled in 1803 for William Beckford, and reused to adorn a pair of secretaires.
3 Museum inventory number 412–1882, V&A.
4 Present whereabouts unknown.
5 See Hutt March 1998, pp. 6–7, for a fuller discussion.
6 Sale of Export Art of China and Japan, Christie's, London, Monday, 7 April 1997, lot 171, p. 176.
7 Museum inventory number 628–1868, V&A.
8 I am indebted to Christiaan Jörg for bringing these to my attention.
9 See Eskenazi 1986, cat. no. 56.
10 The practice of keeping jewellery and coins in ornate lacquered boxes of East Asian origin other than wedding caskets is reflected in various still lifes of the seventeenth century. One such example is a painting by Jan Brueghel the Elder, dated 1618, in the Musées Royaux des Beaux-Arts, Brussels, museum inventory number 5013, and illustrated in Segal 1989, fig. 6.3.
11 Fitzwilliam Museum, Cambridge.
12 Illustrated in Hutt March 1999, p. 23, fig. 4.
13 See forthcoming V&A publication, C. Sargentson et al., *French Furniture 1640–1790 in the Victoria and Albert Museum.*

References

Eskenazi: *Japanese netsuke, inro and lacquer-ware* (exhibition and sales catalogue), London, 12–23 December, 1986
Hutt, Julia: 'A Japanese lacquer chest in the V&A: A seventeenth-century wedding casket for the Dutch market', *Apollo*, vol. CXXXXVII, no. 433, March 1998, pp. 3–9
Hutt, Julia: 'A Japanese export lacquer chest in the Victoria and Albert Museum: Some further observations', *Apollo*, vol. CXLIX, no. 445, March 1999, pp. 22–24
Sargentson, C. et al.: *French Furniture 1640–1790 in the Victoria and Albert Museum,* forthcoming
Segal, Sam: *A prosperous Past: The Sumptuous Still Life in the Netherlands 1600–1700*, 1989

Photo Credits

Fig. 1: Elton Hall, Peterborough, Proby Collection
Figs. 2–5, 7–9: Victoria and Albert Museum, London
Fig. 6: Catalogue of the Sir Trevor Lawrence collection, 1895, frontispiece
Colour plate III.2: Fitzwilliam Museum, Cambridge
Colour plate III.3–5: Victoria and Albert Museum, London

Daniëlle Kisluk-Grosheide

The (Ab)Use of Export Lacquer in Europe

During the sixteenth century a small number of lacquer objects reached Europe through the trade activities of the Portuguese. These rare and early examples of Asian lacquer entered a few select Kunstkammer collections. A good example is a Japanese, so-called, *namban* lacquer cabinet that was in the possession of Archduke Ferdinand II (1525–1595) of Tyrol at the time of his death.[1] Objects of this kind were held in high esteem and were also used as official gifts. In 1616, for instance, the Dutch Republic presented King Gustavus Adolphus II (1594–1632) of Sweden with a Japanese lacquer trunk embellished with mother-of-pearl in *namban* style.[2] By this time the Dutch East India Company (V.O.C.), founded in 1602, played an increasingly important role in the Far East and the Dutch became the only Europeans to be allowed to trade with Japan in 1639. As a result a larger quantity of lacquered goods such as coffers, chests and two door cabinets, so-called *comptoirs*, were shipped to the Netherlands. Mostly supplied in pairs, these cabinets were generally placed on elaborately carved and gilded stands. They continued to be valued furnishings for a long time as is clearly illustrated by a 1861 watercolor of Franz Alt (1821–1914) depicting one of Archduke Ludwig Victor's (1842–1919) rooms at the Hofburg in Vienna which includes four of such Japanese lacquer cabinets (colour plate IV.2).[3]

Despite the fact that Japanese lacquered goods, which were more highly valued than similar Chinese objects, were in great demand in the West, these products were never very profitable for the Dutch East India Company. Due to the labor-intensive procedure of making high quality lacquer, these cabinets and coffers were costly. In addition, they were also bulky and occupied a lot of space in the ships that could be better used for other, more lucrative, wares. As a result, the quantity of Japanese lacquered objects was small compared, for instance, with the large number of imported porcelain pieces. This discrepancy is also clearly reflected in contemporary paintings; while there are many still lives depicting blue and white porcelain, lacquered items are rarely illustrated in seventeenth-century Dutch paintings.[4] One such exception is an undated 'Allegory of the Vanities of Human Life'[5] by Harmen Steenwyck (1612– after 1656) which includes a Japanese sword in a black lacquer scabbard inlaid with mother-of-pearl, that recurs in at least one other of his Vanitas still lifes.[6] This sword, symbolizing the transitory nature of power, may have belonged to one of Steenwyck's patrons. It is, however, also possible and even tempting to think that the artist acquired it himself while traveling in the East Indies and used it as an exotic prop in his paintings after his return in 1655.[7]

Two small lacquered coffers are barely visible on top of the cabinet in a painting by Pieter de Hooch (1629–1684), showing a family in an elegant and well-appointed home (fig. 1).[8] The painting dates to 1663 when de Hooch had moved to Amsterdam from his native Delft. In Amsterdam de Hooch would have had a greater access to such luxury objects. The city's thirty or more East India shops sold a variety of imported goods and the city's officials of the East India Company and many other wealthy merchants had porcelain and lacquer objects in their collections.[9] The inventory of such a successful Amsterdam merchant and art collector Jean Niquet, for instance, drawn up a few years after his death in 1608, already listed a red East Indian cabinet and another inlaid with mother-of-pearl which may well have been made in the Far East.[10] A variety of lacquer goods, some embellished with mother-of-pearl, were also in the residences of the Dutch stadholder in The Hague. The 1632 inventory included various boxes and cabinets, some placed on gilded stands, said to be either from the East Indies, China or Japan.[11]

It was at Huis ten Bosch, the summer palace of Stadholder Frederick Henry, Prince of Orange (1584–1647) and his wife Amalia of Solms-Braunfels (1602–1675) that lacquer was used in a completely new and stunning manner shortly after 1654. Several large Namban coffers from the Stadholder's collection were dismantled and their lacquer panels were used to line the walls of a small room or cabinet, perhaps to create a suitable background for Amalia's collection of Asian art.[12] Travelers mentioned this unusual interior in their diaries, frequently confusing the Japanese lacquer with that from China. In 1677, the brothers Guido and Giulio de Bovio, visitors from Bologna, described the cabinet as 'very grand and sumptuous, completely covered with Chinese wood and painted in the manner of that country, even mother-of-pearl is not wanting, all of which gives the interior a look of considerable extravagance'.[13] Nearly twenty years later, in 1695, another traveler William Montague, pointed to the origin of the lacquer panels when he described this room in his book *The Delights of Holland* as a closet 'of all True Indian Japan, made of Cabinets or Chests taken in pieces'.[14]

Fig. 1. A Family Making Music. Oil on canvas. Pieter de Hooch, 1663

1 Vienna, Schönbrunn Palace, Vieux Laque Zimmer

2 Archduke Ludwig Victor's Salon in the Hofburg, Vienna. Watercolor. Franz Alt, 1861

During the 1680's several rooms, made with Chinese incised, so-called Coromandel lacquer panels cut from screens, were commissioned by Mary Stuart (1662–1695), wife of the Dutch stadholder William III of Orange (1650–1702) and future Queen of England.[15] Today these rooms are only known through the descriptions of impressed visitors. At the palace at Honselaarsdijk outside The Hague, for instance, the Swedish court architect Nicodemus Tessin the Younger (1654–1728) admired a lacquer cabinet in 1687 that was 'sehr kostbahr aussgemacht mit Chineser Arbeit und Tafeln'.[16] It had a mirrored ceiling, according to Tessin 'in welches man die Cammer wieder von neuen sahe…' and was appropriately furnished with lacquered furniture and porcelain.

The dismantling of lacquer objects was not met with general approval and in 1685 Princess Mary received a letter from one of the stadholder's advisers, Constantijn Huygens (1608–1687), that was supposedly written on behalf of the entire Chinese nation. Huygens criticized the cutting up of a Chinese lacquer screen the panels of which were reused as wall decoration at the court. Lamenting the insensitive destruction of Mary's screen Huygens wrote: 'This illustrious monument has been sawed, divided, cut, clift and split asunder by some most ignorant barbarous and malicious people and has thus been reduced to a heap of monstruous shivers and splinters for the sole purpose of serving as a wall decoration of some miserable cabinet'.[17] Typically, no attention had been paid to the images of the screen so that the scenes did not make any sense and that several of the figures were placed upside down. Despite such objections, lacquered screens continued to be dismantled for the decoration of walls until the middle of the nineteenth century.

The only seventeenth-century room of this kind to survive is on display at the Rijksmuseum in Amsterdam and comes from the court of the Stadholder in Leeuwarden (fig. 2).[18] The wall paneling was created from the leaves of three different Coromandel screens, mounted above a low dado and surmounted by a gilded cornice. The residence was renovated for one of the granddaughters of Frederick Henry, Henriëtte Amalia of Anhalt Dessau (1666–1726) who in 1694 had several lacquer screens in her possession. These screens were no longer listed in the inventory drawn up two years later, which gives a good indication of the date of the room. Fitted with a painted ceiling, this lacquer cabinet was originally furnished with carved and gilded etagères that were lined with mirror glass and held costly porcelain on their shelves. Additional porcelain was placed on red or black lacquered drum-shaped tables.

Fig. 2. Cabinet with Coromandel lacquer paneling, originally from the Stadholder's court in Leeuwarden, ca. 1694–96

Fig. 3. Design for a wall elevation with fireplace incorporating lacquered panels and porcelain by Daniel Marot, print from *Nouvelles Cheminées*, Amsterdam 1712

Fig. 4. Design for the wall elevation of an anteroom from Paul Decker's *Fürstlicher Baumeister*, Augsburg 1711

Panel of red Chinese lacquer, originally part of the wall decoration of the *cabinet de travail* at the Hôtel du Châtelet, Paris

From contemporary descriptions it is known that similar rooms were also created in England, France and Germany during the last quarter of the seventeenth century. The English diarist John Evelyn (1620–1706), for instance, described in 1682 the house of his 'good neigbour', Mr. Bohun, a wealthy Spanish merchant, as 'a cabinet of all elegancies, especially Indian; in the hall are contrivances of Japan screens, instead of wainscot. (...) The landscapes of the screens represent the manner of living, and country of the Chinese'.[19]

The indefatigable traveler Celia Fiennes (1662–1741) mentions in her journals similar interiors at Burghley House and at Hampton Court.[20] The one at Hampton Court, 'pannell'd all with Jappan' was created for Queen Mary and must, therefore, antedate the Queen's death in 1694.[21] At Chatsworth, Miss Fiennes admired the Duchess's closet that was 'wanscoated with the hollow burnt japan' [Coromandel lacquer].[22] Having framed, moulded and cut the 'Japan' and joined it into panels, the cabinetmaker Gerrit Jensen (d. 1715) was paid for 'japanning' this closet in 1692.[23] Eight years later, the Coromandel paneling of this room was dismantled and the lacquer was most likely recycled for the second time by being used for the two cabinets on stands that are still in the State Drawing Room at Chatsworth today.

In France, the English doctor and naturalist, Martin Lister (c. 1683–1712), saw in 1698 a cabinet at the Château de Saint Cloud which was decorated with panels of 'laque du Japon' that were combined with paintings and mirrors.[24] Coromandel screens were also taken apart for the wall paneling of cabinets in the residences of the Electors in Berlin and in Dresden.[25]

Despite the stylistic changes that were to take place, the fashion for such luxury rooms, often combining both lacquer and porcelain in their décor, continued during the eighteenth century and may well have been stimulated by the work of the influential designer Daniel Marot (1661–1752). One of Marot's well-known engravings, dating c. 1700, shows a wall elevation, incorporating lacquered panels and a decorative display of porcelain (fig. 3). A similar design, most likely based on those by Marot, was also included in the *Fürstlicher Baumeister* of 1711 by the Nuremberg architect Paul Decker (1677–1713) (fig. 4). A cabinet at Tsar Peter the Great's (1672–1725) *Monplaisir*, in the gardens of Peterhof outside St. Petersburg, with its late Baroque wall elevation is very close to such designs.[26] As this last example shows, japanning could, and often was, substituted for true lacquer and a fair number of imitation lacquer rooms was created during the eighteenth century.[27] In other instances, tapestries[28], and embroidered or leather hangings,[29] clearly inspired by imported lacquer, were used to create a similar effect (fig. 5).

Six Chinese black and gold lacquer panels, however, were inserted in a beautiful early Rococo *boiserie* that was originally part of the Hôtel d'Evreux on the Place de Vendôme in Paris (c. 1715–1725).[30] Coromandel lacquer was part of a sumptuous room decoration in Palazzo Reale, Turin. The architect Filippo Juvarra (1678–1736) had seen the lacquer while in Rome in 1732 and had written to the Prime Minister of King Charles Emmanuel III of Savoy (1730–1773) that these panels, combined with porcelain, would make a splendid décor for a small room.[31] Executed according to the ideas of Juvarra, the so-called Chinese cabinet was completed with japanned designs by a local artist, Pietro Massa, in ca. 1736. A number of lacquered stools, part of the original furnishings, are still at the royal palace.[32]

Chinese lacquer was also used for a cabinet in Falkenlust, a small hunting retreat near Schloss Brühl (c. 1736), that was built for the Elector and Prince Bishop of Cologne, Clemens August of Bavaria (d. 1761).[33] The lacquer panels, specifically acquired for this purpose in Paris in c. 1736, were placed within white and gold Rococo paneling and are supplemented with japanned scenes. The carved brackets surrounding the lacquer panels were intended to hold porcelain figures. A lacquered table and an armchair with Indian decoration were in the room at the time of Clemens August's death in 1761.[34]

Practicing the popular pastime of japanning, Margravine Wilhelmina of Bayreuth (1709–1758), the older sister of Frederick the Great, participated in the decoration of the so-called Japanese room in the Hermitage in Bayreuth (1738–40) (fig. 6). Its colorful décor is composed of European chinoiseries as well as of several Coromandel lacquer panels that came from an eight-leaf screen given to the Margravine by her brother. With a sense of pride the Margravine described the room as: Das 'kleine ... Kabinett mit japanischer Täfelung ... hat grosse Summen gekostet und ist, glaube ich, in ihrer Art die einzige, die es in Europa gibt ... alle, die es sahen, sind davon entzückt gewesen'.[35]

Despite the fact that Chinese painted wallpapers and silk hangings became more readily available during the eighteenth century, lacquered goods continued to be used for the wall decoration of intimate rooms all over Europe.[36] The sumptuous Brussels residence of Johann-Karl Philipp, Comte de Cobenzl (1712–1770), for instance, a diplomat in the service of Empress Maria-Theresa (1717–1780), included a salon mounted with lacquer panels.[37] In the Paris Hôtel of the Maréchal-Duc de Richelieu (1696–1788) one admired a 'salon revêtu de panneaux de vieux laque avec des peintures chinoises, dont les formes toutes variées et ornées de glaces offrent un coup d'oeil tout à fait séduisant'.[38] Extant examples can be found in Russia at Peterhof, where the two, so-called, Chinese Lobbies were redecorated in the 1760's.[39] Incorporating both entire Chinese screens and Russian imitation lacquer, these rooms were intended for the display of the Imperial collections of Asian art and seem to foreshadow the exuberant interiors of the Royal Pavilion in Brighton. More traditional is a small corner cabinet, situated behind the bedroom in the South wing of Schloss Nymphenburg in Munich, that was paneled with Coromandel lacquer and japanning in 1763–1764 (fig. 7).[40]

Almost a decade after it had been built as a birthday present for the Swedish Queen Louisa Ulrica (1720–1782) in 1753, the Chinese Pavilion was replaced by a more permanent structure. Situated in the gardens of Drottningholm Palace outside Stockholm, this new Chinese Pavilion was fitted with several lacquer and japanned interiors. The leaves from a Chinese lacquer screen depicting the seaport of Canton decorate the walls of a brightly colored yellow room.[41] Supplementing the Chinese scenes are European chinoiserie depictions based on compositions by the French painter François Boucher (1703–1770) and on sketches by the English architect William Chambers (1723–1796) included in *Designs of Chinese Buildings, Furniture, Dresses, Machines, and Utensils* of 1757.

Red Chinese lacquer, which was first exported to Europe around the middle of the eighteenth century and became quickly fashionable in France,[42] once lined the walls of the *cabinet de travail* at the Hôtel du Châtelet (colour plate V).[43] Built for Louis-Marie-Florent, Duc du Châtelet (d. 1793), in c. 1770, the hôtel was situated at 127 rue de Grenelle in Paris. An 1812 inventory shows that the room was completely color coordinated.

Fig. 5. The Concert. Wool and silk tapestry, English, late 17th – early 18th century

The case furniture, consisting of four armoires, a commode, and a cylinder bureau with *cartonnier*, was mounted with similar red Chinese lacquer.[44] Gilded seat furniture, upholstered in crimson silk velvet, and matching draperies completed this elegant décor.

At Schönbrunn Palace, Vienna, several rooms were decorated with lacquer among them the famous Vieux Lacque Zimmer designed by the French architect Isadore Canevale in a late and opulent Rococo style, for which lacquer panels were bought in 1770 (colour plate IV.1).[45]

More restrained is the so-called Japanese audience chamber at Huis ten Bosch, The Hague, which was redecorated in 1790–1791 by the cabinetmaker Mathijs Horrix (1735–1809), who specialised in mounting furniture with lacquer panels.[46] Executed in Neo-classical taste, the room combined satinwood veneer with white Japanese silk hangings and black and gold Chinese lacquer, and was furnished with black painted seat furniture.[47]

Although no lacquer rooms from the first half of the nineteenth century are known, a double door fitted with black Chinese lacquer and painted panels may indicate that similar interiors were created later, during the Second Empire.[48] One of the galleries of the Musée Chinois, established in 1863 by Empress Eugénie (1826–1920) at the Château de Fontainebleau, was lined with the lacquer panels from two Chinese screens that had been in the French royal collections since the eighteenth century.[49] The panels were mounted in such a way that the black background of the one screen alternated with the gold lacquer of the other. They created an appropriate décor for art works that had either been looted from the Summer Palace in Peking by the French army during the 1860 military campaign, or given to Napoleon III by the Siamese ambassadors during their offcial visit to Paris the following year.

The desire to furnish lacquer rooms in an appropriate manner often resulted in the demand for japanned or lacquered furniture. It must also have stimulated the decoration of furniture with Japanese or Chinese lacquer panels that were taken from objects that were no longer fashionable, reusing lacquer that could be a hundred years old.[50]

In 1667, Pierre Gole (c. 1620–1684), cabinetmaker to King Louis XIV (1643–1715), delivered a two meter high, pyramid-shaped, cabinet consisting of nine layers, that was 'tout couvert d'ouvrages du plus fin de la Chine'.[51] Although Gole is known

Fig. 6. So-called Japanese or Lacquer Cabinet, Hermitage, Bayreuth, c. 1738–40

Fig. 7. Coromandel Lacquer Cabinet, Schloss Nymphenburg, 1763–64

to have made imitation lacquer, the description of this imposing piece clearly points to the reuse of Asian lacquer and is perhaps the earliest reference to this practice for furniture.

Triads, sets of furniture consisting of a table, pier glass and a pair of candlestands, were frequently decorated with Coromandel lacquer.[52] The mirror and matching table (c. 1685) at Boughton House are good examples.[53] They have been attributed to Gerrit Jensen who was responsible for wainscoting the closet at Chatsworth with panels from a Coromandel screen. The convex curving mirror frame also indicates that seventeenth-century English cabinetmakers were successful in bending Asian lacquer before their French colleagues who excelled in this difficult technique during the Rococo period. The mirror frame at Boughton consists of a hodgepodge of figures and trees of which Constantijn Huygens would not have approved.

Without fully understanding the lacquer decoration with its underlying references to Asian poetry or literary classics, most eighteenth-century cabinetmakers paid some attention to the depictions and tried to match the scenes in a reasonable manner, although this was not always the case. An unsigned commode at Château de Versailles, for instance, is veneered with Coromandel lacquer that has clearly been placed sideways (fig. 8). A panel of Japanese lacquer, showing a delicate floral arrangement, was cut in a rather insensitive way right through the middle. Switching left and right, both pieces were mounted on the fall front of the famous secretary supplied by Jean-Henri Riesener (1743–1806) for use of Queen Marie Antoinette (1755–1793) in c. 1783 (fig. 9).[54]

Fig. 9. Secretary mounted with Japanese lacquer by Jean-Henry Riesener for use of Queen Marie-Antoinette, c. 1783

Fig. 8. Commode veneered with Coromandel lacquer. French, mid 18th century, Château de Versailles

Fig. 10. Coromandel Lacquer cabinet, Schloss Nymphenburg, 1763–64, pair of unusual guéridons with Japanese lacquer bowls and other objects incorporated into their design. French?, c. 1720

Occasionally a complete seventeenth-century Japanese lacquer cabinet was transformed into a modern piece of furniture as happened with a comptoir that was inset into the carcass of a French commode by Bernard van Risenburgh (after 1696–c. 1766) in c. 1730–1735.[55] The export Japanese lacquer cabinets usually enclosed ten drawers of varying sizes. A set of such drawers, retaining their original mounts, was divided between a pair of *secrétaires à abattant,* made by the cabinetmaker Bernard Molitor (1755–1833) in the early nineteenth-century.[56]

Entire objects, Japanese bowls, dishes and trays, were frequently mounted in France in exquisite gilt bronze to form small luxury items such as pot pourri's, inkstands or candlesticks.[57] Good examples are the chamber candlesticks formed of a red and gold and a black and gold lacquer dish with elaborate Neo-classical mounts of c. 1770–1780 (fig. 11).[58] These fashionable products were sold by the Parisian *marchands-merciers* who also played a role in their design supplying the craftsmen with the lacquer they needed.[59] Lacquer bowls and other objects were also incorporated in a highly unusual pair of French guéridons (c. 1720) on display in the lacquer cabinet of Schloss Nymphenburg (fig. 10).[60] Since high quality Japanese lacquer was expensive and hard to find during the eighteenth century,[61] the customer sometimes provided the cabinetmaker with the pieces to be mounted. This was the case with two particularly fine Japanese lacquer plates, showing the coat of arms of Joan van Hoorn (1653–1711), Governor General to the Dutch East Indies from 1704–1709, that were used to embellish a Dutch commode.[62] Having inherited his collection of lacquer, Van Hoorn's descendants decided to sacrifice several plates for the decoration of this Neo-classical piece, not unlike plaques of Sèvres porcelain that were mounted on French furniture.[63]

As the Molitor secretaries mentioned above already indicated, Asian lacquer continued to be used as veneer for furniture early in the nineteenth century. Another example is the pair of secretaries supplied by the firm of Benjamin and Benjamin Lewis Vulliamy to the author and dilletante William Beckford (1760–1844) who was a serious collector of Japanese lacquer. For this purpose they dismantled several important early pieces, including the so-called Buys box, from Beckford's collection. The 1803 bill specified the work as follows: 'For cutting into several pieces (at a very great risque) a very fine Old Japan Box and tray and making the design for two Cabinets in which the different parts of the box and tray are introduced (...).'[64] Generally, however, japanning or the popular technique of papier-mâché was used to embellish furniture instead of lacquer.

Whether preserved in pristine condition or dismantled and cut up, lined along walls, mounted on furniture or transformed into small luxury items, export lacquer continues to enchant us today for its exotic nature and the perfection of its brilliant surface.

Fig. 11. Pair of candlestícks incorporating Japanese lacquer dishes. French, c. 1770–80

Notes

1 This cabinet, listed in the inventory of Schloss Ambras made after the death of Ferdinand II in 1596, is now at the Kunsthistorisches Museum, Vienna. It is illustrated by JOHN WHITEHEAD and OLIVER IMPEY in 'Les laques du Japon dans les arts décoratifs français aux 17e et 18e siècles', *Connaissance des Arts*, no. 432, February 1988, p. 88.

2 IMPEY 1984, p. 125. This coffer is at Gripsholm Castle.

3 These cabinets are still at the Hofburg today. Two are in the office of the Austrian President in the Leopoldinischen Trakt, the other two are in the Kaiserliche Hofmobiliendepot. I am grateful to Eva B. Ottillinger for this information. See also HANZL/OTTILLINGER/RIZZI 1997, p. 615, fig. 732.

4 The *Allegory of Vanity* by Paulus Moreelse (1571–1638) of 1627, now in the Fitzwilliam Museum, Cambridge, includes a small lacquer jewelry box. See HUTT 1999, pp. 22, 24, figs. 1, 5. A lacquer casket is also illustrated in a French still life painting by Simon Renard de Saint-André (1613–1677) in the collection of the Staatsgemäldesammlung, Munich. This painting is illustrated by PETER THORNTON in *Seventeenth-Century Interior Decoration in England, France and Holland*, New Haven/London, 1978, p. 251, fig. 239.

5 This painting is in the collection of the National Gallery in London, see MACLAREN 1991, vol. I, pp. 434–435, pl. 359.

6 WURFBAIN 1983, pp. 319–320.

7 MACLAREN 1991, p. 434. KOOZIN 1990, pp. 43–44.

8 SUTTON 1998, no. 26, pp.142–145.

9 NOORDEGRAAF/WIJSENBEEK-OLTHUIS 1992, pp. 48.

10 FOCK 1992, pp. 78, 296, n. 30.

11 The 1632 inventory of Het Stadhouderlijk Kwartier and Palace Noordeinde in The Hague includes a number of lacquer pieces, see DROSSAERS/LUNSINGH SCHEURLEER 1974, pp. 193, nos. 259, 263, 264, 269; 194, nos. 275–277; 195, no. 332; 204, nos. 530, 533, 534.

12 LUNSINGH SCHEURLEER 1970, pp. 166–167. FOCK 1997, pp. 83–84.

13 'il gabinetto contiguo è nobile e magnifico, essendo tutto coperto di legno della China e dipinto alla foggia di quel paese, nè vi manca la madreperla che lo rende interamente sontuoso', G. BROM, 'Een Italiaansche reisbeschrijving der Nederlanden (1677–1678)', *Bijdragen en mededelingen van het Historisch Genootschap* 36 (1915), p. 119 quoted by FOCK 1997, pp. 84, 256, n. 59.

14 MONTAGUE 1696, p. 42.

15 LUNSINGH SCHEURLEER 1970, pp. 164–165.

16 Ibid. p. 165.

17 JACOB A. WORP, *De briefwisseling van Constantijn Huygens (1608–1687)*, The Hague, 1917, p. 456.

18 LUNSINGH SCHEURLEER 1970, pp. 167–171.

19 BRAY 1850, p. 168.

20 MORRIS 1949, pp. 59, 69. The room at Burghley House was described as: 'my Ladyes Closet is very fine the wanscoate of the best Jappan'.

21 The lacquer room of Queen Mary at Hampton Court was in the Water Gallery, a small Tudor building on the Thames. A Thomas Rymel, 'Japanner', submitted several bills after the Queen's death for dismantling various pieces of lacquer and making new objects out of them. See TURPIN 1999, p. 5, 13, note 16.

22 MORRIS 1949, p. 100.

23 BEARD/GILBERT 1986, pp. 486–487.

24 'A la suite des appartemens de Monsieur, sont de très-jolis cabinets. Le premier où vous entrez est rempli d'une quantité d'ouvrages en cristal de roche, de coupes, d'agates disposés sur des consoles. Les murs sont couverts de glaces du haut en bas, avec, entre elles, des panneaux de laque du Japon & de peintures d'égale largeur, qui font d'un effet admirable'. *Voyage de Lister à Paris en MDCXVIII*, Paris, 1873, p. 182. The painter Jean Lemoyne received 600 livres on 19 February 1690 for the painting and gilding done in the cabinet de la Chine at Saint-Cloud. HAVARD 1887, p. 839.

25 YAMADA 1935, pp. 40–41, pl. XIV, fig. 38.

26 WAPPENSCHMIDT 1990, pp. 38–39, figs. 11–12.

27 Japanned rooms can be found in the Neue Residenz at Bamberg and at Schloss Ludwigslust near Stuttgart. A good example is also in the Haags Gemeentemuseum, The Hague. See KISLUK-GROSHEIDE 1987, pp. 379–399.

28 A number of late seventeenth-, early eighteenth-century tapestries with Indo-Chinese scenes were woven in England. The general decoration showing floating islands with exotic figures was derived from Coromandel lacquer screens. See STANDEN 1981, pp. 119–142. STANDEN 1985, pp. 717–725, no. 127.

29 The Chinese cabinet at the Residence in Munich has black embroidered wall coverings dating to c. 1730 that must also have been inspired by lacquer panels. See BRUNNER/HOJER/SEELIG 1998, p. 107, no. 63.

30 Illustrated in *Chefs-d'oeuvre de la curiosité du monde*, exhib. cat., Musée des Arts Décoratifs, Paris, 1954, cat. no. 127, pl. 65; and in color by STÉPHANE FANIEL (ed.), *French Art of the Eighteenth Century*, London, 1957, p. 134. This paneling was in the collection of the late Stavros Niarchos in Paris.

31 According to Juvarra's letter of 8 March 1732 written to the Prime Minister, Carlo Vincenzo Ferrero marchese d'Ormea, he described the lacquer as 'certe tavole a vernice della China dello Gappone che V.E. potrà far vedere a S.M. che sarebbe cosa galante ornare qualche gabinetto o stanza'. D'Ormea, in his response dated 19 March, said that the king was interested in seeing one or two of these lacquer panels. In return, Juvarra suggested to the minister on the 29th of March to consider acquiring all the panels to decorate 'bellissimi gabinetti combinandole con porcellane che S.M. abonda nelle sue guarderobbe'. ROVERE/VIALE 1937, pp. 95–96. The room is illustrated in MARZIANO BERNARDI, *Il palazzo reale di Torino*, Torino, 1959, pp. 90–95, pls. XVII-XIX.

32 HUTH 1971, p. 58, pl. 138.

33 BADER 1961, p. 216, pls. 37–39.

34 WAPPENSCHMIDT 1990, p. 89: a 'Lehnsessel verguldet mit Indianischem gemähl, gleich dem Paneel des zimmers'; p. 90, fig. 36.

35 Ibid., pp. 144–145, figs. 69–70.

36 Good examples of eighteenth-century Oriental textiles and wallpaper can still be found at the Chinese Pavilion outside Stockholm. See SETTERWALL/FOGELMARCK/GYLLENSVÄRD 1972, pp. 113, 140–143.

37 AUGARDE 1987, p. 40.

38 HAVARD 1887, p. 840. This salon was probably in the Hôtel d'Antin at 34 rue Louis-Le-Gand, Paris, the residence bought by maréchal-duc de Richelieu in 1756. HILLAIRET 1963, pp. 54–55.

39 RASKIN 1978, pp. 86–95, figs. 49–56.

40 HOJER/SCHMID 1986, p. 26, pl. 6.

41 SETTERWALL/FOGELMARCK/GYLLENSVÄRD 1972, pp. 86–89.

42 The Parisian *marchand-mercier* Lazare Duvaux (c. 1703–1758) sold five red lacquer commodes between 1754 and 1758. IMPEY/KISLUK-GROSHEIDE 1994, pp. 56, 58.

43 LEDOUX-LEBARD 1968, pp. 62–65. The nine panels from this cabinet are now in the Musée des Arts Décoratifs in Paris. A red lacquer room was also part of the apartment of Madame de Pompadour on the ground floor of Château de Versailles. Ibid., p. 65.

44 The armoires and bureau are in the music room of the Château de Compiègne. They are illustrated by MADELEINE JARRY in *Chinoiserie: Chinese Influence on European Decorative Art 17th and 18th Centuries*, New York, 1981, pp. 163–165, 167, figs. 179–180, 182. The commode is in the collection of the Moblier National de France and is illustrated by Ernest Dumonthier in *Le Mobilier Louis XVI*, Paris, 1922, p. 10, no. 14.

45 Illustrated by GEORG J. KUGLER in *Schönbrunn farbig*, Vienna, 1986, nos. 56–57.

46 BAARSEN 1993, pp. 176–177.

47 LOONSTRA/BROEKEMA 1989, pp. 70–71, fig. 6. The Japanese wall hangings are described by NICOLE EX in *The Brocadian Paradise: The Restored Walls of the Japanese Chamber in Huis ten Bosch Palace*, Rotterdam, 1997.

48 This door was sold at Sotheby's, Monaco, 19–20 June 1988, lot 1784.

49 SAMOYAULT-VERLET 1994, pp. 19–21, fig. 14, pp. 24–25, fig. 17.

50 IMPEY/KISLUK-GROSHEIDE 1994, pp. 49–51.

51 LUNSINGH SCHEURLEER 1980, pp. 386, 389.

52 A good example of such a triad is at Ham House, see THORNTON/TOMLIN 1980, pp. 113–114, fig. 103.

53 The matching candlestands are missing. HARDY 1992, pp. 117, 132–133, pl. 78, fig. 131.

54 Impey/Kisluk-Grosheide 1994, pp. 53–57, pl. V, figs. 12–13.
55 This commode is in collection of the Musée du Louvre. This and several other commodes incorporating Japanese export lacquer cabinets are illustrated by Daniel Alcouffe in *Musée du Louvre, Nouvelles acquisitions du département des objets d'art*, Paris, 1995, pp. 130–133, no. 46.
56 Alcouffe/Dion-Tenenbaum/Lefébure 1993, pp. 316–319, no. 109.
57 See, for instance, a mid eighteenth-century inkstand, combining Chinese porcelain with a red lacquer tray, mounted in gilt bronze, in the collection of the J. Paul Getty Museum, Malibu. Illustrated in Sargentson 1996, color pl. 13.
58 *The Jack and Belle Linsky Collection in the Metropolitan Museum of Art*, New York, 1984, p. 246, no. 152. Similar candlesticks were sold at Sotheby's, Monaco, 15 June 1996, lots 110–111.
59 For the role of the *marchands-merciers* see Sargentson 1996, pp. 44–58.
60 Langer 1995, pp. 81–83, no. 12.
61 Watson 1963, pp. 103–104.
62 This commode is in a Dutch private collection. Rappard-Boon 1991, p. 80, no. 47.
63 The Groninger Museum voor Stad en Lande, Groningen also has a late eighteenth-century commode mounted with a lacquer tray and other lacquer panels. See Jörg 1989, p. 47, fig. 5.
64 These secretaries are at Elton Hall, Peterborough. See Roberts 1986, pp. 338–341, pls. XIII-XIV.

References

Alcouffe, Daniel/Dion-Tenenbaum, Anne/Lefébure, Amaury: *Le mobilier du musée du Louvre*, vol. I, *Moyen-Age, Renaissance, XVIIe-XVIIIe s. (ébénisterie), XIXe s.*, Dijon, 1993

Alcouffe, Daniel: *Musée du Louvre, Nouvelles acquisitions du département des objets d'art*, Paris, 1995, pp. 130–133

Augarde, Jean-Dominique: '1749 – Joseph Baumhauer ébéniste privilegié du roi', *L'Estampille*, no. 204, June 1987, pp. 14–45

Baarsen, Reinier J.:'"In de commode van Parijs tot Den Haag": Matthijs Horrix (1735-1809), een meubelmaker in Den Haag in de tweede helft van de achttiende eeuw', *Oud Holland*, vol. 107, no. 2, 1993, pp. 161–255

Bader, Walter: *Aus Schloss Augustusburg zu Brühl und Falkenlust*, Cologne, 1961

Beard, Geoffrey/Gilbert, Christopher (eds.): *Dictionary of English Furniture Makers 1660–1840*, Leeds, 1986

Bernardi, Marziano: *Il palazzo reale di Torino*, Torino, 1959

Bray, William (ed.): *Diary and Correspondence of John Evelyn*, vol. II, London, 1850

Brom, G.: 'Een Italiaansche reisbeschrijving der Nederlanden (1677-1678)', *Bijdragen en mededelingen van het Historisch Genootschap* 36 (1915), pp. 87–226

Brunner, Herbert/Hojer, Gerhard/Seelig, Lorenz (eds.): *Residence Munich*, Munich, 1998

Drossaers, Sophie W. A./Lunsingh Scheurleer, Theodoor H.: *Inventarissen van de inboedels in de verblijven van de Oranjes en daarmede gelijk te stellen stukken 1567–1795*, vol. I, The Hague, 1974

Ex, Nicole: *The Brocadian Paradise: The Restored Walls of the Japanese Chamber in Huis ten Bosch Palace*, Rotterdam, 1997

Faniel, Stéphane (ed.): *French Art of the Eighteenth Century*, London, 1957

Fock, C. Willemijn: 'Kunst en rariteiten in het Hollandse interieur', *De wereld binnen handbereik: Nederlandse kunst- en rariteitenverzamelingen, 1585–1735*, Zwolle, 1992, pp. 70–91

Fock, C. Willemijn: 'Frederik Hendrik en Amalia's appartementen: Vorstelijk vertoon naast de triomf van het porselein', *Vorstelijk Verzameld: De kunstcollectie van Frederik Hendrik en Amalia*, Zwolle, 1997

Hanzl, Lieselotte/Ottillinger, Eva B./Rizzi, Wilhelm Georg: 'Wohnen in der Hofburg. Das Appartement Kaiser Franz' II. (I.)', *Österreichische Zeitschrift für Kunst und Denkmalpflege*, no. 3–4, 1997

Hardy, John: 'The English Furniture', in: *Boughton House, the English Versailles*, Tessa Murdoch (ed.), London, 1992, pp. 128–141

Havard, Henry: *Dictionnaire de l'ameublement et de la décoration*, vol. I, Paris, 1887

Hillairet, Jacques:*Dictionnaire historique des rues de Paris*, vol. II, Paris, 1963

Hojer, Gerhard/Schmid, Elmar D.: *Nymphenburg Palace, Park, Pavilions: Official Guide*, Munich, 1986

Huth, Hans: *Lacquer of the West: The History of a Craft and an Industry 1550–1950*, Chicago/London, 1971

Hutt, Julia: 'A Japanese Export Lacquer Chest in the Victoria & Albert Museum: Some further Observations', *Apollo*, vol. CXLIX, no. 445, March 1999, pp. 22–24

Impey, Oliver: 'Japanese Export Lacquer', *Lacquer: An International History and Illustrated Survey*, New York, 1984

Impey, Oliver R./Kisluk-Grosheide, Danielle O.: 'The Japanese Connection: French Eighteenth-Century Furniture and Export Lacquer', *Apollo*, vol. CXXXIX, no. 383, January 1994, pp. 48–61

Jarry, Madeleine: *Chinoiserie: Chinese Influence on European Decorative Art 17th and 18th Centuries*, New York, 1981

Jörg, Christiaan: 'Japanese Export Lacquer: Trade and Imitation', *Imitation and Inspiration: Japanese Influence on Dutch Art*, Stefan van Raay (ed.), Amsterdam, 1989, pp. 39–51

Kisluk-Grosheide, Daniëlle: 'De verlakte kamer uit het Huis Buitenrust te 's-Gravenhage', *Achttiende-eeuwse kunst in de Nederlanden, Leids Kunsthistorisch Jaarboek*, vol. IV, Delft, 1987, pp. 379–399

Koozin, Kristine: *The Vanitas Still Lifes of Harmen Steenwyck: Metaphoric Realism*, Lewiston, 1990

Kugler, Georg J.: *Schönbrunn farbig*, Vienna, 1986

Langer, Brigitte: *Die Möbel der Residenz München*, vol. I, *Die französischen Möbel des 18. Jahrhunderts*, Munich/New York, 1995

Ledoux-Lebard, Denise: 'La découverte remarquable d'un cabinet complet en laque rouge du XVIIIe siècle', *Connaissance des Arts*, July/Aug. 1968, pp. 62–65

Loonstra, Marten/Broekema, Saskia S.: 'Japanese Art at Court', *Imitation and Inspiration: Japanese Influence on Dutch Art*, Stefan van Raay (ed.), Amsterdam, 1989, pp. 61–71

Lunsingh Scheurleer, Theodoor H.: 'Stadhouderlijke lakkabinetten', in: *Opstellen voor H. de Waal*, Amsterdam/Leiden, 1970

Lunsingh Scheurleer, Theodoor H.: 'Pierre Gole, ébéniste du roi Louis XIV', *Burlington Magazine*, vol. CXXII, June 1980, pp. 380–394

MacLaren, Neil: *The Dutch School 1600–1900, National Gallery Catalogues*, 2nd rev. ed., London, 1991

Montague, William: *The Delights of Holland*, London, 1696

Morris, Christopher (ed.): *The Journeys of Celia Fiennes*, London, 1949

Noordegraaf, Leo/Wijsenbeek-Olthuis, Thera: 'De wereld ontsloten. Aanvoer van rariteiten naar Nederland', *De wereld binnen handbereik: Nederlandse kunst- en rariteitenverzamelingen, 1585–1735*, Zwolle, 1992, pp. 39–50

Rappard-Boon, Charlotte van: *Imitation and Inspiration, Japanese Influence on Dutch Art from 1650 to the Present*, exh. cat. Rijksmuseum Amsterdam, 1991

RASKIN, ABRAM G.: *Petrodvorets (Peterhof): Palaces and Pavilions, Gardens and Parks, Fountains and Cascades, Sculptures*, Leningrad, 1978

ROBERTS HUGH, 'Beckford, Vulliamy and Old Japan', *Apollo*, vol. CXXIV, no. 296, October 1986, pp 338–341

ROVERE, LORENZO/VIALE, VITTORIO/BRINCKMANN, ALBERT ERICH: *Filippo Juvarra*, vol. I, Milan, 1937

SAMOYAULT-VERLET, COLOMBE: *Le Musée Chinois de l'Imperatrice Eugénie*, Paris, 1994

SARGENTSON, CAROLYN: *Merchants and Luxury Markets: The Marchands Merciers of Eighteenth-Century Paris*, London, 1996

SETTERWALL, ÅKE/FOGELMARCK, STIG/GYLLENSVÄRD, BO: *The Chinese Pavilion at Drottningholm*, Malmö, 1972

STANDEN, EDITH A.: 'English Tapestries "After the Indian Manner"', *The Metropolitan Museum Journal*, vol. XV, New York, 1981, pp. 119–142

STANDEN, EDITH A.: *European Post-Medieval Tapestries and Related Hangings in The Metropolitan Museum of Art*, vol. II, New York, 1985

SUTTON, PETER C.: *Pieter de Hooch, 1629–1684*, exhib. cat., Wadsworth Atheneum, Hartford, 1998

THORNTON, PETER/TOMLIN, MAURICE: 'The Furnishing and Decoration of Ham House', *Furniture History*, vol. XVI, 1980, pp. 1–194

TURPIN, ADRIANA: 'A Table for Queen Mary's Water Gallery at Hampton Court', *Apollo*, vol. CXLIX, no. 443, January 1999, pp. 3–14

WAPPENSCHMIDT, FRIEDERIKE: *Der Traum von Arkadien: Leben, Liebe, Licht und Farbe in Europas Lustschlössern*, Munich, 1990

WATSON, FRANCIS J. B.: 'Beckford, Mme de Pompadour, the Duc de Bouillon and the Taste for Japanese Lacquer in Eighteenth Century France', *Gazette des Beaux Arts*, vol. LXI, February 1963, pp. 101–127

WHITEHEAD, JOHN/IMPEY, OLIVER: 'Les laques du Japon dans les arts décoratifs français aux 17e et 18e siècles', *Connaissance des Arts*, no. 432, February 1988, pp. 86–97

WORP, JACOB A.: *De briefwisseling van Constantijn Huygens (1608–1687)*, The Hague, 1917

WURFBAIN, MAARTEN L.: *Catalogus van de schilderijen en tekeningen, Stedelijk Museum De Lakenhal,* Leiden, 1983

YAMADA, CHISABURO: *Die Chinamode des Spätbarock*, Berlin, 1935

Photo Credits

Fig. 1: The Cleveland Museum of Art, Cleveland

Fig. 2: Rijksmuseum, Amsterdam

Figs. 6, 7, 10: Bayerische Verwaltung der staatlichen Schlösser, Gärten und Seen, Munich

Figs. 3, 4, 5, 9, 11, colour plate IV.2: The Metropolitan Museum of Art, New York

Fig. 8: Réunion des Musées Nationaux, Paris

Colour plate IV.1: Schloss Schönbrunn Kultur- und BetriebsgmbH/ Alexander Koller, HG.115.015

Colour plate V: Musée des Arts Décoratifs, Paris, Photo Laurent-Sully Jaulmes

Christiaan Jörg

Japanese Export Lacquer for the Dutch Market

The Dutch-Japanese relationship, which started in 1600 and will celebrate its 400-year anniversary in 2000, was for a long time based on mutual profits. In particular after 1641, when the Dutch were the only Europeans left to trade with Japan and had settled on the fan-shaped artificial island of Decima in the bay of Nagasaki, the Dutch East India Company (VOC) became a provider for the Japanese of exclusive Western commodities, of Indian silk and chintzes, of spices and woods and, probably most important, of information on the West. In turn, the Dutch were keen to buy Japanese copper, silver and gold, camphor and articles of lesser importance such as porcelain and lacquer.[1]

Already in the early 17th century, the Dutch and the English regarded Japanese lacquer as far superior to Chinese lacquer, its quality justifying its higher price. The records of the VOC also tell us that even in this early period the Dutch ordered special objects. In 1613, for instance, 2 small caskets, 6 lacquer cups and 12 saucers were sent to Holland. Hendrik Brouwer, Head of the VOC settlement in Japan, commented on this shipment of lacquer as follows: 'This stuff is very expensive but it is exceptionally beautiful and the process to make it is very protracted as I have seen by experience. One can put water in it without it receiving any damage. Suchlike cups and saucers have never before been made in Japan'.[2]

Japanese export lacquer had already been made to order for the Portuguese and the style of this *namban* lacquer, with its lavish use of pearlshell, is well-known.[3] This contribution will concentrate on the Dutch orders, by the VOC as well as by private individuals, and how these orders gradually changed the shapes and decorations of Japanese export lacquer.

The first Company's shipment of lacquer from Japan arrived in the Netherlands in 1610.[4] More lacquer arrived in the years thereafter, presumably all of it pieces in the *namban* style. In the beginning, the directors had high expectations of these exotic luxuries, but unfortunately lacquer proved difficult to sell at auction.[5] It is not mentioned why, but it is likely the imported lacquer was too expensive. This is also indicated by the fact that even at that early date Dutch imitations of lacquer were already being made, for instance by Willem Kick in Amsterdam. His work must have been of high quality, because in 1612 a lacquered chest of his hand was given by the States General to the Sultan of Turkey, together with pieces of real Oriental lacquer.[6]

In the 17th century communications were slow between Holland and Japan and therefore it took some time before the merchants in Japan were informed of the negative results of the auctions. They ceased buying lacquer for the Company in 1616.[7] However, they may not have done so privately, and much *namban* lacquer in old Dutch collections must have arrived as the result of this private trade.

It took some time before the Company resumed interest in lacquer, but when in 1634 orders went out to Japan to buy cabinets and domed coffers of all kinds[8], this must have been a reaction to a growing popularity of lacquer in Holland where it had been supplied by private trade. Dutch inventories from this period, too, prove that lacquer was appreciated in upper-class circles. For instance, nine pieces specified as 'Japanese' lacquer are mentioned in 1632 in the inventory of Noordeinde Palace, home of the Dutch Stadholder, such as 'a small square cabinet from Japan decorated with pearlshell and gilt scrollwork' or 'two small Japanese tables inlaid with pearl-shell and gilded' and even 'two Japanese salts' of which no examples are known today, but it is to be hoped they will once be found in the attic of some country house.[9]

As can be expected lacquer was also prominently displayed in Batavia. The 1627 inventory of the bankrupted Gilles Venant, a former Company's merchant, mentions no less than 20 pieces of Japanese lacquer, including a lacquered bed, several cabinets and coffers and, most extraordinary in these protestant surroundings, a lacquered shrine.[10]

The Company resumed its trade in lacquer with full energy and was now willing to spend substantial sums of money to its acquisition. In 1635, for instance, no less than 233 boxes filled with a variety of lacquer were bought for a total of 4442 tael or 13.882 florins. Apart from coffers, chests and cabinets we also find backgammon boards, dishes with jugs and shaving bowls.[11]

These new Company orders resulted in a change of shapes and decorations; in fact, I think the Company actively stimulated the shift from the *namban* to the 'pictorial' style. For why would a commercial body like the VOC resume trade in lacquer, if it was not for wares of a new style? They would not think of importing the old *namban* wares, because these did not sell well in the Netherlands. New items were wanted, a new style was promoted and in the late 1630s and in the 1640s the new assortment of 'pictorial' lacquer emerged due to this Dutch demand.

Prominent on the shipping lists are the *comptoirs*, the two-door cabinets that developed from the front-fall cabinet in the mid 1630s, exactly the period when the Company resumed her trade in lacquer. These *comptoirs* had a multi-purpose function, from travel chest to a miniature cabinet of curiosities. According to 17th century inventories and some rare paintings they had a prominent place in the interior and must have enhanced the status of the owner (see p. 49, colour plate VI.1).

On decorations, too, the growing interest of the Dutch for lacquer had its impact. The *namban* style with its lavish use of pearlshell, intricate geometric borders and abstracted motifs of foliage and animals apparently did not appeal to the Dutch taste. Most of the 17th century lacquer made for the Dutch is decorated in the 'pictorial style' as described by Oliver Impey in his contribution, a style which developed rather quickly in the 30s and 40s and reached its maturity in the early 50s, coinciding with the Dutch trade monopoly in Japan.

But why did it develop that way? Why was this particular style promoted by the Dutch? Maybe one should look at the art that was produced in the Netherlands to see the basic elements of the preferences of the Dutch buyers. This is best illustrated from seventeenth-century Dutch paintings. Better than anything else these show that it was the depiction and suggestion of reality in

Fig. 1. Pentagonal saucer, Japanese lacquer decorated in the 'pictorial' style with a landscape. On the border ginkgo leaves. Early 18th century, diameter 32.7 cm. Ex Welbeck Abbey collection. Groninger Museum, Groningen

its many appearances that captured the interest of Dutch burghers. This fondness for recognisable and realistic scenes was also mirrored in the things the Dutch wanted from the Far East. It is very remarkable that Chinese 'transitional' porcelain of the 1630s and 40s, too, is an example of this taste: it shows elaborate depictions of landscapes, detailed figural scenes and very naturalistic flowers, plants and animals.[12] Japanese lacquer, too, should depict similar realistic decorations, preserving, of course, its exotic and mysterious Far Eastern charm. It certainly is no coincidence that Chinese porcelain and Japanese lacquer both decorated in naturalistic styles were developed for the Dutch market at the same time, and had such immediate success.

I think this is the reason why during the 1630s and 40s the *namban* style faded away and made place for the 'pictorial' style. First, the geometric *namban* borders became thinner, cartouches became larger, Oriental human figures made their entry. By the mid 17th century border designs function only as small frames for the scene, or have disappeared at all, leaving the whole surface as a ground for the Japanese scene. This ground itself changed as well: it became a large, shiny black surface, like a canvas, on which the decoration was painted in gold and silver. This really was the thing the wealthy Dutchmen liked: a rich and contrasting surface, a detailed exotic decoration, elaborate craftsmanship, in short, an object fit for kings and noblemen which he, just a Dutch burgher, could afford. Lacquer as one of the means to enhance the new Dutch identity and status. Of course, the Dutch would not be the Dutch if they had not haggled over prices again and again when ordering lacquer in Japan, because paying too much was against their nature, even for such exclusive lacquer.[13]

It is interesting to see how the 'pictorial' style on export wares reached the heights of the Van Diemen and the Buys boxes already so early. In their contributions Oliver Impey and Julia Hutt discuss this style, which I think became so sought-after because the Dutch liked its naturalistic character so much. Also the taste of one man, François Caron, a merchant who served the Company in Japan with intervals from 1619 until 1641, might have

Fig. 2. A Japanese lacquer bowl and its model of Japanese kakiemon porcelain, both decorated with a flower spray. Both *c.* 1700, both diameter 13.5 cm. Count of Schönborn collection. Weissenstein Castle, Pommersfelden

stimulated the shift in export style and most probably it was him who had a hand in sending the Van Diemen and Buys boxes to Batavia.[14] To please the Dutch client and comply with his taste, Japanese lacquer makers might first have tried-out their traditional Japanese style of detailed representations for this new market and did their utmost to please the barbarian customers. Soon, however, when it became clear that the Dutch were not willing to pay for this extremely delicate work, they shifted to less elaborate, but still high-class work which pleased the Dutch as well. However, for private orders, the best work in the Van Diemen box style could be revived, like the 'FC' box, which was probably ordered by or for François Caron himself, when he was head of the factory in 1639 and 1640.[15]

The 'pictorial' style had its heyday in the second half of the 17th century, but when the Company ceased orders around 1700 things changed again. By the way, it is interesting to note that at the same time the VOC also stopped buying Chinese and Japanese porcelain for the Netherlands, so apparently it economised on luxury merchandise at that time.[16] Private trade, however, continued, in porcelain as well as in lacquer, but for both articles the assortment changed. The grand and expensive lacquer cabinets and coffers were largely replaced by objects for daily use, such as bowls, dishes, saucers, tea and coffee ware (fig. 1). Middleclass people, too, could afford these items now, and due to large private imports such Japanese lacquer became more common and less status-like. Some of these new lacquer items do even closely resemble Japanese porcelain shapes, as is illustrated by a lacquered bowl and its Arita counterpart from the Count of Schönborn collection (fig. 2).

This private trade in lacquer is not documented, and we have to deal with the objects themselves to get an idea of the assortment and decorations. Apparently the 'pictorial' style with its raised details was continued, but the lacquer is of less quality. New Western shapes, such as knife boxes are introduced (colour plate VI.2), but all export lacquer is decorated in Japanese style. It really is surprising that Western motifs do not occur at all in this phase, quite contrary to the growing popularity of such motifs on 18th century Chinese and Japanese porcelain. Again, this change in lacquer production was caused by Dutch preferences and shifting ideas on the use of lacquer in the interior.

A third example of such Dutch influence can be seen at the end of the 18th and in the early 19th century. As I said, Japanese export lacquer was decorated in Japanese style, but about the 1780s Dutch merchants suddenly became aware of the possibilities of ordering lacquer with Western designs.[17] The first examples of this new trend seem to be the well-known plaques depicting portraits of famous Europeans and Roman emperors (fig. 3).[18] These oval plaques are lacquered on copper and have a ring to hang them. The portraits are done in slightly raised gold lacquer and copy in detail prints from a 6-volume French publication, named *L'Europe Illustré*, published in Paris between 1755 and 1765 by Dreux du Radier. This book clearly was in line with the European interest of that time in famous persons, famous historical events, famous sights and other outstanding famous things. The series of 593 engraved portraits in *L'Europe Illustré* was a cheap art gallery, imitating the grand painting galleries of the past. It is interesting to see that apart from such prints, smaller but comparable series of portraits were also made in other materials in Europe, for instance the portrait of Shakespeare of black basalt Wedgwood ware. It is possible that such ceramic plaques triggered the initiative of a Dutch merchant in Decima to have series of portraits done in Japanese lacquer. One of them, Mr. Reede van de Parkeler, who was Head in Decima in 1783, is known to have done so because in a letter to his father of 1793 he mentions sending over two plaques with 'the oval portraits or busts of Frederick II or the Great, one of which is lacquered with colours and a ditto inlaid with pearlshell or nacre'.[19] Several examples are known that match this description. Lacquer plaques proved to be extremely popular, several extensive series were made and individual plaques are still not rare. However, when European portraits could be done by the Japanese, other Western motifs and scenes could be lacquered as well. Within a few years this became a fashion and all kinds of plaques were ordered, for instance those with sea battles or those with famous buildings and city views.

Fig. 3. Three plaques of Japanese lacquer on copper, the portraits those of the Roman emperor Gordianus, of Catherina de Medici and of the Frankish king Childebert I. Late 18th century, dimensions 14.5 x 12.3 cm. Groninger Museum, Groningen

Fig. 4. Tabacco box of Japanese lacquer on copper, on the inside of the lid a dedication in Dutch, excecuted in gold lacquer. C. 1830, dimensions 8 x 23.5 x 2.5 cm. Groninger Museum, Gronigen

Unfortunately, the Napoleonic Wars disrupted the development of this privately ordered lacquer with European designs. The Dutch factory in Decima was cut off from the world for a long period and trade was not resumed until 1817. Lacquered objects with European designs still were made as souvenirs for the Dutch merchants, for instance card boxes with Dutch scenes derived from prints. Other fashionable souvenirs were tobacco boxes of lacquered copper, some of them decorated with European scenes or names written on the inside (fig. 4). A third item were large lacquered trays, for instance one from a private collection, dated 'Japan 1823' on the reverse and decorated with the view of a Dutch village in pearlshell on front.

Generally speaking, however, the new 19th century fashion was the 'Nagasaki' style with its exuberant Japanese-style decoration of flowering plants and butterflies in colourful pearlshell. Pearlshell and floral styles again: the circle had come round, from *namban* to 'Nagasaki'.

The Dutch were proud on their exclusive contacts in Japan. Their taste and preferences largely dictated the development of Japanese export lacquer for the Dutch market in shape and decoration and lacquer remained an excellent example of Dutch-Japanese interaction.

Notes

This paper resulted from the research undertaken for the forthcoming book *Japanese Export Lacquer* by Oliver Impey, Christiaan Jörg and Cynthia Viallé. I am grateful to both my colleagues for allowing me to use their work.

In the following notes 'VOC' means: the archive of the Dutch East India Company, which is housed in the General State Archives in The Hague. 'NFJ' (Nederlandse Factorij Japan) means the archive of the Decima factory, which is a separate part of the VOC archive.

1 Of the many introductions to the subject of the Dutch in Japan I only mention the classic by C. R. Boxer, *Jan Compagnie in Japan, 1600-1850*, The Hague 1950, and the exhibition catalogue *Japan und Europa 1543–1929*, Martin-Gropius-Bau, Berlin 1993, pp. 72–106, 272–305, 316–337, 369–390 and the many up-to-date references given there. See for lacquer in particular pp. 147–154, 266–271.

2 Letter of Henrick Brouwer to the Governor-General in Banten, 28 January 1613, VOC 1056.

3 A good survey is M. H. Mendes Pinto, *Namban lacquerware in Portugal. The Portuguese presence in Japan (1543–1639)*, Lisbon 1990.

4 Th. H. Lunsingh Scheurleer, 'Aanbesteding en verspreiding van Japans lakwerk door de Nederlanders in de zeventiende eeuw', in: *Jaarverslagen Oudheidkundig Genootschap*, 82–83 (1939–1941), Amsterdam 1941, p. 56.

5 See, for instance, the decisions of Heren XVII with regard to the sale results, 19 March 1614, VOC 7293.

6 Th. H. Lunsingh Scheurleer 1941, p. 57.

7 Letter of Heren XVII to Banten, November 1614, VOC 312. This instruction did not reach Japan until August 1616.

8 The order was promptly met by the VOC merchants in Japan: see the shipping list of 24 November 1634 for the ship *'T Wapen Van Delft*, NFJ 762, and the list of 15 February 1635 for the *Bredam*, NFJ 763.

9 S. W. A. Drossaers/Th. H. Lunsingh Scheurleer, *Inventarissen van de inboedel in de verblijven van de Oranjes en daarmee gelijk te stellen stukken 1576–1793*, vol. 1, The Hague 1974, pp 179–237, items 259, 263, 264, 269, 275, 277, 530, 534, 567.

10 A list of the auctioned goods, mentioning buyers and prices, dated Batavia 20 September 1627, is in VOC 1093. The document is discussed by A. M. Lubberhuizen-van Gelder, 'Een oude Indische inventaris', in: *Cultureel Indië*, 8, Leiden 1946, pp. 211–220.

11 Shipping lists of 13 November 1635 for the *Nieuw Amsterdam* and of 31 December 1635 for the *Wassenaer*, NFJ 763.

12 See for a survey of Chinese transitional porcelain: R. S. Kilburn, *Transitional Wares and their Forerunners*, exhibition catalogue Hong Kong Museum of Art, Hong Kong 1981; S. Little, *Chinese ceramics of the transitional period: 1620–1683*, exhibition catalogue China House Gallery, New York 1983.

13 C. J. A. Jörg, 'Japanese Export Lacquer-Interactions between the Japanese and the Dutch in the 17th century', in: *Western Influence on Japanese Art – 16th century – 19th century*, exhibition catalogue Fukuoka Art Museum, Fukuoka 1995, pp. 55–64.

14 See for the life and career of Caron: C. R. Boxer, ed., *A True Description of the Mighty Kingdoms of Japan & Siam by Caron & Schouten*, Amsterdam/New York 1971, pp. xv–cxxix.

15 This box is now in a private collection. It was auctioned at Sotheby's London, 12/13 June 1986, lot 727.

16 C. J. A. Jörg, 'Chinese Porcelains for the Dutch in the Seventeenth Century: Trading Networks and Private Enterprise', in: R. E. Scott, ed., *The Porcelains of Jingdezhen. Colloquies on Art & Archaeology in Asia No 16*, Percival David Foundation of Chinese Art/SOAS, London 1993, pp. 194–197.

17 C. J. A. Jörg, 'Japanese lacquer for the Dutch. Models and decorations in Western style', in: *Glorious Past of The Netherlands and Japan*, exhibition catalogue Kobe City Museum, Kobe 1993, pp. 138–148, 199–205.

18 C. J. A. Jörg, 'Japanese lacquerwork decorated after European prints', in: *Collection of Essays in Commemoration of the 30th Anniversary of the Institute of Oriental and Occidental Studies, Kansai University*, Osaka 1981, pp. 57–80.

19 Ibid., p. 61. The letter is in the Royal Library, The Hague, MS 133 M 36/2, no 17, dated Souracarta 15 August 1793.

Photo Credits

Figs. 1, 3, 4: John Stoel, Haren
Fig. 2: author
Colour plate VI.1, 2: John Stoel, Haren

Nicole Judet Brugier

From Asia to Europe: Asian Lacquerware applied to French Furniture

This report will concentrate on the use of Oriental lacquers by French 18th century furniture makers, that I have been able to study in detail in the course of various restorations at the Atelier Brugier[1], and in public and private collections in Paris.

First contacts between the Chinese and the Europeans developed from Marco Polo's travels. China appeared as a vastly different place with unknown customs. The mystery increased as Chinese works of art started to be imported and stimulated a fascination and a taste for Chinoiseries. We do not know exactly, when the first pieces of Chinese lacquerware appeared in Europe. In the inventory list of Schloss Ambras near Innsbruck in Austria from the 16th century we find the earliest mentioning of pieces of lacquerware, which gives us a starting point. In the 17th century, collectors of lacquerware were already numerous and in 1658, the great collector cardinal Mazarin organized a lottery, that included several cabinets from China. The taste for the exotic continued to develop during the 18th century. At that time any serious amateur had to possess a curiosity cabinet with works of art in the 'Indian or Chinese style'.

But even in the 18th century it was not that easy to find Eastern lacquers, as we learn from the writings of the most famous *marchand-mercier* Gersaint, whose shop in Paris was called 'A la Pagode'. In 1745, Gersaint who often travelled to Holland wrote: 'Lacquer is still a rather unknown curiosity and therefore not well spread. Good quality pieces are extremely rare, when they are old. They reach prices, that amaze everyone, even in Holland.'

Traders took great care as to the quality of lacquer and asked for panels which were lacquered on both sides in order to make several pieces of furniture out of one. It was at this time that the idea was born to transform Oriental lacquerwork in order to adapt it to European interior decoration and to ornate Western furniture with Oriental lacquer panels. Contrary to what was often said and written, European furniture was not sent to China or Japan to be lacquered. The imported wares such as cabinets, screens, chests and cupboards were transformed in Europe to fit into Western furniture. In proof of this we have numerous sales archives from English, Dutch and French vessels, which also give us an idea of the importance of the trade as listing was done with extreme accuracy. The fact that none of the Oriental parts were varnished in Europe gives another proof for this.

The different types of lacquers and techniques in use during the late Baroque and Rococo period, when Paris was the center for the manufacturing and sale of luxurious furniture and interior decoration in Europe, will be illustrated by three different examples: A commode in Coromandel lacquer by Jacques-Philippe Carel; a chest of drawers in Japanese lacquerware by Bernard II Vanrisamburgh, preserved in the Musée du Louvre, and a red and gold lacquered ensemble from the Hôtel du Châtelet in Paris, now at the Musée des Arts Décoratifs, luxurious pieces of furniture and interior decorations made in Paris between 1730 and 1770 from Chinese panel screens and a Japanese chest.

1. A Commode in Coromandel Lacquer by Jacques-Philippe Carel

The Louis XV commode in Coromandel lacquer by Jacques-Philippe Carel illustrated in colour plate VI.3 once belonged to an ensemble of two corner cabinets, which can be traced back to the property of Valençay castle, and was probably separated only during the auction of the Duke of Talleyrand collection in 1899.

There is little known about Jacques-Philippe Carel. He was active from 1724 to 1750 and gained his mastership in 1723. Looking at the diversity of his work it is most probable that he also acted as a salesman on behalf of his fellow furniture-makers. He worked with François-Antoine Gaudreaus, who produced and provided furniture for Louis XV.

The commode opens by two doors. Its interior is made of natural fruit wood and amaranth and shows three rows of oak-wood drawers. The panels used are probably coming from a twelve panels screen of the Kangxi period showing classical palatial scenes. The twelve panels were once corresponding to the twelve months of the year. Each panel was divided into two parts, thinned out and applied to the structure of the Louis XV commode.

Engraved lacquer called Coromandel lacquer was applied to the commode. Chambers wrote about this kind of lacquer in 1753: 'That kind of Indian painting and carving on wood looks like Japanese work only more fun.' We believe Coromandel lacquer appeared first in 1685 in Versailles. Louis XIV received three screens including a twelve panels one from the famous Siamese embassy as gifts from the Chinese emperor. The new Chinese fashion spread and soon many courtesans had their own Chinese screen. The Chinese word for Coromandel lacquer is *ke hui* and is of purely Chinese origin. In England this technique became to be known as 'Bantam work' according to the name of a trading center of the English East India Company in Java.

After having lost their trading center in Java, the English went to the Coromandel coast in Java. From this time on Bantam lacquer became Coromandel lacquer. It appeared in China during the Ming period at the end of the 15th century, but no piece was dated before the Kangxi period. On the front, one can still recognize two out of four Chinese liberal arts: 'music' on the upper left side and 'painting' on the right door. The two other arts 'writing' and 'chess' (or Go) were originally on the other side. The rich gilded bronze mounts were applied to enhance this magnificent decor. The most frequent decors on the twelve panels screens are palatial scenes, flowers and birds, scenes from the Taoist Paradise and European hunting scenes. Chinese craftsmen generally used some kind of pine wood pieces maintained together by bamboo nails. The panel was covered up with a thin layer of clay and a layer of mixed fibers. Once the layer was dry it was sanded down between 8 to 15 times. Finally, layers of black lacquer were applied following the same process. At this stage the craftsman would outline the drawing and carve out the

Fig. 1. Red and gold lacquer panel from the Hôtel du Châtelet, Paris, before 1770 (Paris, Musée des Arts Décoratifs)

lacquer along the lines in 'intaglio'. The different parts were then coloured with pigments, mixed with a sand to create a mat effect contrasting to the shining appearance of the lacquer background.

2. A Chest of Drawers in Japanese Lacquerware by Bernard II Vanrisamburgh, Paris 1730–1735 (Paris, Musée du Louvre)

The chest of drawers by Bernard II Vanrisamburgh, illustrated in colour plate VI.4, is among the first recorded works using Oriental lacquer. Bernhard II Vanrisamburgh (1696–1766) was received master before 1730. Being of Dutch origin, Vanrisamburgh worked for thirty years at the Faubourg Saint-Antoine, the center of Parisian cabinet making. He produced a large number of luxurious furniture fitting in lacquerware or porcelain panel for important Parisian *marchands-merciers* or traders like Darnault and Poirier. Lacquer was provided by the traders and was seldom to be found in the stock of furniture makers, as we know from their inventory lists.

The style of Bernard II Vanrisamburgh is highly specific and exceptional as can be seen from this chest of drawers. His great speciality became furniture decorated with panels of Japanese lacquer. This piece of furniture bears the label of François-Charles Darnault, who was furnisher of the crown from 1738 on. Lacquer was amongst his specialities. As the taste for chests of drawers and commodes developed since the end of the 17th century, traders often transformed Japanese cabinets into commodes.

Japanese cabinets were also amongst the gifts Siamese ambassadors brought to the royal court of Louis XIV. Pieces like that were also bought by *marchands-merciers* to give them to the furniture makers for further workmanship. The chest of drawers is built from a Japanese cabinet of common shape with two doors opening to ten drawers of various size. The cabinet doors have been thinned down to two or three millimeters and applied on the slightly incurved sides of the commode. The first lacquer panels to be applied on incurved structures are dated approximately 1724. Parts which are not made of lacquer have been painted with black varnish and parts left out by the Japanese locks are filled out and also painted with black varnish. The bronzes precisely fit the drawers and side panels. They are very plain. On the sides they divide Japanese work from varnished parts. The decoration is made of gold *hiramakie* on a *roironuri* ground with pavilions in the landscape.

3. A Red and Gold Lacquered Ensemble from the Hôtel du Châtelet (Paris, Musée des Arts Décoratifs)

The Hôtel du Châtelet, property of Louis-Marie Florent, Duc du Châtelet was built in 1770 by the architect Cherpitel in the heart of the most fashionable part of Paris. It included a *cabinet des laques*. Duc du Châtelet was the son of the famous Marquise du Châtelet, a very close friend of Voltaire, and one of the most sophisticated ladies of her time.

In 1793 the Duke was arrested and beheaded. The Hôtel was seized by the revolutionaries. The ensemble was saved by a miracle: nine panels, four cupboards a desk and a commode. Everything stayed in place until the 19th century. Two out of nine panels are still within their mahogany frames. In 1907 the panels were given to the Musée des Arts Décoratifs in Paris were they remained since then (fig. 1, cf. colour plate V). The cylinder desk and its *cartonnier* are of satinwood and lacquer as well as the four cupboards. In 1860 the cylinder desk and the four cupboards were sent to Compiègne following the instructions of the empress Eugenie. They stayed there and were often believed to be late 19th century works. The commode went to the Palace of l'Elysée in 1877 and is now part of the Mobilier National. It opens with two doors and its upright mounts are decorated with garlands of leaves.

These pieces of lacquerwork seem to be created earlier than the construction of the Hôtel in 1770 and could have been the property of the Marquise du Châtelet, who surrounded herself with lacquerware. None of these pieces bears a stamp. It seems obvious that the whole ensemble was produced from the same screen or the same series of panels of red and gold Qianlong Chinese lacquer. The decor is made of classical scenes with pagodas amongst gardens with walking figures. There are also scenes showing country life, family life, fishing parties, riding and plays on water.[2] When the cabinet was described in 1842, it is interesting to note that its lacquer was considered to be from Japan, which reminds us that the difference between Chinese and Japanese lacquer was not altogether clear at that time.

1 Cabinet or *comptoir*, Japanese lacquer decorated in the 'pictorial' style with a landscape. The stand is European. Third quarter 17th century, dimensions 76 x 89 x 50.5 cm. Groninger Museum, Groningen (see C. Jörg, in this publication, p. 43)

2 Knife box, Japanese lacquer after a European model, decorated with a landscape in Japanese style. Mid 18th century, height 37.9 cm. Groninger Museum, Groningen (see C. Jörg, in this publication, p. 45)

3 Commode in Coromandel lacquer by Jacques-Philippe Carel, Paris 1724–1750 (Paris, Musée du Louvre)

4 Chest of Drawers in Japanese lacquerware by Bernard II Vanrisamburgh, Paris 1730–1735 (Paris, Musée du Louvre)

The French artist Louis Cane, born in 1943, lives and works in Paris. He designs furniture with ancient lacquer panels. The Coromandel cabinet (fig. 2) is made out of a Kangxi period panel. It opens with two doors and is set on a bronze stand. The decor of the palace on the front has been used as an abstract element of architecture. The sides show usual items and vases known as the 'Hundred Antiques'. Still today, a taste for the exotic is inspiring contemporary artists to combine Oriental lacquers with modern furniture design.

Notes

1 The Atelier Brugier was founded by my father André Brugier in 1920; I am in charge of it since 1987. We are specialized in the restoration of Chinese and Japanese lacquerware as well as European lacquers, Vernis Martin and Art Deco lacquers. Our clients are museums, private collections and antique dealers. Amongst many other things we were lucky enough to restore for the Musée du Louvre the most famous blue and white chest of drawers realized by the furniture-maker Criard for the Comtesse de Mailly. Furthermore, we acquired a large collection of historical lacquerware: screens, panels, chests and cupboards.

2 I am most grateful to Madame Ledoux Lebard for her research on those red lacquers.

Acknowledgment

I would like to thank Mr. Daniel Alcouffe, chief curator of the Musée du Louvre for his help, his patience and his knowledge.

Photo Credits

Fig. 1: Atelier Brugier, Paris
Fig. 2: Atelier Brugier, Paris, B. Keller
Colour plate VI.3, 4: Réunion des Musées Nationaux, Paris

Fig. 2. Coromandel cabinet by Louis Cane, private property

Filip Suchomel

Early Examples of Japanese Export Lacquerware in Czech Collections

This is probably the first time for many experts to get acquainted with the Czech collections of Japanese lacquerware. The former Czechoslovakia spent many years in isolation from the outside world and the collections of Asian art deposited in our cultural institutions could not until recently be ranked among the well-known treasures of the world's cultural heritage. This situation is hopefully history now and the Czech collections of Asian art and their presentation and promotion will soon help throw light on major problems which experts in Japanese art face today.

The Czech lands used to be part of the West European culture for centuries, developing together with the cultures of our Western neighbours and as part of the Habsburg monarchy from 1526 onwards. Therefore, it is not surprising that the works of art found on the Czech territory are identical with those in the neighbouring states, such as Austria, Germany, Poland and Hungary. Consequently, the Czech collections of Japanese lacquerware play an important role in Central Europe and could be instrumental in comprehending Central European cultural trends. Although the Habsburg monarchy, a part of which the Czech lands remained until 1918, was not among the great powers with a multitude of colonies, many collections of Japanese art, unique in terms of quantity and quality, were amassed there, including lacquerware by Japanese masters. As it would be difficult to describe all the items in our collections in detail, we have selected just a few examples representing individual types of lacquerware, which had been imported to the Czech lands in the oldest period. The National Gallery in Prague plans to launch a representative exhibition of all major pieces of lacquerware and to publish a voluminous catalogue in 2001. We would like to display all of our important pieces of lacquerware, from the oldest examples to those dating from the early 20th century, and present this material still unknown to most of the professional and lay public.

It is common knowledge that Europe first encountered Japanese lacquerware in the second half of the 16th century. This was when the first products were imported to Europe, but those were earmarked especially for European clients. That is why it is so difficult to find examples of Japanese lacquerware made for the Japanese market before the 16th century. Also the pieces dating from the early Edo period are rarely found in the old European collections and the same was true in Bohemia. The first pieces of lacquerware probably reached its territory from Japan under Rudolf II at the turn of the 16th and the 17th centuries. In his unique collection deposited in his residence in Prague, the Emperor assembled a huge quantity of rare Oriental artifacts, including lacquerware, as we know from contemporary inventories. Due to Rudolf's many contacts with Spain and Portugal, we believe that some of the products in the style were made by lacquermasters in Kyoto for Portuguese and Spanish traders. Many items of Rudolf's unique collection were purloined during the Thirty Years' War and some of the rarest ones were taken away from Prague Castle even in the following centuries. We have retained a large lacquer coffer, but this artifact probably does not come from Rudolf's Kunstkammer and was added to the collection later in the late 17th century. There are also numerous artifacts of Japanese origin in the palaces of the former aristocracy; palace house lacquerware in the *namban* style as well as products dating from the second half of the 17th to the early 19th centuries, which were earmarked for Dutch clients. Among the many, we want to mention at least a small collection of Japanese artifacts assembled by the Lichnowsky family, which is now deposited at the castles in Hradec nad Moravicí and Raduň, the well-known collection of Chancellor Lothar Klemens Metternich from Kynžvart Castle, some of the pieces from the collection of the Schwarzenberg family, which are housed at Hluboká Castle, those of the Lichtenštejn family at Lednice Castle, the Lobkowicz family at their chateaux in Nelahozeves and Mělník, and the Mensdorf-Poully family at Boskovice Castle. Apart from these castle collections, similar products can be found in Czech museums. Perhaps the most significant among them is owned by the Náprstek Museum in Prague, including four pieces of *namban* lacquerware and examples of the Japanese lacquerware production from the 18th century.

Let us briefly describe the major examples of the oldest pieces of Japanese lacquerware in the Bohemian and Moravian collections. We shall focus only on pieces dating from the late 16th to the first third of the 17th century. This is the period of trade contacts to Portugal and Spain, whereas products of a later date were undoubtedly imported by Dutch traders whose ships were the only connection between isolated Japan and Europe after the expulsion of the Spanish and Portuguese from Japan in 1625 and 1639, respectively. We shall not deal with any products made later than that.

In principle, it can be said that the Czech collections comprise only two types of Japanese lacquerware produced in the former period, i.e. while Spain and Portugal played a major role in trade contacts. One is a large rectangular chest with a half-cylinder upper lid and the other is a 'cabinet', the shape of which undoubtedly imitates the Spanish inlaid *varqueno* or miniature writing desk. Whereas its shape is undoubtedly European, its decoration is a mixture of various influences and it is not easy to tell from where the anonymous Japanese artists drew inspiration. Nevertheless, it is certain that this decoration is neither genuinely European nor Japanese. It often bears traces of Moorish and Gujarati ornamentation. At that time, the Portuguese had a fashion of Gujarati 'pseudo-lacquerware-style' products imitating Japanese decoration. It seems likely that the Portuguese commissioned a type of similar decoration, which fully suited them also from Japanese artists. This may be why this early lacquerware is so difficult to define and why we find so many different principles and patterns in its decoration.

Colour plate VII.1 shows the first of the chests found in the collection of the Náprstek Museum in Prague. It is 70 cm long, 37 cm high and 46.5 cm wide. As it was the custom for this type of lacquerware, the decoration was made in gold and silver *hi-*

ramakie and *raden* techniques, but fragments of mother-of-pearl are mostly missing on the lid. The decoration is very typical for the early period between about 1570 and the year 1600. Lacquerware artists did not yet separate individual panels or cartouches, but played with the effects of full, elegant and undivided areas. Only the edges are plainly decorated with a typical undulating line enveloping the entire scene.

The decoration depicts typical Japanese flowers. That seems to give credit to the assumption that the artists interpreted the familiar fauna and flora although it was a rather unusual pattern for them. On the lid, there are the blossoming *sakura* and *tachibana* citrus, the minutely executed vine on the front and rear parts, and the blossoming prunus on the sides in addition to the motifs on the upper lid. The inner surface of the lid is also decorated, but the lacquermasters did not use the lavish decoration like on the other parts of the chest, but contented themselves with a kind of sketched branch in the gold *hiramakie* technique and sparingly used mother-of-pearl. The simple brass fitting is decorated with a fine, stylized floral design.

The similar piece (colour plate VII.2) also comes from the Náprstek Museum in Prague. This chest is much smaller (24 cm high, 37.5 cm long and 18.5 cm wide). Its size is reminiscent of the well-known artifact from the Irving Collection, which was displayed at the Metropolitan Museum in New York City in 1991[1]. Its decoration in the gold and silver *hiramakie* technique and *raden* mother-of-pearl inlay is separated into panels trimmed with mother-of-pearl. This suggests that the piece was produced later than the previous one, probably between 1600 and 1620. Notable are the detailed bodies of phoenixes made in the silver *makie* technique in two square panels on the lid. The front face is decorated with mountain goats and birds among the *sakura* blossoms, mythical unicorns under the camellia and plant motifs continuing on rectangular panels on the sides and rear face. All the panels are trimmed with spiral ornaments. The inside of the chest is decorated in simple black lacquer, while the inner surface of the lid is adorned with a simply stylized scroll design.

Colour plate VII.3 shows an artifact which represents lacquer products with frugal and simple decoration. This miniature box (10 cm high, 16.5 cm long and 9 cm wide) which originally comes from the Schwarzenberg estate at Hluboká Castle is adorned in stylized pearl curved in a net-like pattern with an inscribed lozenge-shaped rosette. The inside is decorated in simple black lacquer. The piece is undoubtedly one of the smallest *namban* lacquer-decorated boxes in the world.[2] In all probability, it was used for jewellery or other valuables.

Now we shall focus on the largest artifact of the same shape (fig. 1) which was already mentioned in the beginning. It is a property of Prague Castle. The production of similar chests culminated in 1620–1640. The size of this one (130 cm long, 63 cm high and 59 cm wide) ranks it among the largest pieces of this type known to date. Its lid is decorated with two cloud-shaped cartouches in the upper section. The first uses a motif of landscape with the lake, bridge, architecture, peasants, rabbits and paulownia trees with long-tailed birds. The main decoration is complemented with the pine, prunus, willow and fancy ducks on the lake. The other cartouche employs a similar decoration of landscape with architecture, phoenixes, a shika deer, ducks, pine, chrysanthemum and vine. The right side of the lid is of a semi-circular form and is adorned with a medallion with rabbits and Chinese bellflowers, whereas the medallion on the left side of the lid bears a motif of herons in the landscape. The inner part of the lid is decorated with a packhorse, straw under the pine tree and birds flying all around. The front side of the chest is also decorated with two cloud-shaped cartouches: the one on the left depicts two owls in the landscape and a gate of the *torii* Shinto shrine, huts and plants – hortensia, fern and chrysanthemum. The right cartouche depicts a little fence and a man with draft oxen but this main motif was completed with birds and plants, bellflowers, chrysanthemums and bamboo. The right side of the chest bears a square-shaped disk with a motif of Chinese bellflowers, a peach tree, bamboo, butterflies and birds. The left side of the chest depicts a square-shaped disk with a painted decoration of a hut under hortensia and chrysanthemum. The rear side is decorated with two squares with a motif of morning glory on the fence, and another motif of vine.

The inside and bottom of the chest are covered in black lacquer. The additional decoration on the sides is shaped as a triple wave called *tomo-e (mitsutomo-e)* and a string of endless pearls (*shippotsunagi*) in lacquer and mother-of-pearl. In Europe, the chest was fitted with a rectangular-shaped mount on short legs, which is adorned with carved rosettes and covered in lacquer with a gold decoration of pearl.

Now we shall concentrate on the other two pieces of *namban* lacquerware of later date. One of them (colour plate VII.5) comes from the estate of the Lichnowsky family and their chateau in Hradec nad Moravicí and the other (colour plate VII.4) from the Lobkowicz estate in Mělník near Prague. These artifacts are dated 1620 to 1630. We can see the change in style, which the decoration of export lacquerware for the Europeans underwent. In the earlier period it was customary to use mother-of-pearl that sometimes covered a substantial part of the surface. In the younger products, however, the mother-of pearl decoration played a minor role as it was used only for marginal geometric patterns as part of the frames of cartouches and panels bearing the main design without any mother-of-pearl inlay. In this piece, too, the absence of mother-of-pearl is obvious. The main cartouches of the Mělník artifact depict views of garden retreats with the pine, bamboo, bamboo fences, birds or merely

Colour Plate VII ▷

1 *Namban* chest (l. 70 cm, h. 37 cm, w. 46.5 cm), *c.* 1570–1600, collection of the Náprstek Museum, Prague

2 *Namban* chest (l. 37.5cm, h. 24 cm, w. 18.5 cm), *c.* 1600–1620, collection of the Náprstek Museum, Prague

3 Miniature *namban* box (l. 16.5 cm, h. 10 cm, w. 9 cm) with frugal and simple decoration, c. 1600, originally from the Schwarzenberg estate at Hluboká nad Vltavou Castle

4 *Namban* chest (l. 45.7 cm, h. 30.4 cm, w. 25 cm), *c.* 1620–1630, estate of the Lobkowicz family, Mělník Chateau

5 *Namban* chest (l. 37.5 cm, h. 24.6 cm, w. 22 cm), *c.* 1620–1630, formerly property of the Lichnowsky family, Hradec nad Moravicí Castle

6 *Namban* cuboid chest with upper lid (l. 89 cm, h. 64.2 cm, w. 44.6 cm), *c.* 1570–1600, Kynžvart Chateau

7 *Namban* jewellery box (l. 34.9 cm, h. 39.3 cm, w. 32 cm), *c.* 1600–1620, varqueno, formerly property of the Lichnowsky family, Hradec nad Moravicí Castle

8 *Namban* cabinet (l. 37.2 cm, h. 26.2 cm, w. 25 cm), dated *c.* 1600–1620, collection of the Náprstek Museum, Prague

9 *Namban* cuboid chest with upper lid (l. 47 cm, h. 34.3 cm, w. 31.7 cm), *c.* 1600, Lednice Chateau

10 *Namban* cabinet (l. 50.3 cm, h. 32.8 cm, w. 31.3 cm), classic example of *namban* varqueno, dated c. 1600–1620, collection of the Náprstek Museum, Prague

△ 1 2 △ 3 △

△ 4 6 ▽ ▽ 7 5 △

▽ 8 9 ▽ 10 ▽

Fig. 1. Namban coffer (l. 130 cm, h. 63 cm, w. 59 cm), *c.* 1620–1640, Prague Castle

jardinières with Japanese flowers. The lacquer piece from Hradec is similarly decorated with herons, camellias, peonies and chrysanthemums. In addition, the upper lid employs vivid lacquer tones that we know from the products of later times made for Dutch traders. Only the rear sides of these chests are reminiscent of the original decoration – they are always designed in a somewhat subdued manner echoing the well-known scroll design or vine enclosed in a lozenge-shaped panel like in the piece from Hradec Chateau.

Two cuboid chests with upper lids are perhaps the most interesting items made by Japanese lacquermasters in the Czech collections. The small chest (colour plate VII.9) comes from the chateau in Lednice and the larger one (colour plate VII.6) is deposited at Kynžvart Castle. Both of them were assembled in Europe and furnished with new massive fittings. In addition, the inside was inlaid in Europe, as customary. Nevertheless, the Japanese parts can be unambiguously classified as the oldest *namban* artifacts dated 1570 to 1600. The front face, sides and lid of the chest from Kynžvart were undoubtedly part of the Japanese original designed for Portugal or Spain; impressive is the minute execution of geometric décor of the *shippotsunagi* type, which encircles the cartouches with plant patterns. The rear side of the chest, however, is decorated with a design of undoubtedly non-Japanese origin, with a motif of Chinese men and jardinière. The piece was certainly completed with its rear side and equipped with the metal fitting in Europe. The same is true for the other piece, although its rear side may be of Japanese origin.

Three pieces of lacquerware representing the other type of Japanese *namban* lacquerware, cabinets or writing desks, are focussed here. The first (colour plate VII.10), in the custody of the Náprstek Museum in Prague, is a classic example of *varqueno* (50.3 cm long, 32.8 cm high and 31.3 cm wide). Its inner walls are decorated with rectangular panels depicting scenes in the flowers-and-birds style in the low *makie* technique and inlaid with mother-of-pearl. The motifs employed are in line with the classical style of decorating products earmarked for export: Chinese bellflowers, *tachibana* citrus, prunus and *sakura* bushes and flying birds. When opened, the front lid exposes ten drawers decorated with similar arabesques. The arrangement of the drawers with a gate-shaped drawer in the middle almost faithfully imitates European originals. The second smaller piece (colour plate VII.8) (37.2 cm long, 26.2 cm high and 25 cm wide) which is also a property of the Náprstek Museum in Prague demonstrates a different decorative style. The artist mostly used mother-of-pearl cut and arranged in a lozenge-shaped lattice-like pattern. This decoration covers all the outer walls as well as inside of the drawers. The typical gate-shaped drawer in the middle is missing. Just the inner part of the lid bears decoration typical of the *namban* lacquerware in the *makie* and *raden* techniques with scroll design and vine. The third piece of this type (colour plate VII.7) – formerly a property the Lichnowsky family – is also a *varqueno*. This jewellery box is one of the smaller artifacts. Very interesting is its almost cuboid shape (the box is 30.3 cm high, 34.9 cm long and 32 cm wide). Even here, mother-of-pearl played a major role as a decorating

Fig. 2. Desk, top decorated in *namban* style (l. 97 cm, h. 79 cm, w. 68 cm), *c.* 1600, estate of the Lobkowicz family, Mělník Chateau

element. Unlike the previous piece, however, the lacquermasters employed a technique of chipping the mother-of-pearl in tiny irregular fragments with which they covered large surfaces on the front face, sides and upper side. Then, cartouches with motifs of plants, birds and wild animals were embedded in the surfaces inlaid with mother-of-pearl. The inner part of the face is similar to that of the previous artifact, but its drawers are decorated sparingly, only with geometric patterns.

Quite exceptional among the objects decorated in the *namban* style are tables or desks and chairs. Only very few have survived, however, as furniture was not a common article in the lacquer workshops of Kyoto. The Czech collections do include one example of such a desk, its top decorated in the *namban* style. The item is part of the collection of the Lobkowicz family at Mělník Chateau (fig. 2).[3] The decoration of the top is designed as a square medallion in a massive mother-of-pearl frame adorned with bamboo and paulownia sprays and two phoenixes executed in the *makie* and *raden* techniques. In addition, the medallion is encircled with a lattice-like 'necklace'. In the corners of the dark brown top there are four fan-shaped medallions executed in the same technique, with motifs of hexagonal lattice or endless tortoise shell *kikkotsunagi*. While the top of the desk is lavishly decorated, its sides and legs are unadorned. This is what distinguishes this piece in the Lobkowicz collection from another well-known desk deposited in the Wilanów Palace in Warsaw.

Our last example, a *namban* artifact (fig. 3), is interesting in terms of shape. Its form imitates that of a traditional circular rice container. This form clearly shows that not all the *namban*-style products necessarily had to be made in European moulds. This one is decorated in the gold and silver *hiramakie* and *raden* techniques. The central motif depicts three herons in the *sakura* bush, and typical Japanese flowers – chrysanthemums and Chinese bellflowers – on the edge. Inside and on the bottom decoration is missing and the wooden skeleton is covered in brown and black lacquer only. This piece, property of Kynžvart Castle,

Fig. 3. *Namban* round box (d. 53.1 cm, h. 20.8 cm), *c.* 1600, Kynžvart Chateau

is fitted with a European mount, suggesting that it served as a miniature table. Unlike cabinets, chests and suitcases that can be found in the world's collections in huge quantities, lacquerware of this shape is very rare.

The origin of the oldest examples of Japanese lacquerware in the Bohemian and Moravian collections is related to the period, when Portuguese and Spanish trading ships were still allowed to land on the Japanese shores. The examples shown here suggest that it is possible to find still unknown and interesting pieces in the Czech Republic. They indicate that such works of art were very popular among many Bohemian and Moravian aristocratic families. It is disappointing, however, that we have not succeeded in finding enough archival material, which would give us an idea of when exactly these artifacts became part of our collections and disclose routes through which such products reached Bohemia. Let us hope that such research will be carried out one day and we shall learn more about the origin of these unique works of art.

Notes

1 See James C.Y Watt/Barbara Brennan Ford: *East Asian Lacquer: The Florence and Herbert Irving Collection,* New York, The Metropolitan Museum of Art, 1991.
2 A similarly decorated coffer survives in The Netherlands. Christiaan Jörg personal communication.
3 For comparison see: Exh. Cat. *Japan und Europa 1543–1929*, Berlin, Berliner Festspiele, 1993, p. 269.

Photo Credits

Fig. 1: Photograph courtesy of the Prague Castle Administration
Fig. 2: Photograph courtesy of the Lobkowicz family
Fig. 3: Photograph courtesy of the Kynžvart Chateau Museum
Colour plate VII.1, 2, 8, 10: Photographs courtesy of the Náprstek Museum in Prague; VII.3: Photograph courtesy of the Hluboká nad Vltavou Castle Museum; VII.4: Photograph courtesy of the Lobkowicz family: VII.5, 7: Photographs courtesy of the Hradec nad Moravicí Castle Museum; VII.6: Photograph courtesy of the Kynžvart Chateau Museum; VII.9: Photograph courtesy of the Lednice Chateau Museum

Namiko Takeuchi

Two Examples of Japanese Export Lacquer Chairs

Studies on Japanese export lacquer have been started in Europe, where many export lacquer objects and documents concerning them have remained, like e. g. the typical Western style chest or chest of drawers. Until recently, it was hardly possible to find other information than the year of completion and the origin of the shape. In this article I want to present two export lacquer chairs, which are now in Japan again. For these two objects I want to determine the period, when they were made from their shape and decoration. First of all, I want to concentrate on the design and the decoration techniques.

1. Decoration

A landscape makie armchair

The armchair (fig. 1), that was acquired by the Tokyo National Museum in 1997, is lacquered in black except for the seat, and decorated in *hiramakie* and *takamakie*. On one part of the U-shaped back there is a peony scroll in *hiramakie*. On the rail below the seat at the front of the chair there are sprays of flowers in *hiramakie*. On the four legs flowers, grasses, birds and a dragonfly are drawn inside a cartouche in *hiramakie,* and on the four supports there are geometrical patterns also in *hiramakie*.

The most remarkable part is the back board. On the front a landscape is drawn in *takamakie* technique (fig. 2). There are *kirikane* (small metal plate) inlays in the rocks, and distant mountains and clouds drawn in *togidashi makie*. Various techniques are used to make the composition clear. The reverse side has two parts (fig. 3): On the upper side autumn grasses and rocks are drawn, on the lower side there is a landscape in *takamakie*.

This type of pictorial style *takamakie* and geometric patterns, flower sprays, grasses within a cartouche in *hiramakie* are often found on Japanese export lacquerware from the mid or the second half of the 17th century.

Fig. 1. Landscape *makie* armchair, Tokyo National Museum; width 66.0, depth 63.5, height 105.5 cm

Fig. 2. Front side, drawing of a landscape in *takamakie*

Fig. 3. Reverse side with autumn grasses and rocks (upper side), and a landscape in *takamakie* (lower side)

1

2

3

A flower arabesque makie raden folding chair

The other object is a folding chair (fig. 5), which has entered a private collection in Kyoto after the sale at Christie's in London in 1993. It was displayed at an exhibition at the Kyoto National Museum and the Fukuoka City Museum in 1995.

On the sides there are phoenixes in *takamakie* and mother-of-pearl inlay (fig. 4). On the rails and turned balusters of the back and posts there are chrysanthemum scrolls and geometric patterns in *hiramakie* and mother-of-pearl inlay (fig. 6). On part of the rail patterns are inlaid in very fine mother-of-pearl or drawn in gold and silver *hiramakie* (fig. 7). The baluster also shows mother-of-pearl inlay (fig. 8). The side is decorated with a phoenix. This type of long-tailed phoenixes is also seen on the well-known Mazarin chest at the Victoria & Albert Museum, which was made around 1640.

Fig. 6. Chrysanthemum scrolls and geometric patterns in *hiramakie* and mother-of-pearl inlay on the rails and turned balusters of the back and posts

Fig. 4. Folding chair (cf. fig. 5), phoenixes in *takamakie* and mother-of-pearl inlay on the sides

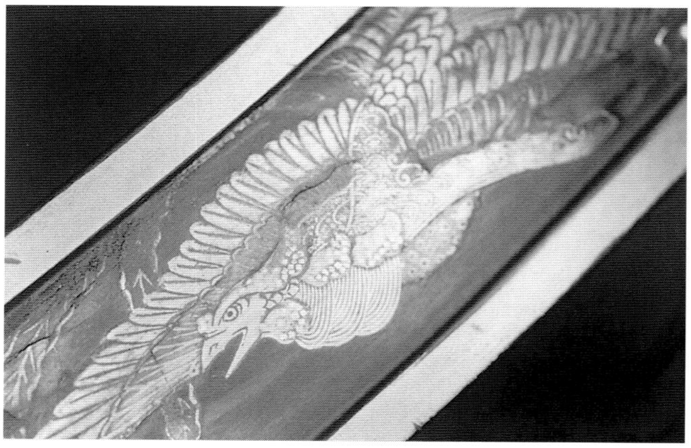

Fig. 7. Patterns in very fine mother-of-pearl inlay and gold and silver *hiramakie* on part of the rail

Fig. 5. Flower arabesque *makie raden* folding chair, private collection, Kyoto; width 36.0, height 67.0 cm

Fig. 8. Mother-of-pearl inlay on the baluster

Fig. 9. Folding chair *kyokuroku* with U-shaped back, Kodai-ji temple, Kyoto

Fig. 10. Armchair *kyokuroku* with U-shaped back and four legs, Myoshin-ji temple, Kyoto

Though this type of fine mother-of-pearl inlay is very rare on export lacquerware, I think this kind of an overall decoration in *hiramakie* and mother-of-pearl inlay is one of the general characteristics of export lacquerware in the first half of the 17th century.

The decoration style can be used to attribute the two chairs to different periods. It is generally acknowledged, that an overall decoration in *hiramakie* with mother-of-pearl inlay, generally called *namban* style, disappeared before the middle of the 17th century, and was then followed by the socalled 'pictorial' style with *takamakie*. Therefore, I think I can say, that according to its decoration the folding chair was made in the first half of the 17th century and the armchair in the second half of the 17th century.

Fig. 11. Armchair, Kohki period (1662–1722), Palace Museum, Beijing

Fig. 12. Armchair, 18th century, Palace Museum, Beijing

2. Shape and structure

Armchair

This type of chair with a U-shaped back is called *kyokuroku* in Japanese, but this word includes two types with different structures. One of them has four legs, the other type is a folding chair. Both forms were mainly used for rituals at temples. In pre-modern Japan people usually sat on the floor and did not use chairs in daily life. Only from the Momoyama period in the early 17th century onwards did they start using this type of chair at parades, festivals, kabuki performances or during cherry blossom festivities. This tradition was for example preserved at the Kodai-ji temple in Kyoto, which is an example of the Momoyama period (fig. 9).

Most of the Japanese U-shaped back chairs are folding chairs. Only two four-legged examples are known. The chair at the Myoshin-ji temple in Kyoto (fig. 10) has an U-shaped back and four legs, nevertheless, it is quite different from the export lacquer chair in proportion and details. But in China lots of four legged chairs with an U-shaped back were made during the Ming and Qing dynasty. The form of the export lacquer armchair seems to be more similar to Chinese than to Japanese chairs. The chair (fig. 11) from the Palace Museum in Beijing from the Kohki period (1662–1722) is very similar to the export lacquer chair in proportion, the shape of the posts at the back and there is a rail below the front seat. Another example (fig. 12), also in the Palace Museum in Beijing and from the 18th century, shows a different shape and more decorated parts. Particularly the way of joining the seat and legs is a new feature typical for the 18th century.

The export armchair has the same structure and form as the examples from the late 17th or early 18th century. But this is no contradiction for the dating of the decoration, which is characteristic for the second half of the 17th century.

Folding chair

Folding chairs are not only seen in the Far East but also in Europe. Figure 13 shows a Dutch chair of the Rijksmuseum in Amsterdam from the 17th century. The shape of the legs and rails are very similar to the export folding chair. In the back of the folding chair there are rails with five arches between turned balusters. On top of the posts there are lions carrying shields. These are all well known features of Dutch chairs of the 2nd quarter of the 17th century. You can also see the rails with arches, balusters and lions on another example from the Rijksmuseum (fig. 14). This Dutch chair is of the same period as the one before. So the shape of the export chair is the same as Dutch chairs of the 2nd quarter of the 17th century which corresponds with the period found for the decoration.

3. Conclusions

In documents of the Dutch East India Company there is a record that in 1640 they sent a chair decorated with *makie* lacquer to the Governor General of Dutch East India from Hirado, Japan. I believe this chair was in European form just like the export folding chair referred to before. But a complex structure and carvings were needed to make a chair in European form and I suppose the Japanese had difficulties with this and also with the larger size. I think, that they began to make export chairs based on the Chinese form or that they were ordered to decorate chair frames, which had been sent from China, with a *makie* decoration.

But the European chair might still have been in demand, because it fitted into European interiors. In documents of the English East India Company there is a record from 1687 which says, that they sent chair frames from Europe to Tonkin to be lacquered there. So in the 18th century the Chinese began to make chair frames by copying the models sent from Europe and then lacquered them.

From these two examples I draw the conclusion, that export lacquer chairs changed in the 17th century in both: shape and decoration. The export folding chair with a decoration style from the first half of the 17th century also has a shape based on a Dutch chair from the same period and the armchair with the decoration style from the late 17th century has a form based on Chinese chairs from the same period.

Photo Credits

All photographs by the author

Fig. 13. Dutch folding chair, 17th century, Rijksmuseum, Amsterdam

Fig. 14. Dutch chair, 17th century, Rijksmuseum, Amsterdam

Ostasiatische Lacke
East Asian Lacquer

Abb. 1. Grabkammer von Grab 1 Hunan, Changsha, Mawangdui. HUNANSHENG BOWUGUAN (HG.): *Changsha Mawangdui yi hao mu*, Bd. 1-2. Peking 1973, Bd. 1, Abb. 36

Margarete Prüch

Zum Dekor eines Sarges aus Grab 1 von Mawangdui

Seit der Entdeckung der drei großen Gräber des Marquis Dai, Li Cang, seiner Frau und deren Sohn von Mawangdui, Changsha in der Provinz Hunan, VR China, im Jahre 1973, ist viel über die Grabanlage und besonders über das reiche Inventar geforscht worden. Bis heute gehört vor allem das zur Zeit der Ausgrabung noch vollkommen intakte Grab 1 zu den spektakulärsten Funden Chinas. Es konnte anhand von Siegelfunden auf das Jahr 168 v. Chr. datiert werden.[1]

Bei der Anlage handelt es sich um ein Schachtgrab mit einer Rampe, die oberhalb der eigentlichen Grabkammer (*guo*) endet. Fünf Stufen führen von der Mündung in den sich nach unten leicht verjüngenden, 16 m tiefen Schacht. Auf der Sohle ruht, umgeben von einer dicken Schicht grau verfärbten Tones, die hölzerne Grabkammer (Abb. 1). Sie schützt vier ineinander geschachtelte, unterschiedlich lackierte Särge (*guan*).[2] Während der äußere Sarg nur mit Schwarzlack ausgekleidet ist, sind die inneren drei Särge zusätzlich mit Dekor überzogen. Um den äußeren dieser drei bemalten Särge (Länge 2,56 m, Breite 1,18 m Höhe 1,14 m) soll es in der vorliegenden Untersuchung gehen (Abb. 7).

Schwungvoll sind auf den schwarzen Lackgrund Wolken gemalt. Sie werden vom Wind getrieben, schweben in langen Bahnen, verdichten sich dann zu einem Wolkenknäuel, wechseln abrupt die Richtung und laufen in zipfligen Endungen aus. Rote und gelbe, an „Strömungspfeile" erinnernde Motive unterstützen noch diesen fließenden Eindruck. In den „Ruhezonen" der Wolken oder auf den Ausläufern der Wolkenzipfel tummeln sich verschiedene Fabelwesen.[3]

Im Folgenden sollen nicht die mythologischen Deutungen der Ornamente und Motive im Vordergrund stehen, sondern der technische Aspekt der Bemalung und der Schaffensprozess der Künstler, deren Aufgabe es war, eine Fläche, das heißt fünf Seitenteile – die Unterseite bleibt undekoriert – eines rechteckigen Holzsarges zu bemalen.

Die Vorläufer

Bisher sind nur wenige gut erhaltene lackierte Särge aus der Zhou-Zeit (867–255 v. Chr.) ausgegraben worden.[4]

Eines der frühesten Beispiele eines lackierten Sarges stammt aus Henan, Guangshan, Baoxiangsi (datiert auf das 8.–7. Jh. v. Chr.).[5] Dort werden die Seitenpaneele des einfarbig schwarz lackierten Sargs von einem breiteren Ornamentband umschlossen. Die sich wiederholenden Motive lassen eindeutige Verbindungen zu den zeitgenössischen Bronzen erkennen.

Bei den beiden Särgen aus dem Grab des Marquis Yi von Zeng in Hubei, Suixian, Leigudun, das aufgrund von Inschriften auf das Jahr 433 v. Chr. datiert werden kann, sind zum ersten Mal die großen Flächen der Seiten und des Deckels in kleinere rechteckige und quadratische Felder und breitere Ornamentbänder unterteilt. Szenen aus der Mythologie, Wächter, gemalte Fenster- oder Türkonstruktionen und Ornamente aus dem Bereich der Bronzen wechseln sich hierbei ab.[6]

Diese frühen Beispiele sind noch sehr an das Musterrepertoire der Bronzen angelehnt. Vor allem die Felder unterteilen in einer strengen Ordnung die Seitenpaneele oder den Deckel.

Ab der Mitte des 4. Jh. v. Chr. ist ein Wandel in der Bemalung von Särgen zu beobachten. Die frühesten Beispiele dafür stammen wahrscheinlich aus Hunan, Xiangxiang, Niuxingshan Grab 1 und 2.[7] Leider existieren keine klaren Aufnahmen von diesen Särgen, so dass nur anhand der Detailfotos und der Beschreibung in dem Ausgrabungsbericht auf die Bemalung geschlossen werden kann. Geschwungene Drachenkörper (bei dem Sarg aus Grab 2 handelt es sich um Phönixvögel) sind intermittierend auf den Seitenpaneelen und Deckeln angeordnet, wobei der Dekor über die gesamte äußere Fläche des Sarges gelegt wird. Es entsteht so der Eindruck, der Sarg sei mit einem kostbaren Seidentuch bedeckt.[8]

Eines der noch erhaltenen Beispiele für die Imitation eines Sargtuchs aus feinem Stoff durch Lackbemalung ist auf dem Sarg aus Grab 2 von Hubei, Jingmen, Baoshan zu sehen[9] (Abb. 3). Der Sarg aus Baoshan war zur Zeit der Ausgrabung noch sehr gut erhalten. Seitenteile und Deckel, der mit Nut und Feder in den Sarg eingepasst und zusätzlich mit Rohlack verklebt war, sind mit dem gleichen Dekor überzogen. Auf jedem der Paneele sind über dem schwarzen Lackgrund ineinander verwobene Drachenkörper so angeordnet, dass sich ihre Köpfe an der Längsachse treffen. Darüber wurden insgesamt acht Phönixvögel – jeweils paarweise – intermittierend entlang der Längsachse gespiegelt. Deutlich sind die Köpfe und langen Schwanzfedern zu sehen, die direkt an gestickte Textilien erinnern. Der Dekor der Seitenpaneele wird über den Deckelabsatz weitergeführt und trifft dann auf den in gleicher Weise gestalteten Deckel, so dass der Eindruck eines geschlossenen, fortlaufenden Musters entsteht. Nur die beiden Stirnseiten sind anders dekoriert. Bestimmend sind hier geometrische Ornamente, aus denen teilweise zoomorphe Motive, wie Drachenköpfe, wachsen.[10]

Funde von Seiden- oder Brokatstoffen mit ähnlichen Motiven bestätigen die Annahme, dass es sich um die Nachahmung von Textilien gehandelt hat. Aus dem reich ausgestatteten Grab 1 von Hubei, Jiangling, Mashan, wurden zahlreiche Stoffe ausgegraben, in die die Bestattete eingewickelt war[11] (Abb. 2). Sie zeigen in ihrem Aufbau und den verwendeten Ornamenten große Ähnlichkeit mit dem Dekor der lackierten Särge.

Die Zhou- und Zhanguo-zeitlichen Särge mit Lackbemalung können so in drei Kategorien unterteilt werden:

- Die Motive stammen aus dem Musterrepertoire der Bronzen.
- Die Bemalung der Särge erfolgt nach einem bestimmten ikonographischen Programm, wie zum Beispiel bei dem Sarg von Suixian.
- Der Dekor der Särge orientiert sich an Textilien, hier besonders an Stickereien, und imitiert sie.

△ 2

Der Sarg von Mawangdui

Die drei bemalten inneren Särge von Mawangdui Grab 1 markieren einen Wendepunkt in der Bemalung von großen Lackgeräten.

Die vier Seitenteile und der Deckel des schwarz lackierten und mit Wolkenornamenten (*yunwen/yunqiwen*) bemalten Sargs werden zunächst in Bänder und Felder unterteilt (Abb. 7). Ein konzentrisches Ornamentband begrenzt jedes Seitenpaneel und den Deckel und umschließt somit ein zentrales Mittelfeld. Durch diese Vorgabe sind die Dekorzonen klar definiert, dort müssen die Ornamente eingepasst werden. Nur der Außenrand des 0,13 cm dicken Deckels ist zusätzlich mit einem weiteren Ornamentband verziert.

Der Deckel und die Seitenteile werden von drei konzentrischen Ornamentbändern umrandet. Das mittlere, etwas breitere Band ist in drei unterschiedlich schmale Bänder mit verschiedenen Mustern unterteilt. Ein Wolkenband bildet das Zentrum. Einzelne Wolkenmotive werden dabei versatzstückartig, jeweils um 180° gedreht, aneinandergefügt.[12] Diese Beobachtung ist vor allem für die Ornamente der zentralen Felder von besonderer Bedeutung. Zwei schmale Bänder mit unterschiedlichen geometrischen Motiven schließen sich direkt an das Wolkenband an. Etwas abgesetzt davon sind die gleichen geometrischen Ornamentbänder, hier allerdings vertauscht, angefügt. Diese drei um-

Abb. 2. Umzeichnung eines mit Drachen- und Phönixmotiven bestickten Seidenstoffs aus Grab 1 von Hubei, Jiangling, Mashan. HUBEISHENG JINGZHOU DIQU BOWUGUAN (HG): *Jiangling Mashan yi hao mu*. Peking 1985, Abb. 45

Abb. 3. Umzeichnung des Dekors der Seitenpaneele des Sargs aus Grab 2 Hubei, Jingmen, Baoshan. HUBEISHENG JINGSHA TIELU KAOGUDUI (HG.): *Baoshan Chu mu*. Peking 1991, Bd. 1, Abb. 45

3 ▽

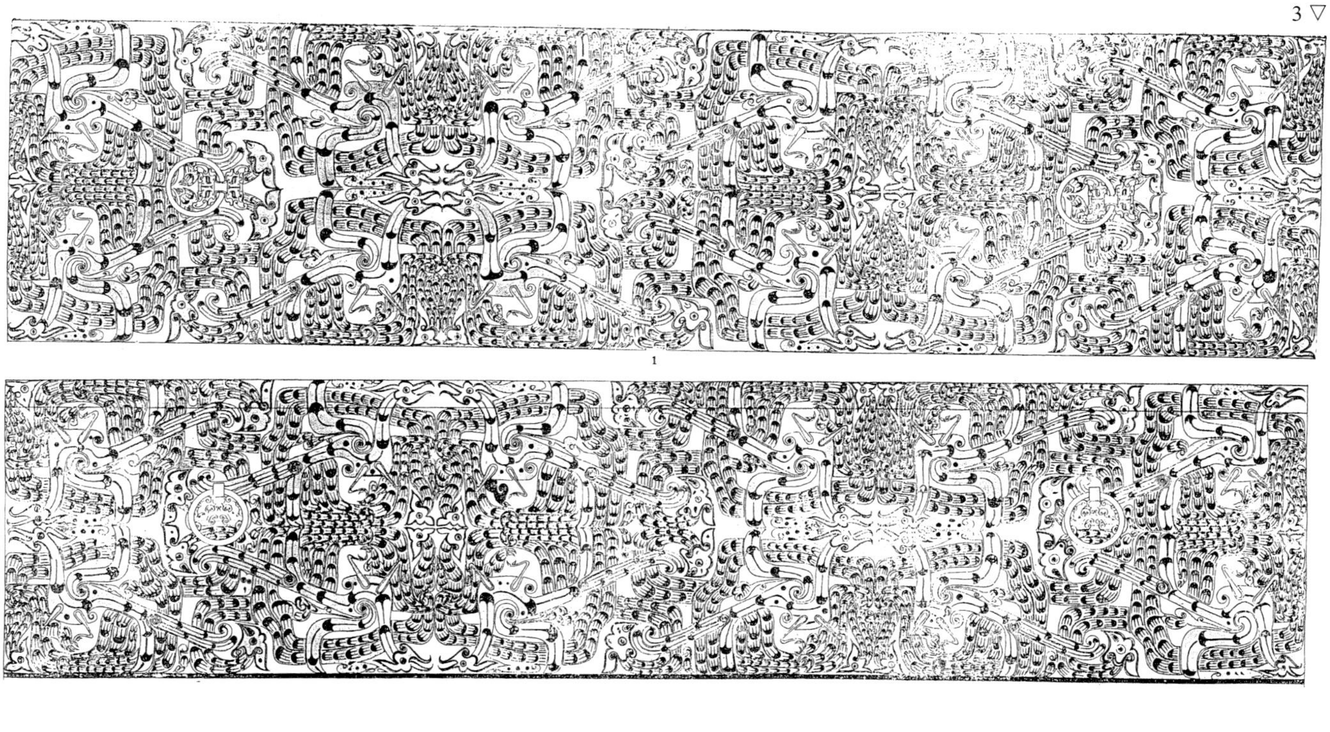

△ 4

▽ 6

5 △

Abb. 4–6. Lacksarg (wie Abb. 7), Details

Abb. 7. Bemalter äußerer Lacksarg von Mawangdui Grab 1. HUNANSHENG BOWUGUAN (HG.): *Changsha Mawangdui yi hao mu*. Peking 1973, Bd. 2, Abb. 25

7 ▽

laufenden Bänder rahmen das Mittelfeld, in dem sich – scheinbar frei – Wolkenornamente den Platz erobern. An einigen Stellen „legt“ sich der Rahmen über die Wolken. Der Betrachter erhält so den Eindruck, als bewegten sich die Wolken hinter den Eingrenzungen weiter. Dieser Eindruck wird zum einen durch das Anschneiden einiger Wolkenzipfel oder -rundungen am Feldrand erreicht. Zum anderen schaffen sich an einigen Stellen die Wolken über die Feldgrenze hinaus Raum, indem sie die vorgegebene Grenze durchbrechen und sich über das äußere Band legen. Erst durch die kleinen Fabelwesen, die sich zwischen oder auf den Wolken tummeln, und die wolkenbegleitenden „Strömungspfeile“ entsteht ein Eindruck von Raumtiefe (Abb. 4–6).

Wie organisierten die Handwerker den Dekor des kastenförmigen Sarges mit flachem Deckel und Seitenflächen? Welche Technik und eventuell welche Hilfsmittel benutzten sie, um die relativ großen Flächen zu gestalten? Welche Rolle spielte dabei die Verteilung der Ornamente in die vorgegebenen Zonen von Band und Feld?

Zum ersten Mal werden Wolken in dieser Form und vor allem auf einem so großflächigen Format dargestellt. Sie wirken zunächst wie eine „Bühne“ für die zoomorphen Gestalten und Fabelwesen aus der chinesischen Mythologie. Häufig findet sich auch in der beschreibenden Literatur die Bezeichnung „Wolkenlandschaft“ als Andeutung auf eine erste Darstellung von Landschaft (*shanshui*) in der chinesischen Malerei.[13]

Im Folgenden soll diese Behauptung einer freien Gestaltung der Sargpaneele genauer untersucht und revidiert werden.

Meine These ist:

Die die zentralen Felder füllenden Wolkenornamente wurden mit einer einzigen Schablone auf den Schwarzlackgrund aufgetragen. Auf den Längsseiten und dem Deckel des Sarges sind je sechs, auf den Stirnseiten je zwei dieser Ornamente eingepasst. Alle anderen Motive, wie zum Beispiel die „Strömungspfeile“ oder Fabelwesen und Tiere, konnten dann nachträglich ergänzt werden.

Die Ornamentschablone hat eine annähernd rechteckige Umrissform und besteht aus zwei Motiven (Abb. 8): einem oberen, in drei zur Mitte hin offenen S- oder C-förmigen Schwüngen verlaufenden Teil und einem unteren, das sich exakt in die Freizonen einfügt, die Schwünge aufnimmt, ergänzt und nach unten hin gerade abschließt. Langgezogene, annähernd parallel verlaufende Linien bilden die Umrisse der Wolken. An den abrupten Wendepunkten verdicken sie sich zu bauschigen Knäueln, die mit kleinen Spiralen oder C-Häkchen angedeutet werden. Ähnliche Verdickungen, die zusätzlich noch in Spitzen auslaufen, bilden die zipfligen Wolkenenden. Die so entstandene Grundform wird dann in unterschiedlichen Rot- und Brauntönen, die einer Schattierung gleichen, ausgefüllt.[14]

Sechsmal findet diese Schablone im zentralen Feld der Seitenpaneele und des Deckels, zweimal auf den Stirnseiten Platz (Abb. 9–12). Dazu wird sie, um sich der rechteckigen bzw. annähernd quadratischen Form der vorgegebenen Felder anzupassen und vor allem in die Aus- und Einbuchtungen der nächsten Schablone einzufügen, jeweils um 180° gedreht. Das regelmäßige Aufbauprinzip innerhalb der Felder ist erst auf den zweiten Blick zu erkennen. Entlang einer imaginären Mittelachse (in der Abbildung durch eine schwarze Linie hervorgehoben), die durch die waagerecht verlaufenden Linien der Wolken entsteht, werden die oberen nebeneinander angeordneten Ornamente (hier mit A gekennzeichnet) noch einmal exakt nach unten verschoben, das heißt durch Translation verdoppelt (hier mit A_1 gekennzeichnet). Allerdings reicht der Platz im Rahmen der vorgegebenen Felder nicht mehr ganz für die gesamte Höhe der drei oberen Ornamente aus, sie werden von den feldumspannenden Ornamentbändern beschnitten.

Das rechteckige Mittelfeld des Deckels (Breite 1,18 m) ist annähernd so breit, daß zwei Schablonenreihen untereinander Platz finden (Abb. 9). Hier sind nur die äußeren Linien der Wolken beschnitten. Kein Wolkenzipfel ragt in die Ornamentbänder hinein. Viele feine „Strömungspfeile“ begleiten die Wolkenschwünge und füllen gleichzeitig die bestehenden Freiräume. Die Zahl der Fabelwesen und Tiere ist im Gegensatz zu den Seitenpaneelen eher gering.

Abb. 9–11. Umzeichnung des Deckels und der Seitenteile des Sargs von Mawangdui Grab 1. HUNANSHENG BOWUGUAN (HG:): *Changsha Mawangdui yi hao mu.* Peking 1973, Bd. 1, Abb. 17–21 ▷

Abb. 12. Stirnseiten, wie Abb. 9–11 ▷▷

Abb. 8. Schablone des Wolkenornaments. HUNANSHENG BOWUGUAN (HG.): *Changsha Mawangdui yi hao mu.* Peking 1973, Bd. 1, Abb. 17, Detail

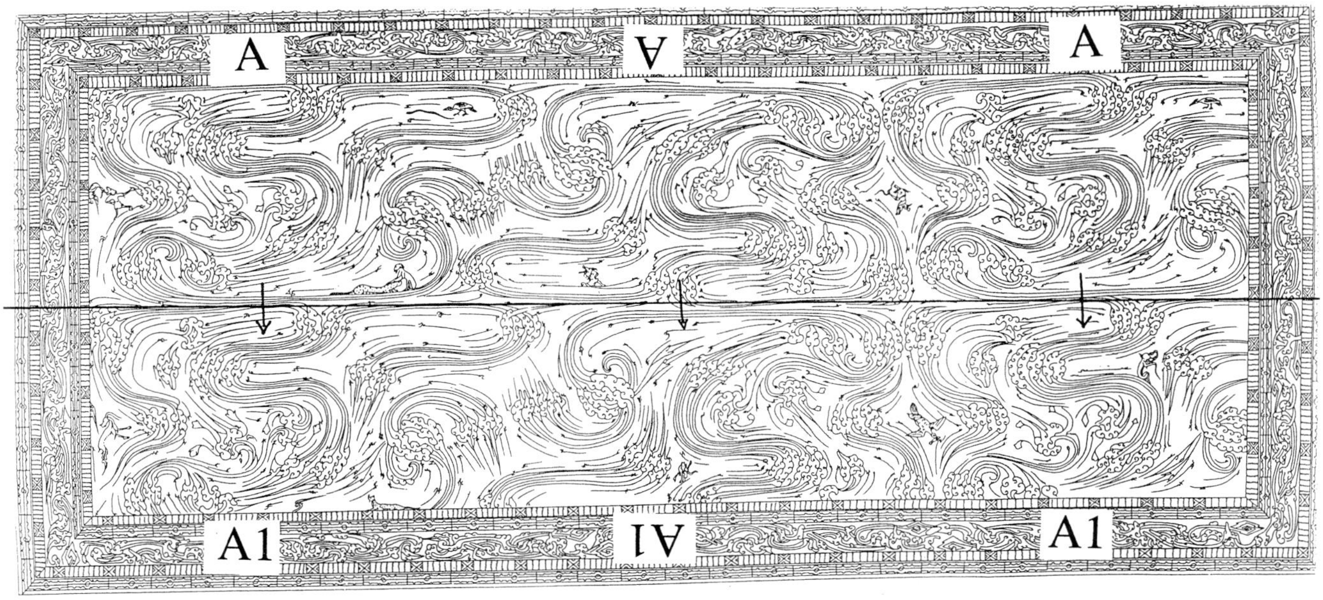

△ 9

10 ▽

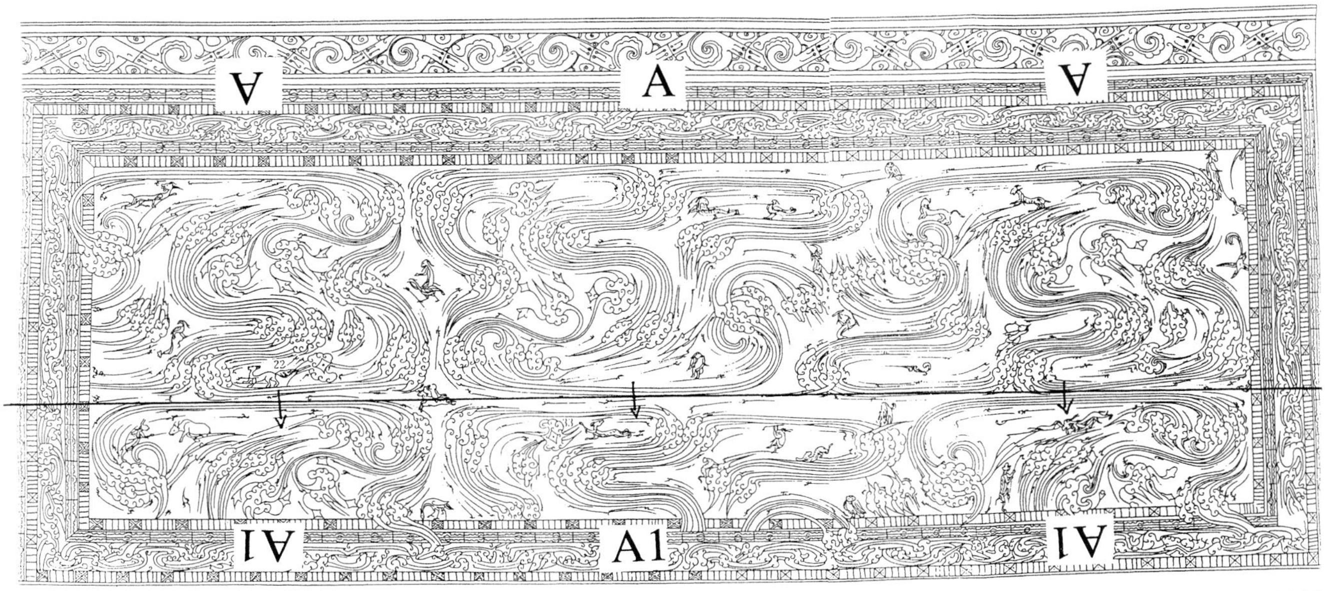

11 ▽

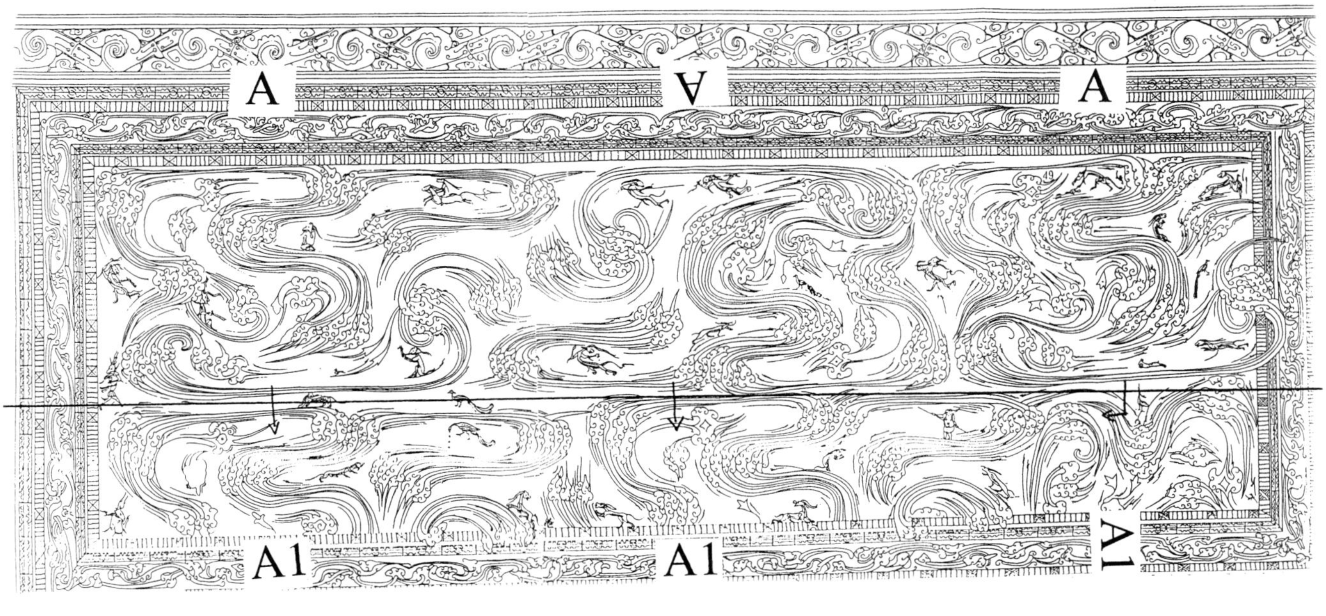

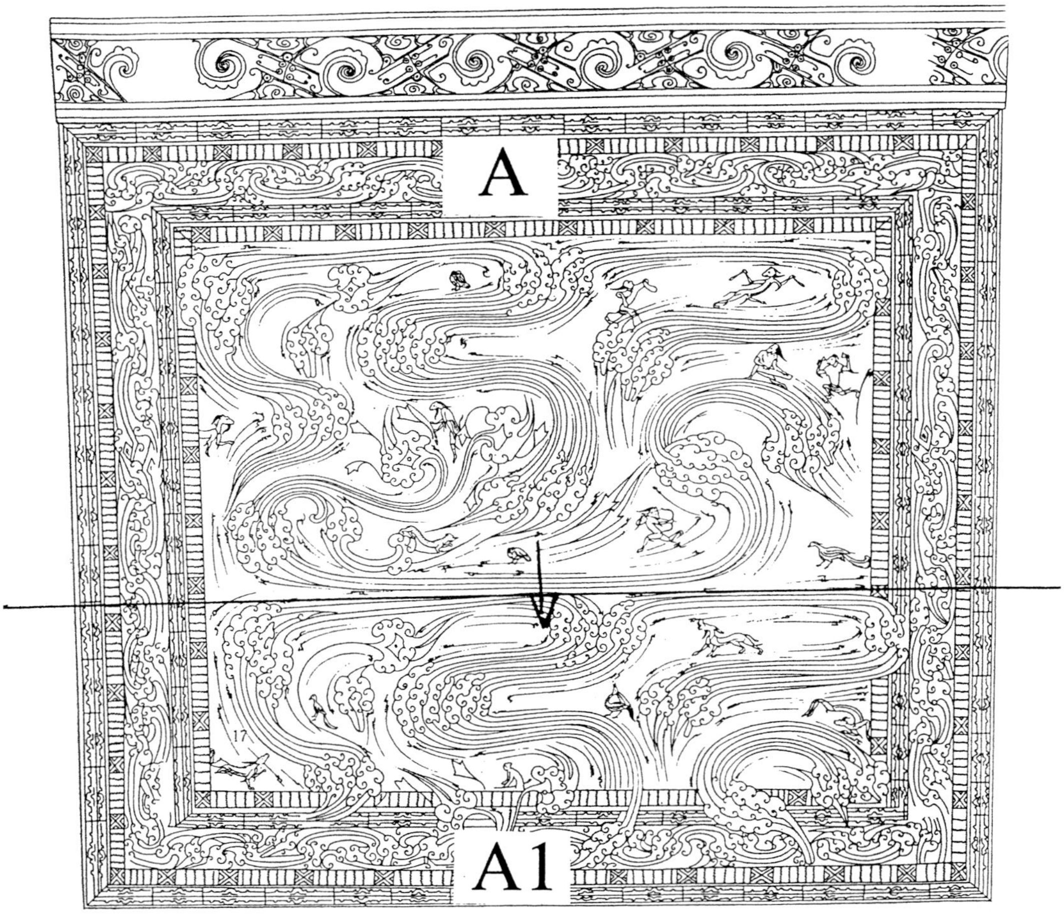

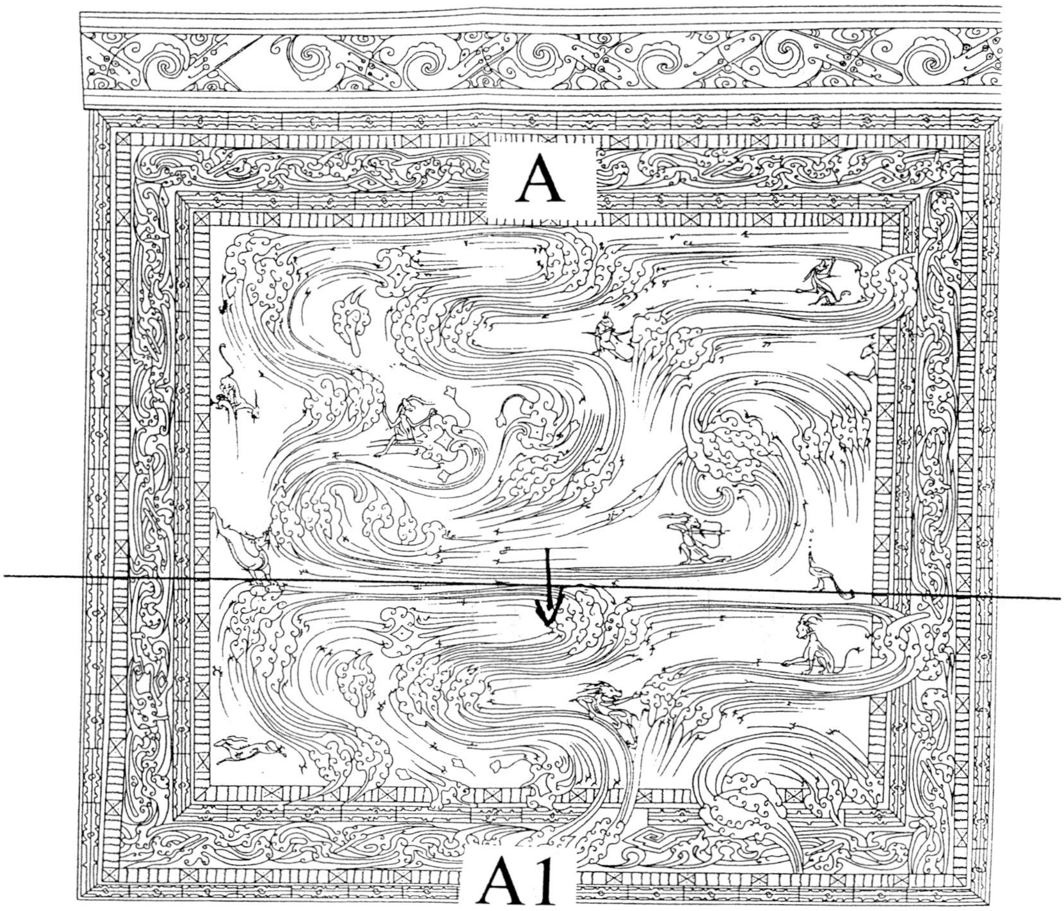

12

Die beiden Seitenteile sind, Deckel und Boden eingerechnet, insgesamt 1,14 m hoch. Während der Deckel seitlich mit einem roten umlaufenden Ornamentband (Phönix-Motiv-Band *fengniaowen*) abgesetzt ist, sind die Seitenflächen des Bodens (die Stärke der Bodenplatte beträgt 0,11 m) in das Gesamtmuster eingebunden. Dem Handwerker standen so aber nur 1,03 m zur Gestaltung zur Verfügung. Die Breite der konzentrischen Bänder blieb unverändert, das zentrale Feld wurde dafür kleiner. Bei dem rechten Seitenfeld wurde das linke Ornament um 180° gedreht und den folgenden angepasst und durch Translation verdoppelt (Abb. 10). Allerdings passte die Schablone hier nicht mehr so gut in das vorgegebene Feld, so dass die Hälfte des Ornaments am unteren Rand beschnitten wird. Um die Illusion eines raumübergreifenden Musters zu schaffen, ragen einige Wolkenzipfel über das umlaufende Ornamentband hinaus. Die den Wolken beigefügten „Strömungspfeile" werden seltener eingesetzt, dafür steigt aber die Zahl der Fabelwesen.

Das Aufbauprinzip des linken Seitenpaneels entspricht dem des Deckels (Abb. 11). Allerdings ist in der unteren Reihe das erste Ornament etwas zur Mitte hin verschoben und beim zweiten die 180°-Drehung vergessen, so daß die letzte Schablone nur noch um 90° gedreht in die untere rechte Ecke „eingezwängt" werden konnte. Zwischen den Wolken gibt es keine „Strömungspfeile" mehr, dafür ist die Zahl der Fabelwesen hier am höchsten.

Jeweils nur zwei Ornamente passen in die Felder der beiden Stirnseiten (Abb. 12). Durch eine leichte Verschiebung der Schablonen sind mehr oder weniger Teile des Ornaments beschnitten bzw. über die Ränder gelegt.

Die Tabelle (Abb. 13) zeigt noch einmal zusammenfassend die Anordnung und Drehung der Schablonen auf allen Seitenteilen.

Sargdeckel		
A	∀	A
A1	Ɩ∀	A1
Rechtes Seitenteil		
∀	A	∀
Ɩ∀	A1	Ɩ∀
Linkes Seitenteil		
A	∀	A
A1	A1	A1
Stirnseiten		
A		
A1		

Abb. 13. Tabelle des Aufbauprinzips der Ornamente (Tabelle M. Prüch)

Bisher wurden keine Schablonen für Lackmalereien ausgegraben.[15] Vorstellbar ist eine Schablone – hier vielleicht aus Leder – die, ähnlich wie für die europäische Freskomalerei der Karton, zur Vorzeichnung diente. Mit dem so entstandenen „Gerüst" ließen sich dann die einzelnen Linien mit Lack nachziehen und die entstandenen Zwischenräume ausmalen.

Dieser Sarg aus dem Grab 1 von Mawangdui ist so ein sehr frühes Beispiel für die Verwendung von Schablonen in der Lackmalerei.

Anmerkungen

1 HUNANSHENG BOWUGUAN 1973. Im Frühjahr 1993 wurde nordöstlich von Changsha in Wangchengpo, Gufenyuan, eine große Grabanlage entdeckt, die nach bisherigen Erkenntnissen die Gräber von Mawangdui in den Schatten stellt. Bei den mehr als 2000 geborgenen Objekten handelt es sich zum größten Teil um Lacke, Gold, Silber, Jade und Musikinstrumente. Ein ausführlicher Ausgrabungsbericht fehlt bislang. Für eine Kurznotiz siehe PANKENIER 1993, S. 33; siehe auch PRÜCH 1997. An dieser Stelle möchte ich Frau Dr. Jorinde Ebert, Frau Dr. Helen Loveday und Herrn Dr. Hermann-Josef Röllicke für viele wertvolle Anregungen zum Thema danken. Falls nicht anders angemerkt, werden die Ortsangaben in der Reihenfolge Provinz, Kreis, Stadt/Ausgrabungsort, angegeben.

2 Zur symbolischen Bedeutung und der Beziehung der drei Särge zueinander siehe KARKOW 1989, S. 22–34.

3 Sehr gute Abbildungen der lackierten Särge und der wichtigsten Funde aller Gräber finden sich in FU JUYOU/CHEN SONGCHANG 1992. Über die Bedeutung von Wolken *yunqi* wurde in den letzten Jahren und vor allem seit der Entdeckung eben dieses Sarges viel spekuliert. Hierbei interessierten aber vor allem die verschiedenen Formen von Wolken, die als Teile der „beobachtbaren Naturphänomene" Vorhersagekraft für schlechte und gute Omen hatten. Siehe dazu auch HULSEWÉ 1979, S. 40–49. Im Grab 3 von Mawangdui fand sich ein Manuskript mit Einträgen zu „Phänomenen des Himmels". So konnten zum Beispiel Wolken in Form von Tieren den Ausgang bevorstehender militärischer Ereignisse prognostizieren. Siehe dazu unter anderem LOEWE 1994; MAJOR 1993.

4 Eine tabellarische Zusammenstellung der Zhanguo-zeitlichen Gräber und Särge findet sich bei TENG RENGSHENG 1992, S. 87–90. Siehe auch HELEN LOVEDAY 1989.

5 Von dem Sarg gibt es nur eine Aufnahme, die während der Ausgrabung entstand. Lediglich der Deckel ist deutlich zu erkennen. LAWTON 1991, S. 32, Fig. 11.

6 THOTE 1991, S. 23–46. Gemalte Tür- oder Fensteröffnungen sind bis zur Mitte des 4. Jh. v. Chr. vor allem auf den Innenwänden von lackierten Grabkammern nachweisbar, wie zum Beispiel auf der großen Grabkammer aus Hubei, Jiangling, Tianxingguan (datiert auf ca. 340 v. Chr.), deren Bemalung an die Vorläufer aus Suixian erinnert. Siehe dazu: HUBEISHENG JINGZHOU DIQU BOWUGUAN 1982, S. 71–116, T. 11–24.

7 DAN XIANJIN 1980, S. 98–112.

8 Grobe Hanftücher oder Bambusmatten als Schutz von Grabkammern oder Särgen sind aus der Literatur bekannt. So heißt es im Ritenkapitel des Xunzi: „Mit dem Anblick des Grabbaus unter dem Erdhügel schafft man das *xiang* (Abbild) eines Hauses und seiner Zimmer. Mit dem Anblick des inneren und äußeren Sargs schafft man das *xiang* der Planken des Daches ... Mit dem Anblick des grobleinenen Sargtuchs, des fischnetzartigen Fadenüberzugs und der mit Fäden eingezogenen Federn schafft man ein *xiang* der oberen und seitlichen Vorhänge des großen Ausflugswagens. ..." Übersetzung nach RÖLLICKE 1996, S. 386. Ein sehr gut erhaltenes Beispiel von Hanftüchern, Bambusgeflecht und einem feinen gestickten Tuch aus der Westlichen Han-Zeit wurde aus Grab 167 von Hubei, Jiangling,

Fenghuangshan ausgegraben. Siehe dazu FENGHUANGSHAN 167 HAO HANMU FAJUE ZHENGLI XIAO ZU 1976, Abb. 1.

9 HUBEISHENG JINGSHA TIELU KAOGUDUI 1991, Bd. 1, Abb. 45.

10 Eine ähnliche Gestaltung mit geometrisiertem Dekor ist auf zwei Särgen aus Henan, Xianyang (ca. 300 v. Chr.), von denen nur noch Fragmente erhalten sind, zu sehen. Das strenge geometrische Aufbauprinzip ließ in diesem Fall eine Rekonstruktion des gesamten Dekors zu. HENANSHENG WENWU YANJIUSUO 1986, T. I und VII.

11 HUBEISHENG JINGZHOU DIQU BOWUGUAN: *Jiangling Mashan yi hao mu*. Peking 1985. Der Sarg war nicht lackiert. Lediglich drei in Lack getränkte Hanfbänder wurden zur Stabilisierung um den Sarg gespannt.

12 Es wäre falsch, an dieser Stelle von einer Ranke zu sprechen, dazu müßten die einzelnen Ornamente des Musters fortlaufend verbunden sein. Siehe dazu auch PAUSE 1976.

13 Siehe dazu unter anderem STURMAN Vol 20/2 (1985), S. 1–17; 3 (1985), S. 1–12; 4 (1985), S. 1–16.

14 Dieser Vorgang ist an einigen Stellen des Sarges, besonders dort, wo ein Teil der Farbe schon abgeblättert ist, deutlich zu erkennen. Siehe dazu die farbigen Detailfotos in FU JUYOU/ CHEN SONGCHANG 1992, S. 8–10.

15 In Mawangdui und auch in dem Grab des Königs von Nan Yue, 122 v. Chr. datiert, im heutigen Guangzhou, Provinz Guangdong, wurden zwei kleine Schablonen aus Bronze für den Textildruck gefunden. Siehe dazu auch GUANGZHOUSHI WENWU GUANLI WEIYUANHUI et. al. 1991; PRÜCH UNTER MITARBEIT VON STEPHAN VON DER SCHULENBURG 1999. Zur Verwendung von Schablonen in der Textilkunst siehe die neuesten Untersuchungen von LOTHAR LEDDEROSE: *Ten Thousand Things – Modul and Mass Production in Chinese Art*. The A.W. Mellum Lectures in the Fine Arts, 1998. The National Gallery of Art. Washington, DC. Princeton University Press 2000, besonders S. 158 ff.

Literaturverzeichnis

DAN XIANJIN: *Hunan Xiangxiang Niuxingshan yi, er hao mu daxing Zhanguo muguo mu*, in: Wenwu ziliao congkan 3 (1980), S. 98–112

FENGHUANGSHAN 167 HAO HANMU FAJUE ZHENGLI XIAO ZU: *Jiangling Fenghuangshan 167 hao Han mu fajue jianbao*, in: Wenwu 10 (1976), S. 31–37

FU JUYOU, CHEN SONGCHANG: *Mawangdui Han mu wenwu*, Changsha 1992

FU JUYOU, CHEN SONGCHANG: *The cultural relics unearthed from the Han tomb at Mawangdui*, Changsha 1992

GUANGZHOUSHI WENWU GUANLI WEIYUANHUI et. al.: *Xi Han Nan Yue wang mu*. 2 Bde. [Zhongguo tianye kaogu bagaoji Serie D, Nr. 43], Peking 1991

HENANSHENG WENWU YANJIUSUO: *Xinyang Chu mu*, Peking 1986

HUBEISHENG JINGSHA TIELU KAOGUDUI: *Baoshan Chu mu*, Peking 1991

HUBEISHENG JINGZHOU DIQU BOWUGUAN: *Jiangling Mashan yi hao mu*, Peking 1985

HUBEISHENG JINGZHOU DIQU BOWUGUAN: *Jiangling Tianxingguan yi hao mu fajue jianbao*. In: Kaogu xuebao 1 (1982), S. 71–116

HULSEWÉ, A. F. P.: *Watching the vapours; an ancient chinese technique of prognostication*, in: Nachrichten der Gesellschaft für Natur- und Völkerkunde Ostasiens (Hamburg), 125 (1979), S. 40–49

HUNANSHENG BOWUGUAN: *Changsha Mawangdui yi hao mu*, Bd. 1–2, Peking 1973

KARKOW, C.: *Three Decorated Lacquer Caskets from Tomb No. 1, Mawangtui*, in: Oriental Art Vol. 35/1 (1989), S. 22–34

LAWTON, THOMAS (Hrsg.): *New Perspectives on Chu Culture During the Eastern Zhou Period*, Washington, Princeton University Press 1991

LEDDEROSE, LOTHAR: *Ten Thousand Things – Modul and Mass Production in Chinese Art*. The A.W. Mellum Lectures in the Fine Arts, 1998. The National Gallery of Art. Washington, DC. Princeton University Press 2000

LOEWE, MICHAEL: *Divination, mythology and monarchy in Han China*, Cambridge 1994

LOVEDAY, HELEN: *A Study of the Regional Styles Present in the Material Culture of the State of the Warring States Period,* unveröffentlichte Dissertation Oxford, 1989

MAJOR, J. S.: *Heaven and Earth in Early Han Thought: Chapters Three, Four and Five of the Huainanzi*, Albany/New York 1993

PANKENIER, D. W.: *Outstanding Early China Archaeological Discoveries of 1993*, in: Early China News 6 (Herbst 1993)

PAUSE, GISELA: *Die Ranke in der chinesischen Kunst des I. Jahrtausends n. Chr.*, Dissertation Heidelberg 1976

PRÜCH, MARGARETE UNTER MITARBEIT VON STEPHAN VON DER SCHULENBURG: *Schätze für König Zhao Mo – Das Grab von Nan Yue*, Heidelberg 1999

PRÜCH, MARGARETE: Die Lacke der Westlichen Han-Zeit – Bestand und Analyse, Frankfurt 1997

RÖLLICKE, HERMANN-JOSEF: *Der Ursprung des Gedankens von der Selbsterweisung (ziran) in der chinesischen Philosophie des 4.–3. Jh. v. Chr.*, Frankfurt 1996

STURMAN, P. C.: *Wild beasts and winged immortals: Early portrayals of landscape in chinese art*, in: National Palace Museum Bulletin Vol 20/2 (1985), S. 1–17; 3 (1985), S. 1–12; 4 (1985), S. 1–16

TENG RENGSHENG: *Lacquerwares of the Chu Kingdom*, Hong Kong 1992

THOTE, ALAIN: *The double coffin of Leigudun tomb no. 1: Iconographic sources and related problems*. In: LAWTON, THOMAS (Hrsg.): *New Perspectives on Chu Culture During the Eastern Zhou Period*, Washington, Princeton University Press 1991, S. 23–46

Abbildungsnachweis

Abb. 4–6, 13: Verfasserin
Alle übrigen Abbildungsnachweise sind in den Bildunterschriften vermerkt

Summary

The discovery of the large tombs of the Marquis Dai and his family in Mawangdui, near Changsha, Hunan province, in 1973 has endowed us with a more complete picture of the structure and inventories of Early Han-Dynastie Tombs. Tomb No. 1 is perhaps best known for the perfect state of preservation of the body of the Marquis Dai (died in 168 B.C.) a result of the tomb construction. Wooden caskets were nested one into the other and sealed with layers of charcoal and clay. The innermost three caskets were elaborately decorated with lacquer painting.

This study focusses on the outer casket, which is decorated with cloud patterns and hybrid creatures, animals and immortals, on the technical aspects of their arrangement and the positioning of the 'cloud-landscape' on the casket. It turned out, that the craftsmen obviously used stencils to apply the cloud ornaments in the center of the black lacquered panels. One of the stencils was of rectangular shape. To increase the illusionistic impression of the 'cloud-landscape' some of the stencil motifs overlap the border ornaments.

The casket of Mawangdui must therefore be considered as one of the earliest examples for the use of stencils in the history of lacquer painting and marks a turning point in the decoration of lacquer objects of this size.

Barbara Piert-Borgers

Dekor und Technik von Lackarbeiten der westlichen Han-Zeit am Beispiel eines Kosmetik-Sets *(lian)* aus dem 2. bis 1. Jh. v. Chr.

Neben Ohrenschalen gehören Kosmetikdosen (*lian*) zu den in der westlichen Han-Zeit (206 v. Chr. – 6 nach Chr.) sehr beliebten Grabbeigaben, die man nach Prüch[1] in sehr vielen Gräbern fand. Zu einem vollständigen Set gehören fünf, sieben oder neun Dosen (*he*), die in einer großen runden Dose aufbewahrt wurden. Die pferdehufförmige Dose enthielt Kämme, die anderen Schminke oder Puder.

Ein komplettes Set solcher Kosmetikdosen aus dem Bestand des Idemitsu-Museums in Tokyo[2] besteht aus der großen Dose (*lian*), je zwei unterschiedlich großen rechteckigen und runden Dosen, einer quadratischen, einer pferdehufförmigen und einer ovalen Dose. Bei einem ähnlichen *lian* mit den sieben dazugehörigen Dosen aus dem Besitz der Galerie Kaikodo, New York[3] (Ø 21,9 cm, H. 17,4 cm, 2. – 1. Jh. v. Chr.), wird das Bild der Dosen durch die Silberringe und die vierblättrigen oder pfeilförmigen Silberauflagen der Dosendeckel bestimmt (Abb. 1). In einem der Blätter dieses *lian* hat sich ein Carneol erhalten. Die Lackfelder zwischen den Silberbändern sind mit den für die Han-Zeit typischen Wolkenmustern in schwarz, rot und grau bemalt.[4] In diese Wolkenlandschaften sind einzelne Tiere hineingesetzt.

Darstellungen von Vögeln, – z. B. eine Gans mit langem Hals, ein Gänsepaar, ein langschwänziger Vogel (Pfau oder Phönix), – von wilden Tieren – z. B. einem Tiger mit seinem Jungen – aber auch menschliche Figuren wie z. B. eine sitzende Gestalt, die an spätere Lohan-Darstellungen erinnert, eine *qin* spielende Figur und eine mit Pfeil und Bogen nach rückwärts schießende Figur – sind in Gold- und Silberfolie (*pingtuo*) eingelegt (Stärke ca. 0,01 mm). Die Silbereinlagen sind zerfallen, die erhaltenen Goldeinlagen weisen Binnenzeichnungen in schwarzem Lack auf. Die Innenwandungen der Dosen sind rot lackiert, die Innenseite des Deckels des *lian* zusätzlich mit Wolkendekor bemalt. Die Innenränder ziert ein einfaches geometrisches Bandmuster in Schwarzlack.

Sieben Lackdosen, die nachfolgend näher beschrieben werden und ebenfalls aus dem Besitz der Galerie Kaikodo stammen, haben die gleichen Formen und Maße, wie die aus dem gezeigten vollständigen Set (Abb. 2). Die Maße der Dosen, deren Höhe 6,3 cm beträgt, sind wie folgt: rechteckige Dose, L. 15,0, B. 3,4 cm; kleine rechteckige Dose, L. 7,8, B. 3,5 cm; quadratische Dose, L. 4,1, B. 4,0 cm; ovale Dose, L. 6,9, B. 4,2 cm; runde Dose, Ø 7,9 cm; kleine runde Dose, Ø 5,1 cm; pferdehufförmige Dose, L. 9,1, B. 6,5 cm. Die Dosenwandungen stehen im rechten Winkel auf der verschiedenartig geformten Grundfläche. Der Stülpdeckel ist stufig abgesetzt, seine Wandung bedeckt nahezu die gesamte Dose.

Abb. 1. Kosmetik-Set (*lian*) mit sieben Dosen (*he*), westliche Han-Zeit, 2. bis 1. Jh. v. Chr.

Zur sogenannten Trockenlack-Technik

Die Dosen sind in der in der westlichen Literatur allgemein als Trockenlack (chin. *jiazhu* oder *tuo tai*) bezeichneten Technik gearbeitet. Bei dieser auch heute noch gebräuchlichen Technik werden bei der in Japan üblichen Ausführung über eine Ton- oder Gipsform entsprechend dem schichtweisen Aufbau einer traditionellen Lackarbeit zunächst Lackschichten, dann Grundierungsschichten aufgetragen. Auf diesen Untergrund wird Ramie- oder Leinengewebe aufgeklebt. Dabei werden die Tücher

Abb. 2. Sieben Lackdosen zu einer Kosmetikdose (*lian*) gehörend, westliche Han-Zeit, 2. bis 1. Jh. v. Chr.

nicht, wie vielfach angegeben, in Lack getränkt, sondern mit einer Mischung aus Kleister und Rohlack aufgeklebt. Von der beabsichtigten Stärke der Wandung hängt die Anzahl der Textilauflagen ab, wobei die inneren gröber sind als die äußeren. Dann werden wiederum Grundierungsschichten aufgebracht, und darüber in der Regel eine Rohlackschicht und zwei pigmentierte Lackschichten. Da die Gipsform mit einem Trennmittel behandelt wurde, kann der Lackkörper relativ leicht abgehoben und die Form wiederverwendet werden. Die Technik wird im Westen allgemein als *kanshitsu* bezeichnet. Nakazato unterscheidet *soku* als Technik zur Herstellung von Dosen und Gefäßen von *dakkanshitsu* als Technik zur Herstellung von Skulpturen.[5] Die *soku*-Technik ist in China durch Grabfunde und Inschriften bis ins 3. Jh. v. Chr. belegt. Die *dakkanshitsu*-Technik wurde im 7. Jh. n. Chr. aus China nach Japan übernommen und gelangte ab der Mitte des 8. und im frühen 9. Jh. zu großer Blüte. Wang[6] nennt die Technik *jia zhu* (ältere Schreibweise *chia chu)*, was der Wortbedeutung nach „gedoppeltes Hanfzeug" bzw. Hanfzeug in mehreren Lagen meint.[7] Wang unterscheidet *buxin zhitai* (body of cloth and paper), eine Technik, bei der mehrere Lagen von Gewebe mit Lack und einer Mischung aus Lack und Asche übereinandergeklebt werden und deren oberste Schicht mit Papier abgedeckt ist, von *zhong butai* (heavy cloth body). Hierbei werden nur Gewebeschichten mit Lack übereinandergeklebt. Nach Wang bezeichnet *tuotai* eine Technik, bei der ein Holz- oder Blechkern benutzt wird. Demgegenüber haben nach Lee[8] in *jiazhu*-Technik hergestellte Lacke Gewebeschichten über einem Holz- bzw. Metallkern und *tuotai*-Lacke einen reinen Textilkern. Nach Brandt heißt *tuotai* „körperlos" und beschreibt „Lackarbeiten mit einem Kern aus mehreren mit Lack getränkten Textilschichten."[9] Die zitierten Autoren machen für die chinesischen Objekte keine direkten Unterscheidungen zwischen Techniken an Skulpturen und solchen, die für Gefäße und Geräte verwendet werden, wie das in Japan üblich ist.

Dem die Textilschichten miteinander verklebenden Lack-Kleister-Gemisch können Füllstoffe, wie Ziegelmehl, Pflanzenfasern, zerschnittene Watte, Haare, Holzmehl oder Knochenasche zugesetzt sein. Durch diese Zuschläge wird das Volumen erhöht, die Klebekraft des Gemisches aber herabgesetzt. An chinesischen Skulpturen aber auch an Lacken der Ming-Zeit ist häufig eine sehr geringe Haftung zwischen Textil- und Zwischenlagen zu beobachten.

Der Kern der Han-zeitlichen Kosmetikdosen besteht sehr wahrscheinlich aus Ramie (*Boehmeria nivea*, „Chinagras“). Marie Therese Worch konnte nach einer ersten Untersuchung definitiv pflanzliche Fasern feststellen.[10] Eine Lage des relativ groben Textilgewebes ist in eine graue Grundierungsschicht eingebettet. Querschliff 04 (Abb. 4) zeigt in 100-facher Vergrößerung die in Lack eingebetteten Textilfasern und die beiden darüber liegenden Grundierungsschichten. Die über der Textilschicht liegende Grundierungsschicht enthält relativ große schwarze, braune und weiße Partikel, die darüberliegende Schicht feinere Partikel. Diese Probe ist am Dosenrand (Abb. 3) unter einer Silberfassung entnommen und weist keine weiteren Abschlusslackierungen auf.[11] Schliff 01 (Abb. 5) ist der inneren Wandung einer Dose im Bereich des Randdekors entnommen und weist folgende Schichten auf:

- Schwarzlackdekor (Beinschwarz)
- Roter Lack (kein Zinnober)
- Schwarzlack (Beinschwarz)
- Schwarze Linie (?)
- Braune Lackschicht
- Grundierungsschicht (Lack mit feinen Einschlüssen von Knochenasche)
- Grundierungsschicht (Lack mit groben Einschlüssen von Knochenasche)
- Textilgewebe in diese Schicht eingebettet.

Schliff 02 (Abb. 6) zeigt ebenfalls zwei verschieden gekörnte Fassungsschichten, die durch eine schwarze Linie getrennt sind. Die obere feinere Grundierungsschicht wird von einer schwarzen Schicht abgedeckt. Darauf liegt die Lackschicht.

Okada[12] identifiziert als Grundierung vergleichbarer Objekte eine Mischung aus Lack, Knochenasche und Mineralien, in zwei Schichten aufgetragen. Strahan kam bei der Untersuchung einer Lackskulptur der Walters-Collection aus dem späten sechsten Jahrhundert zu ähnlichen Ergebnissen. Aufgrund von mikroskopischen Analysen und Untersuchungen mit dem Rasterelektronenmikroskop (SEM) und von Elementanalysen (SEM-EDS und XRD) wurden gemahlene Knochen unterschiedlicher Korngröße und in verschiedenen Farben gefunden: rohe Knochen – weiß, gebrannte Knochen – schwarz und partiell gebrannte Knochen – grau.[13] Schon Garner hat die Frage aufgeworfen, inwieweit der Typ der verwendeten Asche die Polymerisation des Lacks beeinflusst. Er verweist in diesem Zusammenhang auf die Verwendung von Asche aus Reishülsen in Burma.[14] Eine chinesische Quelle des 16. Jahrhunderts nennt u. a. die Verwendung von Hirschhornasche, Kuhhornasche, Porzellanasche, Knochenasche, Schweineblut, gebrannten Muschelschalen und gemahlenem ausgehärtetem Lack.[15]

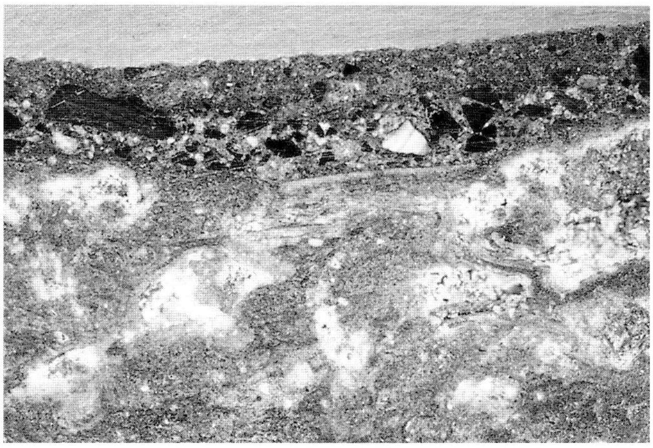

Abb. 4. Querschliff der in den Lack eingebetteten Textilfasern und der beiden darüber liegenden Grundierungsschichten, 100-fache Vergrößerung, am Dosenrand unter Silberfassung entnommen, keine Abschlusslackierung

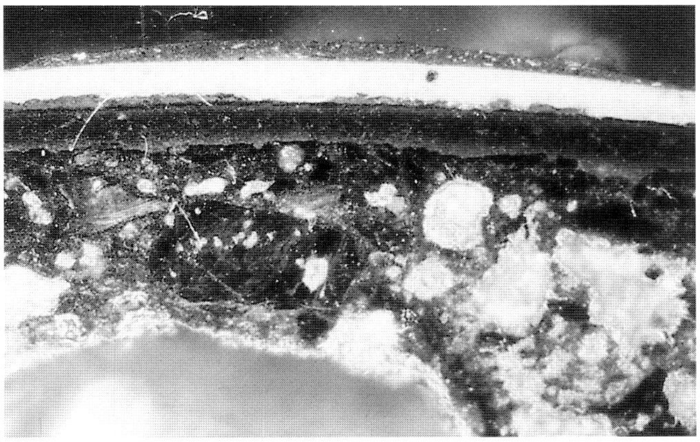

Abb. 5. Querschliff, im Doseninneren im Bereich des in Schwarzlack gemalten Dekors entnommen, 200-fache Vergrößerung

Abb. 3. Detail aus einem Dekorstreifen, darüber unlackierter Dosenrand unter Silberfassung

Abb. 6. Querschliff, Außenwandung, 100-fache Vergrößerung

Zu den Dekorationstechniken

Der Dekor der Deckel und Außenwandungen dieser Dosen wird bestimmt durch eine Fülle von Metalleinlagen. Die mittleren Flächen der Dosendeckel (Abb. 7, 8), in die pfeilförmige oder vierblättrige Silberbleche eingelegt sind, sind mit Goldfolie belegt, die mit einer wasserlöslichen Malerei eingefasst und in einem Wellendekor bemalt ist (Abb. 9, 10). Das zweite dominierende Dekorband auf den Deckeloberflächen besteht aus friesartigen Einlagen von Gold- und Silberfolien. Der Rapport besteht aus jeweils zwei sich folgenden Tieren (Füchsen, Bären, Löwen, Elefanten, Tigern) und einem Dekorabschnitt aus aufgetürmten Bergen. Die Wandungen der Dosen werden durch ein rechtwinkelig gebrochenes Ornament mit regelmäßig integrierten Wolken- und Vogelmotiven in Goldfolie bestimmt (Abb. 11). In die Zwischenflächen sind menschliche Figuren, stehend oder kniend, wie Bogenschützen oder Trommler, und Tiere wie Kranich, Pfau, Phönix, Wolf, Reh usw. in Silberfolie eingelegt (Abb. 12, 13). Alle Bandmuster sind fortlaufend über den gesamten Mantel der Dosen gelegt, was zur Folge hat, dass einige der figürlichen Darstellungen über die Ecken der Dosen geknickt sind.

Die Dosen sind innen rot lackiert und am oberen Innenrand mit einem feinen, geometrisch gemusterten Streifendekor in Schwarzlack bemalt (vgl. Schliff 01, Abb. 5). Auf den Schwarzlackgrund der Außenwandung wurden die breiten Silberbänder und die Gold- und Silberfolien aufgeklebt. Die Metallfolien sind nicht in vorher in den Lack geschnittene „Gräben" eingelegt worden, eine Idee, die in der neueren deutschsprachigen Literatur verbreitet wird, sondern als papierkaschierte Streifendekore aufgeklebt worden. Nach Entfernung des Papiers wurde die gesamte Fläche überlackiert und die Metalldekore freigeschnitten. Die Silberbänder, die Fassungen und die zentralen Deckelmotive haben eine Stärke von 0,1 bis 0,13 mm. Es handelt sich „um verhältnismäßig reines Silber mit geringen Kupferanteilen, außerdem etwas Quecksilber. Im korrodierten Bereich verstärkt Kupfer und zusätzlich Schwefel." Die Goldeinlagen haben eine Stärke von 0,02 mm. „Sie bestehen aus hochkarätigem Gold. Da der Blechstreifen der Probe auf beiden Seiten gleich aussieht und beide Seiten identische EDX-Spektren liefern, kann sogenanntes Zwischgold ausgeschlossen werden."[16] Die Dosen wurden nach dem Aufbringen der Gold- und Silberdekore lackiert, die Außenwandungen vermutlich mit mehreren Schichten Transparentlack überzogen, wodurch eine Oberfläche entstand, die möglicherweise Schildpatt imitiert.[17] Die *pingtuo*-Technik, in japanischer Lesung *heidatsu*, ist von japanischen Kollegen an Hand von Quellen und an Objekten des Shôsô-in erforscht worden. Man unterscheidet die Technik des Freischneidens und die des Abpolierens der gesamten Fläche. Der silberne Dekor eines Spiegelkastens aus der Nara-Zeit (710–794 n. Chr.) ist demnach freigeschnitten, erst später setzte sich die Technik des Abpolierens, als *hyomon* bezeichnet, durch.[18]

Abb. 7. Pferdehufförmige Dose vor der Restaurierung

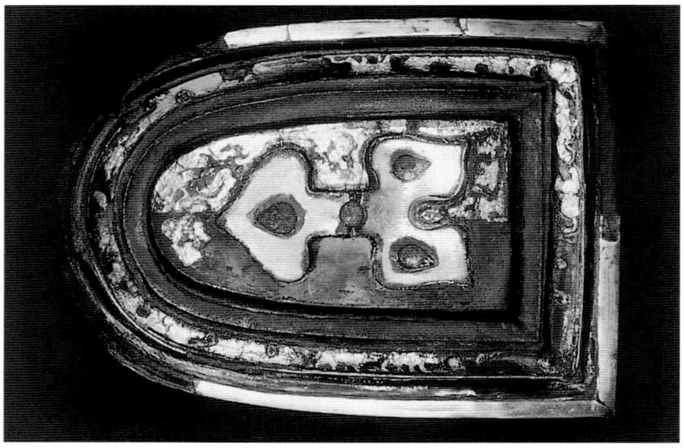

Abb. 8. Pferdehufförmige Dose nach der Restaurierung

Abb. 9. Deckelfläche der rechteckigen Dose

Abb. 10. Deckelfläche der runden Dose, rechts ein Bärenpaar in Silberblech, Wellendekor in Goldblech

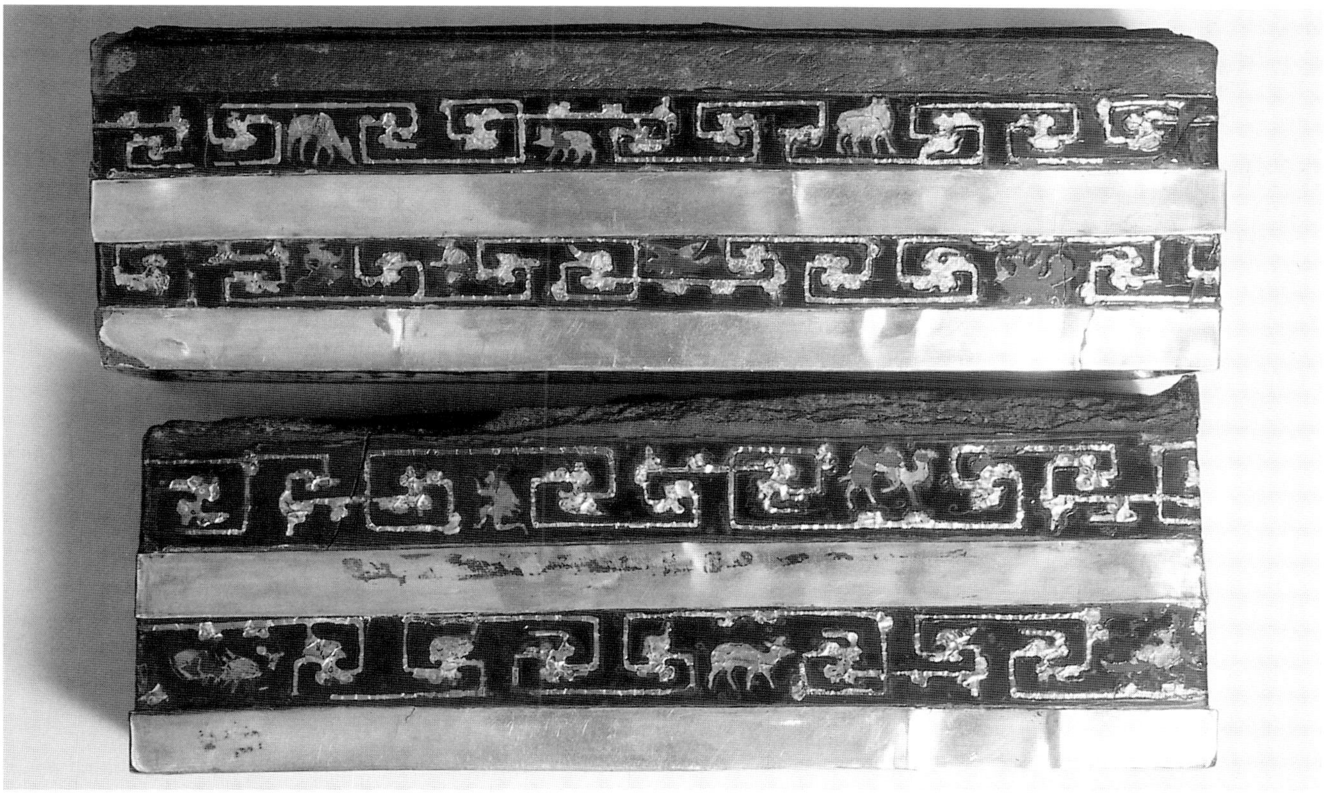

Abb. 11. Seitenwandung der großen rechteckigen Dose

Abb. 12, 13. Details der Metalleinlagen, schwarz und rot eingefasst

13

Um einen geschlossenen Eindruck der Fläche zu erzielen, aber auch, um die dünnen Folien vor Abrieb zu schützen, wurden bei den Han-Kosmetikdosen die Konturen der Einlagen schwarz ummalt. Im vorliegenden Fall entstand ein zusätzlicher Dekoreffekt, indem die Linie nicht nur den Konturen der Goldeinlagen folgt, sondern auch zu kleinen Schnörkeln und Verzierungen ausschwingt. Bei dieser Gelegenheit wurden offenbar in einem Arbeitsgang auch die schwarzen Binnenzeichnungen auf die Metallfolien aufgebracht (Abb. 12, 13). Auf den Flächen um die Einlagen herum findet sich sowohl schwarze als auch rote und silberne Malerei. Der rote Lack ist vermutlich mit Zinnober pigmentiert.[19] Ob es sich beim schwarzen Lack um schwarzen Zinnober handelt, oder um Lack, der mit Rapsöl-Lampenruß eingefärbt wurde, konnte an diesem Stück nicht geklärt werden.[20]

Betrachtet man die Malerei unter dem Mikroskop, wird deutlich sichtbar, dass in den roten Lack Silberpartikel eingestreut sind (Abb. 14). Aufgrund der Korrosionsanfälligkeit ist vielfach aber nur die rote Untermalung erhalten geblieben.

Dieser Silber*makie*-Dekor an einem chinesischen Lack der westlichen Han-Zeit wäre damit das früheste Vorkommen einer Technik, deren erste Varianten bisher an einer Schwertscheide aus dem Shôsô-in, an Speerspitzen aus dem Horyu-ji und an einem Pinselgriff, der in der Nara-Provinz ausgegraben wurde, für Japan belegt sind.

Dieses Set von Dosen wäre damit das früheste im Westen bekannte Beispiel für die *makie*-Technik und würde beweisen, dass auch diese in der Regel als japanisch geltende Lacktechnik aus China übernommen wurde.

Abb. 14. Detail, Silber*makie*-Dekor

Abb. 17. Niederlegen der losen Metalleinlagen mittels *rose-urushi* und Japanpapier

Abb. 15. Von der Innenwandung gelöste Rotlackschicht

Abb. 16. Große runde Dose vor der Restaurierung

Zur Restaurierung

Bei der Restaurierung der gezeigten Lackobjekte traten insbesondere folgende Probleme auf, die ich hier nur kurz vorstellen will:

1. Das Befestigen der sich lösenden, roten inneren Lackhaut von der Dosenwandung (Abb. 15)
2. Die Befestigung der gestauchten Metalleinlagen (Abb. 16)
3. Das Trocknen der nassen Bodenfunde.

Zu 1: Die rote Lackschicht im Inneren der als nasse Bodenfunde vorliegenden Dosen ist häufig lose[21] und reagiert in Sekundenschnelle auf Feuchtigkeitsschwankungen. Sie biegt sich von der Wandung weg nach innen und schmiegt sich nach einem Besprühen mit Wasser wieder an die Innenwandung an. Unter Verwendung von PVA-Leim wurden die gelösten Lackpartien wieder an die Wandung geleimt. Nasses Japanpapier wurde zur Fixierung aufgelegt und mit dünnen Plexiglasfolien, die dem Innenumfang der Dosen entsprechend zugeschnitten wurden, angedrückt. Zwei Schichten Plexiglas, die nahtversetzt übereinandergelegt wurden, erzielten bei den kleinen Dosen einen ausreichenden Druck. Das große *lian* wurde zusätzlich mit senkrecht angebrachten Holzstäben gepresst.

Zu 2: Zur Befestigung der Metalleinlagen wurde *rose-urushi*, eine Mischung aus Rohlack und Schwarzlack verwendet. Bei der Auswahl des Klebers war die Eigenschaft des asiatischen Lackes, bei hoher Luftfeuchtigkeit auszuhärten, entscheidend, da die Objekte im feuchten Zustand konsolidiert werden müssen. Die Metallfolien wurden mit nassem Japanpapier fixiert und umwickelt. Das Papier zieht sich beim Trocknen zusammen und drückt die Metallfolien an die Wandung des Objektes (Abb. 17).

Zu 3: Um den Textilkern zu konsolidieren, wurde in Abständen von zwei Tagen in häufiger Wiederholung eine Lösung von Mehlkleister und Rohlack (*mugi-urushi)* in Petroleumbenzin infiltriert. Beim zweiten Set wurden der Mischung Micro-Glaskügelchen zugesetzt.[22] Damit sollte die Fließfähigkeit und das Materialvolumen im Inneren erhöht werden. Die Glaskügelchen haben allerdings den Nachteil, dass die Verwendungszeit der Lösung reduziert wird. Der Lack flockt nach einiger Zeit aus.

Bei dem *lian* entstand bezogen auf den Umfang eine Schrumpfung von 2,08 %. Dies ist sehr gering, hat aber die Konsequenz, dass es zu Stauchungen und Aufwerfungen der Metalleinlagen kommt und die Bänder sich lösen.

Im Rahmen dieses Beitrags konnten nur einige Probleme der äußerst langwierigen und komplizierten Restaurierung ausgegrabener Lackobjekte angerissen werden. In erster Linie ging es darum, den vom üblichen Wolkendekor der Lacke des 2.–1. Jahrhunderts v. Chr. abweichenden *pingtuo*-Dekor aufzuzeigen und das Vorkommen von Silber-*makie* in dieser Zeit zur Diskussion zu stellen.

Anmerkungen

1 Prüch 1997, S. 117.
2 Yatsunami 1998, Abb. S. 8, Nr. 5 u. 6.
3 Rogers 1996, S. 124 u. 202–203, Pl. 125.
4 Nach Prüch 1997, S. 456, sind Wolkendekore auf ungefähr 80 % der Lackobjekte zumeist als Haupt- oder als Kontaktmotiv in Feldern, seltener als Hauptmotiv in Feldern zu finden. Vgl. zu Wolkendekor auf *lian* auch: Brandt 1988, S. 50–51, Kat. Nr. 8 u. S. 56–57, Kat. Nr. 15; Löw-Beer 1948, S. 266–273, Abb. 1–8; Yatsunami 1997, S. 41–81, S. 2–3 (English Summary).
5 Vgl. Nakazato 1993, S. 211–236.
6 Wang 1983, S. 26, zit. nach Strahan 1993, S. 107 f.
7 Vgl. Gabbert 1972, S. 474.
8 Vgl. Lee 1972, S. 26.
9 Brandt 1988, S. 159.
10 Vgl. Garner 1979, S. 34. Garner betont, dass die Textilauflagen an Lacken des 1. Jh. v. Chr. bis 1. Jh. nach Chr. aus Ramie bestehen, und verweist auf die diesbezüglichen Inschriften auf Grabungsfunden. „The inscriptions invariably refer to the fabric as ramie, and no hemp [...].“ „Hemp“ wird normalerweise mit „Ramie“ übersetzt. Dieses Übersetzungsbeispiel zeigt ein typisches Problem der Lackterminologie auf. Vgl. auch Rein Bd. 2, 1886, S. 424. Rein z. B. spricht vom Material der Textilauflage als Ramie, in der Beschreibung des Arbeitsablaufs vom Aufkleben der Leinwand. Auch Plenderleith identifizierte bei dem *lian* des Britischen Museums als Trägermaterial Ramie. Vgl. Gray 1955, S. 50.
11 Vergleichbare Struktur findet sich bei Okada 1995, S. 22, Schliff 94 116. Der auf S. 28 abgebildete Schliff 137 zeigt die Rekonstruktion einer Grundierung mit Rinderknochenasche. Okada fand Grundierungen, die Knochenasche enthielten, an luxuriösen Lackobjekten mit Textilkern aus Hebei und Henan.
12 Okada 1995, S. 3–8.
13 Vgl. Strahan 1993, S. 112 f.
14 Vgl. Garner 1979, S. 23.
15 Wang 1983, S. 44, zit. nach Strahan 1993, S. 111.
16 Für die Untersuchung der Metallproben danke ich Martin Mach und Christian Gruber vom Bayerischen Landesamt für Denkmalpflege, Zentrallabor.
17 Vgl. hierzu auch: Okada 1995, S. 3–8. „The surface of the lacquer coatings looks slightly reddish amber [...].“
18 Kimura 1988, S. 37–44. Vgl. zur *pingtuo*-Technik auch: Brinker/Louis 1994, S. 58; Zhang 1991/2, S. 81–85; Feng 1961.
19 Das *lian* aus der Sammlung Eumorfopoulos im Britischen Museum weist ebenfalls Lackmalerei in Zinnober auf, die grünlich verblasst ist. Vgl. Gray 1955, S. 51.
20 Zu den in der Han-Zeit verwendeten roten und schwarzen Pigmenten vgl. Okada 1995, S. 3–13.
21 Ein ähnliches Schadensbild ist häufig auch an Schnitzlacken zu beobachten. Hier löst sich die gesamte Dekorschicht von der ockerfarbenen untersten Lackschicht. Vgl. Piert-Borgers 1987, S. 9.
22 Die Verfasserin dankt Jutta Minor, Forchheim, für die Anregung.

Literaturverzeichnis

Brandt, Klaus Joachim: *Chinesische Lackarbeiten*, Ausstellungskatalog Linden-Museum Stuttgart, Stuttgart 1988

Brinker, Helmut/Louis, François: *Gold und Silber im alten China*, in: Museum Rietberg Zürich (Hg.): Chinesisches Gold und Silber. Die Sammlung Uldry, Zürich 1994

Feng, Han-chi: Ping-tó Lacquer and Silver Inlaid Lacquer Excavated from the Tomb of Wang Chien of Former Shú, in: Wenwu, Nr. 11, 1961, S. 46–47

Gabbert, Gunhild: *Buddhistische Plastik aus China und Japan*, Köln 1972

Garner, Sir Harry: *Chinese Lacquer*, London 1979

Gray, B.: *The Eumorfopoulos Lacquer Toilet Box and Blue Tang Horse*, in: British Museum Quarterly, Vol. XIV, 1955

Kimura, Norimitsu: Heidatsu *and* Hyomon *in the Nara Period*, in: Urushi. Proceedings of the Urushi Study Group, Tokyo 1988, S. 37–44

Lee, Yu-Kuan: *Oriental Lacquer Art*, New York 1972

Löw-Beer, Fritz: *Two Lacquered Boxes, part II*, in: Artibus Asiae XI, 1948, S. 266–273

Nakazato, Toshikatsu: *Brief Instruction of Technical Terms of Urushi Techniques*, in: Preprints. The International Symposium on the Conservation and Restoration of Cultural Property. Conservation of Urushi Objects, Tokyo 1993, S. 211–236

Okada, Fumio: *Kodai shutsudo shikki no kenkyu (Studium von ausgegrabenen Lackwaren des Altertums). Kenbikyo de saguru zaishitsu to gihô (Mikroskopische Untersuchungen von Material und Technik,* Tokyo 1995

Piert-Borgers, Barbara: *Restaurieren mit Urushi*, Köln 1987

Prüch, Margarete: *Die Lacke der Westlichen Han-Zeit (206 v.– 6 n. Chr.)*, Frankfurt 1997

Rein, J. J.: *Japan nach Reisen und Studien*, Bd. 2, 1886

Rogers, Howard: *Lacquered Lian Cosmetic Case with Seven Small Boxes*, in: Kaikodo Journal, Spring 1996, S. 124 u. 202–203

Strahan, Donna K.: *The Walters Chinese Wood-and-Lacquer Buddha: A Technical Study*, in: The Journal of the Walters Gallery, H. 51, 1993, S. 103–120

Wang, Shixiang: *Xiushilu Jieshuo,* Beijing 1983

Yatsunami, Hirokazu: *Some Thoughts on Lacquerware in the Museum's Collection (1). Small Lacquered Boxes and a Lian or Cosmetic Boxes with Lacquer Decoration of Clouds on Black Lacquer Ground with Applied Cut Gold and Silver Designs of Animals and Human Figure*, in: Idemitsu Museum of Arts Journal of Art Historical Research, Vol. 3, 1997, S. 41–81, S. 2–3 (English Summary)

Yatsunami, Hirokazu: *Some Thoughts on Lacquerware in the Museum's Collection (2). Two Sets of Lian or Cosmetic Boxes with Lacquer Decoration of Clouds on Black Lacquer Ground and Small Lacquered Boxes and Cosmetic Utensils*, in: Idemitsu Museum of Arts Journal of Art Historical Research, Vol. 4, 1998, S. 37–52, S. 8–10 (Farbabb.), S. 4–5 (English Summary)

Zhang, Guangli/Xu, Tingyun: *Man hua Tang dai jin yin pingtuo (Random Talks on Burnished Works with Gold-Silver Inlay of the Tang Dynasty)*, in: Wenwu, 1991/2, S. 81–85

Summary

The article presents the technique, decoration and conservation of a set of seven small boxes (*he*) originally belonging to and fitting into a cosmetic case (*lian*) originating from a tomb of the Western Han dynasty (2nd–1st century B. C.). The dry lacquer technique of the body is analysed and described. The gold and silver decoration executed in *pingtuo*-technique covering large areas between the wide silver bands anticipates lacquer objects from the Tang dynasty in its abundance. A silver *makie*-decoration was found within the painted decorations surrounding and partly covering the gold and silver inlays. For the first time this technique, usually ascribed to the Japanese Nara period seems to appear on a Chinese lacquer object of the Western Han dynasty.

Abbildungsnachweis

Abb. 1: Kaikodo, New York, Axel Thünker
Alle übrigen Photographien von der Verfasserin

Fig. 1. Lacquerware decorated with mother-of-pearl, dated about 18–19th century A.D.

Somtawin Nilvilai

The Techniques of Producing Ancient Thai Lacquerware

Introduction

Lacquerware is a general term for an utensil made of a woven bamboo substructure or a wooden substructure coated with lacquer derived from the tree of the family *Anacardiaceae.* Lacquerware was probably first made in China.[1] An early technique of making lacquerware was to apply lacquer directly on the substructure. The technique was gradually developed with multi-layer lacquer coatings and the use of fabric to reinforce and strengthen the substructure. The surface decoration on lacquerware was later embellished by using colored lacquer, gold and silver ornament or mother-of-pearl inlay (fig. 1). Gradually the technique used by the Chinese to produce lacquerware spread to other countries in East and Southeast Asia. The manufacturing of lacquerware in most of the countries of Southeast Asia, including Burma, Vietnam, and Thailand is well established at the present time, but the origins of the production process are quite obscure.

There is no reliable evidence on how and when lacquerware was first made in Thailand. It is believed that the technique of making lacquerware was brought to Thailand by the tribe 'Thai Kern'.[2] The 'Thai Kern' originally lived in Chiang Tung in the southern part of China and later migrated to northern Thailand, Chiang Mai. They made and used lacquerware as household utensils and the Thai natives learnt how to produce lacquerware from them. This is the reason why we use the term 'Kreung Kern' for Thai lacquerware. Lacquerware became popular throughout this region. It declined in popularity after ceramics, aluminium wares and plastic wares were introduced.

The techniques of producing lacquerware was passed from generation to generation. There was no record of the extraction process and the technique was gradually changed due to the limited raw materials, the influences of new technologies and commercialization. The technique of producing lacquerware is still practised in Chiang Mai, but now it has lost its own traditional character. The objective of the present work is to investigate the manufacturing techniques of ancient Thai lacquerware by interviewing craftsmen in the lacquerware manufactories in Chiang Mai and the examination of a number of chosen pieces of ancient lacquerware found in the province Chiang Mai by scientific methods using X-ray radiography and microscopic analysis.

Experimental Materials

Wat Chiangmun is the first temple in Chiang Mai. It is located on Rachapakinai road inside the old city near Chang Phuak Gate. In former times it used to be the palace of King Mengrai the great, who ruled Lanna Thai in 1296 A.D. After he established the city of Chiang Mai, he turned the palace into a temple. This temple has a large collection of antiquities and art objects donated by the local people and a monastery museum open to the public. Seventeen ancient pieces of lacquerware in various shapes were selected from Wat Chiangmun for this study.

Equipment and Experimental Conditions

X-ray radiography was carried out using an Andrex CMC 402 X-ray instrument operating condition 60–200 kVp and 0–8 mA with Fuji X-ray films 100x, 10 x 12 inch and developed with Fuji Hi-Rendol 1 and Hi-Renfix 1. Microscopic analysis was performed using a Nikon Labophot-2 microscope equipped with a Nikon Photomicrographic equipment Model H-III. Small samples were taken from the ancient lacquerware for the preparation of cross sections.

Results and Discussion

Two lacquer masters, Mrs. Peeya Piyasak, aged 78, and Mrs. Chumjai Chantawong, 85 years old, were interviewed. Both of them live in Ban Kern village, Tambol Hai Ya, in the province of Chiang Mai, and know well about the traditional process of making lacquerware. They explained, that in former times woven and coiled bamboo strips were mainly used for lacquerware substructures. Wooden substructures were only used more recently.

The lacquering process consists of four steps: The first step, the residue of raw lacquer, is applied on the substructure and then it is placed in a humid underground chamber, which is built by digging into the ground to make a room with a dimension of about 2 x 2 x 2 metres covered with a roof. When lacquer is cured, it is polished with an abrasive stone followed by the second coating of *smook* (a coarse undercoat) made by mixing clay, paddy ash and lacquer. The object is again placed in the humid underground chamber. After it has dried, it is polished again with an abrasive stone and *bai nod* (streblus asper) a leave of plant. The third step, *smook oon* (a fine undercoat) made by mixing grinded paddy ash with lacquer is applied layer after layer at least three times on the object. When it is dried, it is carefully polished with *bai nod*, followed by the final coat of clear lacquer (a filtrated lacquer). In the case of colored lacquerware, a pigment such as cinnabar is mixed with lacquer and is applied on the lacquerware before adding the final coat of clear lacquer.

There are two traditional techniques for the decoration of ancient Thai lacquerware known as *lai kud* and *lai rod nam.* The process of making *lai kud* or incised design, is starting from the engraving of the design with the free hand on the lacquerware using a sharp iron stylus. Then, grinded pigment mixed with lacquer is applied. After rubbing gently, the color remains in the engraved designs. Then, a final coating of clear lacquer is applied. On the other hand, the process of making *lai rod nam* consists of drawing the design and covering all their smallest details which have to remain black with a yellow gummy paint made by mixing Mongosa sap with *ho radan* (Orpiment) and a solution made by soaking a fruit of *Acacia concina* in water. Subsequently, a thin coat of lacquer is applied onto the surface. When it is half way dried, gold leaves are applied on the whole surface. After twenty-four hours the object is washed with water. Water detaches the gold leaves adhering to the yellow gummy paint. This will allow the design to appear in all details. The technique is therefore called *lai rod nam,* which means ornaments washed with water.

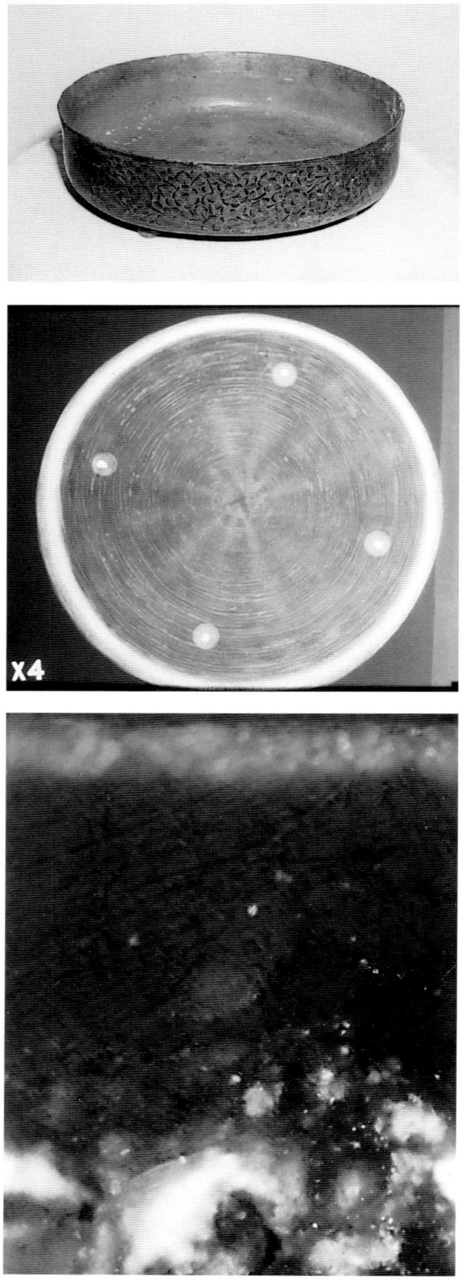

Fig. 2 a–c. Red shallow tray, *lai kud* design

X-ray radiography has proved to be useful for the study of lacquerware substructures[3], as well as microscopic analysis showed useful for the study of the composition and the layer structure of the lacquered objects[4]. We now employ the same techniques for the study of seventeen pieces of ancient Thai lacquerware from the museum of Wat Chiangmun. Some examples showed significant features and characteristic results.

Fig. 3 a, b. Red shallow bowl, *lai kud* design

Sample 1

Red shallow bowl, *lai kud* design, width 20.5 cm, height 3 cm, Wat Chiangmun museum collection. Technical data: 64 kV, 2.4 mA, 20 seconds, distance from tube 74 cm. Result: The substructure is made from woven bamboo strips in twill style at the bottom of the bowl. Bamboo strips are coiled to form the shape of the vessel. There are thick coiled bamboo strips to strengthen the vessel at the top, middle and bottom of the vessel. Under the microscope 3 significant layers become visible: a coarse layer, a fine layer, and a red colored layer (colour plate VIII.1, 4, 7).

Sample 2

Red shallow tray, *lai kud* design, dimension 22.2 cm, height 5 cm, Wat Chiangmun museum collection. Technical data: 64 kV, 2.4 mA, 20 seconds, distance from tube 74 cm. Result: The substructure uses bamboo strips as the warp and bamboo in a wire shape as the weft. It has four hard wood legs at the bottom. Under the microscope 4 lacquer layers become visible: a coarse layer, a fine layer, a red colored layer and a clear lacquer finish at the top (fig. 2 a–c).

Sample 3

Red shallow bowl, *lai kud* design, dimension 20.5 cm, height 6.8 cm, Wat Chiangmun museum collection. Technical data: 64 kV, 2.4 mA, 15 seconds, distance from tube 74 cm. Result: The substructure uses bamboo strips as the warp and wired bamboo as the weft to shape the bowl. The incised design is very sharp (fig. 3 a, b).

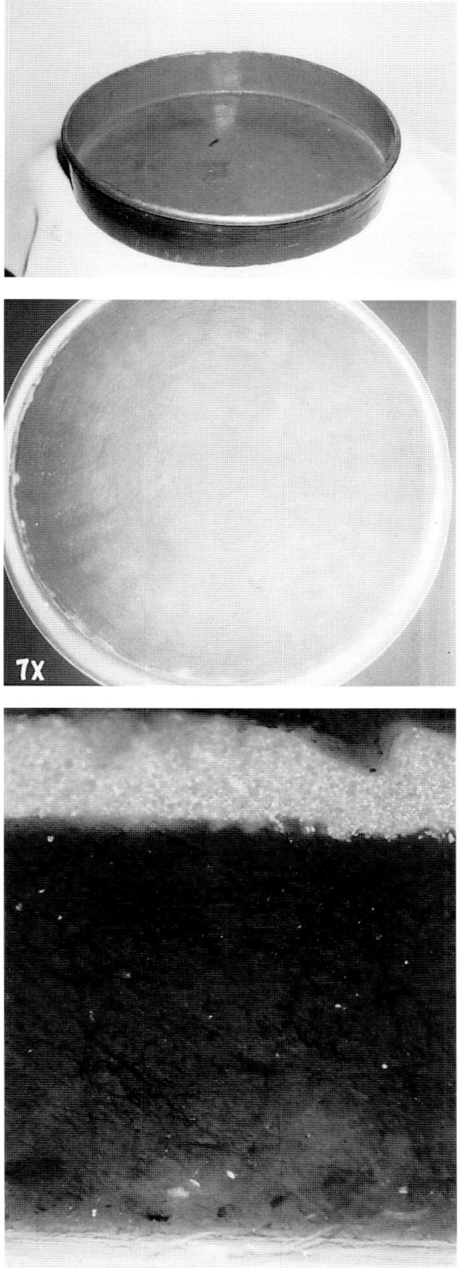

Fig. 4 a–c. Red shallow tray, *lai kud* design

Sample 4

Red shallow tray, *lai kud* design, dimension 20.5 cm, height 4.5 cm, Wat Chiangmun museum collection. Technical data: 64 kV, 3.0 mA, 10 seconds, distance from tube 74 cm. Result: The substructure consists of bamboo strips as the warp and wired bamboo as the weft of the bottom. The coiled bamboo strips are used to shape the vessel. Hard wood is used to strengthen the rim of the vessel. Under the microscope the structure of the cell wall of the wood becomes visible. The coating consists of 4 layers: a coarse layer, a fine layer, a red colored layer and a clear lacquer finish (fig. 4 a–c).

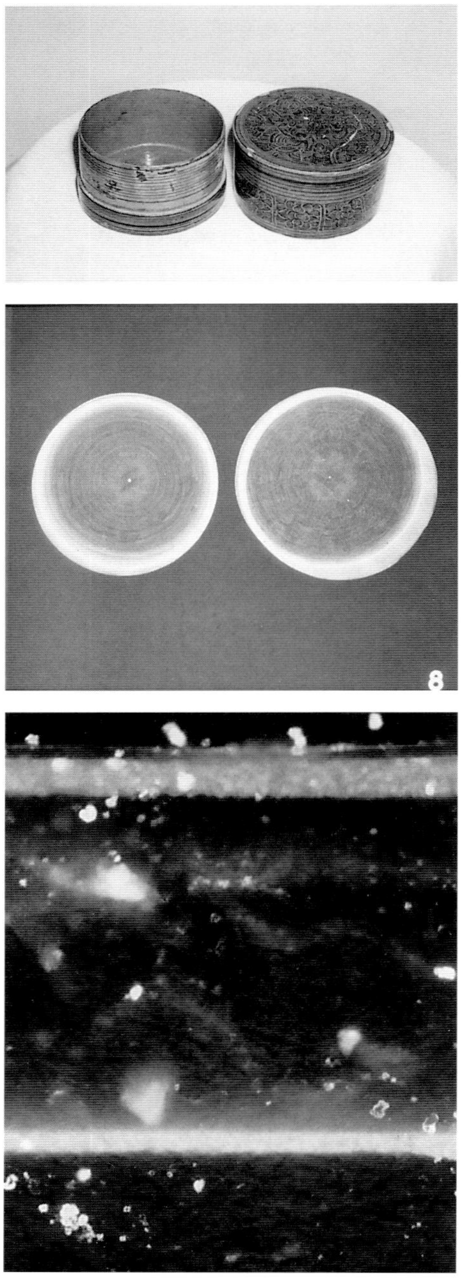

Fig. 5 a–c. Cylindrical box with cover, *lai kud* design

Sample 5

Cylindrical box with cover, *lai kud* design, dimension 10.0 cm, height 5.7 cm, Wat Chiangmun museum collection. Technical data: 64 kV, 2.4 mA, 15 seconds, distance from tube 74 cm. Result: The substructure consists of bamboo strips as the warp and weft of the body and the lid of the box. This example has several lacquer layers. There is a coarse layer, a fine and a colored layer, followed by the same layer sequence and a clear lacquer finish. The final layer is heightened with gold (fig. 5 a–c).

Sample 6

Cylindrical box with cover, *lai kud* design, dimension 12.0 cm, height 7.3 cm, Wat Chiangmun museum collection. Technical data: 64 kV, 2.4 mA, 15 seconds, distance from tube 74 cm. Result: For the substructure bamboo strips are used as a warp and wired bamboo as the weft to shape the cover and the body of the box. Both apply the same technique, but some thick bamboo is used for strengthening the bottom and the rim of the box. This sample has 4 layers: a coarse layer, a fine layer, a yellow colored layer and a clear lacquer layer (colour plate VIII.2, 5, 8).

Sample 7

Pedestal vessel, *lai rod nam* design, width 17.5 cm, height 36.3 cm, Wat Chiangmun museum collection. Technical data: 64 kV, 2.4 mA, 20.0 seconds, distance from tube 47.0 cm. Result: The substructure is made of lathed wood. The microscope shows 7 layers: one coarse layer, one red colored layer, followed by a coarse layer, a fine layer, a red colored layer, a clear lacquer layer and a gilded layer (colour plate VIII.3, 6, 9).

Sample 8

Betel case, *lai kud* design, width 7.0 cm, height 10.5 cm, Wat Chiangmun museum collection. Technical data: 100 kV, 2.4 mA, 15 seconds, distance from tube 74.0 cm. Result: The substructure is made from a thin sheet of zinc and coated with red lacquer and decorated with incised design (fig. 6 a, b).

Fig. 6 a, b. Betel case, *lai kud* design

1 Red shallow bowl, *lai kud* design

2 Cylindrical box with cover, *lai kud* design

3 Pedestal vessel, *lai rod nam* design

4–6 Substructures of objects 1–3 (x-ray-radiography)

4

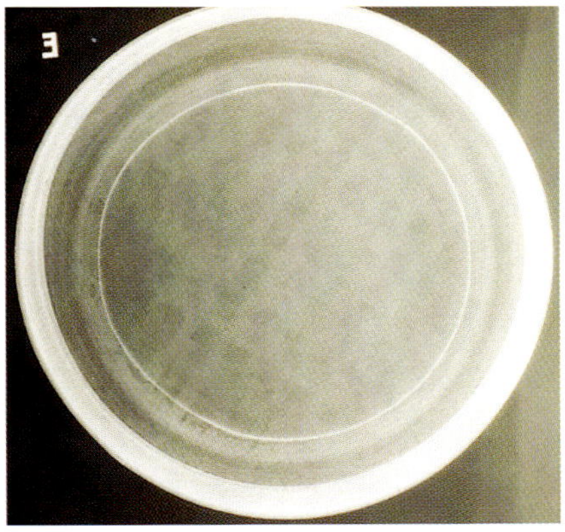

5

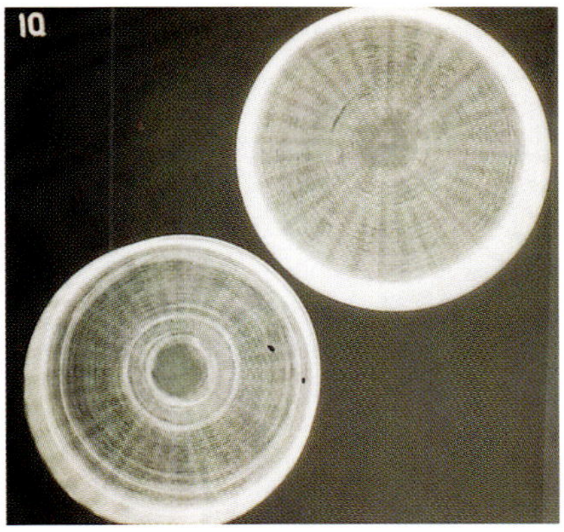

6

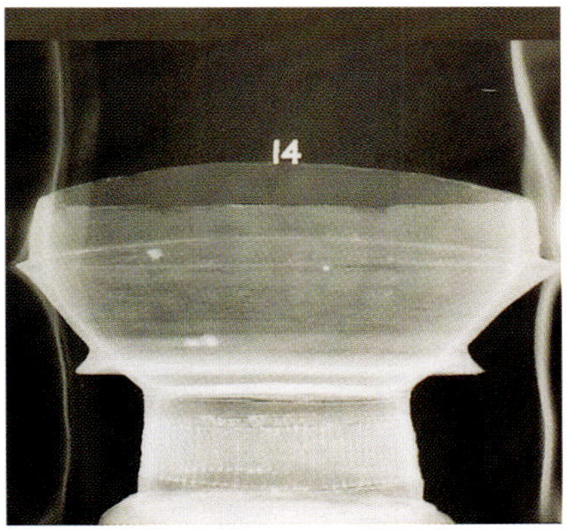

7–9 Cross sections of objects 1–3

7

8

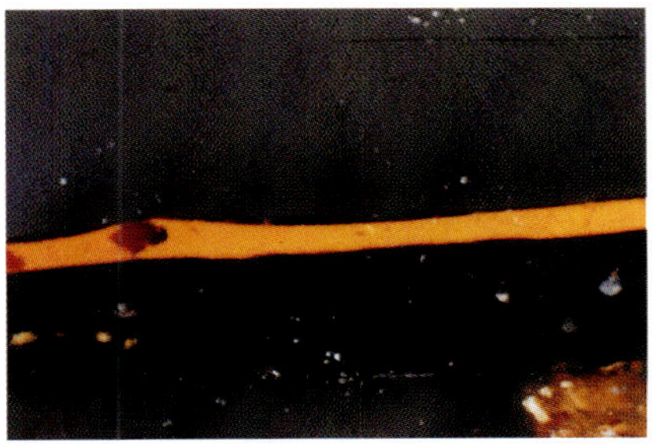

9

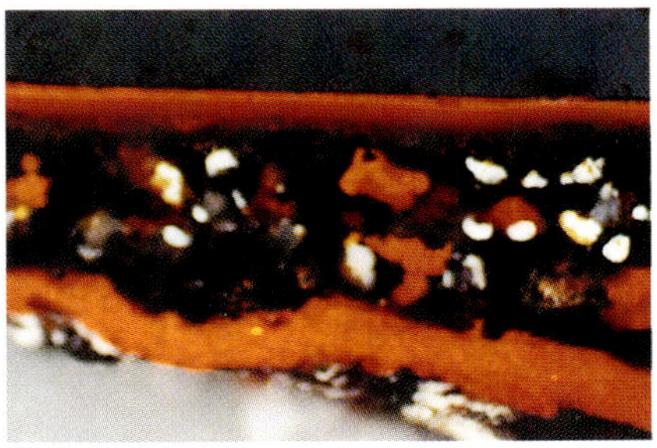

Fig. 7 a–c. Cups, *lai kud* design

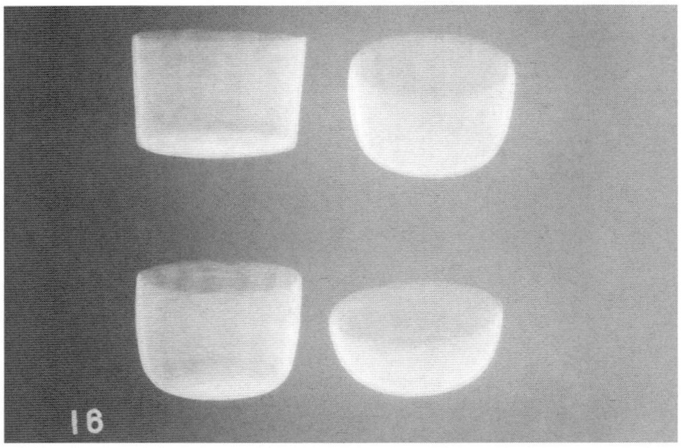

7b △

Sample 9

Cups, *lai kud* design, width 7.2, 7.0, 7.5 and 7.1 cm, height 5.1, 5.0, 5.6 and 4.0 cm, (from right to left), Wat Chiangmun museum collection. Technical data: 64 kV, 2.4 mA, 7 seconds, distance from tube 74.0 cm. Result: The substructures are made in two techniques: Bamboo strips are used to coil the cups or as warps and wired bamboo to shape the cups. Test samples have been taken out from the cup at the right top for microscopic analysis. The microscope reveals 4 layers: two large bands show the coarse and the fine final layers. On top are a colored layer and clear lacquer finish (figs. 7 a–c).

Conclusion

Woven bamboo and coiled bamboo strips were used as substructures of ancient Thai lacquerware; wooden substructures were only used more recently. The traditional Thai lacquering processes basically consist of at least four steps: first a residue of raw lacquer, followed by a coarse undercoat (*smook),* then several layers of fine undercoat (*smook oon)* and, finally, a clear lacquer finish. The coarse layer is mostly composed of clay, particles of mineral become visible under the microscope. The fine layer and the coarse layer become visible as a large band, but it could not be identified how many times the lacquer was applied. There is no evidence for the use of fabric for the strengthening of the substructure of Thai lacquerware. There are two traditional techniques used to decorate ancient Thai lacquerware: *lai kud* and *lai rod nam*. Seventeen examples of ancient Thai lacquerware from the collections at the Wat Chiangmun museum in the Chiang Mai province were examined for this study. The results show twelve pieces of ancient lacquerware made of a woven bamboo substructure, four samples made of wooden substructures and one made of a metal substructure. Different layers of lacquer coating were found. Coarse and fine *smook* layers, colored lacquer and clear lacquer.

The result of this study suggests that the techniques of producing Thai lacquerware have changed considerably during the centuries. Woven bamboo substructures, which were used in the past, have been replaced by coiled bamboo strips and wood in recent times. The lacquering process employs a similar technique to the past but the number of coats of lacquer is less than in the past. In former times lacquerware with mother-of-pearl inlay was not to be found in the north of Thailand, but exclusively in the central part of Thailand, especially in Ayuthaya.

7c ▽

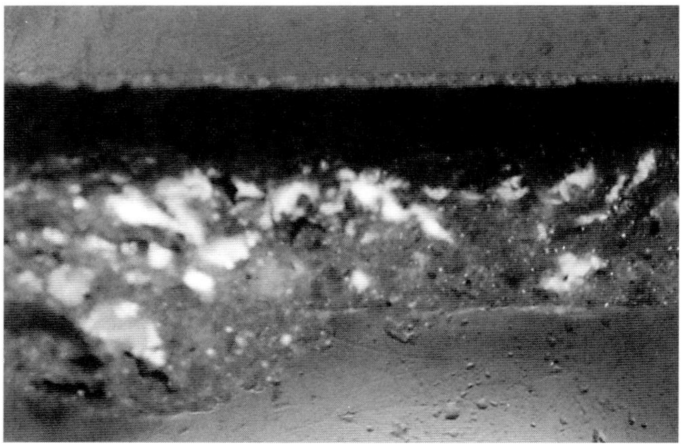

Acknowledgements

The author would like to thank Wat Chiangmun for granting permission to examine the collection of the ancient Thai lacquerware. Thanks are due to Mrs. Peeya Piyasak and Mrs. Chumjai Chantawong for their valuable information. Financial support from the Thailand Research Fund is also gratefully acknowledged.

References

1 GARNER, HARRY: *Chinese Lacquer,* London, 1979
2 THE THAI DEPARTMENT OF INDUSTRIAL PROMOTION (ed.): *Lacquerwares*, Bangkok, 1978
3 MILAM, BILLIE/GILETT, HÉLÈNE: 'X-ray Radiography in the Study of Oriental Lacquerware Substructures', *Urushi. Proceedings of the Urushi Study Group*, June 10–17, 1985, Tokyo, 1988
4 BURMESTER, ANDREAS: 'The Scientific Investigation of Two Japanese Dance Masks', *International Symposium on the Conservation and Restoration of Cultural Property. Conservation of Urushi Objects,* November 10–12, 1993, Tokyo, 1995

Photo Credits

All photographs by the author

U Yu Thein

Myanmar Lacquer Techniques

Introduction

The making of lacquerware is one of the traditional arts, which can look back onto a long cultural heritage in Myanmar. For centuries, Myanmar lacquer techniques have been passed from one generation of Myanmar craftsmen to the next. Lacquer art is renowned in Myanmar as 'Pan-yun'. The art or craft, which creates aesthetic beauty, is prefixed with the word 'Pan', which literally means 'flower'. The ten traditional arts in Myanmar are: 'Pan-chi' (painting), 'Pan-pu' (wood, ivory carving), 'Pan-tain' (gold- and silversmith work), 'Pan-tei' (bronze and copper casting), 'Pan-pei' (blacksmith work), 'Pan-taw' (stucco), 'Pan-tamaw' (stone sculpture), 'Pan-put' (lathe turning), 'Pan-yan' (masonry), 'Pan-yun' (lacquerware).

Archaeological findings have proven, that the art of lacquering had its origins in Myanmar in the 12th century. The lacquerware production in Myanmar is still run on cottage scale, and the techniques differ slightly depending upon location. The lacquerware production centers in Myanmar are: Bagan and Nyaung U in Nyaung U township, Myingaba in Nyaung U township, Kyauk Ka in Monywa township, Maung Daung in Budalin township, Inwa in Tada U township, Lei Cha in Kyaing Ton township, Eastern Shan State (fig. 1).

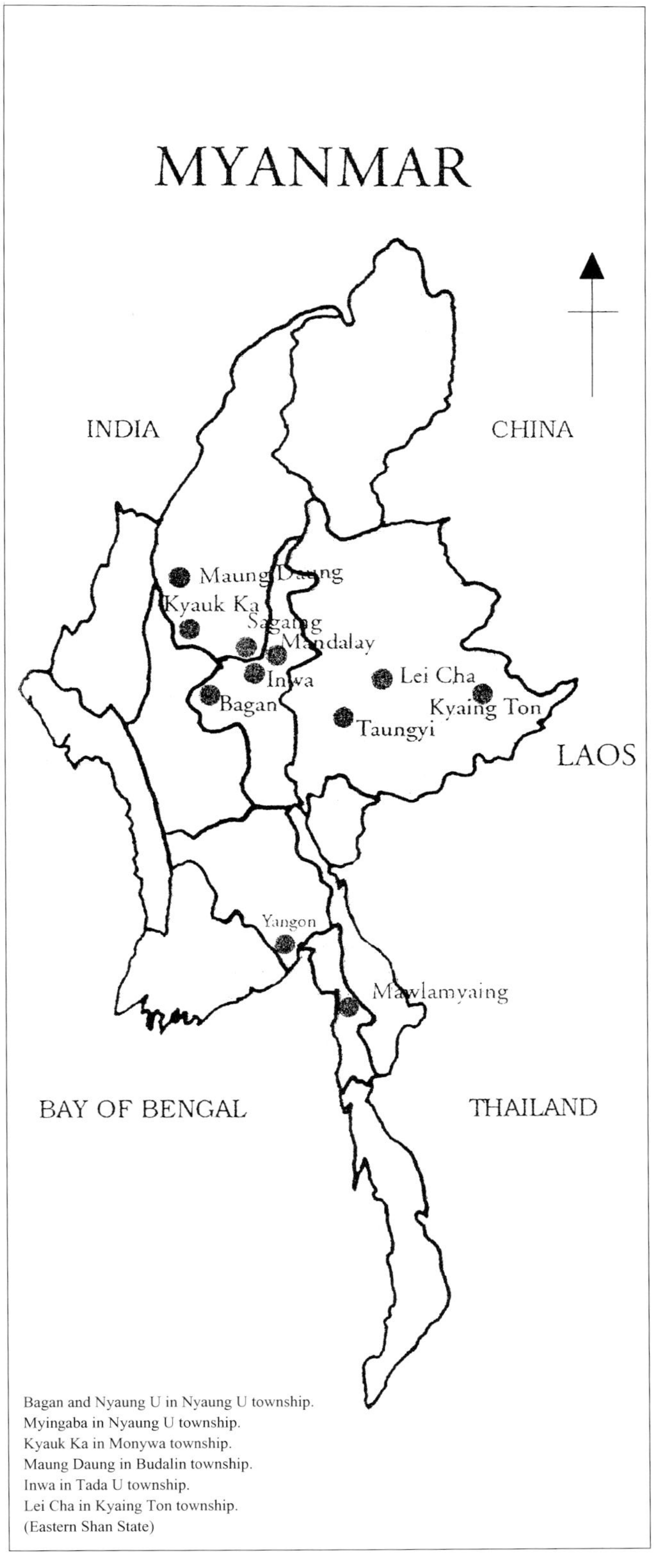

Fig. 1. Map of the Union of Myanmar, showing the lacquer production centers

Myanmar Lacquerware

In Myanmar, the 'Thit-si pin' or lacquer tree (*Melanorrhoea usitata*, genus *Anacardiaceae*) grows in native form in areas up to 3000 ft. above sea level such as Shan, Chin, and Kachin States. The 'Thit-si' or lacquer sap is tapped from the V-shaped incision in the trunk of the lacquer tree. The sap is strained to remove the dirt and solid impurities, resulting in the liquid 'Thit-si', which is stored in tin or usually in wooden containers. The unique colour of Myanmar 'Thit-si' in its original forms is red, brown or black. The best quality grade is termed in Myanmar as 'black variety', and comes from the Moe Nae area in the Shan States.

Because of its excellent spreadibility in painting, 'Thit-si' serves as a natural form of lacquer. The 'Thit-si' film, when coated on an article, has elegant charm and indoor weatherability. One of the salient features of 'Thit-si' is, that it attains maximum hardness when dried in a moisturous surrounding. The dried film of 'Thit-si', despite the well-knit and highly cross-linked structure, is both, flexible and rigid, having high frictional resistance. And, it is on these unique features of 'Thit-si', that the art of lacquerware has developed.

Production of Myanmar Lacquerware

The materials needed and the process and techniques involved in the production of Myanmar lacquerware will be discussed in the following paragraphs, as well as some of the unique features of this traditional Myanmar art (Myanmar 'Pan-yun').

1. Materials

The materials used for the manufacturing of lacquerware are:

1.1. Materials for the Body

Bamboo, wood, straw, horse-hair, cloth, 'Maing Kaing' paper (hand made bamboo paper from the Shan States).

1.2. Materials for an Undercoating

'Thit-si' (lacquer sap), paddy-husk ash, charcoal powder, cow dung (rarely used in the present days).

1.3. Materials for a Decorative Coating

'Thit-si' (lacquer sap), vermilion red (occurs naturally as cinnabar), Prussian blue, chrome green, chrome yellow, Orpiment (natural mineral form of Arsenic(III) sulphide), 'Htanaung' glue (gum Arabic), Neem tree resin (gum of dragon), bone ash.

2. The Process of Lacquerware Production

The manufacturing process of Myanmar lacquerware consists of: The forming of the body, which is either bamboo-based or wood-based 'plain body' making; 'black body' making, the coating of the plain body with 'Thit-si'; the decoration of the surface of the black body by either painting, gilding, engraving or embossing.

2.1. The Formation of the Body

Depending on the design of the body, either bamboo or wood is used. 'Thin wah' (*ephalostachyun bamboo*) and 'Mae-tin-kha wah' are used because of the lightness and the pliable features of these bamboos. These bamboos are obtained from Katha and the Upper Chindwin areas. For wooden bodies a softwood known as 'Baing' or the famous hardwood 'Teak' are used depending on the design of the framework. Bamboo is first sliced and split in-

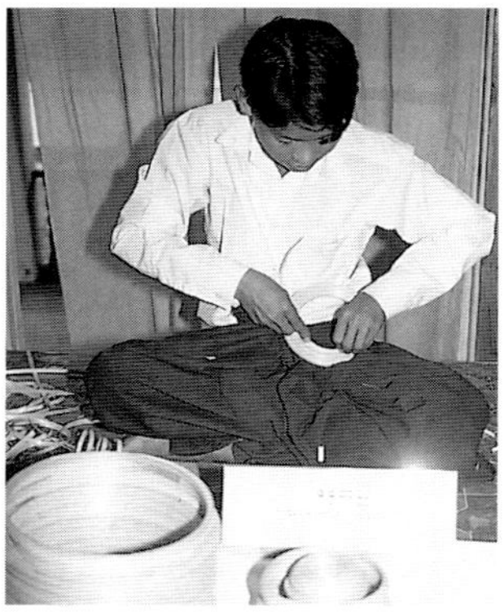

Fig. 2. Bamboo is sliced into narrow pieces and cleaned thoroughly before a body can be formed

Fig. 3. Sliced bamboo stripes are manually wound to form a round body as shown in the foreground

Fig. 4. Completed bodies of bamboo ready for lacquering

Fig. 5. Lacquered boxes made out of bamboo stripes

Fig. 6. Finishing the surface of bamboo bodies

Fig. 7. Sliced bamboo stripes are woven to form a rectangular body

Fig. 8. Sliced bamboo stripes are wound to form a body with the support of a wooden mold

Fig. 9. First stage of lacquer coating

Fig. 10. Last stage of lacquer coating. The lacquer coating is finished when a shining black surface is obtained as shown to the right

Fig. 11. After the body was covered with Neem tree resin and the ornament was designed it is covered with red colour so that the incised lines are filled with red pigment. The red motif appears on the black lacquered surface on the object to the right after the resin has been washed away

Fig. 12. After the red ornament has been finished the same procedure is repeated with yellow pigment

to narrow pieces (fig. 2), which are then thoroughly cleaned. They are next wound or woven into the desired shape, which may be done with or without any support on a wooden mold (figs. 3–8). The wooden body is formed from the dried and seasoned wood pieces.

2.1.1. The Technique of 'Mann' Image Forming

A technique known as 'Mann' image forming or wickerwork frame making needs to be mentioned here. This technique is also known as 'dry lacquer' technique. Well-kneaded clay is shaped into a rough form, usually the image of Buddha. A plaster of straw, ash and water is smeared over the clay image. Pieces of cloth and 'Maing Kaing' paper are soaked in lacquer sap and applied over the lacquer smeared image. For extra flexibility of the wickerwork frame, horse-hair can be fabricated in this process. The paste known as 'Tha-yo' may have a thickness up to half an inch in places wherever it is necessary. Details of the image are executed with an iron implement called 'Than-let'. When the image has dried and hardened, the clay is removed by washing and cutting, and the openings are sealed.

2.2. Black Body Making

This process comprises the coating of the plain body. The whole surface of the body is coated with a thin and even coating of 'Thit-si' and then dried in a cellar. The cellar may be either one above ground, called 'Yay-taik', or a basement cellar, called 'Myay-taik'. To attain maximum hardness of the 'Thit-si' coating, the cellars are kept at the relative humidity of 80–85 %. In about four days the 'Thit-si' coating becomes dry. The coating process is repeated until a good quality is obtained (figs. 9, 10).

2.3. Decorating the Black Body Surface

Various methods are known for decorative coatings on the surface of the black body. Depending upon the method, the following types of lacquerware can be distinguished: Plain lacquerware ('Kyauk-ka' ware; fig. 10), incised lacquerware ('Yun' ware; figs. 13, 23), gilded lacquerware ('Shwe-za-wa' ware; fig. 16), relief molded lacquerware ('Tha-yo pan-kywa' ware; fig. 20), glass mosaic and gilded lacquerware ('Hman-si shwe-cha' ware; fig. 21).

Fig. 13. 'Yun' ware with red and yellow design on the black background

Plain undecorated lacquerware or 'Kyauk-ka' ware is an indigenous product of Myanmar. Successive coatings of 'Thit-si' are applied on the surface of the black body, and the surface is smoothed with whet stone powder. The 'Kyauk-ka' wares come out in classic plain black or a characteristical two-toned black outside and a bright vermilion red inside. 'Kyauk-ka' wares are appreciated for their utility, durability and simplicity in design (figs. 9, 10).

In the production of incised lacquerware or 'Yun' ware, the black body is first coated with 'Hta-naung' glue (gum Arabic) to a considerable thickness. Next, the decorative design or motif is traced lightly on the surface with a steel stylus. The traced lines are then incised and the incised area covered with pigment. The lacquerware is then dried in the drying chamber for about five days. The treated surface is next washed and scrubbed with a powdered paddy husk. The body with the pigmented lines is then masked with 'Hta-naung' glue again using a fine paintbrush. The lacquerware is then dried. Again, the lines, which are to be pigmented with the second colour, are incised and filled with the respective pigment (figs. 11, 12). The process of scrubbing and masking is repeated. In these steps a multicoloured incised lacquerware ('Yun' ware) is produced (figs. 13, 22).

Fig. 14. The outline of the motif depicted on the lacquered body is sketched with a pen using a paste made of Orpiment

Fig. 15. Washing away the resin mask with clean water. After the removal of the mask the ground colour (black or red) reappears forming a contrast to the gilded design

Fig. 16. Gilded object ▷

In the production of gilded designs, the surface of the black body is first coated with 'Thit-si' to a considerable thickness. The surface is next smoothed with whet stone powder. The outline of the desired motif is then sketched with a pen, using a paste made of Orpiment, Neem tree resin (dragon's gum) and water (fig. 14). Next, those parts of the object on which no gilding is required, are masked by covering them up with the same paste. After drying, the painted figure is treated with a thin layer of 'Thit-si' and gilded. This type of lacquerwork requires a special skill.

After the gilded lacquerware has dried in the drying chamber, the Neem resin mask is washed away with clean water (fig. 15). The result is extremely regal and strikingly beautiful. 'Shwe-zawa' wares, which used to be the ornaments exclusively for royal and religious affairs, are now the most costly lacquerwares because of the soaring price of gold (fig. 16).

A very good quality 'Tha-yo' is essential for the production of the relief-molded lacquerware. 'Tha-yo', which literally means bone ash, is a plastic paste, a mixture of bone ash, paddy-husk ash, teakwood sawdust and the lacquer sap. Fine threads are made out of this 'Tha-yo' paste (fig. 17). By means of an iron or wooden stylus, these threads are stuck on the outlines already sketched on the lacquered surface of the object to form a relief design.

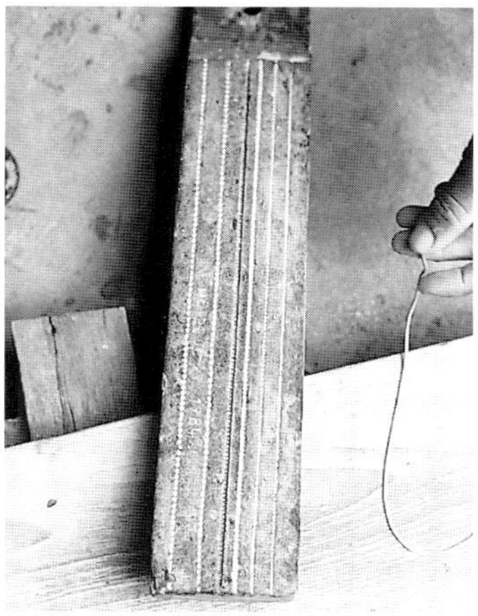

◁ Fig. 17. Fine threads made out of 'Tha-yo' paste

Fig. 18. Threads of 'Tha-yo' paste are stuck on the outlines sketched on the lacquered surface by using an iron stylo. A relief design is formed at the bottom of the object

18 △

Fig. 19. Gilding of the surface with gold leaves

Fig. 20. Example of 'Tha-yo pan-kywa' ware with relief design and gilding

Fig. 21. 'Hman-si shwe-cha' ware ▷

The lacquerware is next kept in the drying chamber for about three days. It is coated with lacquer or given two light coatings of 'Thit-si' and then gilding is done as mentioned previously, using gold leaves (fig. 19), Orpiment and Neem resin. The whole process of producing relief molded lacquerware ('Tha-yo pan-kywa' ware takes about two to three months (fig. 20).

For the production of glass mosaic and gilded lacquerware ('Hman-si shwe-cha' ware), pieces of mirror, coloured glass or mother-of-pearl are cut into different sizes and shapes to fit into the inlaid pattern (fig. 21). Next, these pieces are inlaid onto the surface of the ('Tha-yo' ware) relief molded lacquerware, using a high-grade 'Thit-si' as adhesive. This process of inlaying is followed by the process of gilding. This type of lacquerware can be very costly, not only for the materials, but also for the skill and amount of labour involved. A variety of museum pieces of glass mosaic and gilded lacquerware ('Hman-si shwe-cha' ware), using genuine gems can be seen as the epitomes of Myanmar's cultural heritage.

The 'Mann' image forming or hollow 'dry lacquer' technique has been mentioned before in the context of the formation of Buddha's image ('Mann pha-ya yot-tu-taw'), employing the wicker framework. After the framework of the image is completed, 'Tha-yo' plaster is applied to work out the details of the image. The techniques of ('Yun' ware) incised lacquerware, ('Tha-yo pan-kywa' ware) relief molded lacquerware, ('Hman-si shwe-cha' ware) glass mosaic and gilded lacquerware are all involved in this process.

Fig. 22. Motifs and designs of 'Kauk-kyaung' drawings: 'Kanou', 'Kapi', 'Gaza', 'Nari'

3. The Design and Decoration on Myanmar Lacquerware

Myanmar lacquerware designs, motifs, and decorations are based on Myanmar traditional line drawing techniques known as 'Kauk-kyaung' (curve lines) drawing. The motifs and designs usually associated with the 'Kauk-kyaung' drawings are: 'Kanou", 'Kapi', 'Gaza', 'Nari' (fig. 22). All of these are Pali words.

'Kanou" is the traditional style of depicting convoluted lotus stems, buds, and blossoms. It may also be a scrollwork on floral motifs, or floral arabesques. Any beautiful floral drawing of intricate design can be called 'Kanou". 'Kapi' is the traditional style of depicting apes, monkeys and the like. In a broader sense, the actions and the movements of these animals can also be taken as 'Kapi'. 'Gaza' is the traditional style of depicting elephants, horses or cattle (fig. 23). Again, any massive object such as a mountain, a rock and a tree trunk can be classified in this category. The traditional style of depicting a female figure or all human figures can be categorized as 'Nari'. Motives are lotus, orchids, mythical creatures, demons and divas. Scenes and episodes from Buddhist Jatakas and Buddisatva, Pagoda legends, Myanmar folk tales and mythical tales are also depicted. Myanmar festivals, traditional sports, the twelve signs of the Zodiac are the artists favourite. In the 'Kauk-kyaung' drawings, perspective is needed. The required effect is achieved by adding lines and colours. Here, the artist has a free hand to express his objectives.

Production and Sales

A rough estimation of the total number of lacquerware craftsmen in Myanmar is about 2500, of which 60 % are working in Bagan. The lacquerware trade is so thriving, that almost every household in Bagan is engaged in either the production or the trading with this handicraft. At least 10 main registered companies and cooperatives are active in this trade. The Ministry of Trade, Government economic enterprises, cooperatives and private companies are engaged in promoting the national and international marketing of Myanmar lacquerware.

Promotion of the Lacquerware Production and Quality Improvement

For the enhancement of the lacquerware production, it is imperative that there should be no lack of raw materials. Myanmar's 'Thit-si', renowned for its high quality, is in constant and great demand both locally and abroad. Thus, forestation campaigns to guarantee the proper maintenance of 'Thit-si pin' (lacquer trees) are in progress.

A lacquerware product takes about 3 months to finish. The main factor being the slow drying and hardening process of the 'Thit-si' coating. Research is underway for a better technique of drying 'Thit-si' coatings more quickly without bringing any adverse effect on its salient properties. Modern methods of preservation of bamboo and wood, the basis for the lacquerware products, are also imperative for a further enhancement.

Fig. 23. Tablet with an elephant in Gaza-style

The Myanmar Lacquerware Institute

The importance of maintaining a national cultural heritage can never by overemphasized. Accordingly, Myanmar 'Pan-yun', the lacquerware technique, has been maintained through generations as a pride of Myanmar. A Government Lacquerware Training School was founded in Bagan in 1924, as a seat of systematic training for the craftsmen. More than 600 trainees have been trained since then. In April 1995, the Government of the Union of Myanmar had authorized the upgrading of the Government Lacquerware Training School to The Myanmar Lacquerware Institute with an annual intake of 60 students for a two-year diploma course in lacquerware techniques. Curriculum includes, in addition to the basic crafts in lacquerware, subjects such as natural sciences, history, as well as culture and business management.

Acknowledgments

The author, on behalf of the Cottage Industries Department, Ministry of Cooperatives, Union of Myanmar, would like to put on record his appreciation to the following institutions and individuals: The Bavarian State Department of Historical Monuments in Munich and the German National Committee of ICOMOS, in collaboration with the Tokyo National Research Institute of Cultural Properties providing the opportunity to participate in the international congress of 'East Asian and European Lacquer Techniques'. Dr. Than Htaik, Director General, and U Khin Tun, Deputy Director of the Department of Cottage Industries, Ministry of Cooperatives, Union of Myanmar, for their support in conducting this study. The lacquerware entrepreneurs and artists of the country for the expert contributions for this paper. Dr. Maung Kyaw, retired Professor of Chemistry and Principal of Pathein Degree College, for his invaluable advice during this work.

Photo Credits

Figs. 1–3, 6–12, 14, 15, 22: Author
Figs. 4, 5, 13, 16–21, 23: Michael Kühlenthal, Munich

Abb. 1. Ankauf eines chinesischen Stellschirms (Inv. Nr. E 1) durch Frieda Fischer, der Frau des Gründers und spätere Direktorin des Museums für Ostasiatische Kunst in Köln, 1902

Barbara Piert-Borgers

Untersuchungen zum Fassungsaufbau von Koromandellacken – Vorüberlegungen zu einem Projekt

Im Zusammenhang mit Untersuchungen von chinesischen Lackarbeiten an französischen Möbeln[1] wurde deutlich, wie unterschiedlich und ungenau die Beschreibungen des Fassungsaufbaus von sog. Koromandellacken sind. Beim Vergleich von drei chinesischen Lackarbeiten in Koromandel-Technik mit Querschliffen eines chinesischen Lackfurniers mit farbigem Dekor von einer französischen Encoignure und mit Querschliffen des Fassungsaufbaus eines Stellschirmes mit plastischem Dekor wurden materialtechnische Ähnlichkeiten festgestellt. Diese wurden durch Röntgendiffraktometrie-Untersuchungen (XRD) und durch energiedispersive Analytik im Rasterelektronenmikroskop (EDX) bestätigt. Die Identifizierung einer Probe des asiatischen Lacks als *Rhus succedanea*, einer Spezies des Lackbaumes, die in Südchina verbreitet ist, und Inschriften eines Stellschirms aus dem Museum für Ostasiatische Kunst in Köln[2] (Abb. 1–3, Farbtafel IX–XII), die dessen Herstellung in Südchina belegen, lassen die Vermutung zu, dass ein bestimmter Fassungsaufbau mit den entsprechenden Materialien typisch für Südchina sein könnte.

In seiner Abhandlung *Une promenade dans Canton. La manufacture de laques d'Hip-Qua et l'atelier de tabletterie de Ta-Yu-Tong* über die Herstellung von Kanton-Lacken hebt Rondot[3] die regionalen Unterschiede der Grundierungsmaterialien in Südchina im Vergleich zu den von d'Incarville für Peking überlieferten hervor.[4] Nach Rondot verarbeitete man in Kanton in der Werkstatt Hip-Qua für die Grundierung fein pulverisierten roten Sandstein, gebunden in Ochsen- oder Schweinegalle.[5]

Exkurs:
Arbeitsschritte bei der Lackierung im Atelier Hip-Qua in Kanton im Jahre 1845 (Übersetzung aus dem Französischen*)*

1. *Ein Arbeiter glättet das Holz mit Sorgfalt, beseitigt die Fugen des Zusammensetzens und bedeckt sie mit einem kleinen Messer mit feinem Werg von mâ. Danach klebt man auf die Verbindungen und die Fugen Bänder aus Broussonetia-Papier, und man verstärkt die gesamte Oberfläche, indem man Seidentuch oder ein Blatt Papier aufbringt.*
2. *Auf einem hölzernen, lackierten Tisch mit Randleisten von etwa einem Meter Länge und Breite mischt man mit einem Spatel aus Ebenholz sunn-chi, Ochsen- oder Schweinegalle und sehr fein pulverisierten und gesiebten roten Sandstein (Rotliegendes). (FN: Dieser rote Sandstein ist der old red sandstone der englischen Geologen. In Canton liegt er unmittelbar auf dem Granit, an bestimmten Stellen tritt er kaum an die Oberfläche des Bodens, sondern man findet ihn normaler Weise bedeckt von einem feinkörnigen sehr quarzhaltigen Gestein. Ein wenig weiter im Norden ist der alte rote Sandstein überlagert von Marmor aus kohlehaltigem Kalk. Man versichert uns, dass man durch Grabungen das Vorhandensein von Vorkommen in der Stadt festgestellt hat, deren Ausbeutung allerdings außer in Zeiten der Belagerung nicht erlaubt war.) Dieser Arbeitsgang muss sehr langsam ausgeführt werden und dauert einen ganzen Tag. Es wird ein sehr starker Geruch von Ammoniak frei, weswegen man die Mischung auf der Straße machen muss.*
3. *Man breitet auf dem Möbel eine dicke Lage dieses Überzuges (FN: Hier die Art, wie man nach P. d'Incarville, pag. 124, in Peking diesen Überzug bereitet: „Man nimmt Ziegel, Fichtenholzkohle oder Asche von Hirschhorn und verrührt das jeweilige, zu feinem Puder vermahlene Material mit Lack oder mit Schweineblut [das vorher geschlagen, gesiebt und mit einem Viertel Kalkwasser vermischt wurde] mit einem breiten flachen, kurzborstigen Pinsel von ca. 15 cm Breite, indem man darauf achtet, ihn gleichmäßig auszubreiten. Man lässt ihn an der Luft trocknen, und er nimmt ein körniges Aussehen und eine braun-rötliche Farbe an.")*
4. *Das Glätten dieses Überzugs ist leicht und schnell. Es genügt mehrere Male mit einem Polierstein aus rotem Sandstein darüberzufahren. Um das kleine Möbel für die Lackierung vorzubereiten, genügt es, es mit einer Schicht in Wasser gelöster Kreide zu überziehen oder, wie man es in Japan macht, es mit Wachs abzureiben, um zu verhindern, dass der Lack ins Holz eindringt.*

Abb. 2. Stellschirm (wie Abb. 1), Inschrift

Zur Begriffsgeschichte

Die Bezeichnung Koromandellacke, die auf die südostindische Koromandelküste Bezug nimmt, ist in Europa seit dem 17. Jahrhundert gebräuchlich. Die so bezeichneten Lackobjekte wurden auch mit dem Begriff *Bantam Work* belegt nach der Handelsniederlassung der Holländischen Ostindischen Kompanie in Bantam auf Java.

Zunächst verband man mit der Bezeichnung, zumindest im englischen Sprachraum, auch Arbeiten mit plastischem und malerischem Dekor. Der Begriff Koromandellack als spezifische Bezeichnung für die Lacktechnik wurde in England 1913 zum ersten Mal in einem Katalog einer Ausstellung chinesischer Kunst in der Kunstgalerie der Stadt Manchester verwendet.[6]

Im Inventar der Möbel des Schlosses Versailles von 1708, in dem mehr als zwanzig chinesische Paravents aufgelistet sind, findet sich die Bezeichnung *creusé*[7] bei Stellschirmen mit ausgegrabenem Dekor, und im *Livre Journal* des Pariser Kunsthändlers Lazare Duvaux[8] taucht zwischen 1750 und 1753 in elf Fällen *vernis de Coromandel* auf, wobei allerdings noch keine Spezifizierung auf die Technik ausgeschnittener Bildflächen vorliegt.

Nach Garner taucht der Begriff *vernis de Coromandel* als Terminus technicus für die unten erläuterte Technik in französischer Sprache zum ersten Mal 1922(?) bei Séguy auf.[9] Der in Frankreich im 19. Jahrhundert gebräuchliche, von Jaquemart geprägte Begriff *laque champlevé* setzte sich nicht durch.[10]

Heute bezeichnet man als Koromandellack einen Lackdekor, bei dem über einem Träger aus Holz zunächst Grundierungsschichten aufgetragen sind. Auf dem Holz bzw. zwischen den Schichten können sich Papier- oder Textilauflagen befinden. Nach der Lackierung wird der Dekor bis in die Grundierungsschichten hinein relativ flach und mehr oder weniger großflächig ausgeschnitten und mit Farben oder Gold ausgemalt. Innerhalb der Bildfläche bleiben Lackstege stehen, und der Kontrast zwischen ausgeschnittenen Flächen und den Lackstegen erinnert an Druckplatten asiatischer Holzschnitte (vgl. Abb. 3).

Wang macht 1959 mit seiner kommentierten Neuausgabe des *Xiushilu Jieshuo,* eines Textes des Ming-zeitlichen Lackkünstlers Huang Cheng, der 1625 von dem Lackkünstler Yang Ming kommentiert wurde, den die oben beschriebene Technik bezeichnenden Begriff *kuancai* für die Kunsttechnologie eindeutig.[11] Er bezieht sich dabei insbesondere auf eine Textstelle im Kommentar von Yang Ming: „Der Dekor wird vertieft eingeschnitten, genauso wie bei einer Holzdruckplatte. Dann werden die Farben eingefüllt, und daher kommt der Name."[12] Gleichzeitig bestätigt er damit die Vermutung, dass es Koromandellacke bereits im 16. Jahrhundert gab. Bei Huh findet sich für *kuancai* die Übersetzung *„polychrome carving"*.[13]

Bei Mayer wird für *kuancai* die Übersetzung *„eingeritztes Bunt"* benutzt und diskutiert.[14] Die chinesische Bezeichnung *kehui* für Koromandellack wird bei Huh mit *„carved ash"* übersetzt.[15] Lee beschreibt *kehui* als: *„Coromandel. Carving sandlike putty that is painted with lacquer and filling the carving with coloured lacquer."*[16] Der in der Zeitschrift der Pekinger Archäologischen Gesellschaft *Wenwu* für Koromandellack ebenfalls benutzte Begriff *da diaotian* wird bei Huh mit *„bold carving and filling"* übersetzt und bei Wang als im chinesischen Antiquitätenhandel gebräuchlicher Begriff qualifiziert.[17] Nach den zitierten Untersuchungen von Mayer und Wang erscheint es sinnvoll, parallel zu dem im Westen eingebürgerten Begriff Koromandellack die chinesische Bezeichnung *kuancai* zu verwenden.

Vergleich von historischen Quellen und vorliegenden Untersuchungsergebnissen

Textil- oder Papierauflage

Nach d'Incarville wird auf die mit Kreide vermischtem Gummiwasser abgelöste Holzschicht Seide (*kiuen*) oder Papier (*chetan-tchi*) mit Rohlack aufgeklebt. Rondot nennt zur Abdeckung der Fugen Broussonetia-Papier, zur Verstärkung der gesamten Oberfläche Seide oder Papier. Bei Hornby wird eine Schicht aus Grasfasern als Verstärkung in der Grundierung genannt.[18] Wahrscheinlich ist Ramie gemeint, das fälschlicher Weise auch als Chinagras bezeichnet wird.[19] Garner betont, dass die Textilauflagen an Lacken des 1. Jh. v. Chr. bis 1. Jh. n. Chr. aus Ramie bestehen, und verweist auf die diesbezüglichen Inschriften auf Grabungsfunden. „The inscriptions invariably refer to the fabric as ramie, and no hemp [...]."[20] *„Hemp"* wird allerdings häufig mit „Ramie" übersetzt. Dieses Übersetzungsbeispiel zeigt ein typisches Problem der Lackterminologie auf.[21] Auch Plenderleith identifizierte bei einem *lian* des Britischen Museums als Trägermaterial Ramie.[22] Worch konnte an den Objekten Nr. IV, V und VI (siehe Übersicht) Ramie (*Boehmeria nivea*) nachweisen (Abb. 4–6). Von den anderen untersuchten Objekten wurden bis jetzt keine Textil- bzw. Papierproben entnommen.

Abb. 3. Stellschirm (wie Abb. 1), Koromandellacktechnik

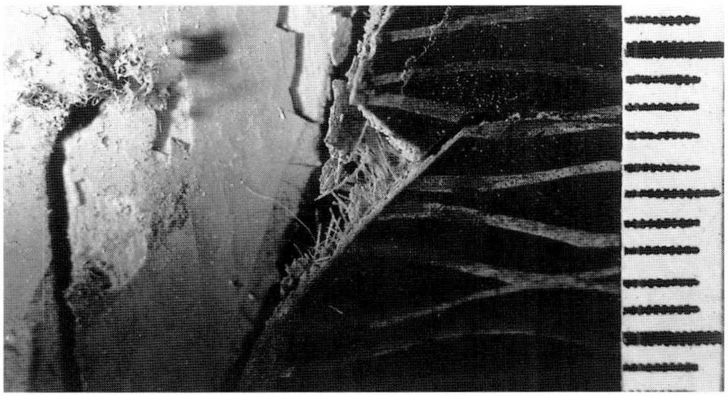

Abb. 4. Encoignure, gestempelt MCRIAERD; freiliegende Rami-Fasern an einer Schadstelle des chinesischen Lacks

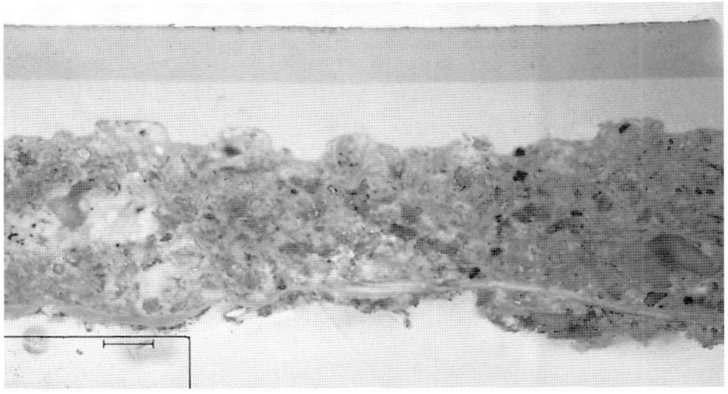

Abb. 5. Encoignure (wie Abb. 4); Querschliff, refl., 100-fach, Schwarzlack mit Rami-Fasern

Abb. 6. Stellschirm, Herzog Anton Ulrich-Museum, Braunschweig, Inv. Nr. CHI 1600; feine und grobe Grundierungsschicht mit Resten von Textilfasern

Grundierung

In dem von Mänchen-Helfen wiedergegebenen Auszug aus dem *Nan-ts'un-cho-keng-lu* des T'ao Tsung-yi (Vorwort aus dem Jahr 1366) findet sich folgende Beschreibung für die Grundierung von Lacken:

„Die Lackarbeiter [...] kaufen von den Drechslern die aus dünnen Weichholzbrettchen zusammengeleimten Körper, schaben die Fugen glatt und füllen kleine Unebenheiten mit einem Gemisch von Naturlack und Leim aus, was man shao-tang nennt. Sie überziehen den Körper mit einer Lackschicht. Auf diese legen sie ein Leinentuch. Über dieses breiten sie die erste Aschenschicht. Im ganzen trägt man drei Aschenschichten auf, Gemenge von Asche, zerstoßenen Ziegeln und Lack, und zwar immer feinere Asche. Jede Schicht wird, sobald sie trocken ist, mit Sandleder (gleich unserem Glaspapier) abgeschliffen. Für billige Ware nimmt man ein Gemisch von Schweineblut und Reiskleister und an Stelle von Leinen ein Hanfgewebe. Auf die letzte Aschenschicht kommt wieder Lack, tsao ch'i, womit das Gefäß fertig grundiert ist. Beim Rotlacken entfällt tsao ch'i.“[23]

In dieser Quelle aus dem 14. Jh. werden die Grundierungsschichten als Aschen bezeichnet und „als Gemenge von Asche, zerstoßenen Ziegeln und Lack“ spezifiziert. Für die billigeren Arbeiten wird ein Gemisch aus Schweineblut und Reiskleister beschrieben. Bei d'Incarville werden als Grundierungsmaterialien Ziegelmehl, Tannenholzkohle und als beste Alternative Hirschhornasche genannt, die in Lack oder Schweineblut, das geschlagen und mit Kalkwasser vermischt wurde, gebunden wurden.[24] Zu der Qualitätsrangfolge der Grundierungsmaterialien bei d'Incarville passt auch die Beobachtung von Okada, der Knochenasche nur an luxuriösen Han-Lacken fand. Rondot führt roten Sandstein, gebunden in Ochsen- oder Schweinegalle an (s. o.).

Burmester wies an einer Reihe von Ming-Lacken mineralische Zusätze in der Grundierung nach. Hohe Konzentrationen von Silicium, Calcium, Magnesium, Aluminium, Titan und Eisen deuten auf die Verwendung von dunklen Erden, Aschen und Ton.[25] Die Untersuchungen und Querschliffe[26] stimmen mit den Ergebnissen zum Stellschirm des Museums für Lackkunst in Münster (Farbtafel XIII) weitgehend überein.[27] Okada identifiziert als Grundierung eines Han-Lackes eine Mischung aus Lack, Knochenasche und Mineralien, in zwei Schichten aufgetragen.[28] Strahan kam bei der Untersuchung einer Lackskulptur der Walters-Collection aus dem späten sechsten Jahrhundert zu ähnlichen Ergebnissen. Auf Grund von mikroskopischen Analysen und Untersuchungen mit dem Rasterelektronenmikroskop (REM) und von Elementanalysen (REM-EDX und XRD) wurden gemahlene Knochen unterschiedlicher Korngröße und in verschiedenen Farben gefunden: rohe Knochen – weiß, gebrannte Knochen – schwarz und partiell gebrannte Knochen – grau.[29] Schon Garner hat die Frage aufgeworfen, inwieweit der Typ der verwendeten Asche die Polymerisation des Lacks beeinflusst. Er verweist in diesem Zusammenhang auf die Verwendung von Asche aus Reishülsen in Burma.[30] Im schon erwähnten *Xiushilu* wird u. a. die Verwendung von Hirschhornasche, Kuhhornasche, Porzellanasche, Knochenasche, Schweineblut, gebrannten Muschelschalen und gemahlenem ausgehärtetem Lack erwähnt.[31] Miklin-Kniefacz fand an chinesischen Lacktafeln aus dem Vieux Lacque-Zimmer des Schlosses Schönbrunn als Füllstoff eine „rötliche Sandsorte“, die als Aluminiumsilikat mit Kreide- und Eisenoxidanteilen analysiert wurde.[32]

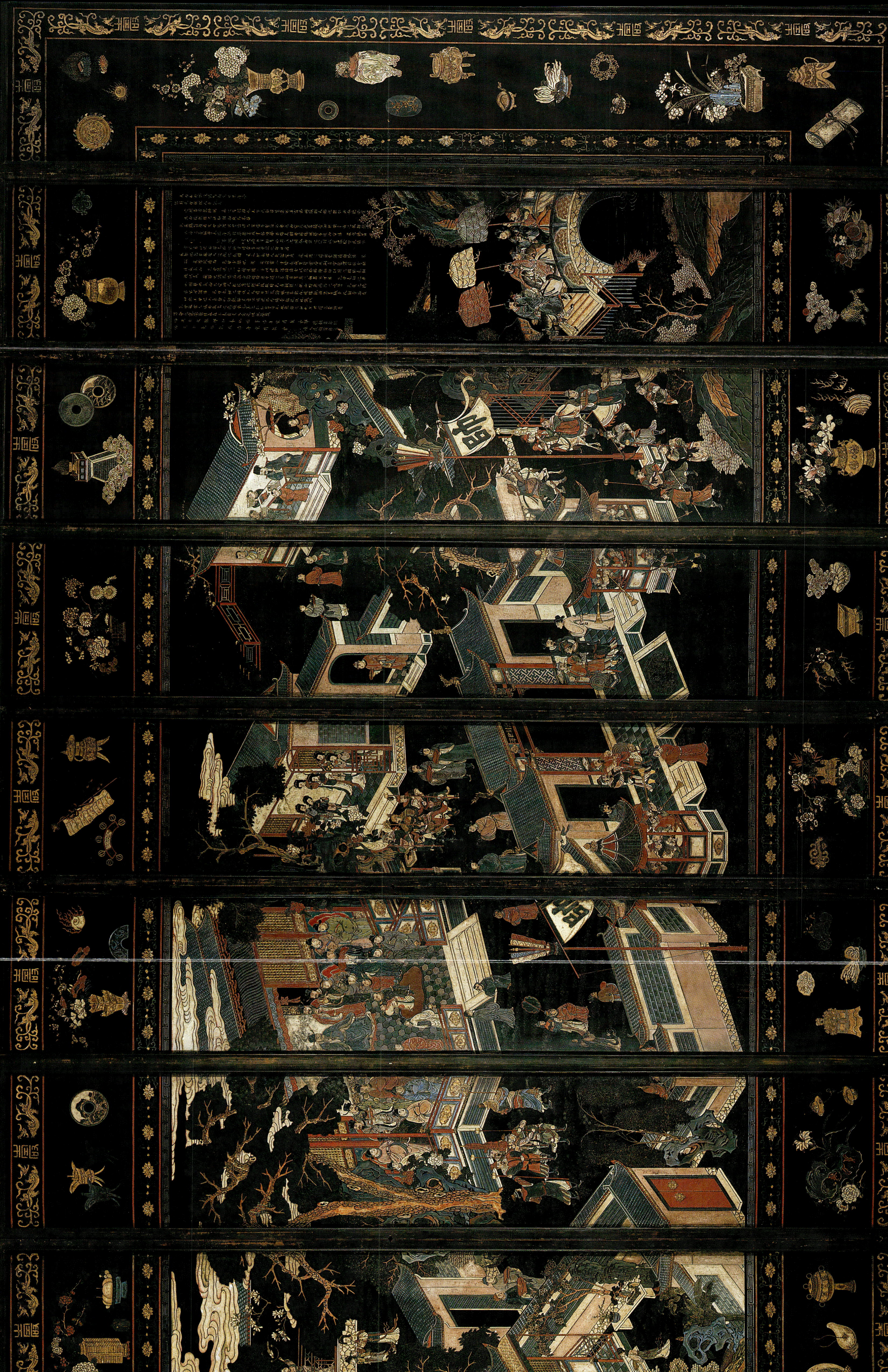

Objekt	I. Kabinettschrank, Koromandellack, MOK Berlin, Inv. Nr. 6515 II.	II. Stellschirm, Koromandellack, MOK Köln, Inv. Nr. E 1
Lit./Abb.	REIDEMEISTER, L.: *Der Große Kurfürst* *als Sammler Ostasiatischer Kunst,* in: Ostasiatische Zs. 8(1932), S. 175–188, T. 22.	SHONO-SLADEK 1994, S. 100–103.
Schliff		
Schliff UV	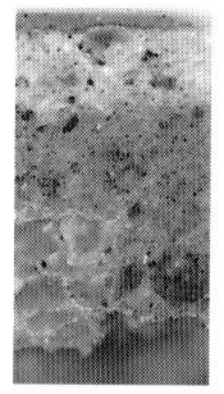	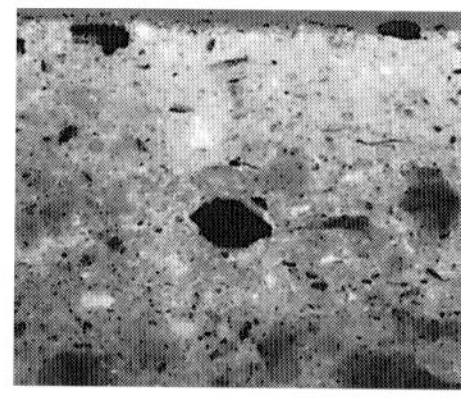
Grundierungsmaterial/ Schichtenfolge	Steinmehl, grobe Quarzpartikel, rote Partikel, feine schwarze Partikel	Steinmehl, grobe Quarzpartikel, rote Partikel, feine schwarze Partikel
	1 grobe Grundierung 2 feine Grundierung 3 feine Grundierung 4 schwarze Linie 5 pigmentierter asiatischer Lack 6 gelblich fluoreszierender Lack	1 grobe Grundierung 2 feine Grundierung 3 Textilauflage im UV-Licht nicht erkennbar 4 feine Grundierung 5 dunkle Lackschicht 6 gelblich fluoreszierende Lackschicht 7 schwarze Linie (Schmutzsc 8 Überzug
Grundierung Probe	Pulver sandfarbig, gelbbraun XRD: Quarz, Calcit, Kalifeldspat	Pulver sandfarbig, gelbbraun visuell: wie I.
Textil/Papier		
Lack		

Objekt	IV. Stellschirm, plast. Dekor, Herzog Anton Ulrich- Museum, Braunschweig, Inv. Nr. Chi 1600, schwarzes Panneau	V. Stellschirm, plast. Dekor, Herzog Anton Ulrich- Museum, Braunschweig Inv. Nr. Chi 1600, rotes Panneau	VI. Encoignure, M. CRIAERD, Paris, Lackmalerei, Graf von und zu Hoensbroech
Lit./Abb.	DIESINGER, G. R.: *Ostasiatische Lackarbeiten,* Kat. d. Slg. des Herzog Anton Ulrich-Museums, Braunschweig 1990, S. 239–240.	DIESINGER 1990, S. 239–240.	PIERT-BORGERS 2000, S. 478–515.
Schliff			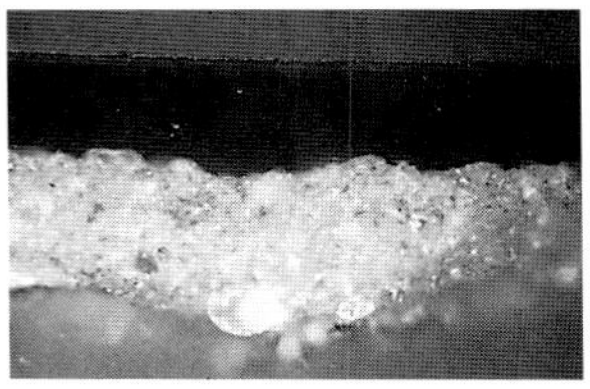
Schliff UV	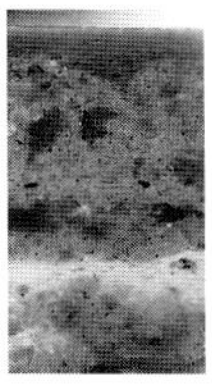	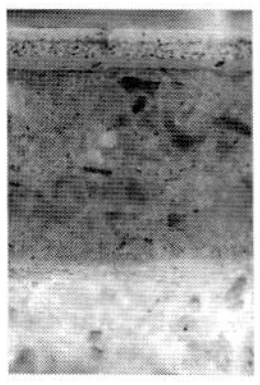	
Grundierungsmaterial/ Schichtenfolge	Steinmehl, rel. große weiße (im UV-Licht schwarze) Einschlüsse	Steinmehl, rel. große weiße (im UV-Licht schwarze) Einschlüsse	Steinmehl, größerer Anteil roter amorpher partikel, entspricht der groben unteren Grundierung von V.
	1 grobe Grundierung dunkelbraun (im UV-Licht hell fluoresz.) asiat. Lack als Bindemittel? 2 Textilauflage, braun (im UV-Licht hell fluoresz.) asiat. Lack im Klebemittel? 3 feinere Grundierung 4 asiat. Lack 5 hell fluoresz. Schicht (neuzeitl. Öllack) 7 feine schwarze Linie, Schmutz Steinmehl, relativ große weiße (im UV-Licht schwarze) Ein- schlüsse	1 grobe Grundierung dunkelbraun (im UV-Licht hell fluoresz.) asiat. Lack als Bindemittel? 2 Textilauflage, braun (im UV-Licht hell fluoresz.) asiat. Lack im Klebemittel? 3 feinere Grundierung 4 schwarze Linie 5 asiat. Lack 6 rot pigment. Lack 7 weiß fluoresz. Lack (Öllack m. Bernstein?) Steinmehl, größerer Anteil roter amorpher Partikel, entspricht der groben unteren Grundierung von V.	1 grobe Grundierungsschicht (im UV-Licht schwarze Partikel) 2 asiat. Lack, helle 3 asiat. Lack mit (durch Lichtein- fluss (?) bedingtes) Oberflächen- craquelé 4 europäischer Glanzlacküberzug
Grundierung Probe	Pulver rotbraun, vereinzelt schwarze Partikel XRD: Quarz, Kalifeldspat PY-GC/MS: Öl, Naturwachs	Pulver rotbraun XRD: Quarz, Kali- und Natronfeldspat PY-GC/MS: Öl, Naturharz	Pulver rotbraun visuell: wie IV
Textil/Papier	Durchlicht-Mikroskop: Ramie REM: Fasern nicht identifizierbar	Durchlicht-Mikroskop: Ramie	Durchlicht-Mikroskop: Ramie
Lack		PY-GC/MS: Öl	PY-GC/MS: *Rhus succedanea*

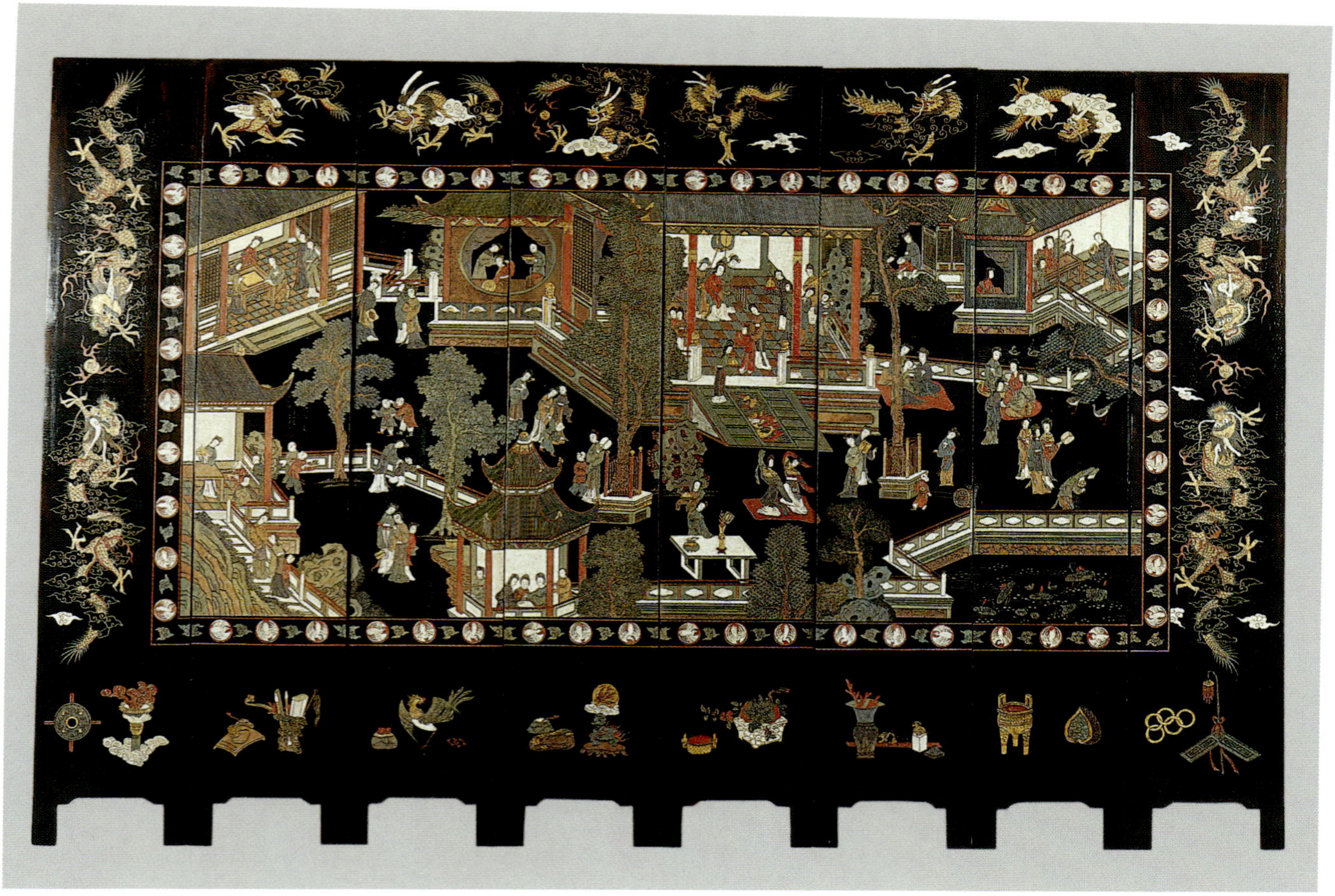

1, 2 Stellschirm, Museum für Lackkunst, Münster, Inv. Nr. AS-CH-a-8, Vorder- und Rückseite

Abb. 7. Kabinettschrank, Koromandellack, China, 17. Jh., geöffnet; ehemaliges Beutegut, Zustand nach Rückführung (Museum für Ostasiatische Kunst, Berlin, Inv. Nr. 6515)

Zur Kreide- bzw. Kalkschicht

Nach Rondot wird die geglättete Sandsteingrundierung mit einer Schicht in Wasser gelöster Kreide überzogen. In einigen Veröffentlichungen wird die Grundierung allgemein als weiße Kreidegrundierung bezeichnet, in die dann der Dekor eingeschnitten worden sei. Brandt nennt als Grundierungsmaterial von Koromandellacken Kreide- oder weißes Schiefermehl.[33] An den uns bekannten Objekten konnte keine weiße Schicht erkannt werden. Selbst beriebene Lackflächen lassen den roten Grund durchscheinen. Wohl finden sich weiße Fassungen unter der farbigen Malschicht. Sie wurden als Bleiweiß identifiziert. Eine der vielen Bezeichnungen für Bleiweiß ist Schieferweiß, wogegen weißes Schiefermehl nicht bekannt ist.

Pigmente

Die Pigmente von Koromandellacken sind nach Wang in Lack oder Öl gebunden,[34] nach Garner ist eher Öl als Bindemittel anzunehmen.[35] Shôno-Sladek nennt Wasserfarben[36] und Brandt Wasserfarben und „mit Leim vermischte" Wasserfarben und Goldpulver.[37] Im Rahmen dieser Vorüberlegungen konnten leider keine Bindemittelanalysen durchgeführt werden. Einige Pigmente wurden von dem Berliner Kabinettschrank (Objekt Nr. I; Abb. 7, 8) entnommen. Hierzu liegen folgende Ergebnisse vor (Tabelle 2):

Abb. 8. Kabinettschrank (wie Abb. 7), geschlossen

Nr.	Probe 1, braun	Probe 2, grün	Probe 3, blau	Probe 4, rot	Probe 5, weiß
Konsistenz	Pulver, vereinzelt Schollen mit der Schichtenfolge: gelbbraun, weiß, rotbraun	Pulver, hellgrün, durchscheinend	Pulver, vereinzelt Schollen mit der Schichtenfolge: dunkelblau über gelbbraun	Pulver, vereinzelt Schollen mit der Schichtenfolge: rotbraun über gelbbraun	Pulver, gelb bis braun und weiß
XRD	Bleiweiß, Quarz	keine auswertbaren Reflexe	basisches Bleicarbonat (Bleiweiß), Bleicarbonat Quarz	Quarz	Bleiweiß, Quarz
EDX	nur rotbraune Schicht: Blei, Aluminium, Silicium, eine Spur Calcium	Aluminium, Silicium, Blei, Calcium, Kupfer	Silicium, Blei, Spuren von Kalium, Calcium, Eisen, Cobalt	Blei, Calcium, Aluminium Silicium, eine Spur Kalium	vorw. Blei, weniger Silicium u. Calcium, Spuren von Aluminium und Kalium
IR		gute Übereinstimmung mit Kupferresinat-Vergleichsspektrum			

Tabelle 2. Proben der Farbfassung von Objekt I

Proben der Farbfassung von Objekt I

Zur Probenentnahme

Die Probenentnahme für die Untersuchung erfolgte als Schabeprobe in mehreren Schichten. Dies hatte zur Folge, dass Fasern unter dem Rasterelektronenmikroskop nicht identifiziert werden konnten. Asiatischer Lack wurde außer beim Objekt VI als Lackschicht nicht nachgewiesen. Die Ursache dafür kann in der zu geringen Menge des zur Verfügung stehenden Materials liegen, oder mit dem alterungsbedingten Abbau des Lackanteils zusammenhängen. Die Analysen der Schabeproben von Objekt IV und V durch T. Miyakoshi (Gaschromatographie/Massenspektrometrie) ergaben für die Grundierung und den roten Lack Ölanteile, für die Grundierungsschichten Anteile von natürlichem Harz bzw. Wachs (s. Tabelle 1).

Schlussbemerkung

Der vorläufige Charakter der hier vorgelegten Voruntersuchungen und die noch rudimentären Ergebnisse lassen es sinnvoll erscheinen, die in westlichen Sammlungen und Schlössern überlieferten Koromandellacke in einem systematisch angelegten Projekt unter Berücksichtigung verwandter Lackobjekte mit plastischen und gemalten Dekoren einer eingehenden Analyse zu unterziehen. Dieses Projekt müsste Untersuchungen in folgenden Bereichen einschließen:

- Bestimmung der Holzträger
- Untersuchung der Papier/Textilauflagen
- Analyse der Grundierungsmaterialien und Bindemittel
- Analyse der Lackschichten (Spezies des Lacks, Zuschläge)
- Untersuchung der Verarbeitungstechnologie
- Pigmentanalysen
- Erstellung von Musterbrettern.

Neben diese naturwissenschaftlich und technologisch ausgerichteten Untersuchungen müssten kunsthistorische und quellenkundliche Studien treten, die auch chinesische Sprachkenntnisse erfordern, um Inschriften auf den Objekten und auf deren Herstellungstechnik bezogene Quellen auswerten zu können. Eine Zusammenarbeit mit chinesischen Fachkollegen wäre wünschenswert. In der praktischen Restaurierungsarbeit erfahrbare Übereinstimmungen des technologischen Aufbaus des Lackgrundes chinesischer Lackstellschirme und die dabei ebenfalls beobachteten Differenzen zu japanischen Techniken könnten durch solche Analysen auf der Grundlage einer größeren Anzahl von Proben und Untersuchungen objektiviert werden.

Da diese Voruberlegungen als Anregung zu weiterer Forschung einem größeren Kreis von Fachkollegen im Rahmen einer Publikation der vom Bayerischen Landesamt für Denkmalpflege veranstalteten Lacktagung erreichen sollten, musste aus Zeitgründen auf eine Untersuchung von weiteren (u. U. an lichtgeschützten Stellen entnommenen) Proben verzichtet werden. Die Lackuntersuchungen von Prof. Tetsuo Miyakoshi sind noch nicht vollständig abgeschlossen.

Danksagung

Marie Therese Worch vom Bayerischen Landesamt für Denkmalpflege ist die Identifizierung der Ramie-Fasern zu danken. Die Analysen der Grundierungsmaterialien und der Pigmente wurden von Martin Mach und Christian Gruber, Bayerisches Landesamt für Denkmalpflege, durchgeführt. Beim Fotografieren der Querschliffe halfen Christa Steinbüchel und Birgit Wessel, Restauratorinnen am Wallraf-Richartz-Museum/Museum Ludwig in Köln.
Prof. Tetsuo Miyakoshi, Department of Industrial Chemistry, Meiji University Kawasaki, sind die GC/MS-Analysen zu danken.

Für ihre Bereitschaft, Objekte für die Untersuchungen zur Verfügung zu stellen, danke ich:
Godehard Graf von und zu Hoensbroech
Dr. Monika Kopplin, BASF Museum für Lackkunst, Münster
Dr. Regine Marth, Herzog Anton Ulrich-Museum, Braunschweig
Dr. Adele Schlombs und Lukas Krämer, Museum für Ostasiatische Kunst, Köln
Prof. Dr. Willibald Veit und Dr. Herbert Butz, Museum für Ostasiatische Kunst, Berlin.
Dr. Michael Kühlenthal, Bayerisches Landesamt für Denkmalpflege, sei für die Förderung dieser Vorüberlegungen gedankt.

Anmerkungen

1 Piert-Borgers 2000, S. 478–515.
2 Dittrich 1970, S. 1–8, T. I–VII.
3 Rondot 1848, S. 43–44.
4 Bei der Untersuchung eines chinesischen Stellschirms aus Schloss Wilhelmsthal und bei der Beschreibung der Technologie kantonesischer Goldlacke wird bei Breidenstein (vgl. Breidenstein 2000, S. 563–565) vorwiegend auf d'Incarville zurückgegriffen. Garner weist allerdings daraufhin, dass es sich bei d'Incarvilles Beschreibungen der Details der Herstellungstechniken um Informationen aus zweiter Hand handelt, die er von den präzisen Informationen des Botanikers selbst abhebt, da sie durchaus einige Unsicherheiten enthalten. Vgl. Garner 1979, S. 21. D'Incarville seinerseits hat die Seriosität seines christianisierten chinesischen Informanten, dessen Beichtvater er war, betont. Vgl. d'Incarville 1767, S. 128.
5 Rondot 1848, S. 43.
6 Vgl. Garner 1979, S. 260.
7 Vgl. Belevitch-Stankevitch 1910, Reprint 1970, S. 137–138.
8 Livre Journal de Lazare Duvaux, marchand-bijoutier ordinaire du roy. Neudruck, Paris 1965, zit. nach Mayer 1990/91, S. 15 f.
9 Vgl. Garner 1979, S. 260. Garner verweist auf Séguy 1922, wo der Begriff in der Einleitung als „sanctioned by use and of commercial origin" bezeichnet werde.
10 Jacquemart 1859, S. 210 ff. u. VI, 1860, S. 3 ff.
11 Huang 1625. Neuausgabe und Vorwort von Wang Shixiang, Peking 1959.
12 Zit. nach Mayer 1990/91, S. 1.
13 Huh 1993, S. 208.
14 Mayer 1990/91, S. 2 u. S. 58.
15 Huh 1993, S. 208.
16 Lee 1972, S. 364.
17 Vgl. Wang 1986, S. 316.
18 Hornby 1985, S. 102.
19 Vgl. Wülfert 1999, S. 278.
20 Vgl. Garner 1979, S. 34.
21 Vgl. Rein 1886, S. 424. Rein z. B. spricht vom Material der Textilauflage als Ramie, in der Beschreibung des Arbeitsablaufs vom Aufkleben der Leinwand.
22 Vgl. Gray 1955, S. 50.
23 Mänchen-Helfen 1937, S. 215.
24 d'Incarville 1767, S. 122.
25 Vgl. Burmester 1985, S. 174.
26 Vgl. Burmester 1985, Nr. 22, S. 182 und den Querschliff auf S. 171.
27 Nach Ansicht von Monika Kopplin handelt es sich bei dem Stellschirm des Museums für Lackkunst wohl um eine Arbeit des 19. Jh. im Stil der Kangxi-Zeit.
28 Okada 1995, S. 3–8.
29 Vgl. Strahan 1993, S. 112 f.
30 Vgl. Garner 1979, S. 23.
31 Wang (ed.) 1983, S. 44. zit. nach Strahan 1993, S. 111.
32 Miklin-Kniefacz 1995, S. 23.
33 Brandt 1988, S. 24.
34 Wang 1986, S. 316.
35 Garner 1979, S. 259.
36 Shôno-Sladek 1994, S. 101.
37 Brandt 1988, S. 26.

Literaturverzeichnis

Belevitch-Stankevitch, H.: *Le goût chinois en France au temps de Louis XIV*, Paris 1910, Reprint 1970

Brandt, Klaus Joachim: *Chinesische Lackarbeiten,* Ausst. Kat. Linden-Museum Stuttgart, Stuttgart 1988

Breidenstein, Irmela: *Konzeptionelle Überlegungen zur Restaurierung eines chinesischen Lackparavents (Considerations Regarding the Restoration of a Chinese Lacquer Screen),* in: Japanische und europäische Lackarbeiten/Japanese and European Lacquerware, München 2000, S. 561–585 (Arbeitshefte des Bayerischen Landesamtes für Denkmalpflege, Bd. 96)

Burmester, Andreas: *Technical Studies of Chinese Lacquer*, in: Bromelle, N.S./Smith, Perry (ed.): Urushi. Proceedings of the Urushi Study Group June 10–27, 1985, Tokyo, Tokio 1988, S. 163–188

Dittrich, Edith: *Ein chinesischer Geburtstagsparavent aus dem 17. Jahrhundert im Museum für Ostasiatische Kunst in Köln,* in: Festschrift für Heinz Ladendorf, Köln 1970, S. 1–8

Garner, Sir Harry: *Chinese Lacquer*, London/Boston 1979

Gray, B.: *The Eumorfopoulos Lacquer Toilet Box and Blue Tang Horse*, in: British Museum Quarterly, vol. XIV, London 1955, S. 49–53

Hornby, Joan: *Koromandellack*, in: Europa und die Kaiser von China 1240–1816, Ausst. Kat. Berliner Festspiele, Horizonte 85, Frankfurt/M. 1985, S. 102–104

Huang, Cheng: *Xiushilu Jieshuo (Account of Decoration of Lacquer)* mit einem Vorwort und Kommentaren von Yang Ming, 1625, Neuausgabe und Vorwort von Wang, Shixiang, Peking 1959

Huh, Shih-chang: *Screen, black lacquer with* kuancai, *dated 1673,* in: Peter Y.K Lam (Hrsg.): 2000 Years of Chinese Lacquerware, Hong Kong 1993, S. 208–211

d'Incarville: *Abhandlung von dem chinesischen Lacke,* in: Allgemeines Magazin der Natur, Kunst und Wissenschaften, zwölfter und letzter Theil, Leipzig 1767, S. 109–143

Jacquemart, Albert: *Les Lacques,* in: Gazette de Beaux Arts IV, 1859, S. 210 ff., 1860, S. 3 ff.

Lee, Yu-kuan: *Oriental Lacquer Art,* Tokio 1972

Mänchen-Helfen, Otto: *Materialien zur Geschichte des chinesischen Lacks,* in: Ostasiatische Zeitschrift 13/1937, S. 215–222

Mayer, Martina: *Koromandellacke (kuancaiqi). Überblick über den bisherigen Stand der Forschung und Untersuchungen zu ausgewählten figürlichen Motiven*, Magister-Arbeit an der Philosophisch-Historischen Fakultät der Ruprecht-Karls-Universität Heidelberg, WS 1990/91

Miklin-Kniefacz, Silvia: *Lacktafel aus dem Vieux-Lacque-Zimmer, Schloss Schönbrunn, Musterrestaurierung Juli '93,* in: Zur Restaurierung der Vieux-Lacque-Tafeln in Schönbrunn. Grundlagen und Vorarbeiten, Schönbrunn 1995, S. 22–31

Okada, Fumio: *Kodai shutsudo shikki no kenkyu (Studium von ausgegrabenen Lackwaren des Altertums). Kenbikyo de saguru zaishitsu to gihô (Mikroskopische Untersuchungen von Material und Technik),* Tokio 1995

Piert-Borgers, Barbara: *Ostasiatische Lackarbeiten an französischen Möbeln (East Asian Lacquerwork on French Furniture),* in: Japanische und europäische Lackarbeiten/Japanese and European Lacquerware, München 2000, S. 478–515 (Arbeitshefte des Bayerischen Landesamtes für Denkmalpflege, Bd. 96)

Rein, J. J.: *Japan nach Reisen und Studien*, Bd. 2, 1886

RONDOT, NATALIS: *Une promenade dans Canton. La manufacture de laques d'Hip-Qua et l'atelier de tabletterie de Ta-Yu-Tong,* in: Journal Asiatique XI/1848, S. 34–64
SÉGUY, E. A.: *Les Lacques de Coromandel*, Paris o. J. (1922)
SHÔNO-SLADEK, MASAKO: *Der Glanz des Urushi (The Splendour of Urushi). Die Sammlung des Museums für Ostasiatische Kunst der Stadt Köln,* Köln 1994
STRAHAN, DONNA K.: *The Walters Chinese Wood-and-Lacquer Buddha: A Technical Study,* in: The Journal of the Walters Gallery, H. 51, 1993, S. 103–120
WANG, SHIXIANG: *Classic Chinese Furniture,* London 1986
WANG, SHIXIANG (ed.): *Xiushilu Jieshuo*, Peking 1983
WÜLFERT, STEPHAN: *Der Blick ins Bild. Lichtmikroskopische Methoden zur Untersuchung von Bildaufbau, Fasern und Pigmenten,* Ravensburg 1999

Abbildungsnachweis

Abb. 1–3: Rheinisches Bildarchiv, Köln
Abb. 5 und Aufnahmen der Schliffe zu Objekt VI (Tabelle 1): Katharina Walch, Bayerisches Landesamt für Denkmalpflege, München
Abb. 7, 8: Prof. Dr. Willibald Veit, Museum für Ostasiatische Kunst, Berlin
Farbtafeln IX–XII: Museum für Ostasiatische Kunst, Köln, Inv.-Nr. E1, Aufnahmen: Rainer Gärtner, Köln
Farbtafel XIII: Museum für Lackkunst, Münster, Inv.-Nr. AS-CH-a-8
Alle übrigen Aufnahmen von der Verfasserin

Summary

The article presents some preliminary results of examinations of Chinese Coromandel lacquer and other related objects. After an insight into the history of the different terms used for Coromandel lacquers in western languages and in Chinese is provided, the article compares descriptions of the priming (ground layers, cloth and paper) in historical sources with results of published investigations. Cross sections taken from five objects (three Coromandel screens, a screen with raised decoration and a painted Chinese lacquer taken from a French encoignure of the middle of the 18th century) were examined by reflected light and ultraviolet light microscopy. The XRD- and EDX-examinations of the ground layers and of the pigments of the polychrome painting of one object are presented in tabulated form.

The article is understood as a preparatory study for a project that should be based on data from a broader variety of objects and should also try to include art historical expertise, especially on dated objects, and results of the investigations of Chinese colleagues. The assumption that certain types of Coromandel and related lacquers were produced in South China may be backed by these investigations.

Yukio Kamiya, Tetsuo Miyakoshi

The Analysis of Urushi by Pyrolysis-Gas Chromatography and Mass Spectrometry

1. Introduction

The identification of oriental lacquer types in ancient coatings is very important for conservation and restoration studies. Therefore, various examples of ancient lacquerware were analyzed by means of pyrolysis-gas chromatography and mass spectrometry, and the results were compared with the characteristics of natural lacquer films.

Oriental lacquer is produced from the sap of the lacquer tree, specifically *Rhus vernicifera* in Japan and China, *Rhus succedanea* in Vietnam and Taiwan and *Melanorrhoea usitata* in Thailand and Burma. The saps are mainly used as a surface coating for wood, porcelain and metalware in Asian countries. The sap of *Rhus vernicifera* is a water/oil type emulsion. The oily portion consists of about 60 % urushiol. The sap consists of about 30 % water, about 10 % water soluble plant gum, such as mono-, oligo-, and polysaccharides, and water-insoluble glycoproteins as shown in table 1. The sap also contains small amounts of enzymes such as peroxidase and stellacyanin, but most important, *Rhus laccase*.

To prepare the lacquer sap for the actual coating material, the sap is stirred in an open vessel at room temperature for about one or two hours until the water content is reduced to about 2 %. The temperature cycle must be carefully controlled in order to retain the activity of the enzymes. At this point the sap has become clear, has changed in color, and has increased in viscosity. The resultant liquid, known as *Kurome* lacquer, consists of urushiol, oligo urushiol, and a small amount of water, and is ready for application. The unprocessed sap is sometimes used as the base coat of the substrate and the treated sap *(Kurome urushi)* is applied as the top coat. The lacquer is now applied to the substrate, dried for one day at 20 °C and at a relative humidity of 70 %. The curing of the urushiol is due to oxidation of the urushiol and other components of the raw lacquer by the enzymes present in the sap. Laccase is the most important enzyme for the polymerization of urushiol.

Table 1. Constituents of the sap from *Rhus vernicifera*

Component	Content (%)
Urushiol	55-65
Glycoproteins	2-3
Polysaccharides	5-7
Laccase	< 0.1
Water	20-30

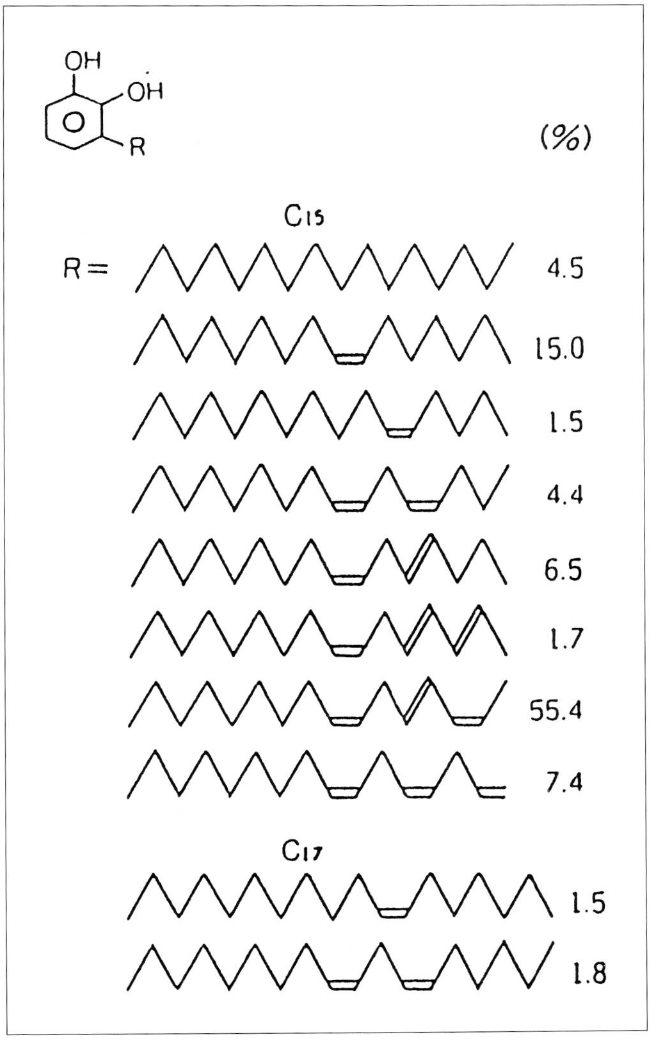

Fig. 1. Constituents of urushiol

Urushiol from *Rhus vernicifera* consists of about 60–70 % of a mixture of catechol substituted in the 3-position with a C-15 hydrocarbon side chain. About 60 % are trienes, about 20 % are monoenes and some dienes are also present as shown in figure 1. The average number of olefins in the side chain of urushiol is 2–2.5. The composition of the urushiol may vary depending on the growing conditions of the lacquer tree and on variations in the seasons. Constituents of the Japanese and Chinese lacquer urushiols appear to be the same. The major constituents of *Rhus vernicifera* are the olefinic isomers, which are the important constituents for the high degree of polymerization of urushiol by the action of *Rhus laccase* in the film-making process or drying process from the sap or lacquer.

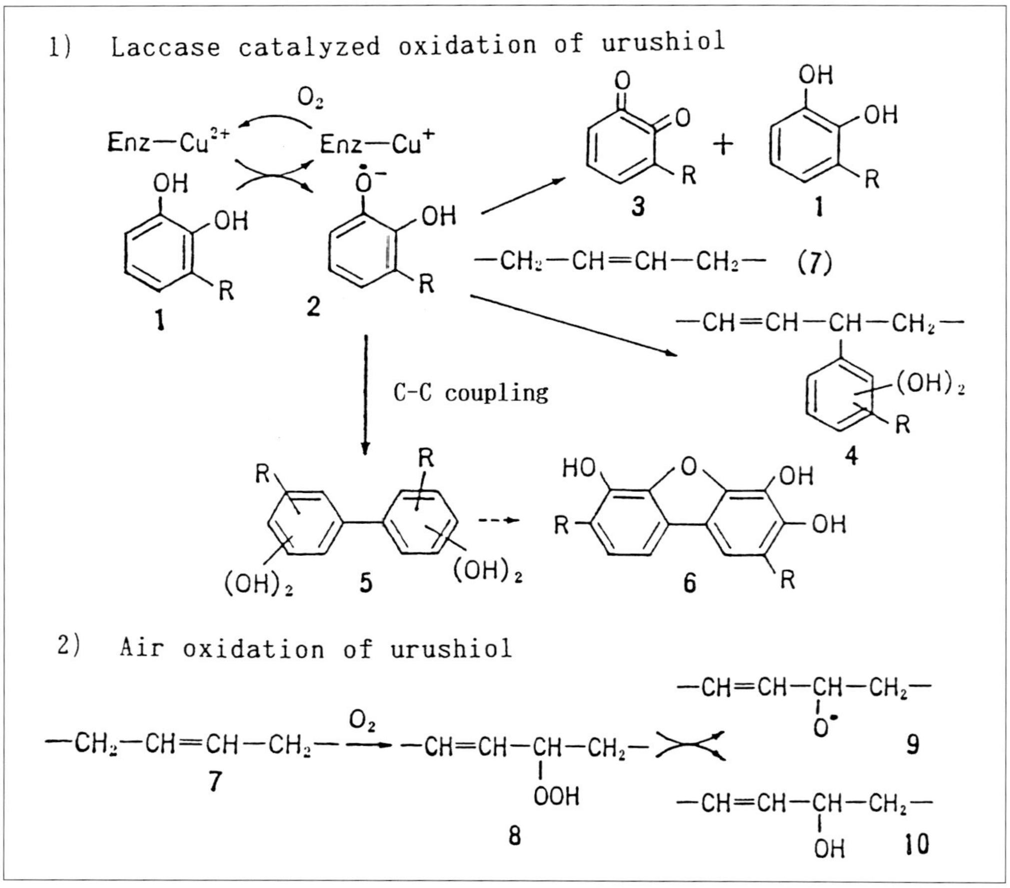

Fig. 2. Polymerization mechanisms of urushiol

Fig. 3. Constituents of phenolic lipids in the sap from Asian lacquer

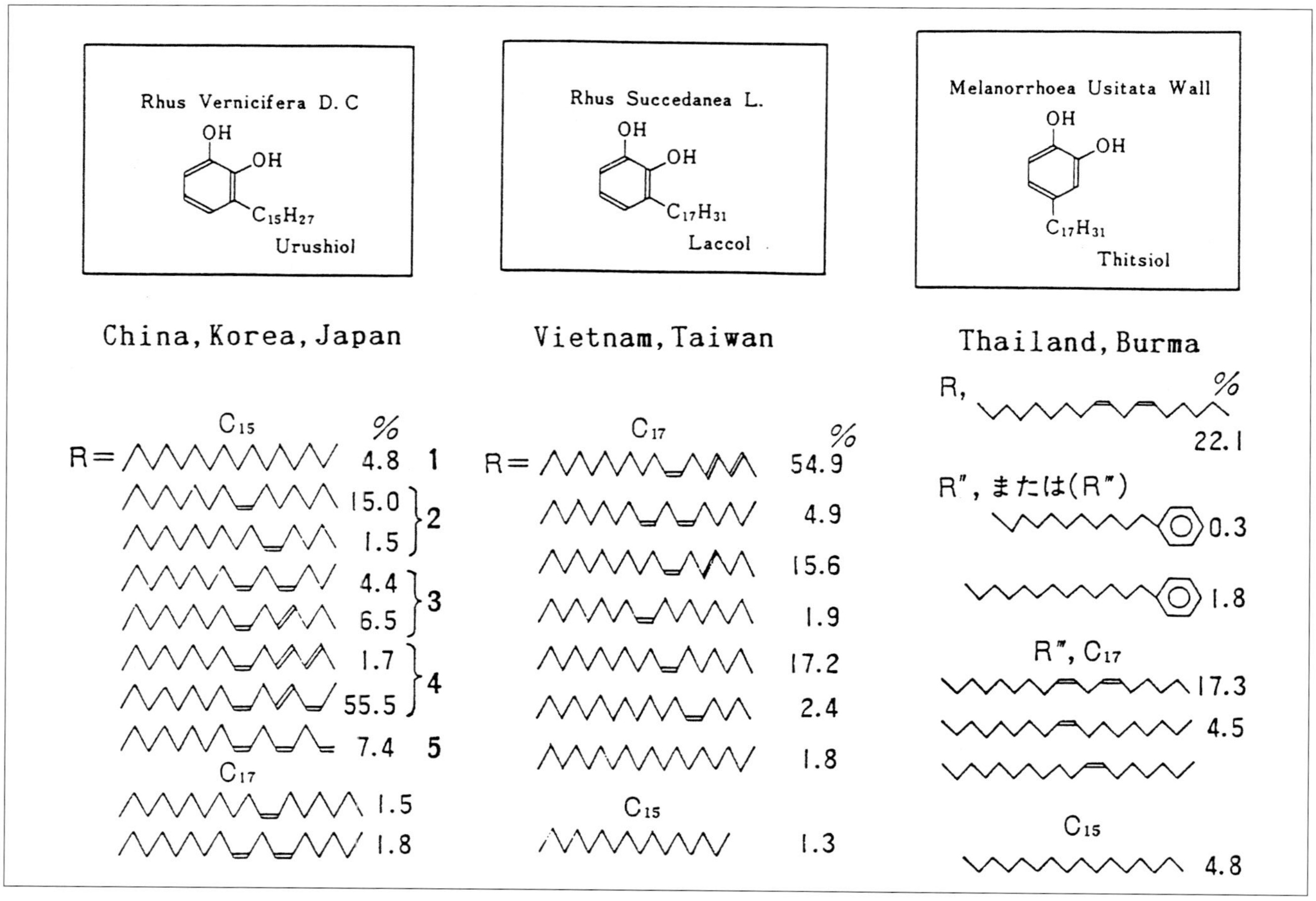

The dimerization of urushiol proceeds through the laccase-catalyzed C-C and C-O coupling reactions. The detailed mechanism has been reported by Professor Kumanotani. The reaction scheme for the laccase-catalyzed oxidation and air oxidation of urushiol is shown in figure 2. The polymerization probably proceeds through these types of couplings. Finally, a tough and brilliant film is produced.

As already indicated, there are three kinds of oriental lacquers: *Rhus vernicifera* from Japan and China, *Rhus succedanea* from Vietnam and Taiwan, and *Melanorrhoea usitata* from Thailand and Burma as shown in figure 3. The saps of the oriental lacquer latex are composed of phenol derivatives, water, plant gum, glycoprotein, and the laccase enzyme. The phenol derivatives of the *Rhus vernicifera* lacquer are urushiol, those of the *Rhus succedanea* lacquer are laccol, and those of the *Melanorrhoea usitata* lacquer are thitsiol.

Although chemists usually use chemical symbols and chemical formulas to represent chemical structures, chemical equations and chemical reaction schemes, these formulas are generally too complicated for conference presentation such as this, which are attended by researchers from various fields.

The formulation of the structure was developed for us in 1865 by the German chemist August Kekulé. He dreamt of a snake that was curled in a circle and bit its tail. Applying the image in his dream to the structure of benzene, he proposed that benzene had a cyclic structure, with the ends of the chain bending around to form a hexagon (scheme 1).

In Japan, the benzene ring is often represented by a turtle shell. The patterns on turtle shells look like benzene rings. An old Japanese proverb says that 'a crane lives a thousand years, and a turtle lives ten thousand years.' Both animals are symbols for long life. Similarly, lacquer has been used for more than 5000 years in Asia. In the Shosoin temple in Japan, a great number of cultural treasures that are coated with oriental lacquer are exhibited, which have all been preserved for more than a thousand years without having lost their original elegance and beauty.

In this paper we will use the sketch of a turtle instead of the chemical formula of the benzene ring. Urushiol is a benzene derivative with two hydroxyl groups and a long side chain. Urushiol of a white turtle has two special hands for the two hydroxyl groups and a long tail for the side chain as shown in scheme 2. The molecular weight of urushiol is 320, which is the weight of the turtle. The length of the long tail for the side chain is carbon 15. The unsaturated side chain and two hydroxyl groups have a very high oxidative reactivity. They are involved in the enzymic and air oxidative polymerization. A turtle forms a double bond by grasping the tail of another turtle using his hand. The C-C double bond at the tail of the turtle is easily caught by other turtles. The polymerization of urushi is represented by several turtles linked together, hand in hand or tail in hand (scheme 3). The striped turtle represents laccol that has two special hands for hydroxyl groups and a long tail for the side chain. The molecular weight of laccol is 348, which is the weight of the striped turtle. The length of the long tail for the side chain is carbon 17. The dotted turtle represents thitsiol and has two special hands for the hydroxyl groups and a long tail for the side chain. The molecular weight of thitsiol is 348, which is the weight of the dotted turtle. The length of the long tail is carbon 17, and it winds around the side (scheme 4).

Urushi films are a cross-linked polymer. Because the lacquer film is insoluble in most solvents, it has only been analyzed

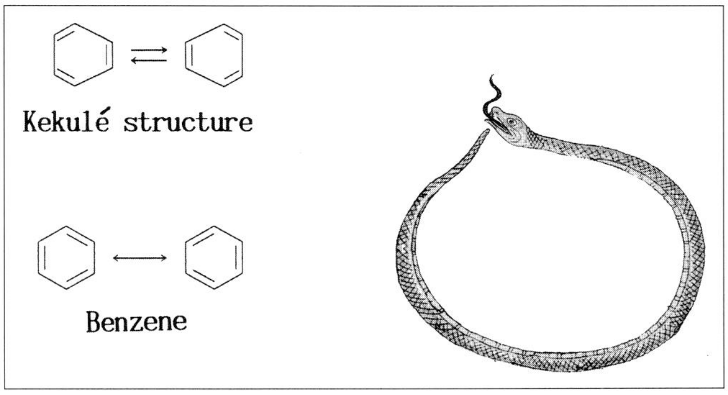

Scheme 1. Benzene structures

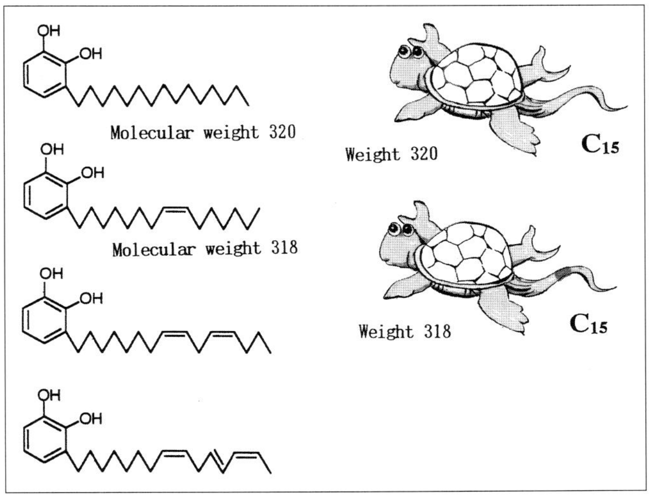

Scheme 2. Urushiol structures

Scheme 3. Polymerization of urushiol

Scheme 4. The typical phenolic lipid of oriental lacquer saps

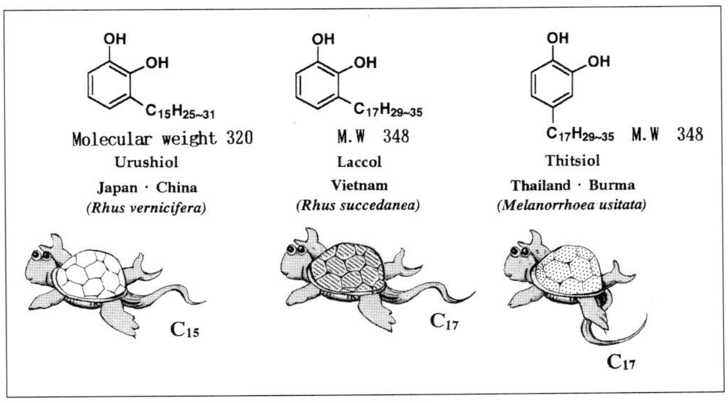

using solid-state methods. However, most of these conventional techniques are time-consuming, demand large amount of sample and frequently require several pretreatments. The pyrolysis-gas chromatography and mass spectrometry method is effective for analyzing the lacquer film, because this method can distinguish between the pyrolysis products of the lacquer samples.

2. Experiment

2.1 Instruments

Pyrolysis-gas chromatography and mass spectrometry measurements were carried out using a vertical micro furnace-type pyrolyzer PY-2010D, HP 6890 gas chromatograph and HP 5972A mass spectrometer as shown in figure 4. A stainless steel capillary column coated with methylsilicon was used for the separation. The sample was placed in a platinum sample cup. The cup was set on top of the sample. It was pyrolyzed near ambient temperature. The sample cup was introduced into the furnace at 500 °C, then the temperature program of the gas chromatograph oven was started. The gas chromatograph oven was programmed to provide a constant temperature increase of 20 °C per min from 40–280 °C, then held for 10 min. All pyrolysis products were identified by mass spectrometry. The mass spectrometer ionization energy was 70eV (EI-MS).

2.2 Materials

Rhus vernicifera lacquer sap from Japan, *Rhus succedanea* lacquer sap from Vietnam and *Melanorrhoea usitata* lacquer sap from Burma were treated using the traditional Nayashi and Kurome methods, and coated on glass plates followed by hardening in a humidity controlled chamber with a RH of 70–90 % at 20 °C for 12 hrs. The respective lacquer films were then removed from the chamber and stored for 3 years.

The ancient lacquer film was obtained from the surface of a wooden dish, which was excavated from layers dating back to the 17–18th century A. D. at the Kinenkanmae iseki on our university campus in the Tokyo prefecture of Japan. A *namban* lacquer film from the 17th century A. D. and an old lacquer film exported from an Asian country during the 17–18th century A. D. were obtained from the surface of the wooden crafts.

The Rococo lacquer film was obtained from the wooden surface of the Rococo Church St. Alto in Altomunster, near Munich, Germany.

3. Results and Discussion

3.1 Pyrolysis-gas chromatography and mass spectrometry of Rhus vernicifera *and* Rhus succedanea *lacquer films*

Rhus vernicifera and *Rhus succedanea* lacquer films were pyrolyzed at 500 °C. The total ion chromatogram (TIC) and mass chromatogram (m/z 320) of the *Rhus vernicifera* lacquer are shown in figure 5. Peak u-1 was identified as the urushiol (MW 320) based on the mass spectrum. The white turtle representing urushiol is found in the pyrolysis products. The TIC and mass chromatogram of m/z 320 and 348 from the *Rhus succedanea* lacquer film are shown in figure 6. Peak l-1 was identified as a striped turtle for laccol (MW 348) by the mass spectrum. Laccol is a typical component of Vietnamese lacquer.

Urushiol (MW 320) was detected in both the *Rhus vernicifera* and the *Rhus succedanea* lacquer films. In contrast, laccol (MW 348) was detected only in the *Rhus succedanea* lacquer film. The pyrolysis products clearly show a good correlation with the constituents of the respective lacquer saps.

Alkylcatechols and alkylphenols are mainly observed as the thermally decomposed components from the terminal alkylcatechol-side chains of the lacquer films. Based on the results for these two specimen, it was possible to differentiate between the species.

Alkylcatechols were detected in the mass chromatograms (m/z 123) at 500 °C of the *Rhus vernicifera* and *Rhus succedanea* lacquer films as shown in figure 7. The alkylcatechols that have the longest side chain are the pentadecylcatechols in the *Rhus vernicifera* lacquer film, whereas those in the *Rhus succedanea* lacquer film are heptadecylcatechols. In addition,

Fig. 4. Analytical system of pyrolysis-gas chromatography and mass spectrometry. 1: Pyrolyzer, 2: Gas chromatograph, 3: Mass spectrometer

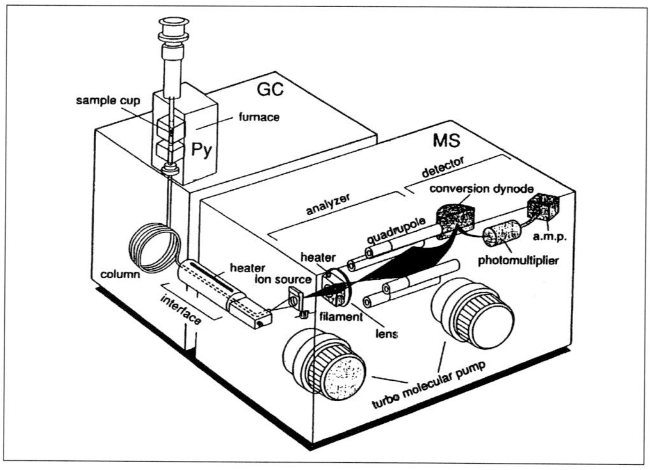

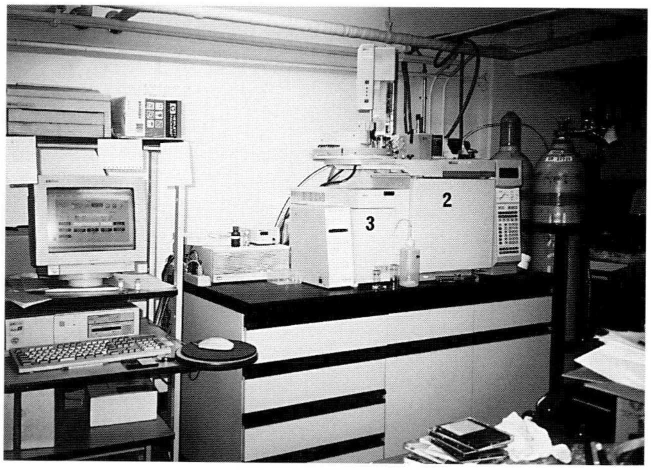

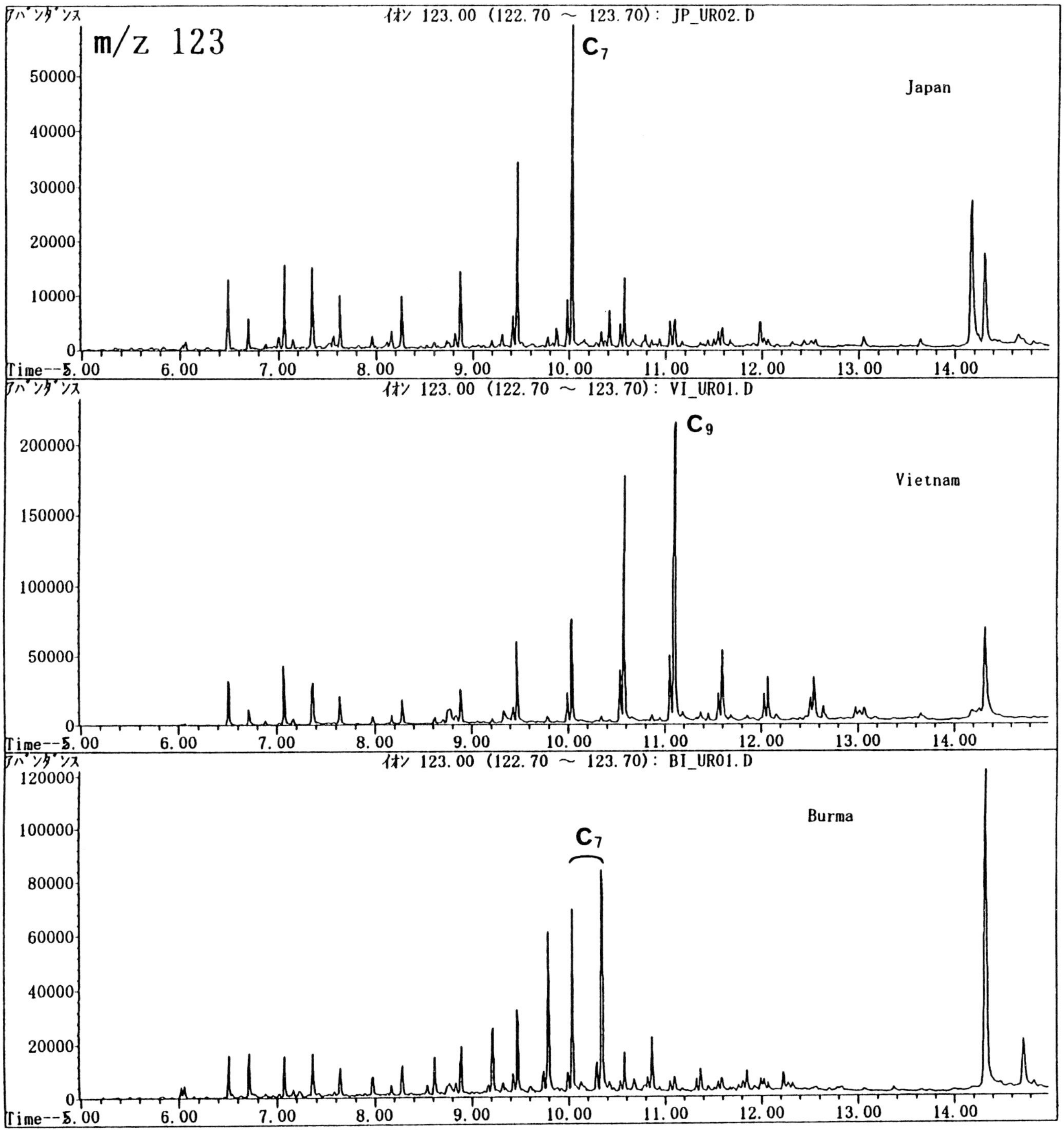

Fig. 7. Mass (m/z 123) chromatograms of lacquer films
Japan C_7 = 3-heptylcatechol; Vietnam C_9 = 3-nonylcatechol; Burma C_7 = 3- and 4-heptylcatechol

alkylphenols using pyrolysis-gas chromatography and mass spectrometry.

3.2 Pyrolysis-gas chromatography and mass spectrometry of Melanorrhoea usitata *lacquer films*

Melanorrhoea usitata is a lacquer tree planted in Thailand and Burma. The sap of *Melanorrhoea usitata* is a latex composed of thitsiol, water, plant gum, glycoprotein and laccase enzyme. The *Melanorrhoea usitata* lacquer sap contains 3- and 4-heptadecadienylcatechols, as well as a series of ω-phenylalkylcatechols.

The *Melanorrhoea usitata* lacquer film was pyrolized at 500 °C. Figure 9 shows the TIC and the individual mass chromatograms at m/z 346, 348, 310, 326, 338 and 354. Peaks 1, 2, 3, 4, 5 and 6 of the mass chromatograms were identified as being due to 4-heptadecenylcatechol (MW 346), 4-heptadecenylcatechol (MW 348), 3-(10-phenyldecyl)phenol (MW 310), 3-(10-phenyldecyl)catechol (MW 326), 4-(10-phenyldodecyl) phenol (MW 338) and 4-(12-phenyldodecyl)catechol (MW 354), respectively, based on the mass spectra. Since the C-O coupling

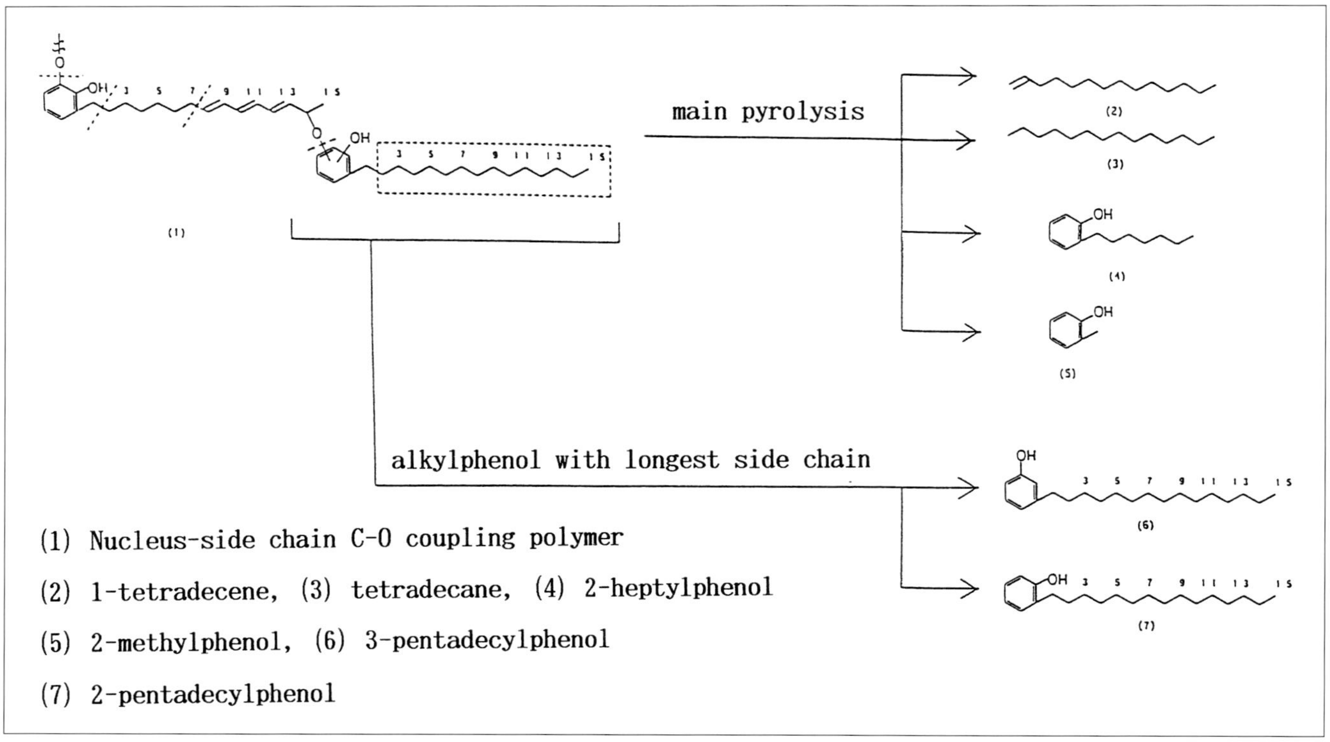

Fig. 8. Pyrolysis mechanisms of urushiol polymer

Fig. 9. Mass (m/z 108) chromatogram of lacquer films

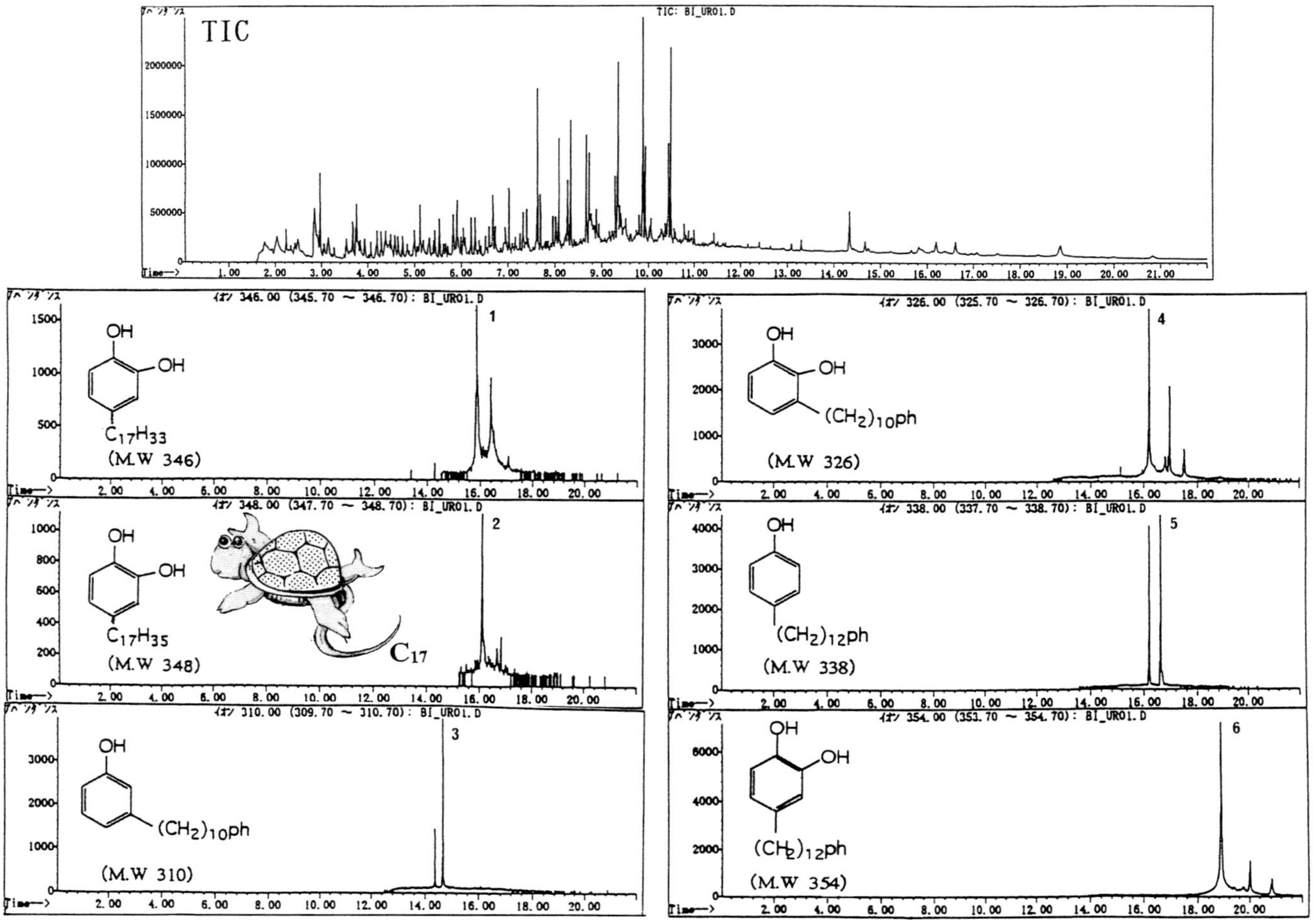

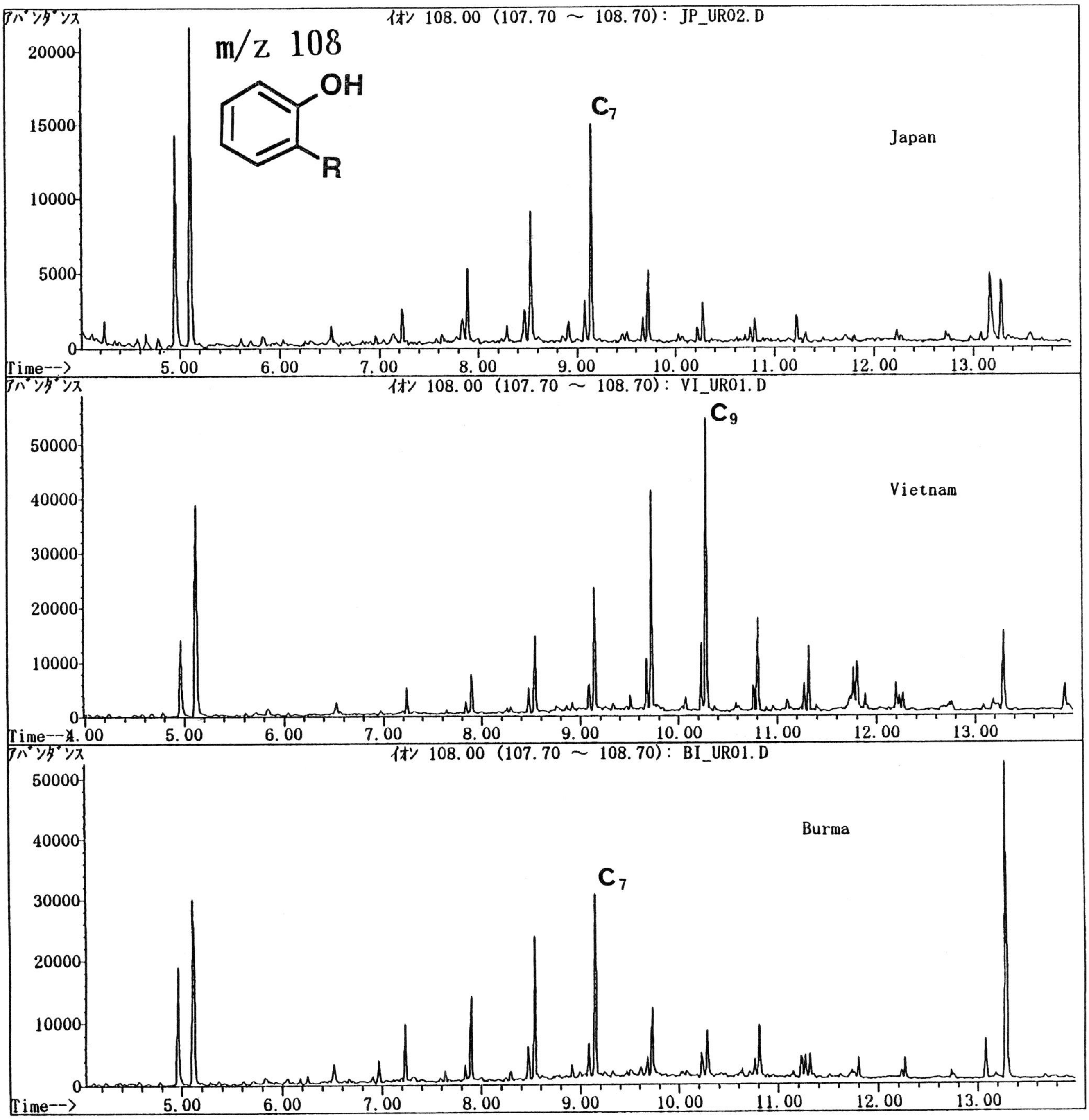

Fig. 10. TIC, mass (m/z 346, 348, 310, 326, 338 and 354) chromatograms of *Melanorrhoea usitata* lacquer film
Japan C_7 = 2-heptylphenol; Vietnam C_9 = 2-nonylphenol; Burma C_7 = 3- and 4-heptylphenol

polymers should be terminated with ω-phenylalkylcatechols, these compounds can be formed from such terminal groups. The molecular weight of laccol is 348, which is the weight of the dotted turtle with the long C 17 tail, that winds around one side.

As shown in figure 7, the peak pairs of the 3- and 4-alkylcatechols were detected in the mass chromatograms (m/z 123) at 500 °C of the *Melanorrhoea usitata* lacquer films. The relative intensity of the 3- and 4-heptylcatechols (C7) is the highest in the pyrolysis products of Burmese lacquer. The highest yield of the 3- and 4-heptylcatechols is thought to be mainly due to cleavage at the α-position of the double bonds of the nucleus-8th and 12th chain C-O coupling for the thitsiol polymers. The detected alkylphenols are likely to be the pyrolysis products of the nucleus-side chain C-O coupling the thitsiol polymers. The dimerization of the lacquer monomers is thought to proceed through the laccase-catalyzed nucleus-side chain C-O coupling as well as the C-C coupling. The yields of the 2- and 3-heptylphenols (C7) are the highest as shown in figure 10. The α- and β-positions of the double bonds of the olefin are susceptible to thermal cleavage so that these highest yields are thought to be primarily produced due to cleavage at the α-position of the double bonds of thitsiol such as the 3- and 4-(heptadeca-8,11-dienyl)catechols.

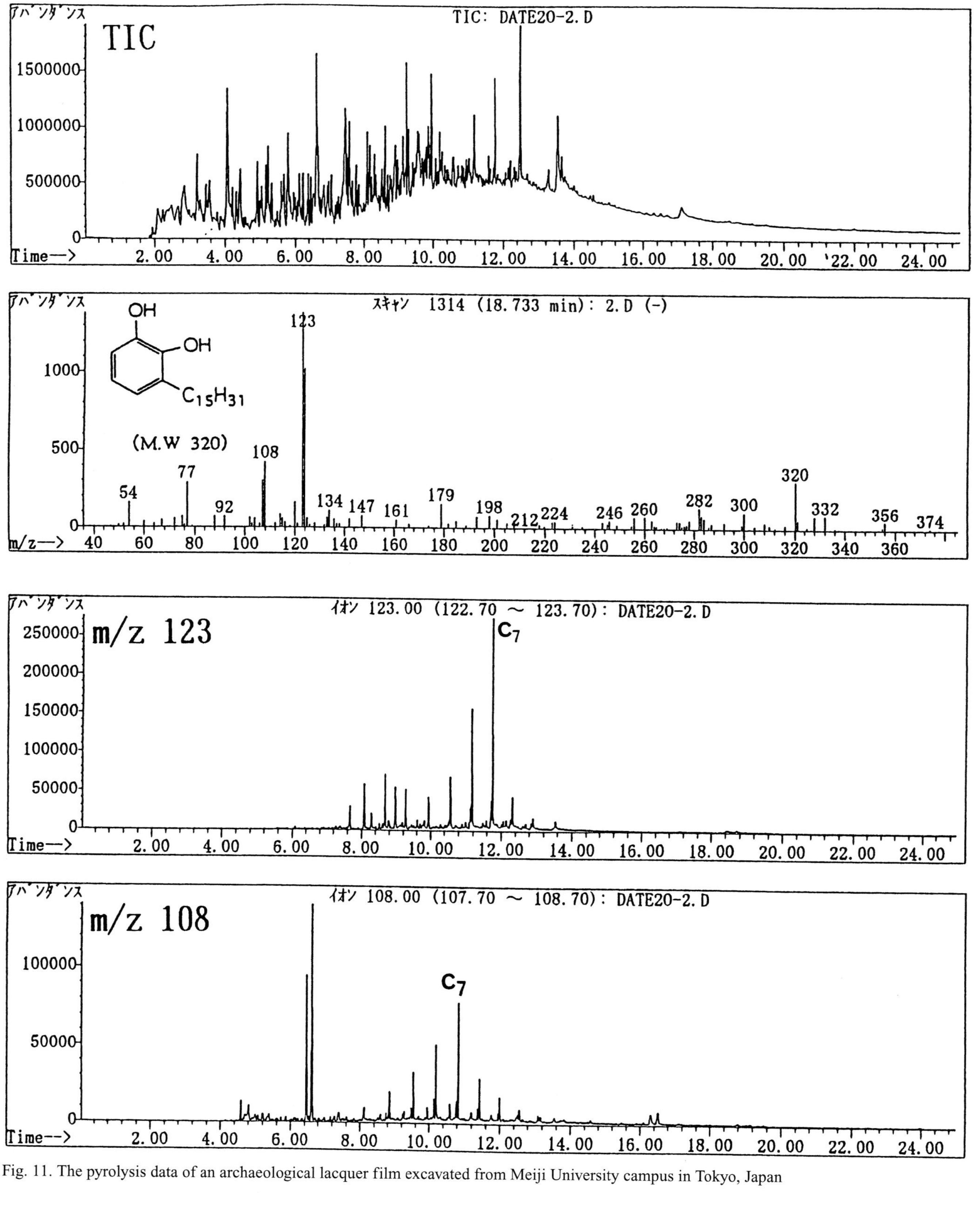

Fig. 11. The pyrolysis data of an archaeological lacquer film excavated from Meiji University campus in Tokyo, Japan

Lacquer film	Rhus vernicifera	Rhus succedanea	Melanorrhoea usitata
Country	Japan, China	Vietnam, Taiwan	Thailand, Burma
Pyrolysis products			
Monomer	Urushiol	Laccol	Thitsiol
Alkylcatechol	3-Heptylcatechol	3-Nonylcatechol	3-Heptylcatechol 4-Heptylcatechol
Alkylphenol	3-Heptylphenol	3-Nonylphenol	3-Heptylphenol
Main component of the lacquer sap	Urushiol	Laccol	Thitsiol

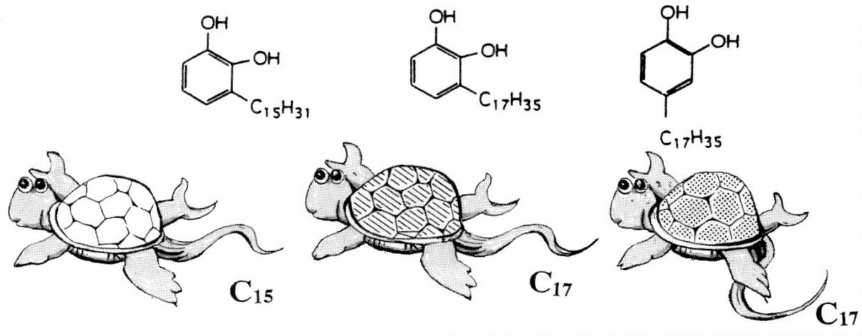

Table 2. Pyrolysis products of oriental lacquer films

The existence of the white, striped or dotted turtles in the pyrolysis products agrees with the characteristic components of the three kinds of lacquer saps as shown in table 2. Furthermore, the data acquired for the alkylcatechols and alkylphenols in the pyrolysis products allow the determination of whether lacquerware is actually produced from urushi or some other resins.

3.3 Pyrolysis-gas chromatography and mass spectrometry of a lacquer sample from an archaeological site

An analytical sample of lacquerware, obtained from an archaeological site, was identified using this method by comparison with oriental lacquer films. This is a rapid technique that does not require large amounts of sample or sample preparation. The lacquer films were pyrolyzed at 500 °C. The TIC and mass chromatograms of m/z 320 of the lacquerware are shown in figure 11. Urushiol, 3-pentadecylcatechol (MW 320) was identified as the monomers of the lacquer film based on the mass spectrum and retention time. This result was compared to those of the three types of oriental lacquers. 3-Pentadecylcatechol of MW 320 is the saturated urushiol component, which is the monomer of the *Rhus vernicifera* lacquer. The monomers of the *Rhus succedanea* lacquer are laccol components such as 3-heptadecylcatechol of MW 348. This was not detected in the ancient lacquer film, except for 3-pentadecylcatechol of MW 320. The monomers of the *Melanorrhoea usitata* lacquer are thitsiol components with saturated and monoenyl side chains such as 4-heptadecylcatechol (MW 348) and 3- and 4-(ω-phenylalkyl)phenols and catechols. These components, except for 3-pentadecylcatechol of MW 320, were not detected in the ancient lacquer film.

In the TIC and mass chromatograms (m/z 108) of the *Rhus succedanea* lacquer film, alkylphenols were also detected in the old lacquer film. However, two differences were found. The longest side chain of the alkylphenols is C 17, and the relative peak intensity of 2-nonylphenol (C9) is the highest in this film. The TIC and mass chromatograms (m/z 108) of *Melanorrhoea usitata* are different from those of the old lacquer film, because phenylalkylphenols are detected in this film, but not in the old lacquer film. It is concluded that the lacquer film obtained from the archaeological site is the *Rhus vernicifera* lacquer.

3.4 Pyrolysis-gas chromatography and mass spectrometry of a lacquer sample from namban *lacquerware*

An analytical sample of *namban* lacquerware was identified using this method by comparison with the oriental lacquer films. The TIC and the mass chromatograms of m/z 60, m/z 123 and m/z 108 from the pyrolysis products of the sample are shown in figure 12. From the mass chromatograms of m/z 60, the *namban* lacquerware was found to include drying oil, which was definitely added to retard the rate of hardening and affect the physical properties of the film. The mass chromatograms of m/z 108 and m/z 123 of the pyrolysis products of the lacquerware are shown in figure 12. The highest abundance of peaks were 2-heptylphenol (C7) and 3-heptylcatechol (C7) as revealed by the mass spectra. It was concluded that *namban* lacquer was made from *Rhus vernicifera* lacquer sap. Urushiol was not detected, because the surface of the *namban* lacquerware was oxidized by oxygen and light. A type of wax was detected in the mass spectrum of the TIC of the pyrolysis products. The wax was used to polish the surface of the lacquerware.

3.5 Pyrolysis-gas chromatography and mass spectrometry of an analytical sample of old lacquerware exported from Asia

An analytical sample of the lacquerware exported from Asia was analyzed using pyrolysis-gas chromatography and mass spectrometry at 500 °C. The lacquerware was identified by comparison with the oriental lacquer films. The TIC and mass chromatograms of m/z 123 and m/z 108 for the pyrolysis products of the sample are shown in figure 13. Alkylcatechols and alkylphenols were detected in the mass chromatograms. The higher abundance of peaks by comparison with nonylcatechols and nonylphenol were the 3- and 4-heptylcatechols (C7) and 2-heptylphenol (C7) as determined by mass spectra. It is concluded

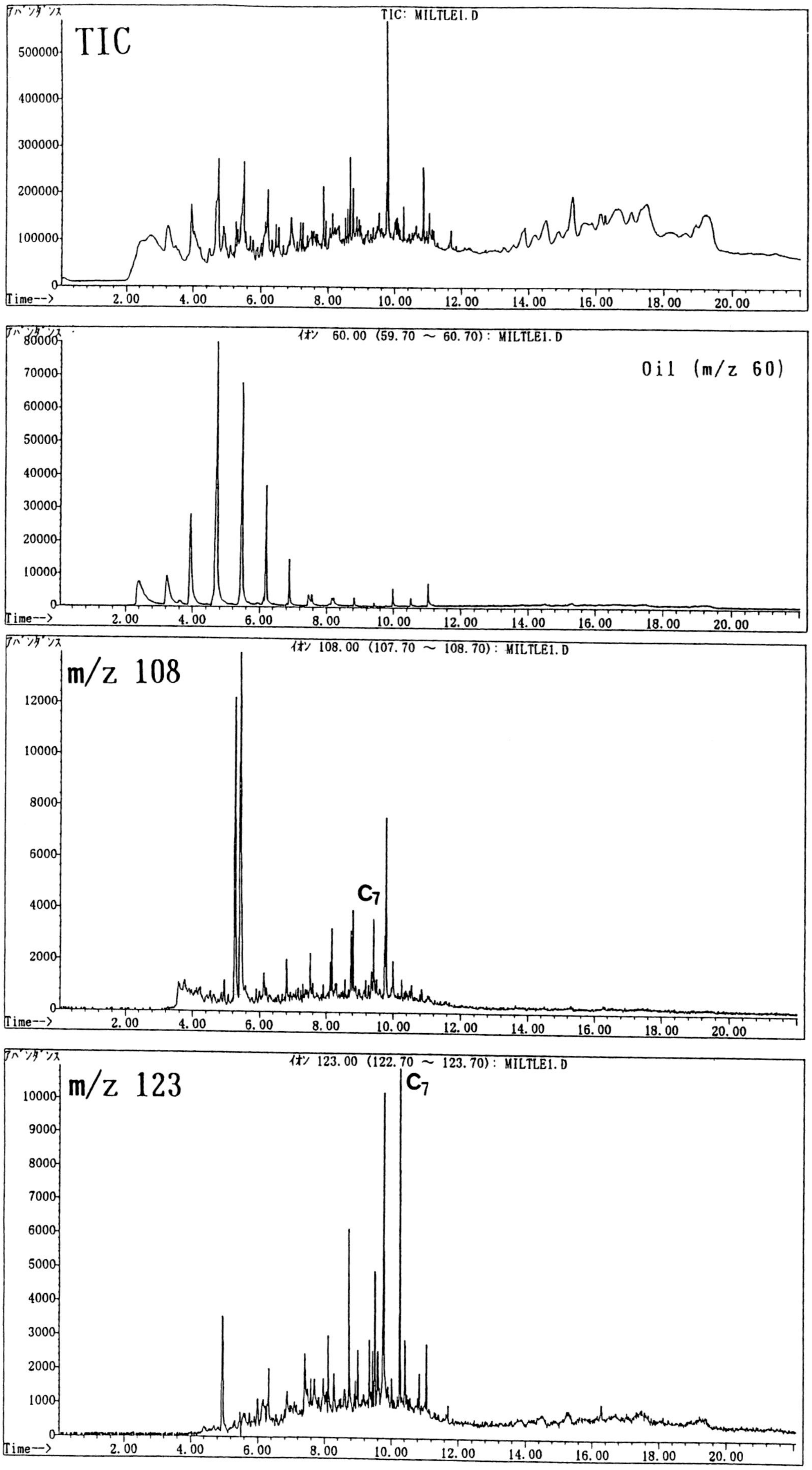

Fig. 12. The pyrolysis data of the *namban* lacquer film

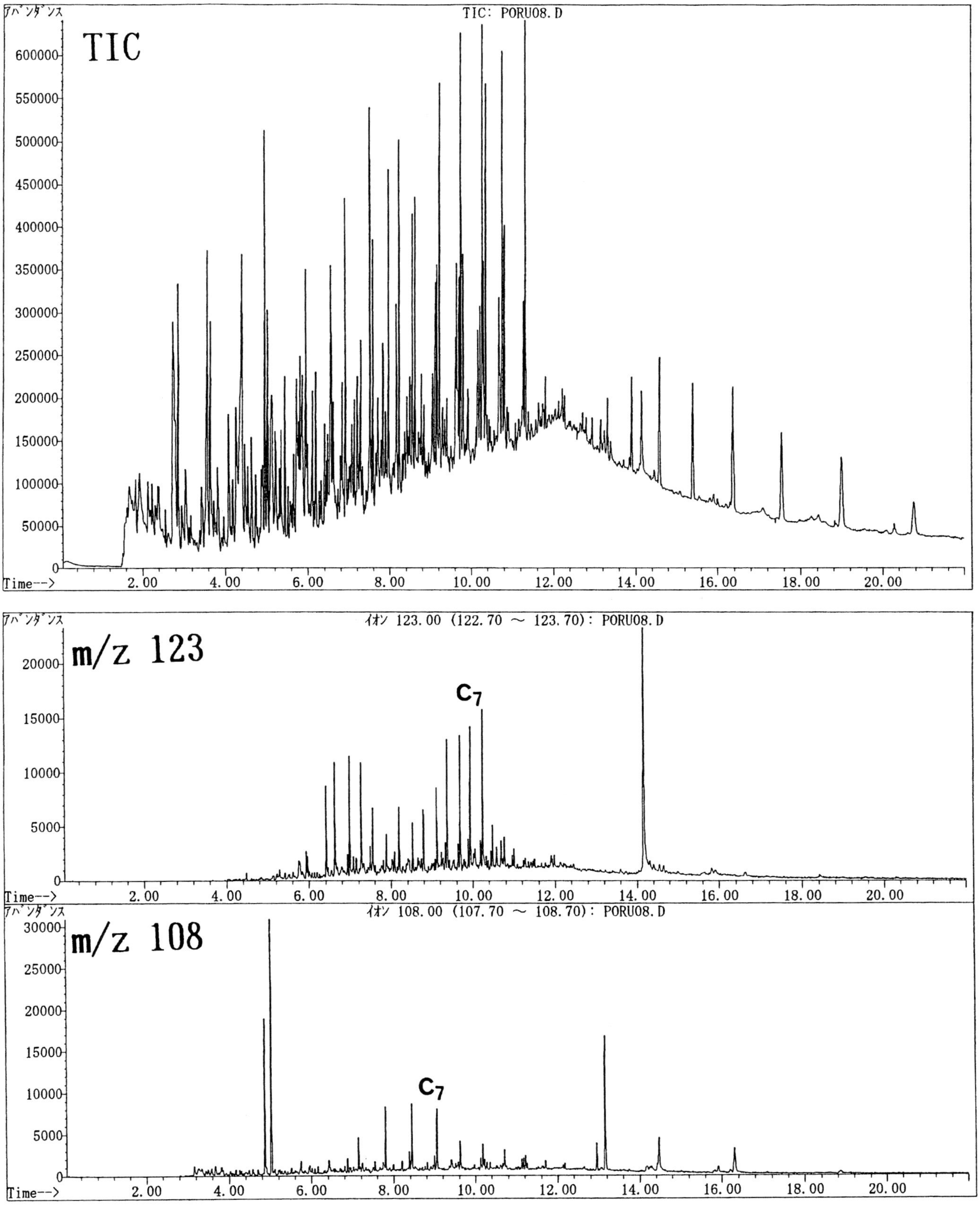

Fig. 13. The pyrolysis data of an old lacquerware exported from Asia

that the lacquerware was produced using *Melanorrhoea usitata* lacquer sap. Thitsiol was not detected from the pyrolysis data, because the surface of lacquerware was oxidized by oxygen and the effect of light. From the TIC and mass spectra of the pyrolysis products, a type of wax was detected. The wax was determined to be a type of bees wax, as revealed by the mass spectra. The bees wax was used to protect and polish the surface of lacquerware.

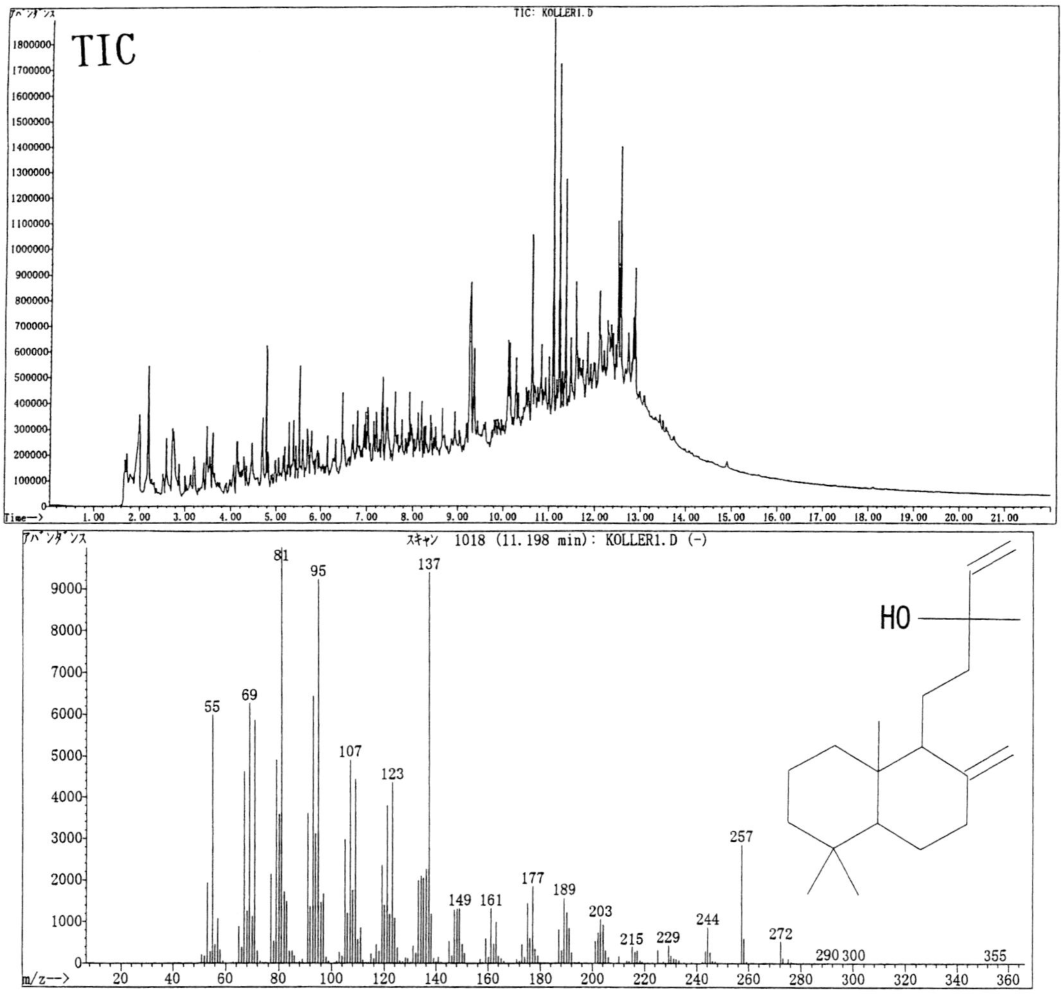

Fig. 14. The pyrolysis data of the Rococo lacquerware

3.6 Pyrolysis-gas chromatography and mass spectrometry of an analytical sample from Rococo lacquerware

An analytical sample of Rococo lacquer was analyzed using pyrolysis-gas chromatography and mass spectrometry at 500 °C. The lacquer sample was identified by comparison with the oriental lacquer films. The lacquer components were not detected from the TIC on the mass chromatograms of alkylcatechol of m/z 123 and alkylphenol of m/z 108 for the pyrolysis products. Monoterpene components and sesquiterpene components were detected in the pyrolysis products of the lacquerware as shown in figure 14. It is concluded that the lacquerware was made from natural resins. The pyrolysis products of the Rococo lacquer and natural resins using this method are under further investigation.

4. Conclusion

The pyrolysis-gas chromatography and mass spectrometry analysis is effective for easily identifying lacquer components and the origin of different types of lacquers. Furthermore, this method can be used for discriminating between lacquer and other resins for the conservation or restoration of lacquerware.

Photo Credits

All illustrations by the author

5. Acknowledgements

We thank Dr. Michael Kühlenthal of the Bavarian State Department of Historical Monuments in Munich, Germany, and Prof. Dr. Sadatoshi Miura of the Tokyo National Research Institute in Tokyo, Japan, for their invaluable suggestions and discussions. We are grateful to Dr. Johann Koller at the Doerner-Institute in Munich, Germany, for the donation of a Rococo lacquer film and Mr. Kazumi Murose from the Mejiro Urushi Institute of Research & Restoration in Tokyo, Japan, for the donation of ancient Japanese lacquer films.

References

KUMANOTANI, JU: *Progress in Organic Coating*, 26, 163–195, 1995

NIIMURA, NORIYASU/MIYAKOSHI, TETSUO/ONODERA, JUN/HIGUCHI, TETSUO: *J. Chem. Soc. Jpn. Chem. & Chem. Ind. Chem.*, Nippon Kagaku Kaishi, 1995, 724–729

NIIMURA, NORIYASU/MIYAKOSHI, TETSUO/ONODERA, JUN/HIGUCHI, TETSUO: *J. Anal. Appl. Pyrolysis*, 37, 199–209, 1996

NIIMURA, NORIYASU/MIYAKOSHI, TETSUO/ONODERA, JUN/HIGUCHI, TETSUO: *Rapid Comm. Mass. Spectrometry*, 10, 1719–1724, 1996

NIIMURA, NORIYASU/MIYAKOSHI, TETSUO/ONODERA, JUN/HIGUCHI, TETSUO: *International J. Poly. Anal. Charact.*, 4, 309–322, 1998

NIIMURA, NORIYASU/MIYAKOSHI, TETSUO/ONODERA, JUN/HIGUCHI, TETSUO: *Archaeometry*, 41, 137–149, 1999

Ingo Rogner

Characterisation of East Asian Lacquers by Laser Desorption Mass Spectroscopy (LD-MS)

Abstract

Lacquer samples from five different Chinese dynasties (Warring States period, Qin, Han, Tang and South Song) were investigated with matrix-assisted laser desorption mass spectroscopy (MALDI) and laser desorption mass spectroscopy (LD-MS). Until now reported mass spectra of original aged lacquer were acquired with the pyrolysis gas chromatography mass spectroscopy (Py-GC/MS) technique only. Both methods presented here are used for the characterisation of urushi lacquer for the first time. The evaluation of the LD mass spectra shows the distribution of 3-catechols with different side chain lengths. It can be determined whether the lacquer was made from the sap of Rhus vernicifera or from Rhus succedanea.

Qi or urushi lacquer is a water in oil type emulsion[1]. In its raw state it is partly soluble in solvents like acetone. After polymerisation however the hardened lacquer is insoluble. It can now be imagined to consist of macromolecules with very high molecular masses.

Therefore, characterisation or spectroscopical evaluation is difficult. Most of the physico-chemical methods commonly applied to gain structural information of the macromolecule have the prerequisite that the analyte is in solution. Differences in the molecular structure can be attributed to various causes: origin of the lacquer, type of the lacquer tree, pretreatment of the raw lacquer and application technique.

Infra-red spectroscopy does not restrict itself to solutions, therefore lacquer can be investigated. This is done with pulverised samples in a KBr disk or with a diamond anvil cell in a thin film with ATR (attenuated total reflection) technology. Therefore, most of the papers concerning lacquer analysis focus on this technology.

If lacquers can be distinguished by a certain method, this method has to have the ability to somehow break up the natural lacquer polymer. All methods with the need to have a solution of the analyte cannot be used, because of the insolubility of the polymerised lacquer. Pyrolysis destroys the polymer by strong heating, the determination is then carried out by gas chromatography (Py-GC). During this process the sample is constantly heated, side reactions among the already pyrolysed fragments can take place. If oxygen is present, the fragments are readily oxidised.

Py-GC measurements on East Asian lacquers from the Qin and Han dynasties were carried out at the Rathgen Forschungslabor by Dr. Herm in 1995. The gas chromatograph was not connected to an IR- or mass spectrometer, thus analyses were difficult to interpret.

The constituents of the qi- or urushi lacquer are presented in the contribution by Tetsuo Miyakoshi. He presents the Py-GC method coupled with a mass-spectrometer to analyse monomeric urushiol. He used a refined acetone fraction of the sap of the lac tree and analysed an ancient Japanese lacquer in a two step pyrolysis[2]. Thus he obtained fragments in the mass spectrum up to about 320 u (atomic mass unit).

MALDI (matrix assisted laser desorption and ionisation) is a new and promising method to generate mass spectra (MS) of high molecular substances, especially biomolecules and technical polymers. Ionised molecular fragments are generated by directing a laser pulse onto the sample. The sample substance is dispersed in a material which is easy to sublime (matrix) and which is supposed to take up the laser energy. In the quick evaporation process of the matrix the sample fragment ions are formed in the desorption plume. In the MALDI process fragments with a high molecular mass are formed predominantly.

For laser desorption a XeCl excimer laser LPX-100 Lambda Physik (308 nm, 30 ns pulse width) was used. The positively charged ions generated were separated by a non-commercial reflectron time-of-flight mass-spectrometer[3] (RETOF-MS, fig. 1) with a mass resolution of $m / \Delta m = 2000$. In contrast to most commercial systems, the laser desorbed ions were allowed to drift for ca. 2 cm before being extracted by a pulsed electric field. The ions were detected by dual multi-channel plates and the signal was collected by a digital oscilloscope. The spectra were then transferred to a PC for further evaluation. The delay between laser pulse and ion extraction allows one to pre-select the mass of the ions detected.

Fig. 1. Section of the laser desorption mass spectrometer

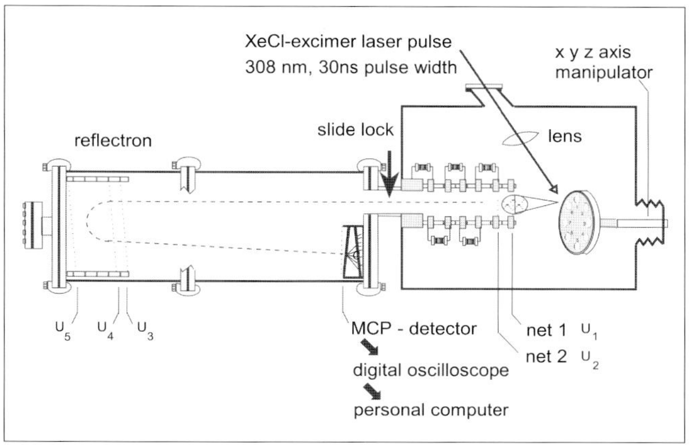

This method was tested in order to find out whether it can be used as an independent method for identifying and analysing Oriental lacquer material. Initial experiments were conducted to find the best matrix for qi-lacquer. Among the matrix materials tested 5-methoxy-salicylic acid gave the best results. Another promising matrix seems to be graphite[4]. The powdered lacquer sample was thoroughly mixed with the solid matrix in a concentration of approx. 1–2 vol.%. The matrix/sample mixture was pressed into a thin layer and onto a carrier pellet (13 mm diameter) made from KBr.

The evaluation of 137 recorded mass spectra found that the sample spectra and the matrix spectrum overlap to such an extend that a deconvolution of the lacquer spectra is not possible. With MALDI we could not obtain a spectrum that is characteristic for each sample.

Table 1. Antique lacquers investigated by LD-MS

One sample of each of the following Chinese dynasties:
Warring States period (481–221 BC)
Qin/Lintong (221–206 BC)
West Han (206 BC–8 AD)
Tang (618–907 AD)
South Song (1127–1279 AD)

Therefore, experiments without matrix were performed, the method of analysis is then called laser desorption mass spectroscopy (LD-MS). With LD-MS it is possible to see smaller fragments of the lacquer, with MALDI larger fragments can be detected (matrix peaks have to be eliminated). However, the advantages of MALDI (fragments of higher mass, gentle desorption process, reduced thermal stress during analysis) cannot be used with LD-MS. Table 1 shows the antique lacquers which were investigated.

During the laser desorption the polymer is broken up by a strong laser pulse at a wavelength of 308 nm (UV, XeCl excimer laser). This laser pulse lasts for only 30 ns (30 x 10^{-9} seconds). Thermal stress of the lacquer is thus minimised. The investigation is carried out in vacuum, therefore no interaction of fragments with oxygen is possible. The mass spectrum will only show unadulterated mass peaks. In contrast to the aforementioned Py-GC the LD-MS method can be carried out within a quarter of an hour. Recorded mass spectra are summed over 100 single mass spectra to ensure a spectrum representative of the investigated sample. Figure 2 presents a LD-MS mass spectrum together with a fingerprint of the peaks of highest intensity.

The correct assignment of mass units to a molecule requires a high degree of structural assumptions. Unassigned peaks are attributed to lacquer additives and degradation products.

Mass spectra were transformed to a kind of fingerprint for easier presentation and evaluation. Figure 3 depicts the compiled results of the analysed qi-lacquer samples.

Fig. 2. LD-MS mass spectrum and fingerprint of a Tang dynasty lacquer sample

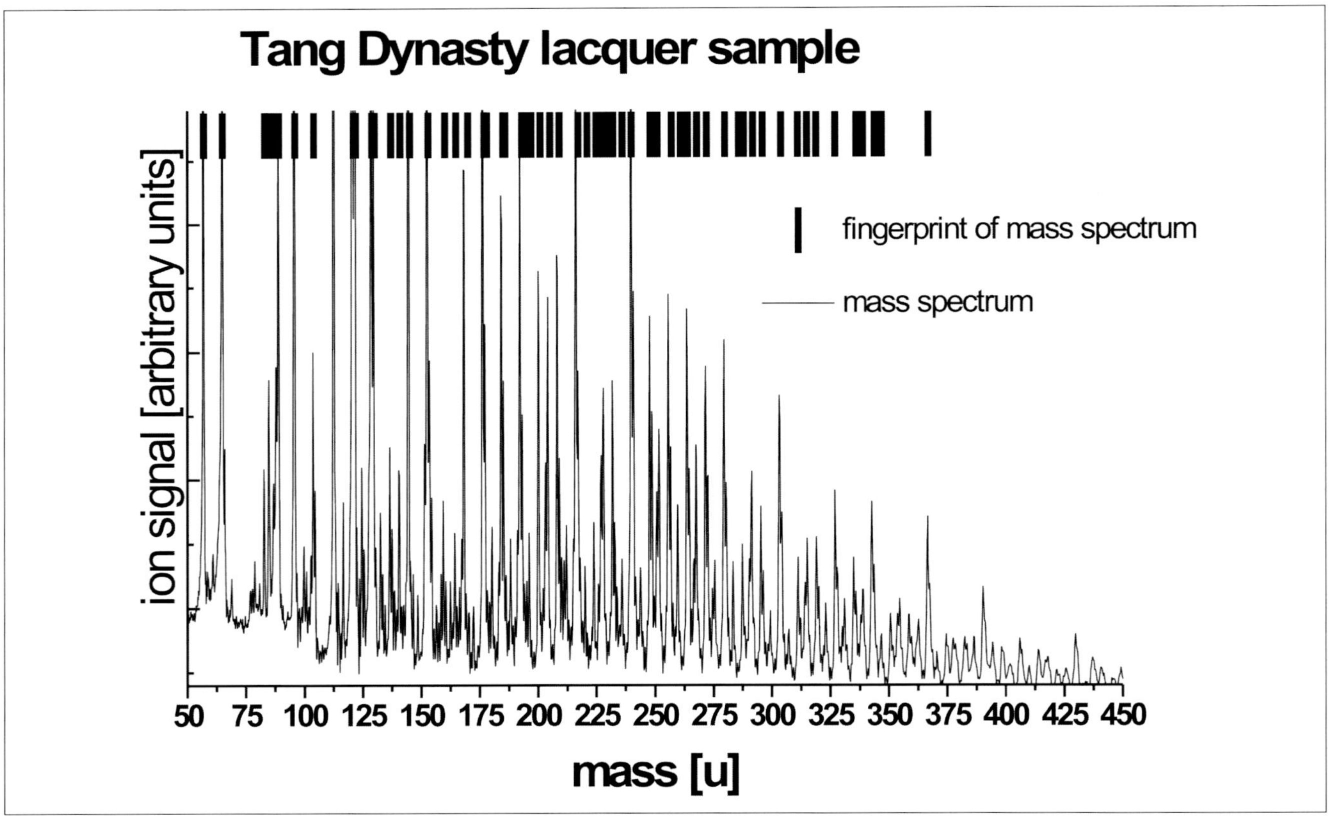

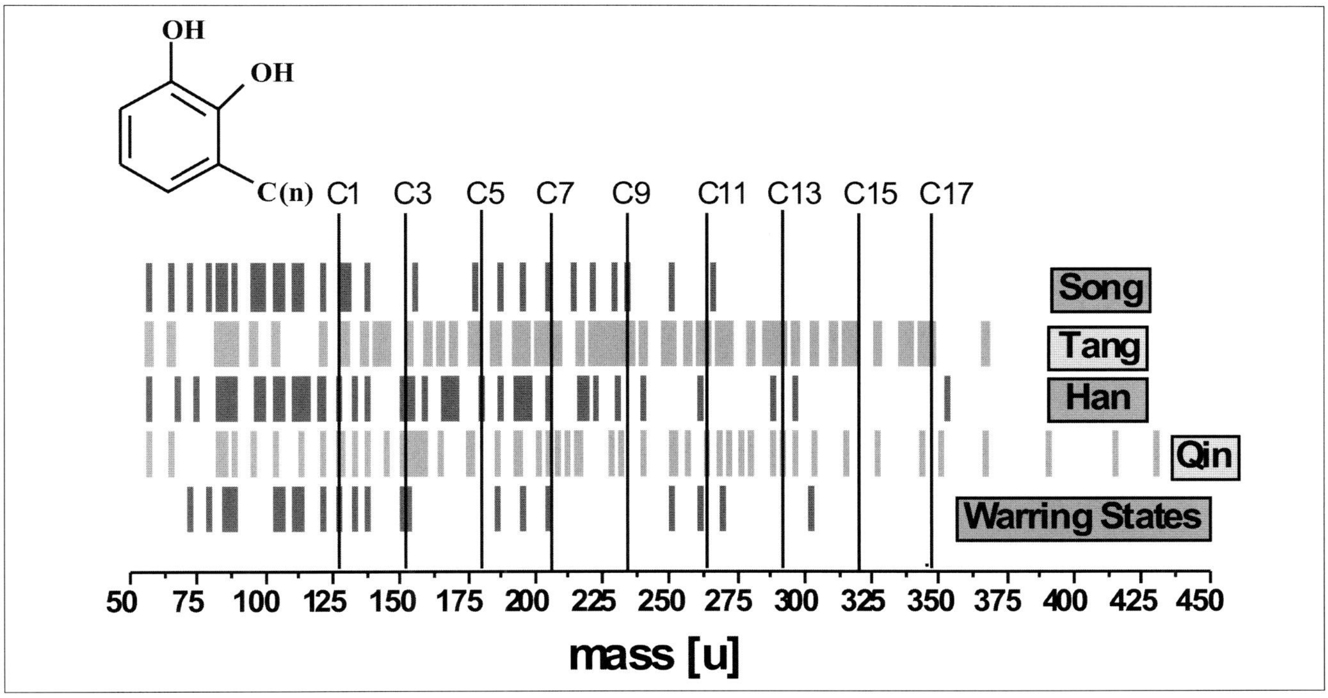

Fig. 3. Fingerprints of the laser desorption mass spectra

For all depicted spectra it can be said that fragments with shorter side chain lengths of urushiol/laccol dominate the spectra. Urushiol and laccol are a mixture of 3-alkylcatechols comprising one or more double bonds. The alkyl side chain of laccol mainly consists of 17 C-atoms ($C_{17}H_x$) whereas urushiol has side chains with 15 C-atoms ($C_{15}H_x$). Taking this into consideration one can conclude that the lacquer samples from the Warring States period, the Han and the South Song dynasty are urushiol based and thus made from *Rhus vernicifera* (Toxicodendron vernicifluum (Stokes) F. A. Barkl.). According to this LD-MS investigation the two samples from the Qin and the Tang dynasty are based on laccol which is the main component of *Rhus succedanea.*

Warring States period lacquer sample: For this sample catechols with side chain lengths of C1–C14 were detected, dominant were peaks for C7 and C11.

Qin lacquer sample: Catechols with C1–C17 were found, C6 side chains are prominent.

Han lacquer sample: Side chains with C1–C13 were evident in the mass spectrum, dominant peaks are found for C11 and C13.

Tang lacquer sample: In this sample C1–C17 side chains were found for the catechols.

Song lacquer sample: Peaks were detected in the mass spectrum for C1–C10 catechol side chains, a dominant peak was found for C7.

In order to distinguish between different East Asian lacquers one has to take into consideration the different factors during the manufacturing process: Which kind of lacquer was used concerning quality, occurrence and method of drying. Additives have to be taken into account. The spectra presented here do not allow to attribute certain patterns in the mass spectrum to a specific dynasty.

Nevertheless, it was found that the laser desorption mass spectroscopy is a technique which is quick in acquiring mass spectra of qi/urushi lacquer. The method allows to use samples without further preparation, small artefacts can be put into the sample chamber directly. Only minute samples are needed to obtain spectra of artefacts which are too large to be put into the apparatus. The evaluation of spectra allows to determine whether the lacquer is laccol or urushiol based. Further evaluation has not been undertaken yet.

LD-MS can be seen as an alternative to pyrolysis gas chromatography mass spectroscopy. The information contained in the mass spectra of both methods is similar but not identical. Therefore, the choice between both analytical techniques depends on the information one wants to obtain from using mass spectroscopy on ancient lacquers.

Notes

1 KUMANOTANI, JU: 'Urushi (oriental lacquer) – a natural aesthetic durable and future promising coating', *Progress in Organic Coatings*, 26, 1995, pp. 163–195.

2 NIIMURA, NORIYASU/MIYAKOSHI, TETSUO et al.: 'Characterization of Rhus vernicifera and Rhus succedanea lacquer films and their pyrolysis mechanisms studied using two-stage pyrolysis-gas chromatography/mass spectrometry', *Journal of Analytical and Applied Pyrolysis*, 37, pp. 199–209.

3 ROGNER, INGO/BIRKETT, PAUL/CAMPBELL, ELEANOR E. B.: 'Hydrogenated and chlorinated fullerenes detected by "cooled" modified matrix-assisted laser desorption and ionisation mass spectroscopy (MALDI-MS)', *Mass Spectrometry and Ion Processes*, 156, 1996, pp. 103–108.

4 ZUMBÜHL, STEFAN et al.: 'A graphite-assisted laser desorption/ionization study of light-induced aging in triterpene dammar and mastic varnishes', *Analytical Chemistry*, 70, 1998, pp. 707–715.

Photo Credits

All illustrations by the author

Figs. 1,2. Examples of wooden lacquerware excavated in China and treated with the higher alcohol method at the Yoshida Biological Institute Inc., Kyoto

Fig. 1. Wooden doll decorated with black lacquer, Han dynasty

Fig. 2. Lacquered tiger pedestal (detail), Warring States period

Fumio Okada

Consolidating Layers of East Asian Lacquer on Ceramics and Waterlogged Wood

This paper deals with the consolidation of excavated lacquerware films on ceramics and waterlogged wood. First, the differences of lacquer coats in Japan and China are discussed. Second, several conservation methods for the treatment of excavated lacquerware, lacquered pottery and wooden substrates are presented.

1. Introduction

Over the past 20 years, I have been engaged in the conservation of lacquerware excavated at historical sites in Japan. During the last 5 years, I have also been involved in a conservation project dealing with Chinese lacquerware from the Warring States period through the Han dynasty. These objects had been removed from China and stored in a waterlogged state.

In addition, I have studied the relationship between the nature of the lacquerware coatings on objects belonging to a wider range of periods in Japan and China and the results of several methods used to conserve these objects. I have found, that there is a close relationship between the nature of the coating on the lacquerware and the results of the conservation techniques. I have concluded that, in order to conserve excavated lacquerware in good condition, it is essential to obtain a solid background of the history of the coating techniques used in various areas and at various times.

In this paper, I would like to present the results of my analyses of the structure of lacquer layers through optical microscopy and some examples of conservational treatment I used on excavated pieces of lacquerware. In addition, I would like to draw attention to some points, that should be kept in mind in order to preserve lacquerware in good condition, as well as during the procedure of conservation and the development of new conservation techniques.

2. Lacquer coating techniques for pottery and wooden objects

2. 1 The structure of lacquer layers applied to pottery

From about 5500 to 2000 years ago, most part of the Japanese pottery excavated until today has obviously been separately coated with either black or red lacquer.[1] During this period, the coating technique remained essentially the same. The surface of the respective piece of pottery was usually carefully polished and then coated with lacquer (colour plate XIV.1). In most cases the black-looking single layer turned out to be a transparent lacquer when observed in the cross-section (colour plate XIV.6). When a red lacquered piece was made, first a transparent lacquer layer was applied (which looks black on the surface) and only then a red lacquer layer was applied on top. Red lacquer was usually applied in a single thin layer (colour plate XIV.2, 7). In the course of my research I found, that most of the pottery excavated in China was coated in this manner.

2. 2 The structure of the lacquer coat on wooden objects

2.2.1 Variation of the wooden substrate

Lacquerware with a wooden substrate date back as far as about 5500 years ago in Japan.[2] Most such objects are made from a single piece of wood. The sources of wood used include broadleaved, diffusely porous trees, such as horse chestnut, zelkova and cherry tree. Although lacquerware from the Warring States period in China was also mostly made from a single piece of wood such as cinnamon tree etc., those from the Han dynasty seem to have been mass-produced by laminating thin sheets of wood veneer.[3] After the Han dynasty, lacquerware with a cloth substrate appears first.

2.2.2 Changes in lacquer coating techniques

Generally speaking, lacquerware coats are made from foundation layers and lacquer layers. The technique used to make foundation layers in East Asia varied with the period. This understanding was gained by analyses of lacquerware excavated in Japan and China.[4]

1) Foundation layer

Two types of wooden lacquerware have been excavated in Japan and China. There are objects with a wooden substrate directly coated with lacquer, and there are others with a foundation layer applied to the wooden substrate, that is then coated with lacquer. Six types of foundation layers have been found on ancient lacquerware from Japan and China:

a) A mixture of lacquer and clay:
This type of foundation layer is found on Japanese lacquerware from about 5500 years ago.[5] In China, similar examples are found on lacquerware from the Han dynasty.[6]

b) A mixture of lacquer and powdered charcoal (colour plate XIV.3, 4):
In Japan this type of foundation layer is found on lacquer containers from about 5500 years ago.[7] In China, similar examples are seen on lacquerware from the Eastern Han dynasty.[8]

c) A mixture of lacquer and sawdust (colour plate XV.1, 5):
In Japan, this type of foundation layer was used to make combs about 4000 years ago.[9] In China, many examples with a similar foundation layer are found among objects from the Eastern Han dynasty.[10]

d) A mixture of lacquer, clay and bone ash (colour plate XV.2, 6):
In China, this type of foundation layer is found on lacquerware from the Han dynasty onwards.[11] In Japan, a similar foundation layer is found on lacquerware from the 7th century.[12]

e) A foundation layer using other materials than lacquer (colour plate XV.3, 7):

△ 1

2 ▽

▽ 3

▽ 4

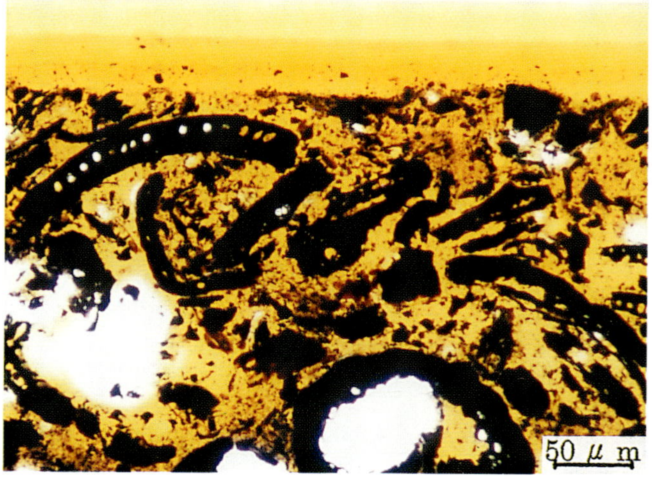

△ 5

6 ▽

7 ▽

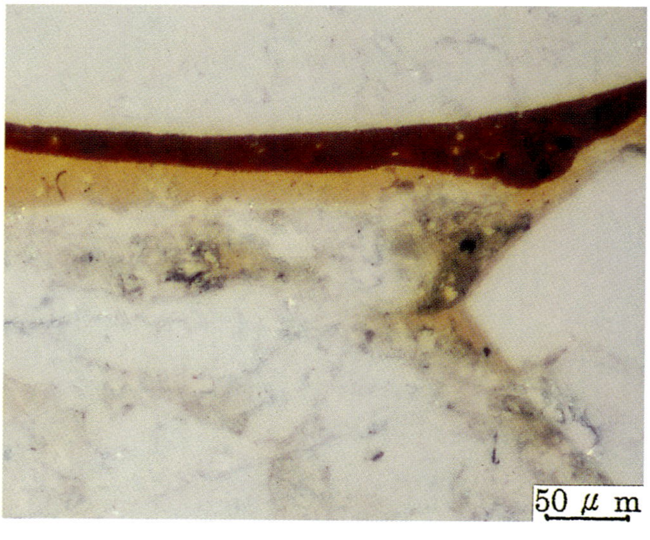

△ 1

2 ▽

▽ 3

▽ 4

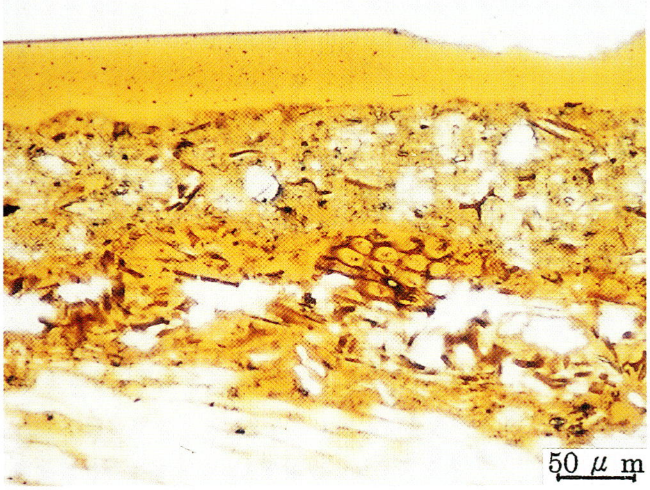

5 △

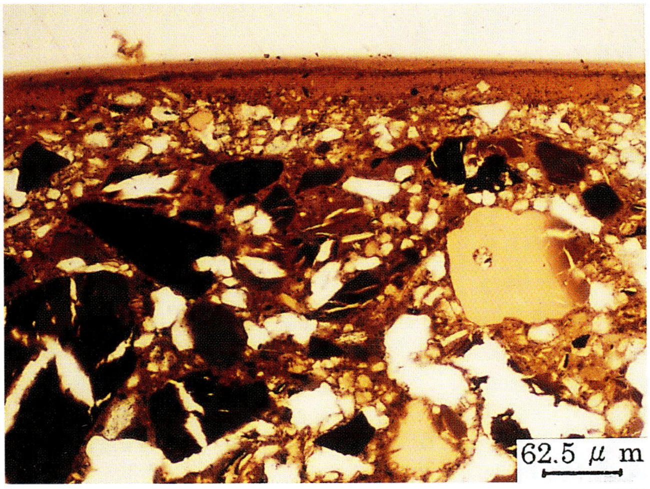

△ 6

7 ▽

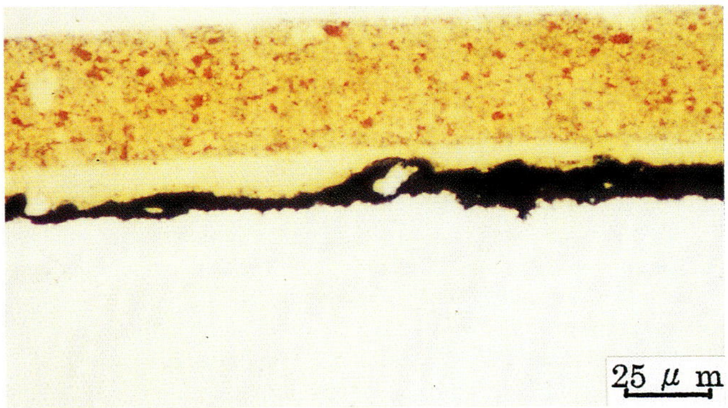

8 ▽

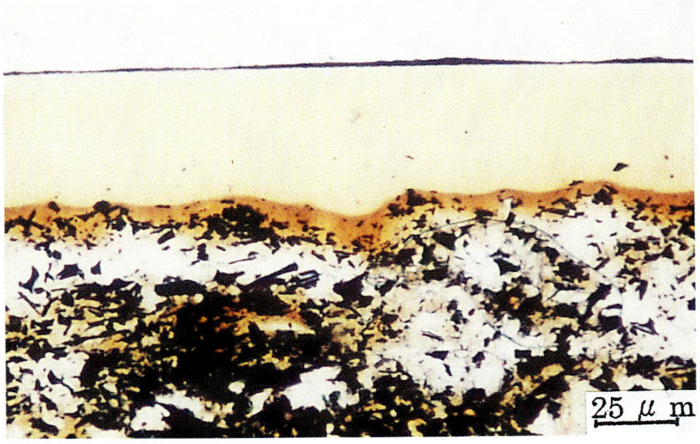

In China, some lacquer-coated wooden objects from the Eastern Han dynasty have a foundation layer of black clay.[13] However, the bonding agent is not yet known.

f) A persimmon tannin foundation layer (colour plate XV.4, 8): The foundation of a popular type of lacquerware from Japan's Medieval period shows persimmon tannin as a bonding agent instead of lacquer.[14]

The types of lacquerware numbered a) c) and d) have often maintained their original shape after being exposed to the air thanks to a stabilizing foundation layer. On the other hand, the types of lacquerware numbered b) e) and f) require special attention when they are treated for conservation.

2) Lacquer coat

There are two types of lacquer coats:

a) Objects with a very thin coat:
In both, Japan and China, this type of lacquer coat is widely found in all periods. In Japan, this type was often placed on lacquerware from the Medieval period and after.[15] In China, lacquerware with this type of coat is found since the Warring States period. Frequently these objects are found included among the possessions buried with a corpse.[16]

b) Objects with a very thick coat due to repeated applications of lacquer:
In Japan, this type of lacquer coat is often found on lacquerware made 5500 to 2500 years ago.[17]

3. Treatments for conserving excavated lacquerware

3.1 Lacquer coat on a pottery surface

When a very thin lacquer coat on the surface of an excavated pottery piece is air dried, it is liable to flake off. Therefore, the lacquer coat on the surface of a piece of damp excavated pottery needs to be reinforced. At the same time, drying out of the object must be prevented to the extent possible. Here are some actual procedures for reinforcing lacquer coats.

1) Using water-soluble emulsion resin
Water-soluble acrylic emulsion resin is diluted to a 5 % solution. This solution is brushed on, so that it will penetrate into the gap between the pottery and the lacquer coat. If pieces of the coating flake off during the application of the resin, they should be pressed down against the object until they stick. The solution is applied until it is clear that all of the coating is well attached to the pottery base.

2) Using non-water-soluble resin

a) Using butyral resin:
The water is drawn from the damp pottery with ethyl alcohol and butyral resin, which can be diluted in alcohol. Butyral resin is diluted with ethyl alcohol to a 3 % solution and this solution is applied to the surface to reinforce the lacquer coat (colour plate XIV.5). If pieces flake off, the resin solution should be applied so that it penetrates to the base, and the chips should be pressed down against the object. The process is repeated until the whole lacquer coat is well attached.[18] Butyral resin does not become so glossy.

b) Using acrylic resin:
Paraloid B72 is used as non-water-soluble acrylic resin. However, Paraloid B72 is liable to turn glossy and a solvent is required to deal with this.

3.2 Wooden-substrate lacquerware

The wooden substrates of lacquerware excavated in Japan are often severely deteriorated and may have moisture contents 400 % to 800 % higher than usual. They are in a waterlogged state.

◁◁ Farbtafel XIV / *Colour Plate XIV*
1 5500 years old pottery, decorated with red and black lacquer, excavated at Torihama Kaiduka, Fukui prefecture
2 3000 years old pottery with a red lacquered surface (fixed with butyral resin), excavated at Tobiragawa, Akita prefecture
3 Lacquered pillow (dried naturally), Eastern Han dynasty, excavated from the tomb of Wang-Hsu in Ro-Rang: its foundation consisting of a mixture of lacquer and powdered charcoal
4 Cross-section of lacquer layers (cf. 3): underneath carbonized segments which seem to be of herbal origin
5 Lacquered pottery, fixed with butyral resin, Han dynasty, excavated from China
6 3000 years old pottery with a black lacquered surface (fixed with butyral resin), excavated at Tobiragawa, Akita prefecture. Microphotograph of a cross-section: the uppermost layer looks black when viewed from above, but looks transparent under the microscope
7 Cross-section of the lacquer layers (cf. 2): a transparent lacquer layer on the pottery substrate is followed by a red layer above

◁ Farbtafel XV / *Colour Plate XV*
1 Lacquered cylindrical vessel (dried naturally), Eastern Han dynasty, excavated from the tomb of Wang-Hsu in Ro-Rang: its foundation consisting of a mixture of lacquer and sawdust mixed with minerals
2 Lacquered box (dried naturally), Han dynasty, excavated in China: its foundation consisting of a mixture of lacquer and bone ash mixed with clay
3 Lacquered plate (dried naturally), Eastern Han dynasty, excavated from the tomb of Wang-Hsu in Ro-Rang: the foundation consists of a mixture of clay and other materials than lacquer
4 Lacquered plate (PEG) treatment), Japan, 12th century, excavated at Kyoto: its foundation consits of a mixture of persimmon tannin and powdered charcoal
5 Cross-section of lacquer layers (cf. 1): under the microscope some wooden tissue becomes visible in the bottom layer
6 Cross-section of lacquer layers (cf. 2): the small semi-opaque mass in the center is bone ash (its color ranging from semi-opaque to blackish brown), with remains of bone tissue and colorless minerals
7 Cross-section of lacquer layers (cf. 3): the black layer at the bottom seems to be a mixture of clay and an agglutinative agent and is characterized by rough upper and lower edges
8 Cross-section of lacquer layers (cf. 4): a mixture of powdered charcoal and persimmon tannin is found in the bottom layer

The conservation of the wooden substrates of lacquerware with extremely high moisture content must be prioritized. On the other hand, some wooden lacquerware excavated from tombs in China (they were buried deep under the ground and protected by several layers of shielding material) are not so badly deteriorated.[19] After air drying, they may remain in relatively good condition (see colour plate XIV.3, XV.1, 2). Therefore, the condition that wooden lacquerware was in when it was just excavated needs to be taken into account, so that the appropriate conservation method is used to conserve it. I will explain the advantages and disadvantages of some of the conservation methods we are now using for wooden lacquerware with severe deterioration of the wooden substrate.

1) Conservation method using water-soluble resin

a) PEG method
The PEG method has been widely used in Japan since the 1970s as a conservation method for deteriorated waterlogged wood.[20] The damp lacquerware is submerged in a solution of polyethylene glycol (average molecular weight: 4000, melting point: 55 °C). At the beginning of the process, the concentration of the PEG solution is about 10 % and the temperature is about 60 °C. The concentration of the solution is gradually increased while the temperature is maintained at the same point. The moisture in the object is completely replaced by the synthetic resin over a period of 6 months to a year, depending on the size of the object.

Since lacquerware pieces can absorb the PEG solution readily, this method produces good results in many cases (colour plate XV.2). Another advantage of this method is that many lacquerware objects can be treated at one time. Nevertheless, there are still some other problems. If the object is entirely coated with lacquer, for example if it is in almost perfect and unblemished condition, it is difficult for the resin to penetrate through the coating and contact the substrate. Also, if the concentration of the solution is increased notwithstanding the degree of penetration into the lower layers, rapid dehydration may occur. The wooden substrate and the lacquer layers may shrink at different rates, leading to cracks or delamination.

In addition, in the PEG method the temperature of the solution must be maintained at 60 °C for a long period. When the object is taken out of the impregnating tank, if its temperature drops rapidly to room temperature the expanded lacquer coat may shrink due to the temperature change. The lacquer coat may flake off the substrate of some lacquerware pieces with a persimmon tannin foundation layer, made from the Medieval period onward, if they are immersed in water after excavation. If they are treated using the PEG method and subjected to the changes in temperature it requires, their surfaces may get wavy (figs. 3, 4).

b) Glyoxal method
This method was developed in China as a new room temperature impregnation method.[21] In this method, the object is impregnated in glyoxal for a long period. To increase the concentration of glyoxal, phosphorus pentoxide is sometimes used as a catalyst. I have used this method for a few years, to conserve wooden lacquerware from China's Warring States period and from Japan's Medieval period. I have obtained relatively good results when the wall thickness of the object is around 3 mm, even if the substrate is wood. This method seems to be more effective than the other methods for preserving colors, such as yellow, created by other substances. I have the feeling that this method is also effective for preserving the special gloss of lacquer objects from the Warring States period. However, when the wall thickness of an object was greater than 1 cm, a great degree of deformation resulted. An additional problem was that the black looking lacquer turned gray after treatment, which is undesirable.

c) Other room temperature method (Polyglycerin method)
I have tried to develop a new room temperature impregnation method using polyglycerin as the principal component.[22] Using this method, the object is impregnated in the agent at room temperature. The liquid is changed three times, at about 10 day intervals. Thus the moisture content in the wooden substrate is replaced by the agent. Then the object is taken out of the bath and air dried at room temperature. This method is still being carried

Fig. 3. An example of a surface lacquer layer that became wavy: wooden substrate, foundation consisting of persimmon tannin and powdered charcoal, excavated from Kyoto City, 12th century

Fig. 4. Cross-section of the lacquer layers (cf. fig. 3): the lacquer layers appear very thin under the microscope

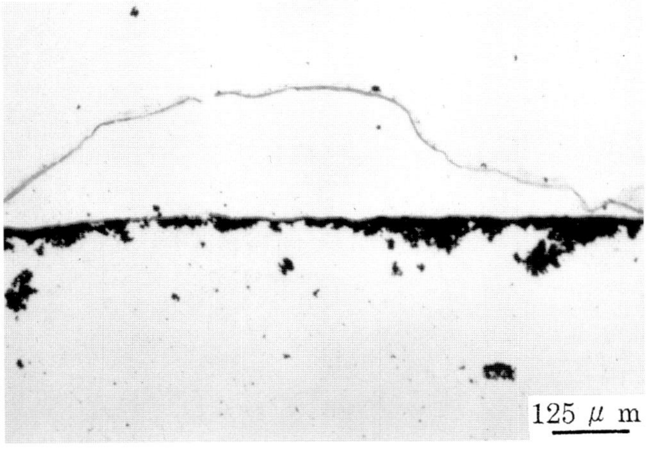

out on a trial basis, but one result up to now is that the gloss of the lacquer is not reduced.

2) Conservation using non-water-soluble resin
It is generally possible to shorten the treatment period by using non-water-soluble resin.

Higher alcohol method
This new conservation treatment method for excavated wooden artefacts was developed in Japan in the early 1990s.[23] To conserve lacquerware, cetyl alcohol (molecular weight: 242, melting point: 50 °C) is used. The impregnation takes about one week for lacquer bowls. The process is as follows:

1) A water-logged lacquerware object is put in a plastic container and bathed in methyl alcohol until the water is replaced.

2) The object is heated to about 50 °C and the methyl alcohol in the object is gradually replaced with cetyl alcohol.

3) After all the methyl alcohol has been replaced by cetyl alcohol, the object is taken out of the container and dried at room temperature.

4) The surface of the object is washed with methyl alcohol. Though some criticize the use of solvents for lacquerware conservation, I think the results of this method are good (figs. 1, 2).

4. Conclusion

To solidify lacquer that is coated on the surface of pottery or wooden objects, and render it stable, the following points must be observed:

1. One should know the different structures of lacquer coats on lacquerware from area to area, and period to period.

2. To solidify a lacquer coat on a pottery object, it is essential to prevent the object from being air dried after excavation. The degree of attachment of the lacquer to the base must be taken into account.

3. When reattaching the lacquer coat to a wooden object, the reinforcement of any fragile wooden substrate must be prioritized.

4. To avoid the destabilization of a lacquer coat on a wooden surface, stresses such as temperature change and the use of organic solvents should be avoided whenever possible.

Notes

1 Kuraku 1988.
2 *Corpus of Excavated Wooden Artifacts* 1993.
3 Harada 1930.
4 Okada 1995.
5 Okada/Naruse/Amitani 1997.
6 Okada 1995.
7 Okada/Naruse/Amitani 1997.
8 Okada/Naruse 1994.
9 Kobayashi/Mino 1979.
10 Okada/Naruse 1994.
11 Okada 1995.
12 *Asuka* 1996.
13 Okada 1995.
14 Yotsuyanagi 1993.
15 *List of Excavation Sites* 1984, 1991.
16 Okada 1995.
17 Nagashima 1985.
18 Yano/Okada/Taniuchi 1997.
19 Harada 1930.
20 Sawada 1973.
21 Chen 1994.
22 Okada/Taniuchi 1997.
23 Okada et al. 1994.

References

Asuka, and Fujiwara Imperial Palace Site Excavations Report IV: Investigations of the Asuka Mizuochi Site, Nara National Research Institute of Cultural Properties (ed.), 1996

Chen, Zhongxing: 'Conservation of Waterlogged Lacquered Wood from Archeological Excavations (abstracts)', *Lacquerware of Qin and Han Periods Excavated from Hubei*, Hubei Province Museum and Museum of The Chinese University of Hong Kong, 1994, pp. 56–58

Corpus of Excavated Wooden Artifacts in the Kinki District. Jomon to Kohun Period, Nara National Research Institute of Cultural Properties, 1993

Harada, Yoshito: *Ro-Rang*, Department of Literature, Tokyo Imperial University, 1930

Kobayashi, Yukio/Mino, Nori: 'On the Structure of Jomon Combs in Lacquer Excavated at Misawagawa Site Hokkaido', *Annual Report of the Historical Museum of Hokkaido*, no. 7, Historical Museum of Hokkaido, 1979, pp. 71–82

Kuraku, Yoshiyuki: 'Origins of the Use of Urushi in Japan and its Development', *Urushi. Proceedings of the Urushi Study Group*, June 10–27, 1985, Tokyo, The Getty Conservation Institute, 1988, pp. 45–50

List of Excavation Sites for Urushiware I, II, Nara National Research Institute of Cultural Properties (ed.), 1984, 1991

Nagashima, Masaharu: 'Lacquerware Techniques of the Jomon Period Seen in Ornamental Bowl Excavated from Juno Bog Site', *Report on the Excavation of Juno Bog Site*, Saitama Prefecture Board of Education and Saitama Prefecture Museum, 1985, pp. 125–130

Okada, Fumio: *A Study of Ancient Excavated Lacquerware*, Kyoto Shoin, 1995

Okada, Fumio/Naruse, Masakazu: 'Scientific Investigation of Lacquerware from Wang Hsu's Tomb in Ro-Rang', *Scientific Papers on Japanese Antiques and Art Crafts*, no. 39, 1994, pp. 61–66

Okada, Fumio/Naruse, Masakazu/Amitani, Katsuhiko: 'A Study on the Structure of the Lacquer Coat of Torihama Kaiduka', *Proceedings from Lectures at the 14th Congress of the Japanese Society for Scientific Studies on Cultural Property*, 1997, pp. 102–103

Okada, Fumio/Sawada, Masaaki/Koeduka, Takao/Yoshida, Hideo: 'The Higher Alcohol Method for the Conservation of Waterlogged Wood', *Scientific Papers on Japanese Antiques and Art Crafts*, no. 37, 1992, pp. 12–20

Okada, Fumio/Taniuchi, Akira: 'Conservation Treatment of Excavated Wooden Lacquer Artifacts Using Polyhydric Alcohol', *Proceedings from Lectures at the 19th Congress of the Japanese Society for the Conservation of Cultural Property*, 1997, pp. 80–81

Sawada, Masaaki: 'Scientific Research into Conserving Ancient Artifacts Part 1', *Collection of Research Papers*, vol. 1, Nara National Research Institute of Cultural Properties, 1973, pp. 1–38

Yano, Kenichiro/Okada, Fumio/Taniuchi, Akira: 'Using a New Type of Resin for Treating a Heavily Deteriorated Wooden Artifact', *Proceedings from Lectures at the 19th Congress of the Japanese Society for the Conservation of Cultural Property*, 1997, pp. 52–53

Yotsuyanagi, Kasho: 'Transition of Urushiware from Ancient to Medieval Periods and Methods of Coating', *Bulletin of Ishikawa Archaeological Society*, 34, 1991, pp. 49–80

Photo Credits

All photographs by the author

Marianne Webb

Preliminary Investigations into Thermochromatic Changes in Asian Lacquer

Overview

There are numerous ways for lacquer to discolour. Conservators are most familiar with the fading of lacquer due to light. The lighter colour of faded lacquer on the surface of boxes for instance can easily be compared with the original surface where the lid has protected part of the lower box.

Most conservators, however, are not quite as familiar with the discolouration of lacquer by exposure to the combination of heat and moisture. The most prevalent example of this type of discolouration is seen on the interior of lacquer soup bowls. The original dark lustrous black of the lacquer has turned to a light brown on the interior.

This discoloured lacquer has been observed by many conservators but not examined in detail or even published. There are only two known references to the phenomenon. In 1995 Shôsai Kitamura gave a lecture at the Tokyo National Research Institute of Cultural Properties in which he mentioned three types of discolouration of lacquerware. The first was discolouration by light; the second he described as fading by heat, moisture and salt; and the third was discolouration by unknown causes – most likely exposure to other substances. The second type he described as typically found on the interior of soup bowls.

Another conservator, Vladimir Simonov, also wrote briefly about the thermochromatic change in his paper on the conservation of a Vietnamese lacquer sculpture in the ICOM-Committee for Conservation 1990 Preprints. He stated in this case that care had to be taken when using a hot wax resin mixture because the lacquer could change colour around 100 degrees Celsius.

Further examples of this phenomenon exist. On the Japanese sake pot (fig. 1) the exterior of the lid remains a dark lustrous brown but the interior of the lid has changed to a light beige colour due to the combination of heat and moisture.

The Japanese tea tray (fig. 2) is another example. It can be clearly seen how the hot tea cups have caused a dramatic change in the colour of the lacquer.

This type of colour change is not gradual such as happens with exposure to light. It happens rapidly once the right conditions are reached. This sudden and dramatic change of colour was observed at the Royal Ontario Museum (ROM) on at least one particular (and dramatic) experiment. In this instance the painting conservator was trying to 'help' the decorative arts conservator flatten some curled lacquer. The experiment involved using BEVA 371 in mineral spirits to flatten the curled lacquer on a vacuum hot table as if it were a painting. However, the adhesive which had been applied from the back did not penetrate the ground. The attempt to force BEVA 371 through the ground layer by softening the adhesive with a hot air gun resulted in an instantaneous change in the lacquer from black to brown. On the left (fig. 3), the original black colour can be seen and on the right is the lighter colour that resulted from the excess heat. Fortunately, the piece was not an artifact but a sample for experiments. These illustrations clearly show that the flattening experiments were not very successful either.

Although, for many years, there has been some curiosity about this phenomenon, it did not seem necessary to explore it further. It was a simple matter to avoid situations where lacquer was exposed to excess heat. Only after several inquiries about the use of heat for pest eradication it was realized, that the exact temperature of this thermochromatic change had not been clearly established. At that time, a series of experiments was undertaken, mainly to answer a recurring question: 'Can heat be used to eradicate insects in lacquer objects?'

Initial experiment

In the initial experiment a number of small chips of lacquer from sample boards or unaccessioned low quality artifacts were exposed to rising temperatures and observed under the microscope. A thermal heating sheet controlled by a rheostat provided heat.

Since previous literature mentioned a change around 100 degrees Celsius, these samples were exposed to temperatures ranging from 90 to 105 degrees Celsius. They shrunk, they turned darker, but they did not exhibit the expected colour change. It was apparent that as they were exposed to the heat, they dried out. Evidently, the moisture must be kept in contact with the lacquer for the thermochromatic change to occur. This makes the phenomena less likely to happen naturally, since both conditions must be present for the colour change. However, these two conditions may still possibly occur during the proposed pest eradication. Objects bagged in polyethylene, a common procedure for pest control, might trap moisture. These conditions could also occur during treatment using heat and adhesives.

In the first attempt each sample was sealed in a mylar envelope to maintain the humidity. Unfortunately, as the samples were heated, the increased air pressure caused the sealed mylar envelope to leak in every instance. Many of the samples dried out before reaching the critical temperature for visible colour transformation. Although some of them changed colour between 90 and 100 degrees Celsius, the results were not consistent. At this juncture it was determined that in order to confirm or deny the hypothesis two things were needed: better equipment to determine the exact temperature and a more efficient method of maintaining the moisture.

Fig. 1. The interior of the lid of this Japanese sake pot has turned from lustrous black to opaque beige in colour

Second set of experiments

The first problem regarding better equipment was solved by a trip to the Canadian Conservation Institute in Ottawa to use their Mettler hot stage. Their hot stage for the microscope not only offers one superior control over the temperature but allows one to set the rate of temperature increase. This makes it much easier to find the exact temperature that the colour change takes place. The microscope can also be hooked up to a video camera allowing the entire procedure to be filmed. It is very important to ensure that the light levels during filming are brilliant enough in order to produce a useful videotape.

The second problem of maintaining the moisture was solved by enclosing the sample in a glass ring covered with a watch glass. This enclosure was filled with wheat starch paste to supply a continuous source of moisture.

The purpose of this second set of experiments was the same as the first: to find the exact temperature at which the colour change takes place.

It was suspected that the colour change might also be related to light damage, therefore a number of samples was used from experiments on light degradation performed more than a decade ago. Each of these samples had been exposed to measured amounts of light. In addition to the controlled light samples, small samples from other lacquer artifacts were used to compare their reactions.

The samples from the original light degradation experiments included: a) black lacquer from a small plate made in the 1950s; b) red lacquer coloured with cinnabar from a nineteenth century bowl; and c) a film of Chinese raw lacquer made in 1986. All of the above were exposed to ultraviolet light in 1986. As well, the original unexposed controls were still available for comparative use. The samples had all been stored in sealed envelopes for the intervening decade. During this set of experiments the reaction of several other artifacts were being tested. All of these artifacts had been exposed to unknown amounts of light. These artifacts included an eighteenth century palanquin that had been exposed to uncontrolled light levels for many years of display. Also used were some small fragments that had lifted off a Han dynasty spear handle. Since this spear handle had never been displayed, it was unlikely to have been exposed to much light at all.

Observations

For the samples of the translucent lacquer film, the hot stage was set to run from 70 degrees to 90 degrees rising at three degrees per minute. The intention was first to do a run below the temperature at which the thermochromatic change would occur. The sample, which had been exposed to the ultraviolet light for four weeks, was enclosed in the paste capsule. For this first sample it was difficult to determine the exact temperature at which the change took place, but by 90 degrees the sample had turned to an opaque beige colour (fig. 4).

The next step was to run the control through the same process. In this instance, the lacquer turned darker but did not exhibit the same colour change. To ensure that the change was not by exposure to the moisture alone, a third sample of degraded lacquer was enclosed with wheat starch paste for two hours. In this third instance, there was no change to the appearance of the sample. From this initial samples it became clear that the colour change was also related to light degradation.

As with all good experimentation, answers to initial questions only create further questions. These are the questions which came to mind: Would the results be the same if black lacquer were used since the black pigment gives some measure of protection against light degradation? The sample from a black lacquer plate that had been exposed to ultraviolet light for four weeks was tried next. The hot stage was set to raise the temperature from 70 to 90 degrees at four degrees per minute. The results were the same. The degraded sample changed to a beige colour by the time it reached 90 degrees. The undegraded sample that had been stored in the dark remained unchanged in appearance when exposed to heat and moisture. Also the degraded sample did not change colour when exposed to the moisture alone.

Fig. 2. The discolouration caused by hot tea cups is readily apparent in the photograph of a Japanese tray

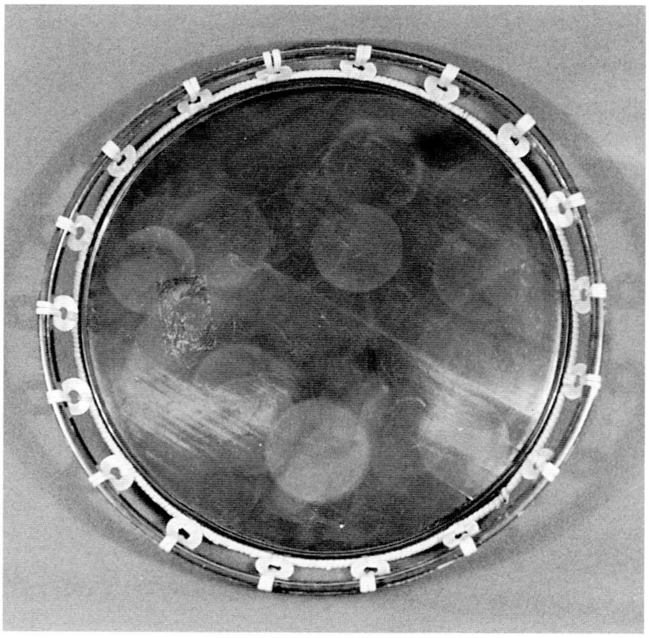

Fig. 3. An experiment in flattening lacquer on a vacuum hot table resulted in the instantaneous change in the colour from black to brown on the right hand side of this sample board. The use of a facing which held moisture against the surface played a part in the thermochromatic change

Fig. 4. The upper sample was exposed to moisture and heat of 70 degrees Celsius to effect this colour change. The change in colour can be seen when compared to the unexposed control in the lower part of the picture

The results for the 19th century red lacquer bowl were slightly different. The control, unexposed to light, remained unchanged when exposed to heat and moisture. The samples that were exposed to ultraviolet light were already dark in colour due to the effect of the light on the cinnabar pigment. The depth of the light degradation could easily be seen on the side of the sample. When this sample was exposed to the wheat starch and paste without heat there was some change in the degraded surface layers. Under the heat and moisture, again using a range of 70 to 90 degrees Celsius, rising at two degrees per minute, there was the same colour change noted as the black and clear sample. This colour change was not as dramatic as the others, however, the change was visible only on the degraded surface layer.

Thus far all of the samples used had been exposed to four weeks of ultraviolet light. What would be the effect of an unknown sample? The next sample was taken from an 18th century Japanese palanquin. The hot stage was set to run from 70 to 80 degrees Celsius at a two degree increase per minute. After a few minutes exposure to heat the colour began to change. By 76 degrees Celsius the sample was completely opaque as seen in figure 5. Since the colour began to change very soon after the beginning of the run, a second sample was run at a lower temperature. The hot stage was set for 60 to 70 degrees Celsius rising, again, at a rate of two degrees per minute. The colour change became evident soon after the exposure to the heat. By 69 degrees Celsius colour had completely changed.

Further samples were run setting the temperature parameters ten degrees lower, beginning at 50 and going to 60 degrees Celsius. Again, the colour changed after a few minutes. The hot stage was then set for 40 to 50 degrees Celsius. At the end of this run the sample remained unchanged. Using short runs from 50 to 55 degrees Celsius, then 50 to 52, the colour change was finally established at a temperature of 51 degrees Celsius.

Fig. 5. The sample on the left was exposed to heat and moisture resulting in a colour change. The control is on the right

This final figure is surprisingly low. This temperature might easily be encountered during a conservation treatment. Without knowing the total light exposure to an object it is difficult to estimate whether this thermochromatic change would occur at even lower temperatures if the object was exposed to more light.

In this set of experiments, the final sample to be exposed came from the Han dynasty spear handle. The hot stage was set, as in previous experiments, to rise from 70 to 90 degrees at a rate of three degrees per minute. After the entire run there was no visible change to the lacquer. It was concluded that, since the appearance of the sample was also very good, there was insufficient light exposure to cause the colour change phenomenon.

Conclusions

In the end, it was found that this set of experiments raised as many questions as it answered. The question of heat treatment for pest eradication seems a qualified no. Heat treatment for pests is usually about 60 degrees Celsius. There is probably no danger of a colour change if there is no moisture in contact with the surface. However, there are circumstances where this contact might occur. Other objects resting against the surface or where the object is stored in polyethylene bags might result in a situation where the moisture cannot escape. The same danger exists, if facings are used to hold detached lacquer in place.

From the observations of these experiments it is clear, that the sudden colour change of lacquer when exposed to heat and moisture is also related to the amount of light degradation encountered by the object. However, what is still not clear is the exact temperature at which this change occurs. It can occur at a temperature as low as 51 degrees Celsius, however most samples changed colour at a higher temperature. What is the difference? Clearly, it must be the amount of light degradation.

Unfortunately, these experiments are far from complete. The next experiments to perform will include new created lacquer films using clear, red and black lacquer. These films will be exposed to known amounts of light; and the samples will then be run through the same heating experiments to determine more accurately, if there is a correlation between the amount of light degradation and the temperature, at which the colour change takes place. If this hypothesis proves true, this information will be valuable for the calculation of the total past light exposure of an object. This would be very useful to know in setting display restrictions for a particular object.

Reference

SIMONOV, VLADIMIR: 'The method for the Conservation Treatment of the Vietnamese Lacquer Sculpture "Donatur"', in *Preprints, ICOM-CC 9th Triennial Meeting,* V., Dresden, 1990, p. 658

Photo Credits

All photographs by the author

Sirichai Wangchareontrakul

Quality Improvement of Lacquer from *Melanorrhoea usitata*

Introduction

Oriental lacquer has been used as a surface coating and embellishment on tableware and interior decoration for several thousand years in the Far East.[1] Lacquer can be applied to a number of materials such as wood, bamboo, paper, metal, porcelain, hide and cloth etc. In Thailand lacquerwork is classified as the applied arts. The design in gold leaves applied over black lacquer is used to decorate many objects for religious purposes and common use. The art of lacquering may protect and decorate small boxes, as well as entire wooden panels (cf. colour plate XVI.2). An extravagant example of lacquerwork (colour plate XVI.1) is preserved in the Royal State palanquin (*Rachentarayan*) for King Rama I (1782–1809 AD). It is made of wood, covered with lacquer and gold leaves, and decorated with glass. Inside the temple of Wat Pra Keaw Don Tao, in the province of Lampang, the ceiling and the walls are decorated with gilded lacquerwork and glass mosaic (colour plate XVI.3).

In the *Anacardiaceae* family, there are various kinds of lacquer trees used as a source for lacquer. *Rhus vernicifera* is the most important source of lacquer in China and Japan, whereas *Melanorrhoea usitata*, which is called *Huk Laung* in Thai, has been used as a source of lacquer in Burma and Thailand.[2] Investigations on the chemical composition of lacquer from *Huk Laung* showed, that the major constituents were (*Z,Z*)-3-heptadeca-8′,11′-dienyl) benzene-1,2-diol (1) (48 %) and its 4-isomer (2) (26 %). Eleven minor components (3–13), summarized in table 1[3–5], could be observed.

The nature of the hardening or setting reaction, usually referred to as 'drying', is known as a polymerization process with cross linking. In the past two decades, a few papers have been published concerning the polymerization of urushiol from *Rhus vernicifera*[6-7]. It has been suggested that the reaction involves an enzyme laccase and oxygen. It proceeds best in a humid atmosphere at a relatively low temperature. The polymerization mechanism of lacquer is quite complicated since it involves enzymic reactions. At present, there is no clear explanation for the behaviour of lacquer in the polymerization process.

After drying the lacquer coating does not only serve as a decorative finish, but also as a preservative and a protective coating. This surface coating has many advantageous properties, because it is water proof, rot proof and weather proof. However, the disadvantage of lacquer is, that it requires a long time for drying. Therefore the objective of the present study is to seek a method that could accelerate the drying process of lacquer.

Experiment

Lacquer of *Melanorrhoea usitata* was collected from the Chiang Mai province. The crude lacquer (1 kg) was dissolved in methanol. The mixture was stirred and standed for 48 hrs. It was filtered and the filtrate was evaporated under reducing pressure to produce a viscous black oil, which was used as a starting material in the next step. Adhesion measurements were carried out using the Tape Test (ASTM D3359–93). A sample

Table 1. Chemical Structures of Individual Components in Lacquer from *Melanorrhoea usitata*

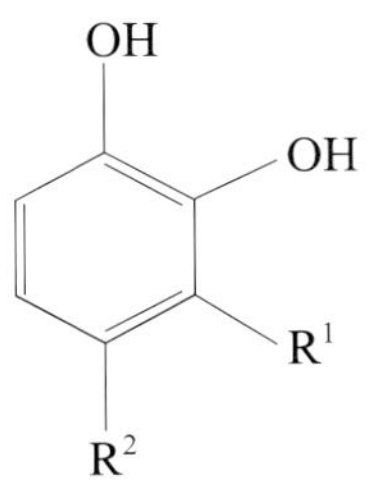

	R 1	R 2
(1)	(*Z,Z*)-heptadeca-8′,11′-dienyl	H
(2)	H	(*Z,Z*)-heptadeca-8′,11′-dienyl
(3)	(*Z*)-pentadec-7′-enyl	H
(4)	pentadecyl	H
(5)	H	pentadecyl
(6)	(*Z*)-heptadec-8′-enyl	H
(7)	(*E*)-heptadec-8′-enyl	H
(8)	H	(*Z*)-heptadec-8′-enyl
(9)	heptadecyl	H
(10)	10′-phenyldecyl	H
(11)	H	10′-phenyldecyl
(12)	12′-phenyldodecyl	H
(13)	H	12′-phenyldodecyl

was applied onto a wooden surface and dried for 7 days before testing.

A water resistancy test was carried out by applying the sample onto a thin stainless sheet (10 x 15 cm and about 1.2 mm thickness). After complete drying, it was immersed in water. The water temperature was kept at 40 ± 1 °C and the water was continuously stirred with air blowing. After 24 hrs the observation was continued.

Evaluation of the Optimum Temperature

Lacquer (10 g) was mixed with ammonium hydroxide (20 ml) and formaldehyde (30 ml) was slowly added in order to keep the temperature constant at 30 °C. The reaction mixture was continuously stirred at room temperature for 2 hrs. The organic layer was separated from the aqueous layer and washed with water until it was free from base. The product was dried under vacuum. Solubility tests showed, that the product did not dissolve in water and ethanol but dissolved in hexane, acetone and ethyl acetate. The surface drying time of the product was 24 hrs.

Lacquer (10 g) was mixed with ammonium hydroxide (20 ml) and formaldehyde (30 ml) and was refluxed on the oil bath at 130–140 °C for 1.5 hrs. The organic layer was separated and it soon solidified at room temperature. The product was washed with water until it was free from base and was dried under diminished pressure. Solubility tests showed, that the product did not dissolve in water and ethanol, but partly in hexane, acetone and ethyl acetate. The surface drying time of the product was 1 hr.

Evaluation of the Optimum Reagents

In this experiment the reaction was performed under the same conditions by reflux at 130–140 °C for 1.5 hrs. The mole of lacquer was kept constant while the mole of reagents, formaldehyde and ammonium hydroxide was varied from 0.25, 0.5, 1.0, 2.5, 5.0, 7.5, to 10.0 respectively. The product obtained from each experiment was subjected to the following tests: solubility, surface drying time, adhesion and water resistancy. The results of the tests are given below.

Lacquer: Reagents (1 : 0.25)
The product did not dissolve in water, but proved partly soluble in ethanol and soluble in hexane, acetone and ethyl acetate. Surface drying time of the product was 2 hrs. The adhesion on wood was classified as 4B and the product passed the water resistancy test.

Lacquer: Reagents (1 : 0.5)
The product did not dissolve in water and ethanol, proved partly soluble in hexane, but soluble in acetone and ethyl acetate. The surface drying time of the product was 1.5 hrs. The adhesion on wood was classified as 4B and the product passed the water resistancy test.

Lacquer: Reagents (1 : 1)
The product did not dissolve in water and ethanol, proved partly soluble in hexane and acetone and soluble in ethyl acetate. Surface drying time was 1 hr 20 min. The adhesion on wood was classified as 4B and the product passed the water resistancy test.

Lacquer: Reagents (1 : 2.5)
The product did not dissolve in water and ethanol, and proved partly soluble in hexane and acetone and soluble in ethyl acetate. The surface drying time of the product was 1 hr 10 min. The adhesion on wood was classified as 4B and the product passed the water resistancy test.

Lacquer: Reagents (1 : 5.0)
The product did not dissolve in water and ethanol, was partly soluble in hexane, acetone and soluble in ethyl acetate. The surface drying time was 50 min. The adhesion on wood was classified as 4B and the product passed the water resistancy test.

Lacquer: Reagents (1 : 7.5)
The product did not dissolve in water and ethanol, was partly soluble in hexane and acetone and soluble in ethyl acetate. The surface drying time was 40 min. The adhesion on wood was classified as 4B and the product passed the water resistancy test.

Lacquer: Reagents (1 : 10)
The product did not dissolve in water, ethanol and hexane, was partly soluble in acetone and soluble in ethyl acetate. The surface drying time was 35 min. The adhesion on wood was classified as 4B. The product passed the water resistancy test.

Lacquer
Lacquer did not dissolve in water, but proved soluble in ethanol, hexane, acetone and ethyl acetate. The surface drying time was more than 24 hrs. The adhesion on wood was classified as 4B. The lacquer passed the water resistancy test.

Results and Discussion

The main constituents in lacquer of *Huk Laung* are alkyl/alkenyl benzene-1,2-diols. The structure of the molecule is constructed with an aromatic nucleus and a long olefinic side chain. From the point of chemistry, polymerization can occur at both positions. An attempt was then made to accelerate the polymerization at the aromatic nucleus. Formaldehyde and ammonium hydroxide, a commercially available reagent, were used as a cross link agent. The lacquer was treated with formaldehyde and ammonium hydroxide to supply a product, which has the same physical properties as crude lacquer, but a 20 times faster surface drying time. When the reaction was carried out at ambient temperature, the surface drying time of the product was about 24 hrs. On the other hand, when increasing the temperature of the reaction up to 130–140 °C, the product needed a surface drying time of about 1 hr. Hence the optimum temperature of the reaction was 130–140 °C. Studies on the evaluation of the optimum reagents indicate, that when the amount of reagents was increased, the drying time of the product was decreased. However, a comparison of the physical properties of the products shows, that products prepared by using the mole ratio of lacquer and a reagent between 1 : 2.5–5.0 were suitable for the reaction. When the mole ratio was greater than 1 : 7.5, the product provided a faster drying time, but it lost its gloss after the water resistancy test.

Acknowledgements

Financial support from the Thailand Research Fund is gratefully acknowledged.

1 Royal State palanquin decorated with lacquer, gold leaves and colored glass

2 Bangkok, Wat Po, black lacquered door with gilded decoration

3 The temple of Wat Pra Keaw Don Tao, Lampang province, interior decorated with gilded lacquer and glass mosaic

References

1 PLESCH, PETER H.: *Chinese lacquer: an age-old polymer,* Shell Polymers, 1982, **6**, 7

2 WANGCHAREONTRAKUL, SIRICHAI: *Oriental Lacquer and Its Care,* SPAFA Digest, 1990, **11**, 53

3 JEFFERSON, ALAN/WANGCHAREONTRAKUL, SIRICHAI: *Long-chain Phenol: Urushiol, Laccol, Thitsiol and Phenylalkyl Catechol Compounds in Burmese Lac from Melanorrhoea usitata*, J. Chomatogr., 1986, **367**, 145

4 JEFFERSON, ALAN/SARGENT, MELVYN V./WANGCHAREONTRAKUL, SIRICHAI: *Synthesis and Identification of w-Phenylalkylcatechols in Burmese Lac*, Aust. J. Chem., 1988, **41**, 19

5 SARGENT, MELVYN V./WANGCHAREONTRAKUL, SIRICHAI/JEFFERSON, ALAN: *The Synthesis and Identification of Alkenyl and Alkadienyl Catechols of Burmese Lac*, J. Chem. Soc. Perkin Trans. I, 1989, 431

6 OSHIMA, RYUICHI/YAMAUCHI, YOSHIO/WATANABE, CHUICHI/ KUMANOTANI, JU: *Enzymic Oxidation Coupling of Urushiol in Sap of the Lac Tree, Rhus vernicifera,* J. Org. Chem., 1985, **50**, 2613

7 KUMANOTANI, JU: 'Traditional Japanese Urushi Techniques – Kurome and roiro-shiage – A Preface of Urushi Cultural Properties Conservation', *International Symposium on the Conservation and Restoration of Cultural Property: Conservation of Urushi Objects*, November 10–12, 1993, Tokyo, 1995

Photo Credits

Colour plate XVI.1, 3: Photographs by the author;
2: Michael Kühlenthal, Munich

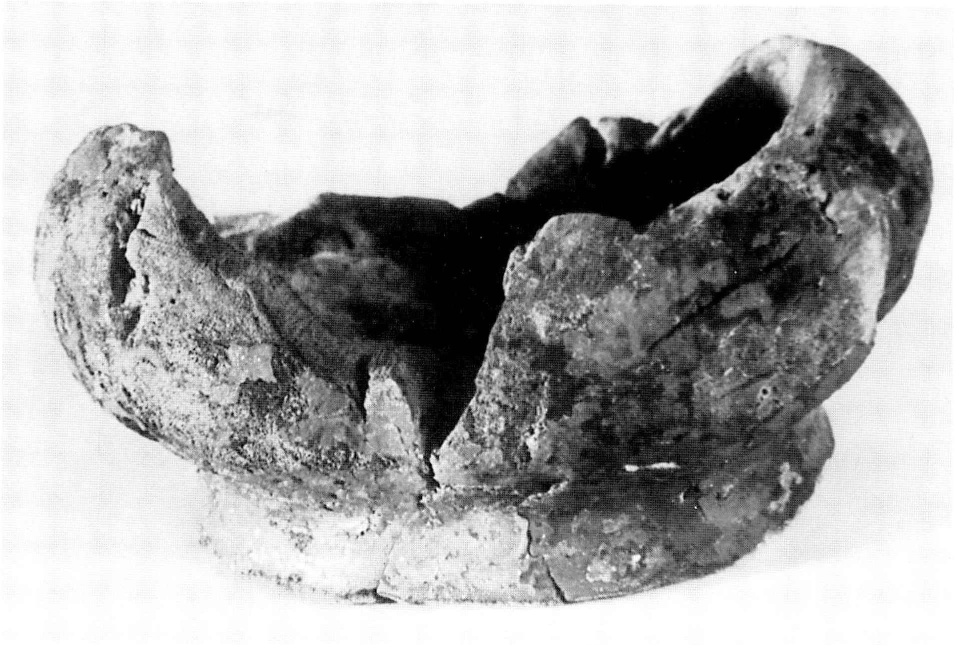

Fig. 1. Red painted wooden bowl, c. 6000 years old

Yuansheng Chen, Yulin Xie

A New Method for Treating Ancient Chinese Lacquer on Waterlogged Wood

1. Introduction

Chinese lacquer (raw lacquer, urushi) has a long history. According to Chinese literature, the legendary emperors Shun and Yu are said to have used lacquer painted wooden vessels for food. This is an indication that lacquerware was in use even before the Xia dynasty (c. 21st century B.C.).

Chinese lacquer has undergone a long process of development. It can be traced back at least to the Neolithic period. In 1978, a red painted wooden bowl (fig. 1) was found at a Neolithic site at Hemudu in Yuyao in the Zhejiang province, which has been dated to about six thousand years ago.[1] We studied the red painting by PY/GC-FTIR analysis.[2] The result confirmed that the red material was vermilion lacquer. The lacquer painted bowl must be considered so far as the earliest piece of lacquerware in China. Other Neolithic sites in China have also yielded examples of early lacquerware. At Changzhou in the Jiangsu province, for instance, two wooden objects were excavated: one was painted in black and the other in red and black lacquer. At least during the Shang dynasty, around the 14th century B.C., the lacquer handicraft must have made a considerable advance. Lacquers from the Shang dynasty found in higher quantities show rich and colourful designs. The decorative patterns were dragons and scrolls, similar to those found on Shang bronzes.

In the history of Chinese lacquer there are two golden periods: The first is from the Warring States period to the Han dynasty (4th century B.C. – 2nd century A.D.). The second golden period is from the Song to the Ming dynasty (9th–16th century A.D.). During these two periods, the lacquer production had reached its peak, in quantity as well as in technique. Especially during the first golden period lacquerware was made in a rich assortment of shapes, the art of lacquer painting flourished and reached heights of brilliance.

During the Han dynasty, official lacquer workshops were established. Under the control of the central government, the manufacturing of lacquer articles was provided for the imperial household. A great number of lacquers were discovered during archaeological excavations at a dated Han dynasty tomb. They confirmed the existence of a vital lacquer craft at that time.

1.1 The condition of unearthed lacquer

Large quantities of lacquerware have been excavated at different places in China. For example, there are thousands of pieces of lacquerware found at Tianchang in the Anhui province and at Jiangling in the Hubei province. Besides these, a great number of lacquers dated from the Warring States period to the Han dynasty were discovered in the provinces Hunan and Jiangsu. The lacquerware found in tombs was usually situated in water. The tombs were sealed without air, therefore the lacquers could be kept so long.

The cores of the lacquerware were made from various materials: For instance, the core of a lacquered scabbard was made of wood and fabric, the cores of lacquered arrows were made from iron and bamboo stripes, and even the back of a bronze mirror was painted and decorated with lacquer (figs. 2a–c). Sometimes other materials such as pottery, rattan, leather or the like were also used as lacquer cores.

1.2 The importance of the task

Among the unearthed lacquers, the number of wooden cores are in the absolute majority. The wooden cores were waterlogged. Up to now, most of them are still soaked in water. It is therefore an important task to study the dehydration and consolidation of waterlogged wooden cores of ancient lacquerware in China.

The wooden core of the ancient lacquerware may be made from various sorts of trees, such as fir, three bristle, cudrania or poplar. It should be noted, however, that the permeability of woods is very variable. At the same time, the structures of wooden cores are different, some are solid wooden sculptures, some heavier or thinner, and even more fabric-strengthened thin wood cores.

Besides this and due to the great difference in burial environments, the waterlogged wooden cores might be deteriorated to different degrees, and the amount of water contents may therefore differ widely. Most wooden cores may have maintained their original appearance and shape, in spite of the weakened condition due to the penetration of water into the wood structure. If these unearthed lacquers are taken out of their original environment without any treatment, the wooden core might split or brake along the grain and the lacquer would therefore shrink or be deformed (figs. 3 a, 3 b), the lacquer film layers be wrinkled or cracked. How these ancient Chinese waterlogged lacquered wooden cores can be preserved is the topic of this study.

2. The treatment methods used until today

During the last two decades, the Chinese conservators have made great efforts to study the preservation of unearthed lacquers and could gain some progress. The situation of unearthed lacquer is so different in the degree of deterioration and in the materials used. It is therefore not suitable to develop a treatment method which can be effective for all waterlogged lacquers. For this reason different methods have been studied.

2.1 Dehydration

A useful way of dehydration is to dry the waterlogged wooden core lacquer slowly, so that the moisture can be redistributed as evenly as possible during drying to reduce the drying stresses. Drying stresses are caused by the greater shrinkage of the outer part of the wood, which dries first compared to the interior, which looses water more slowly and thus remains in an expanded condition for a longer time.

Fig. 2a. Core of laquered scabbard made of wood and fabric

Fig. 2b. Core of laquered arrows made of iron and bamboo stripes

The natural drying method is used to put the waterlogged objects in a high and constant humidity environment, drying step by step over a longer period of time, until the water content of the object is constant. The other way of natural drying is to embed waterlogged objects in a sand- or saw-dust bath. This way the water contents can be balanced and the dehydration process can proceed slowly enough. The sand and sawdust is used to stabilize the objects and prevent their deformation. The natural drying method is simple and practical. It is suitable for lower water contents of waterlogged wooden cores, ramie fabric cores or cores made of fir tree. This treatment has achieved some practical successes.[3]

Fig. 2 c. Core of lacquered mirror made of bronze

Fig. 3 a, 3 b. Shrinkage and deformation of lacquer after the excavation

3 b

2.2 Dehydration and consolidation

Most waterlogged wooden cores of lacquerware are rather weak in their mechanical strength. In this case, the percentage of moisture content of the waterlogged wooden core is higher and the treatment must involve the dehydration as well as the consolidation of the piece of lacquerware. The high water content of the wooden core calls for a bulking agent to fill the micropores within the cell wall of the wood. Thus, the cell wall is strengthened and more resistant to collapse and even the shrinkage of the wood can be reduced. Certain successes have been achieved with sugar or PEG as a bulking agent.

2.2.1 Sugar treatment

The molecular structure of sugar allows to build up a hydrogen-bond with the cellulose molecules and the decomposition products of the wood. The treatment of waterlogged wooden lacquerware with sugar has been studied for many years. According to recent reports this method has shown good results. As for the waterlogged wooden bodies coated with lacquer excavated at Cheng Tai Guan in the Henan province, the water content of the wooden core was more than 600 %. The highest one was about 1600 %, based on the dry weight. After treatment, the percentage of shrinkage is about 2 %.[4]

2.2.2 PEG treatment

PEG is well known as a good bulking agent for waterlogged wood. The molecular weight of PEG of about 4000–6000 is useful to replace the water within the wood.[5] The high water content of the wooden cores of lacquerware should be treated with a highly concentrated PEG solution. The heating impregnation of PEG is often used to decrease the viscosity of highly concentrated PEG. A batch of waterlogged wooden lacquerware found in the Mawang Dui tomb was treated with a PEG solution. After the dehydration and consolidation process the lacquerware had kept its original appearance. The beautiful colours had hardly changed.

3. A new method: mono-glyoxal

Though the conservation methods for waterlogged wooden lacquerware have made some advances, it has not been able to find a single method that could be used in all circumstances for unearthed lacquerware.

It might seem at first, that there is no difference between treating waterlogged wooden objects or waterlogged wooden lacquerware. But in practice, the latter is more difficult not only in hydration, but also in consolidation. There are several reasons: First, the thickness of the lacquer film on the wooden core is about 0.2–0.8 mm. It is impermeable if the lacquer film is in an intact condition and does not show any cracks or fissures on the surface. This will be of disadvantage for the progress of dehydration and consolidation of waterlogged wooden lacquerware. Second, the percentage of shrinkage must be as small as possible after the dehydration and consolidation, otherwise the lacquer film will turn wrinkly and crack, or the lacquer be deformed. Third, we cannot see the degree of degradation of the wooden body and the sort of wood with the naked eyes and the construction of lacquered wooden bodies can hardly be shown by soft x-ray when the lacquer is painted with a red pigment i. e. vermilion (HgS). In order to solve these problems, the lacquer film and a bulking agent that can easily enter the cell wall of the wood must be studied.

3.1. The surface state of the lacquer film

The modern and unearthed lacquer films are examined by SEM (figs. 4 a, 4 b). We find that there are many micropores dispersed in the surface of the unearthed lacquer film and only a few micropores in the modern lacquer film. The diameter of a micropore is about 100 nm. The micropores may be caused by the lacquer layers eroded under the burial environment over thousand years. Perhaps the origin of the micropores is the gum. The raw material of lacquer contains some gum, the gum is degradated and formed micropores. These micropores provided the passway for the dehydration and the bulking agent entering the wooden body of the lacquerwork.

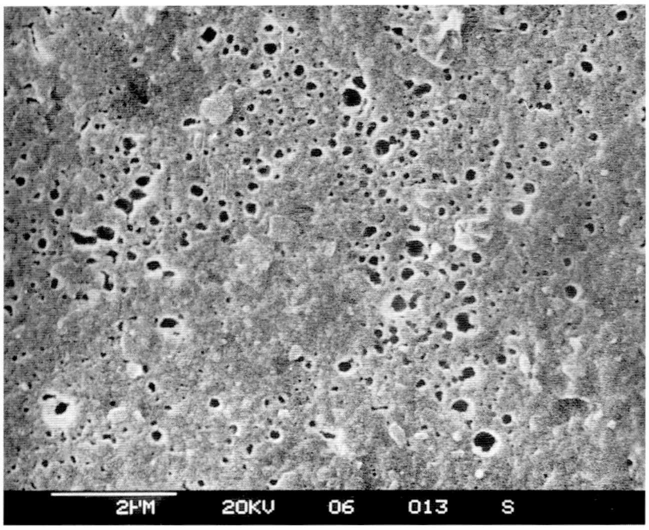

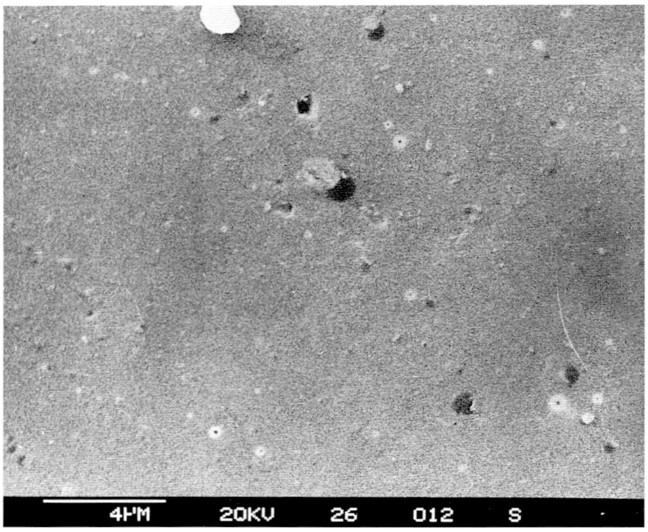

Figs. 4 a, 4 b. Unearthed and modern lacquer film examined by SEM. There are many micropores dispersed in the surface of the unearthed lacquer film and only a few micropores in the modern lacquer film

3.2 The bulking agent mono-glyoxal

The molecular of the bulking agent needs to be small enough to penetrate the micropores of the lacquer film and to diffuse into the cell wall in order to be effective. The molecular structure of mono-glyoxal is a plane type structure. The chemical structure is as follows: The distances between C–C, C–H, C=O is 0.147 nm, 0.109 nm, 0.12 nm respectively. The volume of the molecular is small enough to diffuse into the microcapillaries and fills the cell walls (capillaries =10–100 nm). Since the cell walls are to be filled, it will be effective to control the shrinkage of the waterlogged wooden body of the piece of lacquerware.

3.3 Penetrating test and treatment

3.3.1 Penetrating test

A waterlogged wooden body immersed the solution of glyoxal, a month later, after drying, the cell wall is examined by SEM. The thickness of the cell wall is increased from the original 1–3 nm to over 5 nm. These experiments have proven, that glyoxal entered into the cell wall.

3.3.2 The treatment method using mono-glyoxal

The procedure is as follows: The waterlogged lacquered wooden body is immersed in a solution of mono-glyoxal and some additional agent. The concentration of the solution is successively increased from 40 % to 65–70 % until the weight of the immersed objects is not increasing any more. The objects are taken out of the solution and the surface blotted, then drying slowly in a suitable environment. When the weight of the objects remains constant, the processes of dehydration and consolidation are finished. Poly-oliga glyoxal will be formed and the cell walls are strengthened. The treatment of some waterlogged lacquered wooden bodies with glyoxal proved successful (figs. 5 a–c).

5a

Fig. 5 a–c. Waterlogged wooden bodies of lacquer after treatment with mono-glyoxal and additional agents

5b

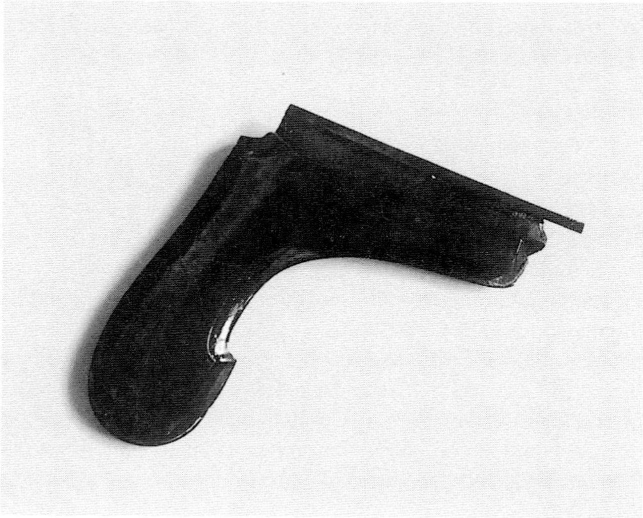

4. Discussion and conclusion

Discussion

1. During the treating periods it is advantageous to maintain more mono-glyoxal in the solution, the small moleculars will help to penetrate and transport a high percentage of bulking agent into the cell wall.
2. White crystal poly-oliga hydrated glyoxal is easily formed in the glyoxal solution. This will retard the passway of replacement water from the waterlogged wooden body of the lacquerwork. It is important to prevent the production of white crystal, and small crystals like crystal seed. A large number of crystals will be produced in a few days.
3. The aqueous of glyoxal is an acidic solution. The PH value is about 1–3. It must be denatured.
4. When the waterlogged wooden body of lacquerwork is treated with PEG, sometimes the lacquer film may bulge and blister. This phenomenon is probably due to the exchange passway retarded by the big molecular PEG in the lacquer film. In order to prove this interference, the blistered lacquer is taken out of the PEG solution and cleaned, then replaced in the bulking agent of the glyoxal solution. After a few weeks, the blisters on the lacquer will disappear so the treatment using glyoxal can avoid occasionally the blistering phenomenon.

Conclusion

As the molecular size of mono-glyoxal is so small that they can easily pass through the lacquer layers and enter the cell wall of wood, the cell wall of waterlogged wooden lacquerware is strengthened and thus the collapse and shrinkage of the wooden body much reduced. Glyoxal is an excellent bulking agent for waterlogged wooden cores of lacquerware. Some waterlogged wooden bodies of lacquerware are treated by using a mono-glyoxal solution and proved successful. The works need to be studied continuously.

Notes

1 Zhijiang Museum, Zhijiang Wen Wu, 1987.
2 Chen, Yuansheng/Xie, Yulin/Lu, Heng et al.: 'Studies on the analysis and identification of prehistoric Chinese lacquers', *Sciences of Conservation & Archaeology*, vol. 7, no. 2, 1995, pp. 12–30.
3 Wu, Jugao: 'Talking about the conservation of lacquerwares unearthed', *Wen Wu*, no. 3, 1986, pp. 28–33.
4 Chen, Jinliang/Cui, Zhanhua: 'Dehydrolyzing and shaping investigation of unearthed, waterlogged, painted woodenware at Changtaiguan of Xinyang in Henan', *Sciences of Conservation & Archaeology*, vol. 6, no. 2, 1994, pp. 1–5.
5 Grattan, D.W.: 'Conservation of waterlogged wood', *Conservation of Marine Archaeology Objects*, 1987, pp.15–16.

Photo Credits

All photographs by the author

5c

Inside of Konjikido of Chusonji Temple at Hiraizumi

Sadatoshi Miura

The Conservation of the Golden Hall (Konjikido) of Chusonji Temple at Hiraizumi

Abstract

The Golden Hall (Konjikido) of Chusonji Temple located at Hiraizumi, Iwate Prefecture, was built between 1109 and 1124 by Fujiwara Kiyohira as a mausoleum for himself and as an Amida Hall. It was named Konjikido, because it is covered with gold leaf. Konjikido is sheltered in a room and separated from the visitors' area by a large glass showcase. The showcase was replaced in 1989, because the inside had become humid (more than 70 % RH through a year). After the improvement, the climate inside has been kept at almost 65 % RH. But cracks occurred on the urushi coating. Researches were conducted since 1992 to study the reasons for these cracks by monitoring temperature, humidity, moisture content and displacement of wooden boards, and strains within the urushi coating. The results showed that a gap between two wooden boards changed about 0.2 mm in a year due to seasonal temperature changes and that the gap had broadened about 0.4 mm in these seven years. Based on this calculation, the total increase of the gap after the improvement would be more than 1 mm, probably enough to cause cracking on the surface of the urushi coating. It has taken the wooden boards a long time to dry after the improvement, because they are coated with urushi which inhibits the passage of moisture. The wood shrinkage seems to have come to an end in recent years. But a careful observation is still required, because there is some strain at the cracks of the urushi coating.

1. Introduction

Chusonji Temple, located at Hiraizumi/Iwate Prefecture, was founded in 1105 by Fujiwara Kiyohira, governor of the northern province. He intended Hiraizumi to be the northern capital, a new Kyoto, so that the culture of Hiraizumi (or Chusonji) has often been called the 'mirror of Kyoto'. Although the twelfth century was a period of wars, and the samurai class was beginning to replace the old aristocracy, the culture of Hiraizumi flourished under Fujiwara, because Hiraizumi is far from Kyoto.

The golden hall (Konjikido), a small wooden building, was built between 1109 and 1124 by Kiyohira as a mausoleum for himself and as an Amida Hall. Konjikido, gorgeously covered in gold leaf, was also a symbol of the prosperity of Hiraizumi culture. In the twelfth century, Chusonji had about 340 buildings and several hundreds of people – monks and aristocrats – lived there. But many of the buildings were burned down or laid waste by war in the fourteenth century. Fortunately, Konjikido remained over the centuries. The remains of Kiyohira, his son and grandson are still mummified beneath the three altars of the golden hall. Konjikido now receives about a million visitors a year as one of the most famous historic sites in Japan (colour plate XVII).

2. Conservation facilities for Konjikido

Konjikido is a one storey, 5.5 m long, 5.5 m wide and 8.0 m high building. In order to protect it, a wooden shelter was built in 1288.

From 1962–1968 a reinforced concrete shelter was constructed and restoration was carried out on its entire exterior and interior (figs. 1, 2). Due to this restoration, it regained its glitter of gold as we see it now.

Konjikido is settled in a large glass showcase to avoid unexpected damages, which means it is separated from the visitors' area by glass screens.

After the construction of the concrete shelter, the humidity inside the glass showcase increased and many dewdrops were observed on the glass screens particularly in early summer (fig. 3). So the following countermeasures were proposed[1] and improvement was made between 1986 and 1990.

a. The reason for the high humidity inside was moisture that had risen from the ground into the glass showcase. A dehumidifier and a moisture barrier under the floor were necessary.

b. The reason for the many dewdrops on the glass screens facing the outside was assumed to be the chilled inside air due to the delay of about one month in the change of ground temperature following that of outside temperature. The dewdrops occurred whenever the surface temperature was lower than the dew point of the outside air. Heat insulation of the ground and air-conditioning of the shelter were necessary.

The glass showcase was also replaced in the campaign of 1986–1990. The new glass showcase was designed to have sufficient air-tightness and to keep the relative humidity inside stable. A moisture barrier and insulation layers were laid under the gravel on the ground. All gaps in the glass showcase were sealed thoroughly with silicon rubber. Inorganic moisture-buffering material was used for the back and side walls of the showcase to prevent a rapid RH change while the dehumidifier was working.

Four electric dehumidifiers were used in place of the former air-conditioning unit. They were set in an antechamber open to the glass showcase. They were controlled individually; that is, each dehumidifier had its own humidity sensor. The four humidity sensors were fixed at the four corners of the veranda of Konjikido. The temperature within the showcase was not controlled, because daily temperature change was estimated small enough due to air-conditioning of the shelter (fig. 4).

Because of the improvement of the conservation facilities, rising moisture from the ground and dewdrops on the glass screen were completely controlled. The dehumidifiers kept a stable level of relative humidity inside (about 65 % RH) through a year.[2] But torsion of the boards and cracks of the urushi coating occurred so that researches were conducted since 1992 to study the reasons.

3. Measurements

Temperature, humidity, moisture content and displacement of wooden boards, and strain of the urushi coating were measured.[3] All data were stored in data loggers (Hakusan Corporation, LT2001 or HLS-200) and transferred occasionally to a personal computer for analysis.

a. The temperature was measured below the left (south) veranda every hour (24 times/day) by a Pt resistance thermometer since July 1992.

b. The humidity was measured at the same point by an electric resistance hygrometer since July 1992.

c. The moisture content was measured at a wooden board (31 mm wide, 84 mm thick and 1.160 mm long) of the left (south) veranda every hour (24 times/day) by an electric resistance wood moisture meter (Kett, MT-8S) since August 1993.

d. The shrinkage of wood was measured by monitoring the width of a gap between two boards of the left (south) veranda every hour (24 times/day) by an inductance displacement transducer (Kyowa, DT-10F) since July 1992.

e. Strain was measured at a crack of the urushi coating on the back (west) wall every 12 hours (2 times/day) by a foil strain gauge (Showa Measuring Instruments, N11-FA-5-120-11-VM3T) from December 1995. Control data were also taken at a sound urushi surface nearby.

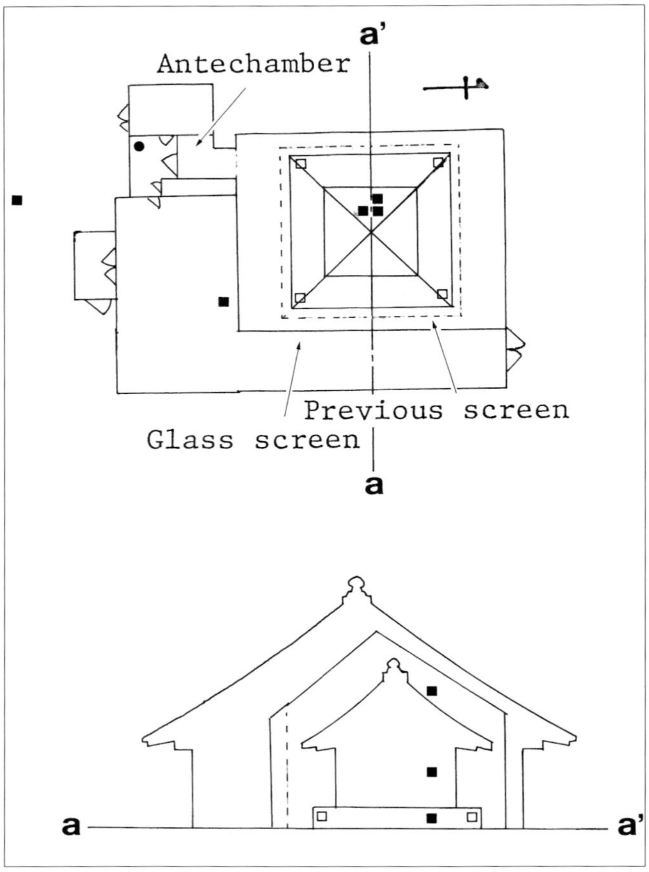

Fig. 2. Plan of the present shelter

Fig. 1. View of the present shelter

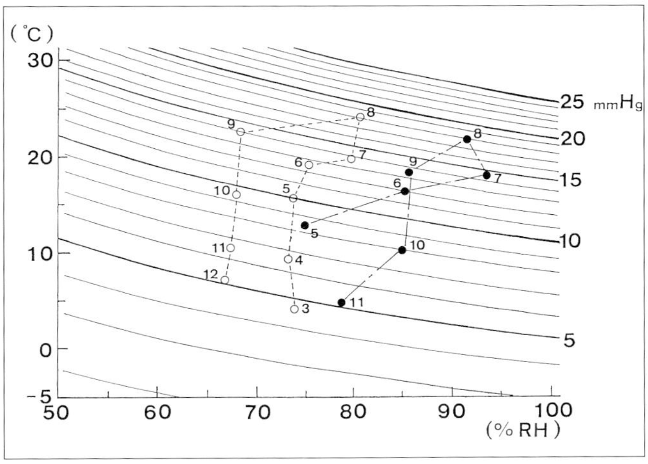

3 △

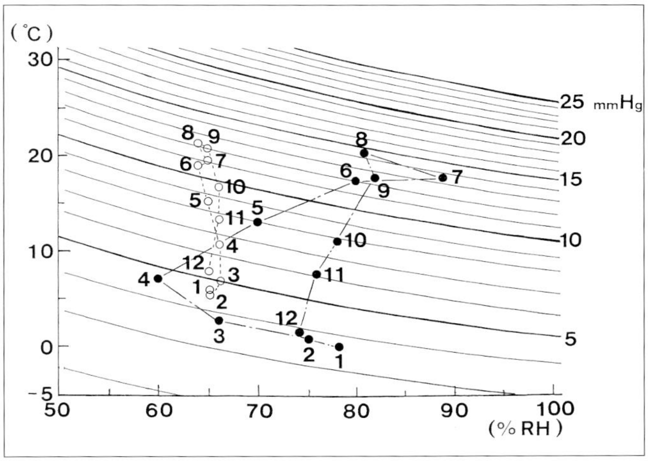

4 △

Fig. 3. Climate of Konjikido (1986, before improvement)
○ inside the glass showcase
• outdoors

Fig. 4. Climate of Konjikido (1993, after improvement)
○ inside the glass showcase
• outdoors

4. Results

Figures 5–8 show the results indicating evident trends in spite of some missing data. The gap width became larger with seasonal changes of about 0.2 mm (fig. 7). The output of a moisture content meter is showed as the vertical axis of fig. 6, because the relation between the output and the real moisture content of the wooden board was not calibrated. But the manual of the moisture meter says that the output range 0–10 mV usually corresponds to a moisture content of 0–30 %. The strain gauge measuring the gap width seemed to be broken because it expanded too much (fig. 8).

Fig. 5. Temperature inside the glass showcase from July 1992 to January 1999

Fig. 6. Moisture content of a wooden board from August 1993 to January 1999

Fig. 7. Gap width between two wooden boards from July 1992 to January 1999

Fig. 8. Strain of the urushi coating from December 1995 to January 1999 large change: measured at a crack
small change: at a sound urushi surface nearby

5 ▽

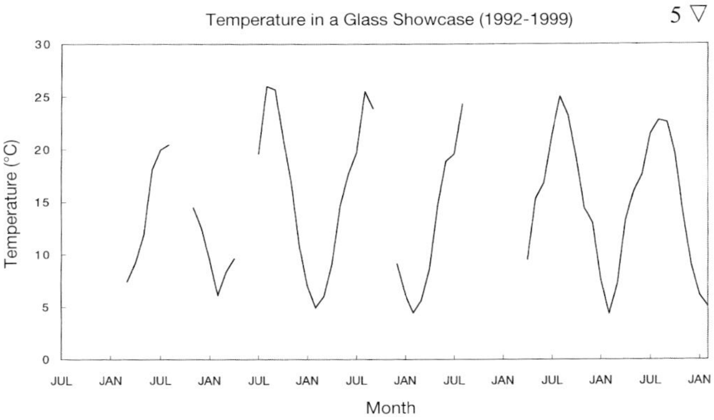

6 ▽

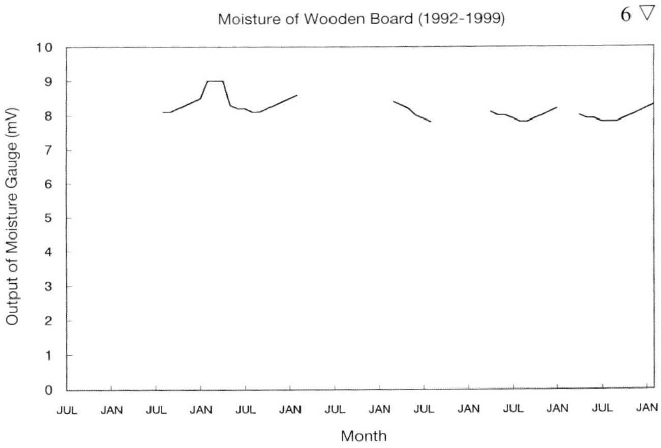

7 ▽

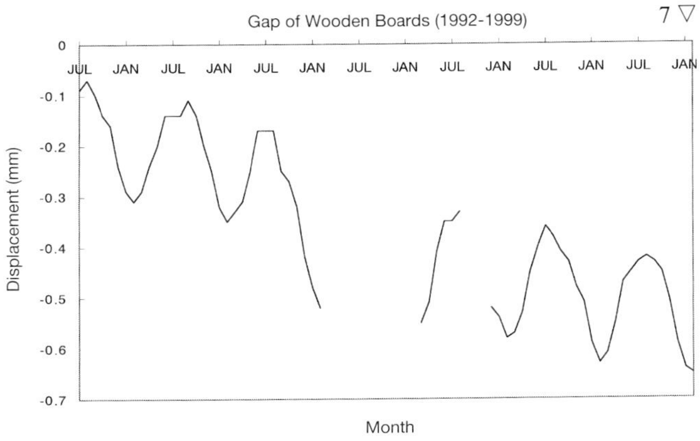

8 ▽

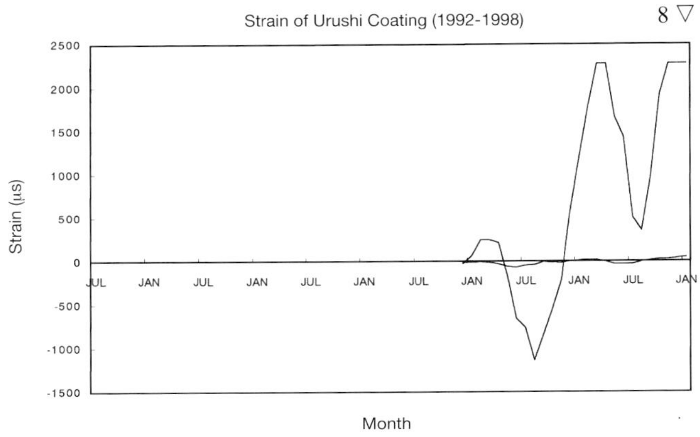

5. Discussion

The gap width varied seasonally by temperature change. The reason was thought to be as follows. Wood expands perpendicularly to its fibers with the ratio of $35–60x10^{-6}$/°C against temperature change. The temperature inside the glass showcase varies about 20 °C annually, also raising the seasonal moisture content change of the board (fig. 6). As the width of the board is 310 mm, movement by annual temperature change was estimated to about 0.2–0.4 mm. This figure corresponded approximately to the seasonal variation of fig. 7.

The continuous expansion of the gap (fig. 6) was due to the climate change caused by the improvement of 1986–1990. Usually wood moves much more by humidity than by temperature. Japanese cypress expands or shrinks with ratios of 0.12 % (straight grain) and of 0.23 % (cross grain) against 1 % change of moisture content. Using these figures, the boards were estimated to move about 0.6 mm against 1 % moisture content change. Figure 7 indicates that the board may have lost about 1 % moisture content during the observation of 1992–1999. Since this monitoring started two years after the improvement, the board should have lost more due to the change of environment. The difference of the equivalent moisture content between 70 % RH and 65 % RH is evaluated at about 2–3 %, which should cause a large shrinkage of more than 1 mm. An urushi film moves much less than wood. The ratio is $15x10^{-6}$/°C against temperature and $2.92x10^{-4}$/% RH against relative humidity. If wood shrinks or expands much by climate change, urushi film can't follow it. The resulting large stress causes cracking. This may happen even if the shrinkage seems to have become stable from 1998, because strain is found still remaining between urushi film and wood (fig. 8). This means that it takes a long time after improvement for wooden boards to dry because they are coated by urushi which inhibits the passage of moisture.

6. Conclusion

The glass showcase for Konjikido was replaced in 1989 because the inside had become humid. By improvement, the climate changed from more than 70 % RH to 65 % RH, but cracks of the urushi coating occurred. Researches since 1992 showed that a gap between two wooden boards of a veranda changed about 0.2 mm in a year due to seasonal temperature changes and that the gap had broadened about 0.4 mm in these seven years. The total increase of the gap after the improvement would be more than 1 mm, probably enough to cause cracking on the surface of the urushi coating. The wood shrinkage seems to have finished in recent years. But a careful observation is still required because there is strain still remaining at the cracks of urushi coating.

Acknowledgement

The author thanks Mr. Haseki of Chusonji, Mr. Kobayashi of Hakusan Corporation and Mrs. Matsubara of Tokyo National Research Institute of Cultural Properties for their help.

Notes

1 SADATOSHI MIURA: 'Temperature and humidity in a large glass showcase for a temple hall', *Preprints for the 8th Triennial Meeting of ICOM-CC*, (1987, Sydney), pp. 897–900.
2 SADATOSHI MIURA: 'Temperature and humidity in a large glass showcase for a temple hall', Part 2, *Preprints for the 9th Triennial Meeting of ICOM-CC* (1990, Dresden), pp. 592–595.
3 SADATOSHI MIURA and T. OGAWA: 'Study on the relation between the occurrence of cracks of Urushi coating and a climate change after the improvement of shelter for Golden Hall of Chusonji', *Conservation Science*, 38, 1999, pp. 31–38 (in Japanese).

Photo Credits

Figs. 1–8 by the author
Colour plate XVII: Chusonji Temple, Hiraizumi

Fig. 1. Portable *namban* altar, front view of altar top with initials of the Society of Jesus I.H.S. before treatment

Kazumi Murose

An Example of Conservation Work: A Portable *Namban* Style Altarpiece with *Makie* Design from the Nagoya Municipal Museum

This report is concerned with the process of conservation of a portable *namban* style altarpiece done at the Mejiro Institute of Urushi between June 1997 and March 1998.

What is *namban* lacquerwork?

In 1549, Francisco Javier landed in Kagoshima and started his missionary work in Japan. While propagating the Catholic religion, the Jesuits had the ritual implements decorated with a traditional Japanese technique: *makie*. Many pieces of lacquerware were brought home by the Jesuits, and can now be seen in Portugal. Very few remained in Japan, for Catholicism was banned in 1619.

Liturgical implements in lacquer technique such as portable altars, host boxes and reading stands were exported to Europe in the early years and highly appreciated. Therefore, more and more lacquered products, such as chests and cabinets, were produced and shipped abroad. The term *namban* lacquerwork is used for lacquerwork made for export as well as for domestic use, which was decorated with patterns and exotic motifs such as foreign people and dogs. A typical design of the *namban* style is a scene with animals and plants framed with geometrical patterns and scrollwork. Motifs are usually inlaid with *hiramakie* or mother-of-pearl. These technical and decorative characteristics may have derived from the popular *Koudaiji makie* style and matched the taste of the Europeans.

1. Introduction

Portable altars of this type with hinged double doors and a picture of the Virgin and Christ inside is called '*seigan*' in Japanese (colour plate XVIII.1). It is one of the typical examples of *namban* lacquerwork made in the sixteenth century in Japan. The outside of the doors shows a design of cherry blossoms, camellias and birds (colour plate XVIII.2); the inside shows wild pinks, maple trees and deer (fig. 2). The pictures are framed with designs of *namban* scrolls and geometric patterns. All the designs are applied with gold and silver *makie* and mother-of-pearl. The sides of the altar are decorated with gourds. The top of the altar is shaped like a Chinese style gable, and is decorated with religious symbols of the Jesuits: the initials I.H.S. (fig. 1), a cross and a heart with three nails. An oil painting of Christ on wood is held in place by two frames lacquered in black and one with *namban* scrolls. The measurements are 45.5 x 31.3 x 4.8 cm.

2. Present Condition

A vertical crack from the shrinkage of wood is seen on the backside of the main body and caused a difference in level (fig. 3). The structure of the altar is unsteady because of cracks also seen at the joint of the body and the top part which is shaped like a Chinese-style gable, and a lacquer coating near the cracks is lifting. There are many dents from the side to the bottom of the

△ 2

3 △

Fig. 2. Right door inside in *makie* with supplements before treatment
Fig. 3. Overall view of altar back before treatment
Fig. 4. Hinge, outer edge, right side, after treatment
Fig. 5. Hinge, left bottom, before treatment

△ 4

5 ▽

body, some of which have been restored in Europe with white material like putty. The center of the right door is seriously damaged and coating and *makie* are inlaid in later restorations with unknown materials.

The panel of the painting is strongly warped. Dryness also added a long crack in the center which runs to the frame. Too much adhesive and animal glue has been stuffed into the crack in later restorations and now spoils the outward appearance of the piece of lacquerwork. Nails used to attach the metal hinges have become loose and prevent doors from opening smoothly. The right upper hinge is broken in two, only held with two nails (fig. 4). The left bottom hinge is also cracked in the corner. Two of the nails have been applied later, as many are missing and new ones need to be supplied (fig. 5).

3. Policy

The present policy of restoration carried out by the Agency for Cultural Affairs is, as is the general trend, conservation rather than restoration of works of art. Therefore, most restoration and conservation measures are undertaken using the same materials and techniques as were originally used for each individual item.

4. Conservation

4.1 Preparatory research

The first step was to photograph and measure the item and to develop a concept for the conservation procedure. Photographs and records were also taken at each step of the conservation process, so that the condition before and after can easily be compared. A report was made later. Conservation work was concentrating on the altar, whereas the panel of Christ was left untouched. Before starting, the altar had to be taken into parts by removing the doors, the frames and the panel in order to repair the crack, make the backside even and to restore the broken hinges.

4.2 Disassembly

Separating the altar into its component parts has originally begun by removing the metal hinges. However, as the copper nails holding the hinges were bent open inside the main frame, the oil painting of Christ and the frame were taken out before removing the hinges. An excessive amount of animal glue and adhesives covering the outer frame had to be removed first.

Animal glue, which struck the inner and outer frame, was softened with warm water and cut away with a very thin blade. The greatest care was taken not to peel off the lacquer coating together with the glue covering it. Once the glue was removed, the panel of Christ came off easily since it had not been glued. At this point an under-panel was discovered. This panel was blackened with charcoal, and held in place by the outer frame. The under-panel and the outer frame were also fixed to the main body with excessive animal glue, which was removed in the same way as before.

It was found, that the reverse side of the under-panel was decorated with a *makie* and mother-of-pearl design unrelated to the rest of the altar. The under-panel had once been broken in two and had been joined together with animal glue. However, the two halves were rejoined with a thin strip of wood in between using much animal glue, and the design was not aligned. The glue and wooden strip used for the restoration were kept. The panels and frames were successfully taken out. This cleared the way for the nails to be straightened and pulled out, thus removing the hinges and the doors.

4.3 Cleaning

After all the basic parts were disassembled, each part was carefully cleaned. A cotton cloth very slightly dampened with water not to scratch the surface was used to wipe away oil strains and dust on the lacquer coating. If the cloth is too wet, moisture may seep through the cracks and weaken the foundation. If the cloth is too dry, dust particles may cause additional scratches on the surface. Cleaning was done except for the previously restored areas of the *makie* design. Lifting and flaking areas were held down with thin strips of *washi* paper and starch to avoid breaking off during the cleaning process.

4.4 Resetting the mother-of-pearl

Since the mother-of-pearl inlay had originally been applied with animal glue, they were reset with the same material. Pressure was applied evenly, and any excessive glue was wiped off. After they were dried, a hairline space between the original lacquer surface and the mother-of-pearl was sealed with *sabi urushi* to protect the mother-of-pearl from relifting and to prevent a seeping through of lacquer during the following process.

4.5 *Urushi gatame*

After the mother-of-pearl inlay was firmly reset, *urushi gatame* was done, a process which is of great importance in conservation work. Lacquer surfaces develop cracks by shrinkage of wooden bodies and exposure to ultra-violet light over a long period of time. Generally speaking, a lacquer surface of about 200 years of age has microscopic cracks; after 300 years or more, they become visible to the eye. The technique of *urushi gatame* aims at preventing further damage of the lacquer surface by seeping natural lacquer into the cracks, and brings back flexibility to the coating. If any other resin is used, the surface becomes unnaturally stiff and causes a cracking of the coating. Natural lacquer is wiped off immediately after it is applied to the surface and seeped into the cracks, leaving the cracks filled. This technique usually needs a week or more to dry the lacquer well.

4.6 Holding down the lifted coating

After the application of *urushi gatame* areas, where lifting pieces had been lightly held down with starch and *washi* paper, were restored. Thinned *mugi urushi* was applied between the lifting pieces and the base, then pressure was evenly applied with pressure distributing plates. Excess *mugi urushi* that was forced out was wiped off. Pressure was reapplied and left for four to five days. It takes a longer time in humid seasons.

4.7 Restoring cracking areas

Cracked areas were set with *mugi urushi* in the same way as the process above. The backside of the altar, where a deep crack was making the surface uneven, was restored by pressuring the surface with a clamp.

4.8 Reassembling the frames

The inner frame had been disassembled into four bars. The top and the bottom wood which were bent were straightened and bonded. Since they had also been carved thinner than the left and the right ones in the previous restoration, four woods were carefully joined in the proper position. The panel underneath, which had once been broken and glued together, was reseparated into two halves and joined together realigned with *mugi urushi*. The outer frame was installed around the inner one. The outer frame and the backside were fixed firmly with wooden nails.

Fig. 6. Altar back: glueing with *mugi urushi*

1 Overall view of the front of the portable *namban* altar after treatment

2 Overall view of the portable *namban* altar before treatment

3 Outer edge, left side below, fault, before treatment

4 Outer edge, left side below, after treatment with *kiwasabi*

4.9 Filling in *kokuso*

Chipped and dented areas were filled with several coats of *kokuso* of different consistencies and set just under the original surface (colour plate XVIII.3, 4). This is to show that the area was conserved rather than restored. White putty-like material used in the previous restoration was removed and replaced with *kokuso* (figs. 7, 8).

4. 10 *Kiwasabi*

After the materials filled in the cracks and underneath the lifting areas were fully dried, very little *sabi urushi* was applied around the restored areas to prevent the recracking and to make a smooth surface.

4.11 Fixing and fittings

Bent hinges were straightened, and the right upper hinge, which had been broken in two, was reinforced with a thin metal plate from the back. New nails were applied to the missing places and in place of the nails of the previous restoration.

4.12 Reassembly

Finally, the parts were assembled. However, because so much animal glue covering the frames and the panel underneath was removed, an empty space of 3 mm remained between the main body and the panel underneath. To compensate the lack of glue, a thin wooden support was installed behind the panel underneath. The oil painting was put back into the main body joined together with the frames.

4. 13 Photographs and records

After all the conservation work was finished, photographs were taken under the same condition as before the work, records were arranged in order and pictures taken during the work were attached to the report.

Fig. 7. Back side, upper left, fault within the wood before treatment

Fig. 8. Back side, upper left: application of *kokuso*, condition after treatment

Photo Credits

All photographs by the author

Europäische Lacke
European Lacquer

Fig. 1. Black lacquered commode attributed to Dubois; detail of the left side (Berlin, Kunstgewerbemuseum)

Johann Koller, Ursula Baumer

Historical Black Lacquers in Europe
Black Lacquers of the 17th and 18th Century

Black in Japanese and European Culture

Black and red, as well as the characteristical natural colour of the urushi-lacquer, are the most important colours of Japanese lacquer art. It is possible to dye urushi-lacquers blue, yellow, green, or even white with the respective pigments or dye-stuffs; but these colours did only play a peripheral role in the long course of its history. Black lacquered objects, like for example black lacquered tableware (fig. 2), have at all times held their position in Japan at official occasions and festivities. Black lacquers have therefore been a main component of Japanese and East Asian art and culture for centuries.[1]

Black did not play any role in the early art of Europe, not even in painting, until around the year 1500. This is equally true for Italian as for Early Netherlandish painting, the supports of early European painting in general. Black has only been used for the drawing of contours, but not as a flat-spread applied paint. It was only Leonardo da Vinci who began to shape shades with black colour.[2] Until that time black was not even considered a colour. Black lacquers are therefore not rooted within the European tradition. In terms of cultural history they constitute a foreign element and are hardly imaginable without the influence of East Asian lacquers in Europe.

Early European Lacquer Recipes and Lacquered Furniture

The history of European lacquers is rather short compared to the thousands-of-years tradition in China and Japan. It were mainly material problems, that were decisive for the late and hesitant development of European lacquers, and above all problems concerning the lacquer binding media. Black lacquers constitute a special problem within the development of European lacquers in so far as additional difficulties occurred due to the bad compatibility of pigments and binding media, especially within oil binding media. These specific difficulties are running through the European lacquer history in general and have only recently been solved in a satisfying way for modern black lacquers, i. e. for car lacquers.

The laborious way to develop a shining and – at the same time – solid black European lacquer is the subject of this article.

Probably the first description of a European lacquer is found in Theophilus (around the year 1100). It is in chapter XXI: 'De glutine vernition',[3] which can be interpreted as an early description of the procedure of making an amber varnish: Even the chapter on glaze painting (chapter XXIX: 'De pictura translucida') can be interpreted as an early source of a 'varnish'. References to decorative coatings on furniture, which can be regarded as varnishes in the broadest sense of the word, are found for the first time in Venice in the 13th century.[4] But even here, the peculiar interest in lacquers, i. e. in coloured or transparent shining coatings, began only in the 16th century, when Venice became - for a short time - the European centre for the production as well as the trade with high-quality, i. e. colourful painted and decorated furniture.[5] This monopolistic position has been installed by a first wave of imported furniture from Near East, which came to Europe exclusively through trade with the Venetians. Nearly nothing is known about the 'lacquers' on these pieces of furniture and it remains doubtful, whether black ones were among them.

The Development of a special European Lacquer Binding Medium

The sources of the 17th and 18th century contain many treatises and books of travels reporting about the strange stuff called 'lacquer'. Even though it was strictly forbidden one has tried secretly to import this 'glue' pouring out of trees in China and Japan and secreting poisonous vapours in liquid condition, which could be dyed with different colours, from theses countries.[6] Sometimes it may have been successful. But one was not familiar with the drying mechanism of this 'glue' with the effect, that the liquid lacquer dried out during the travel on ships due to humidity and reached Europe only as an unusable, worthless material.

The European attempts to produce a proper material for themselves could only slowly proceed. It is known today, that the news about the Martin brothers in Paris who succeeded first in developing a usable lacquer already in 1730 was only an overstatement. But, nevertheless, this assumption is spread again and again.[7] The truth is, that during the 16th century no considerable progress was really achieved. As for the black lacquers this had two reasons: the incompatibility of black pigments, mainly soot pigments, with oil binding media, as well as the lack of appropriate lacquer solvents for non-oil-bound lacquers.

This was the reason why it was hardly possible until about 1670 to produce lacquers everywhere in Europe, that could compete with those East Asian lacquers imported by the Portuguese and the Dutch.

Drying Oils as Lacquer Binding Media?

The hesitant development of lacquered furniture in 16th century Venice has been influenced by a first Eastern wave of import ware, coming – practically without exception – from Near East, i. e. from the Ottoman Empire.[8] The binding media, which were used for these pieces of furniture, are hardly known until now. Not much earlier a change had taken place in the South of Europe, where oil binding media began to substitute the older tempera binding media in painting as well as in the decorative arts. Oil binding media (drying oils) opened new artistic possibilities, but they brought along a lot of risks and new problems, mainly for black pigments.

Drying oils are plant oils, in terms of chemistry liquid fats (triglycerides). But only those among them, which hardened

Fig. 2. Modern Japanese tableware lacquered with urushi in black and red

through autoxidation in the open air when applied in thin layers, were adaptable as lacquer binding media.[9] This process is called 'drying'[10] and is dependent on various factors and influences, for example on temperature and humidity within the lacquer layers. Lead-white pigments, above all in thin layers, are favourable for the drying process and serve as stabilizers. Thick lacquer layers and black pigments (soot) slow it down, and may even hinder the drying process in extreme cases. Soot pigments, furthermore, perform a heavily destabilizing effect on oil layers, making damages almost unavoidable (fig. 3). Other pigments (mainly the reactive copper pigments), to the contrary, accelerate the autoxidation process beyond the necessary degree, thereby degrading the binding medium.[11]

In paints and varnishes only one of the many possible drying oils – linseed oil, poppy-seed oil, (wal)nut oil – has practically been used: linseed oil. Since in Europe at the time (and even later) soot (lamp black) was mostly used as black pigment[12], there was no possibility to produce suitable lacquers with pure linseed oil. Auxiliary measures were taken and temporary solutions were found, oriented on those developed in painting: Small amounts of black copper oxide were added to the black oil lacquer, effecting a faster drying. Or, the direct contact between the (linseed-) oil binding medium and the soot was avoided by 'masquing' the soot. This was done by pasting the black pigment at first with a tempera binding medium – mostly animal glue or egg-yolk – , then stirring it with boiled linseed oil[13] and finally applying it in this form. Since boiled linseed oils show a much faster initial drying (but not hardening!) than rough linseed oil, they were used for black pigments as the only binding medium or as an additive (drier) to rough oils. Extremely durable lacquer layers could, nevertheless, not be reached with this method. These measures resulted in black overcoats, but not always in shining black lacquers, which would allow a comparison to East Asian lacquers.

Shellac (Laksha) as a Basic Component of Black Imitation Lacquers

The old trading routes to India, abandoned and forgotten during the Middle Ages (and even beyond) were searched for well-calculated with the beginning colonialism and imperialism, reestablished and revived. The direct consequence was a second and decisive wave of imported lacquer objects, mainly in the 17th century, this time from Far East. It was the epoche which confronted the cultivated upper class in Europe for the first time with black lacquers. On their way to the Far East the Europeans also came across the stick-lac in India, the raw material for shellac, and became familiar with it; shellac was a historical raw material for lacquer, known since the Neolithic period and the terminological basis for the word 'lacquer'. In the course of the 17th century shellac became the preferred lacquer material for Chinoiseries.[14]

For 'white lacquers', i. e. for clear, transparent gloss lacquers, it could not be used because of its red, resp. yellow-brownish natural colour. But it was perfectly suitable for black lacquers and has also been misunderstood for some time as original Chinese lacquer. This misunderstanding lasted for almost the whole of the 17th century[15], and even though it was corrected towards the end of this century, it has not impaired the great popularity of shellac, favoured for red and black imitation lacquers.

But, at first, problems occurred in the practical application of shellac as a binding medium in lacquers, resulting from the solid aggregate state and the dissolving characteristics of this natural lacquer raw material. For comparison, the urushi raw material flows as a viscous sap from the tapped trunk of the tree and can be used in this form as a binding medium (figs. 4–6). The situation is completely different with shellac, a recent resin of animal provenience, won through cleaning and refining of stick-lac (raw shellac).[16] Stick-lac is the secretion of the lac insects, native from India, which infest certain bushes and trees. The secretion becomes firm rather fast and can therefore be won from the branches coated with it as a resin crust (figs. 7–8). But in this solid form neither stick-lac nor shellac, won from it, can be used

Fig. 3. Damage caused by soot in oil layers

Fig. 4. Urushi plantation

Fig. 5. Winning of Urushi sap

as a lacquer. They have to be, at first, brought into a pasty form, i. e. the shellac has to be made liquid, in some way or the other.

The Indians developed a method of melting shellac onto the objects, that had to be lacquered.[17] Since this method could not be used for black imitation lacquers on furniture, one had to look for a new solution. It was found by bringing shellac into a solution. Nevertheless, the choice of (lacquer-) solvents was very small in the 16th and 17th century. Some essential oils, like e. g. turpentine-, spik-, lavender- and rosemary-oil were at disposal, as well as spirit of wine, later on called spirit or alcohol. Since shellac is not soluble in essential oils, alcohol remained the only alternative. But this was the source of further difficulties during the 16th and the first half of the 17th century. Alcohol could not be produced in pure form, it contained too much water and, therefore, had only a small dissolution capacity. Though it was known since the late Middle Ages, how alcohol could be distilled to brandy or spirits, methods to reduce the high water content have only been developed some time later. Surprisingly modern methods were used and even so called 'drying agents'. These were salts, that could be freed from water by heating. In contact with a humid medium they absorb water and bind it into their crystalline structure. During the 17th century tartar, the deposit of wine, was used to 'dry' alcohols. We do not know until now, to what point of time this method was developed. It is only secured, that it was possible around 1670 to produce spirit lacquers on a shellac or sandarac basis and that this procedure was not to be realized yet around 1600. With the production of a soluble shellac-lacquer the way was open to the development of European black lacquers. Soon afterwards the first black European lacquer cabinets were made.

Practical work shows, that it is indeed possible to produce shining black lacquers with shellac solved in alcohol and black

Fig. 6. Homogenization of the fluid urushi sap

pigments.[18] The production of black lacquers from shellac as the only binding medium is also described in contemporary sources.[19] Nevertheless, our investigations on black lacquered boards from the late 17th and 18th century have – surprisingly – shown so far, that, at least in Central Europe, pure shellac was practically never used. We always found resin mixtures, mostly build on the common basis of shellac and sandarac. Besides, larch turpentine, molten amber, soluble copals, mastic, elemi, camphor and small amounts of oil are to be found, almost the same variety of products known to us from our investigation on gloss lacquers.[20/21] As for the pigments, not only soot (lamp black) was found as referred to in contemporary literatur[22], but also other pigments, like e. g. bone black, wood-tar, bitumina or metal oxides.

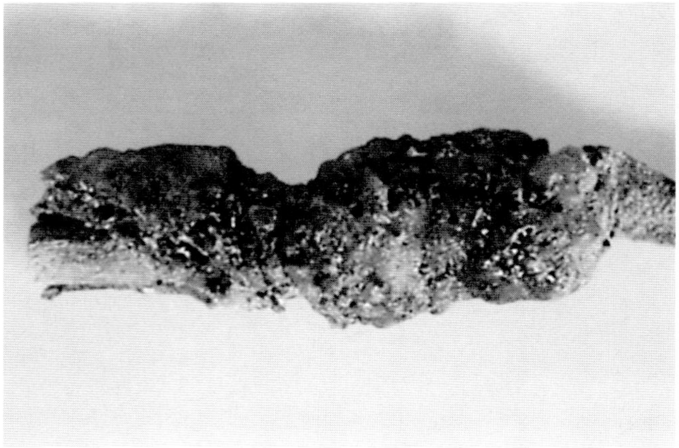

Figs. 7, 8. Stick-lac and dark shellac types won through melting, filtration or extraction. Bright shellac types, won through extraction and afterward bleaching of the stick-lac, have only become a trading good towards the end of the 18th century. The stick-lac (upper left) is taken as a resinous crust from infested branches (cf. fig. 8)

Even though it was possible to produce a shining and polishable lacquer with only one layer of shellac and black pigments, we found at least two main layers in all the investigated objects: one black pigmented fundamental layer and one translucently pigmented or transparent upper layer as a finishing lacquer. The binding media in the pigmented and in the gloss lacquer layer always contained the same components; only their relative amounts were different.

Cheaper Lacquer Versions

For what reason no pure shellac was used in all the investigated black imitation lacquers must be left to speculation. For good reasons it can be assumed, that financial motives have been decisive. Good quality shellac was difficult to buy and expensive. In comparison, all the other listed materials, with the exception of camphor and mastic, were much less costly. In the case of the investigated imitation lacquers we found blended spirit lacquers on a shellac basis.

Furthermore, it speaks in favour of this version, that one has always systematically tried to find cheaper versions of black lacquers. At first, the isolated wooden surface was painted with a black coating with animal glue as a binding medium. The shine and therefore the character of a lacquer was finally achieved in a second step, by coating the coloured paint with a gloss lacquer. This finishing lacquer contained in most cases no shellac components and was oriented in composition on the transparent gloss lacquers ('white lacquers') described before.[23]

The development of highly pure, almost water free alcohol prepared the way not only for lacquers on a shellac basis, but also for spirit lacquers in general. The main representatives of this group are the transparent gloss lacquers, i. e. the spirit lacquers on a sandarac basis. We found them in lacquer binding media in black lacquers and mostly in cases, when we were dealing with minor precious objects.

Spirit Lacquers on a Copal- and Sandarac Basis

The spirit lacquers on a shellac basis as well as the cheaper forms with glue-bound black coating and a finishing sandarac varnish can be found throughout Europe. On French furniture (Deforge and Dubois), to the contrary, special forms could be identified (cf. figs. 1, 9). They contain copal- and sandarac-resins as main components.[24] Besides, varying amounts of natural resins, as they were found in the gloss lacquers, are contained. The compounding of camphor within these lacquers, a natural softener, is extremely high.

The 'copal' has substituted shellac in this rather expensive special form. The speciality of this type of copal is the fact, that it is at least partly soluble in spirit and shows similarities in its composition to the alcohol-soluble Manila- or Kauri-copals. Both types of copal are in use in Europe only since the beginning of the 19th century. The Kauri-copal from New Zealand was only introduced to England in 1841.[25] On the other hand, it is known today, that the distribution area of the Kauri trees as well of the fossile as the more recent Kauri-resins are reaching further than the Kauri-regions of New Zealand and Australia, comprising the whole of Indonesia, the Philippines as well as Malaysia.[26] The proof of spirit-soluble copals of the Kauri- and Manila-type indicates, that this type has been brought to Europe as a trading good in the 18th century already and possibly under another name, e. g. as 'Oriental copal from the East Indies and New Spain'.

The spirit lacquers on a copal- and sandarac-basis are also built in two layers and consist of one pigmented and one finishing lacquer layer. The resin components used in both layers are basically the same and differ only in their relative compounding. Nevertheless, deviations from this scheme have been found within the French pieces of Criard-furniture. Here, the finishing lacquer layer consists of ordinary 'European' gloss lacquers.[27]

Black Oil Varnishes

With only slight temporal delay, compared to the spirit lacquers, black oil varnishes were developed towards the end of the 17th century. As for the oil varnishes we are – in contrast to the terminology – not dealing with pure oil products, but with oil-resin-mixtures, which had to be melted together by cooking. As an oil component linseed oil was used in the historical lacquers. As a resin component amber, different fossile and recent-fossile copals, as well as colophony (= 'resin'), were at disposal. The resulting oil varnishes have been labelled according to their resin-compounding as amber-, copal- and resin-varnishes (= colophony-varnishes). The 'resin-varnish' made from colophony and linseed oil was rather easy to prepare, but it was of minor quality compared to others. The higher-quality amber- and copal-varnishes were, to the contrary, rather difficult to produce, since both resins are insoluble in linseed oil. Therefore, they had to be melted together ('melted in') 'by force' at high temperature (about 300 °C) or brought into a form, that was soluble in linseed oil. The latter occurred, e.g. by 'melting out' the hard fossile copals. 'Melting out' means the heating (or cooking) of copals at an average temperature of 250-300 °C until they melt under steaming off the fugitive components resulting from this process at the same time. The process has to be continued until the copal melt is not smoking any more and a clear melt is left. This leftover, called copal-colophony (or, in the case of amber, amber-colophony), was soluble in linseed oil and could be cooked together with these to a high-quality copal-varnish. Depending from the oil-resin-ratio the results were elastic lacquers with a high oil content or highly shining hard lacquers with a high resin content. The resulting sirup-like products had to be thinned and made more liquid with oil of turpentine before use in order to bring them in an applicable form.

The earliest oil varnishes known until now have been found by us on furniture of the Dagly-workshop in Berlin (around 1700). In the 18th century the best and most elaborate oil varnishes (copal varnishes) have been produced by the Martin brothers in Paris ('vernis Martin').[28] Nevertheless, the oil lacquers remained throughout the 18th century in the shadow of the more brilliant spirit lacquers. Regarded retrospectively they constitute the final step in the development of historical lacquers. They were mechanically more resistant and less affectable by light and environmental influences and therefore they gained ground against the spirit lacquers in the course of the 19th century, to which they were inferior in splendour. Due to their resistance towards weathering they were especially apt as black coach lacquers and did expel all other types of lacquers in this field.

Oil varnishes have been preserved until far into the 20th century and have only been replaced definitively since around 1950 by synthetic resin lacquers. Their complete disappearance from the market was nevertheless not due to a lack of quality. They were exclusively due to the complicated and dangerous production procedure and the high costs caused by them. One further reason was the highly differing quality of the raw materials in use, though resins (copals and amber) as well as those of the oils (linseed-, tung-, castor- and industrial oils). It should not be overlooked in the context of this development, that such an important raw material as amber was practically not available for decades for political reasons.

Acknowledgment

During the six years of research on historical lacquers, carried out within the scope of the German-Japanese cooperation in the field of monument conservation between 1993 and 1998, this paper represents the final contribution and at the same time a sort of conclusion on an important field in the study on historical lacquers. The investigations have been carried out in cooperation with the Bavarian State Department of Historical Monuments.

Our thanks go to the head of the restoration department, Dr. Michael Kühlenthal. Furthermore, we would like to thank especially Katharina Walch, who from the beginnings gave the decisive initiatives and later on contributed important impulses, proposals and questions for our project. From the circle of collaborators of the department of furniture restoration we would like to mention Oliver Morr, Ursula Gassner, Christine Ramsl and Anja Fuchs, who always kindly helped us in the course of our research; we would like to thank them all as well for their continuous support.

Fig. 9. Black lacquered commode attributed to Dubois; front side

Notes

1 Weinmayr 1998, pp. 51–52.
2 Personal communication by Dr. Cornelia Syre, Bayerische Staatsgemäldesammlungen Munich.
3 Anonymous, *Aus der Schedula Diversarum Artium*, in: Technische Mitteilungen für Malerei, 51, 1935, pp. 167–170 and pp. 177–178. Nevertheless, this lacquer has been interpreted by some authors as an early example of a 'vernice liquida', i. e. a sandarac-linseed-oil-varnish. In this chapter Theophilus speaks about 'glue', where we would nowadays say 'lacquer' or 'varnish'. The term 'lacquer' for shining overpaintings has only gradually come into use again after the (re-)introduction of shellac in Europe in the late 17th century.
4 Morazzoni 1954, cited by Huth 1971.
5 Huth 1971, pp. 2 and 16.
6 Baur 1962.
7 Ibid.
8 Huth 1971.
9 Films from oil varnishes are restricted in their thickness because of the hardening mechanism through the reaction with air oxygen. The upper layer diameter lies at 200 µm. Within larger layers the oxygen intrudes too slowly into the lowest areas of the stratum, which therefore tend to remain soft. Since an increase in volume is taking place during the oxidative crosslinking process, the crosslinked 'skin' on top of the soft layer is folded, resulting in the formation of so called 'wrinkles'.
10 The drying is an oxidation process under simultaneous molecular enlargement (oxygen-crosslinking). Besides the first step, the autoxidation, there are only unproven theories up to now about the mechanism of drying. Nevertheless, a polymerization in the sense of macromolecular chemistry is not taking place.
11 Drying oils belong to fats from the point of view of chemistry and can become rancid (deteriorate) just like they do. During this process mainly the unsaturated fatty acids are degraded in an oxidative process. This rancidity process can be accelerated by the presence of certain metals with the lacquer (e. g. cobalt and copper) and slowed down by other metals (e. g. lead).
12 Besides asphalt (bitumen), vegetable black and bone black have been found.
13 Boiled linseed oil is a linseed oil, cooked under the influence of oxygen for several hours at a temperature of about 250–300 °C, under addition of driers, i. e. mixed with metal oxides, which dries much faster than untreated linseed oil. Boiled linseed oils do not show better material characteristics compared to untreated linseed oils, they are even of minor quality. Their advantages in lacquers and paintings lay in the fact, that they dry much faster than untreated linseed oils and that they can be produced in rather varying consistencies, from thin-fluid to viscous. The English term 'heat-bodied linseed oil' in the context of the historical heat-treated oils is not a good choice. It does not clarify, whether stand oils or boiled linseed oils are referred to. Furthermore it gives the impression, that one was dealing exclusively with viscous, thickened (bodied) oils – like in the case of stand oil. Boiled linseed oils, to the contrary could be produced as thickened as well as extremely fluid.
14 Baur 1966.
15 Huth 1971, pp. 21 and 22.
16 Marx 1957.
17 Baur 1966, p. 6.
18 Personal communication by Katharina Walch, Bavarian State Department of Historical Monuments, Munich.
19 Markgräfin Sibylla Augusta, *Die ausführliche und aufrichtige Lack= und Laßurkunst*, in: *Vierfacher Handschrein/Unterschiedlich-angemerkter/Kunst-Speiß-Confitur und Medicinal/Sachen*, personal Manuscript by the Margravine, dated 1688 on the cover. This manuscript is only an example of many contemporary recipes describing pure shellac lacquers. However it is of special interest, because the black lacquer objects commissioned by Sibylla Augusta did not contain pure shellac lacquers.
20 Koller/Walch/Baumer, 'The Lacquers of Margravine Sibylla Augusta' 2000.
21 Koller/Baumer 1997.
22 Stalker/Parker 1960.
23 Koller/Baumer, 'Lacquers of the West' 2000.
24 Koller/Walch/Baumer, 'French Lacquered Furniture' 2000.
25 Trillich 1925.
26 Thomas 1969.
27 Koller/Baumer 1997.
28 Czarnocka 1994.

References

Baur, Paul: 'Abenteuer, China-Moden und Lackmalerei (aus der Geschichte der Lackkunst)', in: *III. FATIPEC Kongreß 1962*, Weinheim, 1962, pp. 3–15

Baur, Paul: 'Aus der Frühgeschichte des Lackes, Laksha + Gummi Forniß', *Farbe und Lack*, 72, 1966, pp. 5–12

Czarnocka, Anna: 'Vernis Martin: The Lacquerwork of the Martin Family in Eighteenth Century France', *Studies in Decorative Arts,* II, 1994, p. 56-74

Huth, Hans: *Lacquer of the West*, Chicago/London, 1971

Koller, Johann/Baumer, Ursula: 'Baroque and Rococo Transparent Gloss Lacquers. II. Scientific Study of Lacquer Systems', in: *Lacke des Barock und Rokoko/Baroque and Rococo Lacquers*, Arbeitshefte des Bayerischen Landesamtes für Denkmalpflege, vol. 81, Munich, 1997, pp. 52–84

Koller, Johann/Baumer, Ursula: 'An Investigation of the "Lacquers of the West". A Methodical Survey', in: *Japanische und Europäische Lackarbeiten/Japanese and European Lacquerware*, Arbeitshefte des Bayerischen Landesamtes für Denkmalpflege, vol. 96, Munich, 2000, pp. 339–348

Koller, Johann/Walch, Katharina/Baumer, Ursula: 'French Lacquered Furniture of the 18th Century: Criard, Deforge and Dubois. A Technical and Scientific Investigation on Imitation Lacquers', in: *Japanische und Europäische Lackarbeiten/Japanese and European Lacquerware*, Arbeitshefte des Bayerischen Landesamtes für Denkmalpflege, vol. 96, Munich, 2000, pp. 537–559

Koller, Johann/Walch, Katharina/Baumer, Ursula: 'The Lacquers of Margravine Sibylla Augusta. Early German Imitation Lacquers in the Palaces of Baden', in: *Japanische und Europäische Lackarbeiten/Japanese and European Lacquerware*, Arbeitshefte des Bayerischen Landesamtes für Denkmalpflege, vol. 96, Munich, 2000, pp. 349–380

Marx, Ernst Ludwig: 'Schellack - seine Herkunft und Verwendung', *Deutsche Farben-Zeitschrift*, 11, 1957, pp. 353–355

Morazzoni, Giuseppe: *Mobili Veneziani Laccati*, 2 vol., Milano, 1954

Stalker, John/Parker, George: *A Treatise of Japanning and Varnishing* [...], Oxford 1688, complete reprint with an introduction by H. D. Molesworth/Alec Tiranti, London, 1960

Thomas, B. R.: 'Kauri Resins – Modern and Fossil', in: G. Eglinton/M. T. J. Murphy (eds.), *Organic Geochemistry*, 1969, pp. 599–618

Trillich, Heinrich: 'Kauriharze', in: *Das deutsche Farbenbuch,* II. Teil, Munich, 1925, pp. 132–133

Weinmayr, Elmar: *Nurimono. Japanische Lackmeister der Gegenwart*, Munich, 1998

Photo Credits

Figs. 1, 9: Munich, Bavarian State Department of Historical Monuments, Katharina Walch
Figs. 2, 6: From E. Weinmayr (1998), Nurimono, with kind permission of the Museum für Lackkunst, Münster
Fig. 3: Munich, Doerner-Institute
Figs. 4, 5: Munich, Bavarian State Department of Historical Monuments, Michael Kühlenthal
Figs. 7, 8: Munich, Bayerische Staatsgemäldesammlungen, Sibylle Forster

Katharina Walch

The Removal of Coatings on Lacquered Surfaces – Possibilities and Limits

Introduction

The restoration of lacquered furniture or interior decorations has increasingly aroused the interest of experts during the past 10–15 years. Indicators for this development include various publications on the topic, as well as the international conferences held in 1985 and 1993 on initiative of the Getty Conservation Center in Los Angeles and the National Research Institute in Tokyo.[1] Despite this increase in awareness, lacquer objects continue to undergo restorations that damage or even decimate the material. Far too often blinded by the splendour of lacquered works, art restorers who are not trained in this field or lack sufficient experience attempt to treat such objects. Precisely because of their complex layer structure and material composition, lacquer surfaces are especially problematic to examine and develop a treatment concept for and – above all – to restore.

As for European lacquers, there are countless instances of damage to sensitive surfaces shortly after their creation, be it a result of technical deficiencies of production, as a consequence of mechanical stresses or because of display under inappropriate climatic conditions. As a result, they have been restored and altered ever since. Additionally, the removal of lacquers from polychromed or veneered surfaces has a tradition at least as old as the art of lacquering. In Europe itself instructions of this kind can be found in manuals on coating techniques from past centuries.[2] These frequent interventions have led to a loss of many original surface textures, be they on chinoiserie, veneered or polychromed decorative objects.

Unfortunately, even today the natural ageing process and therefore the value of historical lacquer surfaces is far too rarely accepted. There is a continued increasing demand for the removal of yellowed and dull original surfaces. Examples for such 'restorations' abound in the very recent past. Colour plate XIX.1 shows part of the surface of the altar of the Rococo decoration of the eminent Swabian monastery church of Roggenburg (Günzburg county). The completely intact original lacquer was removed in 1984, because it had yellowed.

In many instances in the 20th century historical gloss lacquers were replaced by wax, shellac, dammar or synthetic resins. Such materials have nothing in common with the intention of the Baroque or Rococo period, neither in materials, technique nor aesthetics. A prominent example is the socalled 'Chamber of Voltaire' in Schloss Sanssouci near Potsdam. The room was furnished under Frederick II between 1745–1747 and lacquered under Augustin Dubuisson.[3] The restoration of this well-known lacquer room was carried out in the 1970's. The historical gloss lacquers of the surfaces were removed and replaced by alkyd varnishes. The aesthetic transformation which this lacquer cabinet has undergone does not allow the visitor today to experience the former effect of the original, neither in colour nor gloss.

Methods for the Removal of Recent Coatings

Original surfaces have thus repeatedly been removed, inadequately substituted or thoughtlessly overpainted to satisfy the beholder's concept of luster, depth and colour effects. Traditionally, spirit or oil lacquers were used for this and, increasingly since the 1920's and 30's, various synthetic resin lacquers. The removal of such overcoatings belongs to the most complicated topics in conservation. Damage due to unqualified treatments is unfortunately still very frequent.

For the removal of later applied coatings different methods were developed by Richard Wolbers and have been used in conservation for about the last twelve years. With these methods later lacquer layers can be removed much more precisely than with conventional methods, using for example thickened soaps or solvent gels.[4] Nevertheless, lacquer removals have been carried out repeatedly with these methods which – taking the condition of the respective object into consideration – can only be called irresponsible.

In the 1960's and 70's an euphoria over technical advances led to the use of synthetic resin lacquers much too quickly (there are famous collections of lacquered furniture in Germany that were all coated with synthetic resins at that time). Today I have the impression that the decision to remove coatings identified as 'not original' is made much too quickly.

In the Bavarian State Department of Historical Monuments the methods developed by Richard Wolbers have been used with positive results since 1992. Therefore, the opportunity is taken here to report about our experiences with the removal of recent retouchings of historical lacquerwork. In this context only a short summary can be given. It is not the intention to go into too much detail about the materials or methods developed by Richard Wolbers, since various publications have dealt with this.[5]

Instead, through case studies, the general preconditions of each object, which led to the success or failure of the lacquer removal, shall be described. It is not my intention to report about successes, but rather to point to the limits of conservatorial decisions, which were the result of unique surface situations. Furthermore, alternative procedures will be referred to briefly, such as mechanical or laser supported removal of lacquer retouchings.

All the objects referred to have in common that they were submitted to an extremely careful and profound conservatorial and scientific investigation beforehand. The GC/MS analyses for the identification of the binding media was kindly carried out by Johann Koller and Ursula Baumer at the Doerner-Institute in Munich. This procedure made it possible to precisely determine original and recoated areas, which provided the basis for focused conservation procedures.

Practical Prerequisites for Lacquer Removal

There are two basic preconditions for a successful removal of recent coatings: First, the object has to have large, flat surfaces. In this respect lacquered furniture and cabinets or ecclesiastical interiors provide much better conditions than painted surfaces with three-dimensional decoration. Only a flat surface usually shows a regular layer build-up, a basic condition for lacquer removal with chemical means. Second, the lacquer layer should be relatively intact, that is, uniform throughout. Many historical coatings have originally been polished to achieve their characteristic shine. In case such untouched surface structures have not been damaged mechanically or chemically during the recoating, the conditions for a removal are good. In such instances chances are good that the subsequent coat has not bonded well to the original. Complications are to be expected where the original lacquer has developed a fine crackle, degraded or been reduced in its original thickness, allowing the recent coating to intrude deeply into the original. In such situations even the clearing of the media used for lacquer removal poses a problem.

The following survey presents three case studies of objects whose surface characteristics offered such positive preconditions that the removal of the recoatings was possible.

Case Studies:
The Polychromed Altar Ensemble of the Holy Cross Church in Landsberg.
Lacquer Removal with Solvent Gel

The marbled altarpieces at the Church of the Holy Cross in Landsberg/Lech, executed between 1755–60, were created by Franz Anwander. The restoration history of this important ecclesiastical interior decoration is described in this publication by Thomas Schoeller and Andreas Scheuch.[6]

The original, polished lacquer surfaces[7] of the marbling had remained in a more or less satisfying condition, until it was decided to have them inpainted and recoated with shellac during a restoration campaign in the late 1980's. Under UV-light it can be reconstructed, with the help of cross sections, that the historical lacquer layer distinguishes itself clearly from the recent coating. Even if cross sections may sometimes deliver misleading pictures[8], such investigative inquiries are a first basis to gain information about the surface build-up.

The removal of the new coating was not only a matter of aesthetics; it had developed enormous shrinkage cracks, a heavy wrinkling and had turned yellow in a short time (colour plate XIX.2). A solution for this complicated conservation problem was needed since the recent lacquer coating developed increasing inner tensions because of its enormous layer thickness, endangering the original coating – the marbling and the original lacquer – to a degree that could not be stopped any other way.

After intensive research and testing the removal of the shellac mixture was successful with the help of an isopropanol gel on the basis of Carbopol and Ethomeen.[9] The positive precondition, which made a conservation possible, was due to the fact that the new lacquer was still relatively young at the time of its removal, i. e. not older than ten years; its ageing process had evidently not yet accelerated to a degree that it would have resembled the original lacquer too much, eventhough both lacquers contained spirit soluble natural resins. On the other hand, it proved advantageous that the original surface was of considerable layer volume, and its polished and therefore compressed surface was well preserved over most areas. Here, the shellac surface could not intrude too intensively into the original lacquer.

The Veneered Interior Decoration of St. Getreu in Bamberg.
Lacquer Removal with Solvent Gel

Another example for the successful use of solvent gel is the interior decoration of the former convent church of St. Getreu in Bamberg. The exceptional, luxurious marquetry of the altarpieces and the pulpit have been made by the highly appreciated Franconian court carpenters Servatius Brickard and Franz Anton Thomas.

The original coating of the entire interior decoration is still intact today (most unusual). Analyses have shown that different lacquer systems were employed: Besides an oil varnish based on amber and linseed oil, original copal lacquers were also found.[10] These are responsible today for the yellow-toned outward appearance. Additionally, a spirit soluble red dying lacquer had been selectively used as well, mostly on burl veneer. Here several small patches were preserved, which had up to now been covered by applied carvings. The veneers had been ennobled with lacquers of different colour, i. e. of varying composition.

The only retouching that this ensemble had undergone probably took place in the 19th century, when a linseed oil varnish of varying layer thickness had been applied. In the course of time this coating aged such that it developed extreme alligatoring, especially the thicker areas were exposed to a more intensive light in connection with the layer thickness (colour plate XIX.3, fig. 1). For this reason there are some areas, where – due to the high layer thickness of the retouching – the artful variety of the marquetry can hardly be recognized. In addition, the slowly drying linseed oil varnish also bound large amounts of dirt on the horizontal surfaces over an extended period. They cannot be removed by a simple cleaning of the surfaces and deepen the dark-brown natural colour of the linseed oil varnish today.

In such areas we chose test fields for the removal of the linseed oil varnish in 1992 (see colour plate XIX.3). For our purpose the generally well-preserved condition of the original lacquer at the time of retouching proved advantageous. Furthermore, it was helpful that different lacquer systems were lying over one another, and the linseed oil varnish was solvable in polar solvents due to ageing. It could be removed with an isopropanol gel on Carbopol-Ethomeen-basis without damaging the original. Nevertheless, an aesthetic disadvantage remained as the original lacquer had been badly bleached in areas of high light exposure. As a result, the luster of the lacquer surface has survived but the original gold and red toned variations are no longer present.

The Veneered Organ Case in Aich.
Lacquer Removal with Deoxycholate Soap

Frequently, however, nearly insoluble lacquers are laying over original surfaces. An example for this is the veneered organ case in the Catholic Parish Church in Aich, originally made for the Dominican Convent Church in Landshut in 1767.

The gold-toned original lacquer was intact over the entire wood surface. However – as was later discovered – it had been overpainted in the 19th century with a solid coat. This later coat-

Fig. 1. Bamberg, former monastery church St. Getreu. Mensa of a side altar before treatment. The original stained lacquer marquetry has remained, but was overpainted with a linseed oil varnish in the 19th century

ing had turned matt, differentially darkened and was partially alligatored (colour plate XIX.6). It also bound dirt in certain areas due to its extremely slow drying time, which made it almost impossible to recognize the unique and elaborate marquetry. According to the GC/MS analyses a linseed oil-stand oil retouching of the 19th century was found on the intact original natural resin spirit lacquer. Though these were two different binding media systems the problem was that the original lacquer was much more sensitive to all solvents tested than the stand oil coating. Here, not even solvent gels showed any positive results.

Based on an idea by Johann Koller[11], we tried to saponify oil lacquer with deoxycholate soap. After a number of tests which varied the thickness of the soap and the duration of application as well as the relatively complicated method of clearing, the stand oil coating was removed with visibly positive results (colour plate XIX.7).[12] Here, it proved advantageous that the original lacquer surface had remained unbroken and was thick enough, even on the carved elements.

On all three objects described above the original lacquer surfaces were found in such good condition that after removal no new lacquer had to be applied, with the exception of a few severely light damaged patches. The windows of the interiors, responsible for the light damage, were covered with UV-filters to preserve the exposed original surfaces.

As in the cases just described, the following examples present interior decorations from the 18th century whose original lacquers were overcoated, detracting dramatically from the aesthetic intention of the original surface. However, here we decided against a removal of the overcoats with chemical means, for varying reasons.

The Veneered High Altarpiece of the Church of the Guardian Angels in Straubing.
On the Problem of Separating Two Oil Lacquer Layers

The veneered high altar of the Church of the Guardian Angels in Straubing stems from the early 18th century. The original coating of the veneer has been preserved, though partial damage by light was obvious. The analyses showed an amber-containing linseed oil varnish that had been bulked with colophony.

Only in the 20th century had the original lacquer been overcoated with a 'resin lacquer', i. e. linseed oil-stand oil cooked with hardened colophony (colophony neutralized with chalk). This coating had alligatored and even turned brittle in areas damaged by light, disturbing the visual appreciation. Furthermore, its considerable layer thickness hindered the consolidation of the areas covered with veneer cut from a hand plane.

The altar had been relocated to the end of the choir during the secularization in the early 19th century, where large areas of it were exposed to intense light from nearby windows. It was to be expected that the original lacquer had been affected in these areas, even prior to its recoating. Additionally, it may have been

Fig. 2. Cross section of the surface of the veneered high altarpiece at the Church of the Guardian Angels in Straubing under UV-light, 50x magnification. A light-blue fluorescent original lacquer is seen on the wood in the left half of the picture with nearly the original layer thickness. To the contrary, in the right half of the picture it has been reduced to such a degree that it is barely visible on the wood veneer any more. The retouching (yellow fluorescence) lays over both surfaces

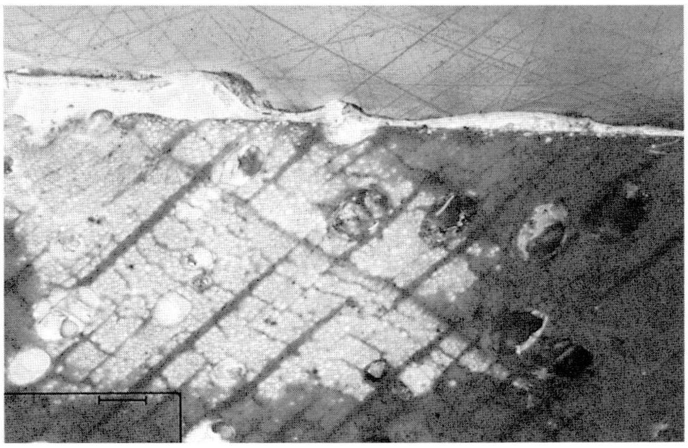

Fig. 3. Side altarpiece of the Catholic Pilgrimage Church at Froschhausen. In the course of earlier restorations it had been partially painted over with a linseed oil-stand-oil lacquer. For this reason the retable shows lacquer runs in several places

mechanically reduced prior to the application of the new lacquer coating. The cross sections of the samples taken seem to support our suspicion (fig. 2). Theoretically this result alone spoke against a removal of the overcoating.

Nevertheless, the conservation needs as well as the absolutely unsatisfying outward appearance made a removal desirable. Therefore several removal test fields were made. However, as both the original amber lacquer and the later applied resin lacquer were oil lacquers, their similarity made the separation trials rather difficult. Furthermore, the more recent lacquer was difficult to dissolve due to its method of production, while the original lacquer reacted very sensitively. As soon as the uppermost lacquer layer began to dissolve, the original lacquer was attacked as well. Even the soaps did not prove successful. As a result of these analyses it was decided to try slow evaporating solvent gels.[13] All efforts failed to bring the desired result: the removal of the 20th century coating without damage to the original lacquer. It was therefore decided to favour a dry cleaning of the surface.

During the tests it was discovered that a visual deepening (saturation) of the finish could be achieved by rolling over the uppermost layer with a swab drenched in isopropanol. Nevertheless, from the side of the Bavarian State Department of Historical Monuments, such a procedure was not recommended, since it enlarged the danger of intermixing the two layers, which would be a severe hindrance for any future restorers that may have improved techniques at their disposal.

The Polychromed Side Altarpieces of the Pilgrimage Church St. Leonhard in Froschhausen. The Difficulty of Removing an Unevenly Applied Linseed Oil-Stand Oil Coating

In the Pilgrimage Church in Froschhausen (county of Weilheim) three marbleized altarpieces from around 1780 have been preserved, with their original highly polished lacquer coatings. The marbling is mostly resin-bound, the spirit soluble gloss lacquer consists mainly of sandarac with an admixture of larch turpentine, mastic and small amounts of elemi.[14] The side altars underwent a first retouching with copaiva balsam, which at least did not lead to any optical effects, but penetrated through the original lacquer into the primer. The second retouching can be dated: it was done in 1935. Linseed oil-stand oil had been applied to only certain areas. This coating was most apparent where it had been unevenly applied, having even run or sagged (fig. 3).

The removal of such uneven retouchings or recoverings is always problematic as the solvent gels can only be applied to the affected areas. Practically, this would be possible on the runs and brush strokes with the aid of a microscope. However, experience has shown that the area affected by the solvent gel often tends to be larger than desired. During cleaning of the gel the neighbouring uncoated areas would most likely also be affected.

For these reasons we decided to leave both overcoats since they did not pose any particular conservation problem. Nevertheless, aesthetically unsatisfying parts, like drips of the linseed oil-stand oil coating from the 1930's, were mechanically removed with the help of a cotton swab and tripoli until they were no longer visually disturbing.

The Polychromed High Altar at Baierbach. On the Difficulty of a Spirit Lacquer Saturated with Synthetic Resin Components

A rather similar problem was encountered with the removal of the retouching of the original lacquered marbling at the high altar of the Catholic Filial Church in Baierbach (county of Landshut, fig. 4).

Fig. 4. Baierbach, district of Landshut, retable of the high altarpiece of the Catholic filial church, the original marbling and its gloss lacquer has been overpainted with a brownish phenolic resin coat in the 20th century

According to the GC/MS analyses the original gloss lacquer of the coating consists of sandarac, larch turpentine resin, mastic and camphor. Additionally, small amounts of copal have been found. The brownish overcoat is a phenol-based synthetic resin lacquer. Components of this coat had penetrated the original lacquer as well as the marbling, which also contained large amounts of lacquer, as it was also bound by resin. For this reason a separation of both layers in the strict sense of the word was not possible; nevertheless, for aesthetic reasons a solution was sought that could reduce the retouching at least superficially. A further problem was that both lacquer layers showed similarities in their composition and solubility. The greatest difficulty was that the lacquer to be removed showed considerable differences in layer thickness, just like in Froschhausen (figs. 5a), 6b), colour plate XIX.4). To compound the problem, there were numerous small areas that had not been coated.

The aforementioned solvent gel and thickened soap that were utilized so successfully affected the surface – due to their nature – uniformly. In the case of the Baierbach altarpiece the retouching covered the original very unevenly. While the gel would still be softening the thicker sections of the lacquer, other areas would already have been dissolved. A deleterious effect on the original lacquer could therefore not be completely excluded. After several tests, it was decided to exclude this method completely.

Removal Attempts with Laser Techniques

In cooperation with Jan Hauptmann and Thomas Heinze at the Fraunhofer-Institute für Werkstoff und Strahltechnik Dresden test series have been carried out with a transportable Nd-YAG-short pulse laser.[15] The samples have been tested under 1064 nm, i. e. in the infrared range, a wave length which has proven its efficiency in comparable fields of conservation.[16] The result of these tests was that the removal was possible without doubts at higher intensities. Nevertheless the exposed original lacquer showed an undeniable yellowing as well as partial losses or punctures, as was later confirmed by cross sections. At lower intensity, which was reached by enlarging the working spot diameter, the removal of the retouching was not possible. In this technique at least one further area was shot, since it could be deducted that at least a certain brittleness of the uppermost layer would be achieved, which could facilitate a subsequent mechanical removal with a scalpel. However, the tests of this hypothesis revealed that this method did not lead to an improvement of the removal technique (see fig. 5c)).

After these tests, which at least showed a partial realization of removal, a laser with OPO-system (optical parametrical oscillator) was used, which allowed an infinitely variable change of the wave length in an area from 400 nm to 700 nm. With this instrument it was possible, due to the different wave length, to test the optical qualities of the lacquer layers that had to be separated. The aim was to find the wave length which would be absorbed by the retouching but reflected or transmitted by the original layer.[17]

With tests in a wave length from 650 nm to 530 nm the laser rays were absorbed by the original lacquer layer, which led to damages of this layer. In contrast, tests in a range from 510 nm to 450 nm succeeded in the originally desired absorption in the uppermost, i. e. the retouching layer. However, its optical parameters resembled those of the original lacquer layer so much, that no possibility existed to affect a separation without damaging the original.

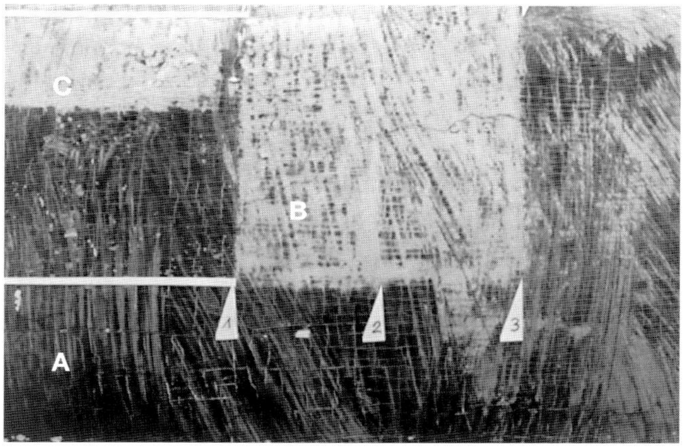

Fig. 5. Detail of a marbled column from the high altarpiece at Baierbach. a) right and lower detail of the picture: The synthetic resin coating shows a brownish colour and an extremely irregular brush stroke. b) upper center: first step in the removal: the uppermost layers of the synthetic resin coat had to be removed mechanically. c) left upper detail: the smaller test field had been pre-treated before with the YAG-laser; the removal of the thereby embrittled lacquer was done mechanically, as can be seen in the detail above

Mechanical Removal Methods

For these reasons the removal was once again attempted with mechanical means. The removal of the relatively stable overlying phenolic resin lacquer with the scalpel was too risky for the original lacquer layer even after pre-treatment with a laser. On the other hand it was possible to maintain control with the swab and abrasive powders (like pumice, tripoli or diamantine). On the other hand, the necessary addition of some drops of distilled water for this technique would have endangered the stability of the original coating, as the original gloss lacquer evidenced a crackle pattern, allowing moisture to penetrate.

Therefore it was finally decided to try a removal in two steps: After thinning of the retouching with abrasive powders

Fig. 6. Fluorescence photograph of a detail of the column with test fields (see fig. 5). From right to left: a) First step: partial mechanical removal, b) Before treatment, c) Nearly complete removal after consolidation; the remains of synthetic resin are visible in daylight (see: colour plate XIX. 4) and are apparent under UV-light

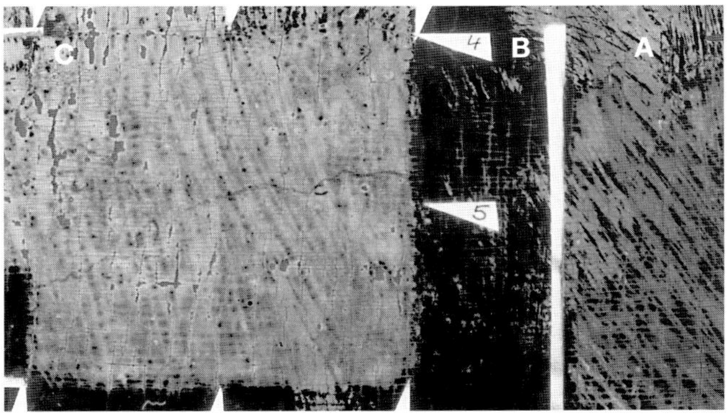

(see fig. 6a)) a consolidation of the mostly exposed crackled lacquer was undertaken. For this purpose a 3 % approx. solution of isinglass as well as a volatile fastening medium cyclododekane, dissolved in mineral spirits, were tested. Both materials proved successful, so that a nearly complete mechanical removal was possible without risk to the polychromy and the original lacquer surface. Minute remnants of the more recent lacquer, which lay imbedded within the original gloss lacquer, were purposely left to minimize the loss of original lacquer by abrasive powders (colour plate XIX.4). A positive side effect of this technique was an enhanced surface gloss, in contrast to its appearance before treatment. In contrast to the above mentioned high altarpiece in Straubing the mechanical removal could be successfully applied in this case only because the surfaces and the original lacquer layer were relatively intact. Furthermore, the synthetic lacquer had the advantage of being rather brittle.

The Lacquer Cabinet in the Residential Palace of Rastatt. On the Problems of a Spirit Lacquer Saturated with Synthetic Components

As a last example the lacquer room in the residential palace at Rastatt shall be presented – a 'japanned' interior, imitating East Asian lacquer, and executed in the first decade of the 18th century.[18]

The lacquer used here was a spirit lacquer, in which mainly shellac, sandarac and amber have been detected.[19] In 1973 the lacquer panels underwent their first comprehensive restoration: The goal was to restore the aged original surface to a 'high gloss'. This was achieved by first mechanically abrading all surfaces, both flat and relief, and afterwards reforming it with E 33, an ester-methanol mixture. This procedure caused heavy losses to the original surface of the lacquerwork. Especially visible is the damage to the chinoiserie decorative painting. The figures have been damaged to such a degree that their original outlines are hardly recognizable today; additionally they have been improperly painted over (colour plate XIX.8). The mechanically as well as chemically reduced and softened original surface has been – according to our latest investigations – retouched and at least recoated twice with a synthetic resin lacquer containing copal- and shellac. Even if the modern coating has until now not led to surface tension problems or the like, its milky natural colour and its extreme lustre caused the colleagues of the Administration of the Castles and Gardens of Baden-Württemberg in Karlsruhe to raise the legitimate question, whether a removal might be both possible and justifiable.

Tests on a small area showed that the surface of the new lacquer was relatively easy to dissolve with polarized solvents. However, an investigation of the painting technique and layer structure dashed our hopes: cross sections showed that the new lacquer had intruded deeply between the original lacquer layers, which had obviously not been consolidated before overcoating.

There is also an additional fundamental problem: During the production of these lacquers a common technique was to apply at least some of the fine drawing of the decoration over the final lacquer layer. As a consequence these parts of the painting are in greatest danger during a restoration. Unfortunately, examples of destruction of these important final decoration drawings are innumerable (fig. 7). Only a fraction of the European imitation lacquers have survived undamaged over the centuries.

The artistic abilities and the refinement of these decorative paintings can therefore only be studied on a few still untouched pieces of furniture or lacquer rooms today.

Farbtafel XIX / *Colour Plate XIX* ▷

3 Detail of the left side of the mensa of a veneered altarpiece at St. Getreu in Bamberg. Alligatored surface of the linseed oil varnish from the 19th century and test window of the exposed original lacquer using isopropanol gel (right detail)

4 Baierbach, district of Landshut, detail of the High altar of the Catholic Filial Church. Right: The original marbling and gloss lacquer was painted over with a brownish phenolic resin coat in the 20th century. Left: Test field for a nearly complete removal of the retouchings of the Baierbach column. Last remains of a brownish synthetic resin have intentionally been left within the original gloss lacquer surface to keep from having to sand it more than absolutely necessary

5 Macro photograph from a detail of a lacquer panel from Rastatt. The lower half of the picture shows the current condition, the surface being coated several times with a glossy synthetic resin lacquer of great thickness. The upper half of the picture shows the condition after the removal of the retouchings with an isopropanol gel in raking light. The fissuring of the original surface – caused by an earlier restoration – can now be seen. A removal would endanger the gold drawings lying on the surface

6 Detail of a side door of the organ case of the Catholic parish church at Aich before treatment. The picture shows the brownish-toned linseed-stand-oil which recovers the original lacquer surface since the 19th century

7 Side door of the organ case after removal of the linseed oil-stand-oil (see 6). The marquetry shows the intact, closed original surface and is of a golden-yellowish colour

8 Detail of the panelling of the Rastatt lacquer cabinet. The original lacquer painting was mechanically and chemically damaged in the course of a more recent restoration, and was only fragmentarily preserved, as the gold painting in the photograph illustrates. The flowers and leaves were subsequently partially repainted in another colour

1 Top of a marbled side altarpiece in the Convent Church at Roggenburg, with remains of the historical gloss lacquer on the left, which has already been removed on the right half. Condition report during the restoration 1983–1985

2 Damage of the historical gloss lacquer on the marbled altarpieces of the Church of the Holy Cross at Landsberg. The details show the extent of yellowing and alligatoring caused by the recent lacquer coating after only six years, additions also caused the here visible delaminating and losses of polychromy

3

4

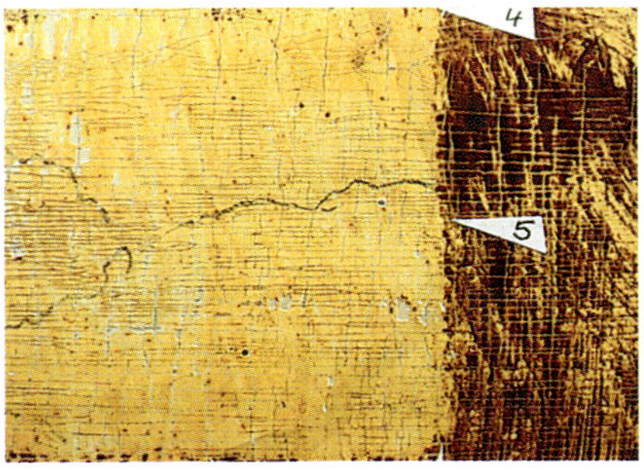

5

6

7

8

Fig. 7. A butterfly on a French secretary by Jean Rhenon, irretrievably lost due to an unprofessional restoration

In the case of the Rastatt lacquer room a major part of the gilded decoration is also on top of the final lacquer layer and has therefore – at least where it survived the restorations of the 1970's – been embedded in the new lacquer. In the cross section under UV-light it is readily apparent that the gold decoration lies between the original lacquer and the retouching. The removal of the retouching lacquer would consequently lead to a further loss of original decorations.

The principles laid down in the beginning of this paper may be recalled here once again: a prerequisite for the separation of lacquer layers is the presence of a compressed, intact original surface. The GC/MS analyses unquestionably proved that the synthetic lacquer from the 1970's had even penetrated the underlying layers of the original lacquer in a characteristic way and did not allow a 'separation' in the strictest sense of the word. Furthermore, the original surface of the lacquer room had been abraded and sanded prior to retouching. In an approximately 1 x 2 cm large test window the completely ruined surface structure could be observed (colour plate XIX.5). Had this surface been exposed it would have urgently required a new coating. Considering the tremendous problems the removal of later overcoats poses, there are good reasons against an overlacquering of original surfaces. This is especially true in cases such as this, where the surface structure has been so badly damaged. The considerations led to the conclusion, in spite of the completely unsatisfying modern coating, not to carry out a removal.

Recent studies by Daniëlle Kisluk-Grosheide and Oliver Impey[20] on French furniture of the 18th century with East Asian lacquer applications have shown that some pieces of furniture were disassembled only shortly after their creation. Their forms already considered unfashionable, they were partially reused in pieces of furniture of the latest fashion. A prominent example is given by a French secretary by Jean-Henri Riesener, dated 1787, in the Metropolitan Museum of Art in New York, integrating – besides the European lacquers – also East Asian lacquer panels of different provenance and date.

Also in German interior decorations from the 18th century it can be repeatedly observed that one object can combine lacquered surfaces of different techniques and from different periods. To recognize this it requires detailed and lengthy examination. When considering the removal of more recent coatings this fact demands an increased sensitivity to the manifold qualities of the original object. Much too often it can be observed that the variety lacquer objects offer is neither expected, respected nor searched for.

Later repairs are not always so easily recognized as in the case of the Riesener secretary at the Getty Museum in Los Angeles, California. Here, a later shrinkage crack in the East Asian lacquer panel has been covered, as can be seen in figure 8, by painting over it with a dragonfly. The preservation of such later additions seems to be increasingly accepted by specialists today, but this view is gaining ground only slowly. To the contrary, subsequent clear lacquer layers, possibly also worthy of preservation, are gaining much less attention. Were this to happen this would most certainly lead more often to the decision not to expose the original lacquer regardless of condition and at any cost.

The preconditions and practical solutions presented in this essay with the aid of case studies – not nearly exhaustive – should reflect the arguments for and against a removal of lacquer retouchings from a technical point of view. They were also meant to illustrate that it is not always sensible nor justifiable to undertake a lacquer removal merely to satisfy our contemporary aesthetic ideals.

Final Remarks

To conclude, a group of European lacquer furniture from the 18th century will be highlighted, which have been decorated with East Asian lacquer panels. It is by now well-known that these East Asian 'implants' have sometimes been over- or inpainted with European lacquers at the time the respective piece of furniture was made. One example is a French *table de toilette* by Criard: the Japanese lacquerwork of the table top is covered with additional French decorations from the period. Such barely recognizable details must first be detected prior to tests for the removal of later retouchings. In such cases the chosen method must not effect the Asian original or the European lacquer. The possibilities for a damage-free removal of later coatings are necessarily reduced in such a case.

Acknowledgment

My special thanks go to Dr. Johann Koller and Ursula Baumer at the Doerner-Institute Munich for the GC/MS analyses for the determination of the binding media, as well as for the most profitable cooperation in finding solutions for the actual problems of lacquer removals. Furthermore, I would like to express my gratitude to Jan Hauptmann and Thomas Heinze at the Fraunhofer-Institute für Werkstoff und Strahltechnik (IWS) in Dresden for the carrying out of a series of experiments with laser technique and, last but not least, Ordinariatsrat Dr. Hans Ramisch for the financial support, which enabled the test series to be carried through. For their cooperation and readiness to help with the translation from German into English I would like to thank Dr. Susan Tipton and Olaf Unsoeld.

Fig. 8. Detail of the front panel of a secretary by Jean-Henri Riesener. A dragonfly has been painted onto it to cover an earlier shrinkage joint

Notes

1 On this topic see: *Urushi, Proceedings of the Urushi Study Group*, June 10–27, 1985, Tokyo and *Preprints, The 17th International Symposium on the Conservation and Restoration of Cultural Property, Conservation of Urushi Objects*, November 10–12, 1993, Tokyo.

2 A remarkable description of this procedure is given by Jean-Félix Watin, *Der Staffirmaler, oder die Kunst anzustreichen, zu vergolden und zu lackieren, ...*, Leipzig, 1774, pp. 297–300: 'Erneuern oder Abputzen einen Firniß, heißt, ihn von allem Schmutz der Fliegen und anderen Insekten, oder von der Fettigkeit, dem Staube, und was sonst darauf gekommen, reinigen, und ihm sein ehemaliges Ansehen geben. Man bedient sich einer Lauge darzu, die auf verschiedene Art gemacht wird. Die beste in dieser Art ist ohnstreitig diejenige, die man von Pottasche und calcinirten Weinhefen verfertigt. ... Wenn die Farben schmutzig sind, so muß man sie mit schwacher Lauge waschen. Bedient man sich obiger Lauge, so gießt man nur $^1/_2$ Nössel davon in eine Kanne Wasser, so ist es stark genug, um den Schmutz abzunehmen. Man muß sich hüten, daß es nicht strichweise läuft, sondern allenthalben gleich ausgebreitet wird, damit es keine Flecken giebt. Wenn diese Lauge 3 oder 4 Minuten darauf gewesen ist, muß man gleich hinter drein mit Flußwasser recht naß waschen, damit der Schmutz und die Lauge abfliessen, sonst würde letztere die Farben und den Firniß anfressen. Die Farben sehen alsdenn frischer wieder aus, und wenn alles recht trocken ist, so giebt man einen oder zwey Anstriche mit Firniß. ... Wenn eine Farbe gänzlich zernichtet oder weggeschaft werden soll, um eine andere an ihre Stelle zu bringen, so ist überhaupt das sicherste, alles durch die Lauge wegzuschaffen, nicht nur den Firniß und die Farbe, sondern auch den Kreidegrund, den Leimgrund, die harten Tinten, und vornehmlich die unterste Grundfarbe, ...' ('Renewing or cleansing a finish means restoring its previous appearance by removing all dirtying flies and insects, or all greasiness, dust and whatever else may have come on it. To do so one uses a caustic solution, that can be made in different ways. The best wash, without a doubt, is made from potash and calcined wine yeast ... If the colors are dirty, they must be washed with a weak solution. Using the above mixture pour only a pint into a can of water, so it is strong enough to remove the dirt. One must be careful that it does not run but rather be spread out evenly so as not to become spotty. After leaving it on for 3 to 4 minutes it should immediately be washed rather wet with river water so that the dirt and caustic solution run off, otherwise the finish and colors would be attacked. The colors will once again appear fresh, and when everything has dried well, coat once or twice with lacquer ... If a color is to be completely removed, to be replaced with another, the most certain method is to remove everything with a caustic solution. Not only the lacquer and color, but also the gesso, glue size, the hard inks, and particularly, the base color.')

3 Württemberg 1998, pp. 97–98.

4 The problem of residues, which may eventually remain on surfaces after clearing of solvent gels based on Carbopol and Ethomeen, is rightly discussed controversially. Recent investigations on this topic, initiated by the Getty Conservation Institute Los Angeles under the working title 'Surface-Cleaning-Systems', will soon be published. See the summary on this research project by Johann Koller: *Restauro*, 3/1999, pp. 216–217.

5 See e. g.: Koller 1990, pp. 106–110. Gilsa 1991, pp. 48–58. Haller 1994. Pelludat 1994.

6 Thomas Schoeller, Andreas Scheuch in this volume, pp. 173–180.

7 The original gloss lacquer consists of 85–90 % sandarac, 5–15 % mastic and max. 1 % elemi. For further details see the scientific analysis results in Koller/Baumer 1997, pp. 70–72.

8 E. g. the plasticizers of synthetic resin retouchings e. g., which penetrate into the underlying historical layers, are usually not visible.

9 For a more detailed description of the removal technique see Schoeller/Scheuch in this volume.

10 More details about the results of the scientific analysis of original lacquers and their retouching in: Koller/Schmid/Baumer 1997, pp. 187–190.

11 Koller 1990.

12 For the removal of the linseed oil-stand oil coating a recipe by Richard Wolbers was used consisting of deoxycholic acid, triethanolamin, hydroxypropylmethyl cellulose and water. For more details about the restoration and the results of the scientific investigation see: WALCH/KOLLER/BAUMER 1997, pp. 335–346.

13 Used were gels based on Carbopol and Ethomeen, with the addition of e. g. Methylacetate, Cyclohexanone and Ethanol, Xylol and Polyvinylether or Buthylacetate and Isopropanol, as well as a mixture of methanol and potassium hydroxide in HPMC.

14 More on the scientific investigations in: KOLLER/BAUMER 1997, pp. 67–70.

15 WAGNER 1998, p. 382.

16 HEILEIN 1998, pp. 410–415.

17 Each sample was begun with a lower intensity, to remain under the intensity threshold value (liminal value) of the lacquer retouching, so as not to cause any damages to the original layer. Gradually the intensity, i. e. the energy per irradiated unit area was increased, or the working distances and the frequency were changed.

18 For more about the lacquer cabinet and its creation see: GRIMM 2000.

19 For the layer structure and the scientific analysis of the binding media used see: KOLLER/WALCH/BAUMER 2000.

20 IMPEY/KISLUK-GROSHEIDE 1994, pp. 48–61.

References

GILSA, BETTINA VON: 'Gemäldereinigung mit Enzymen, Harzseifen und Emulsionen', *Zeitschrift für Kunsttechnologie und Konservierung*, no. 1, annual vol. 5, Worms, 1991, pp. 48–58

GRIMM, ULRIKE :'In einem so weit entfernten deutschen Palast vortrefflichste Seltenheiten so magnific und von einer so hohen Hand so nett rangieret. Zu den Lackarbeiten am Hofe der Sibylla Augusta, Markgräfin von Baden-Baden' ('The finest rarities so magnific and so delicately arranged by such a noble hand in a German palace so distant. On the Lacquerwork at the Court of Sybilla Augusta, Margravine of Baden-Baden'), in *Japanische und europäische Lackarbeiten/Japanese and European Lacquerware*, Arbeitshefte des Bayerischen Landesamtes für Denkmalpflege, vol. 96, Munich, 2000, pp. 237–251

HALLER, URSULA: *Studien zur Herstellung und Anwendung von Lösungsmittel-Gelen, -Pasten und -Kompressen in der Restaurierung*, Dipl. thesis, Institut für Technologie der Malerei an der Staatlichen Akademie der Bildenden Künste, Stuttgart, 1994

HEILEIN, KATHARINA: 'Überzüge auf empfindlichen Malschichten, Untersuchungen zum Abtragen mit unterschiedlichen Lasergeräten', *Restauro*, vol. 6, 1998, pp. 410–415

IMPEY, OLIVER R./KISLUK-GROSHEIDE, DANIËLLE O.: 'The Japanese Connection', *Apollo*, no. 383, London, 1994, pp. 48–61

KOLLER, JOHANN/BAUMER, URSULA: 'Die transparenten Glanzlacke des Barock und Rokoko'('Baroque and Rococo Transparent Gloss Lacquers'), in *Lacke des Barock und Rokoko/Baroque and Rococo Lacquers*, Arbeitshefte des Bayerischen Landesamtes für Denkmalpflege, vol. 81, Munich, 1997, pp. 53–84

KOLLER, JOHANN/SCHMID, EMILIA/BAUMER, URSULA: 'Transparente Lacke auf Holzoberflächen des Barock und Rokoko' ('Baroque and Rococo Transparent Varnishes on Wood Surfaces'), in *Lacke des Barock und Rokoko/Baroque and Rococo Lacquers*, Arbeitshefte des Bayerischen Landesamtes für Denkmalpflege, vol. 81, Munich, 1997, pp. 160–196

KOLLER, JOHANN/WALCH, KATHARINA/BAUMER, URSULA: 'Die Lacke der Markgräfin Sibylla Augusta. Frühe deutsche Imitationslacke in badischen Schlössern'('The Lacquers of Margravine Sibylla Augusta. Early German Imitation Lacquers in the Palaces of Baden'), in *Japanische und europäische Lackarbeiten/Japanese and European Lacquerware*, Arbeitshefte des Bayerischen Landesamtes für Denkmalpflege, vol. 96, Munich, 2000, pp. 349–380

KOLLER, JOHANN: 'Cleaning of a Nineteenth-Century Painting with Deoxycholate Soap: Mechanism and Residue Studies', *IIC Preprints of the Contributions to the Brussels Congress: Cleaning, Retouching and Coatings*, London, 1990, pp. 106–110

PELLUDAT, INGA: *Überlegungen und Versuche zur Anwendbarkeit der sogenannten Wolbersmethode im Hinblick auf die Abnahme von schwerlöslichen Übermalungen auf empfindlichen Malschichten*, Dipl. thesis, Fachhochschule Hildesheim/Holzminden, 1994

SCHOELLER, THOMAS/SCHEUCH, ANDREAS: 'Die Restaurierung der Ausstattung der ehemaligen Jesuitenkirche in Landsberg am Lech. Die Konservierung des Rokokolackes', in this volume, pp. 173–180

WAGNER, WOLF-DIETER :'Reinigen mit dem Nd: YAG-Laser, Funktionsprinzipien', *Restauro*, vol. 6, 1998, p. 382

WALCH, KATHARINA/KOLLER, JOHANN/BAUMER, URSULA: 'Die Restaurierung des Aicher Orgelgehäuses' ('The Restoration of the Organ Case in Aich'), in *Lacke des Barock und Rokoko/Baroque and Rococo Lacquers*, Arbeitshefte des Bayerischen Landesamtes für Denkmalpflege, vol. 81, Munich, 1997, pp. 335–346

WÜRTTEMBERG, PHILIPP HERZOG VON: *Das Lackkabinett im deutschen Schlossbau*, Bern, 1998

Photo Credits

Fig. 1: J. v. Miller, Bad Wiessee
Figs. 2, 5, 6: Author
Fig. 3: E. Wiegerling, Bad Tölz
Fig. 4: R. Neubauer, Bad Endorf
Fig. 7: B. Piert-Borgers, Köln
Fig. 8: Getty Museum, Los Angeles
Colour plate XIX.1: Fa. Bienapfl, Augsburg; 2, 6, 7: H. Huber, Stuttgart; 3: J. v. Miller, Bad Wiessee; 4, 5, 8: Author

Thomas Schoeller, Andreas Scheuch

Die Restaurierung der Ausstattung der ehemaligen Jesuitenkirche in Landsberg am Lech. Die Konservierung des Rokokolackes

Nachfolgender Beitrag ist die Geschichte einer Problemlösung. Sie erläutert die Restaurierung von Lackschichten bei einer Maßnahme, die – selbst für die bayerische Denkmalpflege – ungewöhnlich lange dauerte. Von 1990 bis 1999, also über neun Jahre hinweg, wurden die originalen Lacküberzüge des 18. Jahrhunderts auf den Altären der ehemaligen Jesuitenkirche Heilig-Kreuz in Landsberg am Lech vorab untersucht und anschließend konserviert und restauriert.

Ausgangslage

Im ca. 40 Kilometer westlich von München gelegenen Landsberg errichtete die süddeutsche Jesuitenprovinz eine ihrer zentralen Ausbildungsstätten mit Gymnasium und Noviziat. Zwischen 1580 und 1584 wurde der erste Kirchenbau errichtet. Mit der Weihe 1584 durch Petrus Canisius stellte dieser Bau die erste Jesuitenkirche Bayerns überhaupt dar. An gleicher Stelle wurde dann zwischen 1752 und 1756 ein neuer Kirchenbau errichtet und ausgestattet (Abb. 1). Bei der Bedeutung, welche die Societas Jesu der Kunst und ihrer Wirkung auf religiöse Erziehung und Bildung einräumte, überrascht es nicht, dass hierfür die besten Künstler Augsburgs und Münchens herangezogen wurden.[1] So freskierte etwa der Asam-Schüler Christoph Thomas Scheffler die Kirche mit einem geistreichen Zyklus zur Thematik des Kreuzes als christlichem Symbol des Heils der Menschen. Die sechs Seitenaltäre wurden laut der erhaltenen Rechnungen 1755 von der berühmten Kistlerwerkstatt Dominikus Bergmüllers aus Türkheim geliefert (Abb. 2). Ein Jahr später wurde durch die gleiche Werkstatt auch der nach Entwürfen von Franz Xaver Schmädl gestaltete Hochaltar errichtet. Als Fassmaler der Marmorierungen sind Augustin Aicher, Franz Anton Anwander und Joseph Sibber überliefert.

Was den Retabeln dieser Kirche einen besonderen Rang verleiht, ist die Tatsache, dass an den sieben Altären, der Orgel und der Kanzel die originalen Marmorierungen einschließlich des ursprünglichen Lacküberzuges erhalten blieben.[2] Nur noch sehr selten kann die aufwändige Marmorier- und Lacktechnik des süddeutschen Rokoko in einer solchen Fülle und Qualität studiert werden. Als Beispiel sei die Predellenzone erwähnt, wo auf hellem Farbton unter blau-grün eingefärbten Lackschichten Goldadern aufgetragen wurden.[3] Wie spielerisch diese Fassmaler ihr Metier verstanden, ist allerdings für den normalen Kirchenbesucher nicht erkennbar. An verdeckten Stellen, über Gesimsen oder an Rücklagen finden sich zahlreiche malerische und zeichnerische „Capricci", etwa ein Hundekopf oder ein springendes Pferd.

Mehr als 250 Jahre lang blieb diese Marmorierung samt Überzug unberührt erhalten. Mehr oder weniger große Schäden, bedingt durch einen Abbau des Bindemittels der Malschicht, Lockerungen der Farbschicht und Ausbrüche bzw. Vergilbungen der Lackschicht fanden in einem „natürlichen" Ausmaß statt.

Eine erste „Bearbeitung" erfolgte in den 80er Jahren durch eine örtliche Kirchenmalerwerkstatt.[4] Auf alle Oberflächen der Marmorierung, über die originale Lackoberfläche des 18. Jahrhunderts, wurde ein neuer, z. T. sehr dick gespachtelter Schellack aufgetragen, ohne dass die darunter liegende Fassung zuvor ausreichend gefestigt worden wäre. Dieser neue Überzug enthielt zusätzlich teils kleinere, teils größere Zusätze von Kunstharz. Mit dieser Maßnahme glaubte man die originale Marmorierung und ihren alten Überzug zu konservieren. Der alte Lack wurde also nicht entfernt oder reduziert bzw. abgeschliffen, sondern vollständig durch einen neuen Schellackauftrag „konserviert". In wenigen Jahren aber schrumpfte dieser dick aufgetragene neue Schellacküberzug durch Licht und Wärme krustenartig zusammen und verbräunte stark (Farbtafel XX.1).

Die Spannung des neuen Überzuges bedingte ein Ablösen des Originallackes bzw. der originalen Marmorierung, da dessen Haftung auf der Grundierung nicht mehr hinreichend war und eine Festigung der Grundierungs- und Marmorierungsschichten vor dem Neuauftrag des Schellacks unterblieben war, d. h. es drohte der Totalverlust der originalen Marmorierung und der originalen Überzüge. Die Ablösung der Altarfassung war eine direkte Folge des neuen und viel zu dick aufgetragenen Schellacküberzuges bzw. wurde durch diesen neuen Überzug erheb-

Abb. 1. Innenansicht der ehemaligen Jesuitenkirche Hl. Kreuz in Landsberg am Lech, Blick zum Hochaltar

Abb. 2. Landsberg, Hl. Kreuz, Ignatiusaltar, Zustand vor der Restaurierung 1980

lich beschleunigt. Das Schadensbild nahm in rasantem Maß zu. Der in nur wenigen Jahren eingetretene und rasch fortschreitende Ablöseprozess erforderte ein sofortiges Reagieren und Konservieren der Fassung. Um die Altarfassungen zu retten, wurde auf Anregung des Bayerischen Landesamtes für Denkmalpflege 1990 eine Arbeitsgemeinschaft von Restauratoren aus dem Gemälde- und Möbelbereich eingesetzt. Es galt gemeinsam mit den Werkstätten des Bayerischen Landesamtes für Denkmalpflege eine Methodik der Konservierung und Restaurierung zu erarbeiten und diese anschließend auch praktisch umzusetzen.

Voruntersuchung

1990 begannen die Voruntersuchungen. Dabei wurden die Ursachen der Schäden genau untersucht und definiert sowie erste Überlegungen zur Problemlösung entwickelt.[5] Neben den genannten und gezeigten Schäden fanden sich auch Partien mit kleinteilig muschelig gebrochenem originalem Überzug, einem älteren, lichtbedingten Schaden sowie das charakteristische Craquelé historischer Lacke. Ebenso fanden sich Flächen, an denen die Malschicht durch eingedrungenen Schellack verfärbt war.[6] Während der Voruntersuchungen wurden in den Restaurierungswerkstätten des Bayerischen Landesamtes für Denkmalpflege Querschliffe gefertigt, die Aufschluss über das Materialgefüge gaben (Farbtafel XX.7, 8).

Dabei fiel auf, dass dieser Lack nachweislich eine extrem hohe Schichtstärke aufwies, was die Entwicklung der Schäden sicher begünstigte. Im ultravioletten Licht war zudem deutlich die kompakte Struktur und Konsistenz des neuen, oberen Schellacküberzuges zu erkennen – im Gegensatz zum darunter liegenden Originallack –, der, wie Analysen ergaben, weit gehend aus Sandarak mit Beimischungen von Mastix und Elemi besteht.[7] Insgesamt kristallisierten sich durch die Voruntersuchung drei Problemkreise heraus:

1. Fehlende Bindemittel der Malschicht

Die Bindemittel der Malschicht waren fast vollständig abgebaut. So konnten in der Malschicht der Altarmarmorierung bei Untersuchungen durch Johann Koller, Doerner-Institut der Bayerischen Staatsgemäldesammlungen in München, keine Bindemittel mehr festgestellt werden. Das Bindemittel (weitestgehend ehemals Leim) hatte sich vollständig abgebaut. Dadurch erklärte sich auch die puderige Konsistenz sowie die fehlende Bindung der Malschicht zur Grundierung bzw. zum Holzträger. Der in den 80er Jahren aufgetragene dichte Überzug „schälte“ nun im Wortsinne die alten Farbschichten vom Untergrund ab.

2. Undurchlässigkeit des neuen Schellacküberzuges

Der weit gehend dichte Schellacküberzug verhinderte eine Festigung. Die üblichen Festigungsmaterialien konnten den dichten Überzug an vielen Partien kaum durchdringen. Zusätzlich ergaben sich bei allen getesteten Festigungsmitteln – außer bei tierischen Leimen – starke Verfärbungen der Malschicht.

3. Ähnliches Lösemittelverhalten der Überzüge

Das Lösemittelverhalten beider Überzüge, des originalen Lackes und des neuen Schellacküberzugs, ist nahezu identisch. Beim Abnehmen des neuen Überzuges mit Lösemittel würde ebenfalls der originale Lack gelöst. Deswegen schien eine Abnahme des neuen Überzuges mittels Lösemitteln zunächst nicht möglich, wobei zu Beginn im Wesentlichen Aceton, Aethanol und Isopropanol getestet wurden.

Wegen der pudrig lockeren Konsistenz der Malschicht erwiesen sich auch mechanische Abnahmemethoden (wie etwa Schleifen) vor einer Festigung der Malschicht als unmöglich. Vor allem der letzte Punkt frustrierte zunächst alle Beteiligten. Ohne hinreichende Festigung der Malschicht konnte mit der Abnahme des neuen Schellacküberzuges nicht begonnen werden. Zugleich schien jedoch die Festigung der Malschicht vor Abnahme des dicken Schellacküberzuges zu weiten Teilen nicht möglich. Oder kurz, ohne Festigung keine Abnahme, aber, ohne Abnahme keine Festigung (Farbtafel XX.2).

Es musste also eine, auch auf großen Flächen umsetzbare Methode erarbeitet werden, welche die Festigung der Altarfassung unter Durchdringung des neuen Schellacküberzuges ermöglichte. Weiterhin musste ein Verfahren zur Abnahme des neuen Schellacküberzuges unter Erhaltung des originalen Lackes gefunden werden, sowohl um den weiteren Verlust der Originalfassung zu verhindern, als auch um die extreme optische Erscheinung des modernen Überzuges zu beseitigen oder zumindest zu reduzieren.

Erarbeiten einer Konservierungsmethode

Zunächst musste ein Weg zur Festigung der Schichten gefunden werden. Um dies zu erreichen, galt es vier technische Probleme zu lösen:

1. Finden eines geeigneten Festigungsmittels

Als Erstes war ein geeignetes Festigungsmittel zu finden, welches möglichst keine Verfärbung in der schlecht gebundenen Malschicht hinterlassen durfte. Ausgedehnte Versuche zeigten, dass im Gegensatz zu anderen Festigungsmitteln (wie z. B. Plextol D 360 oder D 498) ausschließlich bei Störleim keine Verfärbungen auftraten und trotzdem eine ausreichende Festigung erzielt werden konnte.

2. Finden eines geeigneten Netzmittels

Als Nächstes erprobte man verschiedene Methoden für das Eindringen der Leimlösung durch die wenig durchlässigen Lackschichten. Bei Versuchen stellte sich heraus, dass an schwierigen Stellen ein Vornetzen mit Toluol besonders effektiv war. In der Praxis musste dieses gesundheitsschädliche Lösemittel jedoch nur selten verwendet werden. Ansonsten funktionierte die Reduzierung der Oberflächenspannung mit Standardmethoden, wie Agepon in Wasser, Triton B oder Ochsengalle.

3. Finden einer Methode zur Festigung

Vor allem musste für diejenigen Stellen eine Festigungsmethode gefunden werden, wo unter dem neuen, noch geschlossenen Überzug bereits Lockerungen der darunter liegenden Malschicht eingetreten waren und die Lackschichten nicht mit der Leimlösung durchdrungen werden konnten. Der Störleim war also unter den völlig dicht schließenden neuen Schellack, unter den originalen Lack und unter die Malschicht zu bringen!

Eine selten angewandte Methode der „ultima ratio" aus der Restaurierung von Tafelgemälden zur Festigung von „Luftblasen" zwischen dichter Malschicht und Träger bzw. Grundierung war Erfolg versprechend und wurde entsprechend modifiziert. Durch die splittrig-spröden Überzüge wurde mit einem selbst konstruierten, ungewöhnlichen Restaurierungswerkzeug, nämlich mit einer zuvor erhitzten Nadel, ein winziges Loch in den Lack geschmolzen (Abb. 3).

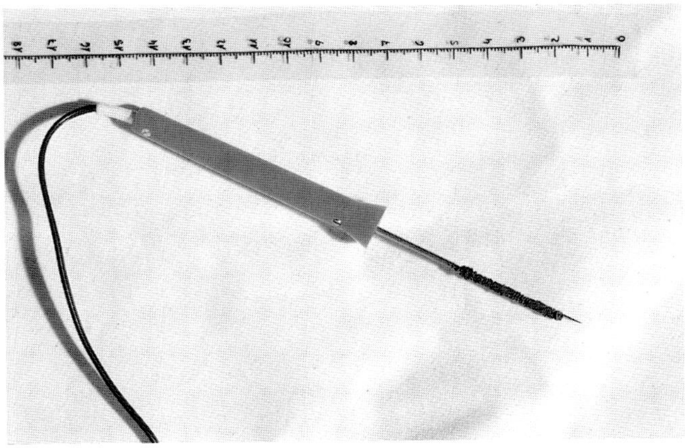

◁ Abb. 3. Ein ungewöhnliches Hilfsmittel zur Fassungsfestigung: Erhitzbare Nadel zum punktuellen Durchschmelzen der Überzüge, um das Festigungsmittel unter die Überzüge fließen lassen zu können

Ein Stich mit der kalten Nadel hätte den Lack zum Splittern gebracht und größere Schäden bzw. Abplatzungen hervorgerufen. Das Festigungsmittel konnte nun durch diese künstlichen Öffnungen an die richtigen Stellen einfließen. Solche extremen Problemzonen waren glücklicherweise nicht allzu häufig. Es wurden also keineswegs Hunderte von Quadratmetern Rokokoaltarfassung kleinstteilig „perforiert" bzw. „durchlöchert".

4. Finden einer Methode zur Abnahme des neuen Schellacküberzuges

Das Schwierigste der zu lösenden Probleme war jedoch die gezielte Abnahme des neuen Schellacküberzuges ohne Beschädigung des darunter liegenden originalen Lackes. Ein komplettes Abschleifen des neuen Schellacks bis auf den originalen Überzug war ohne gravierende Schädigung nicht möglich. Wegen der unzureichenden Bindung der Farbschicht brachen beim Schleifen unvermittelt ganze Schollen samt aller Lack, Farb- und Grundierungsschichten ohne „Vorwarnung" aus und gingen verloren. Durch Schleifen war es zwar grundsätzlich möglich den neuen Schellack zu dünnen und auch einen harten, der ursprünglichen Wirkung vermutlich nahe kommenden Oberflächenglanz zu erzielen, aber eine präzise Freilegung der originalen Oberfläche war nicht möglich. Ebenso war eine Abnahme der neuen Lackschicht mit Skalpell und Stereomikroskop oder Lupe bei den umfangreichen Flächen schlicht utopisch.

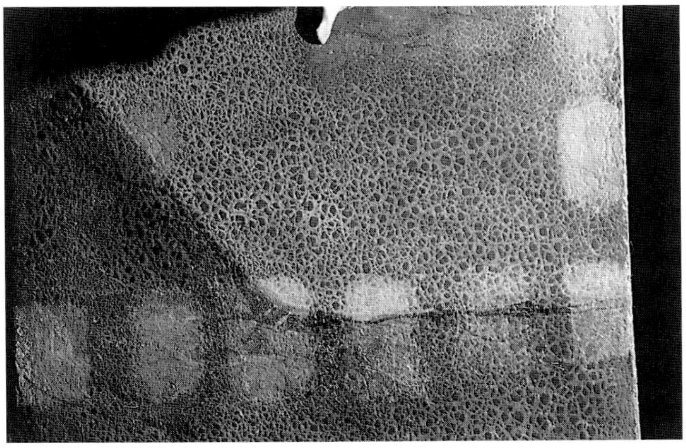

Abb. 4. Landsberg, Hl. Kreuz, Marmorierung eines Seitenaltars, Testreihe zur Abnahme des neuen Überzuges mit verschiedenen Lösungsmittelgelen

Beide Überzüge waren auch mit Lösemitteln unter herkömmlicher Anwendung – da sie ein ähnliches Lösemittelverhalten besitzen – ohne gravierende Schäden nicht voneinander trennbar. Abnahmetestreihen des neuen Überzuges mit Lösemitteln unter herkömmlicher Anwendung lösten auch den Originallack an- bzw. reduzierten sogar teilweise die schlecht oder gar nicht gebundene Malschicht.

△ 1

2 ▽

▽ 3

Zustand des orig. Lackes
nach der Freilegung
intakter Lacküberzug
wenige kleine Ausbrüche
zahlreiche kleine Ausbrüche
durchgehend rauhe Oberfläche (dadurch matt) und großflächige Ausbrüche
fehlender Überzug bzw. Neufassung

△ 4

▽ 5

6 ▽

▽ 7

8 ▽

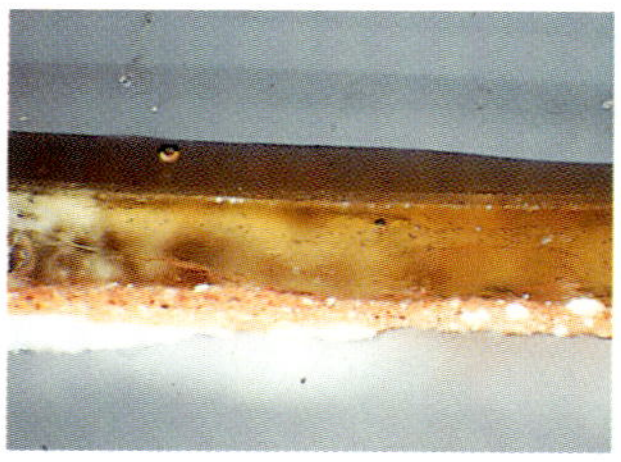

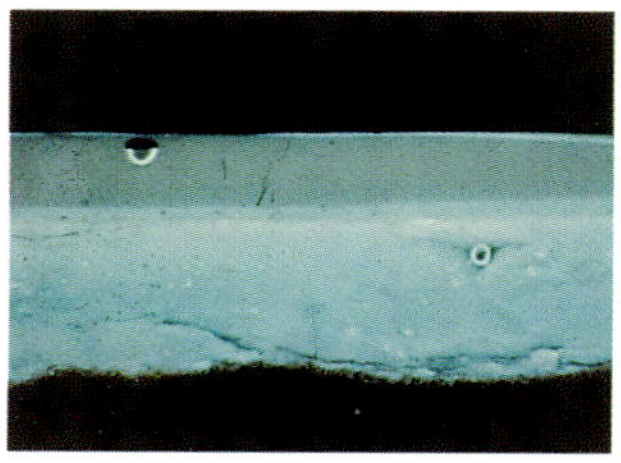

Manchmal braucht es zum Finden von Lösungen einfach Glück und manchmal führt ein an sich falscher Gedanke schließlich doch auf den Weg zur richtigen Lösung. Nachdem alle „Abnahmeversuche" durch Abschleifen und Ähnliches keinen Erfolg brachten, wandten wir uns wieder den Lösemitteln zu. Selbst Versuche mit handelsüblichen Kunstharzlösern erfolgten. Und zum Erstaunen – und anfänglichen Entsetzen – gelang es mit diesen Mitteln an einer Stelle den modernen Überzug vom alten Sandarak zu trennen. Der Beweis war also erbracht, dass es im Prinzip mit Lösemitteln doch möglich war, den alten vom neuen Überzug zu trennen. An anderen Stellen jedoch scheiterte dieses Verfahren und Untersuchungen ergaben, dass die erste erfolgreiche „Trennung" zufällig an einer Stelle stattgefunden hatte, an der wohl der neue Schellack anders gealtert war oder sich andere Harzanteile befanden.

Trotzdem war ein Lösungsansatz gefunden: Die moderne Schellackschicht war grundsätzlich vom originalen Lack ablösbar. Zur „Steuerung" des Löseverhaltens wurden die Lösemittel zunächst in Zellulose gerührt. Das Lösemittel wirkte dadurch nicht so „schlagartig" in die Tiefe. Parallel hierzu unternahm Katharina Walch von den Restaurierungswerkstätten des Bayerischen Landesamtes für Denkmalpflege Testreihen, die auf der Verwendung von Lösemittelgelen nach Wolbers beruhten[8] (Abb. 4) und hinsichtlich des Lösemittels, der Einwirkzeit und der Abnahmemethoden variiert wurden. An einer extrem belichteten und beschädigten Fläche mit besonders stark verbräuntem Schellacküberzug wurden an dicht nebeneinander liegenden Stellen verschiedene polare und unpolare Lösemittelvarianten getestet, um das Freilegungsergebnis im direkten Vergleich auswerten zu können. Als optimales Lösemittel erwies sich hierbei Isopropanol, eingedickt in dem Acrylsäurepolymer „Carbopol 980" (Carboxy Polymethylen) und dem basischen Detergent „Ethomeen C 25" (poly-oxy-ethylen cocamine).[9] Wird zu diesem Gemisch eine kleine Menge Wasser eingerührt, entsteht eine sehr stabile Verbindung in transparenter, gelförmiger Konsistenz. Das so eingebundene Isopropanol ermöglichte ein sehr genaues Abnehmen der jüngeren Lackschicht. Schichtaufnahmen unter UV-Licht zeigten, wie präzise die originale Lackschicht mit dieser Methode freigelegt werden konnte.

Erarbeitung einer Restaurierungsmethode

Nach der Festigung der Malschicht und Abnahme des Schellacküberzuges kam der originale Lack mit seinen alten Schäden wieder zum Vorschein. Je nach Umfang dieser alten Schäden wirkte seine Oberfläche mehr oder weniger matt und die Wirkung der Marmorierung war deswegen teilweise stumpf und leblos. Dies entsprach dem originalen Erscheinungsbild in keiner Hinsicht. Ein wichtiger Punkt im Restaurierungskonzept war es, eine in Farbe und Glanzgrad dem ursprünglichen Aussehen des Rokoko zumindest angenäherte Erscheinung der Altäre wieder zu gewinnen.[10] Es stellte sich also die Frage, wie der matte Originallack wieder zum Glänzen und auch die darunter liegende Marmorierung wieder zum „Leuchten" gebracht werden könne. Auch war die Frage zu beantworten, wie die Farbausbrüche optisch zu integrieren seien, um einen geschlossenen Gesamteindruck der Altarausstattung zu erhalten.

Die Untersuchungen hatten ergeben, dass der originale Lack außergewöhnlich dick aufgetragen worden war und eine gewisse Vergilbung aufweist.[11] Weiterhin zeigten die Untersuchungen, dass durch die Abnahme des Schellacküberzuges auf der Oberfläche des originalen Lackes eine leichte Rauigkeit aufgetreten war. Diese „raue" Oberfläche streut das Licht und lässt die gemalte Marmorierung stumpf und weniger leuchtend erscheinen. Die ursprüngliche künstlerische Absicht war jedoch, den harten Glanz einer polierten Steinoberfläche zu evozieren. Bei Versuchen mit mikrofeinem Schleifpapier der Körnung 1200 konnte an Stellen mit sehr dickem Lack eine Glättung der obersten Schicht des originalen Überzuges erreicht werden. Ansonsten wurde der Überzug mit Tripel – einer Tonerde – poliert.[12] Durch die außergewöhnliche Dicke des Überzuges – bis zu 1,5 mm – erschien dabei ein minimaler Verlust an der Oberfläche des Überzuges als akzeptabel, zumal dadurch die beabsichtigte künstlerische Wirkung wieder nachvollziehbar wurde. Die minimale Reduzierung der originalen Lackoberfläche bewirkt in der Tendenz zugleich eine geringere Materialspannung und damit eine Reduzierung der Gefahr künftiger Lockerungen (Farbtafel XX.5, 6). Außerdem konnten zerklüftete Schichten in der originalen Oberfläche, die sich unweigerlich mit dem Schellack verbunden hatte, mechanisch reduziert werden. Hier war eine reine geltechnische Schellackentfernung nicht möglich.

◁ Farbtafel XX / *Colour Plate XX*

1 Landsberg, Hl. Kreuz, verbräunter und verkrusteter Schellacküberzug auf dem originalen Sandarak des 18. Jahrhunderts an einem Seitenaltar

2 Landsberg, Hl. Kreuz, Abnahmeversuch des neuen Schellacks vom originalen Sandarak mit handelsüblichen Kunstharzlösern

3 Landsberg, Hl. Kreuz, Gebälkzone des Ignatiusaltars nach der Abnahme des neuen Lacküberzuges und der geglätteten Oberfläche des alten Sandaraküberzuges

4 Landsberg, Hl. Kreuz, Stanislausaltar, Kartierung der Verteilung und des Ausmaßes der Lockerungsschäden an der Marmorierung

5 Landsberg, Hl. Kreuz, Josefsaltar, nördliches Postament, Zwischenzustand nach der Festigung der Fassung, Abnahme des neuen Überzuges vom originalen Lack und der Kittung der Fehlstellen

6 Landsberg, Hl. Kreuz, Josefsaltar, nördliches Postament, Zustand nach integrierender Retusche und dem Einstellen des Glanzgrades durch Schleifen bzw. Polieren

7 Landsberg, Hl. Kreuz, Querschliff einer Altarfassung mit dem originalen und dem darüber liegenden neuen Überzug im Normallicht

8 Landsberg, Hl. Kreuz, Querschliff einer Altarfassung mit dem originalen und dem darüber liegenden neuen Überzug im UV-Licht; deutlich wird die große Dicke und gleichmäßige Konsistenz des neuen Schellacküberzuges auf dem Originallack

5

Kleinere Fehlstellen in der Fassung beziehungsweise im Lack konnten mit Aquarell bzw. Tempera retuschiert werden. In Bodennähe wurde, wegen der ständig auftretenden Nässe des Steinbodens, den Retuschiermaterialien Acrylharz zugesetzt, um eine größere Widerstandsfähigkeit der Retuschen zu gewährleisten. Größere Fehlstellen wurden zunächst mit eingeschliffenem Kreidekitt geschlossen, anschließend retuschiert und, wo nötig, mit Mastix überzogen und im Glanzgrad auf die Umgebung eingestellt.

Ausführung

Nachdem 1993 an größeren Flächen die Umsetzung der entwickelten Vorgehensweise an einem Seitenaltar praktisch erprobt worden war, wurden in den vergangenen Jahren die Fassungen sämtlicher Altäre konserviert und restauriert, insgesamt eine Fläche von nahezu 700 Quadratmetern.

Differenzierte Vorgehensweise bei den Konservierungsmaßnahmen

Es zeigte sich, dass je nach Schädigung differenziert zu arbeiten war. An unproblematischen Stellen konnte zunächst gefestigt werden und anschließend erfolgte die Abnahme des neuen Überzuges. An anderen Partien war eine Abfolge der Maßnahmen in umgekehrter Reihenfolge erforderlich. Teils wurde auch vorab partiell gefestigt und anschließend partiell der neue Überzug reduziert.

Differenzierte Vorgehensweise bei den Restaurierungsmaßnahmen

Ähnlich differenziert wurde auch bei der Wiederherstellung des Oberflächenglanzes vorgegangen (Farbtafel XX.5, 6). An vorstehenden Teilen wie Säulen und Gebälk wurde auf höhere Brillanz geachtet, während an Rücklagen und Flächen etwas zurückhaltender verfahren wurde. Durch die Hervorhebung des Glanzes an wichtigen Architekturelementen konnte die unterschiedlich erhaltene Lackoberfläche integriert und insgesamt ein überzeugendes Erscheinungsbild hergestellt werden (Abb. 5). Ebenso differenziert wurde bei den Retuschen vorgegangen.

Lichtschutzmaßnahmen

Bereits früher aufgetretene Schäden durch Licht machten Lichtschutzmaßnahmen durch Vorhänge notwendig.[13] Da die Sonne zu bestimmten Tageszeiten direkt auf die Seitenaltäre scheint, konnte durch die Schadenskartierungen ein deutlicher Zusammenhang zwischen dem Einwirken des Sonnenlichtes und den Schäden aufgezeigt und damit die Notwendigkeit von Lichtschutzmaßnahmen deutlich gemacht werden (Farbtafel XX.4, Abb. 6).

Abb. 5. Landsberg, Hl. Kreuz, Säule eines Seitenaltars nach dem Einstellen des Glanzgrades durch Schleifen bzw. Polieren des Lacküberzuges

Abb. 6. Landsberg, Hl. Kreuz, Stanislausaltar, mittäglicher Lichteinfall

6

Wirkungskontrolle

In den letzten Jahren wurden die bereits bearbeiteten Flächen mehrfach auf den Festigungserfolg überprüft und gegebenenfalls Nachfestigungen durchgeführt. Bei den Kontrollen zeigte sich, dass die Fassungen inzwischen weit gehend stabil sind. Dies belegt, dass die Festigungs- und Freilegungsarbeiten insgesamt erfolgreich waren.

Dokumentation

Selbstverständlich wurden alle Untersuchungsergebnisse, angelegten Muster sowie sämtliche durchgeführten Maßnahmen schriftlich, zeichnerisch sowie fotografisch dokumentiert.[14]

Resümee

Rokokoaltäre gibt es viele in Süddeutschland. Eine in Fassung und Lacküberzug weit gehend komplett erhaltene Altarausstattung des Rokoko ist heute jedoch äußerst selten. Hierin liegt der besondere Rang der Altäre in Hl. Kreuz zu Landsberg (Farbtafel XX.3). Durch die Teamarbeit von Gemälde- und Möbelrestauratoren konnte in Zusammenarbeit mit den Werkstätten des Bayerischen Landesamtes für Denkmalpflege, dem Doerner-Institut der Bayerischen Staatsgemäldesammlungen sowie durch das Verständnis der Auftraggeber eine für die akut gefährdeten Altarfassungen von Hl. Kreuz in Landsberg geeignete Konservierungs- und Restaurierungsmethode entwickelt werden. In den vergangenen neun Jahren gelang es – wofür allen Beteiligten ausdrücklich Dank gesagt sei – eine außergewöhnliche Rokokomarmorierung und ihren originalen Lacküberzug zu erhalten und zugleich seinem ursprünglichen Erscheinungsbild wieder weit gehend anzunähern.

Danksagung

Nach neun Jahren Untersuchung, Forschung und Restaurierung in Landsberg Hl. Kreuz hat sich eine große Dankesschuld angehäuft. Für ihre stete Unterstützung seien gedankt; Herrn Diözesanbaudirektor Dipl. Ing. Werner Köhler von der Diözese Augsburg, der Katholischen Kirchenstiftung Hl. Kreuz zu Landsberg am Lech, insbesondere Herrn Stadtpfarrer Gabriel Beißer, Herrn Kirchenpfleger Bernhard Arnold und dem Mesner Herrn Heinrich Gion, dem Gebietsreferenten des Bayerischen Landesamtes für Denkmalpflege Herrn Hauptkonservator Dr. H. Rainer Schmid, dem Leiter der Restaurierungswerkstätten des Bayerischen Landesamtes für Denkmalpflege Herrn Dr. Michael Kühlenthal sowie den Ltd. Restauratoren Frau Katharina Walch und Herrn Prof. Erwin Emmerling. Für die wissenschaftliche Unterstützung sei dem Doerner-Institut der Bayerischen Staatsgemäldesammlungen, München, Dank gesagt, insbesondere Herrn Dr. Johann Koller und Frau Ursula Baumer. Die untersuchenden und ausführenden Kräfte waren die Restaurierungswerkstätte für Gemälde und Skulpturen Thomas Schoeller, München, und die Werkstätte für Möbelrestaurierung Andreas Scheuch, München, mit folgenden Mitarbeiterinnen und Mitarbeitern: Beatrice Brauckmann, Julia Gens, Gabriele Halbritter, Christine Haunschild, Marion Kast, Manfred König, Alejandra Vela.

Anmerkungen

1 Hierzu sowie zum weiter unten Ausgeführten siehe den 1997 erschienenen, ausführlichen Topographieband zu den Sakralbauten von Landsberg am Lech: DIETRICH/WEISSHAAR-KIEM 1997. Zu Hl. Kreuz siehe S. 338–527 insbesondere S. 371–487 sowie DEHIO 1990, S. 576–578.

2 SCHMID 1997.

3 Zur Methode der Lackiertechnik mit Goldäderung in Landsberg, Hl. Kreuz siehe WALCH, *Transparente Glanzlacke* 1997, S. 39 f. mit Farbabbildungen 2, 3 und 4.

4 Hierzu DIETRICH/WEISSHAAR-KIEM 1997, S. 375–378, insbesondere S. 378.

5 Hierzu WALCH 1997.

6 Bericht der Voruntersuchungen der Altarfassungen in Landsberg, Hl. Kreuz von Thomas Schoeller und Sybille Schmitt, 1990: Archiv des Bayerischen Landesamtes für Denkmalpflege, München. Für ihre Mitarbeit bei den ersten Voruntersuchungen sei Frau Dipl.-Rest. Sybille Schmitt Dank gesagt. Umfangreiche Untersuchungen fanden dann im Zusammenhang mit dem Deutsch-Japanischen Forschungsprojekt des Bayerischen Landesamtes für Denkmalpflege zur Untersuchung und Restaurierung historischer Lacke durch Dr. Johann Koller und Ursula Baumer vom Doerner-Institut der Bayerischen Staatsgemäldesammlungen statt, die zum Teil in KOLLER/BAUMER, *Die transparenten Glanzlacke des Barock und Rokoko. II* 1997, S. 71–73 publiziert wurden. Siehe dort die Abb. 24–26 sowie ein Gaschromatogramm von Lackanalysen vom Ignatiusaltar aus Hl. Kreuz in Landsberg. Vgl. KOLLER/BAUMER u. a., *Mastix* 1997, S. 347 und KOLLER/BAUMER u. a., *Sandarak* 1997, S. 379.

7 KOLLER/BAUMER, *Die transparenten Glanzlacke* 1997, S. 70–72.

8 Bereits 1993 konnte in der kath. Pfarrkirche St. Ulrich in Aich, Landkreis Landshut in Bayern erfolgreich eine Abnahme von sekundären Überzügen nach der Methode von Wolbers an einem Orgelgehäuse durchgeführt werden. Siehe hierzu die Dokumentation der ausführenden Werkstatt für Möbelrestaurierung Andreas Scheuch, München im Archiv des Bayerischen Landesamtes für Denkmalpflege, München. Zu Aich und den Abnahmen von Überzügen nach Wolbers siehe auch: WALCH/KOLLER/BAUMER, *Die Restaurierung des Aicher Orgelgehäuses* 1997, S. 334–345 mit der Angabe weiterer Literatur zur Wolbers-Methode in Anm. 11, 12 und 20. 1994 wurde zur Abnahmemethode nach Wolbers eine Diplomarbeit abgeschlossen: siehe HALLER 1994.

9 Für die Abnahme des neuen Schellacks mit seinen Kunstharzanteilen erwies sich für die Altäre in Landsberg/Hl. Kreuz folgende Mischung als geeignet: 3 gr. Carbopol 980, 10 ml. Ethomeen C25, 100 ml. Isopropanol und 25 ml. Wasser. Die entsprechenden Vorversuche wurden von Katharina Walch, Bayerisches Landesamt für Denkmalpflege, durchgeführt.

10 Zur Bedeutung von Glanz in Kirchenräumen des Rokoko siehe SCHMID 1997.

11 Zur Untersuchung der Dicke von Lacküberzügen siehe WALCH 1992, S. 400–403.

12 Erstmals wurde hier durch Schleifen großflächig ein originaler Rokokolack geglättet bzw. in seiner Oberfläche verdichtet und wieder zum Glänzen gebracht. Auch das Glättungsverfahren des Rokoko bestand aus Schleifen, zum Beispiel mit Schachtelhalmen und Tripel. Zum Schleifverfahren von Lacken im Rokoko siehe WALCH, *Transparente Glanzlacke* 1997, S. 43–44.

13 Zur Problematik des Lichtschutzes und zu Alterungsprozessen von Lacken durch Lichteinwirkung siehe KOLLER/BAUMER, *Die transparenten Glanzlacke* 1997, S. 62 f. und zu dieser Problematik in Landsberg, Hl. Kreuz, ebd. S. 76 sowie die Abb. 24, 25 und die Abbildung eines Gaschromatogramms der Untersuchungen zu Landsberg, Hl. Kreuz, ebd. auf Farbtafel IV, Abb. 5.

14 Nach Abschluss der Arbeiten wird die schriftliche, zeichnerische und fotografische Dokumentation der Maßnahmen im Bayerischen Landesamt für Denkmalpflege archiviert.

Literaturverzeichnis

DEHIO, GEORG: *Handbuch der Deutschen Kunstdenkmäler. Bayern IV. München und Oberbayern,* München/Berlin 1990

DIETRICH, DAGMAR/WEISSHAAR-KIEM, HEIDE: *Landsberg am Lech 2, Sakralbauten der Altstadt,* München/Berlin 1997 (Die Kunstdenkmäler von Bayern, Neue Folge 3)

HALLER, URSULA: *Studien zur Herstellung und Anwendung von Lösungsmittelgelen, -Pasten und -Kompressen in der Restaurierung,* Diplomarbeit am Institut für Technologie der Malerei an der Staatlichen Akademie der bildenden Künste Stuttgart, Studiengang Restaurierung und Technologie von Gemälden und gefassten Skulpturen, Betreuer Prof. Dr. Gerhard Banik, Dipl.-Rest. Ruth Baier, Mai 1994

KOLLER, JOHANN/BAUMER, URSULA u. a.: *Mastix (Mastic),* in: Lacke des Barock und Rokoko/Baroque and Rococo Lacquers, München 1997, S. 347–358 (Arbeitshefte des Bayerischen Landesamtes für Denkmalpflege, Bd. 81)

KOLLER, JOHANN/BAUMER, URSULA u. a.: *Sandarak (Sandarac)* in: Lacke des Barock und Rokoko/Baroque and Rococo Lacquers, München 1997, S. 379–395 (Arbeitshefte des Bayerischen Landesamtes für Denkmalpflege, Bd. 81)

KOLLER, JOHANN/BAUMER, URSULA: *Die transparenten Glanzlacke des Barock und Rokoko. II. Eine naturwissenschaftliche Untersuchung der Lacksysteme (Baroque and Rococo Transparent Gloss Lacquers II. Scientific Study of Lacquer Systems),* in: Lacke des Barock und Rokoko/Baroque and Rococo Lacquers, München 1997, S. 52–84 (Arbeitshefte des Bayerischen Landesamtes für Denkmalpflege, Bd. 81)

SCHMID, RAINER H.: *Licht und Glanz an Kirchenausstattungen des 17. und 18. Jahrhunderts in Altbayern und Schwaben (The Light and Luster of 17th and 18th Century Bavarian and Swabian Church Interiors),* in: Lacke des Barock und Rokoko/Baroque and Rococo Lacquers, München 1997, S. 11–20 (Arbeitshefte des Bayerischen Landesamtes für Denkmalpflege, Bd. 81)

WALCH, KATHARINA: *Transparente Glanzlacke des Barock und Rokoko. I. Rekonstruktion „Weißer Lacke" aufgrund quellenkundlicher Studien und technischer Untersuchungen (Baroque and Rococo Transparent Gloss Lacquers. I. The Replication of 'White Lacquers' on the Basis of Historic Sources and Scientific Investigation),* in: Lacke des Barock und Rokoko/Baroque and Rococo Lacquers, München 1997, S. 21–51 (Arbeitshefte des Bayerischen Landesamtes für Denkmalpflege, Bd. 81)

WALCH, KATHARINA/KOLLER, JOHANN/BAUMER, URSULA: *Die Restaurierung des Aicher Orgelgehäuses (The Restoration of the Organ Case in Aich),* in: Lacke des Barock und Rokoko/Baroque and Rococo Lacquers, München 1997, S. 334–346 (Arbeitshefte des Bayerischen Landesamtes für Denkmalpflege, Bd. 81)

WALCH, KATHARINA: *Firnisüberzüge auf Marmorierungen im 18. Jahrhundert, mit einem Beitrag von Brigitte Hecht-Lang (The Application of Varnish in 18th Century Marbling, with an article by Brigitte Hecht-Lang),* in: Die Wies. Geschichte und Restaurierung/History and Restoration, München 1992, S. 391–410 (Arbeitshefte des Bayerischen Landesamtes für Denkmalpflege, Bd. 55)

Photo Credits

Abb. 1, 2: Bayerisches Landesamt für Denkmalpflege, Restaurierungswerkstätten, Archiv
Abb. 3–5: Arbeitsgemeinschaft Schoeller & Scheuch
Abb. 6: Thomas Schoeller, Sybille Schmitt
Farbtafel XX.1–6: Thomas Schoeller; 7, 8: Katharina Walch, Bayerisches Landesamt für Denkmalpflege, München

Summary

The former Jesuit Church 'Heilig Kreuz' in Landsberg, 40 km west of Munich was built and decorated between 1752 and 1756. The seven retables were made by Dominikus Bergmüller from the Kistler workshop in Türkheim. The polychrome painted marble on the retables is still covered with the original lacquer on the basis of sandarac resin. This original state was left untouched for more than 230 years – an exceptional situation in Bavaria. In the early 1980s the original sandarac-based lacquer was covered with a new shellac coating with synthetic resin additives. A sufficient fixing of loose underlying paint layers did not take place. The result was a considerable surface tension which loosened both old and new lacquer as well as the underlying paint layer from the primer coat. Between 1990 and 1999 a conservation plan was developed by a team of freelance conservators for painting and wood work in collaboration with the conservators at the Bavarian Conservation Trust. After careful research conservation was begun: the newly applied lacquer was removed from the original lacquer with the aid of a solvent gel developed by Wolbers. The underlying chalk-painted marble was fixed with sturgeon glue, which was the ideal material to fix the paint layer and avoid darkening. This penetration of glue through the thick and dense layers of lacquer was an especially difficult problem to solve. The final polishing was accomplished with pasty claydough (tripel with water) and the use of microfine sandpaper for problematic areas. Thus, a reconstruction of the original surface shine of the marble imitation was achieved.

Anna Czarnocka

Ateliers französischer Vernisseure im Paris des 18. Jahrhunderts

Im Paris des 18. Jahrhunderts, einer Stadt, in der das Geschäft mit Luxus- und Galanteriewaren auf Hochtouren lief, treffen wir auf eine ganze Reihe von Händlern und Kunsthandwerkern aller Art, die sich auf die Herstellung von Luxuswaren spezialisiert hatten. Neben Malern, Vergoldern, Bildhauern, Goldschmieden, Uhrmachern und Ebenisten konnten sich die Vernisseure mit eigenen Manufakturen behaupten.

Der Erfolg dieser vergleichsweise jungen Berufsgruppe war dabei von mehreren Faktoren abhängig: Verlangt wurden sowohl handwerkliches Geschick, wie auch Kenntnisse der Chemie und organisatorische Fähigkeiten – weil einige von ihnen mehrere andere Handwerker wie Dreher, Maler oder Vergolder in ihrem Betrieb beschäftigten, und – nicht zuletzt – kaufmännisches Geschick: Ihre Waren mussten Abnehmer finden. Um sich neben erfolgreichen Konkurrenten wie den Gebrüdern Martin behaupten zu können, die mit Erzeugnissen aus ihren Ateliers bereits die besten Kunden, nämlich die königliche Familie und viele Aristokraten bzw. die königlichen Werkstätten der „Gobelins“ versorgten, wo u. a. prunkvolle Kutschen hergestellt wurden, mussten sie selber für Werbung sorgen. Dies geschah durch geschickt formulierte Anzeigen in den renommierten Zeitungen und Magazinen der Zeit und natürlich, soweit vorhanden, über Beziehungen. So tauchen in zahlreichen Ausgaben der „Annonces, Affiches et Avis divers“, einer Zeitschrift, die seit 1751 zunächst einmal, dann zweimal pro Woche gedruckt wurde und schließlich täglich, sogar mit meist umfangreichen Beilagen erschien und das rege Pariser Geschäftsleben widerspiegelte, sowie in der Zeitschrift „L'Avantcoureur“ u. a. die Namen folgender Vernisseure auf: Cazin de la Brosse, Clément mit seiner „Manufacture de vernis sur tôle“, Giros mit seiner „Manufacture de beaux vernis“, Gosse und Samousseau, Watin und Wolff.

Die ersten Werkstätten für Lackarbeiten entstanden in Frankreich im frühen 18. Jahrhundert, im Umfeld der königlichen Tapisseriemanufaktur, die ihre Werkstätten im Pariser Faubourg Saint-Marcel aufgeschlagen hatte. Bereits 1662 hatte Colbert das Grundstück erworben und ein Jahr später wurden hier die Werkstätten der „Gobelins“ angesiedelt.[1] Es folgte 1667 die Einrichtung der „Manufacture royale des meubles de la Couronne“.

Im Oktober 1713 erhielt der Zeichner und Ornamentstecher Claude III. Audran das königliche Privileg zur Gründung einer Manufaktur zur Herstellung von Firnis, der „zumindest so schön wie der aus China“ sein sollte.[2] Dieser Firnis sollte auf biegsame Materialien wie Wolle, Seide und Leder ebenso aufgetragen werden können, wie auf Hölzer und Metalle, und gleichermaßen zur Dekoration wie zum Schutz von Stühlen, Tischen, Kanapees, Kamin- und Wandschirmen, wie von Betten, Tapisserien, Vorhängen oder Wandverkleidungen geeignet sein.[3] Die Aufgaben teilten sich drei Partner: Audran lieferte Ideen für Zeichnungen und Ornamente, die dann von bezahlten Zeichnern sauber ausgearbeitet wurden; der aus Liège stammende Jacques Dagly[4] steuerte das Geheimnis zur Herstellung eines haltbaren, klaren und glänzenden Lacks bei und Pierre de Neufmaison[5] aus Danzig – er war zuvor im Dienst eines polnischen Fürsten Konstantyn tätig gewesen – leitete das Unternehmen. Bereits 1715 verabschiedete sich Audran gegen Auszahlung einer Abfindung aus dem Unternehmen. Er starb 1734, Dagly bereits 1726. Pierre de Neufmaison führte das Unternehmen noch einige Jahre allein weiter, bis er 1746 eine Partnerschaft mit seinem Schwiegersohn Charles-André Tramblin einging. Nach dem Tode von Neufmaison, dem „Directeur des ouvrages de la Chine aux Gobelins“, wurden Möbel und andere Gegenstände im Hôtel Royal des Gobelins zum Kauf angeboten.[6] Die Verantwortung wurde von Tramblin als „Directeur pour le Roi des ouvrages de la Chine à la manufacture des Gobelins“ übernommen.[7] Bereits ab ca. 1746 verkleinerte sich die Tätigkeit des Unternehmens. Neufmaison wurde alt und Tramblin war mit seinen Aufgaben für die Stadt Paris sowie als Maler und Ausstatter für die Oper in Anspruch genommen. 1760 ging er nach Wien und danach nach Russland, wo er sich das Leben nahm.

Zur Haupttätigkeit der Manufaktur gehörten die Herstellung und Verzierung der Equipagen (Abb. 1). Unter den Schuldnern waren viele Adelige u. a. Prince de Conti, Prince de Bouillon, Duc de Caumont, Comtesse d'Egmont und die Königin von Spanien. Diese Namen fanden sich in dem 1733, nach dem Tod der ersten Frau von Neufmaison angefertigten Inventar.[8] Neufmaison und Tramblin versuchten sich auch in anderen Unternehmungen: u. a. im Handel von lackierten und bedruckten Stoffen. Im Depot der Manufaktur befanden sich 42 Stück von dieser „toile peinte et vernie de façon de la Chine“, geschätzt auf 418 Livres.[9]

In den „Annonces, Affiches et Avis divers“ finden wir eine enorme Zahl von Anzeigen über Kutschen, Berlinen, „Berlingot“, Karossen, „Diligencen“, „Vis-à-vis“ und andere Equipagen, die von Neufmaison bemalt, vergoldet und mit Firnis verziert beziehungsweise als Gobelins-Erzeugnisse angepriesen wurden.[10] Sie wurden direkt von ihren Besitzern oder von „selliers“, Sattlern, zum Kauf angeboten. Nur ganz wenige werden näher beschrieben, so z. B. ein „Berlingot“, dessen Paneele mit Darstellungen der vier Jahreszeiten ausgeschmückt waren,[11] eine „en camaïeu“ von Neufmaison bemalte „Berline“,[12] eine „en camaïeu“ in Blau bemalte, vergoldete und von Neufmaison lackierte „Diligence“[13] oder eine „Diligence“, deren Kastenfelder Darstellungen von Kinderspielen schmückten.[14] Ein „Berlingot“ wurde von Neufmaison vergoldet und von Martin lackiert.[15] Unter den Gobelins-Erzeugnissen werden ohne Nennung von Künstlern u. a. eine „Diligence“ mit Aventurinverzierung in Gold auf grünem Grund,[16] eine Kalesche mit Jagdmotiven auf den Paneelen,[17] eine „Berline“, deren Kasten ganz vergoldet war, eine andere schwarze „Berline“ mit goldenen Ornamenten („or haché“) erwähnt[18] bzw. eine „Diligence“, die mit figürlichen Motiven bemalt und vergoldet war.

François A. de Garsault schrieb 1756 in seinem „Traité des Voitures“: „Früher war man mit dem Auftragen eines bemalten Wappens auf die großen Kutschenpaneele von beiden Seiten, vorne und hinten, zufrieden: Alles war mit Ölfarben ausgeführt. Aber seitdem Martin, und nach ihm andere Maler und Lackierer den Firnis wesentlich verbessert haben, verziert man die Karossen mit allerlei Figuren (...), Landschaften, Gottheiten. Einige dieser Malereien sind so schön, dass sie zwischen den besten Bildern Platz nehmen könnten. Der abschließende Glanz des Firnisses ist so fein, dass er einem Spiegel ähnelt, man spiegelt sich darin wider. Oder es wird auch die Karosse mit einem einzigen Farbton bemalt, den der Firnis bestens zur Geltung bringt. Sogar das Schwarz wird dadurch strahlend."[19] Kein Wunder, dass viele europäische Fürsten und Könige ihre Equipagen in Paris bestellten.

Einer der erhaltenen Wagen aus den Werkstätten der „Gobelins" ist der um 1730 hergestellte, prachtvolle Krönungswagen Kaiser Karls VII., der sich in der Sammlung des Marstallmuseums in Schloss Nymphenburg in München befindet (Farbtafel XXI.1).[20] Er ist mit allegorischen Malereien (Justitia, Bellona, Ecclesia und Putten mit Wappen), Rocaillen und Ranken auf glänzendem Grund geschmückt, ähnlich dem um 1750 in Paris hergestellten Brautwagen der Kurfürstin Maria Anna. Letzterer wurde mit allegorischen Malereien im Stil des François Boucher auf blattvergoldeten Feldern verziert.[21] Die Werkstatt arbeitete auf Bestellung, so wie viele Künstler, die in den „Gobelins" tätig waren.

Abb. 1. Chaise à porteurs, Paris, vor 1726 (?); Compiègne, Musée de la voiture

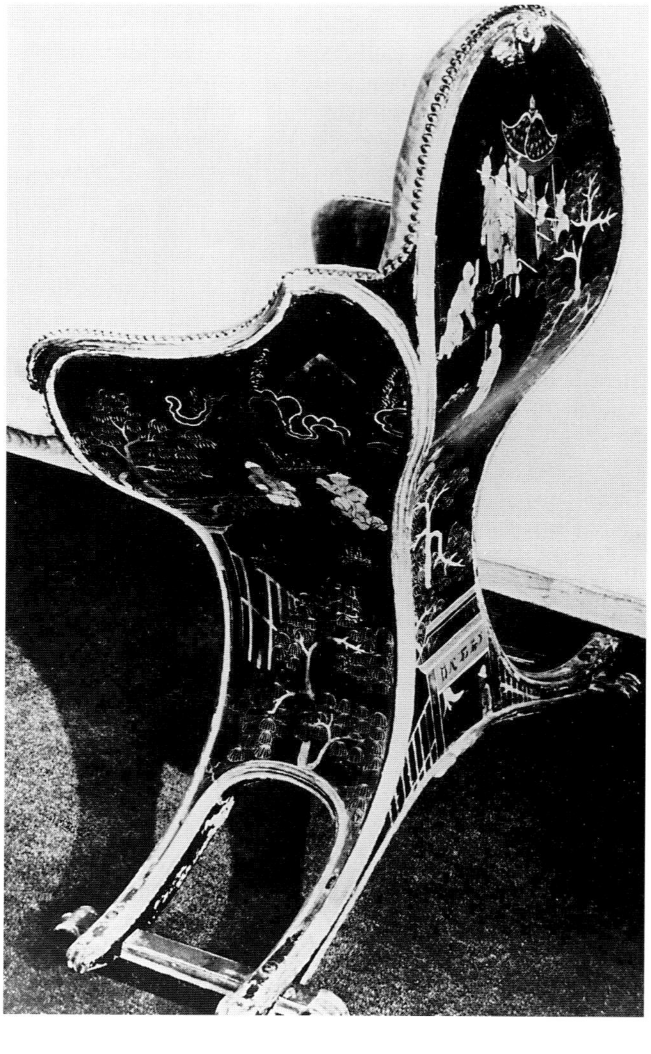

Zur gleichen Zeit wie die „ouvrages de la Chine à la manufacture des Gobelins" waren in Paris aber auch andere Lackkünstler tätig. Einige von ihnen arbeiteten mit den Ebenisten zusammen, andere gründeten eigene Geschäfte. Zu den über Frankreichs Grenzen hinaus berühmten Manufakturen gehörten die der Gebrüder Martin, wo u. a. Kutschen, Möbel und Schmuckwaren aller Art hergestellt wurden. Aber auch andere versuchten ihr Glück.

Die erste Erwähnung des „tablettier-vernisseur" (Kunstdrechsler-Lackierer) Giros stammt aus dem Jahre 1753. Bereits zu dieser Zeit setzte er die Produktion von lackierten Tabakdosen aus Karton, wie man einer Anzeige aus diesem Jahr entnehmen kann, fort. Seine Erzeugnisse bot er in über zweihundert verschiedenen Modellen an. Der Preis lag zwischen 6 Livres und 20 Pistolen pro Stück. Giros verkaufte auch lackierte Tabakdosen aus Schildpatt mit seinem im Boden abgedruckten Namen.[22] Zu Weihnachten 1759 pries Giros noch einmal auf ähnliche Weise seine mit Schildpatt ausgelegten Tabatièren aus Karton an, die jetzt zwischen 3 Livres und 600 Livres kosteten.[23] Offensichtlich hat er seine Dosen gut verkaufen können. 1766 war bereits von der „Manufacture de beaux vernis" von Giros die Rede, der seine Ware in einem Geschäft in Paris, in der rue Neuve Saint Merri im Hôtel Jabach in größeren Mengen anbot.[24] Nur eine Tabatière seiner Herstellung wird genauer beschrieben: Sie ist im Deckel mit einem Medaillon-Bildnis des verstorbenen Dauphin geschmückt.[25] Seine Tätigkeit endete nach 23 Jahren 1776, weil zu dieser Zeit ein gewisser Brosset den Bestand seines Ladens übernahm und weiter seine Tabatièren im Hôtel Jabach verkaufte (Abb. 2).[26]

Aber noch bevor der Name Giros aus dem Pariser Kunsthandel verschwand, nahm man 1767 von einem anderen Geschäftsmann namens Wolff Kenntnis.[27] In seinem Laden in der rue Saint-Martin bot er Tabatièren, Etuis und Schmuckwaren aus Karton an. Seine Erzeugnisse sind mit fein ausgearbeiteten Goldmontierungen geschmückt, seine Dosen mit Bildnissen verziert: Hier ist sogar von einer geheimen neuen Erfindung die Rede, vielleicht handelte es sich bei einigen Tabakdosen um den Doppelboden, eine Dekorart, die frivole Themen mit viel Geschick kaschierte? Zur Ausschmückung seiner Tabatièren trugen die besten Maler mit neuen Motiven bei. Wolff war also ein geschickter Kunsthandwerker, der zur Hebung seiner Produktion eigens Künstler angeworben hat. Was ist aber später aus seiner so vielversprechenden Tätigkeit geworden? Wir wissen es nicht. Vermutlich konnte er der Konkurrenz von Martin, dessen ähnliche Schmuckwaren auf höchstem Niveau sehr gefragt waren, nicht standhalten (Abb. 3).

1759 wird von der Académie Royale des Sciences eine interessante Erfindung vermerkt: ein schöner, glänzender schwarzer Firnis für die Tabakdosen, hart und fest. Seine Anwendung fand er nicht nur auf Karton, sondern insbesondere auch auf Metalloberflächen. So eignete er sich zur Lackierung von Kupfertöpfen oder Pistolenläufen. Der Erfinder ist Gosse, „maître peintre, sculpteur et vernisseur", Meistermaler, Bildhauer und Lackierer. Die Eigenschaften seines Firnisses wurden besonders angepriesen, was aber vor allem für die Tabakdosen wichtig war: sein Firnis war geruchlos.[28]

Erst nach seinem Tode gründeten seine Witwe und sein Schwiegersohn 1767 eine Manufaktur, in der sie einen Firnis herstellten, der sich auch zur Lackierung von Holz, Karton, Metall, für Gewehre und Schornsteine und sogar für Glas und Porzellan eignete. Das Letztere wurde im Journal „L'Avantcoureur" eher mit Skepsis aufgenommen, da Glas und Porzellan keinen

Abb. 2. Tabatière, Paris, um 1750; Paris, Musée Cognacq-Jay

Abb. 3. Etui, Paris, um 1750; Paris, Musée Cognacq-Jay

Abb. 4. Câche-pot, Paris, um 1760; Paris, Musée Carnavalet

zusätzlichen Glanz und Schutz brauchen.[29] Samousseau wurde bei dieser Gelegenheit als Besitzer der Rezeptur des Firnisses „à la façon de la Chine" erwähnt.

Diesen exotischen Namen nutzt auch Cazin de la Brosse, um seine „Manufacture royale des Vernis de Chine" 1777 anzupreisen. Er lackierte, vergoldete und verzierte mit Firnis alle Gegenstände aus Eisen und anderen Metallen für Architektur und Innenausstattung.[30] Sowohl seine Manufaktur, als auch die von Gosses Witwe und Samousseau haben jedoch mit Kunst weniger zu tun.

Zwei Jahre nach der Eröffnung der Manufaktur von Gosse und Samousseau taucht ein anderer Name auf: Clément, „peintre, doreur et vernisseur", ein Maler, Vergolder und Lackierer vermeldete im Sommer 1769 die Gründung seiner Manufaktur. Dabei beschrieb er ausführlich die Vorteile seines neuen Firnisses, der von den Akademiemitgliedern sorgfältig geprüft wurde. Er war nicht nur schön und besaß große Widerstandskraft, er war vor allem gesundheitlich unbedenklich bei der Anwendung.

Abb. 5. Rafraîchissoir à verres, Frankreich, um 1760; Bordeaux, Musée des Arts décoratifs

Clément versuchte eine eigene Klientel gezielt durch Anzeigen für seine Produkte zu interessieren. Wir erfahren daraus, dass er alle Arten geschmackvoller und mit Ornamenten verzierter Gegenstände aus Blech herstellte, nach den „neuesten und best ausgewählten Modellen".[31] Er versah sie mit einem Firnis, dessen Zusammenstellung perfekt chinesischen und japanischen Lack imitieren sollte (Abb. 4). Diesen Firnis konnte er in allen Farben herstellen, ohne dass Schönheit oder Dauerhaftigkeit darunter gelitten hätten. Letzteres zeugt übrigens von den großen Schwierigkeiten, mit denen Lackierer bei der Beigabe verschiedener Farbpigmente während der Firnisherstellung zu kämpfen hatten. Seine Manufaktur hat Clément in „La Petite Pologne" angesiedelt, nahe der Zollschranken von Monceaux, im Norden von Paris. Um sich bekannt zu machen und seine Käufer zu überzeugen, stellte der neue Unternehmer seine Waren auf Märkten aus, u. a. auf dem Markt von Saint Ovide. In einer Anzeige nahm er seine erfolgreichen Geschäfte zum Anlass, sich bei seinen vielen Kunden zu bedanken und informierte darüber, dass seine Erzeugnisse nicht nur direkt in der Manufaktur, sondern nun auch bei dem Juwelier Framery in der rue Saint Honoré im Zentrum von Paris zu kaufen seien.[32] Sein Angebot war erstaunlich umfangreich: Kamingarnituren, Pot-pourris, Wasserbehälter, kleine Brunnen für Esszimmer, Waschschüsseln, Kübel für Flaschen und Gläser, Schreibzeug, Leuchter, Obstkörbe, „déjeneurs", Wasser- und andere Kessel, Karaffen, Büchsen für Seifen und Schwämme, Rasierschüsseln, Teedosen, Tabletts, Tassen und Untersetzer, Dessertteller, Nachtlampen, Vasen (u. a. à l'antique), Urnen, Töpfe, Kannen, Krüge, Schalen, Senftöpfchen, Saucièren, Drahtgestelle zum Eierkochen, Blasebälge, Toilettenkästchen, Tafelaufsätze und vieles andere (Abb. 5). Die Dekore waren vielfältig: Früchte und Blumen in Gold oder bunten Farben, Landschaften, Tier- und Genreszenen, teilweise mit vergoldetem Kupfer geschmückt. Die Ornamente sind in Voll- oder Flachrelief vor einem Hintergrund aus Aventurinlack aufgetragen.

Am 27. März 1770 begann der Ausverkauf der lackierten Erzeugnisse der Manufaktur aus „raisons particulières" und zog sich mehrere Tage hin.[33] Clément setzte jedoch seine Tätigkeit fort, er fertigte die Waren auf Bestellung an und arbeitete sowohl für seine Kunden, als auch für Framery, der weiter seine Erzeugnisse in Paris verkaufte.[34] Mit der Übernahme des Geschäfts durch Dulac, auch in der rue Saint Honoré, änderte sich das Angebot der Manufaktur. Die Kunden, die bis dahin bei Framery bestellt hatten, wurden gebeten, jetzt direkt mit Clément Kontakt aufzunehmen, um Kommoden, Kabinettschränke, Eckschränke, Chiffonnières und andere Möbel nach chinesischer Art sowie Paneele für die Wände der Salons, Galerien oder Kutschen zu bestellen (Farbtafel XXI.2). Da sie ziemlich leicht anzubringen seien, könne man sie beliebig austauschen, wünsche man eine andere Dekoration. Sogar von einer Badewanne war die Rede! Die entsprechenden Muster hat Clément in seiner Manufaktur ausgestellt.[35] Ein wahrhaftig innovatives Denken, das Cléments unternehmerische Kraft bezeugt. Clément betonte mehrmals, dass der Preis der aus Blech von Handwerkern der Manufaktur in Nachahmung von Silber- oder Porzellangegenständen hergestellten Waren viel niedriger sei, als der der Originale. Sogar die Herstellung von Gegenständen aus Blech, die bis dahin nur in Holz angeboten worden waren, wurde angekündigt – mit der Begründung, dass das Blech nicht wie Holz auf Feuchtigkeit oder Temperaturänderungen reagiert. Die Solidität der angebotenen Waren, der Reichtum der Firnisdekorarten und die Schönheit der Ornamente wurden besonders gelobt (Abb. 6).

1 Krönungswagen Kaiser Karls VII., verwendet zur Kaiserkrönung 1742, Paris, um 1730; München, Marstallmuseum, Schloss Nymphenburg

2 Kommode, Frankreich um 1760/70, Pierre Macret (1756 „ébeniste suivant la cour“); Privatbesitz

Trotz ihres Erfolges dauerte die Tätigkeit der Manufaktur nicht lange. 1774 existierte sie nicht mehr und ihre Erzeugnisse waren zum Zwangsverkauf angeboten worden.[36]

An dieser Stelle sollte man noch einen Maler, Vergolder und Großhändler von Farbpigmenten und Firnissen erwähnen, Watin,[37] der als einzig bekannter Lackkunsthandwerker ein Lehrbuch über die Lackkunst für interessierte Amateure und Lackierer geschrieben hat. Die Abhandlung „L'Art de faire et d'employer le vernis, ou l'art du Vernisseur", in der zweiten Auflage als „L'Art du Peintre, Doreur, Vernisseur", erschien 1772[38] und erfreute sich großer Popularität. Dank dieses in mehreren Auflagen erschienenen Buches verkaufte er verschiedene Firnisarten, Pigmente, Utensilien etc. für Anwendungen aller Art. Sehr stolz war er auf eine eigene Erfindung: Ein herausragender Firnis ohne Geruch, der sich besonders zur Dekoration von Wohnräumen eignete.

Die von mir erwähnten Vernisseure haben wesentlich dazu beigetragen, den Ruf von Paris als einer Stadt der Künste und des Luxus im 18. Jahrhundert zu behaupten. So wie ihre Kollegen in England, Deutschland oder Italien gingen sie nicht nur den Errungenschaften der neuesten Mode, sondern auch der neuesten Technik nach, im Rahmen ihrer Möglichkeiten. Sie haben mit ihren chemischen Experimenten wesentlich dazu beigetragen, dass die Lackkunst rasch Fortschritte machte und sich ihre Pracht dank schnell anwendbarer industrieller Techniken auch im 19. Jahrhundert weiter entfalten konnte.

Abb. 6. Verrière, Frankreich, um 1765; New York, Cooper-Hewitt Museum, The Smithsonian Institution's National Museum of Design

Anmerkungen

1 Der erste Direktor war Le Brun (1619-1690). Er machte daraus ein Zentrum der Herstellung von Kunstgegenständen zur Ausschmückung königlicher Residenzen. Viele Künstler und Kunsthandwerker arbeiteten hier zusammen. Als „artistes privilégiés du Roi“ hatten sie einen besonderen Rang. Diese Entwicklung dauerte bis 1694 – in diesem Jahr wurden die Mitarbeiter entlassen. Fünf Jahre später, diesmal unter Jules Hardouin wurde die Manufaktur wiedereröffnet. Vgl. COURAL 1989.

2 Vgl. u. a. SONENSCHER 1989, S. 221 ff. Das Privileg war vom Januar 1714 an für 20 Jahre gültig.

3 A.N. O 1 57 fol. 272 (28. November 1713). Zitiert nach SONENSCHER 1989, S. 221 f.: „une manufacture de verny pour le moins aussy beau que celuy de la chine, pour être appliqué sur touttes sortes de toilles et étoffes de laine, de soye, de cuir et autres matières ployables et de touttes couleurs propres à faire des meubles comme chaises, fauteuils, tabarets, canapez, écrans, paravents, tapisseries, lits, portières, tapis, panneaux de lambris et plat fonds“.

4 Dagly (1665-1728), „entrepreneur des ouvrages du Roy aux Gobelins“ ist im Alter von 63 Jahren in „Les Gobelins“ gestorben. Vgl. LACORDAIRE 1897, S. 27.

5 Pierre de Neufmaison ist offiziell „directeur des ouvrages de la Chine pour le Roi à la manufacture des Gobelins“. Er ist aber auch chevalier de l'ordre de Saint-Jean de Latran und comte palatin. Er stirbt im April 1752, im Alter von ca. 80 Jahren. Vgl. LACORDAIRE 1897, S. 17 und 53.

6 AAA: 3.7.1752, S. 405. Ein Jahr später verkauft wurde ein Altar (devant d'autel), ein sehr schönes „Stück“ von Neufmaison, mit goldenen Ornamenten und Blumengirlanden – gemalt von Fontenay, und einem Lamm und dem Buch der Sieben Siegel – gemalt von Lucas – s. AAA: 30.8.1753, S. 540. Der Maler Lucas arbeitete auch für Martin, vgl. z. B. AAA: 27.9.1753, S. 605; 27.3.1755, S.197 f.; 27.11.1758, S. 732; 15.1.1785, S. 139.

7 Charles-André Tramblin (oder auch Tremblin) wurde als „Peintre du Roy“ und „décorateur de la ville de Paris“ erwähnt. Vgl. LACORDAIRE 1897, S. 52 f. Vermutlich als Nachfolger von Neufmaison war er der Maler einer sehr schönen Sänfte, die in der AAA am 25.8.1757, S. 529 zum Kauf angeboten wurde.

8 A.N. MC XCI 741 (3. Juni 1733), A.N. MC XXXIII 499 (8. November 1746). Vgl. SONENSCHER 1989, S. 223. Ihre Schulden betrugen 27.516 Livres.

9 A.N. MC CXXII 684 (13. Juni 1752), A.N. MC CXXII 692 (23. Oktober und 23. November 1754), A.N. MC LXII 380 (21. November 1740), A.N. MC X 1a 4154 fol. 70 (28. März 1752). Vgl. SONENSCHER 1989, S. 223.

10 Vgl. AAA: 28.2.1752, S. 132; 11.5.1752, S. 292; 8.6.1752, S. 349; 3.7.1752, S. 405; 11.9.1752, S. 565; 2.10.1752, S. 613; 5.4.1753, S. 222; 19.4.1753, S. 253; 7.6.1753, S. 357; 25.6.1753, S. 388; 5.7.1753, S. 413; 30.8.1753, S. 540; 3.9.1753, S. 547; 19.11.1753, S. 717; 10.12.1753, S. 765; 14.1.1754, S. 29; 17.1.1754, S. 36; 31.1.1754, S. 69; 25.2.1754, S. 125; 18.4.1754, S. 237; 20.5.1754, S. 309; 2.12.1754, S. 740; 27.1.1755, S. 61; 13.3.1755, S. 165; 24.3.1755, S. 189; 5.5.1755, S. 277; 17.7.1755, S. 436; 7.8.1755, S. 488 (erwähnt wird der Maler Chastelin, „inspecteur des Gobelins“); 11.9.1755, S. 565 f.; 12.4.1756, S. 238; 16.12.1756; 25.8.1757, S. 529; 3.10.1757, S. 617; 10.7.1758, S. 422; 3.10.1757, S. 617; 20.10.1758, S. 656; 31.10.1758, S. 680; 1.6.1758, S. 334; 10.7.1758, S. 422; 11.2.1760, S. 101; 15.7.1762, S. 442; 13.7.1767, S. 569; 31.8.1767, S. 705; 3.12.1767, S. 945.

11 AAA: 28.2.1752, S. 132 (gemalt und vergoldet in „Les Gobelins“ von Neufmaison).

12 AAA: 20.5.1754, S. 309.

13 AAA: 16.12.1756, S. 781; ein „Vis-à-vis“, in Blau und Gold von Neufmaison gemalt, wurde in AAA vom 15.7.1762, S. 442 erwähnt.

14 AAA: 2.12.1755, S. 740.

15 AAA: 10.12.1753, S. 765.

16 AAA: 5.5.1755, S. 277.

17 AAA: 11.9.1755, S. 565 f.

18 AAA: 17.7.1755, S. 436; AAA: 3.2.1757, S. 76 – diesmal handelte es sich um eine von Neufmaison gänzlich vergoldete „Berline“; AAA: 13.7.1767, S. 569.

19 GARSAULT 1756, S. 73.

20 SCHMID/HAGER 1922, S. 26 f., Abb. 2 und 3.

21 SCHMID/HAGER 1922, S. 11 f. Nicht erhalten haben sich andere von der Werkstatt der „Gobelins“ gelieferte Wagen: der geschnitzte und vergoldete Brautwagen der Maria Amalie von Österreich und fünf weitere Wagen zur Hochzeit des Thronfolgers Karl Albrecht. Im Wagenverzeichnis von 1728 finden wir die Beschreibung eines Pariser Paradewagens, dessen Kasten „aussenher mit feinem Silber gefasst, etwas rothe Figuren, dann das bayerische und österreichische Wappen gemahlen, innenher aber durchaus mit schwefelgelbem Sammet, um den Kranz und Himmel reich mit Silber gestickt und solchen Krepinnen besetzt“ ist. Ein anderer Wagen wurde mit fünf gelben Gläsern ausgestattet und „sonst noch von rot geblümten Sammet, reich mit Gold ausgemacht“. Noch fünf weitere Wagen und ein Gartenwägelchen stammten aus Paris.

22 AAA: 14.5.1753, S. 302. Er wohnte zu dieser Zeit in der rue de Charenton, Faubourg Saint Antoine, im Februar 1758 zog er in die rue Neuve S. Médéric, Hôtel Jabach um.

23 AAA: 20.12.1759, S. 790. Die Preise haben sich seit fast zwei Jahren kaum geändert – 1758 kostete die teuerste Tabatière 500 Livres. Giros bot über 3000 Stücke aus Karton bzw. aus Schildpatt in seinem Geschäft, Hôtel Jabach an.

24 L'Avantcoureur: 24.11.1766, S. 743. Die Anschrift der Manufaktur ist unbekannt, der Laden mit seinen Waren befindet sich immer noch in der rue Neuve S. Merri, Hôtel Jabach.

25 Giros verkaufte auch gravierte Portraits vom verstorbenen französischen Thronfolger in vergoldetem Rahmen. Ähnliche Gravüren hat er vermutlich zur Verzierung seiner Tabakdosen benutzt.

26 AAA: 2.12.1776, S. 1094.

27 L'Avantcoureur: 5.1.1767, S. 7.

28 *Histoire de l'Académie royale des Sciences 1759. Avec les Mémoires de Mathématique et de Physique pour la même Année*, Paris 1765, S. 239 f. VIII (Machines ou Inventions approuvées par l'Académie en 1759). Der üble Geruch war offensichtlich für die Schmuckwarenverzierung ein großer Nachteil – dies war u. a. der Grund, warum z. B. Giros seine Tabatièren mit Schildpatt auslegte. Die Erfindung wurde in den AAA vom 17.1.1760 dem breiten Publikum bekannt gegeben und die Eigenschaften des schönen schwarzen Firnisses, der gegen Kälte, Hitze („moderates Feuer“) sowie Scheidewasser (eau-forte) resistent sei, gelobt. Auch die Anschrift von Gosse wurde für Interessierte mitgeteilt: rue Cimetiere S. Nicolas-des-Champs.

29 L'Avantcoureur: 12.10.1767, S. 644. Die Manufaktur befand sich im Boulevard du Temple in Paris.

30 AAA: 20.3.1777, S. 363. Cazin de la Brosse verkaufte u. a. lackierte Schlösser und Gitter für Häuser und sorgte für deren Anbringung.

31 L'Avantcoureur: 24.7.1769, S. 468 ff.; AAA: 14.8.1769, S. 739.

32 AAA: 18.12.1769, S. 1079. Das erste Depot war bei Monsieur Sayde, quai des Morfondus, vis-à-vis Henri IV. (L'Avantcoureur: 24.7.1769, S. 468 ff.).

33 AAA: 26.3.1770, S. 285; 5.4.1770, S. 329; l'Avantcoureur: 20.8.1770, S. 532f.; 1.8.1774, S. 669.

34 AAA: 19.4.1770, S. 380.

35 AAA: 17.5.1770, S. 491; 2.8.1770, S. 771.

36 AAA: 1.8.1774, S. 669.

37 L'Avantcoureur: 15.6.1772, S. 370 ff.; 20.7.1772, S. 454. Watin bezeichnete sich in der Anzeige als ein Künstler mit dreißig Jahren Berufserfahrung.

38 AAA: 2.7.1772. Die zweite Auflage: „L'Art du Peintre, Doreur, Vernisseur; ouvrage utile aux Artistes et aux Amateurs qui veulent entreprendre de peindre, dorer et vernir toutes sortes de sujets en bâtimens, meubles, bijoux, équipages etc.“, 400 Seiten in 3 Teilen, kam ein Jahr später heraus. Vgl. auch AAA: 8.2.1773, S. 107; 24.5.1773; L'Avantcoureur: 21.6.1773, S. 396 f.; 29.11.1773, S. 762 f.; AAA: 20.1.1777 (dritte Auflage).

Literaturverzeichnis

Coural, Jean: *Les Gobelins*, Paris 1989

Garsault, François A. de: *Traité des Voitures, pour servir de supplement au nouveau parfait*, Paris 1756

Lacordaire, A.-L.: *Etats civils des tappissiers des Gobelins au dix-septième et au dix-huitième siècles*, in: Nouvelles Archives de l'Art français ancien et moderne, 14, 1897, S. 1–60

Schmid, Elmar D./Hager, Luisa: *Marstallmuseum. Schloss Nymphenburg in München. Hofwagenburg und Sattelkammer der bayerischen Herzöge, Kurfürsten und Könige*, Amtlicher Führer, 12. Auflage, München 1922

Sonenscher, Michael: *Work and Wages. Natural law, politics and the eighteenth-century French trades*, Cambridge 1989

Abbildungsnachweis

Abb. 1: Compiègne, Musée de la voiture et du Tourisme, Inv.Nr. CMV-64001

Abb. 2, 3: Paris, Musée Cognacq-Jay, Inv.Nrn. J 456, J 588, Photothèque des Musées de la Ville de Paris

Abb. 4: Stefan Arvay, Köln

Abb. 5: Bordeaux, Musée des Arts décoratifs, Legs Lataillade, Photo: Luc Joubert

Abb. 6: New York, Cooper-Hewitt National Design Museum (Gift of Mr. and Mrs. Talbot J. Taylor), Inv.Nr. 1912-18-17A

Farbtafel XXI.1: Bayerische Verwaltung der staatlichen Schlösser, Gärten und Seen, München; 2: Privatbesitz

Summary

Among the professionals in the production of luxury goods in 18th century Paris we still find a number of well-reknowned *vernisseurs*: besides the Martin family, lacquer artists like Cazin de la Brosse, Clément with his *Manufacture de vernis sur tôle*, Giros with his *Manufacture de beaux vernis*, Gosse and Samousseau, Watin and Wolff. Their activity can be followed through the advertisements in the important French journal *Annonces, Affiches et Avis divers*, which started in 1751.

In October 1713 the painter Claude III Audran was granted a Royal privilege for twenty years to establish '*une manufacture de verny'*. He was joined by Jacques Dagly and Pierre major de Neufmaison. Their *manufacture* in the Gobelins was managed later by Charles Tramblin. The core of their activities was the production and decoration of coaches, carriages or sedan chairs with aventurine lacquer, mythological allegories or painting *en camaïeu*. In the collection of the Marstallmuseum, Munich, there are two carriages produced in the Gobelins, respectively around 1730 and around 1750. The *tablettier-vernisseur* Giros founded his *manufacture de beaux vernis*, where he produced, among other luxury goods, snuffboxes in *papier mâché* (*carton*) with tortoiseshell interior. They were sold in the shop in the rue Neuve Saint Merri, Hôtel Jabach. His activity ended after 23 years in 1776. The *vernisseur* Wolff, active about 1767, produced lacquered snuffboxes, etuis and different types of jewelry in *papier mâché* with gilt mounts. The *vernisseur* Gosse discovered a beautiful black varnish, described 1759 in the records of the Académie Royale des Sciences. His widow and his son-in-law, Samousseau, basing on this discovery, established a *manufacture*, where they produced a varnish for wares made of *papier mâché* and of different metals. Cazin de la Brosse produced around 1777 in his *manufacture* lacquered ironwork and other metals for buildings and furniture. Clément, *peintre, doreur, vernisseur*, established his *manufacture* in 1769 in *La Petite Pologne*, Paris. He produced all kinds of luxury goods of lacquered iron sheet. Later on, he started with the production of lacquered decorations for furniture and coaches. His *manufacture* existed until 1774. The only *vernisseur* who wrote a theoretical work on lacquer art was Jean-Félix Watin. He had a great success with his manual *L'Art du Peintre, Doreur et Vernisseur*, which was dedicated to amateurs and professionals and edited several times (first edition 1772).

Abb. 1. Blechtablett, „Braunschweig von Westen“; Ansicht um 1830; 30,6 x 38,7 cm, H x B; Städtisches Museum Braunschweig

Franz-Josef Christiani

Die Lackproduktion der Manufaktur Stobwasser und ihre lokale Konkurrenz

Motivgruppen der Miniaturmalerei

Lackkunst des 18. und 19. Jahrhunderts von überregionalem Rang in Braunschweig, der Residenzstadt eines kleinen Herzogtums ohne entscheidenden politischen Einfluss? Wie konnten sich hier mehrere Lackmanufakturen entwickeln und im Konzert mit den großen europäischen Lackzentren in England, Frankreich, Belgien und Holland eine wesentliche Rolle spielen?

Braunschweig (Abb. 1) verbindet man mit seinem Gründer, dem welfischen Herzog Heinrich dem Löwen. Ihm gelang es im 12. Jahrhundert ein kunst- und kulturgeschichtliches Zentrum zu gründen, das bald von einem erstarkten selbstbewussten Bürgertum handelspolitisch genutzt und ausgebaut wurde. Das 17. Jahrhundert offenbarte jedoch sozial- und wirtschaftspolitische Fehlentwicklungen, die schließlich dazu führten, dass die welfischen Herzöge ihre ehemalige Residenz zurückeroberten und die bürgerliche Selbstverwaltung stark einschränkten bzw. vollkommen außer Kraft setzten.

Die Zeit des 18. Jahrhunderts stand ganz im Zeichen eines aufgeklärten Absolutismus und dessen Merkantilismus. Das Bestreben der Herzöge richtete sich auch aus Eigennutz auf die Belebung des Handels. Mit dem Versuch, eine staatlich gelenkte Wirtschaft einzuführen, folgte man preußischen Vorbildern. Als Ergänzung zu den starr organisierten Handwerksgilden bildeten sich so genannte Manufakturen, die zwar noch keine Industriebetriebe darstellten, in denen der Fertigungsprozess aber schon Produktzerlegung und Arbeitsteilung kannte. Den Manufakturen wurde gestattet, dazu entsprechende Handwerker unterschiedlicher Gewerbe zu beschäftigen. Das verlieh den Manufakturen die notwendige Unabhängigkeit, ohne die der Erfolg von vornherein vereitelt worden wäre.

Am 18. Mai 1763 erteilte der Herzog dem Lackierer Georg Siegmund Stobwasser und seinem in Abbildung 2 als erfolgreicher Geschäftsmann dargestellten Sohn Johann Heinrich die Genehmigung, nach Braunschweig zu kommen und hier eine Fabrik für lackierte Waren zu gründen.

Als Stobwasser sich 1762 erfolgreich auf eine Zeitungsannonce des Braunschweiger Herzogs Carl I. bewarb, welcher Künstler jeder Art aufforderte, unter großen Begünstigungen in sein Land zu ziehen, schienen die Voraussetzungen gegenüber seiner Heimatstadt Lobenstein im Voigtland um so viel besser, dass die gesamte Familie beschloss, Haus und Hof zu verkaufen, um mit ihrer kleinen Lackierwerkstatt nach Braunschweig überzusiedeln. Bewundernswert, ja leichtsinnig scheint Stobwassers

Optimismus gewesen zu sein, durch den es unterblieb, mit dem Herzog bzw. dem zuständigen „Geheimen Rat“ vorab in weitere Verhandlungen einzutreten, um sich einer entsprechenden finanziellen Unterstützung seitens des Herzoghauses und der Zusage eines dringend erforderlichen Wohn- und Fabrikgebäudes zu vergewissern. So musste Stobwasser sein eigenes Kapital in die Einrichtung einer Lackierwerkstatt investieren und einen ungewissen Anfang wagen.

Erst mit dem Jahre 1769 scheint eine erste mühevolle Epoche in Stobwassers Fabrikgeschichte ihren Abschluss gefunden zu haben. Der Herzog gestand Stobwasser am 3. Oktober das Privileg zu, als einziger „Braunschweiger Lackwaren“ herstellen und sie als solche vertreiben zu dürfen. Es war durchaus üblich, für besondere Erfindungen zeitlich begrenzten Schutz zu gewähren, doch blieb der „Geheime Rat“ gegenüber einer derartigen Monopolstellung grundsätzlich skeptisch eingestellt.

Johann Heinrich Stobwassers guter Ruf als Lackkünstler drang bis an den Hof nach Berlin und ebenso nach Dresden vor. In Berlin hatte er bereits mehrere Staatswagen lackiert und sich damit dem König auf beste Weise empfohlen. Nun wurden die Angebote konkreter. „Wenn sich die Fabrik im nächsten halben Jahr mit Erfolg in Berlin etablieren würde – so hieß es –, wolle man seitens der Regierung freie Reise- und Transportkosten, ein freies Haus, den nötigen Vorschuss auf das Betriebskapital und ein jährliches Gehalt von 400 Reichstalern garantieren.“ Konnte man ein derartiges Angebot ausschlagen? Johann Heinrich hatte schon ähnlich gute Bedingungen aus Dresden abgelehnt und blieb auch jetzt zögerlich. Sein Vater dagegen und alle übrigen Familienangehörigen hätten einem Wechsel liebend gern

Abb. 2. Friedrich Georg Weitsch: Johann Heinrich Stobwasser, um 1780; Öl auf Leinwand; 94 x 76 cm; Städtisches Museum Braunschweig

zugestimmt, hatte doch der Herzog bisher jegliche Unterstützung vermissen lassen. Voller Unverständnis für die Entscheidung ihres Bruders, Braunschweig trotz allem treu bleiben zu wollen, ergriff seine Schwester Louise die Initiative und bat, mit ihrem Mann – dem Franzosen Jean Guérin – eine Zweigniederlassung in Berlin aufmachen zu dürfen. Das geschah im Jahre 1772.

Gleichzeitig schenkte der Herzog Stobwasser in Braunschweig ein Wohn- und Geschäftsgebäude, so dass man die Produktion der Lackwaren in dem Umfang aufnehmen konnte, wie man es sich bereits zu Anfang gewünscht hatte. Dadurch expandierte die Lackmanufaktur in diesen Jahren in überdurchschnittlichem Maße und zählte als wichtiger Wirtschaftsfaktor zu den erfolgreichsten Manufakturen des Braunschweiger Landes.

Landschaften

Die für Stobwasser auf Dosen, Tabletts, Kästen, Kannen, Vasen und Möbeln anfänglich ausgeführten Landschaftsminiaturen (Abb. 3) folgten dem Grundkonzept der modischen Ideallandschaften. Sie wurden abgelöst durch Bildkompositionen, die einen stärkeren Realitätsgehalt erkennen und realistische Einzelstudien nach der Natur spüren lassen. Man konzentrierte sich auf das reine Naturerlebnis, das man in seiner Individualität getreu wiederzugeben wünschte. Typisch sind wilde Gebirgsbäche, romantische Felspartien oder einzelne mit Leichtigkeit gemalte Eichen sowie ganze Baumgruppen vor einem Hintergrund, dessen Partien hell ausgemalt sind und dadurch eine idyllische Durchsichtigkeit erzielen.

Topographie

Mit dem Bedürfnis der genauen Darstellung des Beobachteten stieg der Wunsch der Identifizierbarkeit des Geschilderten. Gefordert wurde eine objektive Wiedergabe, die in der Schilderung geologischer Formationen gleichzeitig zum Erlebnis wird, wie es die Motive von Koblenz mit der Burg Ehrenbreitstein (Abb. 4) sowie andere Rheinlandschaften romantisch verdeutlichen.

Dass bei dieser Beliebtheit topographischer Motive lokale Sujets eine dominierende Rolle spielten, darf vorausgesetzt werden. Doch beschränkten sich die Miniaturen bald nicht mehr ausschließlich auf regionale Motive, sondern gaben auch Motive beliebter Reisen, wie z. B. die Tellskapelle am Vierwaldstätter See (Abb. 5) oder das Brockenhaus (Farbtafel XXII.3) wieder.

Das, was uns heute als lackierter und fein bemalter Behälter mit Deckel überliefert ist, hatte ursprünglich vorrangig die Funktion der Schnupftabakdose. Je nach Geldbeutel reichte die Palette über alle nur denkbar teuren und ausgefallenen Materialien bis hin zum Surrogat Papiermaché. Was die Lackprodukte Johann Heinrich Stobwassers auszeichnete, waren der dunkelsamtige, hochglanzpolierte Bernsteinlack und eine exzellente Miniaturmalerei, die mit einem transparenten Kopallack ihren dauerhaften Schutz erhielt. Die hiesigen Miniaturmaler übertrugen u. a. Motive bekannter Gemälde auf ihre Lackobjekte und trafen somit den allgemeinen Zeitgeschmack.

Bei so viel Erfolg und ungebrochener Nachfrage hochwertiger Lackwaren regte sich natürlich die heimische Konkurrenz. Diese erwuchs anfänglich aus den eigenen Reihen seiner gut ausgebildeten Mitarbeiter, der in der eigenen Fabrikmalschule

Abb. 3. Schnupftabakdose, „Ideallandschaft“; Papiermaché; Durchmesser 10,3 cm; Städtisches Museum Braunschweig

Abb. 4. Schnupftabakdose, „Koblenz mit der Burg Ehrenbreitstein“; Papiermaché; Durchmesser 9,8 cm; Richard Borek Stiftung

Abb. 5. Schnupftabakdose, „Tells Capelle in der Schweiz“; Meyer & Wried, 1839; Blech; 25 x 12,5 x 8,5 cm; Richard Borek Stiftung

1 Schnupftabakdose „Löwenjagd“, Malerei von August Theodor Meyer (1798–1863), Papiermaché, 2,56 x 9,15 x 6,3 cm; Städtisches Museum Braunschweig

2 Schnupftabakdose „Herkules am Scheideweg“, Papiermaché, H = 1,88 cm, Durchmesser 9,64 cm; Städtisches Museum Braunschweig

3 Schnupftabakdose „Ansicht des Brockenhauses“, Papiermaché, H = 1,82 cm, Durchmesser 9,66 cm; Städtisches Museum Braunschweig

ausgebildeten Maler, der Papiermaché herstellenden und verarbeitenden Former und der die Rezepturen beherrschenden Lackierer. Auch Branchenfremde wie der Zinngießer Kraegelius oder der Perückenmacher Evers warben Mitarbeiter ab und produzierten ohne herzogliche Konzession Braunschweiger Lackwaren. Stobwasser versuchte zu Anfang, sein Privileg mit vielen Prozessen zu schützen, um sich so seinen Absatz zu sichern und sich minderwertiger Produkte zu erwehren. Dass Wilhelm Stockmann seine Lackprodukte, vor allem seine auf Blech gemalten Miniaturen nahezu gleichwertig und ohne große Streitigkeiten entwickeln konnte, mag daran gelegen haben, dass er 1811 erst relativ spät auf der Braunschweiger Messe eigene Lackwaren ausstellte. Die Produkte der Braunschweiger Lackfabriken ließen sich dank ihres hohen Qualitätsniveaus kaum noch unterscheiden, was dadurch zu erklären ist, dass die freischaffenden Maler für alle Manufakturen gleichzeitig arbeiteten. Stobwasser, Stockmann und Evers arbeiteten vorwiegend mit Papiermaché, Kraegelius überwiegend mit Zinn und Weißblech. Die Everschen Produkte zeichneten sich durch ihre besondere Malerei und ihre Formenvielfalt aus und Kraegelius' Vorzüge sah man in einem zarten Schmuck mit Vergoldungen.

Firmensignaturen

Während uns die Maler wegen fehlender Signaturen unbekannt bleiben – einige scheinen nur durch den Duktus der Malerei bestimmbar – finden wir in oder an einer großen Anzahl von Lackobjekten die jeweiligen Firmensignaturen. Insbesondere die der beiden Manufakturen Stobwasser und Stockmann sind fast ausschließlich in zinnoberroter Farbe auf Papiermaché-Arbeiten oder in schwarzer Farbe auf Gegenständen aus Blech aufgebracht. Die Innenfläche des Dosenbodens zeigt die Signatur und meist Ziffern, das Deckelinnere ebenfalls die gleichen Ziffern und oftmals, meist in Kursivschrift, den Titel der Malerei und manchmal den Künstler der Vorlage. Die Bedeutung der Zahlen ist bis heute nicht eindeutig geklärt. Gewiss ist, dass Boden- und Deckelinneres die gleiche Zahl tragen, damit die beiden zusammengehörenden Teile nicht vertauscht werden konnten. Die Kennzeichnung der rechteckigen Dosen ähnelt der der runden Arbeiten, für die Schrift wurde bei einigen gelbe Farbe verwendet, während Stockmann für seinen Firmenstempel oft einen Goldton wählte. Sind auf den Tabletts Signaturen und Ziffern nachweisbar, so sind die Ziffern in roter Farbe gemalt, während die Fabrikmarke bei Stockmann in den Farben Rot oder Gold aufgedruckt oder als Aufkleber zu lesen ist.

Bereits Anfang 1775 bat Johann Heinrich Stobwasser den Herzog, seine Lackprodukte mit dem Zeichen eines Rosses und dem unter selbigen stehenden Buchstaben „St“ stempeln zu dürfen. Dieses Zeichen scheint Stobwasser jedoch wenig angewandt zu haben. Eine eindeutige Bestimmung wird außerdem dadurch erschwert, dass die Manufaktur Stockmann in späteren Jahren ebenfalls vereinzelt ein Pferd in das Firmenzeichen integrierte. Von der Manufaktur Stobwasser sind die in Abbildung 6 dargestellten, gängigen Signaturen bekannt.

Nachdem Meyer & Wried 1832 als Nachfolger die Manufaktur Stobwasser übernommen hatten, wurden die Stempeldrucke durch die Namen der ehemaligen Meister erweitert. Daneben sind unterschiedliche gedruckte Firmenschilder bekannt, die rückseitig auf die fertigen Gegenstände geklebt wurden (Abb. 8).

Wilhelm Stockmann produzierte erst relativ spät eigene Lackwaren. Seine Signatur „St“, welche vielleicht auf eine Ver-

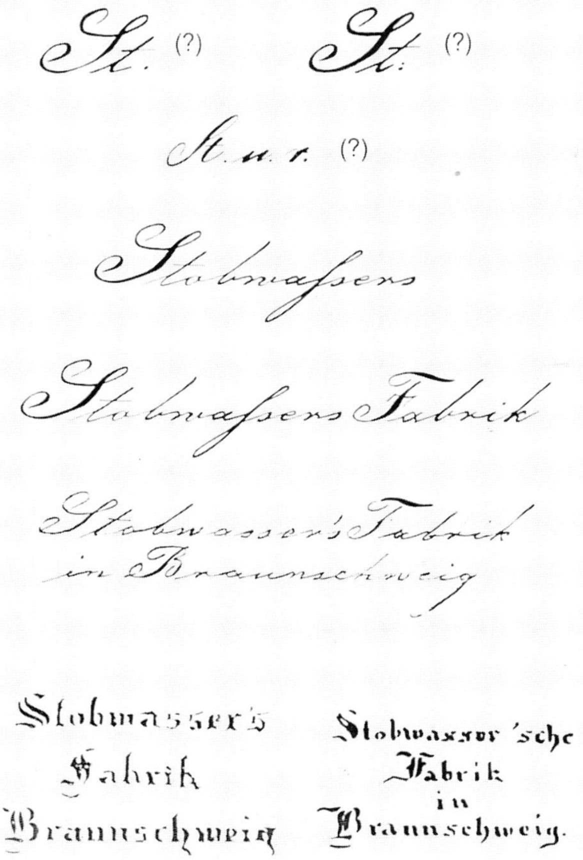

Abb. 6. Kursivschriften und Stempel der Lackmanufaktur Stobwasser

Abb. 7. Signaturen der Lackmanufaktur Stockmann

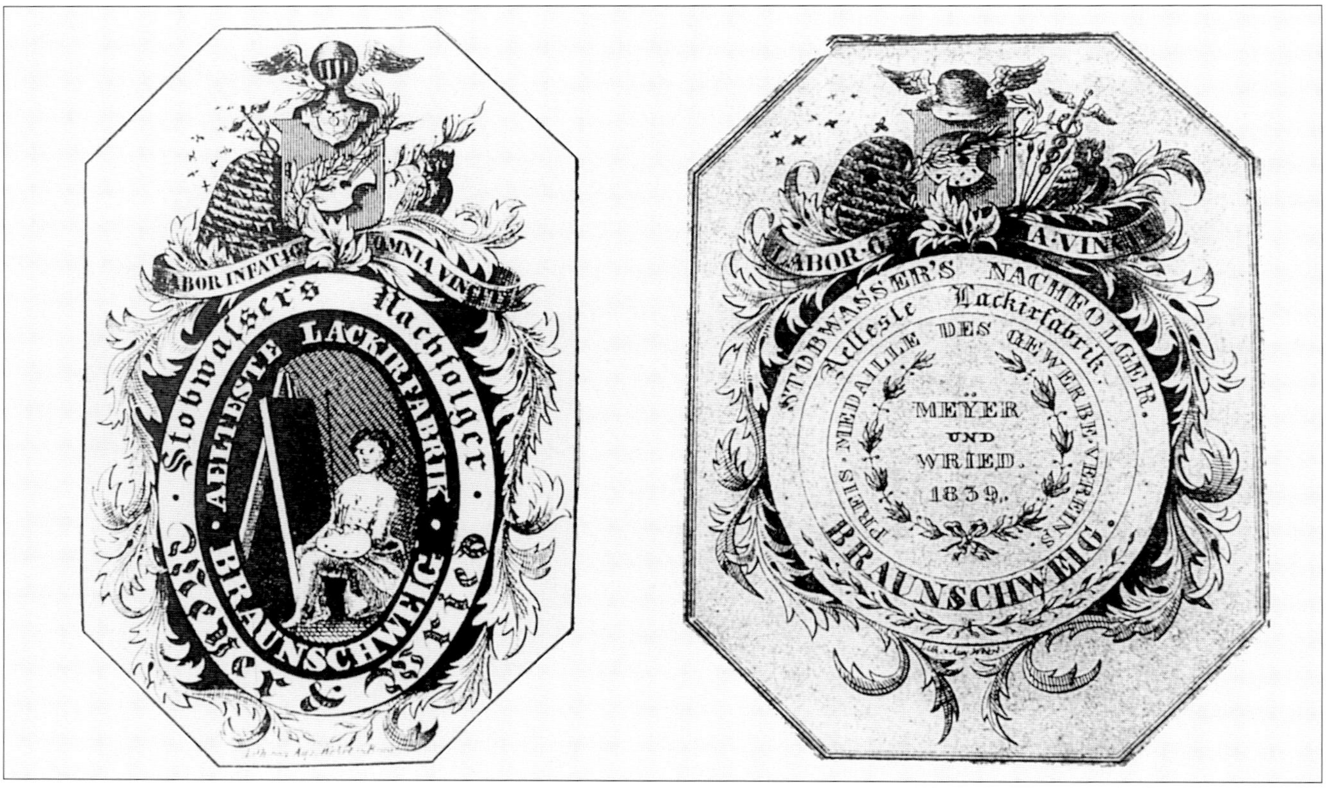

Abb. 8. Etiketten der Stobwasser-Nachfolger Meyer & Wried

Abb. 9. Signaturen der Lackmanufaktur Evers

wechslung mit Stobwassers Produkten zielte, wurde verdoppelt, als sein Bruder Johann Heinrich August als Teilhaber in die Fabrik eintrat. 1836 wurden die Gebrüder Stockmann mit dem Titel „Hof-Lackier-Fabrikant“ ausgezeichnet (Abb. 7).

Heinrich Ludewig Evers lag mit Stobwasser in permanentem Streit. Schließlich wurde ihm die Konzession erteilt, Malerei auf Bestellung herstellen und lackieren zu dürfen. Als er sich mit erstaunlicher Beharrlichkeit auch darüber hinwegsetzte, wurde ihm sein Lackierofen mit einem Ratssiegel verschlossen. Zudem zerstörten ihm die Tischler 1792 seine komplette Werkstatt, weil er unerlaubterweise einen Zimmergesellen mit Tischlerarbeit beschäftigt hatte. Dieser permanenten Auseinandersetzung müde, verlegte er seinen Betrieb nach Wolfenbüttel, wo sich die Fabrik gut entwickelte und von seinem Schwiegersohn G. Bratenahl unter der Bezeichnung „Heinrich Ludewig Evers Nachfolger“ bis 1838 weitergeführt wurde (Abb. 9).

Freiheitskriege

Mit der Rückbesinnung auf die Napoleonischen Kriege erinnerte man sich in der Miniaturmalerei an die Schlachten und ihrer Feldherren. Die Freude über den Frieden und die wiedererlangte Freiheit scheinen so groß gewesen zu sein, dass die Nachfrage nach derartigen Erinnerungsstücken vermutlich nur mit Hilfe der Druckgrafiken gedeckt werden konnte. So zeigt z. B. eine ovale, schwarzlackierte Blechdose aus „Stobwassers Fabrique“ die farbig angelegte Landkarte der Völkerschlacht bei Leipzig am 18. und 19. Oktober 1813, mit der die Vertreibung Napoleons ihren Anfang nahm.

Den Boden dieser Dose zierte eine Karikatur Napoleons, auf dessen Kopf aus Menschenleibern sich der preußische Adler festkrallt. Die Umschrift dazu lautet: „Triumph des Jahres 1813. Den Deutschen zum Neuenjahr“. Der anfänglichen Faszination folgte jetzt die Diffamierung des Usurpators und Tyrannen, den man für den Tod unzähliger Menschen verantwortlich machte. Derartige Karikaturen konzentrierten sich auf die Jahre der Befreiungskriege und auf die später einsetzenden Napoleon-Legenden (Abb. 10).

Nach dem Sieg über Napoleon und dessen endgültiger Verbannung überwog die Freude über den wiedererlangten Frieden. Hiervon zeugt u. a. eine farbig ausgemalte Grafik. Die runde Papiermaché-Dose der Lackmanufaktur Stobwasser trägt als so genannte Friedensdose einen Stich mit einem Portraitkranz der beteiligten Feldherren und dem oberen Teil des Brandenburger Tores, dessen Viergespann mit der Siegesgöttin bekanntlich 1807 von den Franzosen geraubt worden war und 1814 als Symbol des Sieges über Napoleon zurückgeholt werden konnte (s. S. 203, Abb. 10).

Abb. 10. Kolorierte Grafik auf dem Boden der Völkerschlacht-Dose; 9,8 x 13,7 x 2,3 cm; Städtisches Museum Braunschweig

Abb. 11. Schnupftabakdose, „Portrait von Mozart"; Stobwassers Fabrik; Papiermaché; Durchmesser 9,9 cm; Richard Borek Stiftung

Portraits

Ein weiteres herausragendes Thema dieser Zeit waren die Portraits. Hier trat das erstarkte Bürgertum vermehrt als Auftraggeber auf. Ende des 18. Jahrhunderts konnte man von der eigentlichen Blüte der Portraitmalerei sprechen. Von den Künstlern bevorzugten die Maler z. B. angesehene Musiker wie den auf der Höhe seines Ruhmes stehenden Wolfgang Amadeus Mozart, dessen Universalität schon zu seinen Lebzeiten unbestritten war (Abb. 11).

Bereits seit Entstehen der Portraitbildnisse in der Miniaturmalerei genießt das Bildnis von Damen eine große Beliebtheit und begleitet die weitere Entwicklung der Miniaturkunst durch die Jahrhunderte. Seit dem 17. Jahrhundert waren die Portraitisten gefordert, ein Bildnis zu malen, das das gesellschaftlich gültige Schönheitsideal wiedergab. Daher sind seit der zweiten Hälfte des 18. Jahrhunderts die Damenportraits kaum voneinander zu unterscheiden. Die Gesichter auf den Dosen und Zigarrenetuis lassen kaum charakteristische Züge erkennen, der Ausdruck ist vielfach geprägt durch den gleichen Blick, das gleiche Lächeln, die gleiche Wangen- oder Nasenpartie sowie den gleichen Mund. Damenportraits waren meist als Brustbild, in zeitgenössischer Kleidung des Empire oder Biedermeier gemalt und mit mancherlei Accessoires in Form von Schmuck, Blumen, Federn und den unterschiedlichen Variationen von Kopfbedeckungen ausgestattet (Abb. 12–14).

Abb. 12. Schnupftabakdose „Zum Andenken von Friedrich Winkler", Papiermaché, H = 1,05 cm, Durchmesser 10,2 cm, Städtisches Museum Braunschweig

Religion

Ein weiteres Motiv der Miniaturmalerei auf Lackarbeiten ist die Darstellung biblisch-religiöser Inhalte, die in der bildenden Kunst ebenso wie die Darstellung mythologischer Szenen zu den klassischen Themen zählt. Vor allem das umfangreiche Werk Raffaels mit den zahlreichen Madonnendarstellungen diente den Malern der Braunschweiger Lackmanufakturen als Vorlage, wie beispielsweise die berühmte „Macintosh Madonna" der Nationalgalerie London oder die „Madonna della Sedia" im Palazzo Pitti in Florenz (Abb. 15).

Abb. 13. Schnupftabakdose „Mein theurer Ambrosius", H = 1,75 cm, Durchmesser 9,9 cm; Städtisches Museum Braunschweig

Die Qualität einiger Madonnenminiaturen heben sich durch eine außergewöhnlich feine Malerei hervor, die möglicherweise von dem Raffael-Kopisten Johann Christoph Baese, genannt Carlo Baese, geschaffen wurde. Carlo Baese, 1790 in Braunschweig geboren, erhielt zunächst seine künstlerische Lehre in der Stobwasserschen Malschule und war auch als Maler für deren Manufaktur tätig. Später vervollständigte er seine weitere Ausbildung in Wien und Florenz.

Mythologie

Bei den Themen der Mythologie fällt die qualitätvolle Malerei ebenfalls auf. Die bekanntesten Göttinnen, Götter und Figuren der griechischen und römischen Mythenwelt sind als Lackminiaturen für die Zeitgenossen festgehalten und der Nachwelt

Abb. 14. Zigarrenetui, Brustbild einer jungen Frau; Wilhelm Stockmann & Co; Papiermaché; H = 13,8 cm; Städtisches Museum Braunschweig

überliefert (Farbtafel XXII.2. Venus mit ihrem Sohn Amor, Jupiter, Mars, Bacchus, Europa, Juno, Leda, tanzende Amoretten und Putten beispielsweise sind in verschiedenen Episoden vertreten. Die römische Göttin Venus, die sehr früh mit Aphrodite gleichgesetzt wurde und deren Mythologie erhielt, ist die Figur, die mit verschiedenen Begebenheiten ihrer Geschichte am zahlreichsten auf Dosen zu bewundern ist: z. B. „Die Geburt der Venus“ (Abb. 16) oder „Die Toilette der Venus“ nach einer Vorlage von Angelika Kauffmann.

Kleingerät und Möbel

Aus der reichhaltigen Produktpalette der Braunschweiger Lackmanufakturen seien noch zwei Gruppen kurz vorgestellt: die Kleingeräte des bürgerlichen Haushalts und die Lackmöbel. Zum bürgerlichen Biedermeier-Haushalt zählte eine Vielzahl von kunsthandwerklichen Gebrauchsgegenständen. Erhalten ist neben Vasen, Kerzenständern, Tabakdosen, Petroleumlampen, Nähkästchen und Uhren in Vasenform zum Beispiel ein Teekessel mit Stövchen in ziegelrotem Lack, ähnlich dem Rot der Signaturen und Beschriftungen in den Lackdosen (Abb. 17).

Beim vollständigen Interieur eines Biedermeier-Zimmers zählten neben diesen Blech- und Papiermaché-Gegenständen bemalte Lackmöbel zu den Besonderheiten dieser Zeit. Ebene, glatte, hochglanzpolierte Flächen und rechtwinklige Kanten waren das Kennzeichen dieses Geschmacks. Ihre Reduktion auf bisweilen allzu schlichte Möbeltypen wurde von der Wirkung ihrer zarten Bemalung überspielt. Stobwassers Miniaturmalerei fiel auch hier auf fruchtbaren Boden und beeinflusste als lokale Sonderentwicklung und Spezialität seiner Manufakturen in Braunschweig und Berlin weniger die Möbeltypen, sondern mehr die spezielle Oberflächenbehandlung und -dekoration. Kommoden, gradlinige Kästen mit drei Schubladen, sind mit derartig feinlinigen Arabesken und darin eingewobenen Medaillons auf braunrotem Grund bemalt worden. Ihre Abdeckplatten bestehen aus Pappmaché, einem aus vielen Lagen Papier und Leim zusammengepressten Karton. Angefertigt und lackiert wurden sie von Jean Guérin, der eine besonders transluzide, wolkige Art von Lack erfand, der in Anlehnung an das Schildpatt rötlich durchschimmernd aufgetragen wurde und die mythologischen, historischen, topographischen und volkstümlichen Motive der Malerei rahmte.

Ebenfalls ganz im Sinne des Klassizismus erfunden und typisch für ihre Zeit wirken die Schreibmöbel durch ihre klar gegliederten Proportionen. Zum einen ein Rollsekretär in der üblichen, auch von David Roentgen stetig wiederholten Form. Seine Frontflächen sind ausgefüllt mit Landschaftsmalerei und figürlichen Szenen der Mythologie. Zum anderen die Schreibkommode mit Aufsatz, deren kubische Form den barocken Schreibschrank völlig negiert und zum Biedermeier-Sekretär überleitet. Tanzende Mänaden mit Früchte- oder Blumengirlanden oder Bocksköpfe zwischen geflochtenen Bändern schmücken die Füllungen ihrer Kommodenfront und lockern deren Ansicht auf (Abb. 18).

All diese Beispiele vermitteln einen kleinen Einblick in die Fülle der Braunschweiger Lackprodukte über annähernd einhundert Jahre. Man schätzte sie als die Besten in Europa und so ist es nicht verwunderlich, dass der Name Braunschweig und Stobwasser zum Synonym für die deutsche Lackkunst jener Jahre geworden ist. Ein Vertriebssystem mit Verkaufsdepots in verschiedenen Städten förderte den Absatz, so dass die Lackmanufaktur Stobwasser in Braunschweig ein volkswirtschaftlicher Faktor von großer Bedeutung wurde. Die Berliner Fabrik hatte sich anfänglich ebenfalls sehr gut entwickelt, litt dann aber unter der langwierigen Krankheit und dem frühen Tod von Jean Guérin im Jahr 1797. Stobwasser sah sich noch im gleichen Jahr gezwungen, die Leitung der Fabrik vorübergehend zu übernehmen bzw. neu zu organisieren, bis sein Sohn Christian Heinrich 1808 Teilhaber wurde und er nach dem Tode seiner Mutter zwei Jahre später beide Fabriken in Braunschweig und Berlin übertragen bekam. 1818 übersiedelte Christian Heinrich ganz nach

Abb. 15. Schnupftabakdose, „Madonna della Sedia“; Stobwassers Fabrik; Papiermaché; Durchmesser 9,5 cm; Richard Borek Stiftung

Abb. 16. Schnupftabakdose, „La naissance de Venus“; Stockmann; Papiermaché; Durchmesser 10,2 cm; Richard Borek Stiftung

Abb. 17. Teekessel mit Stövchen; rot lackiert mit Goldornamentik; Stobwasser; H = 23 cm; Städtisches Museum Braunschweig

Berlin und verkaufte das Braunschweiger Stammhaus nach dem Tod seines Vaters Johann Heinrich 1832 an A. W. Meyer & Carl Wried, die das Geschäft mit bewährtem Angebot und gleich hoher Qualität bis 1852 und Carl Wried allein bis 1856 weiterführten. Damit erlosch Stobwassers Lackfabrik in Braunschweig nach fast 100-jähriger Firmengeschichte. Berühmt und begehrt wurden die Braunschweiger Lackprodukte letztendlich durch ihre exzellente Miniaturmalerei. Selbst wenn den Miniaturen Vorlagen und Vorzeichnungen bekannter Gemälde zu Grunde lagen, blieben sie trotz der Serienproduktion wertvolle Unikate, die heute wie damals ihren angemessenen Preis haben. Mit Unterstützung der Richard Borek Stiftung präsentiert das Städtische Museum Braunschweig eine ständige Schausammlung von ca. 600 Lackobjekten Braunschweiger Provenienz und verfügt damit über die größte der Öffentlichkeit zugängliche Sammlung.

Literatur

CHRISTIANI, FRANZ-JOSEF/BAUMANN-WILKE, SABINE: *Führer durch die Schausammlung Braunschweiger Lackkunst*, Braunschweig 1999 (Arbeitsberichte aus dem Städtischen Museum Braunschweig, Bd. 64)

RICHTER, DETLEF: *Lackdosen*, München 1988

Abbildungsnachweis

Abb. 1–3, 6–11, 13, 16, 17: Städtisches Museum Braunschweig

Abb. 4, 5, 12, 14, 15: Richard Borek Stiftung

Summary

The exhibition of Brunswick Lacquer Art in the Städtisches Museum Brunswick displays about 600 exponents representing the success story of the Stobwasser lacquer manufacture and its local competitors over a period of almost a hundred years.

The Stobwasser family settled in Brunswick in 1763. Six years later they received an exclusive privilege allowing them to be the sole producers and suppliers of Brunswick lacquerwork.

It was the dark, velvety, highly polished amber lacquer and the excellent miniature painting, protected by a durable transparent copal lacquer, that distinguished the lacquerwork produced by Johann Heinrich Stobwasser from others. Most of the miniatures exhibited can be identified by the company signature instead of the missing signature of the artist.

Apart from the Stobwasser lacquer manufactury, exponents can be attributed to other local competing manufacturers, such as Ludewig Kraegelius, Heinrich Ludewig Evers, Wilhelm and August Stockmann, as well as Stobwasser's successors, A.W. Meyer & Carl Wried.

Brunswick lacquerwork became particularly famous and coveted due to the excellency of their miniatures, the main themes being idyllic landscapes, topography, wars of liberation, portraits, mythology, religious and genre paintings. Sometimes famous works of art were depicted in miniature. Even in those days lacquered products were treasured not only as valuable articles for everyday use, but as collectors pieces as well.

Abb. 18. Schreibkommode mit Aufsatz; schwarz lackiertes Weichholz; Malerei der Füllungen vom Aufsatz: links Minerva und rechts Historia, Friedrich Georg Weitsch, 1794; 143,3 x 89 x 54,2 cm; Städtisches Museum Braunschweig

Silke Schick

Techniken an Tabakdosen der Manufaktur Stobwasser

Runde schwarze Tabakdosen bilden den größten Anteil der uns überlieferten Lackarbeiten der Manufaktur Stobwasser (Abb. 1).[1] Über die Herstellungsverfahren und die verwendeten Materialien ist nur wenig bekannt. Im Rahmen meiner Diplomarbeit wurden deshalb Tabakdosen optisch im Normallicht unter dem Mikroskop und mit Hilfe von Querschliffen sowie durch chemische Analysen untersucht. Für Querschliffe und chemische Analysen musste Material entnommen werden, was sehr schwierig ist, da die Objekte meist in äußerst gutem Zustand sind und eine Beschädigung intakter Objekte selbstverständlich nicht in Frage kam. Es fanden sich aber dennoch einige defekte, zur Untersuchung geeignete Stücke im Depot des Städtischen Museums Braunschweig, im Württembergischen Landesmuseum Stuttgart und im Museum für Lackkunst in Münster. Außerdem wurden zahlreiche Rezeptbücher aus dem 18. Jahrhundert am Institut für Technologie der Malerei in Stuttgart und im Lackmuseum Münster auf Hinweise zu Stobwassers Techniken durchgesehen. Die chemischen Analysen wurden von Johann Koller und Ursula Baumer am Doerner-Institut in München durchgeführt. Die Querschliffe fotografierte Katharina Walch beim Bayerischen Landesamt für Denkmalpflege.

Aufbau des Korpus

Die gängigste Form der runden Tabakdose besteht aus zwei Reifen, den Dosenwandungen und einer planen sowie einer leicht konvexen Scheibe aus Papiermaché. Die Scheiben wurden in den Deckel- oder Bodenreif eingepasst und verleimt. In den Bodenreif wurde ein weiterer Papierring so eingeleimt, dass er den Deckel in sich aufnehmen konnte. Es handelt sich folglich um fünf einzelne Teile, die miteinander verleimt wurden (Abb. 2).[2] Böden und Deckel wurden aus mehrfach übereinander geleimten Papplagen hergestellt. Die Wandungen der Dosen fertigte man aus Papiermaché-Brei, der in Model gepresst, getrocknet und anschließend auf einer Drechselbank in Form geschnitten wurde. Die meisten runden Tabakdosen haben einen Durchmesser von 8–10 cm und variieren alle leicht in ihrer Form.

Lackauftrag

Auf diese Papiermaché-Rohlinge wurde die Lackierung aufgetragen. Die chemischen Analysen, die Ursula Baumer und Johann Koller vom Doerner-Institut durchführten, zeigen, dass in allen Schichten sogenannte Bernsteinlacke vorliegen. Dabei handelt es sich um Produkte, die aus aufgeschmolzenem Bernstein (Bernsteinkolophonium) und Leinölfirnis bestehen. Die Proben, die für diese Analyse gebraucht wurden, konnten aus einem Stück eines einzelnen Dosenreifes entnommen werden, der heute keiner Dose mehr zugeordnet werden kann. Aus diesem Stück Reif wurde auch die Probe für einen Querschliff entnommen. Abbildung 3 zeigt den Querschliff in 200-facher Vergrößerung bei Normallicht.[3] Es handelt sich hierbei um ein geringes Stück Papiermaché, das im Übergang zur ersten schwarzen Schicht etwas dunkler erscheint (einer Schicht, die aussieht, als wäre sie pigmentiert), darüber sind mehrere dünne schwarze Aufträge und schließlich eine durchsichtige, leicht gelbliche Schicht zu erkennen.

Im UV-Licht zeigt sich, dass die im Normallicht so homogene Grundierungsschicht aus zwei Aufträgen besteht (Abb. 4).[4] Die schwarzen Lackschichten kann man in vier unterschiedliche Arbeitsschritte einteilen. Der vorher kaum wahrnehmbare Klarlack erscheint hier verhältnismäßig dick. Es ist anzunehmen, dass es sich bei den untersten Schichten um eine Art Grundierung handelt, die schwarz pigmentiert ist. Das Ergebnis der Analysen verblüfft. Koller schreibt hierzu: „... es wurden keine Pigmente, vor allem keine dunklen Pigmente nachgewiesen." Und weiter: „... die dunkle Farbe kommt durch höhere Schmelztemperaturen und längere Kochzeiten zustande (Bildung von braunen bis schwarzen Verkohlungsprodukten)."[5]

Die Grundierung dieser Dose wurde aller Wahrscheinlichkeit nach mit „verbrannten" Lackresten ausgeführt. Teile des Bernsteinlackes sind in die poröse Struktur der Dose eingedrungen, so dass das Papiermaché am Übergang etwas dunkler erscheint. Die Befunde der Grundierung können anhand von Quellenschriften untermauert werden. Nach Stöckel[6] und Dreme[7] erhalten die fertigen und abgedrehten Dosen zum Härten der Oberfläche den ersten Anstrich mit heißem Leinöl- oder Bernsteinfirnis. Dieser Anstrich wird in einem speziellen Ofen ausgehärtet und anschließend geschliffen. Sieht die Oberfläche des Papiermaché-Korpus in 200-facher Vergrößerung noch nicht sehr glatt aus, so erstaunt die Oberfläche der geschliffenen Grundierung durch ihre genaue, ohne Störungen verlaufende Linie.

Mit äußerster Genauigkeit wurden die Grundierungsschichten nach dem Trocknen geschliffen. In den Quellenschriften des 18. Jahrhunderts, die auf die Verwendung von Schleifwerkzeugen und die Empfehlung von Materialien hin durchgeschaut wurden, wird immer wieder das grobe Schleifen mit Bimsstein, Raspeln, Feilen und speziellen Messern erwähnt. Zum feineren Polieren wird Schachtelhalm verwendet. Stöckel beschreibt es wie folgt: „Der Schachtelhalm wurde zu einem fingerdicken Bündelchen an einem Ende fest zusammengebunden. Dabei muss man darauf achten, dass keine Knoten in die Mitte des Bündels kommen, was beim Schleifen große Nachteile hätte. Wurde zuerst mit Bimsstein geschliffen und dann erst mit Schachtelhalm, so ist dies außerordentlich effektiv, denn die zurückgebliebenen Körnchen des Bimssteins können die Oberfläche sehr verfeinern." [8] Das Polieren konnte aber auch mit Schleifschlamm und einem weichen Lappen erfolgen. Als Schleifpulver diente Bimssteinmehl, Hirschhornsalz,[9] Tripel[10], Haarpuder[11], Stärkemehl oder weiße Kreide[12]. Das Polieren erfolgte auf einem Drehstuhl und nicht aus freier Hand.

Die Aufnahme des Querschliffes im ultravioletten Licht zeigt fünf mehr oder weniger deutlich von einander zu unterscheidende Lackaufträge. Watin, der wohl bekannteste zeitgenössische

Abb. 1. Tabakdose der Manufaktur Stobwasser: „Der Laborant“, Städtisches Museum Braunschweig

Abb. 2. Modell der fünf Einzelteile einer Dose, Städtisches Museum Braunschweig

Autor eines Rezeptbuches, von dem man behauptet, Stobwasser habe diese Rezepte verwendet, beschreibt die Lackaufträge wie folgt: „Mit einem Kopal- oder Bernsteinfirnis von schlechter Qualität werden zwischen 20 und 24 Anstriche aufgetragen. Nach jedem vierten Auftrag wird die Dose auf der Drechselbank geschliffen. Der letzte Anstrich wird nicht mit Bimsstein geschliffen, sondern wegen der besseren Haftung mit einem Messer abgezogen. Mit einem guten Bernstein- oder Kopalfirnis überzieht er anschließend die Dosen 10–12 mal und poliert dann die Oberfläche.“ [13]

Ein anderes Zitat aus der Rezeptsammlung von Bickes schildert den Vorgang auf ganz ähnliche Weise und bezieht sich direkt auf die Arbeiten von Stobwasser. Nur fügt dieser hinzu, dass die mehrfach aufgetragenen Lackschichten eingebrannt wurden: „Das Schleifen erfolgte nicht nach jedem Auftrage, sondern immer nur bei jedem Zweiten oder Dritten. Sie [die Arbeiten aus Papiermaché] erhalten mehr oder weniger Firnisaufträge, je nachdem dem Lack Glanz und Feinheit gegeben werden soll. In den Pariser- oder Braunschweiger Lackfabriken – von deren Letztere den schönsten Lack in Deutschland liefern – werden niemals weniger als zehn bis zwölf Firnisaufträge gegeben. Das Trockenen geschieht im Ofen.“ [14]

Für das Trocknen der Lacke wurden spezielle Öfen entwickelt. In dem Maler und Lackierer- Handbuch von Bonani von 1746 findet sich die Beschreibung eines Trockenofens. Dieser ist aus Mauerwerk aufgebaut und kann von unten bestückt werden (Abb. 5).[15] Höfer beschreibt relativ spät, 1898, einen weiteren Trockenofen speziell für lackierte Ware (Abb. 6). Dieser Ofen ist so konstruiert, dass kein direktes Feuer ins Innere des Ofens dringen kann, ähnlich wie bei dem von Bonani beschriebenen Trockenofen. Die Darstellung zeigt in der linken Hälfte den Durchschnitt eines solchen Ofens. Dabei wird der Feuerraum beheizt und mit dieser Hitze der Kasten umspült. In dem Trockenkasten selbst sind Träger angebracht, auf die eiserne Stangen gelegt werden können, die dann mit den lackierten Gegenständen bestückt werden. In den Öfen wurden häufig Temperaturen von 90–100 °C, das entspricht 190–212 °F erreicht.[16]

Abb. 3. Querschliff 4, 200-fache Vergrößerung, Normallicht

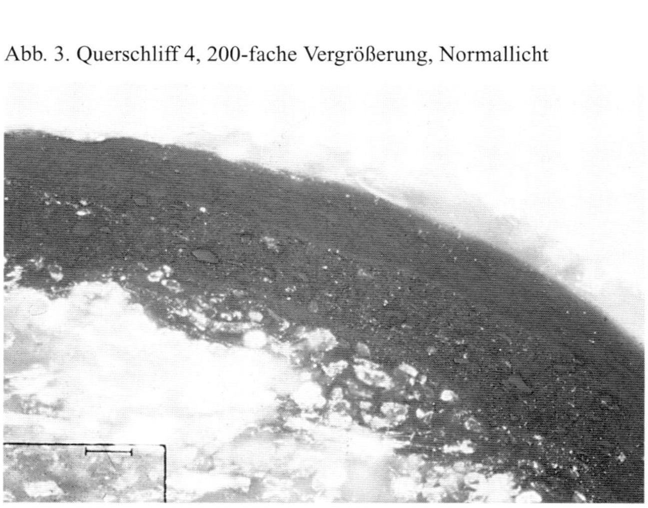

Abb. 4. Querschliff 4, 200-fache Vergrößerung, UV-Licht

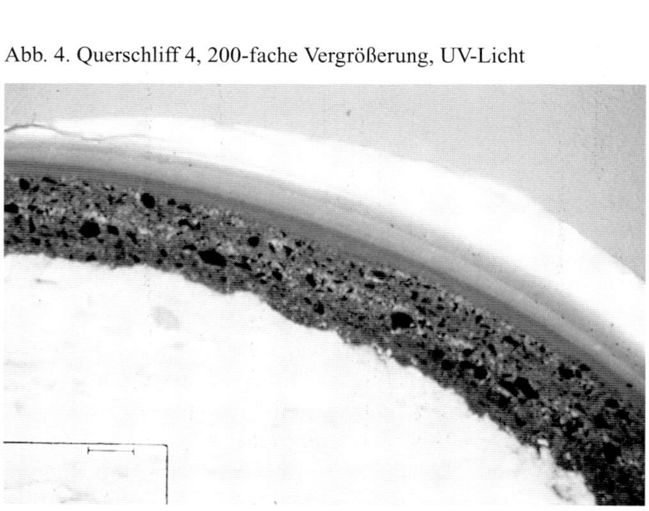

Abb. 5. Gemauerter Trockenofen nach Bonani

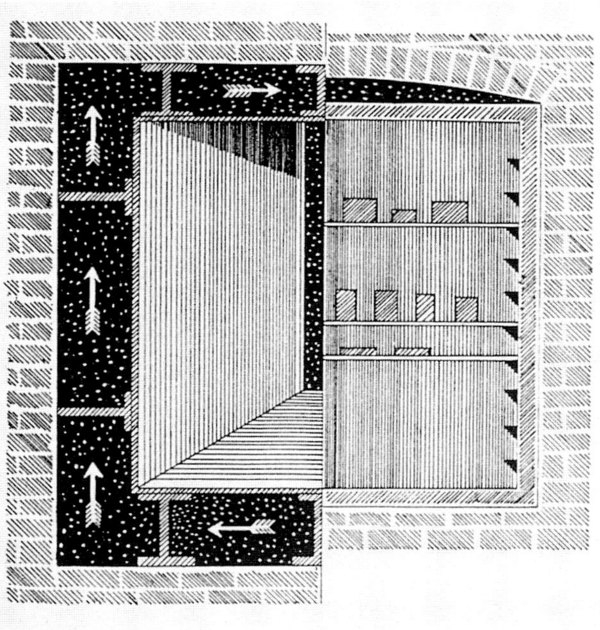

Abb. 6. Trockenofen nach Höfer

Abb. 7. Querschliff 8, 200-fache Vergrößerung, UV-Licht, Probe wurde aus der runden Tabakdose entnommen mit der Darstellung: „Monsieur de la flute", Städtisches Museum Braunschweig

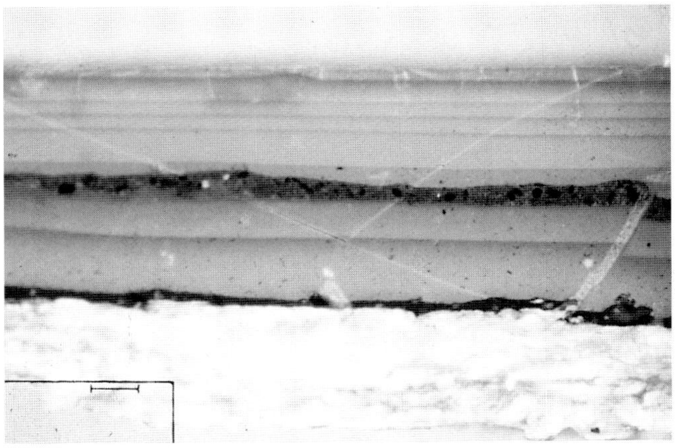

Vergleicht man nun weitere Querschliffe, deren Probematerial aus unterschiedlichen Dosen entnommen wurden, so stellt man fest, dass diese Grundier- und Lackschichten anders aussehen.

Das Probematerial des Querschliffes 8 wurde aus ungefähr der gleichen Stelle entnommen wie das von Querschliff 4 (vgl. Abb. 3, 4), nämlich aus der Außenseite des Bodenreifes (Abb. 7).[17] Bei UV-Licht und gleicher Vergrößerung stellt sich der Querschliff anders dar. Die in Abbildung 4 als Grundierung bezeichnete Schicht fehlt gänzlich. Die untersten Lackschichten sind hier nicht so stark verkohlt. Die durchsichtigen, jedoch braun erscheinenden Lackschichten überwiegen. Es sind mindestens elf Schichten zu zählen.

Vergleicht man nun weitere Querschliffe, deren Probematerial aus unterschiedlichen Dosen entnommen wurde, so stellt man fest, dass diese Grundier- und Lackschichten mit jedem neuen Querschliff auf einen anderen Aufbau schließen lassen. Es ist anzunehmen, dass Arbeitsmethoden im Laufe der Zeit umgestellt und verändert wurden. Aber auch Querschliffe, deren Probematerial aus unterschiedlichen Partien einer Dose entnommen wurden, zeigen im Vergleich einen unterschiedlichen Fassungsaufbau. Eine gegebenenfalls sogar pigmentierte Grundierung wurde zumeist nur auf die Scheibe des Dosendeckels aufgetragen. Wandungen und Bodenplatte sind meist einfacher behandelt und weisen nicht so viele Fassungsschichten auf. Wurden farbige Untergründe gewünscht, so variiert der Aufbau nochmals stark im Gegensatz zu den einfarbig schwarzen Lackierungen.

Bemalungen und Verzierungen

Schildpattimitationen

Die Manufaktur Stobwasser gab sich große Mühe, Schildpatt nachzuahmen. Der schichtweise Aufbau besteht aus einer grauschwarzen, ungleich dicken Grundierung. Darauf folgen eine unregelmäßig dicke, glatt geschliffene, kräftig rote Schicht, anschließend drei Schichten des schwarz wirkenden Lackes und zuletzt ein gelblich durchsichtiger Decklack. Die Spektralanalyse des roten Pigmentes ergibt zweifelsfrei Zinnober für den roten Auftrag. Der wolkige Effekt wurde durch unterschiedlich starkes Polieren und Schleifen der roten Lackschichten erreicht, so dass die rote Schicht mal dick, mal überhaupt nicht erscheint. Der Eindruck dieser Technik wird in der Tabakdose mit der Darstellung „Mann und Frau, den Mond betrachtend" nach Caspar David Friedrich deutlich.[18]

Bunte Marmorierungen

Bunte Marmorierungen finden sich häufig vor allem auf Zigarrenetuis. Diese Technik konnte nicht so genau untersucht werden, da sich keine defekte Dose finden ließ, an der man den Malschichtenaufbau vollständig hätte ablesen können. Dem optischen Eindruck nach wurde auf die grauschwarze oder braune Grundierung der schwarze Lack oder eine Farbe (häufig Dunkelgrün) aufgetragen. Neben bunten Farbspritzern findet man auch „goldene Fusseln" auf dieser Schicht. Dies sind vermutlich Feilspäne aus Messing. Diese Fusseln streute man in die noch nasse Farbe oder den Lack und drückte sie ein. War alles ausreichend getrocknet, malte man die Miniaturen darauf und trug den abschließenden Lack auf.

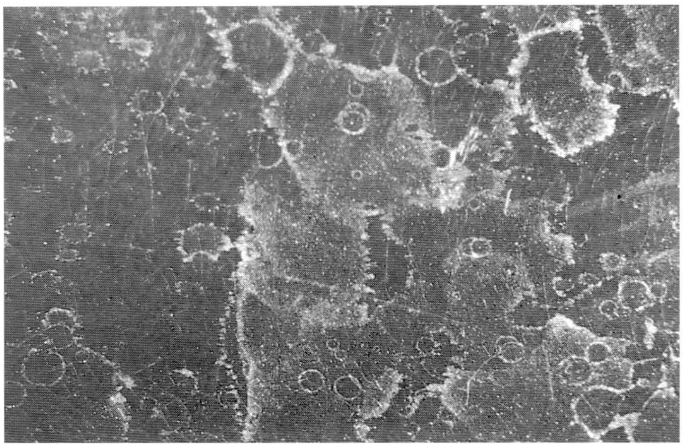

Abb. 8. Melanchthonbecher, goldene Marmorierung auf blauem Untergrund, Württembergisches Landesmuseum Stuttgart

Goldene Marmorierung auf monochromem Untergrund

Marmorierungen mit Gold auf farbigem oder schwarzem Untergrund scheinen dem Zeitgeschmack besonders entsprochen zu haben. Den schichtweisen Aufbau dieser Technik kann man besonders gut am Boden einer beriebenen Dose erkennen: Es handelt sich dabei um den sogenannten „Melanchthonbecher“ aus dem Württembergischen Landesmuseum in Stuttgart (Abb. 8). Auf einer braunen Grundierung liegt der schwarz erscheinende Lack. Wie die goldene Marmorierung aufgetragen wurde, ist nicht ganz klar. Im Mikroskop erkennt man feines Goldpuder. Dieses wurde wässrig gebunden und zog sich dann mit Hilfe von Ochsengalle oder einem ähnlichen Netzmittel selbst in die Kreisform zusammen. Auf dieser Dekoration befinden sich die Miniatur und der Abschlusslack. Abbildung 8 zeigt ein Detail eines blauen Bechers mit goldener Marmorierung.[19]

Bemalung der Dosen: Dosenstücke

Im Nachlass der Firma Stobwasser hat sich noch eine Vielzahl an Vorlagen für die Bemalung der Dosen erhalten. Zum einen sind es Ausschnitte aus Journalen, meist Genreszenen oder zeitgenössische Darstellungen, zum anderen graphische Vorlageblätter, die Reproduktionen beliebter und bekannter Meisterwerke aus den großen Gemäldegalerien zeigen. Die Motive selbst sind mit Bleistift oder einem ähnlichen Stift ausgeführt. Selten gibt es auch mehrfarbige Blätter, lavierte, oder in verschiedenen Rottönen gehaltene Zeichnungen. Teilweise sind die Linien der Zeichnungen locker und frei mit Korrekturlinien oder besonders herausgehobenen Linien versehen. Andere sind sklavisch von einer Vorlage kopiert, oder es sind nur wie beim Durchpausen die notwendigsten Linien wiedergegeben. Diese Blätter sind einzeln oder von Malern in Bücher über- und nebeneinander gezeichnet.

Die Rückseiten vieler Vorzeichnungen wurden mit einer schwach gebundenen, weißen Farbe bestrichen. Dies weist darauf hin, dass die Zeichnung wahrscheinlich mittels der weißen Farbe und einem spitzen Griffel von der Vorderseite her durchgedrückt wurde. Die Zeichnungen pauste man direkt auf die schwarz lackierten Flächen. Bei der weißen Farbe der Rückseitenanstriche konnte Bleiweiß = basisches Bleicarbonat nachgewiesen werden.[20] Es wurde keine Analyse zur Bestimmung des Bindemittels durchgeführt, wahrscheinlich handelt es sich aber um eine wässrige Bindung mit Leim. Die meisten Zeichnungen sehen aus, als seien sie häufig verwendet worden. Sehr sorgsam wurde dabei mit ihnen nicht umgegangen, denn Flecken, Risse und Knicke sind deutliche Gebrauchsspuren.

Abb. 9. Tabakdose, „König Wilhelm I. von Württemberg“, Detail, Württembergisches Landesmuseum Stuttgart

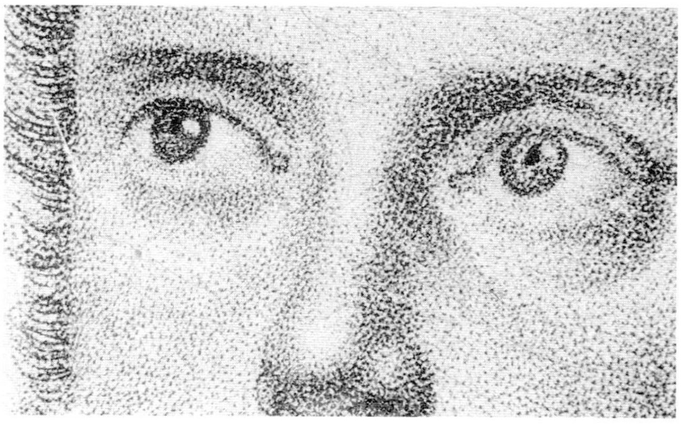

Ausführung der Bemalung

Heinrich Oldenburg, ein Maler, der für Stobwasser gearbeitet hat, hinterließ ein Malerbuch, in dem er erwähnt, dass er Aufträge in Öl ausgeführt hat.[21] Dies ist der einzige direkte Hinweis auf das Bindemitttel der Malerei der Dosen. Tempera-Bindemittel hätten den Vorzug, dass sie kürzere Trocknungszeiten haben und sich durch den Decklack nicht anlösen lassen.

Es ist anzunehmen, dass die zur Bemalung der Dosen verwendeten Pigmente denen entsprechen, die auch für die Ölmalerei des 18. und 19. Jahrhunderts verwendet wurden. Vergleiche der in Quellenschriften speziell für die Lackmalerei beschriebenen Pigmente bestätigen dies.[22] Mit einer leicht fließenden, hellen Farbe zog man die gepausten Konturen nach. Sobald diese getrocknet waren, konnte mit der eigentlichen Bemalung begonnen werden. Zuerst legte man die hellen Partien vor, um den schwarzen Grund abzudecken, anschließend trug man den Lokalton auf, wobei man gleich die Übergänge vom Helleren ins Dunklere berücksichtigte. Zuletzt wurden die Schatten und Lichter gesetzt. Ein Beispiel hierfür ist die eingangs besprochene Dose (Abb. 1).

Durch Graphiken verzierte Tabakdosen

Dosen mit Miniaturmalereien hatten einen relativ hohen Preis. Nicht jeder konnte sich eine bemalte Dose leisten. Um Produktionskosten zu sparen und günstigere Produkte auf den Markt bringen zu können, wurden auch Kupferstiche in den Braunschweiger Lackmanufakturen verwendet. Man klebte sie anstelle der Miniaturmalerei auf und überzog sie mit einem Lack. Wurden die Stiche bemalt, so geschah dieses wahrscheinlich mit Aquarellfarben, da die Farbaufträge lasierend und nicht deckend sind. Ein Beispiel für einen kolorierten Druck auf einer Dose ist die Darstellung von 1815, die sogenannte „Friedensdose“, in die eine kolorierte Graphik eingearbeitet ist (Abb. 10).[23] Es ist die einzige signierte und mit „Evers Fabrique“ beschriebene Dose.

Von diesem Motiv sind außer dieser Dose noch ein Kupferstich und eine Metallplatte mit einem kolorierten Kupferstich im Städtischen Museum Braunschweig erhalten.

Einen völlig anderen Eindruck vermittelt die Dose mit der Darstellung „Wilddiebe vom Förster überrascht" (Abb. 11).[24] Es handelt sich dabei um die gleiche Technik. Der Farbauftrag ist aber wesentlich dicker als bei den oben erwähnten Dosen. Die Graphik ist nicht mehr so deutlich zu erkennen. Man konnte sich auf diese Weise die Übertragung des Motivs mit Hilfe der Pause ersparen. Dass so verzierte Dosen schneller hergestellt werden und damit billiger verkauft werden konnten, ist einleuchtend.

Umdruckverfahren als Ziertechnik

Graphische Blätter wurden nicht nur aufgeklebt, sondern man wendete ein Verfahren an, das als die Übertragung von Kupferstichen auf Glas, Porzellan und Steingut belegt ist. Die schwarze Druckfarbe wurde dabei von einem angefeuchteten Stichabzug durch Anreiben auf eine geleimte oder gefirniste Oberfläche übertragen. Man kann sich dieses Verfahren beinahe wie ein Abziehbildchen vorstellen, bei dem lediglich die Farbe von dem Papier auf die Dose übergeht. Ein Beispiel für diese Technik ist die Dose mit dem Porträt von König Wilhelm I. von Württemberg (Abb. 9).[25] Auf gebundenem goldenem Metallpulver wurde der Druck übertragen. Die Spektralanalyse zeigt, dass es sich hier um Messingpulver handelt. Das verwendete Bindemittel ist wahrscheinlich Kopal- oder Bernsteinlack. Leinölfirnis kann auch nicht ausgeschlossen werden.

Abb. 10. Tabakdose: „Friedensdose", Städtisches Museum Braunschweig

Überzugslack

Auf die Schichten des schwarzen Lackes und die farbigen Verzierungen erhielten die Dosen einen farblosen, glänzenden Überzug. Bei den optischen Beobachtungen konnte festgestellt

Abb. 11. Tabakdose: „Wilddiebe vom Förster überrascht", Städtisches Museum Braunschweig

werden, dass man diesen Schlusslack nicht überall gleich dick, sondern auf den Dosenstücken dick, auf den Wandungen, dem Boden und den Innenseiten dünn aufgetragen hat.

Über den Miniaturen ist der Decklack so dick und gleichmäßig, dass die Unebenheiten der Malschicht nicht zu erkennen sind. Zur Zusammensetzung dieses Lackes gibt es keine direkten Hinweise. Über die Art der Verarbeitung äußert sich Fuhse: „Nachdem das Bild völlig aufgetrocknet ist, wird noch eine Lackschicht darüber gelegt, die aber nicht im Ofen eingebrannt wird, sondern an der Luft trocknen muss."[26] Da die Dosen starken Belastungen durch Abrieb und Gebrauch ausgesetzt waren, beschreibt Dreme Öllacke als geeignet: „Sie (die Fetten- oder Ölfirnisse) sind die solidesten, nehmen durch Politur einen schönen Glanz an, und werden gewöhnlich zum Überziehen solcher Gegenstände angewendet, welche einem starken Gebrauch unterworfen sind."[27]

Häufig bestritten wird von Leuten, die versucht haben, einen Öllack zu kochen, dass man aus dem gelblich bräunlichen Bernstein oder dem Kopal einen so hellen Lack kochen kann, dass man damit die feinen Farben einer Bemalung, wie sie auf den Dosen vorliegt, nicht stört. Sie behaupten, dass durch das Kochen das Leinöl so geschwärzt wird, dass nur dunkle Lacke hergestellt werden können. Rezepte für helle Öllacke findet man aber relativ häufig in Quellenschriften, wie z. B. den weißen Kopalfirnis bei Watin,[28] aber auch die von Bikes[29] und Dreme[30] beschriebenen. Wegen der großen Glätte des Schlusslackes kann man annehmen, daß dieser an den besonders dicken Partien mehrfach aufgetragen wurde und man ihn dann polierte. Ein letzter Firnisauftrag könnte dann, wie bei Dreme beschreiben, erfolgt sein: „War der Firnis recht rein und wurde er gehörig aufgetragen, so braucht dieser Auftrag nicht geschliffen werden. Findet man aber ein Schleifen notwendig, so geschehe es mit abgeschliffener Kreide und Wasser mittels eines Filzes. Nachdem das Abgeschliffene weggewaschen worden, so wird das Geschirr mit einer weichen Leinwand getrocknet und darauf mit einem alten seidenen Tuche gut gerieben."[31]

Die chemischen Analysen des Doerner-Instituts ergaben für den Decklack neben Bernsteinlack, Sandarak, Lärchenterpentinharz und Kolophonium. Angaben über die einzelnen Verhältnisse der Komponenten zueinander konnten nicht gemacht werden.

Anmerkungen

1 Tabakdose, Darstellung: Der Laborant, Besitz: Städtisches Museum Braunschweig.
2 Rekonstruierte Tabakdose, Städtisches Museum Braunschweig.
3 Querschnitt 4, 200-fache Vergrößerung, Normallicht. Probe wurde aus einem Stück Reif einer runden Tabakdose entnommen.
4 Querschnitt 4, 200-fache Vergrößerung, UV-Licht. Probe wurde aus einem Stück Reif einer runden Tabakdose entnommen.
5 Kurzes Protokoll zu Analysen von Johann Koller, Doerner-Institut München.
6 Stöckel 1815, S. 155.
7 Dreme 1821, S. 138.
8 Stöckel 1815, S. 86.
9 Hirschhornsalz, chem. Ammoniumbicarbonatin wird in vielen Schriften erwähnt, z. B. bei Stöckel 1815, S. 86.
10 Tripel, eine gelbliche Tonart, Vorkommen in Böhmen, England und Frankreich. Bickes 1834, S. 57.
11 Schulze 1828, S. 153.
12 Gütle 1793, S. 216.
13 Watin 1774, S. 273.
14 Bickes 1834, S. 126.
15 Bonani 1746, S. 111.
16 Höfer 1898, S. 62.
17 Querschliff 8, 200- fache Vergrößerung, UV- Licht. Probe wurde aus der runden Tabakdose entnommen, mit der Darstellung: Monsieur de la Flute, Städtisches Museum Braunschweig.
18 Tabakdose, Darstellung: Mann und Frau, den Mond betrachtend, nach C. D. Friedrich, Städtisches Museum Braunschweig.
19 Detail: goldene Marmorierung auf blauem Untergrund, Melanchthonbecher, Württembergisches Landesmuseum Stuttgart.
20 Analyse durch das Institut für Technologie der Malerei Stuttgart, H. Härlin.
21 Malerbuch des Heinrich Oldenburg, Städtisches Museum Braunschweig.
22 Croecker 1743, S. 81 ff.; Watin 1774, S. 13 ff.; Le Pileut d'Apligny 1781, S. 113 ff.; Stöckel 1815, S. 10 ff.; Blasche 1847, S. 104; Bickes 1834, S. 21.
23 Tabakdose, Darstellung: Friedensdose, Städtisches Museum Braunschweig.
24 Tabakdose, Darstellung: Wilddiebe vom Förster überrascht, Städtisches Museum Braunschweig.
25 Tabakdose, Darstellung: König Wilhelm I. von Württemberg, Württembergisches Landesmuseum Stuttgart.
26 Fuhse 1925, S. 67.
27 Dreme 1821, S. 115.
28 Watin 1774, S. 220.
29 Bickes 1834, S. 199.
30 Dreme 1821, S. 125.
31 Dreme 1821, S. 147.

Literaturverzeichnis

Bickes, F.: *Das Ganze der Kunst des Lackierens, Vergoldens, Staffirmalens und der damit verbundenen Farbenbereitung*, Heilbronn 1834

Blasche, B.: *Papparbeiter oder Anleitung in Pappe zu arbeiten*, 5. Von J. J. Scherer revidierte Aufl., Stuttgart 1847

Bonani (dt. v. J. J. R.): *Neuer Tractat von Firns- Laquir- und Mahler-Künste*, Breslau/Leipzig 1746

Croecker, J. M.: *Der wohl anführende Mahler welcher curiose Liebhaber lehret, wie man sich zur Mahlerey zubereiten mit Oelfarben umgehen...*, Jena 1743

Dreme, Dr. Georg V. Chr.: *Der Firnis- und Kittmacher*, Brünn 1821

Fuhse, F.: *Vom Braunschweiger Tischlerhandwerk, Stobwasser-Arbeiten, Braunschweiger Werkstücke*, Veröffentlichung aus Museum, Archiv und Bibliothek, Band 1, Berlin 1925

Gütle, J. C.: *Gründlicher Unterricht zur Verfertigung guter Firnisse nebst der Kunst zu Lackieren und zu Vergolden*, Nürnberg 1793

Höfer, J.: *Die Fabrikation künstlicher plastischer Massen sowie der künstlichen Steine, Kunststeine, Stein- und Cementgüsse*, 2. Aufl., Wien/Pest/Leipzig 1898

Le Pileut d'Apligny: *Richtige und vollständige Beschreibung aller Farbmaterialien nebst einer deutlichen Anweisung wie solche zu dem Gebrauch zubereitet. Aus dem Französischen übersetzt mit des Herrn Loriots entdeckten Geheimnis, die Pastellfarben zu fixieren wie auch mit vielen anderen Zusätzen vermehrt*, Augsburg 1781

Schulze, A.: *Praktische Anweisungen zur Lackierkunst*, Quedlinburg und Leipzig 1828

Stöckel, H. F.: *Praktisches Handbuch für Künstler, Lackliebhaber und Ölfarben-Anstreicher*, Nürnberg, 1815

Watin, J.-F.: *Der Staffirmaler oder die Kunst anzustreichen, zu vergolden und zu lackieren (...)*, Leipzig 1774

Abbildungsnachweis

Abb. 3, 4, 7: Katharina Walch, Bayerisches Landesamt für Denkmalpflege, München
Alle übrigen Aufnahmen von der Verfasserin

Summary

The lacquer techniques for snuff-boxes made by the manufactory Stobwasser in Brunswick has been kept a secret ever since. Most of the small boxes were made of papier-maché. Usually, two discs (one of them plane, the other one convex), and three rings were stuck together for a box of an average size between 10 and 12 centimetres. The surface was covered with a varnish.

Tests in normal light, cross-sections of the coatings in normal and ultraviolett light, and chemical tests helped to clarify some of the secrets: all sections prove the use of an oil- lacquer, a combination of linseed oil and amber colophony. For priming, a black carbonized amber lacquer was used. Even the clear, transparent lacquers of the lining contain amber colophony.

In historical manuals, such as Watin's lacquer book, which was probably used by Stobwasser, not less than 20–24 coatings were considered necessary for a good quality lacquer, while in Bickes' book only three to four coatings are mentioned.

After applying the lacquer layers the surface was ground and the lacquer burnt at 190–212 °F. After priming the boxes were coloured, some decorated with a tortoise-shell imitation, and others with coloured marble and gold flitter. Finally the pictures were transmitted. The cheaper boxes were embellished with coloured copperplate prints. Oil colours were used for the small figures.

At the end, 10–12 coats of a clear, transparent varnish were laid all over the box. This varnish contains other components than the black lacquer layers. Chemical tests confirmed the use of amber, linseed oil, sandarac, larch turpentine, and colophony.

Fig. 1. Jean Dunand shortly before his death in 1942, planing wood

Mechthild Baumeister

Jean Dunand – A Master of Art Déco Lacquer

Jean Dunand was one of the most renowned French Art Déco artists, creating lacquer furniture and decorative objects that exemplified the sophisticated taste of his time. His innovative combination of traditional Oriental lacquer techniques with contemporary forms and abstract decorative designs established his international success.

Dunand's development as a lacquer artist is remarkable, especially considering that he was one of the first Western artists working with urushi. Born on May 20, 1877 in Lancy, Switzerland, Dunand started his artistic and crafts-oriented training at the age of 14 at the École des Arts Industriels in Geneva, completing his studies in 1896 with a degree in sculpture and design.[1] The city of Geneva granted the talented young artist a stipend to continue his training in Paris, where Dunand studied with the art nouveau sculptor Jean Dampt. Influenced by Dampt, who believed that a sculptor should also be a good craftsman, Dunand spent his summer vacations as an apprentice to a Geneva coppersmith. There he learned the traditional metalworking techniques for making household wares of hand-beaten copper and brass, known as Dinanderie.[2] Although Dunand found success as a sculptor, participating in major exhibitions of his time, such as the Exposition Universelle 1900 in Paris, commissions for carved furniture and interior decorations demonstrated to him the economic advantages of the applied arts. Consequently, he focused on his decorative metalwork and established himself as a Dinandier. It was in this context that he first experimented with coatings to prevent corrosion. He noticed that the Japanese metal vases sent to his workshop for restoration had a lacquer surface, that was not only protective but added a decorative effect. Fascinated by the Oriental lacquer technique and eager to apply it to his own metalware, Dunand invited several Parisian lacquer specialists to his studio to learn from them the secret of lacquer work. He was astonished by their lack of knowledge and considered them simply varnishers.[3] Pursuing his keen interest in this matter, he then contacted the Japanese lacquer artist Seizo Sugawara, who himself was interested in Dunand's metal working techniques. They agreed to exchange their workshop secrets.

Seizo Sugawara came from the small village of Johoji in the north of Japan, which is famous for its lacquerware. In 1900, at the age of eighteen, he arrived in Paris as part of the Japanese national delegation to the Exposition Universelle, to oversee the lacquerware sent from Japan.[4] Sugawara decided to settle in Paris, where he became an important figure in the art scene, teaching Western artists the Oriental lacquer technique. Dunand and the Irish artist Eileen Gray were his most prominent students.

The thirteen lessons Sugawara gave to Dunand in 1912 are documented in Dunand's personal notebook.[5] He recorded descriptions for preparing the lacquer, the tools and materials, the working procedure, and various decorative techniques, including their Japanese names. The interpretation of Dunand's notes, especially the Japanese terminology, is made easier by comparison with the extensive documentation of Johannes Justus Rein and John James Quin, who independently studied the traditional lacquer techniques in the late 19th century in Japan.[6] Working on behalf of the Prussian government, Rein presented one hundred sample boards and an accompanying report to the Königliche Kunstgewerbemuseum in Berlin in 1874.[7] Quin was commissioned by the British government to collect specimen and tools for the new Museum of Economic Botany at the Royal Botanic Gardens in Kew. By 1882 he had assembled an instructive collection of 170 items, including raw materials and tools, sample boards and objects demonstrating all stages of lacquering and decorative techniques, as well as finished lacquerware.[8] Both reports describe in detail the cultivation of the lacquer tree *Rhus vernicifera*, the extraction of the tree's sap, the refining of the lacquer, the lacquering procedure and traditional techniques of decoration.[9]

Dunand's notes and the sample boards he made during the lessons with Seizo Sugawara reflect the traditional Japanese lacquer technique. The type of lacquer most frequently noted by Dunand is 'Sessimé', which, according to Rein, is a purified, filtered and evenly flowing raw lacquer, rather than the lower quality lacquer by the same name obtained from branches.[10] Dunand describes 'Nashizi' as a high grade transparent lacquer and 'Schuaye', an oil-containing lacquer for use in ordinary and colored lacquerware.[11] Besides heat, Dunand mentions the addition of camphor for thinning and glycerin for thickening the lacquer.

The wooden sample boards made by Dunand during Sugawara's lessons demonstrate a 30 step process of producing a black lacquered surface (figs. 2 and 3). Following ten ground layers of 'Kekso', 'Sessimé', 'Ita', 'Kiriko', 'Dzinoko' and 'Sabi' (the components of which vary from layer to layer and contain different proportions of powdered burnt clay, finely ground clay, chopped hemp or cotton fibers, cloth, 'Sessimé', rice starch and water), three layers of black 'Louero' lacquer were applied and finished with two coatings of 'Sessimé'.[12] Between each application the dried layer was smoothed or polished with a stone, charcoal, finely ground clay, or powdered calcined deer antler.[13] Sugawara must have emphasized the importance of this procedure to Dunand, as indicated by this comment from the notebook: 'Lacquerers who do not know very well how to polish and smooth lacquer with charcoal are called camels, because a camel has two humps, similar to badly polished lacquer'.[14] Dunand describes the 'Louero' lacquer, called 'Ro-iro urushi' in Rein's terminology, as the highest quality black lacquer. It is obtained by the reaction of urushi with iron. A solution of iron filings in vinegar is added to 'Sessimé' and then the lacquer is heated and filtered.[15] In addition, he mentions 'Yuyen', a 'Nashizi' lacquer mixed with lamp black, and a lower grade 'Jôhana' lacquer, which contains oil and is blackened with iron powder. Dunand pointed out that oil-containing lacquers, such as 'Schuaye' and 'Jôhana', used for ordinary lacquer articles were never polished.[16] For colored lacquers various pigments were added, vermilion ('Schu') and iron-oxide ('Benigara') for red lacquer, cadmium and chrome yellow for yellow lacquer,

Fig. 2. Sample boards produced by Dunand during lessons with Sugawara in 1912

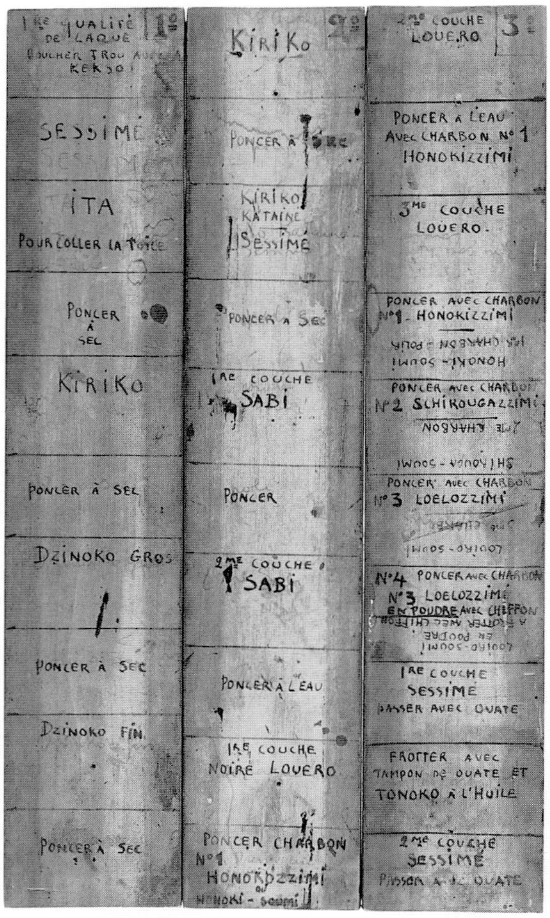

Fig. 3. Backside of sample boards listing the 30 steps for producing a black lacquered surface

Prussian blue for blue lacquer and barium sulfate, lead and zinc white as white colorants. Green lacquer was obtained either from a mixture of yellow and blue pigments or chromium oxide. Brown was achieved by mixing red 'Schu' and black 'Jôhana' lacquer. Sugawara also taught Dunand the application of gold lacquer, which incorporates metal leafs and powder, as well as other decorative techniques. Dunand noted the importance of a dust free environment for the drying of lacquer and that the lacquered object was placed in an armoire. However, he did not comment on the high relative humidity level required for curing lacquer. The use of 'Sessimé' on metal was specifically addressed and special mention was made of the fact that the lacquer applied to metal can be hardened in an oven.[17]

The lessons took place over a period of two months, which can only be considered a crash course.[18] They provided Dunand with an introduction to the Japanese lacquer technique, leaving this immensely talented craftsman with a new fascination that sometimes took on the air of a veritable obsession. When the lessons were completed Dunand continued experiments on his own. After World War I he proceeded with the installation of a lacquer studio in his workshop, located in the Rue Hallé in the fourteenth arrondissement in Paris. He obtained the lacquer from the French colonies in Indochina (now Vietnam), and most of the craftsmen who helped him with the lacquer work in his studio were also Indochinese. In a magazine interview of the early 1920s Dunand explained that he favored Asian assistants because they were experienced in working with lacquer and were not susceptible to the allergic reaction to urushi common among Europeans.[19] The 1920s and 1930s were Dunand's most successful and creative period; lacquer had become the integral element in his artistic oeuvre.[20] René Gimbel, a Paris based art dealer who visited Dunand in his studio on June 8 in 1920 copied Dunand's description of lacquer in his diary: 'Of course there are some art forms which are merely a matter of patience, like the lacquer which I love so much! Just look, and think how much work goes into preparing this stuff and making it. Here you have some trial attempts. On these tablets you can see the various stages of preparation. At the bottom, the first layer of lacquer, then comes the second, and at the top the twentieth. So you have to varnish or paint twenty times – or rather forty, as the job has to be repeated on the other side to keep the wood from warping; otherwise it would crack, for you wouldn't believe how easily the lacquer can twist even the hardest wood into a semicircle. Actually, not forty but as many as a hundred preparations are required, since after varnishing you have to polish and before each varnishing there have to be twenty seasonings, each lasting four days. It'll surprise you to learn that the seasonings require damp conditions, and a dark room where water flows continuously, and that success is more certain at the full moon. So you'll understand that it's positively Oriental labor!'[21]

In his lacquerware Dunand combined traditional techniques with bright colors and modern forms, as well as abstract and figurative designs. Always searching for new applications and expanding the repertoire of his techniques, Dunand applied lacquer to furniture, wall panelings, paintings, portraiture, metal vases, jewelry, and textiles (fig. 11). His extraordinary creativity and his indefatigable stamina lead to an enormous production of lacquerware in the Dunand workshop.

Dunand participated in important art exhibitions of his time. His work was widely shown throughout Europe and the United States and it was acquired by major museums. In 1998 the Metropolitan Museum of Art mounted a small Jean Dunand exhibition showing works drawn mainly from its own collection.[22] This exhibition provided a welcome opportunity to study Dunand's lacquer techniques.

One of the most impressive interiors by Dunand was realized in 1928 for the penthouse of Templeton Crocker, the wealthy grandson of the founder of the Union Pacific railroad company, in San Francisco. Crocker's attention was drawn to Dunand's lacquer work by two exhibitions of contemporary French design shown in the mid-twenties in San Francisco. He commissioned a master bedroom, a dining room, and a breakfast room, all of which were decorated with lacquer.[23] The bedroom furniture is now in the collection of the Metropolitan Museum. The bedroom walls were originally decorated with lacquered panels, depicting a forest landscape (fig. 4).[24] The lacquer surface of the

Fig. 4. Bedroom by Dunand made for Templeton Crocker in 1928. The photograph was taken in 1928 in Paris before the room was shipped to San Francisco

Fig. 5. Bedside table by Dunand from the bedroom made for Templeton Crocker. The Metropolitan Museum of Art, New York, Gift of Mr. and Mrs. Peter M. Brant, 1977 (1977.226.7)

Fig. 7. Detail of 'Fortissimo' screen (cf. colour plate XXIII.5) showing the geometrically abstracted rocks

Fig. 6. Cross section of the mottled lacquer from the bedroom table, showing black laque arrachée applied to the ground layers and filled with a silver-gray lacquer. Microscopic magnification 50 x

Fig. 8. Cross section of marbled side of rock showing black lacquer on ground layer, followed by an unevenly applied pigmented lacquer, which is covered with gold leaf fragments. The irregularities of the surface were filled with a transparent lacquer. The finishing layers vary in thicknesses and continuity, thus creating the speckled appearance of the illuminated side of the rock

furniture features mainly 'laque arrachée', a favored technique of the Dunand workshop in which the freshly applied lacquer was lifted with a flat wooden spatula creating an uneven surface (figs. 5 and 6). In this case the 'laque arrachée' consists of a black 'Louero' lacquer applied to the ground layers.[25] After drying, the surface was lightly smoothed and a silver-gray colored lacquer was applied over the black layer. The metallic effect of this layer was achieved by the addition of aluminum filings mixed with titanium white and cadmium yellow pigments to the lacquer.[26] Surface polishing revealed the raised peaks of the black lacquer within the silver-gray layer, resulting in a mottled effect. Plain silver-leafed and black 'Louero' lacquer were used to accentuate the shape of the furniture, providing a playful contrast to the mottled surface. The analysis of samples from the black and silver-gray lacquer indicated the presence of laccol, a substance found in urushi derived from the lacquer tree *Rhus succedanea*, which is native to Indochina, the present Vietnam.[27] This species is related to *Rhus vernicifera*, which grows in Japan and China and from which an urushiol-based lacquer is obtained.

'Laque arrachée' is the final surface decoration on a series of pictorial wall panels entitled 'Les peuples d'Asie et d'Afrique', which Dunand made for the 1931 Exposition Coloniale in Paris (figs. 9 and colour plate XXIII.4).[28] In this case the uneven texture of the matte brown 'laque arrachée' creates a striking contrast with the smooth and silver-leafed background. Records of a 'laque arrachée' sample board made in Dunand's workshop in 1931 describe the technique as follows: 'On a dried lacquer with gold leaf apply a coat of laque arrachée mixed with clay and draw the design in the freshly applied lacquer. After drying sand lightly with fine sandpaper.'[29]

More elaborate is Dunand's lacquer decoration on a pair of screens 'Pianissimo' and 'Fortissimo', which were made for the music salon of Mr. and Mrs. Solomon R. Guggenheim's residence in Port Washington on Long Island (colour plate XXIII.5).[30] Fabricated in 1925-26, the screens are signed by Dunand and his collaborator on this project, the sculptor Seraphin Soudbinine. The latter was most likely responsible for the design and for carving the relief figures of the angels and the geometrically abstracted rocks. The angels are decorated with an unusual gold-leafing applied to a red vermilion lacquer, juxtaposing smooth and wrinkled metal leafs, creating respectively, shiny and matte effects.[31] Differences in shading in the wrinkled gilding of the angels are achieved by the application of a coating to the darker areas rather than the use of gold leafs with different alloys.[32] The marbling of the towering rocks is achieved by a complex stratification, as illustrated by the cross section of a sample taken from an illuminated side of a rock (figs. 7 and 8). The black 'Louero' lacquer on top of the ground layer represents the side of the rock in shadow and appears as the darkest color in the marbling. A brown, pigmented layer was applied unevenly to the black lacquer and is covered with fragments of metal leaf. The irregularities were filled with a transparent lacquer and the surface was polished until the desired marbled appearance was obtained. Crushed eggshells were used to produce a white lacquer, a color otherwise difficult to achieve due to the dark natural tone of urushi. On the screens crushed eggshells were employed in combination with mother-of-pearl particles to represent the spiral-shaped clouds within the dark blue-green lacquered background, and in the gold lacquer of the angels' drapery.[33]

A technique first introduced by Dunand, which became a specialty of his workshop was the use of crushed eggshells to cover large surfaces. A drop-leaf table from ca. 1925 in the collection of the Metropolitan Museum serves as an example (colour plate XXIII.1). Depending on the desired effect, the eggshell was placed on the freshly applied lacquer either with its convex or concave side facing up. In the latter case the cavities were subsequently filled with lacquer, while in the former the convex eggshell appears mainly white after polishing. The chequered pattern of the table top and drop-leafs is achieved in this manner (fig. 12). The crushed eggshells were selectively positioned on a lacquer ground. Afterwards a grayish lacquer was applied, filling the hollow spaces of the concave eggshell particles and thereby creating a contrast to the adjacent predominantly white eggshell fields showing their convex side facing up. The grayish lacquer also filled the gaps in between the eggshell particles, thus enhancing the craquelure pattern of the eggshell mosaic. Viewing the cross section of an eggshell particle with its con-

Fig. 9. Wall panel from the series 'Les peuples d'Asie et d'Afrique', 1931, Musée des Arts d'Afrique et d'Océanie, Paris

cave side facing up under the fluorescence microscope indicated that the smoothed surface received a final coating of transparent lacquer (colour plate XXIII.2, 3).[34] Dunand's eggshell lacquer became so popular that he maintained a chicken coop in the courtyard of his workshop to guarantee a steady supply of eggs. In order to create different shadings and color contrasts, Dunand also incorporated eggshells of ducks, partridges, and exotic birds.

In a similar way, Dunand also experimented with embedding dried lacquer particles into a freshly applied lacquer, generally of a different color. The dried lacquer was obtained by applying a layer of a colored lacquer to a sheet of paper and heating it in an oven. After removing the paper, the dried lacquer was broken into pieces of the desired size.[35] Sieves with different gauge mesh were used to separate different particle sizes. Dried lacquer particles were also ground to produce a lacquer powder, which was sprinkled on freshly applied lacquer surfaces.

Another technique frequently used in the Dunand workshop was the so-called 'Coromandel' lacquer, in which the lacquered surface was engraved and the incised designs revealed the ground layers, which were either left exposed or were covered with colored lacquers. This technique was mainly applied to screens and wall panels, because 'Coromandel' lacquer provided a relatively simple technique for decorating large surfaces.

Dunand seems to have been more interested in the technical challenges and craftsmanship involved in the surface decoration with lacquer, rather than in the design itself, as indicated by his numerous collaborations with other artists and furniture designers, such as Jean Goulden, Paul Jouve, Seraphin Soudbinine, Jean Lambert-Rucki, Gustave Miklos, Émile-Jacques Ruhlmann, Eugène Printz, and Pierre Legrain. Dunand either executed the pictorial sketches in lacquer or he decorated the surfaces of sculptures and unfinished furniture sent to his workshop. Émile-Jacques Ruhlmann, one of the most important French Art Déco furniture designers, created the 'Chinoise' vanity in ca. 1929 (fig. 13). The dressing table was produced with different finishes, including plain black lacquer, and black lacquer with an abstract eggshell decoration, both executed in Dunand's studio.[36] Dunand's fascination with lacquer and his identification as a lacquer artist is also illustrated by his signature: 'Jean Dunand Laqueur', with which he often signed his work.[37]

Dunand continued to experiment with new ways of using lacquer. Among his most unusual applications were his portraits, which he based on his own photographs and sketches.[38] One of the portraits, in the collection of the Metropolitan Museum, shows Madame Juliette de Saint Cyr (fig. 10). Painted in ca. 1925 it features an eggshell mosaic background and a *laque arrachée* border containing a floral ornament. The fabric of Mme de Saint Cyr's abstractly patterned dress and her jewelry originated from Dunand's workshop as well. Mme Agnès, an influential Parisian milliner and member of the avantgarde had introduced Dunand to the fashion world and encouraged him to experiment with lacquering fabrics and producing jewelry, as well as other fashion accessories with colored geometric decorations in lacquer.

Farbtafel XXIII / *Color Plate XXIII* ▷

1 Drop-leaf table by Dunand, ca. 1925. The table top and drop leafs are decorated with crushed eggshells, arranged in a chequered pattern. The Metropolitan Museum of Art, Gift of Mr. and Mrs. Michael Chow, 1986 (1986.400)

2 Cross section of eggshell with concave side facing up from table top (cf. 1, fig. 12), filled with grayish lacquer and coated with transparent lacquer. Visible light, microscopic magnification 50 x

3 Fluorescence of same cross section (2). UV light, microscopic magnification 50x

4 Detail of wall panel from the series 'Les peuples d'Asie et d'Afrique', Musée des Arts d'Afrique et d'Océanie, Paris, showing the use of matte brown laque arrachée as the final surface decoration, here accentuated with gold leaf to represent ornamental buttons

5 Fortissimo' screen by Jean Dunand and Seraphin Soudbinine made in 1925-26 for Mr. and Mrs. Solomon R. Guggenheim. The Metropolitan Museum of Art, New York, Gift of Mrs. Solomon R. Guggenheim, 1950 (50.102.4)

△ 1

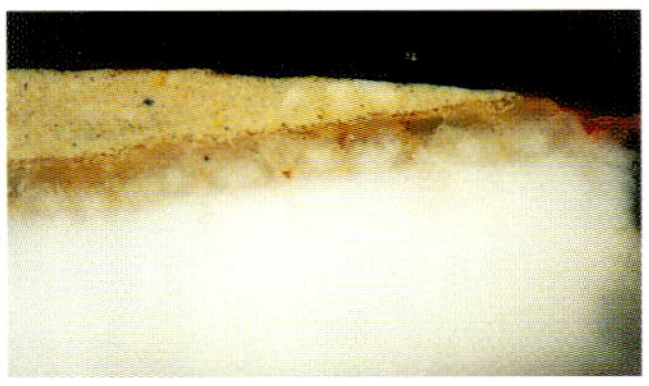

△ 2

3 △

4 △

5

Fig. 10. Portrait of Juliette de Saint Cyr by Jean Dunand, ca. 1925. The Metropolitan Museum of Art, New York, Bequest of Marquise Raoul de Saint Cyr, 1989 (1989.176.2)

Fig. 11. Front of lacquered metal vase by Dunand, ca. 1925. The abstract geometric decoration was created with red and silver lacquer, applied to the black lacquered vase. The Metropolitan Museum of Art, New York, Purchase, Lita Annenberg Hazen Charitable Trust Gift, 1998 (1998.194)

Fig. 13. 'Chinoise' vanity by Émile-Jacques Ruhlmann and Jean Dunand, ca. 1929. The Metropolitan Museum of Art, New York, Gift of Mr. and Mrs. Michael Chow, 1986 (1986.399.3a, b)

Dunand's most extensive commissions were the monumental decorative wall panelings for the luxurious ocean liners: the 'Ile de France' (1927), 'l'Atlantique' (1931), and the 'Normandie' (1935). Their luxurious interiors presented the best contemporary French design. For the 'Normandie' project Dunand was required to use fire resistant materials, which confronted him with yet another new challenge. He developed a gypsum-based material, which contained urushi and which could be cast, carved, and lacquered. The photograph shows Dunand demonstrating with a blow torch the fire resistance of a lacquered table, cast of his newly invented material (fig. 14).

The enormous demand for Dunand's lacquerware and the production of large-scale projects required the constant expansion of his workshop on the Rue Hallé. A ground plan from 1935 outlines his premises, which included a show room, an office, several lacquer studios including one for gilding, as well as designated areas for designing, model making, metal working, cabinet making, casting, and sculpture. For the curing of lacquered surfaces there were several humidity chambers, where water was running down the walls to maintain a high humidity level, and a large kiln for heat resistant substrates.[39] The number of craftsmen and assistants working in Dunand's studio varied depending on the scale of his commissions. In the twenties and thirties, Dunand had about 40-60 employees, nearly half of them Indochinese lacquer workers.[40] During the production of the decorative wall panels for the 'Normandie' Dunand employed more than 100 people to complete this enormous project.

Fig. 12. Detail of table top decorated with crushed eggshells, arranged in a chequered pattern. The eggshells that appear predominantly white were positioned convex side up, while the adjacent eggshells were placed concave side up and the subsequently applied grayish lacquer filled the concavities, thus creating the color contrast

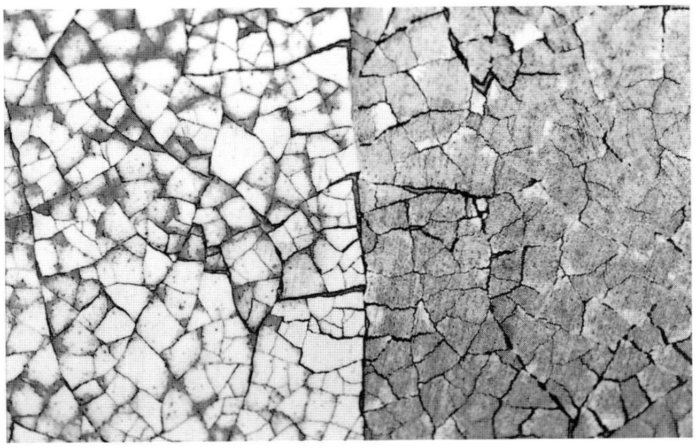

Considering that Dunand's lacquer oeuvre is based on a two months course in the Japanese lacquer technique, his ingenuity in this field is remarkable. Dunand was an extremely open-minded artist and above all an outstanding, multi-talented craftsman, who was constantly looking for new inspirations, and was driven by his own high technical and aesthetic standards. Oriental lacquer presented to him a challenging medium that was difficult to master and provided endless opportunities to develop new techniques and applications. Dunand combined a modern sensibility with a traditional but foreign material, thereby making Oriental lacquer highly fashionable in the Art Déco period. His reputation and mastery of urushi was such that lacquer experts from Tokyo regularly paid visits to his studio to study his innovative techniques and to acquire representative examples of his lacquerwork.[41] His success was also based on the close collaboration with his oldest son Bernard, himself a lacquer artist, and the help of his many Asian assistants, who produced most of the lacquerware under Dunand's supervision.[42]

Dunand died at the age of 65 on June 7, 1942. Although faced with the shortage of materials during World War II, he continued to work and to find new ways to express his creativity. A photograph, taken shortly before his death, shows Jean Dunand planing wood; the resulting shavings were lacquered and applied to hats created by the milliner Mme Agnès (fig. 1).

Notes

1 Dunand was named Jules John, but after settling in Paris he adopted Jean as his first name in 1909. Dunand became a French citizen on May 29, 1922. MARCILHAC, FÉLIX: *Jean Dunand – his life and works*, New York, 1991, p. 26 and p. 37. This major monograph on Dunand was originally written in French: MARCILHAC, FÉLIX: *Jean Dunand – vie et oeuvre*, Paris, 1991.

2 Dinanderie is a term derived from the name of the Belgium town Dinant, which specialized in hand-crafted domestic and ecclesiastical metal objects made of brass, copper and bronze during the 12–15th centuries.

3 GAUTHIER, MAXIMILIEN: 'Vingt minutes avec M. Jean Dunand', in: *La Renaissance politique, littéraire, artistique*, ca. 1923. I would like to thank M. Félix Marcilhac for providing a copy of this article.

4 ADAM, PETER: *Eileen Gray – architect/designer*, New York, 1978, pp. 49–50. MARCILHAC 1991, pp. 28–29, and p. 170. LORAC-GERBAUD, ANDRÉE: *L'art du laque*, Paris, 1973, p. 100. LORAC-GERBAUD, ANDRÉE: *Les secrets du laque*, Paris, 1996, p. 160. Lorac-Gerbaud mentions in his 1996 publication that Sugawara came to Paris with a friend, the ébéniste Inagari, rather than with a Japanese delegation to the Exposition Universelle.

5 Dunand's notebook is preserved in the Dunand family archive.

6 The different phonetic transliterations from Japanese into French, German, and English have to be considered for the interpretation. To complicate this matter Dunand also used various spellings for the same Japanese term.

7 The location of most sample boards (each 20 x 13 cm) and the report is still unknown. Investigations conducted by Hans-Werner Pape, Chief Conservator, Kunstgewerbemuseum Berlin, revealed that the museum's inventory lists the transfer of 100 Japanese lacquer sample boards from Rein's collection, on April 9, 1934 to the Völkerkunde Museum in Berlin. According to Birgit Kantzenbach, Conservator at the Ethnologisches Museum, seven of Rein's sample boards from a later set are preserved in the Museum's collection. During World War II most samples might have been either destroyed or lost. I am grateful to Hans-Werner Pape and Birgit Kantzenbach for this information.
According to Rein, his report formed the basis of his later publication on Japanese lacquer work. REIN, JOHANNES JUSTUS: *Japan nach Reisen und Studien im Auftrage der königlich preussischen Regierung dargestellt. Land- und Forstwirtschaft, Industrie und Handel*, 2nd Volume, Leipzig, 1886, pp. 400–448. Published in English as: REIN, JOHANNES JUSTUS: *The industries of Japan. Together with an account of its agriculture, forestry, arts, and commerce, from travels and researches undertaken at the cost of the Prussian government*, New York/London, 1889, pp. 338–377.

8 Most of the 170 items from the Quin collection are preserved in the Economic Botany Collections, Royal Botanic Gardens Kew. QUIN, JOHN J.: *Report by her Majesty's acting consul at Hakodate on the lacquer industry of Japan*, London, 1882. QUIN, JOHN J.: *Urushi – The technology of Japanese lacquer*, reprint of the 1896 edition, Portland/Oregon 1995. JAESCHKE, HELENA: 'Reflections on lacquer', in: *Kew*, spring 1991, pp. 22–25. I am grateful to Naomi Rumball, Assistant Curator, Economic Botany Collections, Royal Botanic Gardens Kew, for providing a copy of Jaeschke's article.

9 Rein and Quin both identified the Japanese lacquer tree as *Rhus vernicifera*. The currently used and correct botanical name of the species is *Toxicodendron vernicifluum* (Stokes) F. Barkley; *Rhus vernicifera* D.C. and *Rhus verniciflua* Stokes are synonyms. VOGL, OTTO/QIN, MEIFANG AND MITCHELL, JOHN D.: 'Oriental Lacquers. 7. Botany and chemistry of Japanese lacquer and the beauty of the final art objects', in: *Cellulose Chemistry and Technology*, 1995, 29, pp. 273–286. I would like to thank Dr. Dennis Stevenson, Director of the Plant Research Laboratory, The New York Botanical Garden, for his help in clarifying these terms.

10 REIN 1889, p. 350. Dunand also refers to 'Sessimé' as a transparent lacquer and mentions that transparent lacquer is obtained from the tree-trunk.

11 The term 'Schuaye' is spelled in various ways in Dunand's notebook: 'Shuai', 'Schay', 'Shuay', 'Schuay' and 'Schuai'. The oil component of 'Schuaye' is most likely Perilla-oil, which Rein and Quin mention in connection with oil-containing lacquer. REIN 1889, p. 352. QUIN 1882, p. 8.

12 Dunand notes that 'Kekso' is used to fill joints and contains equal amounts of 'Sessimé' and rice starch mixed with hemp or cotton fibers. It is made of the same amount of 'Sessimé' and rice starch and employed for pasting cloth. 'Kiriko' is a mixture of 1/3 'Dzinoko' (powdered burnt clay), 2/3 'Tonoko' (finely ground clay) and water to which an amount of 1/4 'Sessimé' is added. Coarse 'Dzinoko' contains 'Sessimé', a little rice starch diluted with a lot of water and coarse 'Dzinoko' (powdered burnt clay) while fine 'Dzinoko' has the same composition, except using most likely a finer powdered burnt clay, which is not specifically mentioned. Dunand describes that 'Sabi' contains 'Tonoko' (finely ground clay) 'Sessimé', and a little water.

13 In his notebook Dunand mentions two stones by name: 'Arato', which according to Quin is a rough wet stone, and 'Nagato', which could refer to 'Nagura-to-ishi', the finest wet polishing stone. Quin 1882, p. 10. Three different charcoals are used and Dunand specifies that the end-grain direction of the charcoal pieces must be perpendicular to the polishing movement: 1. 'Honokizzimi', 2. 'Schirougazzimi' and 3. 'Loelozzimi'. Afterwards the lacquer is polished with powdered 'Loelozzimi', 'Tonoko' (finely ground clay) and 'Tsinoko' (powdered calcined deer antler) applied with oil and a cloth, cotton wool, or filter paper ('Yossimo Gami', also used for filtering lacquer). The best results are achieved by final polishing with the palm or finger, and women's fingers seem to be extremely suitable as Dunand noted: 'le doigt de femme est très bon pour bien finir.'

14 'Les laqueurs qui ne savent pas bien polir et dresser une laque avec leur charbon, sont dénommés "Chameaux", parce [sic] le chameau a 2 bosses, il est comme la laque mal dressée.' Another note from his booklet addresses the same concern: 'Les laques qui ne sont pas très bien polies sont appelées laques de paresseux.'

15 'Louiro – 1re qualité laque noire. Cette laque est faite avec la laque Sessimé – prendre de la limaille de fer – y mettre un peu de vinaigre – ensuite le mélanger dans la laque et passer sur le feu (avec le filtre).' Quin and Rein both mention, that in the preparation of black 'Ro-iro-urushi/Ro-urushi Haguro', a dye used by women to blacken their teeth, which is a solution formed by boiling iron filings in rice vinegar, is added to the lacquer. QUIN 1882, p. 7 and REIN 1889, pp. 352–353. Dunand mentions the use of 'Yossimo Gami' paper for filtering lacquer.

16 With regard to 'Schuaye', Dunand describes in one occasion the use of 'Honokizzimi' charcoal to smooth each of three layers of transparent 'Schuai' after drying for 2 hours; however, no final polishing is mentioned.

17 The temperature of the oven was noted as 100 °C for the first five hours, followed by 30 minutes at 150 °C and 10 minutes at 180 °C.

18 The lessons started on May 16 and continued until the end of June in 1912.

19 'Pour obtenir un laque réussi, vingt-deux opérations sont nécessaires. Et les matières prémières ne sont pas seulement d'un maniement difficile; leur nocivité ne me permet d'employer, à ce genre de travaux, qu'une main-d'oeuvre elle-même importée, si l'on peut dire; mes ouvriers chinois, japonais, annamites, manipulent impunément des produits qui font, sur l'ouvrier européen, effet de poison.' GAUTHIER ca. 1923.

20 At the 1921 Salon des Artistes Décorateurs in Paris Dunand exhibited for the first time a lacquer panel depicting fishing boats seen against a mountain landscape, which was based on a sketch by his friend, the painter Henry de Waroquier. MARCILHAC 1991, p. 35.

21 GIMBEL, RENÉ: *Diary of an art dealer*, New York, 1966, pp. 137–138. The diary was first published in French: GIMBEL, RENÉ: *Journal d'un collectionneur*, Paris, 1963, pp. 165–166.

22 The exhibition, entitled 'Jean Dunand: Master of Art Deco', took place from May 23 – October 25, 1998 and was organized by J. Stewart Johnson, Consultant for Design and Architecture and Jared Goss, Curatorial Assistant, Department of Modern Art, The Metropolitan Museum of Art.

23 A 1929 article in Vogue magazine, devoted to Crocker's luxurious apartment, praised its modern interior, which also included rooms designed by Jean-Michel Frank, Pierre Legrain and Mme Lipska. MILLER 1929.

24 In the above mentioned Vogue article the bedroom was described as follows: 'In the adjoining bedroom, Dunand has again contrasted his own love for movement and design with Frank's monotones. Here again, laque arrachée on the walls is worked into a modern design in tones of silver and grey with overtones of tan, giving the effect of a woodland. Over the head of the bed, a life-sized deer nibbles a miraculous green bough, and on an adjacent wall, his companion sips calmly from a spring. These deer are made of thin sheets of lead, inlaid with colours. The furniture, low and square, is of black and grey lacquer, with a note of white in the ivory knobs of the commode and the goatskin that covers the chairs. The curtains are of grey chamois in three shades.' MILLER 1929, p. 94. Photographs of the bedroom suite in the Dunand family archive show the following comment written on the back: 'Boiseries en laque arrachée argent, gazelle en plomb incrusté, meuble en laque chine gris et noir.'

25 Elemental analyses of cross sections of lacquer samples were carried out by Mark T. Wypyski, Associate Research Chemist, The Sherman Fairchild Center for Objects Conservation, The Metropolitan Museum of Art, using an energy-dispersive X-ray spectrometer (EDS) attached to a scanning electron microscope. EDS analysis of the black lacquer detected the presence of iron in the layer, indicating the use of 'Louero' lacquer. Fluorescence microscopy of cross sections from samples of the bedroom furniture showed a maximum of 8 ground layers, including cloth, applied to wood and plywood substrates. EDS analyses of the ground layers revealed large amounts of silicon, with lower quantities of magnesium, aluminum, sulfur, potassium, calcium, and iron, apparently a mixture of silica particles and clay. The bottom ground layers also contain bast fibers and wooden particles, the latter most likely in the form of saw dust. I would like to thank Mark T. Wypyski for performing all EDS analyses.

26 The metal filings and pigments were identified by EDS and X-ray diffraction analysis. Some silicon, phosphorus, sulfur, calcium and barium were also detected in the silver-gray lacquer, suggesting the presence of silica, barium sulfate and calcium phosphate particles, the latter possibly in the form of bone or ivory white.

27 The lacquer was analyzed by Prof. Dr. Tetsuo Miyakoshi, Department of Industrial Chemistry, Meiji University, using pyrolysis-gas chromatography/mass spectrometry. I am very grateful to Prof. Dr. Miyakoshi for conducting the analysis of four samples from the Dunand bedroom furniture. MIYAKOSHI, TETSUO: 'The analysis of urushi by pyrolysis-gas chromatography/mass spectrometry', in this publication. *Rhus succedanea* also grows in Taiwan, but because Indochina was a French colony at that time, it is more likely that Dunand imported his lacquer from there.

28 The panels are now in the collection of the Musée des Arts d'Afrique et d'Océanie in Paris, which is housed in the Palais Permanent des Colonies, where Dunand's panels were originally displayed. MARCILHAC 1991, pp. 119–120.

29 'Sur une laque d'or en feuilles sèche passer une couche de laque à la terre arrachée et tracer des décors dedans pendant qu'elle est fraiche. Après séchage passer légèrement en papier de verre fin.'

30 In addition to the two screens, which are now in the collection of the Metropolitan Museum, two double doors decorated with angels sounding horns and a small panel depicting St. Michael and the Dragon were also made by Soudbinine and Dunand for the music salon. Photographs of the original interior of the music room and both screens are published by Marcilhac. MARCILHAC 1991, p. 323, color plate 163.

31 The gilding was probably executed by a craftsman named Zuber, who was the specialist for gold lacquer in Dunand's workshop. EDS analysis of the red lacquer, identified vermilion as the red pigment, based on the presence of mercury and sulfur.

32 EDS analysis characterized the composition of the gold leaves as about 90 % gold, 7% silver and 3% copper by weight. Cross sections of the darker gilding viewed under a fluorescence microscope showed an orange fluorescence of the applied coating, which most likely indicates the use of shellac. It is known that Dunand used shellac, and in this case he might have chosen it because of its orange coloration.

33 The examination of cross sections from the blue green lacquer of the background showed a mixture of coarse blue, fine blue-green and yellow pigments. EDS analysis of the blue-green lacquer detected mainly chromium, aluminum, and cobalt, with traces of silicon, sulfur, calcium, and iron, most likely due to the use of cobalt blue, chromium oxide green and an organic yellow pigment.

34 For the fluorescence microscopy the following filter set was used: excitation filter 365 nm, chromatic beam splitter 395 nm and emission filter 397 nm.

35 Records of a sample board made in 1932 in Dunand's workshop describe the technique as follows: 'Sur une couche de laque noire coller des morceaux de laque à la terre rouge. – Morceaux obtenus en cassant une plaque de laque à la terre faite en passant une couche de cette laque sur du papier et en la faissant cuire au four. La laque à la terre rouge était obtenue avec de l'ocre rouge, de l'eau et moitié laque transparente, moité laque naturelle. Après séchage passer une couche de laque noire. Après séchage poncer et polir.'

36 CAMARD, FLORENCE: *Ruhlmann*, Paris, 1983. The dressing table with the black lacquer and abstract eggshell decoration as well as the matching chair are illustrated on p. 60 and 275.

37 In addition to signing his work, Dunand also stamped pieces produced in his workshop. The heated metal stamp left the following imprint on unexposed lacquered and wooden surfaces of the Crocker bedroom furniture: 'JEAN DUNAND – 72 RUE HALLE – PARIS – MADE IN FRANCE'.

38 In the 1927 October issue of the magazine Arts & Decoration a page was devoted to Jean Dunand's spectacular portraiture, showing four different portraits of famous French women. In Paris you must have a lacquer portrait, in: *Arts & Decoration,* October 1927, p. 134.

39 A-DAYOT, MAGDELEINE: 'Art et technique – une visite à Jean Dunand', in: *L'Art et les Artistes*, November 1936, pp. 57–62. MARCILHAC 1991, p. 172.

40 DUNAND, BERNARD: 'Jean Dunand', in: *Club français de la Médaille*, 1982, No. 77, p. 42–43 and 49.

41 GARNER, PHILIPPE: 'The lacquer work of Eileen Gray and Jean Dunand', in: *The Connoisseur*, May 1973, pp. 3–11. Dunand also participated in an exhibition of French decorative arts shown in Japan. MARCILHAC 1991, p. 72.

42 From 1925 on Bernard Dunand was Jean Dunand's closest collaborator. Thanks to his understanding and appreciation, as well as his own involvement as a lacquer artist, many utensils, materials, documents and sample boards from Jean Dunand's workshop are preserved. I had the honor to meet Bernard Dunand three weeks before he died at the age of ninety. The talk associated with this article was dedicated to Bernard Dunand. I am also most grateful to M. and Mme Christian Dougoud for their strong encouragement of my ongoing research about the lacquer techniques of Jean Dunand.

References

ADAM, PETER: *Eileen Gray – architect/designer*, New York, 1978

A-DAYOT, MAGDELEINE: 'Art et technique – une visite à Jean Dunand', in: *L'Art et les Artistes*, November 1936, pp. 57–62

CAMARD, FLORENCE: *Ruhlmann*, Paris 1983

DUNAND, BERNARD: 'Jean Dunand', in: *Club français de la Médaille*, 1982, No. 77, pp. 42–43, 49

GARNER, PHILIPPE: 'The lacquer work of Eileen Gray and Jean Dunand', in: *The Connoisseur*, May 1973, pp. 3–11

GAUTHIER, MAXIMILIEN: 'Vingt minutes avec M. Jean Dunand', in: *La Renaissance politique, littéraire, artistique*, ca. 1923

GIMBEL, RENÉ: *Diary of an art dealer*, New York 1966 (The diary was first published in French: GIMBEL, RENÉ: *Journal d'un collectionneur*, Paris 1963)

JAESCHKE, HELENA: 'Reflections on lacquer', in: *Kew*, spring 1991, pp. 22–25

LORAC-GERBAUD, ANDRÉE: *L'art du laque*, Paris, 1973

LORAC-GERBAUD, ANDRÉE: *Les secrets du laque*, Paris, 1996

MARCILHAC, FÉLIX: *Jean Dunand – his life and works*, New York 1991 (Originally written in French: MARCILHAC, FÉLIX: *Jean Dunand – vie et oeuvre*, Paris, 1991)

MILLER, MARY ASHE.: 'A twentieth century apartment', in: *Vogue*, August 3, 1929, pp. 30–35, 94

MIYAKOSHI, TETSUO: 'The analysis of urushi by pyrolysis-gas chromatography and mass spectrometry' in this publication, pp. 107–120

QUIN, JOHN J.: *Report by her Majesty's acting consul at Hakodate on the lacquer industry of Japan*, London, 1882

QUIN, JOHN J.: *Urushi – The technology of Japanese lacquer*, reprint of the 1896 edition, Portland/Oregon, 1995

REIN, JOHANNES JUSTUS: *Japan nach Reisen und Studien im Auftrage der königlich preussischen Regierung dargestellt. Land- und Forstwirtschaft, Industrie und Handel*, 2nd Volume, Leipzig, 1886 (Published in English as: REIN, JOHANNES JUSTUS: *The industries of Japan. Together with an account of its agriculture, forestry, arts, and commerce, from travels and researches undertaken at the cost of the Prussian government*, New York/London, 1889)

VOGL, OTTO/QIN, MEIFANG AND MITCHELL, JOHN D.: 'Oriental Lacquers. 7. Botany and chemistry of Japanese lacquer and the beauty of the final art objects', in: *Cellulose Chemistry and Technology*, 1995, 29, pp. 273–286

Photo Credits

Figs. 2, 3, 6–8, 12: Author
Fig. 4: Thérèse Bonney
Figs. 5, 10, 11, 13: The Metropolitan Museum of Art, New York
Fig. 9: Réunion des Musées Nationaux, Agence photographique, Paris
Figs. 1, 14: Dunand family archive
Colour plate XXIII.1–4: Author; 5: The Metropolitan Museum of Art, New York

Fig. 14. Jean Dunand demonstrating with a blow torch the fire resistance of a lacquered table, cast with a newly developed material, 1935

Wolfgang Kippes

Klimamessungen im Vieux Laque-Zimmer im Schloss Schönbrunn

Schloss Schönbrunn, seit 1996 in die Liste des Weltkulturerbes der UNESCO aufgenommen, beherbergt einige der wichtigsten Artefakte aus Österreichs reichem kulturellen Erbe. Eines davon ist das Vieux Laque-Zimmer, bestehend aus Wandvertäfelungen mit originalen chinesischen Lacktafeln (Abb. 1). Soweit bislang bekannt, stammen diese Lacktafeln aus dem Ende des 17. Jahrhunderts aus der kaiserlichen Manufaktur in Peking. Sie wurden Mitte des 18. Jahrhunderts im Auftrag der Kaiserin Maria Theresia am heutigen Standort montiert. Im Original handelte es sich um beidseitig lackierte Lackparavents, die gespalten wurden, um sowohl die Vorder- als auch Rückseite präsentieren zu können. Dabei wurden die dünnen Lacktafeln auf heimische Holztafeln montiert, die Rückseite allerdings blieb offenporig.

Die Schadensbilder, Ergebnisse aus der Quellenforschung, Nutzungsgeschichte und die Erkenntnisse einer Proberestaurierung wurden in einer Publikation zusammengefasst und 1995 im Rahmen der Wissenschaftlichen Reihe Schönbrunn veröffentlicht.[1]

Die raumhohen Lacktafeln (6 m Länge) zeigen mehr und mehr Schäden in Form von Rissbildungen der Lackoberfläche und schollenartige Ablösungen, vor allem an der westlichen inneren Ecke in der Nähe eines inaktiven, alten Warmluftauslasses. Ziel der Untersuchungen zum Raumklima war es, durch ein systematisches Messdatenerfassungsprogramm mögliche Kausalzusammenhänge zwischen Innenklima, Außenklima, Besucherstrom und Schadensbildern zu ergründen.

Die Klimamessungen im Vieux Laque-Zimmer: Überblick über die Messpunkte Querschnittsmessung

Um die vielen offenen Fragen beantworten zu können, wurde eine aufwendige Messmethode entwickelt, die wir „Querschnittsmessung" nannten (Abb. 2).[2] Dafür wurden die Außentemperatur und Außenfeuchte sowie die Windgeschwindigkeit an der Fassade, weiters die Temperatur in der Mitte der Außenmauer, Temperatur und rF im Raum an vielen Punkten gemessen. Dazu gehören Messpunkte an der Oberfläche der Lacktafeln an der Vorder- und Rückseite, im Luftraum zwischen Lacktafeln und der Mauer sowie an der Oberfläche der Mauern selbst. Die Messpunkte waren horizontal und vertikal systematisch gestaffelt, um ein Querschnittsprofil für T und rF erstellen zu können.

Ferner wurden CO_2-Fühler im Raum und in einem Vergleichsraum (Rösselzimmer), zu dem die Besucher keinen Zutritt haben, gesetzt. Dank genauer stündlicher Besucherstatistiken können so die Wirkungen der Besucher auf das Raumklima genau beobachtet werden. Letztlich wurde ein Luftgeschwindigkeitsfühler im Durchgang zum Vieux Laque-Zimmer gesetzt, um mögliche Luftströmungen im Raum zu erfassen und daraus Luftwechselzahlen nachvollziehen zu können.

Diese Untersuchungen waren Teil einer umfassenderen Klimauntersuchung in den Räumen von Schönbrunn, bei der eine laufende Beobachtung der Raumtemperaturen und Raumfeuchte sowie ein permanenter Vergleich mit den Bedingungen des Außenklimas erfolgte. Im Zuge eines internationalen EUROCARE Forschungsprogramms, bei dem Partner aus Schweden, England, Slowenien, Deutschland und Österreich kooperierten, konnten wichtige Vergleichsdaten und Erkenntnisse gewonnen werden.[3]

Die Ergebnisse der Untersuchungen

1. „Hypothese der Wohlmeinenden"

Seit mehreren Jahrzehnten wird von jenen, die es gut mit dem Schloss und seiner Ausstattung meinen, die Hypothese vertreten, der massenhafte Strom der Besucher zerstöre durch seine Wirkungen auf das Raumklima die dort gezeigten Artefakte. Ich nenne daher diese Annahme die „Hypothese der Wohlmeinenden".

Natürlich treten inakzeptabel große Schwankungen des Raumklimas, gemessen an der Raumtemperatur und Raumfeuchte auf. Aber als Schlussfolgerung aus allen bisherigen Untersuchungen kann formuliert werden, dass unter den gegebenen messtechnischen und bauphysikalischen Bedingungen in den Prunkräumen des Schlosses Schönbrunn kein nennenswerter Zusammenhang zwischen dem Besucherbetrieb und den Schwankungen des Raumklimas besteht.

Eine Heizung des Schlosses in der Winterperiode erfolgt nicht, jedoch müssen die Besucher als Energiequelle angesehen werden. Die damit ausgelöste Erwärmung – daneben ist noch die elektrische Beleuchtung als Wärmequelle zu berücksichtigen – würde theoretisch eine Absenkung der Raumfeuchte auslösen, die aber durch die Feuchteabgabe der Besucher überkompensiert wird.

Wesentlich mehr Beachtung ist den Wirkungen des Außenklimas auf das Raumklima zu schenken, das in geschlossenen Räumen gedämpft und leicht zeitverzögert einwirkt, hingegen in Prunkräumen mit intensivem Publikumsbetrieb über das Lüftungsverhalten unmittelbar und radikal Wirkung zeigen kann.

Daran gemessen haben die Besucher nur untergeordnete, nachrangige Bedeutung für das Raumklima. Sie haben aber eine indirekte Wirkung auf das Raumklima, weil sie das Lüftungsverhalten auslösen.

Im Rahmen der Messkampagne ließ sich auch der Nachweis erbringen, dass sich im Zwischenraum zwischen den Lacktafeln und der Wand ein Mikroklima einstellt, das deutlich unterschiedlich zum Raumklima ist. Diese Differenzen sind eine der Ursachen für Verformungen an den Lacktafeln und damit für die Schäden.

Wie kann die Wirkung der Besucher, ich möchte sie „Kontamination" nennen, erfasst werden? Es wäre naiv zu behaupten, die Besucher hätten keinerlei Einfluss auf das Raumklima. Allerdings drückt sich dieses nicht in den üblicherweise gemessenen Standardparametern des Raumklimas, also der Temperatur

Abb. 1. Wien, Schloss Schönbrunn, Vieux Lacque-Zimmer, chinesische Lacktafel

und der Raumfeuchte aus, sondern in Form der Kontamination. Diese wiederum ist Ursache für die, in der Folge noch eingehend zu behandelnden, häufigen Lüftungsmaßnahmen. Wenn zwecks Lüftung der Räume ein Fenster geöffnet wird, erfolgt ein, in der Fachsprache mit „Stoßlüftung“ bezeichneter Vorgang, der einen raschen Zustrom frischer Außenluft in den Raum ermöglichen soll. Dabei wird i. Allg. nicht Rücksicht darauf genommen, welche Außenklimabedingungen gerade vorliegen bzw. wie das Außenklima und Raumklima zueinander in Relation stehen.

Idealtypisches Beispiel aus unserer alltäglichen Praxis wäre ein heißer Sommertag, wenn gleichzeitig besonders viele Besucher im Schloss sind. Nehmen wir z. B. einen üblichen Tag im August: Es ist drückend heiß und schwül. Von den Aufsichten wird das Raumklima als unerträglich empfunden. Wie häufig im August in Wien zieht ein Gewitter auf und plötzlich regnet es in Strömen. Gerade dann wird am liebsten gelüftet, weil endlich die lang ersehnte Abkühlung erfolgt und man wieder frei durchatmen kann. Die Außenfeuchte hat 100 % rF erreicht, innen bestand noch knapp vor dem Lüftungsvorgang eine Raumfeuchte um 50 % rF. Im Falle dieses Stoßlüftungsvorgangs wird die Raumfeuchte innerhalb weniger Minuten auf ca. 70 % hinaufschnellen.

Bevor wir uns aber mit diesem physikalischen Phänomen beschäftigen, möchte ich noch kurz die Frage der Kontamination behandeln. Wie wir am Beispiel des Augusttages gesehen haben, sind die Besucher nicht ursächlich an den Schwankungen der Raumfeuchte beteiligt, sondern nur indirekt Auslöser des Stoßlüftungsvorgangs, weil die im Raum bestehende Luft als „verbraucht“, somit kontaminiert empfunden wird.

Es gibt eine ganze Reihe von Indikatoren für verbrauchte Luft. Der am leichtesten zu messende Parameter, der gleichzeitig einen besonders sensiblen Indikator für die Wirkung der Menschen darstellt, ist CO_2. Die Untersuchungen von CO_2 in der Raumluft sind nicht neu, sie gehen auf Max von Pettenkofer zurück. Er war Professor für Hygiene in München und hat bereits 1859 erstmals den Grenzwert von 1000 ppm CO_2 in einem Kubikmeter Raumluft als gesundheitlich bedenklich definiert. Noch heute gilt dieser Grenzwert in allen Fragen der Raumluftqualität weltweit, allerdings ist sich niemand der Quelle bewusst.

Als Beispiel für die Wirkung der Besucher auf den CO_2-Gehalt in der Raumluft wurde willkürlich der 31.10.1997 herausgegriffen (Abb. 3, 4). In der Darstellung ist erkennbar, dass pünktlich mit Beginn des Besucherbetriebs um 9.00 Uhr morgens der CO_2-Wert von den in Wien üblichen Außenbedingungen um 400 ppm hinaufschnellt, tagsüber Spitzen von mehr als 1000 ppm erreicht und ab 17.30 Uhr in einer typischen exponentiellen Kurve wieder abfällt. Überblendet man diese Kurve mit den Aufzeichnungen der Besucherströme, fällt der Zusammenhang zwischen Besuchern und dem CO_2-Gehalt unmittelbar auf. Die Mittagsspitze der Besucher fällt nicht ganz so stark ins Gewicht wie am Nachmittag, weil gelüftet wurde. Für unsere Untersuchungen über das Raumklima in Schönbrunn ist der Parameter von besonderer Bedeutung, weil mit diesem Parameter der tägliche Luftwechsel berechnet werden kann und weil damit in Hinkunft die mechanische Frischluftversorgung gesteuert wird.

2. Was ist die Ursache für die hohen Raumklimaschwankungen?

Wie wir am Beispiel des Augusttages zuvor gesehen haben, ist der Stoßlüftungsvorgang ein Hinweis auf die möglichen Ursachen für die Raumklimaschwankungen. Physikalisch gesprochen handelt es sich um das Phänomen der „natürlichen Lüftung“. Diese tritt nicht nur im Falle der Stoßlüftung auf, sondern ist ein alltäglicher, für unser Wohlbefinden bzw. für die Raumluftqualität unverzichtbarer Prozess des Austausches von verbrauchter Raumluft mit frischer Außenluft.

Jedes Fenster gewährleistet auch in geschlossenem Zustand permanent einen bestimmten Luftwechsel. Wird dieser Luftvolumenstrom mathematisch auf das Raumvolumen bezogen, spricht man von der Luftwechselzahl (LWZ). Eine LWZ von 1 pro Stunde würde daher bedeuten, dass 1 mal pro Stunde das Raumvolumen an Luft durch Frischluft ersetzt wurde.

Mit welchen LWZ kann nun in historischen Objekten wie Schönbrunn gerechnet werden? Dazu gibt es wiederum eine Reihe von Messmethoden, z. B. über Spurengase. Wir messen die Strömungsgeschwindigkeit der Luft im Eingang zum Vieux Laque-Zimmer und können damit aus dem gegebenen Querschnitt der Türe und der horizontalen Geschwindigkeit der Luft in dieser Türe einen Volumenstrom pro Stunde berechnen. Bezieht man dieses berechnete Volumen auf das Raumvolumen, ergibt sich in etwa die Luftwechselzahl.[4] Dies ist im vorliegenden Beispiel für den Zeitraum vom 17.8.1996 bis 3.9.1996 erfolgt (Abb. 5).

Spitzengeschwindigkeiten der Luft im Bereich von ca. 1,2 m/sec wurden gemessen. Für den gesamten dargestellten Zeitraum ergibt die Berechnung des Luftvolumenstroms eine permanente LWZ von ca. 5,4 pro Stunde. Wählt man das maximale Stundenmittel der Strömungsgeschwindigkeit, also den Extremfall in dieser Kurve, wo Fenster geöffnet waren und die Spitzengeschwindigkeiten auftraten, kann die maximale LWZ mit 14,7 pro Stunde errechnet werden. Das bedeutet also, dass über den beobachteten Zeitraum permanent 5,4 mal pro Stunde die Raumluft gegen Außenluft getauscht wurde und dass im extremen Stoßlüftungsfall die Raumluft ca. 15 mal pro Stunde getauscht wurde. Der Extremfall kann auch anders ausgedrückt werden: Eine LWZ von 15 pro Stunde bedeutet, dass alle 4 Minuten das Raumvolumen an Luft gewechselt wurde. In diesem Fall können die Besucher unmöglich Auswirkungen auf die Temperatur oder Feuchte im Raum haben!

Diese Zahlen bedeuten allerdings noch nicht sehr viel. Die Frage ist nämlich, welche LWZ nötig ist, um für die Besucher ein akzeptables Raumklima zu schaffen. Bewusst wird vorerst nicht auf konservatorische Aspekte des Luftwechsels eingegangen.

In dem Standardwerk für Techniker zur Planung von Lüftungsanlagen, dem „Recknagel“[5], werden Erfahrungszahlen für den stündlichen Luftwechsel bei verschiedenen Raumarten genannt: So wird z. B. für Bibliotheken eine LWZ von 2–5 pro Stunde, für Büroräume von 3–6 pro Stunde, für Toiletten von 4–6 pro Stunde und für Hörsäle von 8–10 pro Stunde empfohlen.

Von größerem Interesse ist es, den Empfehlungen des „Recknagel“ für die Lüftungsplanung von Museen zu folgen. Demnach wäre ein Luftvolumenstrom von $20m^3$ pro Stunde pro Besucher anzustreben, „...und unter besonderen Umständen ist es durchaus zu verantworten, auch 15 oder sogar $10m^3/h$ je Person der Berechnung zugrundezulegen“.[6] In der 68. Auflage dieses Standardwerks der Haustechnikplanung wird nur mehr eine Frischluftmenge von 12–15 m^3/h und Person empfohlen.[7]

Wenn man nun den Tag mit der maximalen Besucherzahl für eine Vergleichsrechnung heranzieht, kann der zuvor gefundene Luftwechsel besser eingeschätzt werden. Wir wissen aus unseren statistischen Daten und aus der durchschnittlichen Verweildauer der Besucher im Raum, dass am maximal belasteten Tag mit einer permanent anwesenden Besucherzahl von 25 zu

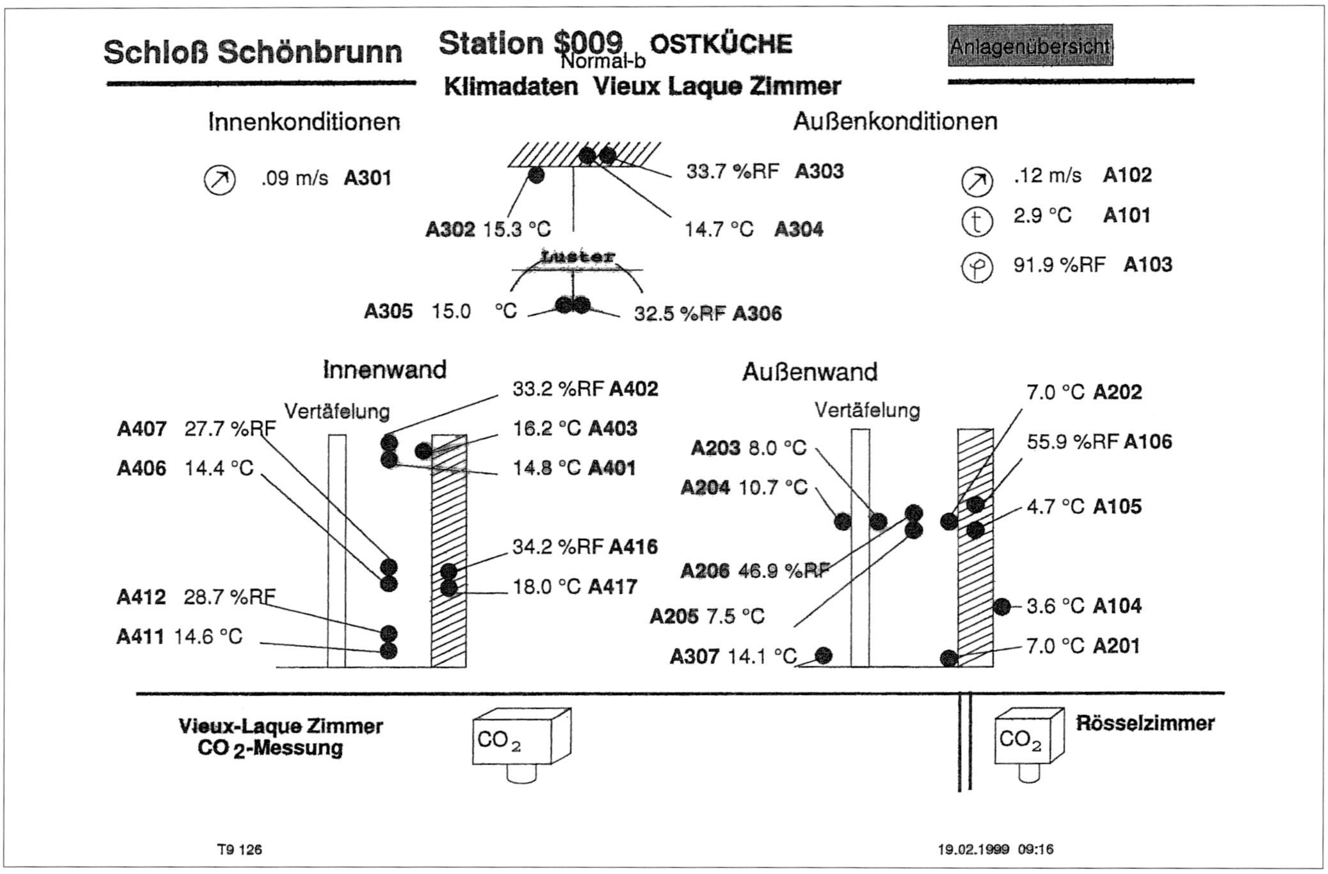

Abb. 2. Das Messprogramm im Vieux Laque-Zimmer

Abb. 3. CO_2-Messungen im Vieux Laque-Zimmer

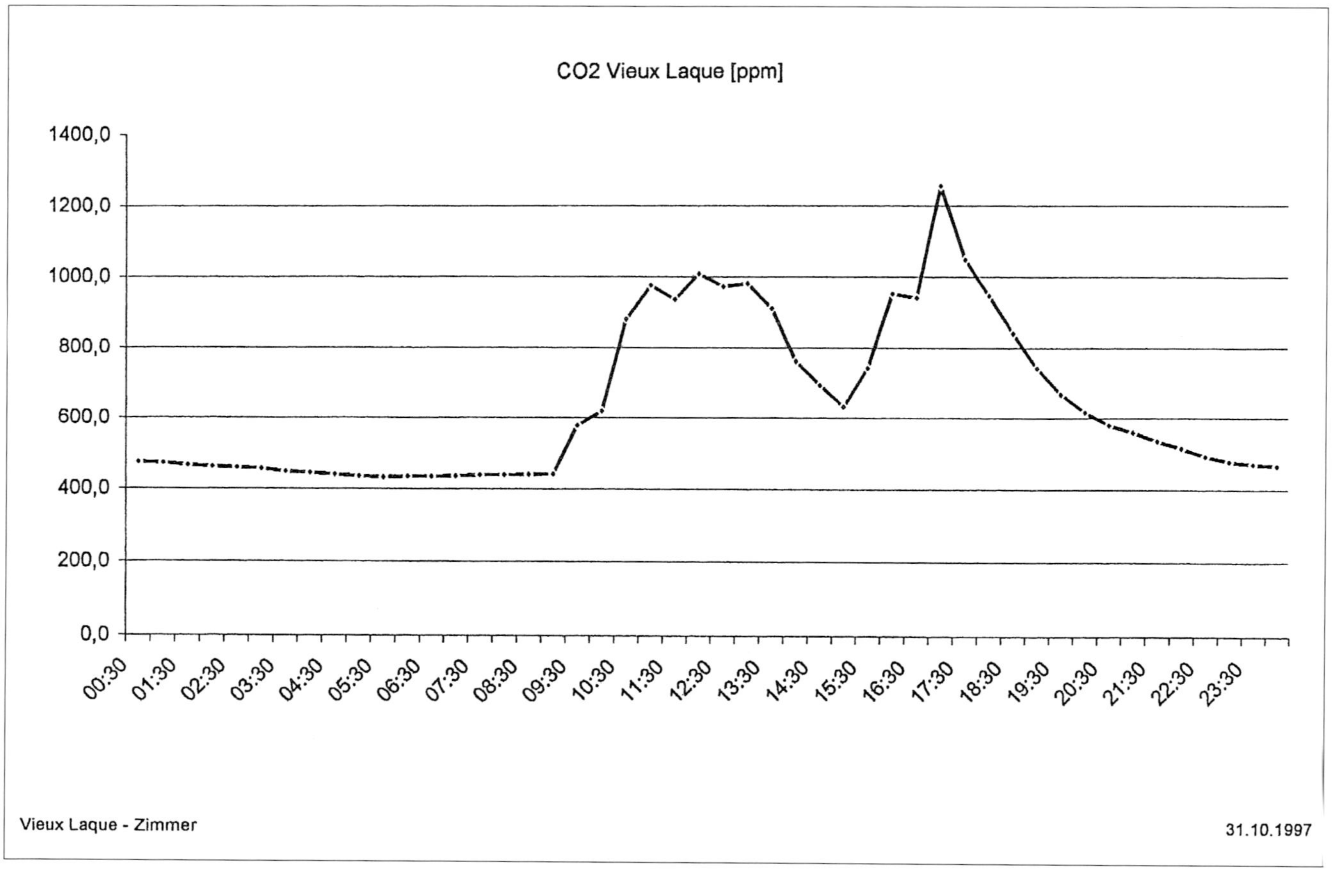

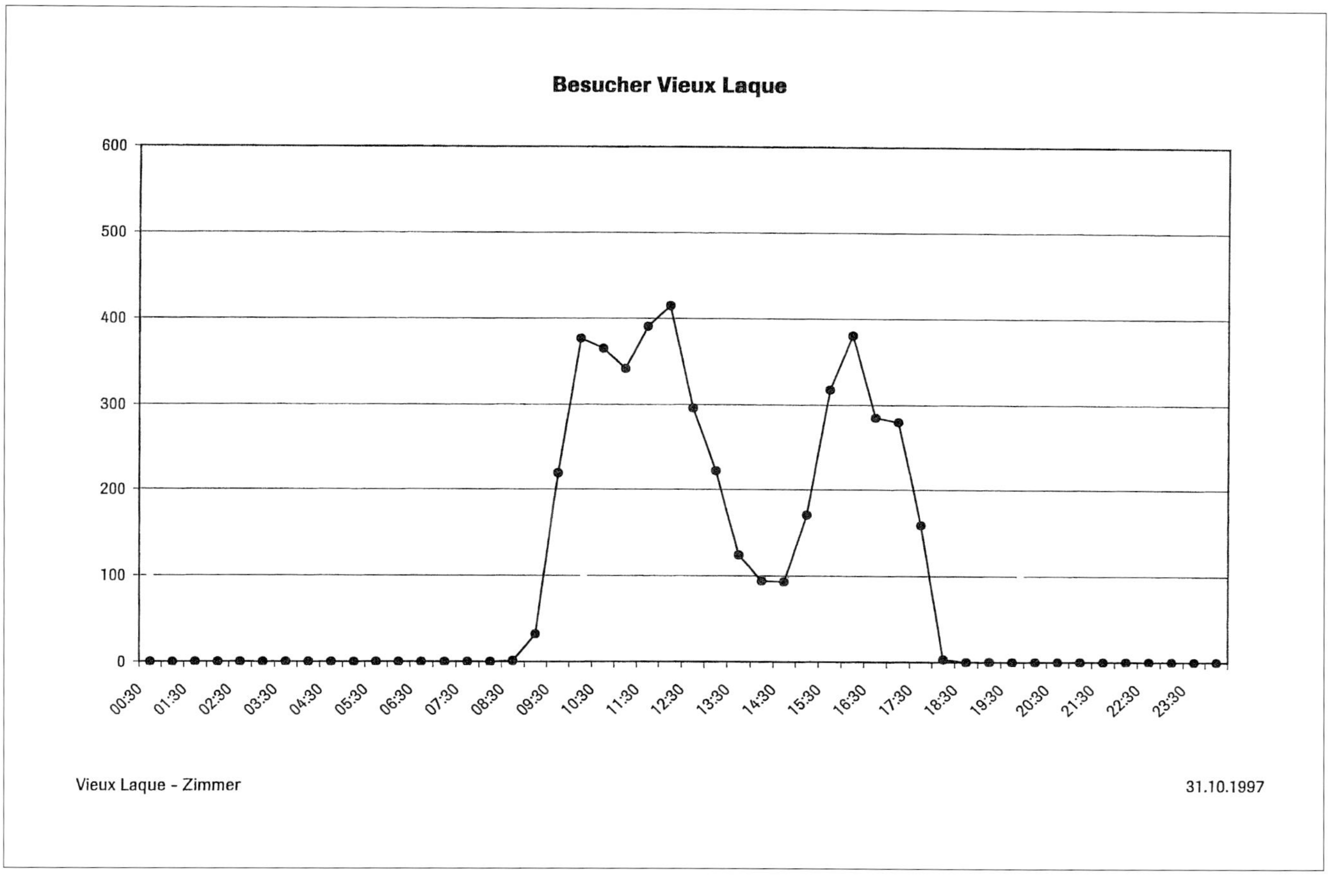

Abb. 4. Besucherziffern im Vieux Laque-Zimmer

Abb. 5. Strömungsgeschwindigkeit der Luft im Vieux Laque-Zimmer (in m/sec)
Zeitraum 17.8.1996 bis 3.9.1996

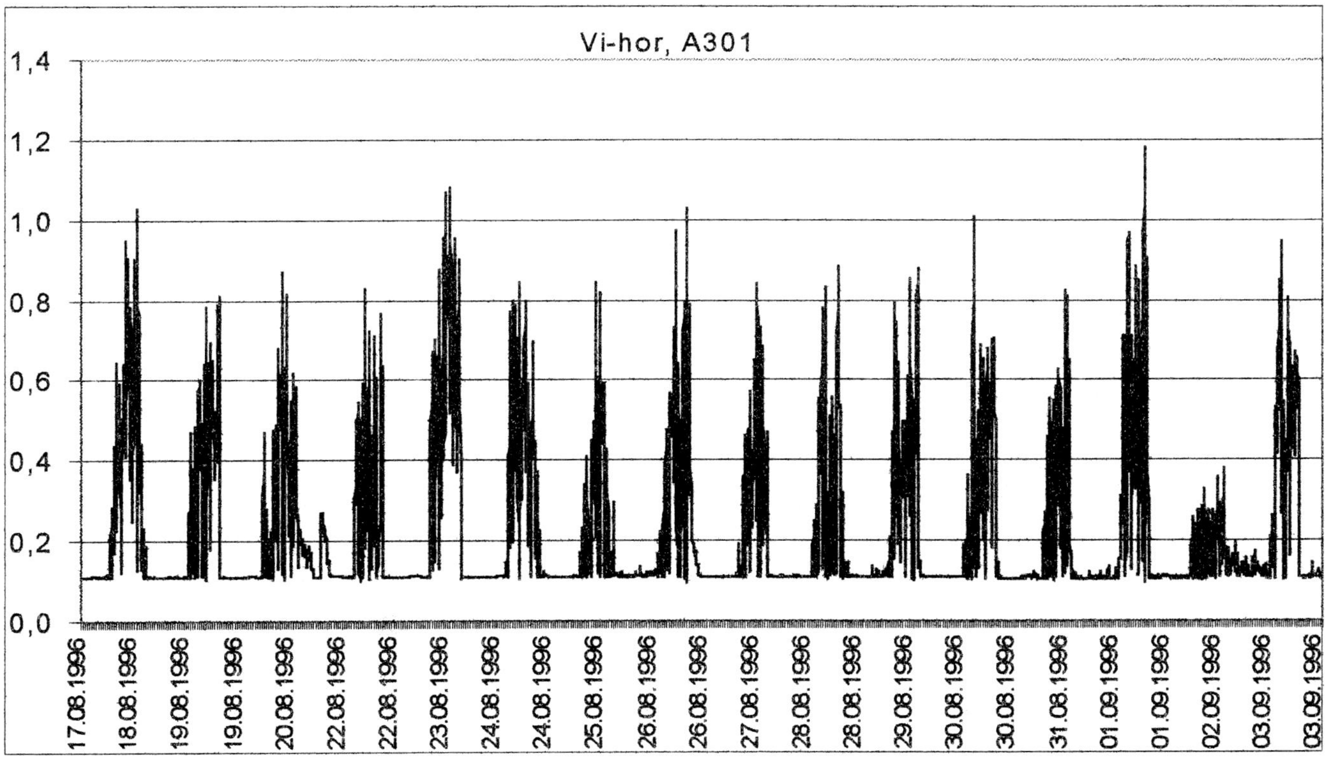

kalkulieren ist.[8] Nimmt man nun einen Frischluftbedarf von 15 m^3/h pro Besucher an, ergibt sich die erforderliche stündliche Frischluftzufuhr von:

$$V = 25 \times 15\ (m^3/h) = 375\ (m^3/h)$$

Bei einem Raumvolumen von 381 m^3 des Vieux Laque-Zimmers entspricht dies einer LWZ von ca. 1 pro Stunde. Wie wir zuvor gesehen haben, sind die berechneten Luftwechselzahlen wesentlich höher. Aus den Spurengasmessungen wissen wir, dass die geschlossenen Kastenfenster im Schloss bei durchschnittlichen Windverhältnissen in Wien einen einfachen Luftwechsel pro Stunde zulassen. Diesen Prinzipien zufolge sollte somit in den Schauräumen des Schlosses Schönbrunn überhaupt keine Lüftung notwendig sein, um die für Besucher erforderliche Raumluftqualität sicherzustellen.

Allerdings sind die treibenden Kräfte für die natürliche Lüftung durch die Undichtheiten der Bauhülle der Wind sowie die Temperaturdifferenz zwischen Innen und Außen. Da wir das Außenklima nicht steuern können, kann auch der natürliche Luftwechsel nicht den jeweiligen betrieblichen Erfordernissen angepasst werden.

Wie wird dieses klimatechnische Problem in Zukunft gelöst? Schritt 1 muss sein, unkontrollierte Luftvolumenströme bzw. Infiltrationen zu erfassen und kontrollierbar zu machen, d. h. den Luftwechsel zu beherrschen. Schritt 2 wird sodann sein, diesen Luftwechsel im Winter und Sommer den aktuellen Anforderungen an Frischluftzufuhr anzupassen. Dies kann, um unabhängig von den gerade herrschenden Außenklimabedingungen zu sein, nur durch eine mechanisch gestützte Lüftung erreicht werden.

Mechanische gestützte Lüftung bedeutet im Falle Schönbrunn die Ausnutzung bestehender Kamine, um den Aufwand an voluminösen Lüftungsleitungen so gering wie möglich zu halten. Lüftungsleitungen in das historische Raumambiente einzubauen hieße, das zu zerstören, was zu erhalten ist, nämlich die Authentizität der Raumerscheinung. Für die Umsetzung dieses technischen Problems greifen wir wieder auf Erfahrungen aus dem 19. Jahrhundert zurück. Es gibt eine Reihe von Beispielen, aus denen geschlossen werden kann, dass man damals schon für die Heizung und Lüftung von großen Bauwerken mit einer LWZ von 1 pro Stunde gerechnet hat und den dafür notwendigen Leitungsbau bereits in die Bausubstanz integriert hat.[9]

Die Frischluft wird nach uraltem Brauch extern angesaugt und unter dem Fundamentniveau in Technikräume im Keller eingebracht und dort gefiltert. Dazu haben wir einen mehr als 200 m langen, gemauerten Schacht im Park reaktiviert, der vermutlich aus dem 19. Jahrhundert stammt, dessen Nutzung allerdings bislang ungeklärt ist.[10] Diesen langen Zulauf der Luft nutzen wir als Energiebrunnen, d. h. es ist zu erwarten, dass sich sowohl im Sommer wie im Winter bereits eine vorkonditionierte Luft, also eine weitgehend hinsichtlich Temperatur und Feuchte gleichmäßige Zuluft ergeben wird.

Mit geringem Überdruck wird die gefilterte Frischluft in das Objekt eingebracht, wofür teilweise ein Quellluftsystem im Foyerbereich, teilweise historische Warmluftkanäle genutzt werden. Um die gewünschte Strömungsrichtung der Luft von der Ansaugung zu den Prunkräumen sicherzustellen, muss in den Prunkräumen ein Unterdruck aufgebaut werden. Dazu erfolgt eine Absaugung der Raumluft durch die historischen Kamine über steuerbare Ventilatoren am Kaminkopf. Gleichzeitig werden die Kastenfenster in klassischer, handwerklicher Art abgedichtet, um Fehlluft und damit den Staubeintrag zu reduzieren. Die Steuerung des Frischluftanteils erfolgt über die Steuerung des Luftvolumenstroms, der durch die Kamine abgesaugt wird, also über das Ausmaß des Unterdrucks. Als Steuerungsparameter dient die Messung von CO_2, mit dem eine maximale LWZ von 1,5 pro Stunde geregelt wird.

3. Schlussfolgerungen für die Konservierung des Vieux Laque-Zimmers

Unter der Voraussetzung, dass das bislang nur teilweise fertiggestellte neue Raumklimakonzept das erfüllt, was wir uns davon versprechen, ist nach Aussage der betreuenden Restauratoren keine unmittelbare Gefahr für die Lacktafeln gegeben. Wir haben für die laufende Beobachtung des konservatorischen Zustands und für die Entwicklung von Konservierungsmaßnahmen ein Team zusammengestellt, in dem Mag. Silvia Miklin-Kniefacz für Lackprobleme und Mag. Stefan Kainz für die Holzfrage verantwortlich zeichnen. Ich zitiere aus dem aktuellsten Gutachten:[11]

„Aus dem oben Gesagten ergibt sich für uns der Schluss, dass eine Demontage der Tafeln zu riskant, eine Beschichtung der Rückseite zudem nicht erforderlich ist und eine Festigung der aufstehenden Lackschollen in situ erfolgen sollte. (...) Weiterhin ist für ein stabiles Klima und möglichst geringe Lichteinwirkung Sorge zu tragen.

In der nächsten Restaurierphase sollten alle in den Schadensplänen vermerkten aufstehenden Schollen (insgesamt ca. 100 Stellen) gefestigt werden. Dazu werden spezielle Zwingenkonstruktionen hergestellt, die nach Abnahme der goldgeschnitzten Zierleisten im darunter verborgenen Falz befestigt werden können. (...)

Für die Oberfläche ergibt sich für uns daher: Reinigung der Oberfläche trocken oder mit Testbenzin, keine Abnahme der Überfirnissung und Übermalungen. Es sollte auch keine neuerliche „Auffrischung" der Oberfläche erfolgen. (...)

Danach sollte in einem Rhythmus von 4 oder 5 Jahren eine Kontrolle und evtl. Nachfestigung der Lackschollen und der Golddekorschollen sowie die neuerliche Reinigung vorgenommen werden."

Plakativ formuliert bedeutet dies für uns: „Do not touch, but watch."

Anmerkungen

1 SILVIA MIKLIN-KNIEFACZ (Hrsg.): *Zur Restaurierung der Vieux Laque-Tafeln in Schönbrunn: Grundlagen und Vorarbeiten*, Wissenschaftliche Reihe Schönbrunn, Band 1, Wien 1995.
2 Vgl. JOCHEN KÄFERHAUS: *Querschnittsmessung im Vieux Laque-Zimmer in Schloss Schönbrunn als mögliches Analyseinstrument zur Klärung der Schäden an den Vieux Laque-Tafeln*; unveröffentlichter Bericht im Rahmen des Projekts EU-1383 PREVENT, Wien 1998.
3 EUROCARE EU-1383 PREVENT: Preventive Conservation. Innerhalb eines dreijährigen Forschungszeitraums sind bislang von den Partnern 20 Einzelberichte vorgelegt worden.
4 Die grob vereinfachende Erfassung des Luftwechsels wird durch die Ergebnisse der Spurengasmessungen sowie über die Berechnung des CO_2-Abbaus der Größe nach bestätigt.
5 HERMANN RECKNAGEL/EBERHARD SPRENGER/ERNST-RUDOLF SCHRAMEK: *Taschenbuch für Heizung+Klimatechnik 1997/98*, München/Wien 1997/98, S. 520 ff. sowie in der 67. Auflage 1994/95, S. 1361ff.
6 Ebd., 67. Auflage, S. 1360.
7 Ebd., 68. Auflage, S. 1525.
8 Die durchschnittliche Verweildauer beträgt 3 Minuten, die Maximalzahl an Besuchern pro Tag ca. 5000.
9 Vgl. JOCHEN KÄFERHAUS: *Reaktivierung der natürlichen Lüftung im Corps de Logis in der Wiener Hofburg*; unveröffentlichtes Gutachten, Wien 1997.
10 Der Schacht wurde aus Ziegeln errichtet und hat ein flaches Gewölbe. Die unterschiedlichen Querschnitte und Verzweigungen lassen vermuten, dass es sich um eine Vorrichtung zur Entwässerung handelte.
11 SILVIA MIKLIN-KNIEFACZ/STEFAN KAINZ: *Gutachten zum Konservierungskonzept im Vieux Laque-Zimmer in Schönbrunn*; unveröffentlicht, Wien 1999.

Abbildungsnachweis

Abb. 1: Schloss Schönbrunn Kultur- u. Betriebsges.m.b.H.: Alexander Koller, Hg. 115.015
Abb. 2–5: Verfasser

Summary

Ancient Chinese lacquerwork in Schloss Schönbrunn needs sensible care. In order to learn more about the reasons of deterioration detailed indoor climate monitoring was performed. In addition to the standard parameters describing the indoor climate (temperature/T, relative humidity/rH) monitoring was extended to air flow and CO_2 measurements indoors, as well as T, rH and air flow measurements outdoors.

The results of the measurement campaign are striking: According to the accumulated data there is no direct relationship between the number of visitors and indoor climate fluctuations. But there is an enormous impact of the outdoor to the indoor climate via natural ventilation, especially when windows are opened to improve indoor air quality (appr. 15 air changes per hour). The CO_2 measurements give detailed information about everyday air changes.

To improve the indoor climate stability and to provide sufficient air supply for the visitors an air change of 1 per hour has to be achieved. A new mechanical ventilation system avoiding air ducts was introduced.

Dießen, ehem. Stiftskirche Mariä Himmelfahrt, Hochaltar

Michael Kühlenthal

Zum Problem der Erhaltung und Restaurierung von Lacken in der Denkmalpflege

In Europa ist man sich lange Zeit nicht bewusst gewesen, dass ein wichtiger Teil unseres kulturellen Erbes durch Oberflächenbeschichtung mit Lacken in ganz wesentlichem Maße bestimmt gewesen ist. Das Finish, die Differenzierung von Glanzgraden, war wesentlicher Ausdrucksträger ganzer Kunstgattungen namentlich im Barock und Rokoko. Dazu gehörten die gesamten Kirchenausstattungen (Farbtafel XXIV) mit ihren farbig gefassten, furnierten oder holzsichtigen Oberflächen wie Altarretabel, Orgelprospekte, Kanzeln, Beichtstühle, Brüstungs- und Kommuniongitter, Leuchter, Chor- und Laiengestühle etc. genauso wie die wertvollen Ausstattungen unserer Schlösser mit den zahlreichen aus China und Japan importierten Lackmöbeln, deren europäischen Imitationen und den Lackkabinetten, die sich viele Schlossherren im Barock und Rokoko einrichten ließen. So wie das schon lange vor der Erfindung Böttgers aus China importierte Porzellan im Englischen als „China" bezeichnet wird, sind in Europa Lackarbeiten so sehr mit der Vorstellung von Japan verbunden worden, dass die Veredelung von Oberflächen durch Lacke als „Japanning" bezeichnet wurde.

Die künstlerische und kulturhistorische Bedeutung dieser heute meist verlorenen Oberflächengestaltungen (Farbtafel XXV.1) geht aus Texten des 18. Jahrhunderts recht eindrucksvoll hervor. In der Zedler'schen Enzyklopädie von 1737 z. B. heißt es: „Lackiren heisset, die hoelzernen Gefaesse und Mobilien, als Tische, Stuehle, Gueridons, Schreib-Contoirs, Schraenke, Schuesseln, Schachteln, der Gestallt mit Farben kuenstlich bemahlen, und alsdenn mit einem sauberen Firniß ueberziehen, daß man es fuer Marmor oder Ostindische Arbeit, oder als wenn es mit Glas ueberzogen waere, ansehen sollte."[1] Watin charakterisiert 1774 Art und Zweck von Firnissen wie folgt:
„ ... er dient die Gegenstaende zu heben, die Lebhaftigkeit der Farbe zu erhoehen, und sie zu erhalten."[2] Solche Äußerungen zeigen ganz klar, wie wichtig transparenter Glanz und Politur, das Licht widerspiegelnde Oberflächen, für die künstlerische Konzeption ganzer Stilepochen gewesen sind. In vielen Fassmalerverträgen und Abrechnungen des 18. Jahrhunderts ist von „Glattschleifen", „Polieren" und „mit bestem Glanzfirnis" verzieren die Rede. Lacke oder Firnisse waren nicht nur Schutzüberzüge, sondern ein wichtiges Element der ästhetischen Wirkung. Und diese die künstlerische Wirkung bestimmende Funktion wurde im 19. Jahrhundert vollkommen verkannt, denn die meisten Lacke hatten den Nachteil nachzudunkeln und zu vergilben, wodurch die ursprüngliche Farbwirkung der Kunstwerke verfremdet bzw. stark beeinträchtigt wurde. Man hat also die vergilbten historischen Lacke entweder entfernt – eine Methode, die bis weit ins 20. Jahrhundert hinein angewandt worden ist, – oder neu überfasst. Bei der späteren Entfernung solcher Überfassungen wurden die oft noch darunter erhaltenen originalen Lacke nicht als solche erkannt, als bedeutungslose und willkommene Trennschicht angesehen und durch Lösungsmittel oder mechanisch zerstört. In den meisten Fällen erhielten die Ausstattungsstücke nach der Lackentfernung keinen neuen Überzug und blieben matt. Die dadurch zwangsläufig verursachte Bindemittelarmut bewirkte eine verminderte Farbintensität.

Um den ausgemagerten Oberflächen wieder ein gewisses Tiefenlicht zu geben und sie zu schützen, ging man schließlich dazu über, dünne Überzüge aufzutragen. Die zu diesem Zweck bis in die 80er Jahre des 20. Jahrhunderts verwendeten Materialien wie z. B. Wachs, Nitrolack oder Schellack entsprachen in keiner Weise den originalen Lackschichten und erreichten auch deren Glanzwirkung nicht. Solche Beschichtungen sind häufig nur unter Gefährdung der noch erhaltenen Originalsubstanz wieder zu entfernen. Äußerst problematisch ist besonders die Abnahme von Kunstharzüberzügen. Heute zieht man wegen der ihnen zugesprochenen Reversibilität und geringen Vergilbung meist Dammar-Überzüge vor. Durch ihre charakteristische Eigenfarbe und Weichheit, besonders aber durch ihren geringeren Glanzgrad unterscheiden sie sich jedoch wesentlich von den barocken Originallacken. Dammar war im 18. Jahrhundert nicht bekannt.

Auf diese Weise sind Ausstattungsstücke mit original erhaltener Oberfläche heute zur Seltenheit geworden. Durch den Mangel an ursprünglichen Zeugnissen ging auch das Wissen über diesen wesentlichen Aspekt der Fasstechnik des Barock und Rokoko verloren. Ungestört erhaltene originale Lackoberflächen sind in der Regel nur mehr unter Applikationen und Beschlägen, die bei den späteren Bearbeitungen nicht entfernt worden sind, oder hinter Altarblättern (Farbtafel XXV.4), soweit diese bei der Erneuerung der Lacküberzüge nicht abmontiert wurden, aufzufinden. Diese kleinen Restflächen zeigen – im Verhältnis zum vorgefundenen Zustand – ganz anders geartete Qualitäten. Die Oberflächen lassen keine Pinselstrukturen erkennen, sie sind glatt wie polierter Stuckmarmor, vermitteln in ihrer Härte ein Gefühl von Stein und haben trotz der Vergilbungen ein ganz anderes Tiefenlicht als die neueren und einfacheren Lacküberzüge. Ihre spiegelnde Härte gibt den Kunstwerken einen veränderten Materialcharakter. So sind diese noch vorhandenen Teilflächen beredtes Zeugnis dafür, wie einem marmorierten Holzaufbau in überzeugender Weise das Aussehen eines Marmor- oder Stuckmarmorretabels verliehen werden konnte. Durch die Oberflächenbearbeitung wurde sozusagen ein „edlerer Schein" kreiert. Diese Intention ist durch zeitgenössische Quellentexte belegt, in denen sehr häufig Ausdrücke wie „auf Marmor-, Porzellan- oder Jaspis-Art" verwendet wurden.

Solche Wirkungen konnten aber nur durch ausgeklügelte Arbeitstechniken erreicht werden. Und damit sind die Probleme der Lackrestaurierung in Deutschland bereits umrissen:
- Historische Beispiele sind fast vollständig entfernt,
- die verwendeten Materialien und ihre Mischungsverhältnisse nicht bestimmt,
- die Verarbeitungstechniken nicht bekannt.

In dieser Situation kam eine Initiative des deutsch-japanischen Komitees für wissenschaftlich-technische Zusammenarbeit zu Hilfe, das in seiner Sitzung am 25./26. Oktober 1990 in Tokio beschlossen hatte, den bereits bestehenden Erfahrungsaustausch zwischen beiden Ländern auf das Gebiet des Denkmalschutzes und der Denkmalpflege auszuweiten. Man ging davon aus, dass der Erfahrungsaustausch zweier Staaten mit langer Kulturtradition und hohem technologischem Standard bei der Lösung von Erhaltungsproblemen fruchtbar sein dürfte. Beide Staaten verfügen über eine Fülle von Denkmälern und gut organisierte Institutionen mit einer nahezu hundertjährigen Erfahrung auf dem Gebiet der Denkmalpflege und des Denkmalschutzes. In beiden Staaten haben auch verstärkt Umweltprobleme dazu geführt, dass mehr und mehr Forschung und moderne Technologie bei der Konservierung des Kulturerbes eingesetzt werden muss. Die finanziellen Mittel wurden auf deutscher Seite vom Bundesministerium für Bildung und Forschung, auf japanischer Seite vom Kultusministerium (Mombusho) bereitgestellt. Die Projektierung und praktische Durchführung wurde den Restaurierungswerkstätten des Bayerischen Landesamtes für Denkmalpflege und dem Tokyo National Research Institute of Cultural Properties übertragen. Das Tokyo National Research Institute of Cultural Properties ist ein praxisorientiertes Forschungsinstitut mit verschiedenen Abteilungen, wie u. a. „Conservation Science" und „Restoration Techniques". Das Bayerische Landesamt für Denkmalpflege verfügt in seinen Restaurierungswerkstätten mit ihren neun Fachbereichen und einem chemisch-physikalischem Labor als einziges Denkmalamt in der Bundesrepublik über eine in Teilbereichen ähnlich geartete Einrichtung. Da der Erfahrungsaustausch und die Zusammenarbeit zunächst auf naturwissenschaftlichem und restauratorisch-technischem Gebiet stattfinden sollte, wurde der Eigenart und Ausrichtung der beiden Institute gemäß, als aktuelles Thema der Zusammenarbeit das „Studium von Verfallsmechanismen und anwendbaren Konservierungsmethoden" gewählt und als erstes Fachthema die Erforschung und Restaurierung von Lacken vereinbart. Die Zusammenarbeit sollte den Austausch von Konservierungskonzepten und Technologien, die Förderung spezieller Forschungen auf dem Gebiet historischer Materialien und Restaurierungsmethoden, die Veröffentlichung der Resultate und die Abhaltung von Kongressen, Symposien und Workshops beinhalten.

Für Japan ist die Beschäftigung mit Lacken ein uraltes Thema und fundamentaler künstlerischer Ausdruck seiner Kultur. Die ältesten Lackarbeiten wurden dort schon 2500 v. Chr. nachgewiesen. So hat in Japan die Lack- bzw. Urushiforschung – Urushi ist der japanische Lack – schon eine längere Tradition. Trotzdem gab es noch keine Methode, Urushi sicher zu definieren. Das hatte namentlich auch für Europa Konsequenzen, denn hier wurden im 17. und 18. Jahrhundert aus Ostasien importierte Lackarbeiten zerlegt, in europäische Möbel integriert und die fehlenden Teile in oft so perfekter Weise dazu imitiert, dass die Imitation nur sehr schwer von den Originalen zu unterscheiden war (siehe Farbtafel VI.3, 4). Für die Restaurierung dieser meist hoch qualitätvollen Stücke hieß das, dass man nicht wusste, mit welchen Materialien man es zu tun hatte. Dementsprechend häufig und gravierend sind auch die Fehler gewesen, die gemacht wurden.

In Deutschland – und man kann ruhig sagen in ganz Europa – mussten der Erforschung und Restaurierung von Lacken neue Impulse gegeben werden, weil hier das ganze Fachgebiet vernachlässigt worden war.

Da die Analysemöglichkeiten europäischer Lacke bisher nur sehr unbefriedigend gewesen sind und nur allgemeine Mischungsverhältnisse oder chemisch übergeordnete Gruppen festgestellt werden konnten, ist im Rahmen des Projekts vom Doerner-Institut ein völlig neues Extraktionsverfahren zur GC/MS-Analyse entwickelt worden, das nun die exakte Bestimmung von unterschiedlichen Bindemitteln wie Harzen, Balsamen und Ölen, erlaubte.[3] Darüber hinaus gelang eine etwaige Quantifizierung der Einzelkomponenten zur Auswertung von Mischungsverhältnissen. So wurde z. B. festgestellt, dass im 17. und 18. Jahrhundert nicht, wie bisher angenommen, Schellack, sondern Sandarak die Basis vieler Lackbeschichtungen war und, dass dem Sandarak in der Regel weiche Harze wie z. B. Mastix oder härtende, zum Schliff besonders geeignete Substanzen wie Kopal beigemengt worden sind. Querschliffe haben gezeigt, dass der Schichtaufbau oft ebenso kompliziert gewesen ist wie bei den ostasiatischen Arbeiten. Tiefenlicht und Glanz der Lackbeschichtungen konnten nur durch mehrfache Arbeitsgänge, d. h. durch mehrfache, oft extra polierte Beschichtungen erreicht werden. Zwischen den einzelnen Lackschichten wurden gelegentlich Goldadern aufgetragen oder zusätzlich Farbstoffe zugesetzt (Farbtafel XXV.4). Bei den 1732/33 angefertigten rot lackierten Türen des Miniaturenkabinetts der Münchner Residenz z. B. wurden innerhalb des Lackaufbaus nochmals unterschiedliche Bindemittelsysteme nachgewiesen. Der Lackaufbau war offensichtlich in 14–16 Schichten vorgenommen worden.[4]

Abb. 1. Bad Wörishofen, Dominikanerinnenklosterkirche, südlicher Seitenaltar

Abb. 2. Moritzburg, Schloss, japanisches Lackkabinett auf europäischem Gestell

Außer der analytischen Bestimmung der Materialien und ihrer Mischungsverhältnisse mussten auch Rekonstruktionen der historischen Lackbeschichtungen erarbeitet werden, um die früher entfernten Lacke auf den ausgemagerten und gefährdeten Oberflächen zu ersetzen. Die erste Rekonstruktion einer historischen Lackbeschichtung wurde bei der Innenrestaurierung der Wieskirche am nördlichen Seitenaltar (Farbtafel XXV.3) mit drei bis vier aufeinanderfolgenden Arbeitsgängen auf Sandarakbasis unter 3-prozentigem Leinölzusatz nach historischen Quellen durchgeführt, weil noch keine erschöpfende Materialanalyse möglich war. Immerhin zeigte es sich, dass – nach einer umfangreichen Versuchsreihe mit unterschiedlichen Materialien wie u. a. auch Dammar und Kunstharzen – nur Sandarak mit anschließender Politur den gewünschten Oberflächenglanz ergab. Spätere Rekonstruktionen wie z. B. bei den furnierten Altären der Dominikanerinnenkirche in Bad Wörishofen (Abb. 1) und den gefassten Altarretabeln in der Alten Kapelle zu unserer lieben Frau in Regensburg (Farbtafel XXV.2) konnten bereits auf genauen Materialanalysen aufbauen.

Bei den überarbeiteten Ausstattungsstücken war das Problem der Abnahme späterer Lackbeschichtungen von den originalen Oberflächen zu bewältigen. Für solche Lacktrennungen mussten in der Abteilung Restaurierung des Bayerischen Landesamtes für Denkmalpflege Spezialtechniken entwickelt werden. Die erste dieser Maßnahmen gelang an dem Orgelgehäuse der Pfarrkirche St. Ulrich von Aich im Landkreis Landshut.[5] Die vorgefundene Situation war typisch für das bisher übliche Vorgehen: Ein Kirchenmaler hatte zunächst in einem Muster alle Beschichtungen bis auf das Holz abgebeizt, um einen neuen Schellacküberzug aufbringen zu können. Die gelungene Trennung des später aufgebrachten Lackes von der originalen Beschichtung hat hingegen eine Wiedergewinnung des früheren Zustandes und eine Erhaltung der originalen Substanz möglich gemacht (Abb. 3). Hierzu wurden von den Amtswerkstätten in Zusammenarbeit mit dem Doerner-Institut entsprechende Testreihen angelegt.

Alle diese neuen Ergebnisse und Errungenschaften sind im Arbeitsheft 81 des Bayerischen Landesamtes für Denkmalpflege von Katharina Walch und Johann Koller: „Lacke des Barock und Rokoko" 1997 veröffentlicht worden.

Ein weiteres Problem war die Behandlung importierter ostasiatischer Lackarbeiten und ihrer europäischen Imitationen. Um 1584 wurden die ersten japanischen Lackarbeiten in Europa bekannt. Die Importe nahmen im Lauf des 17. Jahrhunderts in dem Maße, in dem der Handel an Umfang gewann, sehr rasch zu, denn die glänzenden Lackarbeiten entsprachen, so wie das durchscheinende Porzellan, voll und ganz dem Zeitgeschmack des Barock und Rokoko, d. h. dem Geschmack der oberen Schichten, denn sie waren teuer, exotisch und elitär. Man hat die importierten Stücke unserem Wohnstil entsprechend auf europäische Fußgestelle gestellt (Abb. 2) oder Zeichnungen und Modelle europäischer Möbelformen nach Ostasien geschickt und dort herstellen und lackieren lassen. Dadurch ist bei uns die Bestimmung, welchem Kulturkreis die jeweiligen Stücke zuzuordnen sind, nicht einfacher geworden. Material und Herstellungstechnik der ostasiatischen Lackarbeiten blieben in Europa jedenfalls unbekannt. Auch heute noch kann kaum ein europäischer Restaurator mit ostasiatischen Lackarbeiten umgehen, denn der in China, Japan, Burma und Thailand ebenfalls aus Baumharzen hergestellte Lack hat vollkommen andere Eigenschaften als die europäischen Materialien: er ist giftig, wird hart wie Bakelit, hat eine Oberfläche, die glatt ist wie polierter Marmor und ein ebensolches Tiefenlicht. So bilden in Japan die Lackmeister und Lackrestauratoren, die für ihre Ausbildung viele Jahre benötigen, eine eigene Berufssparte.

Die nach Europa importierten Lackarbeiten wurden vornehmlich in den Palais und Schlössern des Adels aufgestellt. Man wusste nicht, dass die Lacke UV-empfindlich sind und Trockenheit nicht vertragen. So sind die glänzenden Stücke mit der Zeit matt

Abb. 3. Aich, Landkreis Landshut, St. Ulrich, Orgelgehäuse nach Abnahme der späteren Lackierung

1 Landsberg/Lech, ehem. Jesuitenkirche Heiligkreuz, Hochaltar, Detail, restaurierte Originallackierung

2 Regensburg, Basilika Unserer Lieben Frau zur Alten Kapelle, Hochaltar, Detail, Originalfassung mit rekonstruierter Lackbeschichtung

3 Wies, Wallfahrtskirche Zum gegeißelten Heiland, nördlicher Seitenaltar, rekonstruierte Lackbeschichtung

4 Landsberg/Lech, ehem. Jesuitenkirche Heiligkreuz, Rest der barocken Originallackierung

geworden (Abb. 4–6), sie erblindeten und der Lack krakelierte. Da man mit den Materialien nicht umzugehen verstand, hat man sie – und das bis in allerneueste Zeit – mit europäischen Lacken, – auch mit Kunstharzlacken, – überstrichen, um ihnen wieder neuen Glanz zu verleihen. Die Lackarbeiten haben anschließend zwar wieder geglänzt, auch wenn sie ihre Farbigkeit nicht wiedergewonnen haben, waren aber auch gleichzeitig meist irreversibel geschädigt, denn die späteren Lacküberzüge, besonders Kunstharzlacke, sind nur mehr sehr schwer ohne Beschädigung des Originals von den ursprünglichen Oberflächen zu entfernen (Abb. 7). So ist die Behandlung ostasiatischer Lackarbeiten in Europa, in jedem Fall aber in Deutschland, bis heute von Unkenntnis und Dilettantismus bestimmt gewesen. Um einen Ausweg aus diesem Dilemma zu finden, sind manche Museen dazu übergegangen, Teile ihrer Lackbestände in Japan restaurieren zu lassen. Es wurden auch japanische Stiftungen ins Leben gerufen, die solche Aktionen finanzieren.

Dabei haben die ostasiatischen Lackarbeiten in den Museen noch ganz akzeptable Existenzbedingungen. Die Situation ist bei den Schlösserverwaltungen, die einen Großteil dieses Kulturerbes verwalten, häufig anders. Die Ausstattungsstücke sind oft starkem Licht oder direkter Sonnenbestrahlung ausgesetzt, die Depots oft nicht klimatisiert, ja gelegentlich auch im Dachraum der Schlösser untergebracht. Restaurierungsmaßnahmen werden in der Regel Restauratoren anvertraut, die für den Umgang mit ostasiatischen Lacken nicht ausgebildet sind. In Deutschland gibt es vorderhand nur eine einzige Restauratorin, die eine zweijährige Ausbildung im Tokyo National Research Institute of Cultural Properties durchlaufen und einen Restaurator, der eine ähnlich ausgerichtete Ausbildung, wenn auch nicht in Japan, wenigstens ein Dreivierteljahr genossen hat. Dementsprechend wird Urushi als Restaurierungsmaterial auch nicht eingesetzt, ja abgelehnt, und das wohl nur deswegen, weil niemand damit umgehen kann.[6] Natürlich wird nach Alternativen wie Leim oder Kunstharzen (wie z. B. Acryl) zur Konservierung gesucht, die oft bestens geeignet sind, ja auch in Japan verwendet werden. Gelegentlich bietet sich aber, namentlich bei schwarzen Oberflächen oder korrodiertem Streugrund Urushi an, das einem der wichtigen Grundsätze der Denkmalpflege, nämlich der Verwendung historischer Technik und Materialien entspricht und zudem einen sehr guten regenerierenden Effekt hat (Abb. 8). Grundsätzlich muss eben aus der gesamten zur Verfügung stehenden Palette dasjenige Material ausgewählt werden, das für die individuelle Situation am besten geeignet ist.

Abb. 4. Bad Homburg, japanisches Lackkabinett, Schäden des Lackes durch UV-Bestrahlung

Auf diesem Gebiet gibt es in Deutschland noch viel Nachholbedarf. Es mangelt an Restauratoren, die willens sind, einen Teil ihrer Ausbildung in Japan zu absolvieren. Möglichkeiten wären jedenfalls durch Stipendien gegeben. Solange es allerdings den Auftraggebern nicht wichtig ist, von wem ihre wertvollen Stücke bearbeitet werden und keine Fachausbildung nachgewiesen werden muss, um einen Auftrag zu erhalten, kann man von den Restauratoren auch nicht verlangen, eine solche Fachausbildung zu durchlaufen, d. h. die dafür notwendige Zeit und die Kosten auf sich zu nehmen.

Abb. 5. Bad Homburg, japanisches Lackkabinett, original erhaltener Nashijigrund unter einem abgenommenen Beschlag im Vergleich zum UV-geschädigten Bereich

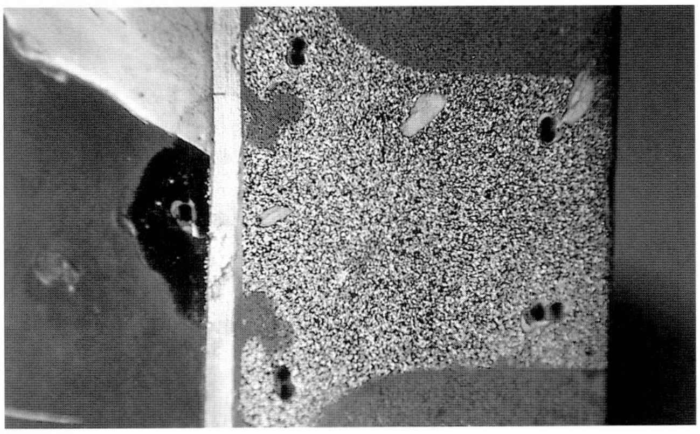

Abb. 6. Bad Homburg, japanisches Lackkabinett, original erhaltene Lackoberfläche im Vergleich zum UV-geschädigten Bereich

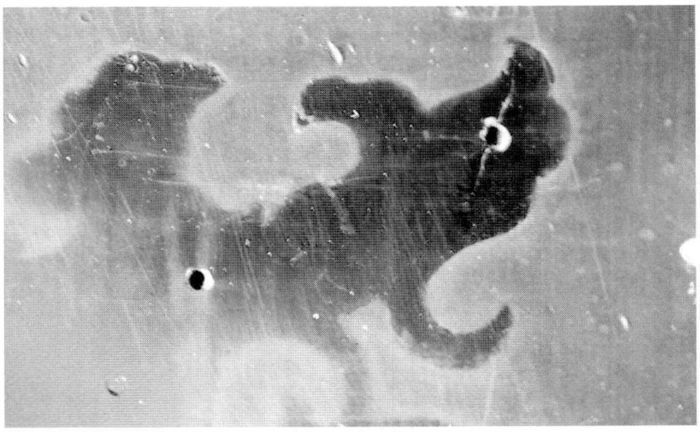

Abb. 7. Rastatt, Residenz, Wandvertäfelung des Lackkabinetts, Detail, Überlackierung mit Kunstharzlack

Genauso groß wie bei den ostasiatischen Lacken ist der Nachholbedarf auch bei der Restaurierung europäischer Lacke. Die Zusammenhänge und Probleme, die sich auf diesem Gebiet stellen, sind kompliziert und ohne naturwissenschaftliche Untersuchungen nicht zu lösen. Es genügt nicht festzustellen, dass „harzige Anteile" vorhanden sind oder dass es sich „wahrscheinlich" um Kopal oder Schellack handelt. Außerdem wurde ein Harz, soweit wir feststellen konnten, nur selten alleine verwendet. Um mit den Restaurierungsmaßnahmen richtig ansetzen zu können, ist es jedoch wichtig, die einzelnen Bestandteile einer Beschichtung und ihr quantitatives Verhältnis zueinander zu kennen. Dies ist nun erstmalig durch die Forschung des Doerner-Instituts ermöglicht worden.

Abb. 8. Tokio, Werkstatt des National Museums, Lackarbeit des 17. Jahrhunderts mit Regenerierung durch Urushi

Wie unterentwickelt das Gebiet der Lackrestaurierung noch ist, zeigt die Tatsache, dass hier die Forderungen, die für andere Fachgebiete selbstverständlich sind, – dass nämlich nur Fachleute zum Einsatz kommen dürfen – nicht erhoben werden; ein großer Fehler angesichts der Tatsache, dass ein großer Teil des Bestandes an gefassten Ausstattungsstücken und vor allem die Bedeutenderen unter ihnen, ursprünglich lackiert gewesen sind.

Ähnlich prekär ist natürlich auch die Situation bei der Behandlung von Lackarbeiten, die in Imitation ostasiatischer Lacke mit europäischen Materialien hergestellt wurden (Abb. 9, 10). Die Bandbreite reicht von den zahlreichen kleinen, dem Gebrauch oder der Dekoration dienenden Gegenständen wie Toilettenartikeln, Kästchen, Dosen, Spiegeln, Tellern, Vasen oder Leuchtern über Möbel wie vor allem Kommoden, Sekretäre, Truhen, Schränke, Etagèren oder auch Cembali und ganze Zimmereinrichtungen bis hin zu den bekannten Lackkabinetten, die sich alle Schlossherren, die etwas auf sich hielten und mit dem Geschmack der Zeit gehen wollten, in ihre Schlösser einbauen ließen. Relativ günstig ist, wie immer, die Situation dann, wenn die Kunstwerke noch keiner Restaurierung unterworfen worden sind. Große Probleme ergeben sich dann, wenn Überarbeitungen, namentlich mit Kunstharzlacken oder anderen schwer löslichen Materialsystemen vorgenommen worden sind.

Während der Laufzeit des gemeinsamen deutsch-japanischen Projektes ist deutlich geworden, dass wir zumindest drei Dinge von Japan lernen können:

- den Respekt vor dem Original, die Wertschätzung der Altersspuren statt Erneuerung, Auffrischung und Renovierung;
- den pfleglichen Umgang mit wertvollen Lackarbeiten, d. h. u. a. keine Dauerausstellung, Schutz vor Licht und Trockenheit (Installation von Lichtzeituhren, Klimatisierung);
- die sachgerechte Magazinierung (in geeigneten Schutzbehältern, dunkel und klimatisiert) (Abb. 11, 12).

Das Fazit, das leider gezogen werden muss, ist, dass Kunstwerke mit lackierten Oberflächen bisher kein ernsthaftes Thema für die Denkmalpflege in Deutschland gewesen sind. Mit dem deutsch-japanischen Forschungsprojekt ist somit ein lange vernachlässigtes Fachgebiet aufgegriffen worden, dessen Ergebnisse nun ein Agieren im Rahmen der Optionen, die wir noch haben, möglich macht:

- Eine Bestimmung des Lackaufbaus durch eingehende optische Untersuchung.
- Eine genaue Materialanalyse, die in dieser Exaktheit allerdings vorläufig nur am Doerner-Institut möglich ist, weswegen eine weitere Verbreitung dieser Technologie ein dringendes Desideratum wäre.
- Eine durch Materialanalyse und historische Rezepturen gestützte Rekonstruktion abgenommener Lacke in historischer Technik und mit historischen Materialien, um einerseits ausgemagerte Oberflächen zu schützen und andererseits den Kunstwerken wieder etwas von ihrer ursprünglichen Wirkung zurückzugeben.
- Eine Trennung von Lackschichten, wenn der originale Lack zu einem späteren Zeitpunkt überstrichen wurde. Bei der Abnahme von Lacken ist allerdings Vorsicht und Zurückhaltung zu empfehlen, weil diese Arbeit große Kenntnis und viel Fingerspitzengefühl erfordert. Zu schnell entstehen Schäden, wenn zu viel abgenommen wird und die gestörte Oberfläche erst recht wieder überlackiert werden muss. Bei Wiederholung kann dieser Vorgang zur völligen Reduktion des Originals führen.[7]

Als Appell an die Denkmalpflege wäre zu formulieren:

- Mehr Aufmerksamkeit den Oberflächen widmen. Genaue Voruntersuchungen fordern, um möglicherweise noch vorhandene Reste originaler Lacke festzustellen, weil durch diese Untersuchungen nicht nur die Basis für eine objektgerechte Restaurierung geschaffen, sondern auch neue Erkenntnisse für die Kunstgeschichte gewonnen werden.
- Augenmerk auf schädliche Umwelteinflüsse richten, d. h. Wert auf Klimakontrolle und Lichtschutz legen.
- Keine Überlackierungen des neuen Glanzes willen durchführen. Mit anderen Worten also, den Alterswert respektieren, wenn die originale Oberfläche noch vorhanden ist.
- Ganz allgemein Bedingungen schaffen, die der langfristigen Erhaltung der Kunstwerke förderlich sind.

Zu warnen ist vor den sogenannten Regenerierungen, die meist doch nur den Wert eines Märchens haben. Eine solche Manipulation ist ohne Einbringen eines neuen Materials bzw. einer neuen Substanz nicht möglich. Entweder handelt es sich um das Einbringen von Lösemitteln, nach deren Verflüchtigung der Lack wieder das ist, was er vorher war, oder es handelt sich um einen Materialauftrag wie Überlackierungen, die in jedem Fall problematisch sind.

Sehr schwierig ist auch das mechanische Ausdünnen vergilbter Lacke, das nur möglich ist, wenn die Lackschicht sehr dick aufgetragen wurde. Größte Vorsicht ist besonders dann geboten, wenn ein dünner Lack über einer Malschicht liegt, die stets ein Mikrorelief aufweist und zu leicht in ihren Höhen beschädigt werden kann.

Durch das deutsch-japanische Projekt, zu dessen Abschluss dieser Kongress veranstaltet wurde, sind wir in den Fragen der Restaurierung, Pflege und Erforschung lackierter Oberflächen einen großen Schritt weitergekommen. Die Ergebnisse wurden publiziert und stehen allgemein zur Verfügung. Man sollte sie nützen und daraus, in Zukunft aber auch voneinander lernen. Meist ist es doch nur eine persönliche Unsicherheit, wenn man nicht bereit ist – von wem auch immer – hinzuzulernen. Jeder Restaurator muss sich schließlich vor Augen halten, dass nachfolgende Generationen oder auch Kollegen, die ihn noch kennen, zu einem späteren Zeitpunkt mit den Ergebnissen seiner Manipulationen konfrontiert werden und ihn unweigerlich danach beurteilen. Unsachgemäße Behandlungen, die momentan noch verschleiert werden können, werden spätestens dann offen gelegt, d. h. Zusammenarbeit und Erfahrungsaustausch tut Not.

Das wichtigste zu empfehlende Kriterium des eigenen Tuns wäre, dem Kunstwerk zumindest kein weiteres Schadenspotential hinzuzufügen, schonende, objektverträgliche Maßnahmen zu wählen und keine Manipulationen vorzunehmen, die Möglichkeiten einer weiteren Behandlung ausschließen. Es wäre also zu hoffen, dass die in dem deutsch-japanischen Projekt erzielten Ergebnisse auch in die Praxis umgesetzt werden, dass der damit gemachte Anfang Anstoß für weitere Bemühungen ist, damit auch dieses spezielle Fachgebiet der Restaurierung den ihm schon längst gebührenden Stellenwert erhält und wir unserer unleugbaren Verantwortung gegenüber diesem Teil unseres kulturellen Erbes auch endlich gerecht werden können.

Abb. 9. Budapest, Nationalmuseum, Lackkabinett von Martin Schnell

Abb. 10. Berlin, Kunstgewerbemuseum, Lackkommode

Abb. 11. Tokushima, Schlossmuseum, Blick in das Depot

Abb. 12. Tokushima, Schlossmuseum, Depot, Behälter für die Magazinierung von Lacktabletts

Anmerkungen

1 ZEDLER, JOHANN HEINRICH: *Großes vollstaendiges Universal-Lexicon Aller Wissenschaften und Künste, welche bishero durch menschlichen Verstand und Witz erfunden und verbessert worden ...*, Bd. XVI, Halle/Leipzig 1737, S. 40.
2 WATIN, JEAN FELIX: *Der Staffirmaler, oder die Kunst anzustreichen, zu vergolden und zu lackieren, wie solche bey Gebaeuden, Meublen, Galanteriewaren, Kutschen usw. ...*, Leipzig 1774, S. 169 f.
3 KOLLER, JOHANN/BAUMER URSULA: *Die transparenten Glanzlacke des Barock und Rokoko II. Eine naturwissenschaftliche Untersuchung der Lacksysteme (Baroque and Rococo Transparent Gloss Lacquers II. Scientific Study of Lacquer Systems)*, in: Lacke des Barock and Rokoko (Baroque and Rococo Lacquers), München 1997, S. 52–84 (Arbeitshefte des Bayerischen Landesamtes für Denkmalpflege, Bd. 81).
4 WALCH, KATHARINA: *Rote Lacke des Barock und Rokoko I. Die rote Lackarbeit im Miniaturenkabinett der Münchner Residenz. Rekonstruktion der Technik durch quellenkundliche Studien und restauratorische Untersuchungen (Baroque and Rococo Red Lacquers. I. The Red Lacquer-work in the Miniaturenkabinett of the Munich Residenz. Replicating the Technique on the Basis of Historic Sources and Scientific Investigation)*, in: Lacke des Barock and Rokoko (Baroque and Rococo Lacquers), München 1997, S. 128–144 (Arbeitshefte des Bayerischen Landesamtes für Denkmalpflege, Bd. 81).
5 WALCH, KATHARINA/KOLLER, JOHANN/BAUMER, URSULA: *Die Restaurierung des Aicher Orgelgehäuses (The Restoration of the Organ Case in Aich)*, in: Lacke des Barock and Rokoko (Baroque and Rococo Lacquers), München 1997, S. 334–346 (Arbeitshefte des Bayerischen Landesamtes für Denkmalpflege, Bd. 81).
6 HAGEDORN, BRIGITTE: *Schadensbilder an asiatischen und europäischen Lackobjekten und Möglichkeiten der Konservierung und Restaurierung*, in: Hellwig, Friedemann (Hrsg.): Vom Umgang mit dem Original, München 1998, S. 79–81.
7 Vgl. den Beitrag „The Removal of Coatings on Lacquered Surfaces – Possibilities and Limits" von Katharina Walch in dieser Publikation.

Abbildungsnachweis

Abb. 1, 3: Horst Huber, Stuttgart
Abb. 2, 4–6, 8, 11, 12: Verfasser
Abb. 7: Bayerisches Landesamt für Denkmalpflege, Abt. Restaurierungswerkstätten, Elke Giermann
Abb. 9, 10: Bayerisches Landesamt für Denkmalpflege, Abt. Restaurierungswerkstätten, Katharina Walch
Farbtafel XXIV: Bayerisches Landesamt für Denkmalpflege, Abt. Restaurierungswerkstätten, Archiv
Farbtafel XXV.1: Verfasser; 2: Horst Huber, Stuttgart; 3: Achim Bunz, München; 4: Thomas Schoeller, Sybille Schmitt, München

Summary

On the Problem of Preservation and Restoration of Lacquers in Monument Conservation

In Europe it has for a long time not been realised that an important part of our cultural heritage has been determined to an important degree by lacquer coatings. The 'finish', the differentiation of lustre degrees, has been namely in the Baroque and Rococo period a decisive element of expression for entire genres of the fine arts. Church interiors with their polychromed, veneered or wooden surfaces like altarpieces, organ prospects, pulpits, confessionals, parapets and communion gratings, chandeliers, choir stalls and pews belong to it, as well as the precious interior decorations of palaces with their numerous pieces of lacquered furniture imported from Japan or China, their European imitations and the lacquer rooms many owners used to install during the Baroque and Rococo period.

Just like the porcelain imported from China before Böttger's invention was called 'china' in English, the art of lacquering was so much connected to the image of Japan in Europe, that the refinement of surfaces with lacquers was called 'japanning'. Lacquers or varnishes have not only been protective coatings, but also an important element of aesthetic impact. As most of the varnishes had the disadvantage of darkening or yellowing, they were to a large extent removed or over-coated in the 19th or 20th centuries. For this reason interior decorations with untouched surfaces have become rare. At the same time the knowledge about historical coating techniques and the original materials disappeared. This circumscribes the problems of lacquer conservation and restoration in Germany today: Historical examples have mostly been completely removed, the materials used and their compounding were not studied, the application techniques not known.

In this situation an initiative of the German-Japanese Committee for scientific and technical co-operation brought help. During a conference on Oct. 25th/26th 1990 in Tokyo it was decided to enlarge the already existing exchange of experience between both countries in the field of monument preservation and conservation. The financial support has been made available on the German side by the Federal Ministry for Education, Science, Research and Technology, on the Japanese side by the Ministry of Culture (Mombusho). The implementation and the practical realization have been entrusted to the Bavarian State Department of Historical Monuments and the Tokyo National Research Institute. As a first topic of co-operation the investigation and restoration of lacquers has been agreed upon. The results of the research project on the German side were among others:

- the insight, that in the 17th and 18th centuries sandarac and not shellac has been the base of most lacquer coatings;
- that also in Europe varnishes and lacquer coatings have mostly been rather complicated and many-layered in their build-up with polishing, painted veins or coloured layers in between the lacquer coatings;
- the possibility of reconstructing baroque lacquers and varnishes on the base of contemporary sources, material analyses and practical test series;
- the development of a procedure for separating lacquers in order to remove later coatings from original lacquer surfaces.

The results on the Japanese side were:

- the discovery of the until now completely neglected export lacquerware in Japan, which shows mostly a different technique, form and iconography than pieces made for the Japanese market;
- the development of an analytical method (GC/MS-Pyrolysis), which allowed for the first time a firm determination of urushi and its country of provenience;
- the installation of a network of Japanese lacquer workshops serving the exchange of experience between masters working up to now mostly isolated from one another.

The numerous Japanese pieces of lacquer ware exported to Germany in the 17th and 18th centuries are a common German-Japanese cultural heritage. Not a single piece of export lacquerware manufactured in Japan has remained there. In order to treat and to preserve them correctly a good deal of joint efforts for their investigation will still have to be made. Regarding restoration the problem is, that there are only a few conservators in Europe who know how to work with urushi. Consequently many mistakes have been made in the past, like for instance the overcoating with modern, differing lacquers, which are partly irreversible. Similarly precarious is the situation regarding the treatment of lacquer work, which have been made in imitation of East Asian lacquers with European materials. There are not even enough laboratories able to carry out exact qualitative and quantitative analyses of the lacquer composition.

In the course of the joint German-Japanese project it has become evident, that we can learn at least three attitudes towards ancient works of art from Japan:

- the respect of the original, the appreciation of the traces of ageing instead of renewal and renovation;
- the careful dealing with these precious pieces of lacquer work, i. e. among others no permanent exposition, protection against light and dryness;
- the proper storing in appropriate boxes and protective containers, in the dark and under fitting climatic conditions.

In the actual situation the appeal must be made to monument conservationists:

- To give more attention to surfaces, i. e. to ask for exact investigations in order to detect possibly still preserved remains of original lacquers, because such investigations are not only the base for an appropriate restoration, but also for a new understanding in the field of art history.
- Not to be content with general statements from the side of the material analysis but to insist on detailed information about the qualitative and quantitative composition of lacquer coatings.
- To draw the attention to harmful environmental influences, i. e. to consider the importance of climate control and on light protection for the objects.
- Not to carry out over-coatings for the sake of a new lustre; in other words: to respect the traces of ageing of the original surfaces.
- Not to add any substances which might have harmful effects on the work of art in the future.
- To choose compatible measures and not to carry out manipulations, that exclude the possibility of a further treatment.

Autoren / *Authors*

Mechthild Baumeister, The Metropolitan Museum of Art, The Sherman Fairchild Center for Objects Conservation, Furniture Department, 1000 Fifth Avenue, New York, N.Y. 10028–0198, USA

Ursula Baumer, Doerner-Institut, Barerstr. 29, 80799 München, Germany

Prof. Yuansheng Chen, Research Laboratory for Conservation and Archaeology, Shanghai Museum, 1118 Long Wu Road, Shanghai, 200232, China

Dr. Franz-Josef Christiani, Städtisches Museum Braunschweig, Am Löwenwall, 38100 Braunschweig, Germany

Dr. Anna Czarnocka, 36, Boulevard d'Angleterre, 78110 Le Vésinet, France

Julia Hutt, Assistant Curator, Far Eastern Department, Victoria & Albert Museum, London SW7 2RL, Great Britain

Dr. Oliver Impey, Ashmolean Museum of Art and Archaeology, Department of Eastern Art, Beaumont St., Oxford OX1 2PH, Great Britain

Prof. Dr. Christiaan J. A. Jörg, Groninger Museum, Museumeiland 1, Postbus 90, 9700 ME Groningen, The Netherlands

Nicole Judet Brugier, 74, Rue de Sèvres (VII), 70700 Paris, France

Yukio Kamiya, Department of Industrial Chemistry, Meiji University, Higashimita, Tamaku Kawasakishi 214–8571, Japan

Dipl. Ing. Dr. Wolfgang Kippes, Schloß Schönbrunn Kultur- und Betriebsges.m.b.H., 1130 Wien, Austria

Daniëlle Kisluk-Grosheide, Associate Curator, The Metropolitan Museum of Art, European Sculpture and Decorative Arts, 1000 Fifth Avenue, New York, N.Y. 10028–0198, USA

Dr. Johann Koller, Doerner-Institut, Barerstr. 29, 80799 München, Germany

Dr. Michael Kühlenthal, Leiter der Restaurierungswerkstätten/*Head of Restoration Department*, Bayerisches Landesamt für Denkmalpflege, Hofgraben 4, 80539 München, Germany

Prof. Sadatoshi Miura, Director of Conservation Science Department, Tokyo National Research Institute of Cultural Properties, 13–27 Ueno Park, Taito-ku, Tokyo 110, Japan

Dr. Tetsuo Miyakoshi, Department of Industrial Chemistry, Meiji University, Higashimita, Tamaku Kawasakishi 214–8571, Japan

Kazumi Murose, Director of Restorations, Urushi Institute of Research and Restoration, 4–23–5 Shimo-Ochiai, Shinjuku-ku, Tokyo 161, Japan

Somtawin Nilvilai, Conservation Science Division, Bangkok National Museum, Na Pra That Road, Bangkok 10200, Thailand

Prof. Fumio Okada, Kyoto University of Art and Design, Research Center for Science and Cultural Property, 2–116 Uriuyama Kitashirakawa, Sakyo-ku Kyoto 606, Japan

Barbara Piert-Borgers, Schnurgasse 74, 50676 Köln, Germany

Dr. Margarete Prüch, Johannisberg, Schloßheide 73a, 65366 Geisenheim, Germany

Ingo Rogner, Emil-Riedel-Str. 11, 80538 München, Germany

Andreas Scheuch, Nymphenburger Str. 106 Rg., 80636 München, Germany

Dipl.-Rest. Silke Schick, Schwalbenring 18, 72555 Metzingen, Germany

Thomas Schoeller M. A., Westermühlstr. 6, 80469 München, Germany

Dr. Filip Suchomel, Director and Chief Curator, Narodni Galerie v Praze, Collection of Asian Art, Zámek Zhraslav, Zbraslav c.p.2, CZ-156 00 Praha 5, Czech Republic

Namiko Takeuchi, Assistant curator, Lacquerware section of Tokyo National Museum, 13–9 Ueno Park, Taito-ku, Tokyo, Japan

U Yu Thein, Principal, Myanmar Lacquerware Institute, Cottage Industries Department, North Okkalapa, Yangon, The Union of Myanmar

Katharina Walch, Ltd. Restauratorin der Abt. Möbelrestaurierung/*Chief conservator in charge of furniture section*, Bayerisches Landesamt für Denkmalpflege, Hofgraben 4, 80539 München, Germany

Dr. Sirichai Wangchareontrakul, Conservation Science Division, Bangkok National Museum, Na Pra That Road, Bangkok 10200, Thailand

Marianne Webb, Royal Ontario Museum, 100 Queen's Park, Toronto, Ontario, Canada M5S 2C6

Yulin Xie, Research Laboratory for Conservation and Archaeology, Shanghai Museum, 1118 Long Wu Road, Shanghai 200232, China

East Asian and European Lacquer Techniques

International Conference
of the Bavarian State Department of Historical Monuments and the German National Committee of ICOMOS
together with the Tokyo National Research Institute of Cultural Properties

Munich, March 11th – 13th, 1999
'Max-Joseph-Saal' of the Munich Residenz

Thursday, March 11th, 1999

9.00 am Welcome address
Prof. Dr. Michael Petzet, President of the German National Committee of ICOMOS and Director general of the Bavarian State Department of Historical Monuments

9.15 am Oliver R. Impey, Oxford: Japanese Export Lacquer, the Fine Period

9.45 am Julia Hutt, London: East and West in Japanese Export Lacquerware: Some Problem Pieces in the Victoria & Albert Museum

10.15 am Daniëlle O. Kisluk-Grosheide, New York: Export Lacquer and its (Ab)Use in Europe

10.45 am Coffee break

11.15 am Nicole Judet Brugier, Paris: From Asia to Europe: Asian Lacquerware Applied to French Furniture

11.45 am Christiaan J.A. Jörg, Groningen: Japanese Export Lacquer for the Dutch Market

12.15 pm Filip Suchomel, Praha: Japanese Lacquerware for Export in Main Czech Collections

12.45 pm Namiko Takeuchi, Tokyo: Two Examples of Japanese Export Lacquered Chairs

1.15 pm Lunch break

2.45 pm Margarete Prüch, Geisenheim: The Lacquerware of the Zhanguo- and Han-Period (5th – 1st Century BC)

3.15 pm Barbara Piert-Borgers, Cologne: A Beauty Set: Décor and Technique of Lacquerwares of the Western Han-Period (2nd – 1st Century BC)

3.45 pm Yuansheng Chen, Shanghai: A New Method for Treating Chinese Ancient Lacquer on Water-Logged Wood

4.15 pm Coffee break

4.45 pm Monika Kopplin, Münster: Korean Raden Lacquers. Migration of a Technique

5.15 pm Winfried Baer, Berlin: Javanese Export Lacquers

5.45 pm Somtawin Nilvilai, Bangkok: The Techniques of Producing Ancient Thai Lacquerware

6.15 pm U Yu Thein, Yangon: Myanmar Lacquer Technique

7.30 pm Reception by the Bavarian State Department of Historical Monuments, Hofgraben 4, Munich

Friday, March 12th, 1999

9.00 am Tetsuo Miyakoshi, Tokyo: The Analysis of Urushi by Pyrolysis-Gas Chromatography/Mass Spectrometry

9.30 am Ingo Rogner, München: Characterization of East Asian Lacquers by Laser Desorption Mass Spectroscopy (LD-MS)

10.00 am Fumio Okada, Kyoto: The Consolidation of East Asian Lacquers on Ceramics and Water-Logged Wood

10.30 am Coffee break

11.00 am Sadatoshi Miura, Tokyo: The Conservation of the Golden Hall in Chuson-ji at Hiraizumi (1124)

11.30 am Kazumi Murose, Tokyo: The Conservation of Urushi Objects in Japan today. The Repair of a Namban Portable Altar

12.00 pm Richard Wolbers, Delaware: Conservation of a Chinese Convert Lacquer of the 18th Century

12.30 pm Sirichai Wangchareontrakul, Bangkok: Quality Improvement of Lacquer from Melanorrhoea usitata

1.00 pm Lunch break

2.30 pm Johann Koller/Ursula Baumer, Munich: Black Lacquers of the 18th Century

3.00 pm Anna Czarnocka-Crouillère, Le Vésinet: Studios of French Lacquer Masters as Shown by Selected Workshops in 18th Century Paris

3.30 pm Thomas Schoeller, Andreas Scheuch, Munich: The Restoration of the Interior Decoration of the Former Jesuit Church in Landsberg/Lech

4.00 pm Coffee break

4.30 pm Katharina Walch, Munich: The Removal of Added Layers from Original Lacquer Surfaces. Possibilities and Limits

5.00 pm Franz-Josef Christiani, Braunschweig: The Lacquer Production of the Stobwasser Manufactory and its Associates

5.30 pm Silke Schick, Metzingen: Techniques of the Stobwasser Manufactory used on Tobacco Boxes

6.00 pm Mechthild Baumeister, New York: Jean Dunand – A Master of Art Deco Lacquer

6.30 pm Snacks

7.00 pm Visit to the Restoration workshops and the Central Laboratory of the Bavarian State Department of Historical Monuments

Saturday, March 13th, 1999

9.00 am Marianne Webb, Toronto: Colour Change of Lacquers Depending on Conditions (Temperature, Moisture etc.)

9.30 am Wolfgang Kippes, Vienna: Climatic Analyses of the Vieux-Lacquer-Room in Schönbrunn Palace

10.00 am Michael Kühlenthal, Munich: Problems of the Preservation and Restoration of Lacquers in Conservation Practice

Excursion

11.30 am Miniature cabinet in the Munich Residenz (Royal Palace)

12.30 pm Lunch break (Traditional Bavarian snack)

1.30 pm Departure from Munich

2.30 pm Visit to St. Leonhard Church in Froschhausen: Altar retables of the 18th century with original lacquer surfaces

4.00 pm The 'Wies' Pilgrimage Church (World Heritage Monument): original and reconstructed lacquers on the furnishings of the 18th century

5.30 pm Benedictine Abbey, Ettal: Visit to the Abbey church

6.00 pm Buffet in the representative rooms of the Abbey

c.9.00pm Return to Munich

Walch/Koller

Lacke des Barock und Rokoko

Baroque and Rococo Lacquers

ARBEITSHEFTE DES BAYERISCHEN LANDESAMTES FÜR DENKMALPFLEGE

Walch, Katharina/Koller, Johann: Lacke des Barock und Rokoko/Baroque and Rococo Lacquers, München 1997 (Arbeitshefte des Bayerischen Landesamtes für Denkmalpflege, Band 81); Karl M. Lipp Verlag, München, Meglingerstraße 60, 81477 München, Fax 089/785808-33, eMail info@lipp.de; ISBN 3-87490-651-5, 398 S. zahlr. SW-Abb., 14 Farbtafeln; DM 68,00; vergriffen

Die vorliegende Publikation ist die erste Veröffentlichung im Rahmen der deutsch-japanischen Zusammenarbeit auf dem Gebiet der Denkmalpflege und des Denkmalschutzes, die am 25./26.Oktober 1990 vom deutsch-japanischen Komitee für wissenschaftlich-technische Zusammenarbeit in Tokio beschlossen wurde. Man ging davon aus, dass der Erfahrungsaustausch zweier Staaten mit langer Kulturtradition und hohem technologischem Standard bei der Lösung von Erhaltungsproblemen fruchtbar sein dürfte. Die finanziellen Mittel wurden auf deutscher Seite vom Bundesministerium für Bildung, Wissenschaft, Forschung und Technologie, auf japanischer Seite vom Kultusministerium bereit gestellt. Die Projektierung und praktische Durchführung wurde der Abteilung Restaurierung des Bayerischen Landesamts für Denkmalpflege und dem Tokyo National Research Institute of Cultural Properties übertragen. Da der Erfahrungsaustausch und die Zusammenarbeit zunächst auf naturwissenschaftlichem und restauratorisch technischem Gebiet stattfinden sollte, wurde der Eigenart und Ausrichtung beider Institute gemäß, als aktuelles Thema der Zusammenarbeit das „Studium von Verfallsmechanismen und anwendbarer Konservierungsmethoden“ beschlossen und als erstes Fachthema die Erforschung und Restaurierung von Lacken gewählt.

Den Oberflächen von Ausstattungsstücken ist bis vor kurzem noch weniger Aufmerksamkeit als Wandfassungen und Putzstrukturen, den Oberflächen von Architektur, gewidmet worden. Krakelierte und vergilbte Überzüge wurden bedenkenlos, ohne nähere Untersuchung ersetzt, weil nur die farbige Fassung, die Furniere oder auch das bearbeitete Holz als originale, das Aussehen der Kunstwerke bestimmende Oberflächengestaltung betrachtet wurden. Durch das Auswechseln gealterter Lacküberzüge konnten schließlich auch die Farbigkeit oder Maserung der Oberfläche wieder besser zur Geltung gebracht werden. Dabei wurde nicht erkannt, dass es sich bei diesen Lackbeschichtungen weniger um Schutzüberzüge, als vielmehr um Glanzlacke handelte, die das ästhetische Erscheinungsbild wesentlich beeinflussten. Die vergilbten Originallacke wirkten so verfremdend, dass sie mit der Zeit fast überall ausgewechselt wurden. In der Regel können heutzutage nur noch wenige Reste unter Applikationen und Beschlägen, oder hinter Altarblättern gefunden werden, die bei der Auswechslung der Lacke nicht entfernt worden waren. Diese kleinen Restflächen zeigen jedoch – im Verhältnis zum vorgefundenen Zustand – ganz anders geartete Qualitäten. Die Oberflächen sind häufig glatt wie polierter Stuckmarmor, vermitteln in ihrer Härte ein Gefühl von Stein und haben trotz der Vergilbung ein ganz anderes Tiefenlicht als die neueren Lackanstriche. Ihre spiegelnde Härte gibt den Kunstwerken einen veränderten Materialcharakter. Einem marmorierten Holzaufbau zum Beispiel konnte so in überzeugender Weise das Aussehen eines Stuckmarmor- oder Marmorretabels verliehen werden. Durch die Oberflächenbearbeitung wird sozusagen ein edlerer Schein kreiert. Die Holzarchitektur tritt mittels ihrer aufwendig gearbeiteten Beschichtung als Imitation des teuren Marmors an die Seite des Stuckmarmors.

Solche Wirkungen waren allerdings nur durch ausgeklügelte Arbeitstechniken zu erreichen, die ausschließlich zur Erzielung bestimmter ästhetischer Effekte entwickelt wurden. Der in der Regel wenig kunstvollen Kistlerarbeit eines Altarretabels konnte durch die Oberflächenbearbeitung des Fassmalers optisch die Illusion eines Marmoraltars verliehen werden. Diese Intention ist durch zeitgenössische Quellentexte belegt, in denen häufig Ausdrücke wie „auf Marmor-, Porzellan-, oder Jaspisart“ verwendet wurden. Diesen kunstvollen Beschichtungen, der für Barock und Rokoko so wesentlichen Kunst des schönen Scheins, die bei den späteren Überarbeitungen zerstört worden ist, galt die Forschung, deren Ergebnisse im vorliegenden Arbeitsheft dargestellt werden. Die gründlich ausgewerteten und zitierten Quellen des 17. und 18. Jahrhunderts zeigen, wie vielfältig und raffiniert die Materialverarbeitung, der Fassungsaufbau und die Oberflächengestaltungen gewesen sind. Viele dieser Überlieferungen sind durch die naturwissenschaftlichen Untersuchungen bestätigt worden. Vor allem wurde durch die Forschung deutlich, wie kompliziert die bis zu zwanziglagigen Oberflächenbeschichtungen aufgebaut waren und, dass man damit stets ein Optimum an Licht und Glanz erzielen wollte.

Wie jede von Untersuchungen begleitete Restaurierung zeigt, war namentlich das Rokoko eine Stilepoche, die eine besondere Raffinesse in Glanzgraden und Oberflächenwirkungen entwickelt hat und ohne die Differenzierung von Matt- und Glanzvergoldungen, matten und polierten Weißfassungen, dem Unterschied farbiger Lüster, der Lackierung nicht nur von Holz, sondern auch von Stuckmarmor, – nur um eine zusätzliche differenzierende Wirkung zu erzielen, – nicht zu denken ist und auch nicht richtig verstanden werden kann.

Die in den Restaurierungswerkstätten des Bayerischen Landesamts für Denkmalpflege schon seit Jahren bestehende Beschäftigung mit Oberflächen von Ausstattungsgegenständen, die in Zusammenarbeit mit dem Doerner-Institut langsam weiterentwickelt wurde, konnte durch das 1993 begonnene deutsch-japanische Projekt intensiviert fortgeführt und nach drei Jahren zu einem vorläufigen Abschluss gebracht werden. Um die Fülle der verschiedenen Einzelobjekte zu systematisieren, wurden zunächst transparente Lacke auf farbig gefassten und ungefassten, d. h. furnierten Ausstattungsstücken, sowie rote Lacke untersucht. Außerdem wurde eine Darstellung der Herkunft, Gewinnung und analytischen Spezifik von drei der wichtigsten, im 18. Jahrhundert gebräuchlichsten Lacke, – Sandarak, Mastix und Lärchenterpentin, – aufgenommen.

Die hier dargestellten Forschungsergebnisse und Restaurierungskonzepte beziehen sich auf individuelle, besonders gelagerte Fälle, da entsprechende Untersuchungen weder großflächig noch zahlreich zur Verfügung stehen. Die angegeben Restaurierungskonzepte können daher keine allgemein gültigen Rezepturen sein, sondern sind als beispielhafte Lösungsansätze für ganz bestimmte, im einzelnen erforschte Fälle zu sehen.

Die Analysen auf dem Gebiet der organischen Chemie sind äußerst schwierig. Ebenso schwierig ist die restauratorische Umsetzung der naturwissenschaftlichen Ergebnisse unter gleichzeitiger Beachtung der historischen Quellen und Rezepturen. Die naturwissenschaftlichen Analysen wurden daher ausführlich und so dargestellt, dass die speziell entwickelten Verfahren in allen Einzelheiten nachvollziehbar sind.

Die zweite Projektphase wird den Herstellungstechniken japanischer Lackarbeiten und deren Restaurierungsmöglichkeiten sowie der Erforschung der europäischen Imitationen an Ausstattungen vornehmlich des 18. Jahrhunderts gewidmet sein.

Michael Kühlenthal (Hrsg./Ed.)

Japanische und europäische Lackarbeiten

Japanese and European Lacquerware

ARBEITSHEFTE DES BAYERISCHEN LANDESAMTES FÜR DENKMALPFLEGE

Kühlenthal, Michael (Hrsg./Ed.): Japanische und europäische Lackarbeiten. Rezeption, Adaption, Restaurierung / Japanese and European Lacquerware. Adoption, Adaptation, Conservation, München 2000 (Arbeitshefte des Bayerischen Landesamtes für Denkmalpflege, Band 96); Karl M. Lipp Verlag, München, Meglingerstraße 60, 81477 München, Fax 089/785808-33, eMail info@lipp.de; ISBN 3-87490-703-1, 604 S., 438 SW-Abb., 22 Farbtafeln; DM 138,00; erhältlich im Buchhandel

Die zweite Publikation im Rahmen des deutsch-japanischen Projektes zur Erforschung und Restaurierung historischer Lackarbeiten ist eine Gemeinschaftsleistung deutscher und japanischer Wissenschaftler und Restauratoren. Sie präsentiert die Ergebnisse, die in der zweiten Phase des sechs Jahre währenden, vom Bundesministerium für Bildung, Wissenschaft, Forschung und Technologie, sowie vom Japanischen Kultusministerium (Bunkacho) unterstützten Projektes gewonnen werden konnten.

Es werden verschiedene japanische Lacktechniken und die derzeit in Japan praktizierten Restaurierungsmethoden von Urushi an Hand von Fallbeispielen vorgestellt. Besonders interessant ist die Tatsache, dass es der japanischen Forschung gelungen ist, Urushi zu bestimmen. Dies ist auch für die europäische Forschung ein wichtiger Fortschritt, weil bei europäischen Möbelstücken, die in Imitation ostasiatischer Lackarbeiten hergestellt wurden und Originaltafeln japanischer Lackarbeiten integrierten, bisher immer Unsicherheiten über die Zuschreibung der einzelnen Bestandteile bestanden haben. Viele europäische Imitationen sind so perfekt, dass nur die Analyse Klarheit schaffen kann.

Eine der wichtigsten Erkenntnisse der zweiten Projektphase war die Tatsache, dass japanische Exportlacke, d. h. ausschließlich für den Export bestimmte Lackarbeiten, ein gemeinsames japanisches und europäisches Kulturgut sind, um das man sich gemeinsam bemühen muss. Sie wurden in Japan hergestellt, sind jedoch nicht in Japan verblieben. Es handelt sich dabei um eine besondere Gattung von Lackarbeiten, die in darauf spezialisierten Werkstätten angefertigt wurden, bei denen andere Herstellungstechniken als bei den für den Binnenmarkt bestimmten Lackwaren, oft auch eine andere Ikonographie verwendet wurden und die nicht nur japanisches Ideengut verarbeiteten, sondern auch durch europäische Anregungen mitbestimmt gewesen sind. Die Tatsache, dass diese Exportarbeiten im Rahmen des Projekts im Mittelpunkt des Interesses gestanden haben, hat in der japanischen Forschung zu der Initiative geführt, sich erstmalig mit der Eigenart dieser für den Export bestimmten Lackarbeiten zu befassen. Für Deutschland und Europa sind diese Lackwaren wichtiger Bestandteil des kulturellen Erbes, die in die Schlosseinrichtungen der gehobenen Schichten integriert und oftmals gesuchte Sammlerstücke waren. Europa hat sich durch diese Exportarbeiten ein Bild von dem fernen Land, das im Barock und Rokoko die eigene Kultur so stark beeinflusste, gemacht, von einem Land, das niemand aus eigener Anschauung kannte und das seit 1638 auch kein Fremder betreten durfte. Diese Stücke hatten somit eine beträchtliche Auswirkung auf den Geschmack der Zeit, ja haben offenbar die Kunst des 17. und 18. Jahrhunderts in entscheidendem Maße mit geprägt.

Darüber hinaus steht vor allem die Rezeption japanischer Lackarbeiten in Deutschland und Europa im Vordergrund. Da japanische Lackarbeiten zur Zeit des Barock und Rokoko in Europa sehr gefragt gewesen sind und das Angebot die Nachfrage nicht befriedigen konnte, haben europäische Meister begonnen, die ostasiatischen Lacke zu imitieren. Dies geschah jedoch nicht nur aus dem Grund die Nachfrage zu befriedigen und am Marktgeschehen teilzuhaben, sondern, weil die relativ kleinen aus Japan importierten Ausstattungsstücke wie Truhen und Kabinettschränke in europäischen Räumen auf extra dafür angefertigten Gestellen, deren Oberflächen an die japanischen Möbel anzugleichen waren, aufgestellt wurden. Zudem waren europäische Möbelformen mit der Zeit gefragter als die japanischen Exportwaren. So kam es, dass japanische Arbeiten zerlegt und die einzelnen auf diese Weise gewonnenen Tafeln als Prunkstücke in europäische Arbeiten integriert wurden. Auch in diesem Fall mussten die übrigen Teile des Möbels an die Exporttafeln angeglichen werden. Europäische Meister waren auf diese Weise zur Imitation gezwungen, entwickelten aber mit der Zeit eine solche Perfektion, dass sie alle europäischen Möbelformen mit ostasiatischem Dekor versehen und auch ganze Lackkabinette auf äußerst raffinierte Weise gestalten konnten. So haben die japanischen Exportwaren in Europa einen neuen Kunstzweig angeregt, der bald zu einer ernsten Konkurrenz für das eingeführte Kulturgut wurde und zahlreiche Kunstwerke hervorgebracht hat. So sind in diesem Band, dem interdisziplinären Charakter des ganzen Projektes entsprechend, außer naturwissenschaftlichen, auch kunsthistorische Beiträge über verschiedene wichtige deutsche Sammlungen der Zeit, als auch Abhandlungen über bedeutende Werkstätten, wie diejenigen der Gebrüder Dagly in Berlin, Martin Schnells in Dresden, die Lackarbeiten am Hofe der Markgräfin von Baden-Baden, oder auch französische Möbel des 18. Jahrhunderts von Criard, Deforges und Dubois enthalten. Sie werfen Licht auf die Art und Weise der Handelsbeziehungen zwischen Ost und West, die Art wechselseitiger Beeinflussung, und den Stellenwert, den die Importe wie auch die Imitationen an den europäischen Höfen besaßen.

Schließlich sind restauratorische Untersuchungen und beispielhaft Restaurierungen von Imitationslacken dargestellt. In diesem Band wurde, nach der Behandlung klarer und roter Lacke im ersten Band, besonderes Gewicht auf die Untersuchung und Restaurierung von schwarzen Lacken gelegt. Zwei besondere Kapitel wurden den blauen Lacken des 18. Jahrhunderts gewidmet. Im Rahmen dieser Bemühungen konnten neue Erkenntnisse über die Fassungstechnik und den Fassungsaufbau, wie auch über die ursprüngliche Erscheinungsweise der Kunstwerke gewonnen werden.

Der Austausch mit japanischen Fachleuten im Rahmen des Projekts hat zudem neue Aspekte für die Urushi-Restaurierung in Deutschland gebracht. Zumindest wurde deutlich, dass es sich bei Urushi um ein ganz spezielles Material handelt, dessen Restaurierung eine lange Ausbildung und Erfahrung erfordert und, dass japanische Lackarbeiten einer ganz besonderen Behandlung durch den Fachmann bedürfen. Als Anhang ist dem Arbeitsheft ein Glossar japanischer Fachausdrücke beigefügt, das sicher nicht Vollständigkeit beansprucht, aber trotzdem eine willkommene Hilfe bei der Lektüre der japanischen Beiträge ist.

Neben Kunsthistorikern verschiedener Museen in Deutschland und Japan wie auch der Schlösserverwaltungen in Bayern, Sachsen und Baden-Württemberg sind Naturwissenschaftler des Doerner-Instituts in München, des Tokyo National Research Institute of Cultural Properties und anderer wissenschaftlicher Institutionen, sowie Restauratoren des Bayerischen Landesamts für Denkmalpflege, des Tokyo National Research Institute of Cultural Properties und freischaffende Restauratoren in Deutschland und Japan mit zahlreichen Beiträgen vertreten.

Arbeitshefte des Bayerischen Landesamtes für Denkmalpflege

1. Inventarisation, Dokumentation und Pflege von Museumsgut, 1978 (vergriffen)
2. Die Lindenhardter Tafelbilder von Matthias Grünewald, 1978 (vergriffen)
3. Vom Glaspalast zum Gaskessel – Münchens Weg ins technische Zeitalter, 1978
4. Steinkonservierung, 1979 (vergriffen)
5. Torsten Gebhard, Denkmalpflege und Museum, 1979 (vergriffen)
6. Konservierung, Restaurierung, Renovierung – Grundsätze, Durchführung, Dokumentation, 1979 (vergriffen)
7. Bauen in München 1890-1950. Eine Vortragsreihe in der Bayerischen Akademie der Schönen Künste, 1980 (vergriffen)
8. Dieter Klein, Martin Dülfer – Wegbereiter der deutschen Jugendstilarchitektur, 1981, 2. erw. Aufl. 1993
9. Denkmalinventarisation in Bayern. Anfänge und Perspektiven, 1981 (vergriffen)
10. Heinrich Habel, Das Bayerische Armeemuseum in München, 1982
11. Der Schwabacher Hochaltar, 1982
12. Michael Kühlenthal/Martin Zunhamer, Der Passauer Dom und die Deckengemälde Carpoforo Tencallas, 1982 (vergriffen)
13. Dagmar Dietrich, Der Kirchenbau und seine Ausstattung, 1982, 2. Aufl. 1983
14. Das Kurhaustheater in Augsburg-Göggingen, 1982
15. Paul Werner, Der Zwiehof des Berchtesgadener Landes, 1983
16. Der Englische Gruß des Veit Stoß zu St. Lorenz in Nürnberg, 1983
17. Schätze aus Bayerns Erde, 1983
18. Denkmalpflege in Bayern, 75 Jahre Bayerisches Landesamt für Denkmalpflege, 1983 (vergriffen)
19. Hans Maier, Denkmalpflege in Bayern – eine Bilanz 1972–1982/Vierter Mehrjahresplan 1983–1985, 1983 (vergriffen)
20. Michael Kühlenthal, Irsee. Geschichte und Instandsetzung des ehem. Benediktiner-Reichsstifts, 1984 (vergriffen)
21. Farbige Architektur – Regensburger Häuser. Bauforschung und Dokumentation, 1984
22. Rolf Snethlage, Steinkonservierung. Forschungsprogramm des Zentrallabors für Denkmalpflege 1979–1983, 1984
23. Das Südportal des Augsburger Domes – Geschichte und Konservierung, 1984
24. Handwerk und Denkmalpflege, 1984 (vergriffen)
25. Rolf Snethlage/Wolf-Dieter Grimm, Adneter Rotmarmor. Vorkommen und Konservierung, 1984
26. Archäologische Denkmalpflege in Niederbayern – 10 Jahre Außenstelle des Bayerischen Landesamtes für Denkmalpflege in Landshut (1973–1983), 1985
27. Die Römer in Schwaben I: Katalog der Jubiläumsausstellung 2000 Jahre Augsburg, 1985 (vergriffen)
28. Die Römer in Schwaben II: Ausstellungsdokumentation der Jubiläumsausstellung 2000 Jahre Augsburg, 1986 (vergriffen)
29. Manfred Schuller, Die Kaskade von Seehof – Bauforschung und Dokumentation, 1986 (vergriffen)
30. Lusus Campanularum. Beiträge zur Glockenkunde, 1986
31. Natursteinkonservierung. Internationales Kolloquium in München am 21./22. Mai 1984, 1985
32. Glaskonservierung, 1985 (vergriffen)
33. Textile Grabfunde aus der Sepultur des Bamberger Domkapitels, 1987 (vergriffen)
34. Umweltbedingte Gebäudeschäden. Eine Bestandsaufnahme der Forschungstätigkeit in der Bundesrepublik Deutschland, 1986 (vergr.)
35. Hans Graßl, Monumente bayerischer Geschichte. Sieben Denkmäler von europäischem Rang, 1987
36. Silvia Codreanu-Windauer, Der romanische Schmuckfußboden in der Klosterkirche Benediktbeuern, 1988 (vergriffen)
37. Bernd-Peter Schaul, Das Prinzregententheater und die Reform des Theaterbaus um 1900. Max Littmann als Theaterarchitekt, 1987
38. Denkmalinventarisation. Denkmalerfassung als Grundlage des Denkmalschutzes, 1989
39. Harald Gieß, Fensterarchitektur und Fensterkonstruktion in Bayern vom ausgehenden 18. Jahrhundert bis zum Ersten Weltkrieg, 1990 (vergriffen)
40. Fritz Buchenrieder, Gefaßte Bildwerke, 1990 (vergriffen)
41. Denkmäler am Münchner Hofgarten. Forschung und Berichte zu Planungsgeschichte und historischem Baubestand, 1988
42. Die Bamberger „Himmelfahrt Mariä" von J. Tintoretto, 1988 (vergriffen)
43. Denkmäler jüdischer Kultur in Bayern, 1994
44. Wolf Schmidt, Das Raumbuch als Instrument denkmalpflegerischer Bestandsaufnahme und Sanierungsplanung, 1989 u. 1993 (vergriffen)
45. Konservierung und Restaurierung von verputzten Mauerflächen, 1990 (vergriffen)
46. Denkmalpflege und Kirche. Jahrestagung 1989 der Vereinigung der Landesdenkmalpfleger in der Bundesrepublik Deutschland, 1991
47. Paul Werner, Der Hof des Salzburger Flachgaus, 1992
48. Das Panorama in Altötting, 1990 (vergriffen)
49. Die Restaurierung der Wallfahrtskirche Vierzehnheiligen, 1990, 2 Bde.
50. Wolf-Dieter Grimm, Bildatlas wichtiger Denkmalgesteine der Bundesrepublik Deutschland, 1990 (vergriffen)
51. Detta und Michael Petzet, Die Hundinghütte König Ludwigs II., 1990
52. Die Barockorgel der Maihinger Klosterkirche, 1991 (vergriffen)
53. Wolf Schmidt, Das Templerhaus in Amorbach, 1991 (vergriffen)
54. Beiträge zur Heimatforschung. Wilhelm Neu zum 70. Geburtstag, 1991
55. Die Wies. Geschichte und Restaurierung/History and Restoration, 1992
56. Beiträge zur Denkmalkunde. Tilmann Breuer zum 60. Geburtstag, 1991
57. Industrie Museum Lauf. Spuren der Industriekultur im Landkreis Nürnberger Land, 1992
58. Forschungen zur Geschichte der Keramik in Schwaben, 1993
59. Helmut Becker, Archäologische Prospektion. Luftbildarchäologie und Geophysik, 1996
60. Michael Petzet, Denkmalpflege heute. Zwanzig Vorträge zu grundsätzlichen Fragen der Denkmalpflege 1974–1992, 1993
61. Hans Zehetmair, Denkmalschutz in Bayern. Zur Verleihung der Bayerischen Denkmalschutzmedaille 1991, 1993
62. Die Deckengemälde der Lindauer Stiftskirche. Rekonstruktion und Restaurierung, 1993
63. Heinrich Habel, Der Marstallplatz in München, 1993
64. Leonie von Wilckens, Der Paramentenschatz der Landsberger Jesuitenkirche Heiligkreuz, 1994
65. Klosterlangheim, 1994
66. Das Buxheimer Chorgestühl, 1994 (vergriffen)
67. Der heilige Alexius im Augsburger Maximilianmuseum, 1994
68. Jagdschlösser Balthasar Neumanns in den Schönbornlanden, 1994
69. Wilfried Lipp/Michael Petzet (Hrsg.), Vom modernen zum postmodernen Denkmalkultus, 1994

70. Michael Petzet/Wolf Koenigs (Hrsg.), Sana'a. Die Restaurierung der Samsarat al-Mansurah/The Restoration of the Samsarat al-Mansurah, 1995

71. Die Restaurierung von Schloß Oberschwappach, 1996

72. Die Restaurierung der Basilika St. Lorenz in Kempten, 1994

73. Holzschutz, Holzfestigung, Holzergänzung, 1995

74. Gerhard Ongyerth, Kulturlandschaft Würmtal, 1995

75. Holzschädlingsbekämpfung durch Begasung/Fumigation as a Means of Wood Pest Control, 1995

76. Brigitte Huber, Denkmalpflege zwischen Kunst und Wissenschaft, 1996

77. Karlheinz Hemmeter, Bayerische Baudenkmäler im 2. Weltkrieg, 1995 (vergriffen)

78. Salzschäden an Wandmalereien, 1996

79. Putzsicherung. Sicherung von Malereien auf gemauerten und hölzernen Putzträgern, 1996 (vergriffen)

80. Rolf Snethlage, Natursteinkonservierung in der Denkmalpflege (Verlag Ernst & Sohn GmbH, Berlin, ISBN 3-433-01248-2), 1996 (vergr.)

81. Katharina Walch/Johann Koller, Lacke des Barock und Rokoko/Baroque and Rococo Lacquers, 1997 (vergriffen)

82. Der Große Buddha von Dafosi/The Great Buddha of Dafosi, 1996

83. Die Terrakottaarmee des Ersten Chinesischen Kaisers Qin Shihuang (in Bearbeitung)

84. Das Antonierhaus in Memmingen, 1996

85. Das Heilige Kreuz von Polling. Geschichte und Restaurierung, 1996

86. König Max I. Joseph. Modell und Monument, 1996

87. Michael Petzet, Die Alte Münze in München, 1996

88. St. Lukas in München, 1996

89. Erwin Emmerling/Cornelia Ringer (Hrsg.), Das Aschaffenburger Tafelbild. Studien zur Tafelmalerei des 13. Jahrhunderts, 1997

90. Susanne Fischer, Die Münchner Schule der Glasmalerei, 1997

91. Gabriele Wimböck, Der Ingolstädter Münsteraltar, 1998

92. Hinterer Bach 3. Bauforschung in Bamberg, 1998

93. Thomas Gunzelmann/Manfred Mosel/Gerhard Ongyerth, Denkmalpflege und Dorferneuerung. Der denkmalpflegerische Erhebungsbogen zur Dorferneuerung, 1999

94. Martin Mach (Hrsg.), Metallrestaurierung/Metal Restoration, 1998

95. Die Schatzkammer von St. Andreas in Weißenburg, 2000

96. Michael Kühlenthal (Hrsg./Ed.), Japanische und europäische Lackarbeiten/Japanese and European Lacquerware, 2000

97. Produkt Denkmal. Denkmalpflege als Wirtschaftsfaktor, 1998

98. Peter Mottner/Martin Mach (Hrsg.), Zinkguß. Die Konservierung von Denkmälern aus Zink, 1999

99. Nikolaus Lang. Spurensicherung, 1999

100. Monumental. Festschrift für Michael Petzet, 1998 (vergriffen)

101. Gerhard Klotz-Warislohner/Martim Saar, Reparatur in der Baudenkmalpflege. Das Bayerische Bauarchiv Thierhaupten, 1999

102. Thomas Gunzelmann/Angelika Kühn/Christiane Reichert, Kulmbach. Das städtebauliche Erbe, 1999

103. Die Gartenkunst des Barock, 1999

104. Konservierung von Wandmalerei (Arbeitstitel)

105. Michael Kühlenthal/Helge Fischer, Petra. Die Restaurierung der Grabfassaden/The Restoration of the Rockcut Tomb Façades, 2000

106. Das Portal der Hl.-Geist-Kirche in Landshut (Arbeitstitel)

107. Heike Fastje/Harald Gieß/Helmut-Eberhard Paulus/Karl Schnieringer, Vom Handelshaus zur Schnupftabakfabrik. Dokumente zur Geschichte zweier Regensburger Patrizierhäuser, 1999

108. Jörg W. E. Fassbinder/Walter E. Irlinger (Hrsg.), Archaeological Prospection. Third International Conference on Archaeological Prospection, 1999

109. Ursula Schädler-Saub, Gotische Wandmalereien in Mittelfranken. Kunstgeschichte, Restaurierung, Denkmalpflege, 2000

110. Michael Petzet, z. A. Presse GK. 25 Jahre Denkmalpflege in Bayern im Spiegel der Presse, 2000

111. The Polychromy of the Terracotta Army of the First Chinese Emperor Qin Shihuangdi (Arbeitstitel)

112. Michael Kühlenthal (Hrsg./Ed.), Ostasiatische und europäische Lacktechniken/East Asian and European Lacquer Techniques, 2000

ICOMOS · HEFTE DES DEUTSCHEN NATIONALKOMITEES

I. ICOMOS PRO ROMANIA
Exposition/Exhibition/Ausstellung Paris, London, München, Budapest, Kopenhagen, Stockholm 1989/1990, München 1989. ISBN 3-87490-620-5

II. GUTSANLAGEN DES 16. BIS 19. JAHRHUNDERTS IM OSTSEERAUM – GESCHICHTE UND GEGENWART
Tagung des Deutschen Nationalkomitees von ICOMOS in der Akademie Sandelmark, 11.-14.9.1989, München 1990. ISBN 3-87490-310-9

III. WELTKULTURDENKMÄLER IN DEUTSCHLAND
Deutsche Denkmäler in der Liste des Kultur- und Naturerbes der Welt, eine Ausstellung des Deutschen Nationalkomitees von ICOMOS in Zusammenarbeit mit der Dresdner Bank, München 1991. 2. erweiterte Auflage von 1994. ISBN 3-87490-311-7

IV. EISENBAHN UND DENKMALPFLEGE I
Erstes Symposium. Eine Tagung des Deutschen Nationalkomitees von ICOMOS, Frankfurt am Main. 2.-4.4.1990, München 1992. ISBN 3-87490-619-1

V. DIE WIES
Geschichte und Restaurierung/History and Restoration, München 1992. ISBN 3-87490-618-3

VI. MODELL BRANDENBURG
Eine Tagung des Deutschen Nationalkomitees von ICOMOS und der GWS – Gesellschaft für Stadterneuerung mbH Berlin/Brandenburg zum Thema Stadterneuerung und Denkmalschutz in den fünf neuen Bundesländern, München 1992. ISBN 3-87490-624-8

VII. FERTÖRÁKOS
Denkmalpflegerische Überlegungen zur Instandsetzung eines ungarischen Dorfes/Műemlékvédelmi megfontaolások egy magyar falu megújításához, hrsg. vom Deutschen Nationalkomitee von ICOMOS mit der Arbeitsgemeinschaft Alpen-Adria, München 1992. ISBN 3-87490-616-7

VIII. REVERSIBILITÄT – DAS FEIGENBLATT IN DER DENKMALPFLEGE?
Eine Tagung des Deutschen Nationalkomitees von ICOMOS und des Sonderforschungsbereichs 315 der Universität Karlsruhe, 24.-26.10.1991, München 1992. ISBN 3-87490-617-5

IX. EISENBAHN UND DENKMALPFLEGE II
Eine Tagung des Deutschen Nationalkomitees von ICOMOS, Frankfurt am Main, 2.-4.4.1992, München 1993. ISBN 3-87490-614-0

X. GRUNDSÄTZE DER DENKMALPFLEGE / PRINCIPLES OF MONUMENT CONSERVATION / PRINCIPES DE LA CONSERVATION DES MONUMENTS HISTORIQUES
München 1992. ISBN 3-87490-615-9 (vergriffen)

XI. HISTORISCHE KULTURLANDSCHAFTEN
Eine Tagung des Deutschen Nationalkomitees von ICOMOS mit dem Europarat und dem Landschaftsverband Rheinland, Abtei Brauweiler, 10.-17.5.1992, München 1993. ISBN 3-87490-612-4

XII. ARCHITEKTEN UND DENKMALPFLEGE
Eine Tagung des Deutschen Nationalkomitees von ICOMOS, des Instituts für Auslandsbeziehungen in Zusammenarbeit mit der Deutschen UNESCO-Kommission und der Architektenkammer Baden-Württemberg, 18.-20.6.1992, München 1993. ISBN 3-87490-613-2

XIII. BILDERSTURM IN OSTEUROPA
Eine Tagung des Deutschen Nationalkomitees von ICOMOS, des Instituts für Auslandsbeziehungen und der Senatsverwaltung Berlin, 18.-20.2.1993, München 1994. ISBN 3-87490-611-6

XIV. Christoph Machat (Hrsg.), DENKMÄLER IN RUMÄNIEN / MONUMENTS EN ROUMANIE
Vorschläge des Rumänischen Nationalkomitees von ICOMOS zur Ergänzung der Liste des Weltkulturerbes / Propositions du Comité National Roumain de l'ICOMOS pour la Liste du Patrimoine Mondial, München 1995. ISBN 3-87490-627-2

XV. Michael Petzet und Wolf Koenigs (Hrsg.), SANA'A
Die Restaurierung der Samsarat al-Mansurah/The Restoration of the Samsarat al-Mansurah, München 1995. ISBN 3-87490-626-4

XVI. DAS SCHLOSS UND SEINE AUSSTATTUNG ALS DENKMALPFLEGERISCHE AUFGABE
Eine Tagung des Deutschen Nationalkomitees von ICOMOS und des Facharbeitskreises Schlösser und Gärten in Deutschland, 5.-8.10.1994, München 1995. ISBN 3-87490-628-0

XVII. DER GROSSE BUDDHA VON DAFOSI / THE GREAT BUDDHA OF DAFOSI
München 1996. ISBN 3-87490-610-8

XVIII. DIE TONFIGURENARMEE DES KAISERS QIN SHIHUANGDI
(in Bearbeitung)

XIX. Matthias Exner (Hrsg.), STUCK DES FRÜHEN UND HOHEN MITTELALTERS
Geschichte, Technologie, Konservierung
Eine Tagung des Deutschen Nationalkomitees von ICOMOS und des Dom- und Diözesanmuseums Hildesheim, 15.-18.6.1995, München 1996. ISBN 3-87490-660-4

XX. STALINISTISCHE ARCHITEKTUR UNTER DENKMALSCHUTZ?
Eine Tagung des Deutschen Nationalkommitees von ICOMOS und der Senatsverwaltung für Stadtentwicklung und Umweltschutz in Berlin, 6.-9.9.1995, München 1996. ISBN 3-87490-609-4

XXI. DAS DENKMAL ALS ALTLAST?
Auf dem Weg in die Reparaturgesellschaft. Eine Tagung des Deutschen Nationalkommitees von ICOMOS und des Lehrstuhls für Denkmalpflege und Bauforschung der Universität Dortmund, 11.-13.10.1995, München 1996. ISBN 3-87490-629-9

XXII. DIE BISCHOFSBURG ZU PÉCS. ARCHÄOLOGIE UND BAUFORSCHUNG
Eine Publikation des Deutschen und des Ungarischen Nationalkomitees von ICOMOS mit dem Ungarischen Denkmalamt, Budapest 1999 (in Bearbeitung)

XXIII. Matthias Exner (Hrsg.), WANDMALEREI DES FRÜHEN MITTELALTERS. BESTAND, MALTECHNIK, KONSERVIERUNG
Eine Tagung des Deutschen Nationalkomitees von ICOMOS mit der Verwaltung der Staatlichen Schlösser und Gärten in Hessen, Lorsch, 10.-12.10.1996, München 1998. ISBN 3-87490-663-9

XXIV. KONSERVIERUNG DER MODERNE?
Über den Umgang mit den Zeugnissen der Architekturgeschichte des 20. Jahrhunderts. Eine Tagung des Deutschen Nationalkomitees von ICOMOS mit der ›denkmal '96‹, der Europäischen Messe für Denkmalpflege und Stadterneuerung, Leipzig, 31.10.-2.11.1996, München 1998. ISBN 3-87490-662-0

XXV. DOM ZU BRANDENBURG
Eine Tagung des Deutschen Nationalkomitees von ICOMOS und des Brandenburgischen Landesamtes für Denkmalpflege, mit Unterstützung des Domstifts Brandenburg und des Fördervereins ›Dom zu Brandenburg‹, Brandenburg, 2.-3.12.1996, München 1998. ISBN 3-87490-661-2

XXVI. LEGAL STRUCTURES OF PRIVATE SPONSORSHIP
International Seminar organized by the German National Committee of ICOMOS with the University of Katowice, Weimar, 17th-19th of April, München 1997. ISBN 3-87490-664-7

XXVII. EISENBAHN UND DENKMALPFLEGE III
Drittes internationales Eisenbahnsymposium des Deutschen Nationalkomitees von ICOMOS, Frankfurt am Main, 14.-16.4.1997, München 1998. ISBN 3-87490-667-3

XXVIII. DIE GARTENKUNST DES BAROCK
Eine internationale Tagung des Deutschen Nationalkomitees von ICOMOS in Zusammenarbeit mit dem Bayerischen Landesamt für Denkmalpflege und dem Arbeitskreis Historische Gärten der Deutschen Gesellschaft für Gartenkunst und Landschaftskultur e.V., Schloß Seehof bei Bamberg, 23.-26.9.1997, München 1998. ISBN 3-87490-666-3

XXIX. Martin Mach (Hrsg.), METALLRESTAURIERUNG / METAL RESTORATION
Internationale Tagung zur Metallrestaurierung, veranstaltet vom Bayerischen Landesamt für Denkmalpflege und vom Deutschen Nationalkomitee von ICOMOS, München, 23.-25.10.1997, München 1998. ISBN 3-87490-665-5

XXX. Michael Petzet, PRINCIPLES OF CONSERVATION / PRINCIPES DE LA CONSERVATION DES MONUMENTS HISTORIQUES
München 1999. ISBN 3-87490-668-X

XXXI. OPERNBAUTEN DES BAROCK
München 1999. ISBN 3-87490-669-8

XXXII. DAS KONZEPT „REPARATUR". IDEAL UND WIRKLICHKEIT
München 2000. ISBN 3-87490-671-X

XXXIII. THIRD INTERNATIONAL CONFERENCE ON ARCHAEOLOGICAL PROSPECTION
München 1999. ISBN 3-87490-670-1

XXXIV. Michael Kühlenthal/Helge Fischer, PETRA. DIE RESTAURIERUNG DER GRABFASSADEN / THE RESTORATION OF THE ROCKCUT TOMB FAÇADES
München 2000. ISBN 3-87490-672-8

XXXV. Michael Kühlenthal (Hrsg./Ed.), OSTASIATISCHE UND EUROPÄISCHE LACKTECHNIKEN / EAST ASIAN AND EUROPEAN LACQUER TECHNIQUES
Internationale Tagung des Bayerischen Landesamtes für Denkmalpflege und des Deutschen Nationalkomitees von ICOMOS in Zusammenarbeit mit dem Tokyo National Research Institute of Cultural Properties, München, 11.-13. März 1999, München 2000. ISBN 3-87490-673-6

Zu beziehen über Karl M. Lipp Verlag, Meglingerstraße 60, 81477 München, Telefon 089/78 58 08-0, Telefax 089/78 58 08 33, E-mail: info@lipp.de